A
Disputation
on
HOLY SCRIPTURE
Against the Papists
especially
Bellarmine and Stapleton

by

William Whitaker, D.D.

Regius Professor of Divinity, and Master of St. John's College,
in the University of Cambridge

Translated and Edited for the Parker Society
by Rev. William Fitzgerald, A.M.

Prebendary of Donoughmore in the Cathedral of St. Patrick, and
Professor of Moral Philosophy in the University of Dublin

SOLI GLORIA PUBLICATIONS
. . . for instruction in righteousness . . .

Soli Deo Gloria Publications
A division of Ligonier Ministries, Inc.
P.O. Box 547500, Orlando, FL 32854
(407) 333-4244/FAX 333-4233
www.ligonier.org

A Disputation on Holy Scripture
was first published in 1588 in London.
Printed in the U.S.A.

Jacket and book design by
DogEaredDesign.com and Ligonier Ministries
This 2005 Soli Deo Gloria reprint is a lithograph of the 1849
edition published by the Parker Society in Cambridge.

ISBN 1-57358-090-2

William Whitaker's
A Disputation on Holy Scripture
(1588, ET 1849)

An Analysis of the Contents
(Compiled by Rowland Ward)

Question 1: The number of the canonical books (p. 25)

The six questions dealt with in this book are outlined (25), and the first question (which books are canonical?) is given (27). As a preliminary, the rejection of parts of Scripture by heretics or the assertion of mistakes in Scripture is discussed (30). The claims of the Apocrypha are then considered and shown from history (and particularly the testimony of Cajetan) to be without canonicity in the strict sense, being at best canon for edification but not for faith (39). The positive case is then advanced: the apocryphal books were not written by prophets (49); councils, fathers and other early writers testify to the apocrypha as not canon for faith. The particular books of the apocrypha are considered in turn: Baruch (67); additions to Esther (71); additions to Daniel (76); Tobit (80); Judith (82); Wisdom of Solomon (86); Ecclesiasticus (90); 1 & 2 Maccabees (93); next, the books Rome admits are apocryphal (102). A review of the New Testament and certain spurious books concludes consideration of the first question (105).

Question 2: The authentic edition and versions (p. 110)

(A) The authentic edition: The state of the question is given: Rome sets up the Latin Vulgate as the authentic version whereas the Protestants affirm the Hebrew and Greek originals (111). The Hebrew Bible is discussed, particularly with reference to the role of Ezra (112); then the translation into Greek known as the Septuagint (117), and then the Greek translations of Aquila, Symmachus, Theodotion and Lucian, which Origen collated with other texts (123); and then the New Testament in Greek is considered, (125). The origin and character of the Latin Vulgate Bible is reviewed and some of its evident corruption noted (128); then five arguments of Bellarmine in favor of the Vulgate are considered and answered (135); then ten arguments of the translators of the Rheims NT of 1582 likewise (141). Eleven arguments showing why the Vulgate is not authentic are then advanced (145); examples of corruptions in the Vulgate translation of Genesis are given (163); likewise in the Psalms (179), and in the New Testament (193).

(B) Translations in the vernacular: The state of the question concerning translations in the vernacular is given: Rome hedges such translation about with many conditions whereas Protestants affirm that all should study the Scriptures and have them in their own language (208). Eight arguments by Bellarmine against vernacular versions are refuted (21), and six positive arguments are set forth (235).

(C) Worship services: State of the question concerning worship services in the vulgar tongue: Rome uses Latin, Protestants the common tongue (250). Five arguments of Rome are considered (251); followed by five positive arguments (258).

Question 3: The authority of Scripture (p. 275)
The state of the question is given: whether or not we should believe the Scripture is canonical solely because of the authority of the church rather than the internal testimony of the Spirit (275). Rome admits the scriptures are true, but says they would not be believed apart from the approval of the church; Protestants acknowledge Scripture because it comes from God, and has authority in itself, which we have assurance of through the operation of the Holy Spirit (275). The relationship of the authority of the church to Scripture is considered (280). A consideration of Stapleton's arguments, namely, that the authority of the church is necessary to know what is canonical (285); what writings of inspired men are intended to be canonical (300); what writings doubted by some became undoubted (304); and why some writings have not been admitted into the canon (312). The same is urged from the connection between the church's judgement of heretics and her judgement what is the canon (316); a saying of Augustine (319) and other sources (323); and by a claimed rule of faith in the church that enables true scriptures to be distinguished; to which the argument from the priority of the church to the written word is appended (327). The Protestant case is then put forth in nineteen arguments (332).

Question 4: The perspicuity of Scripture (p. 359)
The state of the question: It is conceded that there are obscure places in Scripture and that the ministry of the word is necessary, but Scripture is sufficiently clear on the main matters related to salvation, whereas Rome wants to exaggerate the obscurities of the Scriptures so as to keep them from the common people (359). Some reasons why God has placed obscure passages in the Scripture (365). Bellarmine's five arguments for the obscurity of Scripture answered (366); and twelve Protestant arguments set forth (381).

Question 5: The interpretation of Scripture (p. 402)

Rome claims interpretation of Scripture is the privilege of the church and that the true interpretation agrees with "the fathers," yet there are problems of definition (402); Rome's fourfold sense of Scripture rejected in favor of one true and genuine sense, which may have several different applications, Scripture always interpreting Scripture (403).

(A) The authority and supreme tribunal: Rome's many qualifications on learning the sense of Scripture from her teachers means that ultimately they are driven to say that only the Pope can give a sure interpretation; we say that an external persuasion arises from scripture itself but that full assurance comes through the Holy Spirit as the supreme interpreter (410). Bellarmine's argument from seven OT passages reviewed (416); also nine NT passages (425); and the earlier practice of the church (434), and his argument from the nature of the case (444). The positive case (the Holy Spirit speaking in the Scriptures) is affirmed from the conclusion of the 3rd question and 15 further arguments (447).

(B) The means to be used: Prayer, knowledge of the original texts, nature of the language being expounded, context, comparing the obscure with plainer passages, comparison with other passages, the analogy of faith, reference to the more skilled are proper means (466). Three arguments against these means considered (474) and refuted (476), and four means proposed by Rome rejected (484). The interpretation of Scripture by Scripture is proven (488).

Question 6: The perfection of Scripture over against human traditions (p. 496)

The question is proposed whether the books of the OT and NT are a complete and perfect rule of faith or whether unwritten traditions are necessary as well (497). Rome's definition of tradition (497); classifications into divine, apostolic or ecclesiastical and again divided according to their content (500); and rules are given for distinguishing true and false traditions (503). The dogmas Rome bases on the authority of tradition is shown (511).

The state of the question: We say all things necessary to faith and morals may be collected or inferred from Scripture, but Rome denies this (513). Bellarmine's argument that Scripture is not necessary without traditions (515), and a brief response affirming that they are necessary (521). Bellarmine's argument that Scripture is not sufficient without tradition (524); his argument from Scripture in support of some true unwritten traditions (542); his argument from the decisions of certain councils (562), and from the testimonies of the fathers (564), with sundry concluding arguments (610). The positive case is now presented first from Scripture arguments Bellarmine attempted to answer (615), then from Scriptures he did not consider (640), then four arguments based on the nature of the thing (651); and finally on the testimony of the fathers (669).

CONTENTS.

PREFACE.

It seemed desirable that this, the great work of one of the greatest of our early divines upon the cardinal point of difference between the churches of the Roman and the reformed communions, should be comprised in the collection of the Parker Society; not only on account of its intrinsic merits, but also for its historical value; as exhibiting the posture of defence assumed by our schools against that change of tactics in the management of this great controversy, which is to be dated from the institution of the Society of Jesus.

William Whitaker (or Whitacre) was born at Holme, in Lancashire, A.D. 1547, of a good family, nearly related to Alexander Nowel, the celebrated dean of St Paul's. He was bred at Cambridge, where he soon distinguished himself, and was in 1579 appointed the Queen's Professor of Divinity. In 1586, through the influence of Burghley and Whitgift, and in spite of obstinate and powerful opposition, he was made Master of St John's College in that University; soon after which appointment he took his degree of Doctor in Divinity. His delay in assuming the doctorate seems curious, and it was maliciously made the ground of a most unjust imputation of puritanism. How small was his sympathy with the disciplinarian party, appears from the manner in which he speaks of their great leader, Cartwright, in a letter preserved by Bancroft[1] : " Quem Cartwrightus nuper emisit libellum, ejus magnam partem perlegi. Ne vivam, si quid unquam viderim dissolutius ac pene puerilius. Verborum satis ille quidem lautam ac novam supellectilem habet, rerum omnino nullam, quantum ego quidem judicare possum. Deinde non modo perverse de Principis in Rebus Sacris atque Ecclesiasticis auctoritate sentit; sed in papistarum etiam castra transfugit; a quibus tamen videri vult odio capitali dissidere. Verum nec in hac causa

---

[1] Survey of Discipline, p. 379, Lond. 1593.

ferendus, sed aliis etiam in partibus tela a papistis mutuatur. Denique, ut de Ambrosio dixit Hieronymus, verbis ludit, sententiis dormitat, et plane indignus est qui a quopiam docto refutetur."

But though far removed from the disciplinarian tenets of the puritans, Whitaker undoubtedly agreed with them in their hostility to the Arminian opinions, which in his time began to prevail in the Church of England; as appears from the share taken by him in the prosecution of Baret, and the devising of the Lambeth articles. The history of such proceedings is foreign from my present purpose; but the reader will find a full detail of the circumstances connected with them in Strype's Life of Whitgift, Book IV., Chapters 14—18. Shortly after the termination of that memorable dispute, Whitaker died in 1595, in the forty-seventh year of his age. He was married, and had eight children. It was pleasantly said of him, that he gave the world a child and a book[1] every year. Of his children I have nothing to communicate, and his books will speak for themselves. They gained for him in his life-time a high character, not only with friends, but with enemies also. "I have," says the writer of his life, in Lupton's Protestant Divines[2], "I have heard it confessed of English Papists themselves, which have been in Italy with Bellarmine himself, that he procured the true portraiture and effigies of this *Whitaker* to be brought to him, which he kept in his study. For he privately admired this man for his singular learning and ingenuity; and being asked of some of his friends, Jesuits, why he would have the picture of that heretic in his presence? he would answer, *Quod quamvis hæreticus erat et adversarius, erat tamen doctus adversarius:* that, "although he was an heretic, and his adversary, yet he was a learned adversary," p. 359. "He was," says Gataker, "tall of stature and upright; of a grave aspect, with black hair and a ruddy complexion; a solid judgment, a liberal mind, an affable disposition; a

[1] *Librum* et *Liberum* quotannis. See Fuller's Life of Whitaker in the "Holy State."

[2] History of the moderne Protestant Divines, &c., faithfully translated out of the Latin by D. L., London, 1637.

mild, yet no remiss governor; a contemner of money; of a moderate diet, a life generally unblameable, and (that which added a lustre to all the rest) amidst all these endowments, and the respects of others (even the greatest) thereby deservedly procured, of a most meek and lowly spirit." "Who," asks Bishop Hall, "ever saw him without reverence? or heard him without wonder?"

I have only to add, that in the translation I have endeavoured to be as literal as would consist with a due regard to the English idiom. Had I considered myself at liberty to use more freedom, I should have made my task more easy to myself, and the work perhaps less tedious to the reader: for there is a prolixity in Whitaker's style, which contrasts unfavourably with the compactness of his great antagonist, Bellarmine; though he trespasses far less upon the student's patience than Stapleton, whose verbose rhetoric made him admired in his own day, and whose subtlety of logic cannot save him from neglect in ours.

It is proper to apprise the reader, that, besides the Controversy translated in the present volume, the only one published in the Author's life-time, three others are contained in the ponderous volumes of his works, all of which were published after his death by John Allenson, B.D., Fellow of St John's College. The subjects of these are *De Ecclesia*, *De Conciliis*, and *De Romano Pontifice*. He encountered Bellarmine also on the other controversies in succession, *De ministris et presbyteris Ecclesiæ*, *De sanctis mortuis*, *De Ecclesia triumphante*, *De Sacramentis in genere*, *De Baptismo*, and *De Eucharistia*. "Quas," adds his biographer, Obadiah Assheton, a Fellow of his College, "utinam licuisset per otium relegisse, et mandasse typis universas: id enim auditoribus erat in votis vel maxime; quorum cum summa admiratione et acclamatione singulas tractarat controversias. Ceterum studio respondendi Bellarmino in omnibus controversiis religionis provectus, optimum censuit has elucubratas disputationes apud se reponere; ratus (quod postea non evenit) aptius fore tempus eas per otium evulgandi. Sed Deo immortali, cujus consilia sunt abyssus inscrutabilis, aliter visum est."

The following is the list of his works :

1.   Responsio ad decem rationes Edm. Campiani.   8vo. Lond. 1581.

2.   Responsionis ad decem rationes Edm. Campiani Defensio. 8vo. Lond. 1583.

3.   Refutatio Nic. Sanderi, quod Papa non sit Antichristus. 8vo. Lond. 1583.

4.   Answer to W. Rainold's Reprehensions, &c.   8vo. Camb. 1585.

5.   Disputatio de Sacra Scriptura contra hujus temporis Papistas.   4to. Cantab. 1588.

6.   Pro authoritate atque αὐτοπιστίᾳ S. Scripturæ Duplicatio contra T. Stapletonum.   Libri 3. Cantab. 1594.

7.   Prælectiones de Ecclesia, &c., edited after his death by J. Allenson.   4to. Cantab. 1599.

8.   Prælectiones de Conciliis.   8vo. Cantab. 1600.

9.   Concio in 1 Thess. v. 12.   4to. Cantab. 1599.

10.   In Controversiam de R. Pontifice, distributam in quæstiones viii., adversus Pontificios, imprimis R. Bellarminum, prælectiones.   8vo. Hanov. 1608.

11.   De Sacramentis.   Francof. 1624. 4to.

A complete collection of his works in Latin was printed in two vols. folio, at Geneva, 1610.

Besides the above, Whitaker published in 1569 a Greek translation of the Common Prayer; in 1573, of Nowel's larger, and in 1575, of the smaller Catechism.

EPISTLE DEDICATORY.

TO THE MOST NOBLE AND PRUDENT,

WILLIAM CECIL, KNIGHT,

BARON BURGHLEY, HIGH TREASURER OF ENGLAND, AND
CHANCELLOR OF THE UNIVERSITY OF CAMBRIDGE.

THERE have been many heretofore, illustrious Cecil, who
have defended the papal interest and sovereignty with the utmost
exertion, the keenest zeal, and no mean or vulgar erudition. But
they who have played their part with most address, and far out-
stripped almost all others of their own side, are those men who
now, for some years back, have been engaged most earnestly in
this cause; a fresh supply of monks, subtle theologians, vehement
and formidable controvertists; whom that strange—and, in former
times, unheard of—Society of Jesus hath brought forth, for the
calamity of the church and the christian religion. For when,
after that black, deadly, baneful, and tedious night of popish
superstition and antichristianism, the clear and cheerful lustre
of the gospel had illuminated with its rays some portions of
the christian world, attracting, and by its incredible charms at the
same time moving all, to gaze on, admire, and cleave to it; on
a sudden, these men sprang up to obscure with pestilential vapours,
and ravish, if possible, from our view, this light, so hateful to
themselves, so hostile and prejudicial to their interests. So indeed
had John, that holy disciple of Christ, predicted in the Apocalypse,
that a star, which had fallen from heaven, and received the key
of the infernal pit, should remove the covering of the abyss,
and cause a mighty smoke to issue forth, like the smoke of a
great furnace, shedding darkness over the sun and heaven. This

pit, from the time that it was first opened, hath not ceased to
exhale perpetual smoke to blind the eyes of men; and, as the
same prophet had foretold, hath sent forth innumerable locusts
upon the earth, like scorpions, who have wounded with their
deadly stings all men upon whose foreheads the seal of God was
not impressed. The event itself, the best interpreter of prophecies, has illustrated the obscurity of the prediction. For who can
doubt the meaning of the star, the pit, the smoke, the locusts;
who considers the state of the papal power, in which they are
all so pourtrayed to the very life, as to be most readily discerned by any one, who can compare together the past and present, and interprets what was foretold, as about to happen, by
that which is seen to have occurred?

Amongst these locusts,—that is, as very learned men justly
deem, amongst the innumerable troops of monks — none, as we
before said, have ever appeared, more keen, or better prepared
and equipped for doing mischief, than are the Jesuits at this
present day; who in a short space have surpassed all other
societies of that kind in numbers, in credit, and in audacity.
Other monks, following the rule and practice of former times,
lived in general a life of leisure and inactivity, and spent their
time, not in reading and the study of the sciences, but in repeating
by the glass certain offices for the canonical hours, which con-
tributed nothing to the advancement of either learning or religion.
But the Jesuits have pursued a far different course. They have
left the shade of ancient sloth and inactivity, in which the other
monks had grown grey, and have come forth to engage in toils,
to treat of arts and sciences, to undertake and carry through an
earnest struggle for the safety of the common interests. It hath
come to be understood, that the cause of Rome, which, shaken by
the perilous blows dealt on every side by men of ability and
learning, had begun in many parts to totter and give way,
could never be defended or maintained, except by learned and
diligent and active champions.

For just as a dilapidated mansion, unless propped up almost

every day by fresh and firm buttresses, will suddenly fall in a violent and total ruin; so they perceived that the Roman synagogue, tottering as it is and threatening to fall, in its wretched state of decay and dilapidation, hath need continually of new supports and bracings, to maintain any remnant of its state and dignity under the pressure of such vehement assaults. Yet, with all their efforts, shall they never be able to avert the imminent calamity, or rescue themselves from perdition. But as buildings, whose foundations are subverted, their walls pierced, their roofs uncovered, having no part secure, can never be supported long by any multitude of artificial props; so that church of theirs, all rent and torn on every side, in which nor roof, nor pillar, nor foundation remains sound, intrinsically devoid of firmness and integrity, must at length fall headlong, and crush many to destruction in its ruins. We are not to believe that the Roman church is flourishing, because the Jesuits are often able to impose upon inconstant and unskilful persons, and lead them into the popish fraud by the lures and blandishment of their fallacious reasoning, any more than we should think that health and life is restored to the frame that labours in a mortal malady, when it gains, for a moment, some casual alleviation of its pain. Let the Jesuits do their best; let them exert, if possible, still more intense sedulity, and omit nothing that learning and diligence can accomplish without the aid of truth. Yet all they can accomplish will be this,—to prop a falling house with mounds and buttresses, to afford some brief refreshment to antichrist, now gasping in his last long agony,—and, despite of all the rules of physic, apply remedies to a desperate disease.

Amongst these Jesuits, Robert Bellarmine, a native of Italy, hath now for several years obtained a great and celebrated name. At first he taught scholastic divinity in Belgium; but afterwards, having removed to Rome, he treated of theological controversies in such a manner as to excite the admiration and gain the applause of all. His lectures were eagerly listened to by his auditors, transcribed, transmitted into every quarter, and treasured up as jewels and amulets. After some time, for the sake of rendering them more generally useful, they were epitomized by a certain Englishman. Finally, the first volume of these controversies hath been published at Ingolstadt, printed by Sartorius; and the rest are expected in due time[1]. Now, therefore, Bellarmine is cried up by his party as an invincible champion, as one with whom none of our men would dare to engage, whom nobody can answer, and whom if any one should hope to conquer, they would regard him as an utter madman.

When you, honoured sir, demanded my opinion of this writer, I answered, as indeed I thought, that I deemed him to be a man unquestionably learned, possessed of a happy genius, a penetrating judgment, and multifarious reading;—one, moreover, who was wont to deal more plainly and honestly than is the custom of other papists, to press his arguments more home, and to stick more closely to the question. Thus, indeed, it became a man who had been trained in the schools, and who had made the handling of controversies his professed business, to dismiss all circumlocutions and digressions, and concern himself entirely with the argument; and, having read all that had been previously written upon the subject, to select those reasons and replies which seemed to have most strength and sinew in them. In the prosecution of which task, he was led to weigh everything with a profound and anxious solicitude, and has sometimes differed from all his predecessors, and struck out new explanations of his own; perceiving, I suppose, that the old ones were not sound enough to be relied on. We have an instance (Lib. II. de Verbo Dei, c. 16) in his treatment of 1 Cor. 14, where the apostle forbids the use of a strange language in the church. The former popish writers had usually understood that place to speak of exhortations or sermons to the

[1 The first complete edition of Bellarmine's Controversies was printed, according to Bayle, at Ingolstadt, in three Tomes, 1586. The oldest edition which I have seen is that of 1588, printed also at Ingolstadt by Sartorius, in three Tomes. Alegambus states that the first Tome was printed so early as 1581.]

people; or, if they conceded that it might be understood of divine service, interpreted it so as to require that the words of the minister should be understood, not by the whole congregation, but only by him who made the responses in their name. But Bellarmine, having reflected upon the falsehood and weakness of these evasions, hath invented another for himself; and pretends that the apostle is speaking not of the offices of divine service, nor yet of the public reading of the scriptures, but only of certain spiritual songs and canticles. What, however, or what sort of things these were, or why they required to be recited in a known language more than the common prayers or the scripture lessons, it is not so easy to understand. But of this place of the apostle, and this new pretence of Bellarmine's, we have discoursed sufficiently at large in the second question, chap. 18, of this controversy.

So again, (Lib. III. cap. 2) where he is answering an objection drawn from St Peter's calling the prophetic word a lamp, he does not answer, as Hosius did (Lib. III. contra Proleg. Brentii), that in the prophecies there are many things plain, and that what is enigmatically spoken in the prophets is expressed clearly in the gospel; but he says that prophecy is called a lamp, not because it is easily understood, but because it illuminates when it *is* understood. He saw clearly that Hosius' exposition left our doctrine of the perspicuity of scripture in sufficient strength, and therefore excogitated this new one; upon which we have treated, Quest. iv. chap. 4.

In the same way, when we maintain that the mysteries of the faith should be concealed from no one, and allege, in proof, those words of Christ, " What ye hear in the ear, that proclaim ye upon the house-tops;" Bellarmine, (Lib. iv. c. 12) has recourse to a strange and hitherto, I think, unheard of interpretation;— *that is,* says he, *if need so require.* He gives the allegation no other reply whatever; and how proper and apposite an answer this is, I am content that others should determine.

Again, when we urge that the scripture is called canonical, and therefore is, what that very appellation indicates, the rule of faith and of living; Bellarmine answers confidently in the same chapter, that the scripture was not published to be the rule of our faith, but to serve "as a sort of commonitory, useful to preserve and cherish the faith received by preaching." So that, according to this new interpretation of Bellarmine's, we learn that the scriptures are no rule of faith at all, but a certain commonitory,—an honour which they share with many others;—nor yet even a *necessary* one, but only *useful* to the end of preserving the traditions. This is a noble judgment of the value of scripture, and altogether worthy of a Jesuit!—a judgment which leaves the bible only the office of admonishing us, as if we only required to be admonished, and not taught.

Bellarmine hath innumerable such new discoveries; with which he defends the papal cause in a different manner, indeed, from that of its former patrons, but yet is so far from really serving it, that he hath rather done it the greater damage and injury with discreet and attentive readers, who have any care for their faith and religion. For hence it appears that, while Bellarmine cannot approve the answers of others, it is impossible to invent new ones, which are not worse than the old.

I remember, too, that in the course of that same conversation between us, I allowed Bellarmine the merit of dealing less dishonestly with the testimonies of the fathers than is customary with others, and of not captiously or maliciously perverting the state of the question; a fault which, I found, had particularly disgusted you in certain writers; whereas religious disputes and controversies should be managed in such a way as to eschew all craft, and seek truth, and truth alone, with a holy earnestness. I acknowledged that, while our adversaries erred grossly in this respect, our own party stood not so wholly clear of the same fault, as became the investigators of truths so sacred; which, in proportion as they are more heavenly in their nature, and concern us more nearly, should be searched into and handled with so much the more sincerity.

But, since many—more eager for contention than for truth— propose to themselves scarcely any other object than to be able to say something against their opponents, and to be esteemed the champions of a cause, which they love much better than they understand ; so it comes to pass, that the just state of the question is laid aside with a cold neglect, and truth, as usual, is lost in altercation.   Thus Bellarmine himself, where he undertakes to impugn our doctrine of the perspicuity of scripture (Lib. III. c. 1), lays this down as the state of the question, " Whether scripture be so plain in itself as to be sufficient, without any explication, to determine controversies of faith ;" and he imposes upon us the office of maintaining that the scriptures are in themselves most plain and easy, and stand in need of no interpretation :—as if we either thought that every part of scripture was plain, easy, and clear, or ever rejected the exposition and interpretation of the scriptures ! Could Bellarmine really hope to impose upon us in so gross a manner, as to make us confess *that* to be our opinion which had never so much as entered into our thoughts ?   But to this we have given a sufficiently plain answer in our fourth question.

I could wish that this were the only place in which Bellarmine had shewn bad faith, and that he had not elsewhere also played the Jesuit in matters of no small importance.   For there can be no end of writing and disputing, no decision of controversies, no concord amongst Christians, until, laying aside all party feelings, and assuming the most impartial desire and design of investigating truth, we apply ourselves entirely to that point where the stress of the controversy lies.

And now (since I am addressing one who is accustomed both to think of these matters often and seriously himself, and to listen to others delivering their own opinions upon them also), allow me briefly to explain, and commend to your consideration, a thing which I have long wished for, and which I trust might be accomplished with singular advantage and with no great difficulty. Our adversaries have very often demanded a disputation, and declared that they especially wish and long for permission to hold

a scholastical contest with us upon the subject of those questions
which form the matter of our present controversies.   Whether this
demand be made hypocritically, as many suppose, or sincerely, I,
for my part, would desire that they may have their asking.   For,
although they cannot deny that they have often been disputed
with in Germany, France, and England, nay, that those learned
men Melancthon and Brentius repaired to Trent for the sole purpose
of defending the confessions of their churches against the Popish
theologians; yet I would have them made to understand, that they
have no reason for believing that their cause hath become one
whit the better, since it hath been espoused by its Jesuit patrons,
than it was heretofore, when defended by the ancient orders.   Let
the Jesuits be allowed acute, ready, practised, eloquent, and full of
resources; let them be, in a word, whatever they are, or are believed to be: yet truth is ever one and the same; and still, the
more it is attacked, shines out with greater brilliancy and lustre.
Perhaps, indeed, it will be said that none can be found who would
dare to stand a conflict with the Jesuits, or are fit to be matched
with such opponents.   I know well, for my part, how confident and
boastful these men are, and what a look and mien they assume
in disputation; as if they had only learned how most arrogantly
to despise their adversaries, not how to give a better answer to
their arguments.   Yet, since the sacred laws of such conferences
secure to each man just so much advantage, and no more, as he
can win by reason and argument, and whatever is said must be
reduced to the rules of Syllogism; there remains no ground to fear
that painted falsehood will prevail more than simple and naked
truth.   Not to speak of foreign nations and churches, where every
one knows that there is abundance of learned men, this island itself
possesses persons well skilled in every kind of learning, who could
readily, not only explain the truth, but defend it also against any
adversaries.   In both our Universities there are men so practised
and skilled in every portion of these controversies, that they would
rather forfeit their recognisance, than shrink from a dispute so
honourable, just, and necessary.

Nor do I see that any so great inconvenience is to be apprehended from this course, as some suspect. For, although those who are bound to this cause by a blind superstition, will probably be so far from reaping any advantage, that they will rather be rendered still more obstinate, and some fickle people will, perhaps, be even alienated from our side; as, in every disputation, opinions incline different ways, according as the several auditors are capable of judging or inclined to attend and reflect;—yet, we may reasonably augur the following important results: First, it would easily appear, what is the true state of the question in each controversy; which should be pressed, driven home, and discussed, without regard to impertinent and trifling altercations. In the next place, it cannot be doubted, that all who measured religion, not by the decrees of men or their own caprice, but by the standard of the holy scriptures, and were ready to acknowledge and embrace the truth when it was found, would easily reject the rotten devices of the papists, and prefer that sound and wholesome doctrine of the faith, which our churches have drawn from the pure springs of scripture, to their old and idle superstition. Lastly, the wishes of our adversaries would be satisfied; nor could they any longer, with any shew of probability, reproach us openly with cowardice. Yea, the truth itself, which we profess, would rise above the suspicion which it has incurred in the minds of some, and establish itself in the light and conscience of all the world. There is nothing which truth fears so much as to be prevented from appearing in public, and being exposed to the examination of all men. It would rather have any patron that is not absolutely dumb, than go without defence from the unrighteous calumnies of unjust accusers. One thing only I would have carefully provided. Prudent and grave moderators should preside in this disputation; who should restrain petulance, repress clamours, permit no breach of decorum, and maintain order, modesty and discipline. I have now laid before you my thoughts and wishes. The determination rests with those who are at the helm of church and state;—with yourself especially, in regard of that singular wisdom which hath ever distinguished you in every judgment and deliberation. I now return to Bellarmine.

I am rejoiced that these controversies of his, so much celebrated in common report, have now been published by himself; so as that we all may easily judge of their quality, their value, their strength, and their importance, nor believe Bellarmine to be any other than we find him by their evidence. And, although our adversaries' opinions might be collected from the many other writers who have appeared in great numbers on the same side; yet, since there are many points upon which they do not all agree, it hath been a matter of some obscurity hitherto, to ascertain the real judgment of the Roman church. But now that Bellarmine hath been published, we shall know better and more certainly what it is they hold upon every subject, the arguments on which they specially rely, and what is (so to speak) the very marrow of popery, which is thought to be as much in the Jesuits as in the pope himself. Knowing, therefore, how much our party desire that these Jesuits should be answered, and having fallen in with a manuscript copy of Bellarmine's Lectures, I thought it worth my while to handle these same controversies in the schools in the discharge of the duties of my office, to discuss the new sophisms of the Jesuits, and vindicate our unadulterated truth from the captious cavils with which the popish professor had entangled it. Afterwards, being often requested by many persons to publish some of my disputations against our adversaries, and let the whole church share in the benefit of my toil and studies, I determined to commit to the press this controversy concerning SCRIPTURE, which is the first of them; and which, forming, as it does, a sort of vestibule to the rest, and sufficing of itself to fill a reasonable volume, seemed, as it were, to demand that I should not wait until I had completed the remainder, but publish it by itself, and separate from all the others.

In all this I did nothing without the approbation of the most reverend father, the archbishop of Canterbury,—a man of the greatest wisdom and the greatest learning, who, having read and thoroughly considered this whole controversy, declared it worthy of publication. Now that it is published, I dedicate it to you, most noble Cecil, whom I have ever esteemed the great patron and Mæcenas of my studies; you, in whom this college prides herself as a member of her body, and will always, as long as she stands, challenge to herself on this account a just prerogative ; you, whom our university respects as chancellor ; whom the whole state celebrates as the father of your country ; whom the church recognises as a son serviceable both to its interest and safety.   I pray God that he may preserve you ever in safety and prosperity to our church, state, university, and college.   Farewell.

Your most devoted servant,

WILLIAM WHITAKER.

CAMBRIDGE.   From the College of St John
   the Evangelist.   *April* 30, 1588.

PREFACE TO THE CONTROVERSIES,

DELIVERED

TO THE AUDIENCE AT CAMBRIDGE.

I THIS day enter upon a new undertaking, often demanded by many and not unworthy of our university, the attempt to go through those controversies, both numerous and great, as ye all perceive, which are agitated between the Roman popish synagogue and our churches reformed according to the word of God. Accustomed as I have hitherto been to handle a sedate quiet kind of theology, I here come suddenly upon the sternest strifes and most violent contentions. I hope that this will appear matter of surprise or censure to none of you; at least I should desire that the object of my intentions and design should meet with approbation from you all. For I have not been led to this undertaking through any rashness, or unreasonable and fickle impulses and movement of my feelings, through disgust of old subjects to look out for new ones; but have proceeded with thought and deliberation, and not without the authority and encouragement of those who have the greatest influence in our church and university. Upon these grounds, I am confident that I shall undertake the task upon which I am now entering, not only without blame from any one, but with the highest satisfaction to all except the papists: which consideration inspires me with still greater alacrity for these controversies, although I am by no means ignorant that the toil which I shall have to undergo in managing them is at the same time increased and doubled. But for your interests I should willingly do anything, and spare no labour which I can perform. Indeed, if I wished to indulge myself, or had any concern for my own leisure, I should never have launched out upon this most stormy sea of controversies, in which I shall be exposed to such a tossing as I have never yet experienced in fulfilling the duties of my office, and where all the diligence must be applied, which is required by a business of the highest difficulty. But since our undertaking is both noble and necessary, and long and earnestly desired by you, it did not become me to balk your desires on account of the trouble of the task, but to lay out for the common good whatever strength and ability I may possess.

Now of this discourse I perceive that the utility, or rather the necessity, is three-fold. In the first place, we have to treat not of the opinions of philosophers, which one may either be ignorant of, or refute with commendation,—not of the forms of the lawyers, in which one may err without damage,—not of the institutions of physicians, of the nature and cure of diseases, wherein only our bodily health is concerned,—not of any slight or trivial matters; —but here the matter of our dispute is certain controversies of religion, and those of the last importance, in which whosoever errs is deceived to the eternal destruction of his soul. In a word, we have to speak of the sacred scriptures, of the nature of the church, of the sacraments, of righteousness, of Christ, of the fundamentals of the faith; all which are of that nature, that if one be shaken, nothing can remain sound in the whole fabric of religion. If what these men teach be true, we are in a miserable condition; we are involved in infinite errors of the grossest kind, and cannot possibly be saved. But if, as I am fully persuaded and convinced, it is they who are in error, they cannot deny that they are justly condemned if they still persist in their errors. For if one heresy be sufficient to entail destruction, what hope can be cherished for those who defend so many heresies with such obstinate pertinacity? Therefore either they must perish, or we. It is impossible that we can both be safe, where our assertions and belief are so contradictory. Since this is so, it behoves us all to bestow great pains and diligence in acquiring a thorough knowledge of these matters, where error is attended with such perils.

Besides, there is another reason which renders the handling of these controversies at the present time not only useful, but even necessary. The papists, who are our adversaries, have long since performed this task; they have done that which we are now only beginning to do. And although they can never get the better of us in argument, they have nevertheless got before us in time. They have two professors in two of their colleges, Stapleton at Douay, Allen at Rheims, both countrymen of ours, (besides other doctors in other academies,) who have explained many controversies and published books, Stapleton on the Church and Justification, Allen on the Sacraments. But beyond them all, in the largeness wherewith he hath treated these controversies, is Robert Bellarmine, the Jesuit at Rome, whose lectures are passed from hand to hand, and diligently transcribed and read by very many. Indeed I should wish that they were published, and am surprised that they are not. But many copies of these lectures fly about everywhere among the papists, and sometimes, in spite of their precautions, fall into our hands. Shall we then, whilst these men defend their own side with such activity and zeal, lie idle and think nothing of the matter? These things, although they were in a fragmentary manner explained by the papists, in many commentaries and separate books, yet are now handled in one single volume by themselves; the object and design of which proceeding cannot possibly be a secret to any one. Why then should not we do the same, and put a complete body of controversies into men's hands, collecting and compacting into one book whatever hath been disputed in defence of the truth against popery, by writers of our own or of any other party? It is not every one that can at once form a judgment of an argument, or find out a fitting reply in the books of our divines. We must take measures for the security of these persons, and especially at the present time, when so many, partly by the reading of such books as are every day published by our adversaries, partly by too great a familiarity with papists, have fallen under a deplorable calamity, and deserted from us to the popish camp.

Indeed, when I compare our side with the papists, I easily perceive the great truth of Christ's saying, that " the children of this world are in their generation wiser than the children of light." Mark well, I beseech you, with what solicitude, vigilance, and cunning, these men maintain their own kingdom! They prevent their people from reading our books, and forbid them to have any intercourse with us, that so they may provide against the influence of that contagion which they fear. Surely this is wisely done. Who can deny it? For if we be heretics, as they, though falsely, exclaim, it is but a just consequence of that opinion of us to denounce us, as persons to be carefully avoided by all who are under their control. In the meanwhile we buy, read, peruse all the productions of those whom we justly esteem heretics, and never suspect the possibility of any damage accruing from our conduct. Hence unskilful persons are easily deceived; especially if there be any encourager at hand to lend an impulse, as there are at present everywhere too many. We avoid the acquaintance of no one; yea, we take a pleasure in conversing with papists. This is all well, if your aim and desire be to reclaim them from their errors, and if you are able to do this, and see that there is any hope of them remaining. Those who are perverse and desperate should be left to themselves; you can do them no service, and they may do you much damage. I commend courtesy in every one, specially in an academic or man of letters; but courtesy should not be so intent upon its duties towards men as to forget piety and its duty towards God. Bellarmine compares heresy to the plague, and rightly. For the plague does not hang about the outward limbs, but attacks the heart, immediately poisons it with its venom, and suddenly destroys him who but a little before was in health; then it spreads a fatal contagion to others also, and often pervades a whole family, sometimes fills the state itself with corpses and funerals. In like manner heresy especially assails the heart, and expels faith from the mind; then creeps further and diffuses itself over many. If then you tender your salvation, approach not near so deadly a pestilence without an antidote or counterpoison. Speaking of Alexander the coppersmith, Paul gives this admonition, 2 Tim. iv. 5, " Of whom be thou ware also ;" and subjoins as the reason of this caution, " for he hath greatly withstood our words." Those, therefore, who not only cherish in their own minds a perverse opinion in religion, but cry out against and oppose sound doctrine, and resist it to the utmost of their power, with such persons it is perilous and impious to live on pleasant and familiar terms. For, as the same apostle elsewhere directs, Tit. iii. 10, " A man that is a heretic, after the first and second admonition, must be avoided. For he is subverted, and sins against his own conscience, and is condemned by his own judgment." Tertullian, in his Prescriptions against heretics, declares that heresy should be " avoided as a deadly fever." Now " fever," says he[1], " as is well known, we regard as an evil, in respect both of its cause and its power, with abomination rather than with admiration; and, as far as we can, strive to avoid it, not having its extinction in our own power. But heresies inflict eternal death, and the burning of a still intenser fire." And Cyprian, Epist. 40[2], " Fly far from the contagion of

[1 Febrem ut malum, et de causa et potentia sua, ut notum est, abominamur potius quam miramur, et quantum in nobis est præcavemus, non habentes abolitionem ejus in nostra potestate: hæreses vero mortem æternam et majoris ignis ardorem inferent. Præscript. Hæret. c. ii.]

[2 i. e. in Pamelius' edition : but in Fell's (Amstel. 1691) Ep. xliii. p. 82. The words are: Procul ab hujusmodi hominum contagione discedite, et ser-

such men, and shun by flight their discourses as a canker or a
pestilence; since the Lord hath forewarned us, saying, 'They are
blind, and leaders of the blind.'" Similar to this is the admonition
of Jerome, in his Epistle to Pammachius and Oceanus: " Beware,
reader, of reading: fly the viper[1]." Thus it behoves us to fly as
poisonous vipers, not only the discourse, but the books and letters
of heretical persons. For, as Ambrose says in his 80th Epistle,
heretics "shed forth the speech of serpentine discourse, and,
turning catholic truth into the madness of their own doctrine,
traduce it after the example of the devil, and deceive the simplicity
of the sheep[2]." If this be true at any time, surely we have felt it
true of the papists in our time. But let us return to the tenor of
our present discourse.

Besides the advantages of this task already enumerated this
should be added, in the third place, that, when a fixed method of
controversies hath been handled and explained by us, you will be
enabled to set down and assign to its proper place and division
whatever you may read yourselves in the books of ancient or later
divines of any pertinence to these subjects, or whatever arguments
against the papists may be suggested by your private meditations.
Many things escape us in the course of our reading or reflexion,
from our not knowing to what head they should be referred; and
many are ill arranged, so that, although we have noted them down,
yet they do not readily present themselves at the proper time. But
when every thing is duly distributed in meet order, it will be easy both
to copy what we please in its appropriate place, and to find it there
again whenever we chance to have occasion. And perhaps, in this
first essay of ours, some things will be omitted—(though we shall
endeavour not to seem to omit many things and those of principal
importance)—but if any thing be omitted, it will claim its own
place, and (as it were) its proper receptacle, when our work passes
under a second review.

And since the new popery, which in general may be called
Jesuitism, differs widely from the old, and the former scholastic

mones eorum velut cancer et pestem fugiendo vitate, præmonente Domino et
dicente, Cæci sunt et cæcorum duces.]

[1 Cave, Lector, ne legas; fuge viperam.]

[2 Sermonem serpentinæ disputationis effundunt, atque veritatem catho-
licam vertendo ad suæ doctrinæ rabiem diabolico more traducunt, atque
ovium simplicitatem defraudant.]

divinity delivered many things much otherwise than they are now maintained by the Roman church; we must, lest we should seem to construe the doctrines of the papists otherwise than the practice of the Roman church requires, or to take for granted what they grant not, or to ascribe to them opinions which they disclaim, take care to follow this order, namely, first to inquire what the council of Trent hath determined upon every question, and then to consult the Jesuits, the most faithful interpreters of that council, and other divines, and our countrymen at Rheims amongst the rest. And since Bellarmine hath handled these questions with accuracy and method, and his lectures are in every body's hands, we will make him, so to speak, our principal aim, and follow, as it were, in his very footsteps.

Our arms shall be the sacred scriptures, that sword and shield of the word, that tower of David, upon which a thousand bucklers hang, and all the armour of the mighty, the sling and the pebbles of the brook wherewith David stretched upon the ground that gigantic and haughty Philistine. Human reasonings and testimonies, if one use them too much or out of place, are like the armour of Saul, which was so far from helping David that it rather unfitted him for the conflict. Jerome tells Theophilus of Alexandria, that " a sincere faith and open confession requires not the artifice and arguments of words[3]." However, since we have to deal with adversaries who, not content with these arms, use others with more readiness and pleasure, such as decrees of councils, judgments of the fathers, tradition, and the practice of the church; lest perchance we should appear to shrink from the battle, we have determined to make use of that sort of weapons also. And, indeed, I hope to make it plain to you, that all our tenets are not only founded upon scriptural authority, which is enough to ensure victory, but command the additional suffrage of the testimonies of fathers, councils, and, I will add, even of many of the papists, which is a distinguished and splendid ornament of our triumph. In every controversy, therefore, after the sacred scriptures of the old and new Testaments, we shall apply to the councils, the fathers, and even to our adversaries themselves; so as to let you perceive that not only the ancient authors, but even the very adherents of the Roman church, may be adduced as witnesses in the cause. Thus it will be clear, that what Jerome, Epist. 139, applies out of Isaiah to the

[3 Fides pura et aperta confessio non quærit strophas et argumenta verborum. Epist. lxii. ad Theophil.]

heretics, that "they weave the spider's thread," is pertinently applied to the papists. For, as Jerome says, they weave a web[1] " which can catch small and light animals, as flies and gnats, but is broken by the stronger ones." Just thus many stick fast in the subtleties of the papists, as flies do in the spider's web, from which they are unable to extricate themselves, though nothing can possibly be frailer than those threads. Such are the reasonings of the papists, even the Jesuits themselves ; who, although they seem to spin their threads with greater skill and artfulness, yet fabricate nothing but such cobwebs as may easily be broken by any vigorous effort. Be ye, therefore, of good cheer. We have a cause, believe me, good, firm, invincible. We fight against men, and we have Christ on our side ; nor can we possibly be vanquished, unless we are the most slothful and dastardly of all cowards. Once wrest from the papists what they adduce beside the scripture, and you will presently see them wavering, turning pale, and unable to keep their ground. Yet I do not ascribe to myself all those gifts of genius, judgment, memory and knowledge, which are demanded by such a laborious and busy undertaking. I know well and acknowledge how slightly I am furnished with such endowments ; nor can any think so meanly of me as myself. But " I can do all things through Christ who strengtheneth me ;" relying upon whose assistance I enter upon the combat. They come against us with sword, and shield, and armour : we go against them in the name of Jehovah of Hosts, of the armies of Israel, whom they have defied.

But it is now time to distribute the controversies themselves under their proper heads, that we may see beforehand the order in which we are to proceed. Bellarmine hath reduced all the controversies to three articles of the Creed ;—*I believe in the Catholic Church, the Communion of Saints, the Forgiveness of Sins.* In this respect I shall not follow Bellarmine. I have another, and more certain, plan and method of my own. He could not frame to his method the controversy concerning scripture, which assuredly challenges the first place for its nobility and importance. He therefore calls it *a Proem,* and says that he hath set it before the rest in the manner of a preface. But since popery is nothing else but mere antichristianism, it is evident that both must fall under the same rule and method, and that popery must have in it all the

[1 Quæ parva et levia capere potest animalia, ut muscas et culices, a fortioribus statim rumpitur. Epist. cxxxix. ad Cyprianum.]

heresies which belong to antichristianism. Now antichristianism consists not in the open and outward denial of Christ, or in the worn-out defence of obsolete heresies. For who would not immediately recognise, cry out against and explode, the patrons of Cerinthus, Valentinus, Arius, Nestorius, and other heresiarchs of the same complexion? Who could tolerate amongst Christians him who should openly and publicly deny Christ? Antichrist was not so stupid as to hope that he would gain much by such a course as this. It was not fit, therefore, that antichrist should hold those errors which may be generally described as touching the nature of God, the mystery of the Trinity, the person of Christ. But, since antichrist must needs be the opposite of Christ, the same purpose must be gained in a more secret and more artful manner. For it is a certain mystery of iniquity, which in words establishes Christ, but in fact destroys him. This is the very antichristianism of the papists, who leave indeed the natures of Christ intact, but make away with the offices of Christ, and consequently Christ himself. For Jesus cannot be Christ, if he bear not all his offices and merits. Now these offices and benefits are designated by the very names CHRIST and JESUS. All the heresies of the papists (a very few excepted, which relate to his person,) concern these offices and merits of Christ: on which account it will be no inconvenient distribution of the popish errors and heresies, to set them forth as they are tenets opposed to Christ and Jesus.

Survey now, I beseech you, this whole body of antichristianism, as I shall submit it to your inspection, that you may see, as it were in one view, a monster mis-shapen, vast, horrible, and manifold. For I will present to you the very portraiture and lineaments, drawn out and expressed as it were with one stroke of the pencil; and afterwards distribute and describe its limbs more accurately, when we come to speak severally of each. The name of CHRIST denotes three offices, as you know, of *Prophet, King,* and *Priest.* That of JESUS sets before us the benefits of redemption and salvation; and these latter benefits result from the former offices. For he was anointed to be our Prophet, King, and Priest, in order that he might discharge the function of our Saviour. Now, therefore, we should regard in Christ Jesus his offices and merits as well as his person. In the former the papists are wholly astray: in regard of his person they hold not many errors, but they have some. There are then two chief heads of these controversies; concerning the offices and benefits of Christ Jesus, and concerning his person.

Hear, therefore, what particular heresies they maintain against Christ Jesus.

The first office is that of PROPHET, which shews that the function of supreme teacher is to be ascribed to Christ. This saving teaching Christ hath proposed to his church in the scriptures. In defending this office of Christ against the papists we handle these controversies concerning the scriptures; of the number of the canonical books of scripture; of vernacular versions of scripture; of the perspicuity of scripture; of the authority of scripture; of the interpretation of scripture; of the perfection of scripture in opposition to human traditions, upon which our adversaries lay such weighty stress as to equal them even to the scriptures themselves. How far from slight this controversy is, you readily perceive.

The second office of Christ is the ROYAL, which all the heretical opinions of the papists concerning the church impugn. The kingdom of Christ is the church; in it he reigns and is sole monarch. This controversy is complex, and requires to be distributed into its several parts. The church is either militant or triumphant. We must dispute first of the militant, and afterwards of the triumphant church. Our controversies concern either the whole church militant, or the members of it. Of the whole— what it is; of what sort; whether visible; by what notes distinguished; whether it may err; what power it possesses; whether the Roman be the true visible church of Christ. Next, we have to speak of the members of the church. These members are either collected in a council (which is the representative church), or considered separately. Here, therefore, we must treat of councils; whether they must needs be assembled; by whom they should be convoked; of what persons they should consist; what authority they have; who should be the chief president in a council; whether they are above the pope; whether they may err. Next, we come to the several members of the church. Now they are divided into three classes. There is the principal member, or head, the intermediate members, and the lowest. They affirm the Roman pontiff to be the head of the church militant: whereupon the question arises of the form of the church's government; whether it be, or be not, monarchical; whether the monarchy of the church was settled upon Peter; whether Peter was bishop of the church of Rome, and died there; whether the pope succeeds Peter in his primacy; whether he may err; whether he can make laws ecclesiastical; whether he can canonize saints; whether he hath temporal power; whether he be antichrist. The intermediate members are the clergy, of whom they make two sorts, some secular, some regular. Those are called secular, who are engaged in any ecclesiastical function. Now here arise controversies concerning the election and rank of these persons, whether celibacy be necessarily attached to the ministry, whether ministers be exempt from the secular yoke. The regulars are monks and members of religious orders. Here we have to discourse of evangelical counsels, of vows, of retirement, of the dress and labours of monks, of the canonical hours. The lowest members, as they arrange them, are laymen, even kings or emperors. Here we have to inquire concerning the civil magistracy; whether the care of religion appertains to the civil magistrate; whether he may punish heretics capitally; whether he can ever be excommunicated or deposed by the pope; whether civil laws oblige the conscience. And so far of the church militant.

Next follows the church triumphant; which consists of angels and deceased saints. The controversies are, of the hierarchies, ministry, and invocation of angels. When we come to deceased saints, the occasion requires us to dispute, of the *limbus patrum,* of purgatory; whether saints are to be invoked and adored, of the relics of saints, of the worship of images, of the temples of the saints, of their festivals, of pilgrimages to their places: and these controversies are concerning the royal office of Christ.

His third office is that of PRIEST, which includes two functions, intercession and sacrifice. It pertains to intercession to inquire, whether Christ be the sole mediator of intercession. In the question of sacrifice, we shall have to explain the whole body of controversy concerning the sacraments; for by the sacraments, as so many means instituted by Christ, the efficacy of that sacrifice is derived to us. We must treat of sacraments, first generally, and then specially: generally, what a sacrament is, how many sacraments there be, what is the efficacy of the sacraments, what the distinction between the old and new sacraments: specially, concerning each of the sacraments by itself; and first, of baptism, whether those who die without baptism cannot be saved; whether laymen or women can baptize; whether John's baptism was the same as Christ's; whether the popish ceremonies are to be used in the administration of baptism. After the sacrament of baptism, we have to speak of the eucharist, which topic contains most important controversies, of transubstantiation, of the sacrifice of the mass, of communion in one kind. Next follow the five sacraments of the papists, upon which great controversies depend, of confirmation, of penance (where we shall have to treat of contrition, confession, satisfaction, indulgences), of extreme unction, of orders, of matrimony; and all these controversies hitherto set forth belong to those three prime offices, which are signified by the name of CHRIST.

Next we have to handle controversies concerning the benefits of our redemption and salvation, which are indicated by the very name of JESUS. Here first arise questions concerning predestination and reprobation; whether God hath predestinated or reprobated any persons, on what account he hath done so, whether predestination be absolute. Next we have to treat of sin, what it is, how manifold, whether all are born with the infection of original sin, even the virgin Mary; whether all sins be equal; whether any sin be venial of itself; whether concupiscence after baptism be sin; whether God be the author of sin. Next in order, we must speak of the law, whether it can be fulfilled, and even more done than it commands. Afterwards we must explain the controversy concerning free-will; faith, what it is and how manifold; good works and merits; justification.

In the last place, there remain a few questions concerning the person of Christ, as whether he is αὐτόθεος; whether he increased in wisdom; whether he suffered in his soul the pains of hell, and whatever others there be of this sort.

You have now the principal classes and heads of those controversies which are contested with the greatest earnestness between us and our adversaries at the present day. You see almost the whole mass and body of the popish heresies. In considering, revolving, and explicating these matters it becomes us now to be wholly occupied. We must begin from the first, and proceed through the intermediate to the last, at which we hope at length to arrive, and pray that the issue may correspond to our hope and wishes.

THE FIRST CONTROVERSY.

QUESTION I.

CHAPTER I.

WHEREIN THIS WHOLE CONTROVERSY IS DISTRIBUTED INTO ITS PARTICULAR QUESTIONS.

WE will lay the foundation of this controversy in those words of Christ which are to be found in the fifth chapter of St John's Gospel at the thirty-ninth verse : Ἐρευνᾶτε τὰς γραφὰς, SEARCH THE SCRIPTURES. Christ had been commended to the Jews by the testimony of John the Baptist. That testimony was most true and honourable; and could not be despised by the Jews themselves, amongst whom John lived in the highest respect and estimation. Yet Christ declares that he had others greater, more certain and more august than the testimony of John. He enumerates three of them : first, the works which he performed ; secondly, his Father who had sent him ; thirdly, the holy scriptures themselves, which he calls his witnesses. The Jews, indeed, thought honourably of the scriptures, and supposed that eternal life might be found in them. Nor does Christ blame in the least that judgment of theirs concerning the scriptures, but rather praises it. He bids them go on to " search the scriptures ;" he inflames in every way their zeal for the scriptures, and sharpens their industry. For he exhorts them not only to read, but search and thoroughly examine the scriptures : he would not have them content with a slight perusal, but requires an assiduous, keen, laborious diligence in examining and investigating their meaning, such as those apply who search with anxious toil for treasures buried in the earth.

Now since Christ hath bid us search the scriptures without exception, not this part, or that part, or the other, it is manifest that in these words we are commanded to search the whole of scripture ; not to confine ourselves to certain portions of it, while we despise or overlook the rest. All parts give plain testimony to Christ. But the scriptures are praised by the papists, as well as highly esteemed by us; nor is there any controversy, whether the scriptures are to be searched. But concerning the due manner of searching them, and who they are to whom that care appertains, and concerning the scriptures themselves, which we all unanimously affirm should be searched, there is a most important controversy, which I shall now attempt to explain. In order to effect this clearly and methodically, I think it may be all divided into six questions, after the following manner.

We are commanded to search the scriptures: and for that purpose we must first understand, what are those genuine books of scripture, in searching and turning over which it behoves us to be occupied. The first question therefore shall be, *Of the number of the canonical books of scripture.*

We are commanded to search the scriptures: and therefore we must next consider, to whom this precept is addressed; whether only to the learned, and those skilled in the ancient languages, or to all the faithful. The second question therefore shall be, *Of versions of the scripture and sacred rites in the vulgar tongue.*

We are commanded to search the scriptures: whence it appears that the scriptures enjoy a very high dignity and authority, since Christ himself appeals and refers us to them. The third question therefore shall be, *Of the authority of scripture;* whether it have this so great credibility and dignity of itself, and from the Holy Ghost its author, or from the testimony of the church.

We are commanded to search the scriptures: whence some hope appears to be shewn that we shall come to understand them, and gain much profit by the search, if we do as we are commanded. Therefore the fourth question shall be, *Of the perspicuity of scripture.*

We are commanded to search the scripture; that is, to seek and investigate the true sense of scripture, since the scripture lies wholly in the meaning. Therefore the fifth question shall be, *Of the interpretation of scripture;* how it is to be interpreted, and who has the right and authority of interpretation.

We are commanded to search the scripture: and under the name of scripture the written word of God is plainly understood. Here then we must consider whether we are only bound to search the scripture, or whether, beside the scripture, something else be commended to our investigations. Therefore the sixth and last question shall be, *Of the perfection of scripture;* which I shall prove to be so absolutely complete that we should wholly acquiesce in it, and need desire nothing more, and that unwritten traditions are by no means necessary for us.

These questions I purpose to treat in the order in which I have proposed them.

CHAPTER II.

CONCERNING THE STATE OF THE FIRST QUESTION.

THE books of scripture are called *canonical*, because they contain the standard and rule of our faith and morals. For the scripture is in the church what the law is in a state, which Aristotle in his Politics calls a canon or rule. As all citizens are bound to live and behave agreeably to the public laws, so Christians should square their faith and conduct by the rule and law of scripture. So, in Eusebius[1], the holy fathers accuse Paul of Samosata of departing from the rule (ἀποστὰς ἀπὸ τοῦ κανόνος), and becoming the author of an heretical opinion. So Tertullian, in his book against Hermogenes[2], calls the scripture the rule of faith; and Cyprian says, in his discourse upon the baptism of Christ: "One will find that the rules of all doctrine are derived from this scripture; and that, whatever the discipline of the church contains springs hence, and returns hither[3]." Chrysostom too, in his 13th

[1 ὅπου δὲ ἀποστὰς τοῦ κανόνος ἐπὶ κίβδηλα καὶ νόθα διδάγματα μετελή-λυθεν, οὐδὲν δεῖ τοῦ ἔξω ὄντος τὰς πράξεις κρίνειν. H. E. VII. 30. T. 3. p. 391. ed. Heinich. Lips. 1828. But it is most probably the Creed that is there meant.]

[2 Whitaker most probably refers to the famous passage, c. xxii. "Adoro plenitudinem scripturæ," &c. cited below, Qu. 6. c. xvi., and produced also by Cosin (Scholastical History of the Canon, chap. i. §. 1.) in proof that the Church always regarded scripture as "the infallible RULE of our FAITH." Some, however, suppose that Tertullian refers to scripture, and not the Creed, in these words: "Solemus hæreticis compendii gratia de posteritate præscribere: in quantum enim *veritatis regula* prior, quæ etiam *futuras hæreses prænuntiavit*, in tantum posteriores quæque doctrinæ hæreses præjudicabuntur." Adv. Hermog. i. (*Opp.* P. IV. p. 1. ed. Leopold. Lipsiæ, 1841.) For the Creed contains no prediction of heresies.]

[3 This treatise, falsely ascribed to Cyprian, may be found in the works of Arnold of Chartres (Carnotensis) subjoined to Fell's Cyprian (Amstel. 1691). The passage cited is at p. 33 : "Inveniet ex hac scriptura omnium doctrina-

Homily upon 2 Corinthians calls scripture the exact balance, and standard, and rule of all things." For the same reason Augustine affirms, that "whatever belongs to faith and moral life may be found in the scriptures[1];" and he calls the scripture *the scales*, in the following passage: "Let us not apply deceitful scales, where we may weigh what we wish, and as we wish; but let us bring God's own scales from the holy scriptures," &c.

So Basil calls the sacred doctrine "the canon of rectitude and rule of truth," which fails in no part of perfection: and Ruffinus, in his exposition of the creed, after enumerating the books of scripture, adds, "These are the books which the fathers included in the canon, and from which they willed that the assertions of our faith should be demonstrated[2];" and then he subjoins: "From these fountains of the divine word our cups are to be drawn[3]." Aquinas too lays down, that "the doctrine of the apostles and prophets is called canonical, because it is, as it were, the rule of our intellect[4]." Hence it plainly appears why the scriptures are called *canonical ;*—because they prescribe to us what we must believe, and how we ought to live: so that we should refer to this test our whole faith and life, as the mason or architect squares his work by the line and plummet. Hence, too, we may perceive that the scripture is perfect, since otherwise the title of canon or rule could hardly be applied to it; upon which point we shall have to speak under the sixth question.

Now these books, which are called canonical, are comprised in the old and new Testaments, and are therefore styled *Testamentary.* So Eusebius calls these books ἐνδιαθήκους[5]; and Nicephorus often uses the same term. Some also call them διαθηκο-

---

rum regulas emanasse; et hinc nasci, et huc reverti, quidquid ecclesiastica continet disciplina." But Arnold is not speaking of the whole scripture, but of the command to love God.]

[1 See these passages cited more fully below. Qu. 6. c. 16.]

[2 Hæc sunt quæ patres intra canonem concluserunt; ex quibus fidei nostræ assertiones constare voluerunt. Ad Calc. Opp. Cypriani, p. 26, ut supra.]

[3 Hæc nobis a patribus, ut dixi, tradita opportunum visum est hoc in loco designare, ad instructionem eorum qui prima sibi ecclesiæ ac fidei elementa suscipiunt, ut sciant ex quibus sibi fontibus verbi Dei haurienda sint pocula. Ibid. p. 27.]

[4 Doctrina apostolorum et prophetarum canonica dicitur, quia est quasi regula intellectus nostri. Thomæ Aquin. in 1 Tim. vi. Lect. 1.]

[5 H. E. Lib. v. c. 25. οὐκ ἐνδιαθήκους μὲν, ἀλλὰ καὶ ἀντιλεγομένους.]

γράφους. The question, then, between us and the papists is, What books are to be esteemed canonical and testamentary. Concerning many, and indeed the principal ones, we are agreed : concerning some we are at variance. But, in order that the true state of this question may be understood, we must see, in the first place, what the council of Trent hath determined upon this subject. Its words are as follows : "The synod hath deemed it fitting that a catalogue of the sacred books should be subjoined to this decree, lest any should have occasion to doubt what books are received by it[6]." Then it recites the books which are truly canonical, and are received by us without any hesitation. But it subjoins others which we do not acknowledge as canonical. Such are these six books : Tobit, Judith, Wisdom, Ecclesiasticus, two books of Maccabees. These are the books of the old Testament. Afterwards, it enumerates the books of the new Testament, all of which we receive without any controversy, although they were not always alike received in the church, as you shall hear in the sequel. Finally, the council concludes in these words : " Whoever does not receive these books entire with all their parts, as they are contained in the ancient Latin Vulgate, for sacred and canonical, let him be accursed[7]!" Here you have the decree of the Tridentine council, and the terrible sanction of that decree. From these premises it now appears that we are required by the Tridentine fathers, if we would escape their anathema, to receive as authoritative canonical scripture not only those six entire books which we have mentioned, but besides certain parts of and additions to the books, as Baruch, the Hymn of the three Children, the histories of Susannah and Bel and the Dragon, which are attributed to Daniel, and certain apocryphal chapters of the book of Esther : for it is thus that the Jesuits interpret the meaning of this decree. Now, therefore, the state of the question is this ; whether these books, and these parts of books, should be received for sacred and canonical scriptures ? They affirm : we deny. It remains that we should proceed to the discussion. I will first answer their arguments, and then proceed to the defence of our cause ; which course I

[6 Sacrorum vero librorum indicem huic decreto adhibendum censuit, ne cui dubitatio suboriri possit, quinam sint, qui ab ipsa synodo suscipiuntur. Concil. Trid. Sess. IV. Decret. 1.]

[7 Si quis autem hos libros ipsos integros cum omnibus suis partibus, prout in ecclesia catholica legi consueverunt, et in veteri vulgata editione habentur, pro sacris et canonicis non susceperit. . . . Anathema sit. Ibid.]

intend to follow throughout, because I deem it most suitable to the matter we have in hand, and I perceive that it hath been generally adopted by Aristotle. And since, as Nazianzen tells us, "every argument is designed either to establish our own opinion, or overturn the opposite[1]," I will choose first to overturn the opposite opinion, and then to establish my own.

CHAPTER III.

CONCERNING THOSE HERETICS WHO WERE GUILTY OF SACRILEGE AGAINST THE SACRED AND CANONICAL SCRIPTURES.

But, before I proceed, I deem it necessary for you to censure the madness of certain ancient heretics, who impiously removed some certain and undoubted parts of scripture from the sacred canon. Such heretics, indeed, there were in great numbers, as we read in Irenæus, Tertullian, Epiphanius, Augustine, and others. I shall not endeavour to go through them all, but will enumerate for you the principal.

First of all, the Sadducees received no scriptures but the five books of Moses[2]. This many suppose to have been the reason why Christ (Matt. xxii.) refutes the Sadducees denying the resurrection, by the testimony of the Mosaic scripture. Simon, following in their steps, declared that the prophets were not at all to be regarded; as Irenæus testifies[3], Lib. i. c. 20. The Manichees rejected the whole old Testament, as proceeding from the evil God: for they imagined two gods, the one good and the other evil. Epiphanius has treated upon this subject, Hæres. lxvi. So Saturninus rejected the God of the Jews, and consequently the whole old Testament, as Irenæus tells us, Lib. i. c. 22[4]. The impious Marcion insulted with a load of reproaches the God who is preached in the law and the prophets, and held that Christ had come to dis-

[1] Διττοῦ ὄντος λόγου παντός, τοῦ μὲν τὸ οἰκεῖον κατασκευάζοντος, τοῦ δὲ τὸ ἀντίπαλον ἀνατρέποντος. Orat. xxxv. p. 562. A. Nazianz. Opp. T. I. Colon. 1690.]

[2] This common notion is reasonably doubted by many. See Jortin's Remarks, B. xi. Appendix 1, on the Sadducees, Vol. I. p. 439.]

[3] Prophetas autem a mundi fabricatoribus angelis inspiratos dixisse prophetias; quapropter nec ulterius curarent eos hi, qui in eum et in Selenen ejus spem habeant. P. 116. B. ed. Fevard. Paris. 1685.]

[4] Judæorum Deum unum ex angelis esse dixit, et . . . advenisse Christum ad destructionem Judæorum Dei . . . . . . Prophetias autem quasdam quidem

solve the law and the prophets, and the works of that God who made the world. This Irenæus tells us[5], Lib. I. c. 29. Such frantic men Christ himself expressly refutes by his own words, when he says, that he did not come to destroy the law and the prophets, but to fulfil. Matt. v. 17. This heresy Augustine also imputes to the Cerdonians, whom he affirms to hold the old Testament in contempt[6], (*Ad Quod vult Deum*, c. 21), and to the Severians, of whom he writes, " They condemn the resurrection of the flesh and the old Testament[7]," (ibid. c. 24.) Guido Cameracensis reckons this also amongst the heresies of the Albigenses. This heresy is refuted by Epiphanius, in the place which I have already cited, and most copiously by Augustine against Faustus the Manichee, and against the adversary of the law and the prophets.

The Ptolemæans condemned the books of Moses[8], as Epiphanius relates, Hæres. xxxiii. The Nicolaitans and Gnostics ejected the book of Psalms from the sacred canon, as Philaster informs us, (in Lib. de Hær. c. 127); which heresy the Anabaptists have renewed in our times. But all these heretics are refuted by the clearest evidence of the new Testament.

Many formerly, as Philaster relates (in Cat. c. 132, 133), rejected the books of Solomon, and especially Ecclesiastes and the Song of Songs; because in the former Solomon seems to invite men to a life of pleasure, and in the latter, to relate certain amatory discourses between himself and Pharaoh's daughter. But it is plain that these men fell into a manifest and impious error. For in Ecclesiastes Solomon does not allure men to enjoy the pleasures and blandishments of the world, but rather deters them from such pleasures, and exhorts them, with a divine eloquence, to

ab iis angelis qui mundum fabricaverunt dictas; quasdam autem a Satana, quem et ipsum angelum adversarium mundi fabricatoribus ostendit; maxime autem Judæorum Deo. Ibid. p. 118, c.]

[5 Marcion . . . impudorate blasphemans eum qui a lege et prophetis annunciatus est Deus . . . Jesum autem [dicens] . . . venientem in Judæam . . . dissolventem prophetas et legem, et omnia opera ejus Dei qui mundum fecit. Ibid. p. 129, A.]

[6 Resurrectionem mortuorum negat, spernens etiam Testamentum Vetus. Augustini Opp. T. VIII. col. 43, A. Paris. 1837.]

[7 Carnis resurrectionem cum Vetere Testamento respuentes. Ibid. c.]

[8 Παρὰ γὰρ τοῖς εἰρημένοις καὶ τὸν νόμον τοῦ Θεοῦ τὸν διὰ Μωυσέως βλασφημῶν οὐκ αἰσχύνεται. Ed. Petav. Colon. 1682. T. I. p. 216. See the curious epistle of Ptolemæus to Flora, which he there subjoins, given also by Grabe, Spicil. II. 69.]

despise and contemn the present world.   Thus at the very commencement he exclaims, "Vanity of vanities, all is vanity:"
in which words he declares that all those things which are sought
after in this world, are uncertain, transitory, and fallacious. Whence
it necessarily follows that those are mad who acquiesce in the
enjoyment of such objects.   And so (after having disputed through
the whole book against those who pursue these pleasures so
greedily, and desire to satisfy themselves with such goods, whatever they are) he at the close teaches that happiness consists not,
as many suppose, in things of this kind, but in true piety, and
thus concludes: "Fear God, and keep his commandments; for this
is the whole of man."   This is not the judgment of an Epicurus,
but of a holy prophet, withdrawing foolish men from the pursuit
of worthless objects, and recalling them into the true path of a
pious and a happy life.

In the Song, if Solomon had wished to praise his wife, he
would not have used such prodigious and absurd comparisons. For
he compares her to the cavalry of Pharaoh, her head to Carmel,
her eyes to fish-ponds, her nose to a tower, her teeth to a
flock of sheep; and finally pronounces her whole person terrible
as an army.   Such things do not suit the daughter of Pharaoh
and the bride of Solomon.   They must, therefore, be referred
to the mystic bride of another Solomon,—that is, to the Church
of Christ, whose consummate union of faith and love with her
spouse this whole book sets forth; as, indeed, all men of sound
judgment have always determined.   Nor is the fact, that none of
the customary names of God occur in this book, any proof that
it is not canonical.   For, although such names are omitted, yet
others are used of the same kind and importance, as shepherd,
brother, friend, beloved, spouse, which were much more suitable to
the style of such a piece: since he, whom the bride so often
addresses under these names, is no other than Christ, at once the
true Son of God, and the true God himself.

We care little for the impious Anabaptists, who reject this book
with contempt; nor can we at all excuse Castalio[1], if he really wrote

[1 I write the name thus in conformity with Whitaker's usage; but the
correct form is *Castellio*.   See the curious history of the origin of the other
form in Bayle, CASTALIO, Rem. M.   With respect to the imputation mentioned in the text, Varillas charges it upon Castellio more definitely, stating
this injurious opinion of the Canticles to be avowed by him in his argument
to that book. Bayle observes, that in five editions of Castellio's bible which he

what some object to him ;—that this book is nothing but a conversation which Solomon held with his Sulamith.

The Anabaptists are said, at the present day, to reject and ridicule the book of Job, and some have written that it is called by those heretics a *Hebrew Tragi-Comedy*. This they would seem to have learned from the wicked Jews: for certain rabbins, authors of the Talmudic fables, affirm[2] that it is a fictitious story, and no such man ever existed. The impudence of these persons is refuted by other testimonies of scripture. For, in Ezekiel xiv. 14, the Lord says : "If these three men were in the midst thereof, Noah, Daniel, and Job, &c." Whence we perceive that Job must have really existed, as no one doubts that Noah and Daniel did. Paul too cites a clear testimony from this book (1 Cor. iii. 19): "He taketh the wise in their own craftiness ;" which words we find, in Job v. 13, to have been pronounced by Eliphaz. The apostle James, also, hath mentioned this man, James v. 11. Hence it is manifest that this was a true history, and that the book itself is canonical, and that they who determine otherwise are to be esteemed as heretics.

Jerome, in the Proëm of his Commentaries on Daniel[3], relates that Porphyry the philosopher wrote a volume against the book of our prophet Daniel, and affirmed that what is now extant under the name of Daniel, was not published by the ancient prophet, but by some later Daniel, who lived in the times of Antiochus Epiphanes. But we need not regard what the impious Porphyry may have written, who mocked at all the scriptures and religion itself,

examined, he could find no argument to that book whatever. However, in the London edition of the Latin bible (in 4 vols. 12mo. 1726), there is the following : "Colloquium *Servatoris* et *Ecclesiæ*. Domestici in Ecclesiæ (Ecclesia) hostes. Servator, lilium Columba. Solomo Christi Imago. Ad puellas vir, et ad virum puellæ. Ecclesiæ pulchritudo. Servatoris in Ecclesiam Studium. Ecclesia vinea copiosa."]

[2 Nosti quosdam esse, qui dicunt Jobum nunquam fuisse, neque creatum esse; sed historiam ejus nihil aliud esse quam parabolam. Maimonides, Moreh Nevoch. par. III. c. 22. Compare Manasseh Ben Israel, de Resurr. Mort. p. 123.]

[3 Contra prophetam Danielem duodecimum librum scripsit Porphyrius, nolens eum ab ipso, cujus inscriptus est nomine, esse compositum, sed a quodam qui temporibus Antiochi Epiphanis fuerit in Judæa; et non tam Danielem ventura dixisse, quam illum narrasse præterita. T. III. p. 1071, &c. ed. Bened.]

[WHITAKER.]   3

and whose calumnies were refuted by Eusebius, Apollinarius and Methodius[1], as Jerome testifies in the above-cited place. So far concerning the old Testament.

The new Testament, also, was formerly assaulted in various ways by heretics and others. The Manichees shewed themselves no less impious and sacrilegious towards the books of the new Testament than they were towards those of the old. They were not afraid to say that the books of the apostles and evangelists were stuffed full of lies : which madness and frenzy of theirs Augustine hath most learnedly confuted in his thirty-second book against Faustus the Manichee.

Others received no gospel but that of Luke, and hardly any other part of the new Testament; as Cerdon and his disciple Marcion. Tertullian speaks of these towards the end of his Prescriptions[2] : " Cerdon receives only the gospel of Luke, nor even that entire. He takes the epistles of Paul, but neither all of them, nor in their integrity. He rejects the Acts of the Apostles and the Apocalypse as false. After him appeared his disciple, Marcion by name, who endeavoured to support the heresy of Cerdon." These men took away almost the whole contents of the new Testament.

The Valentinians admitted no gospel but that of John, as Irenæus tells us[3] ; (Lib. III. c. 11.) which error the papists charge on Luther also, but most falsely, as they themselves well know. The Alogians[4], on the contrary, rejected all John's writings, and were so called because they would not acknowledge as God the Logos,

[1 Cui solertissime responderunt Cæsariensis Episcopus. . . . . Apollinarius quoque . . . . . et ante hos, ex parte, Methodius. Ibid.]

[2 Solum Evangelium Lucæ, nec totum recipit, Apostoli Pauli neque omnes neque totas epistolas sumit; Acta Apostolorum et Apocalypsin quasi falsa rejicit. Post hunc discipulus ipsius emersit, Marcion quidam nomine... hæresin Cerdonis approbare conatus est. c. 51. This piece, which forms the concluding part of the Prescriptions (from c. 45), seems the work of some later hand.]

[3 Hi autem qui a Valentino sunt, eo quod est secundum Joannem plenissime utentes ad ostensionem conjugationum suarum, ex ipso detegentur nihil recte dicentes. p. 258, D.]

[4 Lardner, History of Heretics, chap. 23 (Works, 4to ed., Vol. IV. p. 690), considers the existence of such a heresy very doubtful; but I cannot see sufficient ground for all his suspicions. However, it is hard to believe that any men in their senses ever ascribed all John's writings to Cerinthus, as Epiphanius seems to say, p. 424.]

whom John declares to be God in the beginning of his gospel.
This is related by Epiphanius (Hær. Lib. I.), who gave them this
appellation upon that account.

Irenæus relates[5] (Lib. I. c. 26.), that the Ebionites received
only the gospel according to Matthew, and rejected the apostle
Paul as an apostate from the law.

The Severians made no account of the Acts of the Apostles, as
Eusebius informs us, Lib. IV. c. 27[6].

The Marcionites rejected both epistles to Timothy, the epistle
to Titus, and the epistle to the Hebrews, as Epiphanius records,
Hær. XLII.[7]

Chrysostom and Jerome[8], in the Preface to the epistle of Paul
to Philemon, testify that it was by some not received as canonical;
which conclusion they were led into by considering that human
frailty could not bear the continual uninterrupted action of the
Holy Ghost, and that the apostles must have spoken some things
by a mere human spirit. Amongst these they classed this epistle,
as containing in it nothing worthy of an apostolic and divine authority, or useful to us. Chrysostom[9] refutes this opinion, with
much truth and beauty, in the Argument of this epistle, and teaches
us that many noble and necessary lessons may be learned from it:
first, that we should extend our solicitude to the meanest persons:
secondly, that we should not despair of slaves, (and therefore, still
less of freemen,) however wicked and abandoned: thirdly, that it is
not lawful for any one to withdraw a slave from his master under
pretence of religion: fourthly, that it is our duty not to be ashamed
of slaves, if they be honest men. Who now will say that this
epistle is useless to us, from which we may learn so many and

[5 Solo autem eo quod est secundum Matthæum Evangelio utuntur, et
Apostolum Paulum recusant, apostatam esse eum Legis dicentes. p. 127, c.]

[6 Βλασφημοῦντες δὲ Παῦλον τὸν ἀπόστολον, ἀθετοῦσιν αὐτοῦ τὰς ἐπιστολὰς,
μηδὲ τὰς πράξεις τῶν ἀποστόλων καταδεχόμενοι.   T. I. p. 409.]

[7 Ἐπιστολὰς παρ' αὐτῷ τοῦ ἁγίου ἀποστόλου δέκα, αἷς μόναις κέχρηται. §. 9.
T. I. p. 309. D.]

[8 Volunt aut epistolam non esse Pauli, quæ ad Philemonem scribitur;
aut etiam si Pauli sit, nihil habere quod edificare nos possit.—Hieron. præf.
in Ep. ad. Philem. T. IV. p. 442.]

[9 The best edition of Chrysostom's admirable Commentary on the epistle
to Philemon is that by Raphelius, subjoined to Vol. II. of his Annotationes
Philologicæ. Lugd. Bat. 1747. The reader will find the passage here referred to at pp. 28, 30, 32.]

such distinguished lessons? Forasmuch, therefore, as this epistle was both written by Paul, and contains in it such excellent instruction, it ought not by any means to be rejected.

Such, then, was the opinion, or rather the mad raving of the heretics concerning the sacred books. There were others also, who either rejected altogether certain books and parts of books of the new Testament, or else allowed them no great authority, whom it is not necessary to enumerate: for we must not spend too much time in recording or refuting such persons. But the Schwenkfeldtians[1] and Libertines, proceeding to a still greater length in their wickedness, despise the whole scripture, and insult it with many reproaches, holding that we should attend not to what the scriptures speak, but to what the Spirit utters and teaches us internally. Of these, Hosius Polonus writes thus, in his book concerning the express word of God: "We will dismiss the scriptures, and rather listen to God speaking to us, than return to those beggarly elements. One is not required to be learned in the law and scriptures, but to be taught of God. Vain is the labour which is expended upon scripture: for the scripture is a creature and a beggarly sort of element[2]." Many passages of scripture condemn this monstrous heresy. Christ says: "Search the scriptures." Paul says: "Whatsoever things were written of old time were written for our learning." Rom. xv. 4. And elsewhere: "All scripture is given by inspiration of God, and is profitable for doctrine, for correction, for reproof, and for instruction in righteousness." 2 Tim. iii. 16. There are innumerable such testimonies, by which the authority of the scriptures is fully proved, and the blasphemy of these men refuted; against which our divines have also written many excellent discourses.

At the same time that we justly condemn the heresies which I have mentioned, we cannot but wholly disapprove the opinion of those, who think that the sacred writers have, in some places, fallen

---

[1 So called from Gaspar Schwenckfeldt, a Silesian knight, and counsellor to the Duke of Lignitz, who died in 1561. See an account of him in Mosheim, Cent. xvi. Sect. iii. part ii. c. 1, §§ 23, 24.]

[2 Nos ... ipsas scripturas ... facessere jubebimus, et Deum loquentem potius audiemus, ... quam ad egena ista elementa nos convertamus. ... Non oportet legis et scripturæ peritum esse, sed a Deo doctum. Vanus est labor qui scripturæ impenditur: scriptura enim creatura est, et egenum quoddam elementum.—Hos. Op. Col. 1584. De express. Dei Verbo. Tom. i. p. 624.]

into mistakes. That some of the ancients were of this opinion appears from the testimony of Augustine, who maintains, in opposition to them[3], "that the evangelists are free from all falsehood, both from that which proceeds from deliberate deceit, and that which is the result of forgetfulness." (De Cons. Ev. Lib. ii. c. 12.) Consequently, Jerome judged wrong, if he really judged, as Erasmus supposes[4], "that the evangelists might have fallen into an error of memory." Erasmus himself, indeed, determines that it is neither impious nor absurd to think so ; and allows it possible that Matthew, for instance, in that place of his 27th chapter, may have put the name of Jeremiah instead of Zechariah. Upon which place Erasmus writes thus : "But although this were a slip of memory merely in the name, I do not suppose that one ought to be so over-scrupulous as that the authority of the whole scripture should seem invalidated on that account[5]." But it does not become us to be so easy and indulgent as to concede that such a lapse could be incident to the sacred writers. They wrote as they were moved by the Holy Ghost, as Peter tells us, 2 Pet. i. 21. And all scripture is inspired of God, as Paul expressly writes, 2 Tim. iii. 16. Whereas, therefore, no one may say that any infirmity could befall the Holy Spirit, it follows that the sacred writers could not be deceived, or err, in any respect. Here, then, it becomes us to be so scrupulous as not to allow that any such slip can be found in scripture. For, whatever Erasmus may think, it is a solid answer which Augustine gives to Jerome : "If any, even the smallest, lie be admitted in the scriptures, the whole authority of scripture is presently invalidated and destroyed[6]." That form which the prophets use so

[3 Omnem autem falsitatem abesse ab Evangelistis decet, non solum eam quæ mentiendo promitur, sed etiam eam quæ obliviscendo.—Aug. Opp. T. iii. P. ii. 1310. B.]

[4 Erasmus (loc. infra citat.) gives Jerome's own words from his epistle *de optimo genere interpretandi:* Accusent Apostolum falsitatis, quod nec cum Hebraico nec cum Septuaginta congruat translatoribus, et, quod his majus est, *erret* in nomine: pro Zacharia quippe Hieremiam posuit. Sed absit hoc de pedissequo Christi dicere, cui curæ fuit non verba et syllabas aucupari, sed sententias dogmatum ponere.—Epist. ci. T. ii. p. 334. Antv. 1579.]

[5 Ceterum etiamsi fuisset in nomine duntaxat memoriæ lapsus, non opinor quemquam adeo morosum esse oporteret, ut ob eam causam totius scripturæ sacræ labasceret auctoritas.—Erasm. Annot. p. 107. *Froben.* Basil. 1535.]

[6 Si mendacium aliquod in scripturis vel levissimum admittatur, scripturæ auctoritatem omnem mox labefactari ac convelli.—This is the quotation as given by Whitaker in his text. The following is probably the passage

often, " Thus saith the Lord," is to be attributed also to the apostles and evangelists. For the Holy Spirit dictated to them whatever things they wrote ; whose grace (as Ambrose writes, Lib. II. in Luc.) " knows nothing of slow struggles[1]." Hence neither can that be tolerated which Melchior Canus has alleged, (Lib. II. c. 18. ad 6) in explanation of a certain difficulty in the Acts of the Apostles, chap. vii. 16; where Stephen says, that Abraham bought a sepulchre from the sons of Emmor, whereas Moses relates that the sepulchre was purchased by Jacob, not by Abraham. Canus thinks that Stephen might have made a mistake in relating so long a history, but that Luke committed no error, since he faithfully recorded what Stephen said[2]. But that answer draws the knot tighter, instead of loosing it : for Stephen was not only full of the Holy Ghost, but is even said to have spoken by the Holy Ghost. Acts vi. 10. Stephen, therefore, could no more have mistaken than Luke; because the Holy Ghost was the same in Luke and in Stephen, and had no less force in the one than in the other. Besides, if we concede that Stephen mistook or was deceived, I do not see how he can excuse Luke for not rectifying the error. Therefore we must maintain intact the authority of scripture in such a sense as not to allow that anything is therein delivered otherwise than the most perfect truth required. Wherefore I cannot understand with what degree of prudence and consideration Jerome can have written that, which he says is to be noted, in his Questions upon Genesis : " Wherever the apostles or apostolical men speak to the people, they generally use those testimonies which had gotten into common use amongst the nations[3]."

intended : Admisso enim semel in tantum auctoritatis fastigium officioso aliquo mendacio, nulla illorum librorum particula remanebit, &c. Epist. xix. Tom. II. p. 14.]

[1 Nescit tarda molimina Sancti Spiritus gratia. c. XIX. Ambros. Opp. T. v. p. 46. Paris. 1838.]

[2 Stephano id quod vulgo solet accidisse, ut in longa videlicet narratione, eademque præsertim subita, confuderit nonnulla et miscuerit, in quibusdam etiam memoria lapsus fuerit ; . . . . Lucas vero, historiæ veritatem retinere volens, ne iota quidem immutavit, sed rem ut a Stephano narrata erat exposuit.—Melch. Cani Loc. Theolog. fol. 89. 2. Colon. Agripp. 1585.]

[3 Ubicunque Sancti Apostoli aut Apostolici viri loquuntur ad populos, iis plerumque testimoniis abutuntur, quæ jam fuerant in gentibus divulgata. —Hieron. Quæst. Hebr. in Genes. T. III. p. 468.]

CHAPTER IV.

WHEREIN THE ARGUMENT OF THE ADVERSARIES IS PROPOSED AND CONFUTED.

HAVING now premised a brief explanation of these matters, we will come to the discussion of the cause and question proposed. And first, we shall have to treat of the six entire books, Tobit, Judith, Wisdom, Ecclesiasticus, and the two books of Maccabees, all together; and then, of those several books taken separately, as likewise of those fragments and parts of books, Esther, Baruch, &c.

Our adversaries have but one argument in behalf of these books, which is derived from the authority of certain councils and fathers. They allege, in the first place, the third council of Carthage, (in which Augustine himself bore a part,) can. 47[4], wherein all these books are counted canonical.   Should any one object, that this council was only provincial, not general, and that its judgment is, therefore, of less consequence; our antagonists proceed to shew, that this council was confirmed by pope Leo IV. (Dist. 20. C. de libellis), and also in the sixth general council held at Constantinople, which is called Trullan, can. 2.   Hence they argue, that although the decree of the council of Carthage might not, perhaps, be strong enough of itself to prove this point, yet, since it is confirmed by the authority of this pope and of a general council, it hath in it as much efficacy as is required to be in any council.   Besides, they adduce the council of Florence under Eugenius IV. (in Epistol. ad Armenos), that of Trent under Paul III. (sess. 4), and pope Gelasius with a council of seventy bishops[5].   Of fathers, they cite Innocent I., who was also a pope, in his third Epistle to Exuperius of Tholouse ; Augustine, Lib. II. c. 8. De Doctrina Christiana ; Isidore of Seville, Etymolog., Lib. VI. c. 1.   So that the argument of our opponents runs thus : these councils and these fathers affirm these books to belong to the sacred canon ; therefore, these books are canonical.   In order to make this argument valid, we must take as our medium this proposition : whatsoever these councils and these fathers determine is to be received without dispute.   We may then add to it, But these councils and these fathers receive these books as canonical ; therefore these books are truly canonical and

[4 *Mansi*, Collect. Concil. Tom. III. p. 891.]
[5 Vide infra, or in Mansi, T. VIII. p. 146.]

divine : otherwise there will be no consequence in the reasoning. Now let us answer somewhat more clearly and distinctly.

In the first place, we deny the major proposition of this syllogism. We must not concede that whatever those councils determine, and whatever those fathers affirm, is always true: for it is the special prerogative of scripture, that it never errs. Therefore, it is manifest that nothing can be concluded from these testimonies which hath the force of a certain and necessary argument.

In the second place, the council of Florence was held one hundred and fifty years ago, and the council of Trent in our own times, and this latter for the express purpose and design of establishing all the errors of the popish church. These both were no legitimate councils of christian men, but tyrannous conventicles of antichrist, held for the object of opposing the truth of the gospel. How general that of Trent was, in its fourth session, may be appreciated from the number of the bishops who were present in that session. The legates, cardinals, archbishops, and bishops, who were then present, and who published this decree concerning the number of the canonical books, made in all about *fifty ;* and those, almost to a man, Italians and Spaniards. Where the attendance was so thin, it was impossible that any general council could be held. Yet Alanus Copus (in Dialog. Quint. c. 16.) says, that there were fewer bishops in many famous councils than at Trent[1]. I allow this to be true of provincial synods ; but no œcumenic council can be named, in which there was such a paucity and penury of prelates. These two councils, therefore, are to be wholly set aside from the dispute.

Thirdly, the council of Carthage was merely provincial and composed of a few bishops ; and therefore hath no authority sufficiently strong and clear for confirming the point in question. Besides, our adversaries themselves do not receive all the decrees of this council. For the papists vehemently and contemptuously blame the injunction most solemnly expressed in can. 26[2], that " the bishop of the chief see shall not be called high priest, or chief of the priests, or by any such title." They cannot then bind us by an authority to which they refuse to be tied themselves.

But, they say, this Carthaginian synod was approved by the

[1 Sed nullam isti habent causam paucitatem istam contemnendi, cum rariore numero multa præclara concilia sint habita.—Alan. Cop. Dialogi VI. Dial. v. c. 16. p. 487. Antv. 1573.]

[2 Ne primæ sedis episcopus appelletur Summus Sacerdos, aut Princeps sacerdotum, aut ejusmodi aliquid. Labb. Concil. T. II. p. 1176.]

Trullan council of Constantinople, which was universal. Be it so.
But, if this decree of the number of the canonical books was legitimately approved, then that also concerning the title of high priest
was confirmed by the same sanction, which yet they will by no
means concede. How, then, will they divide these things? I acknowledge, indeed, that this Trullan synod[3] was œcumenical. But
the papists themselves doubt what should be determined of the
authority of the canons which are attributed to this council. Pighius, in a treatise which he wrote upon this subject, calls the acts
of this council spurious, and by no means genuine; which he seeks
to prove by some arguments. Melchior Canus too (Lib. v. cap. ult.)
declares that the canons of that council have no ecclesiastical authority: which is also the opinion of others. For there are some
things in those canons which the papists can by no means approve;
namely, that the bishop of Constantinople is equalled with the
Roman, can. 36; that priests and deacons are not to be separated
from their wives, can. 13; that the law of fasting is imposed on
the Roman church, can. 55; and others of the same kind. There
is one rule, also, which truth itself disapproves; that which forbids
the eating of blood and things strangled, can. 67. It is, besides,
a strong objection to the credit and authority of these canons, that
eighty-five canons of the apostles are approved and received in
them, can. 2. For pope Gelasius (in Gratian, Dist. 15. C.
Romana Ecclesia) declares the book of the apostolic canons apocryphal[4]. And Gratian (Dist. 16[5]) says, that there are only fifty

[3 Called *Quini-sext* from serving as a kind of supplement to the fifth and
sixth general councils, with the latter of which it is, as here by Whitaker,
commonly confounded. It was held in 691, and its claims to the character
of an œcumenical Synod are generally denied by the Romanists; though
principally, as it would appear, because its canons are repugnant to their
system. See the article in Cave's Historia Literaria, Concil. Constant. IV.
anno 691.]

[4 Liber Canonum Apostolorum apocryphus: which clause is wanting in
Justellus' and two other MSS. The genuineness of this decree, which has
been strongly impeached, is very learnedly defended by Mr Gibbings, in his
Roman Forgeries, p. 93, et seq. To his authorities from Isidore of Seville
(p. 94) he may add another produced by Hody, p. 653, col. 70.]

[5 Isidorus scribit dicens, canones qui dicuntur apostolorum, seu quia eos-
dem nec sedes apostolica recepit, nec sancti Patres illis assensum præbue-
runt, pro eo quod ab hæreticis sub nomine apostolorum compositi dignos-
cuntur, quamvis in eis utilia inveniantur, tamen . . . . eorum gesta inter
apocrypha deputata. Dist. XVI. c. 1.]

canons of the apostles, and they apocryphal, upon the authority of Isidore, who hath related that they were composed by heretics under the name of the apostles. But this synod receives and confirms eighty-five canons of the apostles; whereas pope Zephyrinus, who was five hundred years older than that synod, recognises, as appears in Gratian[1], no more than sixty. Pope Leo IX[2]., who was three hundred and fifty years later than the synod, receives the same number exactly, as Gratian writes in the place just cited. The thing itself, indeed, shews that the canons ascribed to the apostles are spurious. For in the last canon the gospel of John is enumerated amongst the scriptures of the new Testament; which all agree to have been written when all or most of the apostles were dead. Yet they affirm that these canons were not collected by others, but published by the assembled apostles themselves. Thus Peiresius determines in the third part of his book concerning traditions[3]; and so others. For, can. 28, Peter himself says, "Let him be removed from communion, as Simon Magus was by me Peter[4]." If this canon, therefore, be true, Peter was present at the framing of it. But how could Peter, who was put to death in the time of Nero, have seen the gospel of John, which was first written and published in the time of Domitian? For the figment which some pretend, that Peter and the rest foresaw that gospel which John was afterward to write, is merely ridiculous. So in the last chapter all the apostles are made to speak, and the phrase occurs "the Acts of us the Apostles[5]."

It is no less easy to refute the answer which others make, that Clemens published these apostolic canons. For how could Clemens,

[1 Ibid, c. 2.]

[2 Ibid, c. 3. The words are really Cardinal Humbert's, taken from his Reply to Nicetas. See Canisius, Antiq. Lect. T. VI. p. 181. Gratian takes the liberty of attributing them to Leo, on the principle, that the words of the Legate are the words of his employer.]

[3 Peiresius Aiala, De Divinis, Apostolicis, atque ecclesiasticis Traditionibus. Paris. 1550.]

[4 ἐκκοπτέσθω παντάπασι καὶ τῆς κοινωνίας, ὡς Σίμων ὁ Μάγος ὑπ᾽ [ἐμοῦ] Πέτρου. It is numbered 29 by Beveridge, and 30 by Whiston. The word in brackets is omitted by Dionysius Exiguus, for obvious reasons.]

[5 καὶ αἱ πράξεις ἡμῶν τῶν ἀποστόλων. Beveridge here pronounces the word ἡμῶν to be an interpolation; but, as it seems, without any sufficient grounds for such an opinion.]

whom Damasus[6] and Onuphrius[7] testify to have died in the time
of Vespasian, have seen the gospel of John, which he wrote after
his return from Patmos, during the reign of Trajan? For almost
all authors say very plainly, that the gospel was written by John
after his exile. So Dorotheus in the Life of John, the Prologue to
John, Simeon Metaphrastes, Isidorus in his book of the parts of the
new Testament, Gregory of Tours (Glor. Plurim. Mart. c. 30.),
Huimo (Lib. III. de rerum Christianarum Memorabil.), Alcuin upon
John, and innumerable other writers of great authority.

But the matter is clear enough of itself. For these canons of
the apostles approve the constitutions of Clement and his two
epistles. Yet the council of Constantinople, which hath received
the canons of the apostles, condemns the constitutions of Clemens[8],
as, indeed, many others do also; concerning which book we shall
speak hereafter. Besides, these canons of the apostles damage the
papal cause: for they set down three books of Maccabees[9], and
omit Tobit and Judith[10], and direct young persons to be instructed
in the Wisdom of Sirach[11], and make no mention of the Wisdom of
Solomon. If these are the true and genuine canons of the apostles,
then the papists are refuted in their opinion of the number of the
canonical books of the old and new Testaments by the authority of
the canons of the apostles. If they be not, as it is plain they are
not, then the synod of Constantinople erred, when it approved them
as apostolical. Yet these men deny that a general council can err
in its decrees respecting matters of faith. Let the papists see how
they will answer this. Certainly this Trullan synod approved the
canons of the council of Carthage no otherwise than it approved the
canons of the apostles. But it is manifest, and the papists themselves
will not deny, that the canons of the apostles are not to be approved. Hence we may judge what force and authority is to be

[6] i. e. The Liber Pontificalis, which goes under his name: see the article
Damasus (anno 366) in Cave's H. L. and Pearson, de success. prim. Episc.
Rom. Diss. II. c. 4. § 4—6.]

[7] Annotat. in Platinam. p. 13. Colon. Ilb. 1600.]

[8] Canon. II. Beveridge, Pandectæ, Can. I. 158.]

[9] Μακκαβαίων τρία. C. 85. But Cosin (pp. 30—1) endeavours to shew that
the canon in its original state made no mention of any books of Maccabees.
Cf. Gibbing's Roman Forgeries, p. 114.]

[10] Cotelerius, however, found one MS. with the clause ᾿Ιουδεὶθ ἕν, which,
of course, he was glad enough to have any authority for inserting.]

[11] μανθάνειν ὑμῶν τοὺς νέους τὴν σοφίαν τοῦ πολυμαθοῦς Σιράχ. Can. LXXXV.]

allowed to the canons of this council of Constantinople; and what
sort of persons the papists are to deal with, who both deny that
these canons have any legitimate authority, and yet confirm the
sentence of the council of Carthage by the authority of these very
canons. For so Canus (Lib. ii. cap. 9) proves that the authority
of the council of Carthage, in enumerating these books, is not to be
despised, because it was approved by the general Trullan synod;
yet the same man elsewhere (Lib. v. cap. 6. ad argument. 6.)
makes light of the authority of these canons, and brings many
arguments to break it down.

Fourthly, Gelasius with his council of seventy bishops recites
but one book of Maccabees[1], and one of Esdras. Thus he rejected
the second book of Maccabees, which is apocryphal, and Nehemiah,
which is truly canonical. Isidore, too[2], confesses that there are
but two and twenty books found in the Hebrew canon: and that
their canon is the true one will be proved hereafter.

Lastly, before they can press us with the authority of councils,
they should themselves determine whether it is at all in the power
of any council to determine what book is to be received as canonical. For this is doubted amongst the papists, as Canus confesses,
Lib. ii. c. 8.

Let us come now to the minor premiss of the proposed syllogism. We allow that the council of Carthage, and Gelasius
with his seventy bishops, and Innocent, and Augustine, and Isidore call these books canonical. But the question is, in what
sense they called them canonical. Now, we deny that their meaning was to make these books, of which we now speak, of equal authority with those which are canonical in the strict sense; and the
truth of this we will prove from antiquity, from Augustine, and
from the papists themselves.

For, in the first place, if it had been decreed by any public
judgment of the whole Church, or defined in a general council,
that these books were to be referred to the true and genuine
canon of the sacred books, then those who lived in the Church
after the passing of that sentence and law would by no means have
dissented from it, or determined otherwise. But they did dissent,
and that in great numbers; and amongst them some of those
whom the Church of Rome acknowledges as her own children.

[1 In Dominica prima mensis Septembris ponunt librum Machabæorum:
where, however, Ivo reads *libros*. Decret, P. i. Dist. xv. c. 3.]
[2 Offic. i. 12.]

Therefore, there was no such judgment of the Church publicly received.

Secondly, Augustine, in that same place, plainly indicates that he did not consider those books of equal authority with the rest. For he distinguishes all the books into two classes; some which were received by all the churches, and some which were not. Then he lays down and prescribes two rules: one, that the books which all the churches receive should be preferred to those which some do not receive; the other, that those books which are received by the greater and more noble churches should be preferred to those which are taken into the canon by churches fewer in number and of less authority. It will be best to listen to Augustine himself, whose words are these (Lib. II. c. 8. de Doct. Christ.)[3]: "Now, with respect to the canonical scriptures, let him follow the authority of the greater number of catholic churches; amongst which those indeed are to be found which merited to possess the chairs of the apostles, and to receive epistles from them. He will hold this, therefore, as a rule in dealing with the canonical scriptures, to prefer those which are received by all catholic churches to those which only some receive. But, with respect to those which are not received by all, he will prefer such as the more and more dignified churches receive, to such as are held by fewer churches, or churches of less authority." Then follows immediately, "Now the whole canon of scripture, in which we say that this consideration hath place," &c.

Hence, then, I draw an easy and ready answer. We, with Jerome and many other fathers, deny these books to be canonical. Augustine, with some others, calls them canonical. Do, then, these fathers differ so widely in opinion? By no means. For Jerome takes this word "*canonical*" in one sense, while Augustine, Innocent, and the fathers of Carthage understand it in another. Jerome calls only those books canonical, which the church always held for

[3 In canonicis autem scripturis ecclesiarum catholicarum quam plurimum auctoritatem sequatur; inter quas sane illæ sint, quæ apostolicas sedes habere et epistolas accipere meruerunt. Tenebit igitur hunc modum in scripturis canonicis, ut eas, quæ ab omnibus accipiuntur ecclesiis catholicis, præponat eis quas quædam non accipiunt; in eis vero quæ non accipiuntur ab omnibus, præponat eas quas plures gravioresque accipiunt eis quas pauciores minorisque auctoritatis ecclesiæ tenent. . . . . . Totus autem canon scripturarum, in quo istam considerationem versandam dicimus, &c. Aug. Opp. T. III. c. 47, 48. A. B.]

canonical; the rest he banishes from the canon, denies to be canonical, and calls apocryphal.　But Augustine calls those canonical which, although they had not the same perfect and certain
authority as the rest, were wont to be read in the church for the
edification of the people.　Augustine, therefore, takes this name
in a larger sense than Jerome.　But, that Augustine was not so
minded as to judge the authority of all these books to be equal, is
manifest from the circumstance that he admonishes the student of
theology to place a certain difference between the several books,
to distinguish them into classes, and to prefer some to others.　If
his judgment of them all was the same, as the papists contend,
such an admonition and direction must appear entirely superfluous.　Would Augustine, if he held all the books to have an equal
right to canonicity, have made such a distribution of the books?
Would he have preferred some to others?　Would he not have
said that they were all to be received alike?　But now, Augustine
does prefer some to others, and prescribes to all such a rule for
judging as we have seen.　Therefore Augustine did not think that
they were all of the same account, credit, and authority; and, consequently, is in open opposition to the papists.　All this is manifest.
It makes to the same purpose, that this same Augustine (de Civit.
Dei, Lib. XVII. c. 20.) concedes, that less reliance should be placed
upon whatever is not found in the canon of the Jews[1].　Whence it
may be collected that, when Augustine observed that some books
were not received by all, or the greatest and most noble churches,
his remark is to be understood of those books which are not contained in the Hebrew canon: and such are those which our churches
exclude from the sacred canon.

　　Let it be noted too, that in the council of Carthage, and in the
epistle of pope Innocent, five books of Solomon are enumerated;
whereas it is certain that only three are Solomon's.　So, indeed,
Augustine himself once thought that the book of Wisdom and
Ecclesiasticus were Solomon's, though he afterwards changed (but
without correcting) that opinion.　For in the same place of his
City of God he thus speaks of those books: "Learned men have
no doubt that they are not Solomon's[2]."　This was one error in
Augustine.　Another, and no less one, was supposing that the
book of Wisdom was written by Jesus the son of Sirach (de

[1 Sed adversus contradictores non tanta firmitate proferuntur quæ
scripta non sunt in canone Judæorum.—Aug. Opp. T. VII. 766. A.]

[2 Non autem esse ipsius, non dubitant doctiores.—Ubi supra, 765.]

Doct. Christ. Lib. II. c. 8.); which error he retracts, Retract. Lib.
II. c. 4.[3] Yet he allegeth an excuse, which is neither unhandsome
nor trifling, for attributing five books to Solomon ; that "these
books may be all called Solomon's, from a certain likeness which
they bear." Hence, however, it appears that Augustine was in
a great mistake when he thought, first, that these two books were
written by Solomon, and then, that they were written by Jesus
the son of Sirach. Indeed, Augustine himself testifies that these
books were by no means received in all churches (De Civit. Dei.
Lib. XVII. c. 20.); where he says that these books were especially
received as authoritative[4] by the Western church. To this Western church Augustine and Innocent belonged. For the oriental
church never allowed to these books such great authority. But
the mistake of counting Wisdom and Ecclesiasticus amongst the
books of Solomon, although it is a very gross one, was yet, as
we read, entertained and received by many. For pope Mar-
cellinus, in an epistle to Solomon, adduces a testimony from Ecclesiasticus, as from Solomon ; and likewise pope Sixtus II. in
an epistle to Gratus : which shews sufficiently that these persons
must have thought that Solomon was the author of this book. I
know, indeed, that these epistles were not really written by Mar-
cellinus or Sixtus, but are falsely attributed to them : yet still,
by whomsoever written, they indicate that this opinion was a common error.

Thirdly, the papists themselves understand and interpret
Augustine and the rest in the same manner as we do. For so
many persons after Augustine and after those councils would
never have denied these books to be canonical, if they had not
perceived the reasonableness of this interpretation. If then they
blame our judgment, let them at least lend some credit to their
own companions and masters. I will bring forward no man of
light esteem, no mean or obscure doctor, but a distinguished cardinal,—that special pillar of the popish church, Cajetan, who assuredly excelled all our Jesuits in judgment, erudition, and

[3 In secundo sane libro (de Doc. Christ.) de auctore libri, quem plures
vocant Sapientiam Salomonis, quod etiam ipsum, sicut Ecclesiasticum, Jesus
Sirach scripserit, non ita constare sicut a me dictum est postea didici, et
omnino probabilius comperi non esse hunc ejus libri auctorem. Ib. T. I.
86, 87. D. A.]

[4 Eos tamen in auctoritatem maxime occidentalis antiquitus recepit ecclesia. Ut supra, 765.]

authority.   I will recite his words, because they are express and
should always be in remembrance.   Thus, therefore, writes Cajetan at the end of his commentary upon the History of the old
Testament : " Here," says he, " we close our commentaries on the
historical books of the old Testament.   For the rest (that is,
Judith, Tobit, and the books of Maccabees) are counted by St
Jerome out of the canonical books, and are placed amongst the
Apocrypha, along with Wisdom and Ecclesiasticus, as is plain from
the Prologus Galeatus.   Nor be thou disturbed, like a raw scholar,
if thou shouldest find any where, either in the sacred councils or
the sacred doctors, these books reckoned as canonical.   For
the words as well of councils as of doctors are to be reduced to
the correction of Jerome.   Now, according to his judgment, in the
epistle to the bishops Chromatius and Heliodorus, these books (and
any other like books in the canon of the bible) are not canonical,
that is, not in the nature of a rule for confirming matters of
faith.   Yet, they may be called canonical, that is, in the nature
of a rule for the edification of the faithful, as being received and
authorised in the canon of the bible for that purpose.   By the
help of this distinction thou mayest see thy way clearly through
that which Augustine says, and what is written in the provincial
council of Carthage[1]."   Thus far Cajetan ; in whose words we
should remark two things.   First, that all the statements of councils and doctors are to be subjected to the correction of Jerome.
But Jerome always placed these books in the apocrypha.   Secondly,
that they are called canonical by some councils and Fathers, and
customarily received in the canon of the bible, because they propose a certain rule of morals.   There are, therefore, two kinds

[1 Hoc in loco terminamus commentaria librorum historialium veteris
Testamenti. Nam reliqui (videlicet Judith, Tobiæ, et Machabæorum libri) a
Divo Hieronymo extra Canonicos libros supputantur, et inter Apocrypha
locantur cum Sapientia et Ecclesiastico, ut patet in prologo Galeato.   Nec
turberis novitie, si alicubi reperies libros istos inter canonicos supputari, vel
in sacris Conciliis vel in sacris Doctoribus. Nam ad Hieronymi limam redu-
cenda sunt tam verba Conciliorum quam Doctorum, et juxta illius sententiam
ad Chromatium et Heliodorum episcopos libri isti (et si qui alii sunt in Canone Bibliæ similes) non sunt canonici, id est, non sunt regulares ad firman-
dum ea quæ sunt fidei : possunt tamen dici canonici, id est regulares ad ædificationem fidelium, utpote in Canone Bibliæ ad hoc recepti et auctorati.
Cum hac distinctione discernere poteris dicta Augustini, et scripta in Pro-
vinciali Concilio Carthaginensi.   In ult. C. Esther, ad fin.]

of canonical books : for some contain the rule both of morals and of faith ; and these are, and are called, truly and properly canonical : from others no rule, but only of morals, should be sought. And these, although they are improperly called canonical, are in truth apocryphal, because weak and unfit for the confirmation of faith. We may use, if we please, the same distinction which I perceive some papists themselves to have used, as Sixtus Senensis (Bibliothec, Lib. I.), and Stapleton (Princip. Fid. Doctrin. Lib. IX. c. 6), who call some books *Proto-canonical*, and others *Deutero-canonical*. The proto-canonical are those which are counted in the legitimate and genuine canon, i. e. of the Hebrews. These Jerome's accurate judgment hath approved ; these our churches acknowledge as truly canonical. The Deutero-canonical are they which, although they be sometimes called canonical in the sense just now explained, are yet in reality apocryphal, because they do not contain the combined rule of faith and morals[2]. The papists are greatly incensed against their partner Cajetan, on account of this most solid sentence ; and some even vituperate him. Canus says, that he was deceived by the novelties of Erasmus. Let us leave them to fight with their own men. This is certain, that there never was a papist of more learning and authority than Cajetan, whom the pope sent into Germany to oppose Luther. This testimony should be a weighty one against them. Let them shake it off as they best can : and yet they never can shake it off, since it is confirmed by solid reason.

Thus we have seen how weak their argument is. They have none better : for they have none other. Now, since we have answered them, we will proceed to the confirmation of our own cause.

CHAPTER V.

WHEREIN REASONS ARE ALLEGED AGAINST THE BOOKS OF THE SECOND KIND.

I FORM the first argument thus : These books, concerning which we contend, were not written by prophets : therefore they are not canonical. The entire syllogism is this. All canonical books of the old Testament were written by prophets : none of these

[2 A difference of authority is owned also by Lamy. App. Bibl. L. II. c. 5. p. 333. Lugd. 1723 ; and Jahn, Einleitung ind. A. T. Vol. I. p. 141.]

4

books was written by any prophet : therefore none of these books is canonical. The parts of this syllogism must be confirmed.

The major rests upon plain testimonies of scripture. Peter calls the scripture of the old Testament, "The prophetic word," 2 Pet. i. 19, (for it is evident from Luke iii. 4, that λόγος means scripture,) and "prophecy," ibid. ver. 20. Paul calls it, "the scriptures of the prophets." Rom. xvi. 26. Zacharias the priest says, "As he spake by the mouth of his holy prophets, which have been since the world began." Luke i. 70. Where he means that God had spoken in the prophetic scriptures. So Abraham says to the luxurious man, "They have Moses and the prophets," that is, the books of scripture. Luke xviii. 39. And elsewhere Luke says : "Beginning at Moses and all the prophets, he expounded unto them in all the scriptures the things concerning himself." Luke xxiv. 27 ; so Rom. i. 2. Here we see that all the scriptures are found in the books of Moses and the prophets. The apostle to the Hebrews says : "God spake in divers manners by the prophets." Heb. i. 1. Therefore the prophets were all those by whom God spake to His people. And to this refers also the assertion of the apostle, that the Church is built "upon the foundation of the apostles and prophets." Eph. ii. 20. This foundation denotes the doctrine of the scriptures, promulgated by the prophets and apostles. Christ says : "All things must be fulfilled which are written in the law of Moses, and in the prophets, and in the psalms, concerning me :" and then follows immediately, "Then opened he their understanding, that they might understand the scriptures." Luke xxiv. 44, 45. Paul asks king Agrippa, "Believest thou the prophets ?"—that is, the scriptures. Acts xxvi. 27. And when he dealt with the Jews at Rome, he tried to convince them "out of the law of Moses and the prophets." Acts xxviii. 23.

From these testimonies we collect that the assertion in the major is most true ;—that the whole scripture of the old Testament was written and promulgated by prophets. And there are many other similar passages from which it may be concluded, that there is no part of the old Testament which did not proceed from some prophet. But we must remark, that the entire old canonical scripture is sometimes signified by the name of *the prophets*, sometimes of *Moses and the prophets*, sometimes of *Moses, the prophets, and the Psalms*. So Augustine, in his discourse against Cresconius the grammarian : "Not without cause was the canon of the church framed with so salutary a vigilance, that certain books of the pro-

phets and apostles should belong to it[1]." Lib. ii. cap. 31. And in
another place: " Let them shew us their church, not in the rumours
of the Africans, but in the injunction of the law, in the predictions
of the prophets, in the songs of the Psalms; that is, in all the
canonical authorities of the sacred books[2]." De Unit. Eccles. c. 16.
And elsewhere: "Read this in the law, in the prophets, in the
Psalms[3]." We have said enough in confirmation of the major; let
us now proceed to the minor.

That these books, against which we are disputing, were not
written, or set forth to the church, by prophets, is exceedingly
clear and certain. For, in the first place, all confess that Malachi
was the last prophet of the Jews, between whom and John the
Baptist no prophet whatever intervened. But most of the authors
of these books undoubtedly lived after Malachi. This is manifest
in the case of the writers of Ecclesiasticus and the Maccabees; and
even our adversaries themselves are not able to deny it. Besides,
those books were not written in the prophetic tongue, which was
the language of Canaan and the proper language of the church.
But if prophets, who were the teachers and masters of the Israelitish church, had written those books, they would have used, in
writing them, their native and prophetic language, not a language
foreign and unknown to the church; which no right-minded person
will deny. Now that most of them were written not in Hebrew
but in Greek, the Fathers affirm, and the papists concede, and the
thing itself proves fully: concerning the rest, we shall see in the
sequel. Finally, if these books had been written by prophets, then
Christ would have used them as his witnesses. But neither Christ
nor his apostles ever made any use of their testimony. This is
what Augustine says of the books of Maccabees: " The Jews do
not esteem this scripture as the Law and the Prophets, to which the
Lord bears testimony as his witnesses[4]." (Contra Gaudent. Epist.

[1 Neque enim sine causa tam salubri vigilantia canon ecclesiasticus constitutus est, ad quem certi prophetarum et apostolorum libri pertineant.
Aug. Opp. T. ix. 668, 669. D. A.]

[2 Ecclesiam suam demonstrent, si possunt, non in sermonibus et rumori-
bus Afrorum, non in conciliis episcoporum suorum,... sed in præscripto
Legis, in Prophetarum prædictis, in Psalmorum cantibus... hoc est, in omnibus canonicis sanctorum librorum auctoritatibus. Ibid. 585. A.]

[3 Lege hoc mihi de Propheta, lege de Psalmo, recita de Lege. August.
de Pastoribus, c. 14.]

[4 Et hanc quidem scripturam, quæ appellatur Machabæorum, non habent

Lib. II. cap. 23.)   Christ bears no testimony to these books as his
witnesses.   Therefore they are not sufficient or fully credible witnesses of Christ.   But this they would be if they were prophetic.
For all the canonical and prophetic scriptures testify of Christ;
and to them as his witnesses Christ bears distinguished testimony,
when he says, "Search the scriptures," and when he cites so many
testimonies from those books.   So Jerome[1]: "We must have
recourse to the Hebrews, from whose text both the Lord speaks,
and his disciples choose their examples."   But that these books
are not prophetical, we shall hereafter prove still more clearly.

The second argument.   These books were not received by the
church of the Israelites; therefore they are not canonical.   The syllogism may be framed thus: The ancient church of the Hebrews received and approved all the books of the old Testament.   That church
did not receive these books; therefore they are not canonical.

The major proposition is certain, and may be easily demonstrated.   For, first, if that church had rejected a part of the Lord's
Testament,—especially so large a part,—she would have been
guilty of the highest crime and sacrilege, and would have been
charged with it by Christ or his apostles.   For, since the Jews
were blamed for putting wrong senses upon the scripture, they
would never have escaped still greater and sterner reprehension, if
they had taken away the scripture; forasmuch as it is much more
wicked and impious to take away books of scripture than to interpret them ill in certain passages.   But neither Christ, nor his
apostles, nor any others, ever accused the Jews of mutilating or
tearing to pieces their canon of the sacred books.   Nay, the ancient Israelitish church both received all the canonical books, and
preserved them with the greatest care and faithfulness.   On which
point read what Josephus writes, in Eusebius, Lib. III. cap. 10[2].
This is also confirmed by the authority of scripture itself.   For
the apostle says, that to the Jews were committed and delivered in
charge *the oracles of God*,—that is, the scriptures.   Rom. iii. 2.
Whence we learn, that the excellent treasure of the sacred scripture
was deposited by God with the church of the Jews, and by it
received and guarded: which diligence and fidelity of the Jews,

Judæi sicut Legem et Prophetas et Psalmos, quibus Dominus testimonium
perhibet ut testibus suis (Lib. I. §. 38.)   Aug. Opp. T. IX. 1006. c.]

[1 Ad Hebræos revertendum, unde et Dominus loquitur, et discipuli exempla præsumunt.   Procem. in Paralip.]

[2 Contra Apion. L. I. c. 8.   Vide infra.]

in preserving the sacred books, Augustine (Ep. 3, and 59.) and all the other Fathers celebrate. Besides, if so many canonical books had been (not only not received, but) rejected by the ancient church of the Jews, it would follow that many canonical books were never received by any church : for before Christ there was no other church but that of the Jews. If then we grant that that church, which was the whole and sole church at that particular time, could have rejected canonical books, then it is evident that the church may err, which the papists will not be willing to allow. Yet is it not a great error, not only not to acknowledge and receive sacred books, but to repudiate and eject them from the canon of the inspired writings ? But the whole Jewish church rejected these books : which was our assumption in the minor, and may be confirmed by the confession of all the fathers, and even of the papists themselves. For every one understands that these books were never received into the Hebrew canon.

As to Bellarmine's pretence (Lib. i. cap. 10), that these books have the testimony of the apostolic church, and that the apostles declared these books canonical, whence does its truth appear ? The apostles never cite testimonies from these books, nor can anything be adduced to shew that any authority was attributed to them by the apostles. Indeed when Cajetan affirmed, in his commentary on 1 Cor. xii., that only to be sacred and divine scripture which the apostles either wrote or approved, he was blamed by Catharinus (Annot. Lib. i.) on that account ; and Catharinus lays it down in that place, that the church receives certain books as canonical which certainly were neither written nor approved by the apostles. The allegation of Canus, that these books were neither received nor rejected[3], is merely ridiculous. For, surely, if the Jews did not receive these books, what else was this but rejecting them utterly ? He who does not receive God rejects him : so not to receive the word of God, is to refuse and reject it. " He that is not with me is against me ; and he that gathereth not with me scattereth." Luke xi. 23. Besides, how could that church either receive or rather not reject books written in a foreign tongue ?

The sum of both arguments is this : These books are not written by prophets, nor received by the Israelitish church. Therefore they are not canonical.

The third argument. Certain things may be found in these

[3 Negamus hos libros a synagoga esse rejectos. Aliud est enim non recipere, aliud vero rejicere.—Melch. Cani Loc. Theol. Lib. ii. cap. xi. p. 45 a. Colon. Agrip. 1585.]

books which prove them not to be canonical. This argument is very strong, as derived from the nature and genius of the books themselves : and the conclusion will appear with fuller evidence in the sequel of this discourse, when we come to the particular examination of the several books ; whence it will be sufficiently manifest that none of those now called in question have any just claims to be considered as canonical.

CHAPTER VI.

WHEREIN THE TRUTH OF OUR CAUSE IS ILLUSTRATED BY OTHER TESTIMONIES.

LASTLY, it is clear from the testimonies of councils, fathers and writers, that these books deserve no place in the true canon of scripture. Which argument, though it be merely human, yet may have force against them who themselves use no other in this cause.

The synod of Laodicea (c. 59[1]) forbids the reading of any *non-canonical* books in the church, and allows only " the canonical books of the old and new Testament" to be used for that purpose. Then those are enumerated as canonical, which our churches receive ; not Tobit, nor Judith, nor the rest. There is, indeed, a clear error in this council. For Baruch is coupled with Jeremiah, (which former perhaps they thought to be a part of the latter,) and the epistles of the prophet Jeremiah are mentioned[2], whereas there is but one epistle of Jeremiah in the book of Baruch :—unless, perhaps, there may here be a fault in the Greek book, since these words are omitted in the Latin. There is another error with respect to the Apocalypse, which these fathers have not placed in the catalogue of the books of the new Testament. And it is certain that many in the church doubted for a long time concerning that book[3]. However, in the judgment of those fathers,

[1 ὅτι οὐ δεῖ ἰδιωτικοὺς ψαλμοὺς λέγεσθαι ἐν τῇ ἐκκλησίᾳ, οὐδὲ ἀκανόνιστα βιβλία, ἀλλὰ μόνα τὰ κανονικὰ τῆς καινῆς καὶ παλαιᾶς διαθήκης. Mansi, T. II. p. 574.]

[2 Ἰερεμίας, Βαροὺχ, θρῆνοι καὶ ἐπιστολαί. Can. 60. ibid.]

[3 It is to be observed that Canon 60 professes only to give a list of those books ὅσα δεῖ ἀναγινώσκεσθαι—i. e. in the Church. Hence Cosin (Hist. of the Canon, p. 60.) supposes the Apocalypse to be left out, not as uncanonical, but as unfit for popular instruction on account of its mysterious obscurity ; for which reason, he observes, it is omitted likewise in the Calendar of Lessons read in the Church of England, though received in our Canon.]

these books of the old Testament, Tobit, Judith, Ecclesiasticus, Wisdom, and the two books of Maccabees, are not canonical. We form the same judgment of those books. The papists object, that the canon of scripture was not then settled; consequently, that *they* might leave these books out of the canon of scripture, but *we* cannot claim a similar right after this canon of scripture hath been defined by the church. But this is too ridiculous. For who can, without great impudence, maintain that there was no certain canon even of the old Testament for four hundred years after Christ; until, forsooth, the time of the council of Carthage? Was the church so long ignorant what books pertained unto the canon of scripture? A pretence at once false and impious! On the contrary, the fathers who lived before that council testify that they very well knew and understood what books were divine and canonical, as shall presently appear. Besides, that council of Carthage could not determine anything about the canon of scripture, so as to bind the whole church, since it was only a provincial one.

But (it will be said) the universal Trullan synod determined that these books should be received into the canon, and defined this matter by its authority. If we ask, how we are to understand that this is so? they answer, from its approving the acts of the council of Carthage. But that is not enough to make this a clear case. For (besides that we have already sufficiently obviated the force of this argument), in the first place, the Trullan synod does, in the very same place and canon, approve also the acts of the council of Laodicea. If that canon, therefore, of the Trullan synod be genuine, the Laodicene and Carthaginian decrees concerning the canonical books do not contradict each other. Consequently, although these books be called in a certain sense canonical by the council of Carthage, yet they are in strictness *uncanonical*, as they are pronounced to be by the council of Laodicea. But if the judgments of these councils be contradictory, the Trullan synod failed in prudence when it approved the acts of both.

Secondly, the Trullan synod was held six hundred years after Christ. Now, was the canon of scripture unknown, or uncertain, or unapproved for so many ages? Who in his right senses would choose to affirm this?

Thirdly, the later church did not judge that the canon of scripture was in this way determined and defined by these councils; which may easily be understood from the testimonies of those writers who flourished in the church after those councils, as you shall hear presently. First of all, therefore, I will adduce the

testimonies of the ancient fathers, then of the later, from which
the constant judgment of the church concerning these books may
be recognised.   And although it may be somewhat tedious to go
through them all, yet this so great multitude of witnesses must needs
possess the greater authority in proportion to their numbers.
Melito of Sardis, as Eusebius tells us, (Lib. IV. cap. 26) testifies
that he went into the East[1], and learned with exact accuracy all the
books of the old Testament.   He, therefore, considered the matter
by no means doubtful; which would have been impossible without
a fully ascertained knowledge of the canon.   Now this Melito, who
took so much pains in determining these books, recites precisely
the same books of the old Testament as we do, with the single exception of the book of Wisdom.   There are some, indeed, who think
that this Wisdom of Solomon, which Melito mentions, is the book
of Proverbs itself: but I do not agree with them[2], for no cause can
be given why the same book should be twice named.   But though
he might have mistaken in one book, he could not have mistaken
in all, especially when using such diligence as he professes himself
to have used.   The error arose from the circumstance, that this
book was in the hands of many, and was more read and had in
greater esteem than the rest.   Indeed, I acknowledge that of all
Apocryphal books most respect was always exhibited towards this
one : and this is the reason why Augustine seems to defend its
authority[3] (Lib. de Præd. Sanct. c. 14); from which defence it is
evident that this book was publicly read in the church, and that
the church thought very honourably of its character.

[1 ἀνελθὼν οὖν εἰς τὴν ἀνατολήν . . . καὶ ἀκριβῶς μαθὼν τὰ τῆς παλαιᾶς διαθήκης βιβλία, κ. τ. λ. p. 403. T. I. ed. Heinichen. Lips. 1827.]

[2 The clause in question is Παροιμίαι ἡ καὶ Σοφία, or, according to Stephens,
ἡ Σοφία; and the question, whether we should not rather read ἤ or ἥ. ἤ is
the reading of six MSS. confirmed by Nicephorus and Rufinus (who translates quæ et Sapientia), and adopted by Valesius. Stroth and Heinichen agree
with Whitaker in preferring ἥ, in which I think them undoubtedly wrong,
because when the title of a book is given in an index or catalogue, the article
is hardly ever prefixed, and in this catalogue in particular never.   In reply
to Whitaker's objection, I suppose it is sufficient to say that the Book of
Proverbs is twice named, because it had two names. "Certe," says Valesius,
"veteres pœne omnes proverbia Salomonis Sapientiam vocabant, interdum
et Sapientiam panareton."   Cf. Euseb. H. E. IV. 22.]

[3 Quæ cum ita sint, non debuit repudiari sententia libri Sapientiæ, qui
meruit in ecclesia Christi de gradu lectorum ecclesiæ Christi tam longa an-
nositate recitari; et ab omnibus Christianis, ab episcopis usque ad extremos
laicos fideles, pœnitentes, catechumenos, cum veneratione divinæ auctoritatis
audiri.—Aug. Opp. T. x. 1370. c.]

Origen (in Eusebius, Lib. VI. c. 25) enumerates the same books
as are acknowledged by our churches to be canonical, and says,
that the testamentary books of the old Testament are two and
twenty, according to the number of the Hebrew alphabet[4]. And
many others after him have made the same remark. Now, if the
canonical books agree in number with the Hebrew letters, as these
fathers determine, then it is certain that no place is left in the
sacred canon for those books concerning which we now dispute;
otherwise there would be more canonical books than Hebrew letters.
But those books which we concede to be truly canonical correspond
by a fixed proportion and number to the elements of the Hebrew
alphabet.

Athanasius says, in his Synopsis: "Our whole scripture is
divinely inspired, and hath books not infinite in number, but finite,
and comprehended in a certain canon." There was, therefore, at
that time a fixed canon of scripture. He subjoins: "Now these are
the books of the old Testament." Then he enumerates ours, and
no others, and concludes: "The canonical books of the old testament are two and twenty, equal in number to the Hebrew letters."
But, in the meanwhile, what did he determine concerning the rest?
Why, he plainly affirms them to be *uncanonical*. For thus he
proceeds: "But, besides these, there are also other *non-canonical*
books of the old Testament, which are only read to the catechumens." Then he names the Wisdom of Solomon, the Wisdom of
Sirach, the fragments of Esther, Judith, Tobit. "These," says he,
"are the non-canonical books of the old Testament[5]." For Athanasius makes no account of the books of Maccabees. He does not
mention Esther in the catalogue, but afterwards remarks, that this
book belongs to another volume;—perhaps to Ezra, by whom
Isidore and others say that book was written. And some fathers,
when enumerating the books of scripture, do not mention this by
name, either because they thought it part of some other book, or
esteemed it apocryphal on account of those apocryphal additions of
certain chapters.

[4 οὐκ ἀγνοητέον δ᾽ εἶναι τὰς ἐνδιαθήκους βίβλους, ὡς Ἑβραῖοι παραδιδόασιν,
δύο καὶ εἴκοσι, ὅσος ὁ ἀριθμὸς τῶν παρ᾽ αὐτοῖς στοιχείων ἐστίν.]

[5 πᾶσα γραφὴ ἡμῶν Χριστιανῶν Θεόπνευστός ἐστιν, οὐκ ἀόριστα δέ, ἀλλὰ
μᾶλλον ὡρισμένα καὶ κεκανονισμένα ἔχει τὰ βιβλία. Καὶ ἔστι τῆς μὲν παλαιᾶς
διαθήκης ταῦτα . . . . . ἐκτὸς δὲ τούτων εἰσὶ πάλιν ἕτερα βιβλία τῆς αὐτῆς παλαιᾶς
διαθήκης, οὐ κανονιζόμενα μέν, ἀναγινωσκόμενα δὲ μόνον τοῖς κατηχουμένοις . . . .
τοσαῦτα καὶ τὰ μὴ κανονιζόμενα.—Athanas. Opp. ii. 126, sqq. ed. Bened.—The
Synopsis is the work of an uncertain author, falsely ascribed to Athanasius.]

Hilary, bishop of Poitiers, speaks thus in the Prologue to his
Exposition of the Psalms : " The law of the old Testament is considered as divided into twenty-two books, so as to correspond with
the number of the letters[1]." By the term "the Law" he denotes
the whole scripture of the old Testament.

Nazianzen, in his verses on the genuine books of sacred scripture, fixes the same number of the books of the old Testament.
These are the lines of Nazianzen, in which he declares that he
counts twenty-two books in the canon,—that is, so many in number
as the Hebrew letters :

Ἀρχαίους μὲν ἔθηκα δύο καὶ εἴκοσι βίβλους,
Τοῖς τῶν Ἑβραίων γράμμασιν ἀντιθέτους[2].

He omits mentioning Esther ; the reason of which we have before
explained.

Cyril of Jerusalem, in his fourth catechetical discourse, hath
written many prudent and pious directions upon this matter. " Do
thou," says he, "learn carefully from the church what are the
books of the old Testament. *Read the divine scriptures, the two
and twenty books*[3]." Thus he shews that there were no more than
twenty-two divine books. Then he enumerates the same books as
are received by us for canonical, save that he includes in that
number the book of Baruch, because he took it (though wrongly,
as we shall prove anon) for a part of the book of Jeremiah. Now
if any shall affirm that nevertheless there are other canonical books
besides these, Cyril will refute him with this splendid objurgation :
Πολὺ σοῦ φρονιμώτεροι ἦσαν οἱ ἀπόστολοι καὶ οἱ ἀρχαῖοι ἐπί
σκοποι, οἱ τῆς ἐκκλησίας προστάται, οἱ ταύτας παραδόντες. As
if he had said, "Who art thou, that thou shouldest make these
books canonical ? The apostles, the ancient bishops, the governors
of the church, were much wiser than thou art, who have commended these books alone to us as canonical, and no others."
What now becomes of those who say, that these books were approved by the apostles and the apostolic churches ?

Epiphanius (Hær. VIII. contra Epicuræos[4]) counts twenty-seven

[1 Lex veteris Testamenti in viginti duos libros deputatur, ut cum literarum numero convenirent. He adds, however: Quibusdam autem visum
est, additis Tobia et Judith, viginti quatuor libros secundum numerum Græcarum literarum connumerare.]
[2 Carm. XXXIII. L. 28. p. 98. T. II. Opp. Nazianz. Colon. 1690.]
[3 Φιλομαθῶς ἐπίγνωθι παρὰ τῆς ἐκκλησίας ποῖαι μέν εἰσιν αἱ τῆς παλαιᾶς δια
θήκης βίβλοι .... ἀναγίνωσκε τὰς θείας γραφὰς, τὰς εἴκοσι δύο βίβλους τῆς παλαιᾶς
διαθήκης.—Cyril. Hierosol. Catech. IV. 33. p. 67. ed. Tuttei.]
[4 Opp. i. p. 19. ed. Petavii.]

books of the old Testament, which he says were delivered by God
to the Jews; or rather, as he subjoins, twenty-two: ὡς τὰ παρ'
αὐτοῖς στοιχεῖα τῶν Ἑβραϊκῶν γραμμάτων ἀριθμούμεναι. For
so he determines that the genuine books of the old Testament are
equal in number to the letters of the Hebrew alphabet. But some
books (as Epiphanius says) are *doubled*. Hence arises that variety
in the sum; being counted when doubled, twenty-two, and, taking
each book severally, twenty-seven. Then he adds, "There are
also two other books which are doubtful,—the Wisdom of Sirach
and that of Solomon, besides some others which are apocryphal[5]."
He calls some dubious, some merely apocryphal. The same author
writes, in his book of Weights and Measures[6], that the Jews sent
to king Ptolemy twenty-two books transcribed in golden letters,
which he enumerates in a previous passage; although Josephus, in
the beginning of his Antiquities, relates that only the five books
of Moses were sent[7]. In this place he writes thus of those two
books, the Wisdom of Solomon and of Sirach, which he had in the
former citation called dubious: "They are indeed useful books,
but are not included in the canon, and were not deposited in the
ark of the covenant[8]." Which is as much as to say plainly, that
they are not to be counted canonical.

Ruffinus, in his Exposition of the Apostles' Creed, says, that
he intends to designate the volumes of the old and new Testaments,
which are believed to have been inspired by the Holy Ghost himself; and then he enumerates our books in both Testaments, subjoining: "But it should be known that there are other books
also, which were called by the ancients not canonical but ecclesiastical, the Wisdom of Solomon and of Sirach, the book of Tobit, Judith,
Maccabees. These," says he, "they would have to be read in
churches, but that nothing should be advanced from them for confirming the authority of faith[9]." The papist Pamelius praises this

[5] εἰσὶ δὲ καὶ ἄλλαι δύο βίβλοι παρ' αὐτοῖς ἐν ἀμφιλέκτῳ, ἡ σοφία τοῦ Σιρὰχ,
καὶ ἡ τοῦ Σολομῶντος, χωρὶς ἄλλων τινῶν βιβλίων ἐναποκρύφων. Ib. c.]

[6] Opp. ii. p. 100. De Pond. et Mens. cc. 22, 23.]

[7] αὐτὰ μόνα τὰ τοῦ νόμου παρέδοσαν οἱ πεμφθέντες ἐπὶ τὴν ἐξήγησιν εἰς
Ἀλεξάνδρειαν. Procem. §. 3, p. 3. ed. Havercamp.]

[8] χρήσιμοι μέν εἰσι καὶ ὠφέλιμοι, ἀλλ' εἰς ἀριθμὸν ῥητῶν οὐκ ἀναφέρονται,
διὸ δὲ ἐν τῷ Ἀαρὼν ἀνετέθησαν, οὔτε ἐν τῇ τῆς διαθήκης κιβωτῷ. Ib. p. 162.
The passage is corrupt, and should probably be read—διὸ οὐδὲ ἐν τῇ τῆς
διαθήκης κιβωτῷ τῷ Ἀαρὼν [אָרוֹן] ἀνετέθησαν.]

[9] Sciendum tamen est, quod et alii libri sunt, qui non canonici, sed ecclesiastici a majoribus appellati sunt: ut est Sapientia Salomonis, et alia Sa-

book, but blames this single passage in it; which yet did not deserve reprehension, since it is both true and accordant with innumerable judgments of the ancient fathers.   He would not even have praised it, if he had not seen it praised by many, who yet are far from blaming that in it which he disapproves.   That exposition was really made by Ruffinus, though it was attributed to Cyprian.

I come now to Jerome, who most plainly of all rejects these books from the canon, and argues strenuously against their canonical authority, and shews himself a most vehement adversary of these books.   It would be tedious to review all his testimonies. In the Prologus Galeatus to Paulinus, " As," says he, " there are two and twenty letters, so there are counted two and twenty books."   Then he adds : " This Prologue to the scriptures may serve as a sort of helmed head-piece for all the books which we have translated from the Hebrew into Latin, to let us know that whatever is out of these is to be placed amongst the Apocrypha. Therefore the Wisdom of Solomon, and Jesus, and Judith, and Tobit, are not in the canon[1]."   Testimonies of the same sort occur everywhere in his books.

Gregory the Great, in his Commentaries on Job (Lib. XIX. cap. 16), expressly writes that the books of Maccabees are not canonical[2]; and there is no doubt that he thought the same of the other books also.

To these authorities of the ancient fathers, I will subjoin the testimony of Josephus, which exactly agrees with them, as it lies in his first book against Apion the grammarian, and is transcribed by Eusebius in the tenth chapter of the third book of his Eccle-

pientia, quæ dicitur Filii Sirach . . . Ejusdem ordinis est libellus Tobiæ et Judith et Maccabæorum libri. . . . Quæ omnia legi quidem in ecclesiis voluerunt, non tamen proferri ad auctoritatem ex his fidei confirmandam.—Exposit. in Symb. Apost. in Append. ad Cyprian. ed. Fell. p. 26.]

[1 Quomodo igitur XXII elementa sunt . . . ita XXII volumina supputantur. . . . Hic prologus scripturarum quasi galeatum principium omnibus libris, quos de Hebræo vertimus in Latinum, convenire potest, ut scire valeamus, quicquid extra hos est inter Apocrypha esse ponendum. Igitur Sapientia quæ vulgo Salomonis inscribitur, et Jesu filii Sirach liber, et Judith et Tobias et Pastor non sunt in canone.—The prologues of Jerome, being to be found in every common copy of the Vulgate and in a thousand other shapes, are not generally referred to by the page in these notes.]

[2 De qua re non inordinate agimus, si ex libris, licet non canonicis, tamen ad ædificationem ecclesiæ editis, testimonium proferamus. p. 622. A. B. Paris. 1705.]

siastical History : "We have not innumerable books, inconsistent and conflicting with each other ; but two and twenty books alone, containing the series of our whole history, and justly deemed worthy of the highest credit. Of these, five are by Moses ; embracing the laws, and delivering down a narrative from the origin of the human race until his own death; which is a period of nearly three thousand years. From the death of Moses to the reign of Artaxerxes, who succeeded Xerxes as king of Persia, the prophets after Moses have written accounts of the events of their own times in thirteen books. The remaining four contain hymns to God and moral admonitions to man. It is true, that from the time of Artaxerxes to our own particular accounts have been written of the various events in our history : but these latter have not been deemed worthy of the same credit, because the succession of the prophets has not been regularly and exactly maintained in that interval[3]."

Assuredly it is plain enough from this testimony of Josephus, what was the judgment of the Israelitish church concerning these books ; and the testimonies which have been alleged from so many fathers, distinguished both by antiquity and sanctity, evince with the highest certainty that the opinion of the Christian church also could not have been different.

Hitherto, therefore, we have proved by the clearest testimonies of the fathers that these books, about which we contend, are not canonical, but apocryphal; for so they are expressly called. Therefore these fathers plainly agree with us, and confirm our sentiments by their suffrages.

But perhaps the papists may have an answer to allege suffi-

[3 οὐ γὰρ μυριάδες βιβλίων εἰσὶ παρ᾽ ἡμῖν, ἀσυμφώνων καὶ μαχομένων· δύο δὲ μόνα πρὸς τοῖς εἴκοσι βιβλία, τοῦ παντὸς ἔχοντα χρόνου τὴν ἀναγραφὴν, τὰ δικαίως θεῖα πεπιστευμένα. Καὶ τούτων πέντε μέν ἐστι τὰ Μωυσέως, ἃ τούς τε νόμους περιέχει, καὶ τὴν τῆς ἀνθρωπογονίας παράδοσιν μέχρι τῆς αὐτοῦ τελευτῆς. Οὗτος ὁ χρόνος ἀπολείπει τρισχιλίων ὀλίγον ἐτῶν. Ἀπὸ δὲ τῆς Μωυσέως τελευτῆς μέχρι τῆς Ἀρταξέρξου τοῦ μετὰ Ξέρξην Περσῶν βασιλέως ἀρχῆς, οἱ μετὰ Μωυσῆν προφῆται τὰ κατ᾽ αὐτοὺς πραχθέντα συνέγραψαν ἐν τρισὶ καὶ δέκα βιβλίοις. Αἱ δὲ λοιπαὶ τέσσαρες ὕμνους εἰς τὸν Θεὸν καὶ τοῖς ἀνθρώποις ὑποθήκας τοῦ βίου περιέχουσιν. Ἀπὸ δὲ Ἀρταξέρξου μέχρι τοῦ καθ᾽ ἡμᾶς χρόνου γέγραπται μὲν ἕκαστα· πίστεως δὲ οὐχ ὁμοίας ἠξίωται τοῖς πρὸ αὐτῶν διὰ τὸ μὴ γενέσθαι τὴν τῶν προφητῶν ἀκριβῆ διαδοχήν. Δῆλον δ᾽ ἐστὶν ἔργῳ πῶς ἡμεῖς τοῖς ἰδίοις γράμμασι πεπιστεύκαμεν· τοσούτου γὰρ αἰῶνος ἤδη παρῳχηκότος, οὔτε προσθεῖναί τις οὐδὲν, οὔτε ἀφελεῖν αὐτῶν, οὔτε μεταθεῖναι τετόλμηκεν. κ. τ. λ. Contra Apion. L. I. c. 8.]

cient to shew that these testimonies avail us nothing. Indeed I will
not dissemble their answer, nor conceal any thing from you that I
know.   Well then, in order to break the force of these testimonies
and overturn our argument, some of them bring two objections :
the first, that these fathers spoke of the Jewish, not of the Christian
canon : the second, that the canon was not yet fixed ; wherefore
those fathers are not to be blamed for determining otherwise concerning the canon than the church afterwards defined, while we,
nevertheless, are precluded from a similar liberty.   Let us briefly
obviate both objections.

First of all, these fathers whom I have cited do speak of the
canon of Christians, as any one who looks at their words themselves
will readily perceive.   The synod of Laodicea prescribes what
books should be read as canonical in the churches.   Melito declares
that he had taken pains to find out what books should be received ;
and this he did surely not for the sake of the Jews, but for his
own.   Athanasius says that those books which he calls uncanonical
were wont to be read only to the catechumens.   Now the catechumens were Christian catechumens.   Cyril forbids the reading of
those books which he calls apocryphal, and says that the apostles
and old bishops and masters of the church had taken no other
books into the canon than those which are received by us.   Who
does not see that he is speaking of the Christian canon?   Although
perhaps Cyril was too vehement in forbidding these books to be
even read : for the other fathers, although they determine them
to be apocryphal, yet permit their perusal.   Ruffinus says, that
those only which our churches also receive were received into the
canon by the ancients (who doubtless were Christians), but that the
rest were called by those same ancients, not *canonical*, but *ecclesiastical*.   So Jerome, writing to Paulinus a Christian bishop,
makes none others canonical than we do, and briefly describes the
contents of these books, and of no others.   Therefore he acknowledged no other canon of the sacred books than we do now.   In
his preface to the books of Chronicles he writes in these plain
words : " The church knows nothing of apocryphal writings ; we
must therefore have recourse to the Hebrews, from whose text the
Lord speaks, and his disciples choose their examples[1]."   " What is
not extant with them is to be flung away from us[2]," says Jerome,

[1] Apocrypha nescit ecclesia: ad Hebræos igitur revertendum, unde et
Dominus loquitur et discipuli exempla præsumunt.]

[2] Quæ non habentur apud illos, procul abjicienda sunt.]

in his preface to Ezra and Nehemiah. And elsewhere, in his preface to the books of Solomon, he hath these words : " As therefore the church, while it reads Judith and Tobit and the books of Maccabees, yet receives them not amongst the canonical scriptures ; so she may read these two volumes also [the Wisdom of Solomon and Sirach] for the edification of the people, not for confirming the authority of articles of faith[3]." Plainly Jerome speaks of the Christian church, and determines that the canon of the old Testament is no other with Christians than it was with the Hebrews. They are absurd, therefore, who imagine a double canon. Again, in his first book against the Pelagians, he blames a heretic for citing testimonies from the Apocrypha, when proposing to prove something about the kingdom of heaven.

In the next place, whereas they say that the canon of scripture was not then fixed, it is but fair that they should speak out, and teach us when afterwards it was fixed. If it be said, in the council of Florence or of Trent, these are but modern ; and, I am very sure, they will not affirm that it was fixed so late. If in the council of Carthage, that council of Carthage was not general. If in the Trullan, those canons are censurable in many respects, even in the opinion of the papists themselves, as we have shewn clearly above. Will they concede then, either that there was no definite canon of scripture for six hundred years after Christ, or that these books were not received into the canon for so many ages? This indeed would be sufficient to overturn the authority of the books. Let them answer, therefore, and mark the precise time, that we may understand when the canon of scripture was at length defined and described. If they can name any general council in which is extant the public judgment of the church concerning the canonical books, let them produce it. Except this Trullan council, they have absolutely none at all. And this Trullan does not precisely affirm these books to be canonical, but only confirms the council of Carthage ; which is of no consequence, since it also confirms the council of Laodicea, and the papists themselves deny all credit to the Trullan canons. Thus they are left without defence on any side. However, that you may the better see how empty that is which they are wont to urge about the Trullan synod ; I will now shew, by the most illustrious and certain testimonies of those men

[3 Sicut ergo Judith et Tobiæ et Machabæorum libros legit quidem ecclesia, sed eos inter canonicas scripturas non recipit ; sic et hæc duo volumina legat ad ædificationem plebis, non ad auctoritatem ecclesiasticorum dogmatum confirmandam.]

who have governed and taught the church of Christ in more
recent times, that since that council these books were nevertheless
not held to be canonical in the church.

Isidore, who lived almost in those very times, says (in Lib. de
Offic.) that the old Testament was settled by Ezra in two and
twenty books, "that the books in the law might correspond in
number with the letters[1]." John Damascene (Lib. IV. c. 18.) says:
"It must be known that there are two and twenty books of the
old Testament, according to the alphabet of the Hebrew language[2]."
Thus Damascene agrees with those ancient doctors concerning the
number of the canonical books of the old Testament. The Wisdom
of Solomon and Sirach he praises indeed, but puts them out of the
canon: the rest he does not even mention. Yet he lived, as
every one knows, after the Trullan Synod. So Nicephorus (apud
Cyrum Prodromum in versibus):

τῆς μὲν παλαιᾶς εἰσὶν εἴκοσι δύο.

"There are two and twenty books of the old Testament." Likewise Leontius determines, in his book of Sects (Act. 2), that there
are no more canonical books of the old Testament than the twenty-
two which our churches receive. Thus he speaks: "Of the old
Testament there are twenty-two books." Then he goes through
all the books of the old and new Testaments in order, and finally
subjoins, "These are the books, old and new, which are esteemed
canonical in the church[3]." Rabanus Maurus (De Inst. Cler. c. 54)
says, that the whole old Testament was distributed by Ezra into
two and twenty books, "that there might be as many books in the
law as there are letters[4]." Radulphus (Lib. XIV. in Lev. c. 1.):
"Tobit, Judith, and the Maccabees, although they be read for
instruction in the church, yet have they not authority[5]." Therefore
they are not canonical. Hugo S. Victoris (Prolog. Lib. I. de Sacram. c. 7) says, that "these books are read indeed, but not written
in the body of the text or in the authoritative canon; that is, such
as the book of Tobit, Judith, Maccabees, the Wisdom of Solomon,

[1 Ut tot libri essent in lege, quot et literæ habentur.—Isid. de Eccl. Offic.
Lib. I. c. 12.]

[2 ἰστέον ὡς εἴκοσι καὶ δύο βίβλοι εἰσὶ τῆς παλαιᾶς διαθήκης κατὰ τὰ στοιχεῖα
τῆς Ἑβραΐδος φωνῆς.]

[3 ταῦτά ἐστι τὰ κανονιζόμενα βιβλία ἐν τῇ ἐκκλησίᾳ, καὶ παλαιὰ καὶ νέα.]

[4 Ut tot libri essent in lege, quot habentur et literæ.—Rab. Maur. de
Instit. Cleric. Lib. II. c. 54.]

[5 Tobias, Judith et Machabæorum, quamvis ad instructionem ecclesiæ
legantur, tamen non habent auctoritatem.]

and Ecclesiasticus." Again, (Didascal. Lib. IV. c. 8) "As there are twenty-two alphabetic letters, by means of which we write in Hebrew, and speak what we have to say, and the compass of the human voice is included in their elementary sounds; so twenty-two books are reckoned, by means of which, being as it were the alphabet and elements in the doctrine of God, the yet tender infancy of our man is instructed, while it still hath need of milk[6]." Twenty-two letters form the language, and twenty-two books the faith. The same is the opinion of Richardus de S. Victore, (Exception. Lib. II. c. 9). For, after telling us that there are twenty-two canonical books of the old Testament, he presently subjoins: "There are besides other books, as the Wisdom of Solomon, the book of Jesus the son of Sirach, and the book of Judith and Tobit, and the book of Maccabees, which are read indeed, but not written in the canon[7]." In which words he plainly denies them to be canonical. And presently after, in the same place: "In the old Testament there are certain books which are not written in the canon, and yet are read, as the Wisdom of Solomon, &c." So Lyra, (Prolog. in libros Apocryph.); Dionysius Carthusianus, (Comment. in Gen. in princip.); Abulensis, (in Matt. c. 1); Antoninus, (3 p. Tit. XVIII. c. 5). Cardinal Hugo, in his Prologue to Joshua, calls Tobit, Judith, Maccabees, the Wisdom of Solomon, and Ecclesiasticus, apocryphal; and says that the church does not receive them for proof of the faith, but for instruction in life. These are his lines; in metre, poor enough; in sense, excellent.

> Restant apocryphi, Jesus, Sapientia, Pastor,
> Et Machabæorum libri, Judith atque Tobias:
> Hi, quod sunt dubii, sub canone non numerantur;
> Sed quia vera canunt, ecclesia suscipit illos.

But, in what sense the church always received them, the same author explains elsewhere (in Prol. Hieron. in Lib. Regum)[8]: "Such the church receives not for proof of the faith, but for instruction

---

[6 Quomodo ergo viginti duo elementa sunt, per quæ Hebraice scribimus, omneque loquimur, et eorum initiis vox humana comprehenditur; ita viginti duo volumina supputantur, quibus quasi literis et exordiis in Dei doctrina tenera adhuc et lactens viri nostri eruditur infantia.]

[7 Sunt præterea alii libri, ut Sapientia Salomonis, liber Jesu Filii Sirach, et Liber Judith, et Tobias, et liber Machabæorum, qui leguntur quidem, sed non scribuntur in Canone.—Opp. p. 320. Rothomag. 1650.]

[8 Tales recipit ecclesia, non ad probationem fidei, sed ad morum instructionem.—Opp. Venet. 1703. T. I. p. 218. 2.]

in morals." Which other fathers also had said before him. The
Gloss upon Gratian's decree (Dist. 16) affirms that the Bible has
some apocryphal books in it. Erasmus in many places maintains
the same opinion, and Cardinal Cajetan most expressly. Now all
these flourished after the Trullan synod, and some of them after
the Florentine; and the church of Rome acknowledges them all as
her sons and disciples; except perhaps Erasmus, whom she hath
expelled, as he deserves, from her family: although Leo the
Tenth called even him, in a certain epistle, his most dearly beloved
son[1]. Antonio Bruccioli, an Italian, translated the old Testament
into the Italian language[2], and wrote commentaries upon the canonical books, but omitted the apocryphal. Even since the council
of Trent, Arias Montanus, who was himself present in that synod,
and published that vast biblical work, and is called by Gregory
XIII. his son, in an edition of the Hebrew Bible with an inter-
linear version declares that the orthodox church follows the canon of
the Hebrews, and reckons apocryphal the books of the old Testament which were written in Greek.

Thus, therefore, I conclude: If these books either were canonical, or so declared and defined by any public and legitimate judgment
of the church; then these so numerous fathers, ancient and modern,
could not have been ignorant of it, or would not have dissented,
especially since they were such as desired both to be, and to be
esteemed, catholics. But these fathers, so numerous, so learned, so
obedient to the godly precepts of the church, were not aware that the
church had decreed any such thing concerning the canon of scripture, and openly pronounced these books to be apocryphal. Therefore these books are not canonical, and were never inserted in the
sacred canon of scripture by any legitimate authority or sanction
of the church. Whence it follows that our church, along with all
other reformed churches, justly rejects these books from the canon;
and that the papists falsely assert them to be canonical. If they
demand testimonies, we have produced them. If they ask for a
multitude, they ought to be content with these which are so many,
and may well satisfy their desires with them.

[1 See Leo's Epistle "Dilecto Filio Erasmo Roterod." prefixed to Erasmus' Greek Testament, Basil. 1535.]

[2 The first edition was printed in 1530. There were three others printed
in his life-time, in 1539, 1540, 1541. See an account of him in Simon, Hist.
Crit. p. 333.]

CHAPTER VII.

OF THE BOOK OF BARUCH.

ORDER requires that we should now treat particularly of these several apocryphal scriptures: and first of those which are counted parts of the canonical books. Here, in the first place, what is commonly called "the book of Baruch" claims an examination. To confirm the authority of this book, our opponents avail themselves of four arguments. The first is, that there is a quotation made from the last chapter of Baruch in 2 Macc. ch. ii. The second, that the councils of Florence and Trent place this book by name amongst the canonical scriptures. The third, that the church takes some lessons from this book in her anniversary offices. The fourth, that many fathers produce testimonies from this book as canonical. From these premises Bellarmine concludes that this book is truly canonical (Lib. I. c. 8). To these we can answer briefly: for the arguments are, as you see, altogether slight ones, and require no very long reply. Thus, therefore, I answer them severally.

To the first: The second book of Maccabees is apocryphal; as I shall hereafter prove by demonstrative arguments. Now one apocryphal book cannot confirm by its testimony the authority of another apocryphal book. Therefore this is no argument.

To the second: We care nothing for those councils. They were popish and altogether antichristian assemblies. The papists may attribute as much weight to those councils as they please: we refuse to be pressed or bound by any such authority.

As to what is objected in the third place,—although the church used to read, and still does read, certain parts of this book, yet it by no means hence follows that the book is in the genuine and strict sense canonical. For we have shewn above, from Jerome and other fathers, that the church was wont formerly to read books not canonical, for the benefit of the people in forming their morals, but not for confirmation of the faith. Besides, what church is it whose example they object to us as an argument? For we are so far from recognising in the custom of the Roman church the force of so great an argument, that we count it a matter of very slight importance.

To the last: I acknowledge that some testimonies are cited from this book by the fathers; and I add too that some of them believed this piece to be a part of Jeremiah. And, in truth, this book does seem preferable to the rest of the apocrypha : for everything in it, whether we consider the matter or the style, appears more august and suitable to the sacred character than in the other books. Nevertheless, the book is apocryphal, as you shall hear. There is no consequence in this reasoning : Some fathers thought this book a part of Jeremiah, therefore it is a part of Jeremiah. For those fathers were in error, as is manifest. Nor is there force in this inference : Some fathers cited testimonies from this book, therefore the book hath canonical authority. For testimonies are often alleged from other books also, which are by no means to be esteemed canonical. Irenæus cites the book of the Shepherd (as Eusebius relates, Lib. v. c. 8)[1] ; but I suppose he did not deem that book part of the canonical scriptures. Yet, alleging a passage from it, he hath used the expression, " Well spoke the scripture which says, &c." And Eusebius writes of him, "He receives the scripture of the Shepherd." And Nicephorus also attests the same, Lib. iv. c. 14. In like manner Athanasius, in his third oration against the Arians, produces something from the book of Baruch : but the same writer does also, in the same oration, bring forward a testimony, to prove that the word is God, from the third of Esdras, which book our adversaries confess to be apocryphal. Testimonies out of this third book of Esdras are used also by Cyprian (Epist. LXXIV.)[2]; by Augustine (Vet. ac Nov. Test. Quæst. 109[3], and Civit. Dei, Lib. XVIII. c. 36)[4]; and Ambrose (De bono Mortis, c. 10), in order to prove that souls are not extinguished with the body[5]. Now this book of Esdras is not canonical, as the papists themselves allow ; so that it is manifest that the cause is not concluded by this argument.

[1 Οὐ μόνον δὲ οἶδεν, ἀλλὰ καὶ ἀποδέχεται τὴν τοῦ Ποιμένος γραφὴν, λέγων· " Καλῶς οὖν εἶπεν ἡ γραφὴ ἡ λέγουσα, κ. τ. λ." T. II. p. 54. ed. Heinich.]

[2 Scieutes quia et apud Esdram veritas vicit, sicut scriptum est, veritas manet et invalescit in æternum. p. 215. ed. Fell.]

[3 Et audi Zorobabel, qui super omnia ait veritas.—Aug. Opp. T. III. p. 11. 2980, A. The reference is 3 Esdr. iii. 12. But this is not a genuine piece : see the admonition prefixed by the Benedictines.]

[4 Nisi forte Esdras in eo Christum prophetasse intelligendus est, quod . . . . . . veritatem super omnia demonstravit esse victricem.—Ibid. T. VII. 833, A. B.]

[5 De quo tibi Esdræ librum legendum suadeo, qui et illas philosophorum nugas despexerit ; et abditiore prudentia, quam collegerat ex revelatione, perstrinxerit eas substantiæ esse superioris.—Epistt. Class. I. Ep. 34. n. 2. T. VIII. p. 433. Paris. 1839.]

The papists object, that these books of Esdras are not cited by those fathers as sacred and canonical, but that the book of Baruch and the rest are cited and mentioned by them in such a manner as to shew that they thought them to be truly canonical. Therefore there is no analogy between the two cases. I answer, that they are indeed styled by them *sacred*, and *scriptures*, but in a certain general sense. For most of them did not suppose that the books were sacred in such a sense as to leave no difference between them and the books which are truly divine and canonical. This John Driedo, one of the chief popish writers, expressly testifies in the case of this very book of Baruch. For thus he writes (de Cat. Script. Lib. I. c. 4. ad Difficult. 11): "So Cyprian, Ambrose, and the other fathers cite sentences from the book of Baruch, and from the third and fourth of Esdras, not as if they were canonical books, but as containing salutary and pious doctrines, not contrary, but rather consonant to our faith[6]." A papist answers the objection of the papists: for in these words he denies that the book of Baruch is either canonical, or cited as such by those fathers. Melchior Canus too (Lib. XII. c. 6) writes thus of this same book: "For, as we have shewn in the second book, the church hath not placed the book of Baruch in the number of the sacred writings so certainly and clearly, as to make it a plain catholic verity that it is a sacred piece, or a plain heresy that it is not. That book, therefore, or any other, which may be called in question without heresy, can not produce certain and evident verities of the catholic faith[7]." From this testimony of Canus I collect, in the first place, that the book of Baruch is not clearly canonical: in the next, that we may deny its canonicity without heresy: lastly, that no firm and evident verity of the catholic faith can be derived from this book ;—an evident proof that the book itself is apocryphal, since all canonical books are fit to produce certain and evident verities of the catholic faith.

Aquinas, however, in his Commentary upon Jude, says, that it

[6 Sic Cyprianus, Ambrosius, ceterique patres citant sententias ex libro Baruch, et 3 et 4 Esræ, non tanquam ex canonicis libris, sed tanquam ex libris continentibus quædam pia, juvantia et non contraria, sed consona potius fidei nostræ.—Opp. Lovan. 1550. T. I. p. 22.]

[7 Nam, ut in secundo libro docuimus, libellum Baruch non adeo explorate et firmiter in sacrorum numero ecclesia reposuit, ut aut illum esse sacrum fidei catholicæ veritas expedita sit, aut non esse sacrum hæresis expedita sit. Libellus ergo iste, sive quilibet alius, qui in quæstionem citra crimen hæreseos vocari possit, non efficit certas atque constantes catholicæ fidei veritates.— Opp. Colon. Agripp. 1605. p. 588.]

is "lawful to derive a testimony to the truth from an apocryphal book," since Jude the apostle hath cited a passage from the apocryphal book of Enoch, v. 14. But, although I by no means deny that it is just as much lawful to quote a passage from an apocryphal book, as from a profane author,—as Paul cites an Iambic line from Menander, 1 Cor. xv. 33, a hemistich from Aratus, Acts xvii. 28, and an heroic verse from Epimenides the Cretan, Tit. i. 12 ; yet I do not think that this passage, which Jude recites, is taken from an apocryphal book, because Jude uses the term προεφήτευσε, "he prophesied." Consequently, he hath adduced this as a prophetical testimony : unless, perhaps, he used the word *prophet* here in the same sense as Paul when he called Epimenides a prophet ; though, indeed, he does not style him a prophet simply, but a prophet of the Cretans.

We have now sufficiently shaken the authority of this book. For I ask, who wrote it ? Either Baruch himself, or Jeremiah, is counted the author of the book. But neither of them could have written it ; as is clear from hence—that it was written in Greek, not in Hebrew, as Jerome tells us, and as the book itself shews. For Jerome says, in the preface to Jeremiah[1], that this book is not read by the Hebrews, nor extant amongst them, and that it was therefore wholly omitted by him. But if it had been written by that Baruch, or by Jeremiah himself, it would doubtless have appeared in Hebrew, not in Greek : for Jeremiah spoke in Hebrew, and published his prophecies in the Hebrew language ; and Baruch was Jeremiah's scribe, and committed many things to writing from Jeremiah's lips, as we find in Jerem. xxxvi. 4. Besides, the very phraseology and diction is Greek, not so condensed, nervous, sedate, and majestic as the style of scripture is wont to be. In the Epistle of Jeremiah, which is recited in Chap. vi., the expression, "Ye shall be there seven generations," (v. 2), is new and foreign to the Hebrew idiom : for in the Hebrew books the term "generation" is never used to designate a period of ten years, as Francis Junius hath correctly observed. Whoever wrote this book was a Greek, or wrote in Greek. Consequently he was neither Baruch nor any other of the prophets. Thus we prove by inevitable deduction that this book must be necessarily esteemed apocryphal.

[1 Librum autem Baruch notarii ejus, qui apud Hebræos nec legitur nec habetur, prætermisimus.—T. ix. p. 783.]

CHAPTER VIII.

OF THE SEVEN APOCRYPHAL CHAPTERS OF ESTHER.

So much of Esther as is Hebrew, that is, canonical, we receive ; and therefore we raise no question concerning those ten chapters which are contained in the Hebrew books. The whole question and controversy is concerning those seven last chapters, which are of a different family and stamp, as we shall easily make appear. The papists will have those seven chapters joined to the rest, without any distinction in point of authority, because the Tridentine council, which has more weight with them than all reason and scripture together, commands those books to be received with all their parts. Their arguments are nearly the same as were alleged for the book of Baruch. Some passages from these chapters are read in the offices of the church, and the fathers sometimes adduce testimonies from them : the little force of which kind of reasoning we have already sufficiently exposed. They say besides that Josephus (Antiq. Lib. x. cap. 6 [2]) mentions two epistles of Ahasuerus, which are found in these last chapters and not in the previous ones. These are the arguments of our opponents.

I do not choose to reply again to what has been already refuted. But I will observe that the argument which rests upon the authority of Josephus is inconclusive. For, in the first place, what if Josephus took something from these chapters, to enlarge or illustrate his history ? must he therefore have deemed these chapters to appertain to the canonical scripture ? But, concerning this whole matter, let Lyra answer for me, who, in the close of his commentary upon this book, makes use of the following expressions [3]: " The rest which comes after I do not intend to explain, because it is not in the Hebrew, nor belongs to the canonical scripture, but rather seems to have been invented by Josephus and other writers, and afterwards inserted in the vulgar edition." Josephus, therefore, did not take those things from any canonical book, but was himself the first writer of them ; and others afterwards, read-

[2 The reference should be xi. c. vi. § 12. pp. 575, 576. Haverc.]

[3 Cetera quæ sequuntur non intendo exponere, quia non in Hebræo sunt, nec de scriptura canonica, sed magis videntur a Josepho et aliis scriptoribus conficta, et postea editioni vulgatæ inserta.—Nic. Lyrani Comment. Antwerp. 1634. *in fin. Estheræ.*]

ing them in Josephus, copied them into the Bible.   But although
they were, as Lyra says, inserted in the vulgar edition, it does not
therefore follow that they were ever allowed a canonical authority.
Sixtus Senensis (Lib. I.) approves and follows the opinion of Lyra[1].
Lastly, it is certain that Josephus's own judgment concerning the
canonical books was no other than that of Jerome, as appears from
his first book against Apion.   There he determines that no books
are canonical, but such as were written by prophets of ascertained
authority.   Now these chapters were not written by any prophet,
which I will prove by the following arguments.

In the first place, the matters related in the former chapters
are told over again in these following ones; which repeated narra-
tion of the same events sufficiently shews that all were not written
by the same person.   For there was no reason whatever for his
telling the same history twice over.   Nor would the same author
have written the latter part in a different language from the
former.   But if he were another person, why yet, if he were a
prophet, did he not use the Hebrew tongue, the proper language
of prophecy?   Learned men make either Ezra, or Joachim the
priest, or Mordecai himself, the author of this book, and recognise
no other than these.

Secondly.   There are many incongruities and inconsistencies,
which it is impossible to reconcile, in these chapters, of which I
will produce some specimens.   *First*, in chap. xi. 2, Mordecai is
said to have dreamed of the two eunuchs who conspired against
the king, in the second year.   See also chap. xii. 1.   But in
the second chapter, which is canonical, ver. 16, we read that this
conspiracy took place in the seventh year of Ahasuerus.   Bellarmine answers, that the narrative of the plot which is contained in
chap. xii. belongs to the beginning of the book; but that what we
read to have occurred in the second year in chap. xi. is not to be
understood of the plot, but of the dream of Mordecai: for that the
plot was laid in the seventh year, as we are told in the second
chapter.   But all this is said without proofs, and in spite of the
plain declaration of the book itself.   For at the close of chap. xi.
Mordecai says that, when he arose, he pondered many thoughts in
his mind concerning that dream, until the night, ($\H{\epsilon}\omega\varsigma$ $\tau\hat{\eta}\varsigma$ $\nu\nu\kappa\tau\acute{o}\varsigma$);
and that then, as he rested in the court with the two eunuchs, he

[1 Even in our own times, notwithstanding the stringent declaration of
the council of Trent, this seems to have been the opinion of some respectable Roman Catholic divines, e. g. John in his Einleitung in A. T.]

detected their conspiracy. There was not therefore an interval of five years between the dream of Mordecai and the plot of the eunuchs, as Bellarmine fancies, but only of one day, if there be faith in the book itself.

Secondly, the narrative in this book was written many years after the death of Mordecai. For, in chap. xi.[2] mention is made of Ptolemy and Cleopatra, who assuredly lived after the times of Mordecai and of the prophets. Nor can one well understand what the meaning of that passage is intended to be. Lysimachus of Jerusalem, the son of Ptolemy, is said to have "interpreted the present epistle of Phurim," which Dositheus and his son Ptolemy brought in the reign of Ptolemy and Cleopatra. Bellarmine says it may be answered, that the first author of this book, who wrote the history of Esther in Hebrew, drew up only the sum of the story, and that this Hebrew narrative has come down to us; that then, at some other time, the history was written more copiously by some other person, and translated into the Greek language by Lysimachus, as is indicated in chap. xi.; and that not the original book of this later author, but only a translation of it, is now extant.

But, in the first place, Lysimachus is not here said to have translated any Hebrew book into the Greek tongue, but only the epistle of Phurim. And, in the next place, if the assertion that the later author wrote this history more copiously than the former were true, then this history, of which a translation only hath survived, could not be that which the later author wrote: for it is shorter than the Hebrew history, and does not give the series of the narrative at all so fully, as every one may readily perceive. Lastly, who translated this Greek translation of Lysimachus into Latin? Jerome found a certain Latin translation, and subjoined it to his version, though containing, as he tells us, some things which were extant neither in the Hebrew, nor in the text of any other interpreter. Yet this vulgar translation, which Jerome deemed utterly unfaithful, is in the highest sense authentic and canonical with the papists.

[2 The passage referred to is plainly a scholium, or marginal note, as follows: ἐτοῦς τετάρτου βασιλεύοντος Πτολεμαίου καὶ Κλεοπάτρας εἰσήνεγκε Δοσίθεος, ὃς ἔφη εἶναι ἱερεὺς καὶ Λευίτης, καὶ Πτολεμαῖος ὁ υἱὸς αὐτοῦ, τὴν προκειμένην ἐπιστολὴν τῶν φρουραὶ, ἣν ἔφασαν εἶναι καὶ ἡρμηνευκέναι Λυσίμαχον Πτολεμαίου τὸν ἐν Ἱερουσαλήμ. Compare Ussher de LXX. Int. p. 22, and Valckenaër de Aristobulo Judæo, p. 63, who supposes this Lysimachus to have been the author also of what is called the Third Book of Maccabees.]

Thirdly, this pretended author tells us, chap. xii. 5, that a reward was given by the king to Mordecai for his information; whereas, in chap. vi. 3 of the true history, we read that no reward was bestowed upon him. Bellarmine, however, replies that there is no difficulty here; since in chap. xii. that magnificent reward is meant which he afterwards received. But any one who reads the place itself will see, that this interpretation can by no means stand. For in this twelfth chapter Haman is said to have plotted mischief against Mordecai, after the gifts were bestowed upon him; which cannot be understood of those most distinguished honours and gifts with which the king graced him after he had read the annals. For that very morning, as we read in chap. vi., Haman was in attendance to settle with the king about hanging Mordecai; and that very day Mordecai was raised to the highest dignity, and loaded with royal favours. Nor could Haman, after that, attempt anything against him: for Mordecai was then in the highest favour with the king, and Haman himself was presently hanged upon that same day. Therefore here there must be some false-hood upon the other side.

Fourthly, in chap. xii. 6, Haman is said to have been enraged against Mordecai on account of the eunuchs whom Mordecai accused, and whom, upon being arraigned of treason, and convicted by Mordecai's evidence, the king had punished capitally. But it is incredible that Haman, who had received such honour and dignity from the king, should have favoured the treason of the eunuchs; and nothing of the kind is found in the true history, but, on the contrary, a very different cause of his offence and anger is assigned, chap. iii.

Fifthly, in chap. xv. 7, this author says that, when Esther came into the king's presence, the king looked upon her with so angry a countenance, that she fainted through fear. On the contrary, chap. v. 2, she is said to have obtained great favour on coming in to the king.

Sixthly, in chap. xvi. 10, Haman is called a Macedonian; but in chap. viii. 3, we find him to have been an Agagite, that is, of the race of Amalek.

Seventhly, Haman is not only said (chap. xvi.) to have been a Macedonian himself, but also to have designed, after removing Mordecai and Esther, to lay violent hands upon the king, in order to transfer the kingdom of the Persians to the Macedonians. But, first, how could Haman have transferred the kingdom of the Persians to the Macedonians, if he had succeeded ever so well in putting the king to death? For the kingdom of the Macedonians was at that time little or nothing. Besides, the true history contains not a trace of the story told in chap. xvi., that he plotted against Mordecai and Esther, in order that, by their destruction, he might the more easily attack the king, and transfer the kingdom to the Macedonians. For he was not aware that the queen was a Jewess, or related to Mordecai; and he devised all sorts of mischief against Mordecai, not to open himself a way to the kingdom, but simply to satisfy his malice. For Mordecai was not, in the beginning, when Haman first conceived this grudge against him, in any station of authority, so as in any way to eclipse his splendour. But if any one choose to say that Mordecai's information was the means of saving the king from assassination, and that thus an obstacle was set in the way of Haman's ambition, and it was this which kindled such a blaze of hatred; he must be given to understand that he contradicts the sacred narrative. For that conspiracy of the eunuchs and the information of Mordecai took place before Haman had acquired so much favour and power in the royal court, as is manifest from the second chapter and the beginning of the third.

All these things are of such a nature, that they can by no means stand together or be reconciled with each other: whence it follows, that the authority of these chapters must needs fall to the ground. And rightly is it ordered that these chapters are not read in our church.

Thirdly. These chapters are not written in Hebrew. For Jerome says that he had marked these chapters with an *obelus* set before them; which is the mark by which he is wont to indicate apocryphal additions. For the pretence of some that they were once in the Hebrew text, but have now dropped out of it, is easily refuted by what we have observed already. Jerome had no suspicion of this, and the style cries out against it, and reason proves the contrary. For how could they have been better preserved in the Greek than in the Hebrew? or what need is there to give any credit to mere fictions and conjectures of this nature?

Fourthly. Besides other authors, and some papists also, whom I have already alleged, Sixtus Senensis, who wrote his *Bibliotheca* after the council of Trent, in the first book of that work asserts these chapters to be apocryphal; a concession which he never would have made, unless overcome by the very force of truth, since he labours so energetically to maintain the credit of the other apocryphal pieces. Nor did the Tridentine decree, requiring the books there mentioned to be received *with their parts*, avail to turn him from his opinion. For he contends that this is no native and genuine part of the Book of Esther, but that in these chapters all is supposititious. He writes in plain words, that "by reason of these strips appended, inserted by the rashness of certain writers from various quarters[1]," it had come to pass that it was late ere this book acquired a canonical authority amongst Christians. So clearly did pious men see these to be fabulous, that they threw a shade of suspicion over even the canonical portions. And though this papist, Sixtus, is blamed by the Jesuits, yet is he not refuted. But let us leave them to quarrel amongst themselves.

CHAPTER IX.

OF THE APOCRYPHAL PARTS OF DANIEL.

To confirm the authority of these parts, the papists can allege no peculiar argument. For their allegation, that the fathers quote testimonies from these chapters as well as from the others, and call them testimonies of scripture, is devoid of strength. They do indeed quote them, and call them scriptures; but they do not affirm them to be canonical scriptures, such as the Books of Moses and the prophets. They are styled scriptures, because they used to be publicly read in the church, that the people might thence take noble examples of morals, and were preferred (as Augustine says in a certain place) to the treatises of all other discoursers[2]. But this is far from proving the authority of these portions equal to that of the remainder of the book, which is truly canonical. Now, therefore, let us say a few words of that Hymn of the three children which is commonly placed in, and reckoned to the end of the third chapter; and of the History of Susanna, Bel and the Dragon, which are joined in the vulgar Bibles with the prophecy of Daniel, and counted a part of it. These pieces I will prove to be spurious and apocryphal by sound and cogent arguments.

[1 Propter has appendicum lacinias hinc inde quorundam scriptorum temeritate insertas.—p. 20. Paris. 1610.]

[2 Qui sententiis tractatorum instrui volunt, oportet ut istum librum sapientiæ . . . . . omnibus tractatoribus anteponant.—August. de Prædest. Sanct. Lib. I. c. 14.]

First, then, let us hear Jerome expressly pronouncing his judgment concerning these portions. Thus he speaks, in his proem to Daniel, and in the preface of his commentary upon that prophet : " Daniel, as it stands in the Hebrew text, has neither the History of Susanna, nor the Hymn of the three children, nor the fables of Bel and the Dragon ; which we, considering that they are now dispersed over the whole world, have subjoined with an obelus prefixed, and [as it were] striking them through, lest the ignorant should think that we had cut off a great part of the volume[3]." From these words of Jerome we collect : 1. That no part of these pieces was found in the Hebrew, which sufficiently proves them to be spurious. 2. That they seemed to Jerome to deserve the stroke of that obelus by which he uses to distinguish the apocryphal from the canonical passages. 3. That, nevertheless, they were in use and read every where. 4. That he would himself have omitted them, but that he feared the calumnies of certain persons. 5. That it was the unlearned who supposed that these were really any parts of Daniel.

Secondly, John Driedo (de Catal. Scripturæ, Lib. I. cap. ult.) does not say that this history is canonical, but only that it is not to be despised ; and that he who believes these things to be all true, falls into no pernicious error ; " even as we read," says he, " the acts of the martyrs, from which we do not derive arguments for matters of faith[4]." You see what distinguished and honourable opinions the papists themselves entertain of this history. We ourselves can not think more lowly than they do of this class of writings. But that learned theologian saw that it was impossible to frame any more exalted judgment of these fragments, since they are not found in the Hebrew and sacred volumes of the scripture, but are derived from the Greek translation of the worthless and perfidious Theodotion.

Thirdly, that Paronomasia, of which Jerome speaks in the preface to Daniel, ἀπὸ τοῦ σχίνου σχίσει, ἀπὸ τοῦ πρίνου πρίσει[5],

[3 Apud Hebræos nec Susannæ habes historiam, nec hymnum trium puerorum, nec Belis draconisque fabulas : quas nos, quia in toto orbe dispersæ sunt, veru÷ anteposito, eoque jugulante, subjecimus, ne videremur apud imperitos magnam partem voluminis detruncasse.—Hieron. Opp. T. IX. 1362. ed. Vallars. Veronæ. 1738.]

[4 Ut legimus gesta martyrum, ex quibus argumentum non sumimus efficax ad demonstrandum ea quæ sunt fidei.—T. I. p. 22.]

[5 Audivi ego quendam de præceptoribus Judæorum, quum Susannæ derideret historiam, et a Græco nescio quo diceret esse confictam, illud op-

proves that this little story was not written in Hebrew, but in Greek. Daniel asked one of the elders, under what tree he had found Susanna with her paramour. He answered, under a mastick tree, σχίνου. Then Daniel forthwith, alluding to the name of the tree, subjoins, σχίσει σε ὁ Θεός. Afterwards he comes to the other, and asks him under what tree he had seen Susanna committing so foul a crime? He mentions a different tree, and says that it was under a holm-oak, πρίνου. Then Daniel, using a similar play upon the name, brings in his judgment, πρίσει σε ὁ Θεός. This Greek etymology (for so Jerome calls it) shews that the history itself was written in the Greek language: for you will find no allusion of the kind in the corresponding Hebrew names and verbs. Therefore it was not written by Daniel, or any prophet.

The papists object, that this argument was long ago answered by Origen in his Epistle to Julius Africanus, mentioned by Eusebius[1], who alleges that there were words in the Hebrew which contained plainly such an allusion, but that the Greek interpreter had changed the names to preserve the paronomasia. But nothing can be slighter or more futile than that conjecture. For, in the *first* place, though I confess that Origen did write about this matter to Julius Africanus, yet what he wrote is not known. For the piece upon that subject which hath lately appeared hath not yet gained any clear credit[2].

I ask, in the *next* place, what are those Hebrew names of trees which will yield this allusion? a question which must needs bring them to a stand.

Thirdly, the Holy Spirit does not use to affect this change of names, or put a force upon the truth of things, or alter their denominations, especially seeing that the refutation of the charge depends upon the very diversity of the names. For if they answered that they had seen Susanna under an oak or a fig, the story should not have been told as if they had said a mastick or a holm-tree, since that is not true in fact. Effectually to discover the falsehood of these calumnies of the elders, the very names of the trees should have been preserved.

ponere quod Origeni quoque Africanus opposuit, etymologias has ἀπὸ τοῦ σχίνου σχίσαι, καὶ ἀπὸ τοῦ πρίνου πρίσαι, de Græco sermone descendere.—Opp. T. IX. 1364.]

[1 Hist. Eccl. VI. c. 31.]

[2 All doubts, however, were very soon removed by its publication in Greek by Hæschelius. August. Vindel. 1602.]

Fourthly, I cannot understand how it should be taken for a solid proof of the falsehood of the charges, that because different trees were named by the elders, therefore it should be evident that Susanna was undeservedly accused. They might have said that they had not specially observed what kind of tree it was, and so might easily have been mistaken. They who were so wicked in devising the charge would not have been so stupid in proving it.

Lastly, when they object to us in this cause so often the authority of Origen, let them attend to what Jerome hath written of him in the preface to Daniel. " I wonder," says he, " that some querulous persons should be indignant at me, as if I had mutilated the book ; whereas Origen, and Eusebius, and Apollinarius, and other ecclesiastical men and the doctors of Greece, confess, as I have said, that these visions are not extant in the Hebrew, and declare that they are not bound to answer Porphyry in defence of things which have no authority of sacred scripture[3]." If that be true which Jerome writes of Origen, they have no reason to call Origen a patron of this history. For Origen together with the other Greek doctors expressly affirmed, if we believe Jerome, that these pieces were not extant in the Hebrew, nor possessed the authority of sacred scripture.

In fine, the papists cannot agree amongst themselves who that Daniel was who was thrust into the lion's den for slaying the dragon and destroying Bel, and was suffered to remain there six days. Bellarmine, after carefully weighing the whole matter, at length arrives at the conclusion, that this Daniel was not the same person as the distinguished prophet, but a different one. For the great prophet Daniel was of the tribe of Juda, as is manifest: but the Seventy, as Jerome testifies in the preface to Daniel, make that Daniel who had intercourse with Cyrus, a priest of the tribe of Levi; and the more learned papists think that this was the same Daniel who destroyed Bel and the dragon, and was preserved six days in the den of lions. Thus these things cannot be speciously defended, without introducing a second Daniel contrary to the common and general opinion. But what proof have we of the existence of such a Daniel? What credit

[3 Et miror quasdam μεμψιμοίρους indignari mihi, quasi ego decurtaverim librum: quum et Origenes, et Eusebius, et Apollinarius, aliique ecclesiastici viri et doctores Græciæ has, ut dixi visiones non haberi apud Hebræos fateantur, nec se debere respondere Porphyrio pro his quæ nullam scripturæ sanctæ auctoritatem præbeant.—Hieronym. Opp. T. v. 619.]

do the stories which the Seventy tell about this matter deserve? And if what is told in this fourteenth chapter was not done by that great Daniel, but by some other, why is it made a part of that Daniel? why said to be his, and attributed to him? Let all, therefore, understand that the Daniel who subverted Bel, burnt the dragon, and remained six days in the den, was not that great Daniel whose prophetic book is extant, and worthy of all authority, and that by the confession of the papists themselves, but some other unknown, unheard of, and uncertain Daniel. But we have hitherto never heard of more prophets of the name of Daniel than one, and may therefore dismiss this second Daniel without further ceremony.

CHAPTER X.

OF THE BOOK OF TOBIT.

AFTER having proved that those fragments which are stuck upon certain canonical books should be cut off, and plucked out from the body of sacred scripture, it follows now that we should treat of those six entire apocryphal books.

And first let us consider the book of Tobit, for the authority of which the papists adduce no special argument whatsoever. For, though it be quoted by the fathers, it does not thence follow that it is a canonical book, as we have already clearly proved : and as to its being called "divine" by Ambrose, the meaning is not to teach us that the book is undoubtedly canonical and equal in every respect to those which really form part of the canon, but that it is a book by no means to be despised or esteemed lightly. For although it is not truly canonical, yet it may be styled divine, as it was wont to be read in the church, and was joined with the canonical books in one volume, so as commonly to pass under the name of scripture. For that it is not properly canonical, we have shewn by many testimonies of the fathers, and can demonstrate by plain arguments. But here consider how the papists run into a clear contradiction. Bellarmine confesses that Jerome rejects this book, and the rest which are involved in the present controversy, from the canon of scripture ; and pretends that it is no wonder he should do so, since no general council (which hath the regular privilege of determining and defining what should be deemed the canon of scripture) had decreed the canonicity of these books. Yet, in the meanwhile, the papists bring testimonies from Irenæus, Cyprian, Hilary, Ambrose, to prove these books canonical. But how or by what authority could those fathers affirm these books to be canonical, when that matter was not yet certain and clearly known, being as yet not decided by any general council? Therefore, either this is not the exclusive prerogative of a general council, or those fathers followed opinion rather than judgment and reason, when they received (as our opponents imagine) these books for canonical, which the church had not yet approved by its sanction and testimony.

Let us now bring forward some objections against the authority of this book. And first, Jerome witnesses the judgment which the church of old passed upon this book. For he says, in the preface to the books of Solomon, that the church does not receive the book of Tobit into the canonical scriptures [1]. Therefore the catholic church (of which Jerome speaks) hath judged this book not to be canonical. And, in the prologue to the book of Tobit [2], he wonders at the importunity of those by whom he had been induced to translate into the Latin tongue this book, which the Hebrews had cut off from the list of the divine scriptures, and which was only to be read in the Chaldee, a language with which he was unacquainted. Wherefore he confesses that he had availed himself of the assistance of another, and had rendered in Latin words that which some unknown interpreter, skilled both in the Hebrew and Chaldee languages, had dictated to him in Hebrew. So that Jerome hath rather translated some other person's version of this book than the book itself. Besides, the book is now extant only in Greek and Latin, and it is wholly uncertain in what language it was originally written. Jerome writes that he had seen a Chaldaic copy of it, but attributes to it no sort of authority. And the present copies of the book are exceeding various and corrupt, as may be easily detected by a collation of them. What more do we

[1 Judith, et Tobi, et Machabæorum libros legit quidem ecclesia, sed inter canonicas scripturas non recipit. Hieronym. Opp. T. ix. 1296.]

[2 Mirari non desino exactionis vestræ instantiam: exigitis enim ut librum Chaldæo sermone conscriptum ad Latinum stylum traham, librum utique Tobiæ, quem Hebræi de Catalogo divinarum scripturarum secantes, his quæ *Apocrypha* memorant, manciparunt ...... Utriusque linguæ (Hebrææ et Chaldææ) peritissimum loquacem inveniens, unius diei laborem arripui; et quidquid ille Hebraicis verbis expressit, hoc ego, accito notario, sermonibus Latinis exposui.—Opp. T. x. 293. The common reading is *Hagiographa* for *Apocrypha*: but the correctness of the latter is so evident, that it is admitted by the Benedictines and Vallarsius.]

want? The book may speak for itself, the whole character of which shews, as clear as the light, that it hath no claims to canonicity.

CHAPTER XI.

OF THE BOOK OF JUDITH.

OUR adversaries snatch up an argument from Jerome in favour of this book, which goes under the name of Judith. For Jerome tells us, in the preface to the book of Judith, that this book was counted in the sacred scriptures by the Nicene synod[1]. Therefore, say they, Jerome himself testifies that this book at least is canonical. But this testimony injures our opponents' cause more than it helps it. For first, if that synod received this book into the number of the sacred scriptures, it affected those others, which it omitted, with no slight prejudice. For if, as these men will have it, it determined this book to be canonical, why did it not comprehend the others also in the same decree, if they be really canonical?

Secondly, Jerome's words are, " *We read* that the synod of Nice counted this book in the number of sacred scriptures." But where this is read, he tells us not. And if the Nicene synod had determined the canonicity of this book, the council of Laodicea, which was held a short time after that of Nice, would not have left it in the Apocrypha. And Erasmus hath rightly noted, that Jerome does not himself affirm that this book was counted sacred scripture by the council of Nice.

Thirdly, " To be *canonical scripture*" is one thing, and "to be counted in the number of *sacred scripture*" is another thing. For those pieces which are read along with the sacred scriptures for the edification of the people, although not for confirmation of doctrines, are counted in the number of sacred scriptures. And

---

[1] Sed quia hunc librum Synodus Nicena in numero sanctarum scripturarum legitur computasse, &c.—Opp. T. x. 22. Most critics suppose that the council of Nice in some of their documents had quoted some testimony from the book of Judith: but Vallarsius thinks it more probable that Jerome alludes to some spurious index of the scriptures, forged under the name of that council. He appeals, very properly, to Cassiodorus, Instit. Divin. Lit. c. 14, to shew that such indexes existed, and passed under the names of the councils of Nice and Chalcedon.]

that this was the mind and meaning of Jerome, is plain from
Jerome's own words in the preface to the Proverbs. "The
church," says he, "reads this book, but does not receive it amongst
the canonical scriptures[2]." Although, therefore, this book be read,
and counted in the number of sacred scriptures, yet is it not received amongst those scriptures which are canonical and sacred in
the highest sense. This Jerome asserts in plain words; but this
he would never have asserted, if the council of Nice had determined
this book to be canonical. Nay, in this very preface Jerome
shews this book not to be canonical by two arguments:—first, because the Hebrews esteem it apocryphal, and unfit for confirming anything which may be called in question[3]: secondly, because
the book was written in the Chaldee language, and the copies of it
grossly corrupted and depraved. For which reason Jerome, in
translating it, gave the general sense rather than the exact meaning of each word, and only rendered into Latin what he found uncorrupted in the Chaldee[4]. Now, however, even those Chaldee
copies themselves have perished; and the Greek ones differ widely
from Jerome's version. Besides, Josephus, in his commentaries
upon the Jewish antiquities, does not touch at all upon this story
of Judith,—a sufficient proof that Josephus did not consider it
canonical.

But now let us estimate the authority of this book by the
evidence of the book itself, and briefly examine what the times
were of which it professes to be the history. For the opinions of
authors upon this subject are various; nor is it needful that we
should enumerate them particularly. Let us hear, then, the de-
terminations of those who at present sway the Romish schools.
Sixtus Senensis (Lib. VIII. Hær. 11) writes, that he who is called
Nabuchodonosor was Ahasuerus, the son of Darius Hystaspes,
and that he reigned in Babylon after Cyrus was slain. But no
Persian emperor was called Nabuchodonosor; and the Persian
kings fixed the seat of their empire not at Nineve but at Babylon.

[2 Vide supra, p. 81.]

[3 Apud Hebræos liber Judith inter Apocrypha legitur: cujus auctoritas
ad roboranda illa quæ in contentionem veniunt minus idonea judicatur.
Chaldæo tamen sermone conscriptus, inter historias computatur.—Opp. T. x.
p. 22.]

[4 Magis sensum e sensu, quam ex verbo verbum transferens. Multorum
codicum varietatem vitiosissimam amputavi: sola ea, quæ intelligentia integra
in verbis Chaldæis invenire potui, Latinis expressi. Ibid.]

But he who sent Holofernes with an army to subdue the world, is called in the first chapter of this book Nabuchodonosor, and is said to have reigned at Nineve. There are many other incongruities besides, so that Bellarmine refers this history to the times of Manasseh, whom Nabuchodonosor took captive, brought to Babylon, and after a long while set at liberty. He supposes, therefore, that these events happened a little after the return of Manasseh, following Melchior Canus, (Lib. II. c. 16): which opinion (although repugnant to that of all his predecessors, as Eusebius in his Chronicon, Augustine, Philo, Bede, Lyra, Driedo and others,) seems yet much more probable than that of the rest, since it is certain that there was no Nabuchodonosor in existence after the Babylonian captivity. But now let us sift this hypothesis, and prove that these things could not have been done even in the time of Manasseh.

First, in the beginning of the fifth chapter, when Holofernes perceives that the Jewish people were meditating and preparing war, he convokes all his officers and asks them what people this was, and who was their leader. But if Manasseh had been only a short time before taken captive by the king of the Chaldeans, and carried into Babylon, neither Holofernes nor the Chaldeans could have been so ignorant who was their king as to be forced to seek and obtain information upon this subject from Achior the Ammonite. For they are made to inquire concerning the people, the country, the cities, the power of the inhabitants, their mode of warfare, their leader and king, as if they had never heard of such a nation as the Jews. But the Chaldeans had before then made war upon this people, wasted Judæa, taken Jerusalem, and carried away with them Manasseh into Babylon. Therefore these things about which they now inquire could not have been unknown to them.

Secondly, when Holofernes came into Judæa, the temple was overthrown. For these are the very words of Achior, in the Greek text: Ὁ ναὸς τοῦ Θεοῦ αὐτῶν ἐγενήθη εἰς ἔδαφος καὶ αἱ πόλεις αὐτῶν ἐκρατήθησαν. "The temple of the Jews at Jerusalem was overturned and rased to the ground, and their cities occupied." But in the captivity of Manasseh there was no subversion of the temple, nor was the temple levelled to the ground before the reign of Zedekiah, in which (as everybody knows) the great captivity took place.

Thirdly, if these things had happened in the time of Manasseh and after his return, the Jewish people would not have treated the messengers of the king of Babylon so shamefully, or dismissed them so ignominiously, as we are told they did in the first chapter. For the Jews had then experienced both the power and the clemency of the Babylonians.

Fourthly, in the history of the Kings, in which the acts of Manasseh are written, we read nothing of this kind about Holofernes; which being a thing of such a remarkable character, it is surprising that the Holy Spirit should have omitted to mention it.

Fifthly, in the last chapter we read that Judith lived more than 105 years, and that while Judith lived, after this victory no enemy troubled Israel. This peace, therefore, lasted many years. But now, when Holofernes was in Judæa, Judith had not passed the flower of her age; for she was very beautiful, and she pleased Holofernes, and is called a girl, chap. xii.: so that, after this victory, there must have been peace for near a hundred years. For the peace is said to have subsisted many years, both during her life and after she was dead. But Amon succeeded Manasseh, and reigned two years; Josiah succeeded Amon, and held the sovereignty thirty-one years. After the death of Josiah, a mighty mass of trouble fell upon the state, which could not be allayed until it was entirely subverted, and the people carried into captivity. How can we assign that long peace to such times as these?

Sixthly, I should wish to know, (for I am by no means disposed to think it,) whether there was any Nabuchodonosor in Manasseh's time. For Nabuchodonosor the first, whose son was the second and great Nabuchodonosor, began to reign with Josiah, who was 33 years later than Manasseh. Before him, if we believe history, no Nabuchodonosor reigned either at Nineve or Babylon. For, as to the allegation that all the kings of the Babylonians were called Nabuchodonosor, I grant it to have been so after that great Nabuchodonosor, whose greatness was the cause that this name became hereditary in the line of Babylonian kings: but there is no evidence that they all went by that name before him.

We have now shewn plainly enough that this history does not suit the times of Manasseh. And the argument which led Bellarmine to cast it in those times is utterly destitute of force. Eliakim, says he, was at this time high priest, as he is called in the fifteenth chapter of Judith; and in the time of Hezekiah there was a certain Eliakim priest, the son of Hilkiah. But Bellarmine did not observe that that Eliakim, who is mentioned in the history of Hezekiah, was not a priest, but a certain officer, of the tribe of Judah and the family of David, as appears from Isai. xxii. and

2 Kings xviii. For he succeeded Shebna, who was either the royal scribe, as some render it, or the chancellor, as others, or the master of the royal household, as others; but who neither was, nor could have been, a priest. Josephus, in the last book of his Jewish antiquities, gives a list of all the pontiffs of the Jews, from Aaron down to the last, yet names no Eliakim or Joakim about these times. You see what sort of foundation Bellarmine had for his opinion concerning the history of Judith.

Genebrard, in his Chronology, (Lib. II. anno mundi 3560[1]) assigns the date of this history otherwise, but much more rashly. For he says this was the same Nabuchodonosor, who subdued Zedekiah, took Jerusalem, and carried the people into captivity; that he sent Holofernes into Judæa in the 13th year of his reign, and in the 19th transferred the remainder of the Jews to Babylon. But Genebrard hath not made a correct distribution of the times. For how can it be truly said that Judith lived so long after that calamity, and that peace subsisted during her life and a long time after it? Or how could the Chaldeans have failed to be thoroughly acquainted with the people and king of the Jews, when Nabuchodonosor had, but a little before, made Zedekiah himself king of the Jews? No time, therefore, can be found, which suits with these transactions. For it is manifest that none of these three opinions is true, and our adversaries can invent none truer than these.

CHAPTER XII.

OF THE BOOK OF WISDOM.

WE have now to treat of those two books, whereof one is called the Wisdom of Solomon, the other Ecclesiasticus; which pieces we deny not to be replete with very beautiful admonitions, precepts, and sentiments, yet maintain to be deservedly placed amongst the apocryphal scriptures by our churches. Besides the common arguments, which we have often answered already, our adversaries allege one peculiar to the case of that book which is called the Wisdom of Solomon. They pretend that the apostle Paul hath used the testimony of this book, Rom. xi. 34, where he says, Τίς ἔγνω νοῦν Κυρίου, ἢ τίς σύμβουλος αὐτοῦ ἐγένετο; "Who

[1 p. 236. Paris. 1600.]

hath known the mind of the Lord, or who hath been his counsellor?" Likewise that the expression, Heb. i. 3, "Who, being the
brightness of his glory, and the express image of his person," is
borrowed from the seventh chapter of this book.

As to the first place, I answer: The apostle does not intimate
that he is there citing any testimony. For there is no consequence
in the reasoning, that, because similar words to those are found in
this place, therefore the apostle quoted this place. And even if
the apostle recited the words of some prophetic scripture, or alluded
to some scripture, we are not therefore obliged to suppose that it
was to this place in Wisdom. For the same sentiment is found in
Isaiah xl. 13, in these words: "Who hath directed the Spirit of
the Lord, or, being his counsellor, hath taught him?" &c. Thus
Thomas Aquinas, in his fifth lecture upon Rom. xi. says, that the
apostle here brings in the authority of Isaiah[2]. So also Cajetan,
and our countrymen the Rhemist interpreters, in their English
version. Add to this, that, whereas there have been various
indexes of testimonies cited out of the old Testament in the new,
drawn up by many persons, and placed in various editions of the
Bible, no one of these exhibits any testimony from this book of
Wisdom, and all refer this citation by name to Isaiah[3].

As to the second place, the apostle makes no citation, as is
evident. For what though some words be found in the book of
Wisdom not unlike those wherein the apostle describes the person
of Christ? For indeed it cannot be said that the words are iden-
tically the same, but only that they are similar. So that this
argument has but weak force to prove the canonical authority
of this book. But now we, on the other hand, will produce some
considerations which may shew that the book is apocryphal. We
concede indeed, with Epiphanius, that it is a useful book; but we
add also with Epiphanius, that "it is not referred to the number
of the canonical scriptures:" which assertion he extends also to the
following one.

First, this book, as all allow, was written in Greek, and that, as
hath already been proved, is sufficient to exclude it from the canon.

Secondly, Jerome, in the Preface to Proverbs, says of these
two books, Wisdom and Ecclesiasticus: "These two volumes one
may read indeed for the edification of the people, but not to

---

[2 T. xvi. p. 37. 2. Opp. Venet. 1593.]
[3 It is in fact the Sept. translation of that passage, with only the varia-
tion of ἡ for καί.]

confirm the authority of the dogmas of the church[1]." Where also
he calls the book *pseudepigraphal*[2], so as that, although it goes
under the name of Solomon, it is not to be supposed to be really
his ; and observes that it " savours of Grecian eloquence."

Thirdly, most of the ancients determine that this book was
written by Philo, who certainly neither was a prophet, nor could
have written a canonical book of the old Testament. For he
lived after Christ in the time of Caligula, before whom he discharged his celebrated embassy on behalf of the Jews. But then
the time of the old Testament had already passed ; and Christ
says, " The law and the prophets were until John the Baptist."
For the conjecture of some, and Bellarmine among the rest, that
there was some other Jewish Philo, is grounded upon no testimony
of antiquity, and is rejected by Sixtus Senensis, (Lib. VIII. c. 9), and
is at variance with the general opinion of the doctors. For thus
writes Bonaventura in his Commentary upon this book : " The
first efficient cause, in the way of a compiler, was Philo the wisest
of the Jews[3]." So that he determines it to have been written by
Philo, not by Solomon. But by what Philo ? By any other than
him who flourished after Christ, and wrote so many pieces with
so much eloquence? of whom some one said, ἢ Πλάτων φιλω-
νίζει, ἢ Φίλων πλατωνίζει[4]. Bonaventura subjoins, " who lived
in the times of the apostles." It is evident therefore what Philo he
supposed the author of this book. For he recognised no other
Philo ; and he tells us that the same was said by Rabanus. For
Josephus, in his first book against Apion, names a certain older
Philo, but one who was a Gentile and a philosopher, not a Jew
or conversant with the scriptures[5]. Wherefore, since this book was

[1 Hæc duo ecclesia legat ad edificationem plebis, non ad auctoritatem
ecclesiasticorum dogmatum confirmandam. T. IX. 1296.]

[2 Alius ψευδεπίγραφος, qui Sapientia Salomonis inscribitur .... et
ipse stylus Græcam eloquentiam redolet ; et nonnulli veterum scriptorum
hunc esse Judæi Philonis affirmant. T. IX. 1295.—Hence some have endeavoured to explain how it came to be attributed to Solomon, Philo's name
in Hebrew being Jedidiah.]

[3 Proxima causa efficiens per modum compilantis fuit Philo sapientissimus
Judæorum, qui temporibus apostolorum fuit. Opp. T. I. p. 341. Lugd. 1668.]

[4 Hieronym. in Catal. sub voc. PHILO. Photius. Cod. CV. Suidas, Voc.
Φίλων, &c.]

[5 Ὁ μέντοι Φαληρεὺς Δημήτριος καὶ Φίλων ὁ πρεσβύτερος καὶ Εὐπόλεμος
οὐ πολὺ τῆς ἀληθείας διήμαρτον· οἷς συγγινώσκειν ἄξιον· οὐ γὰρ ἐνῆν αὐτοῖς μετὰ
πάσης ἀκριβείας τοῖς ἡμετέροις γράμμασι παρακολουθεῖν.— Josephus, c. Apion.
Lib. I. c. 23. p. 458. ed. Havercamp.]

written by that Philo the Jew in the time of the apostles, it cannot be by any means canonical. For if Philo were a true prophet, or imbued with the prophetic spirit, why did he not receive Christ? Why not believe the gospel? Why was he a stranger to the apostles? Why are not his other books had in similar honour? Certainly none of the ancients ever said that this Philo was a Christian. How then, after Christ, should a man who was not a Christian have written a book worthy to be classed amongst the canonical books of the old Testament? But the most learned of the papists themselves allow that the book was not written by Solomon, so that that point needs not our confirmation. For if Solomon had written this book, it would not have been written in Greek but in Hebrew, as the Proverbs, Ecclesiastes, and the Song. But, as to the notion of some, who make Solomon the author of this book, because Solomon is introduced in chap. ix. making prayers and vows, it has no argumentative validity whatsoever. For that might have been done in the way of imitation by the writer whoever he might be: so that they who argue thence that Solomon must have been the writer himself, are grievously deceived. Jodocus Clitovæus and Sixtus Senensis are chargeable with this ignorance and error. But, with better reason, John Driedo (Lib. i. c. 4, ad 4m. difficult.[6]) concludes that this book was not written by Solomon, and says that the manner of scripture requires, that he who speaks should speak in the person of another. So John Capistranus, in the preface to his *Speculum Clericorum,* says that Philo speaks in the person of Solomon[7].

Fourthly, the church in old times judged no otherwise of this book than Jerome and we do; and this may be collected even from Augustine, whom our adversaries name upon their side. For in his book *de Prædestinatione Sanctorum,* c. 14, when he had cited a testimony from the book of Wisdom, chap. 4, "Speedily was he taken away, lest that wickedness should alter his understanding;" many pious and catholic brethren cried out against him that the book was not canonical[8]. Andradius, in his Defence of the Council of Trent, (Lib. iii.) attacks Chemnitz for using this place and testimony out of Augustine with many reproaches, in which attack

[6 pp. 41. 42. De Eccl. Script. Lovain. 1533.]

[7 Et cum Philone in persona Salomonis divinum præsidium . . . . invocabo. p. 2. Venet. 1580.]

[8 Quod a me quoque positum fratres istos ita respuisse dixistis, tanquam non de libro canonico adhibitum.—Opp. T. x. p. 807. Par. 1690.]

Bellarmine also joins (Lib. I. c. 12), but unreasonably. For, whatever may have been Augustine's own opinion of this book, yet it is
evident that others did not think it canonical, and that their judgment was the received opinion of those churches. Nor does Augustine contend very anxiously or earnestly for the authority of the
book : he only says that it is not "to be despised," since it had
been so long read with great reverence in the church, and that it
was "to be preferred to all the treatises of discoursers[1];" which may
perhaps be conceded to him. But if Augustine had thought that the
book was certainly canonical, he would never have been so slack
and cool in defending its authority, but would have blamed with
much severity those who rejected the book as utterly without claims
to a place in the canon. In truth, what he hath written upon this
subject is much more intended to screen himself from odium than to
fortify the authority of this book. But we understand already that
the book is not canonical, and we want nothing more.

CHAPTER XIII.
OF THE BOOK OF ECCLESIASTICUS.

OUR adversaries can allege no special argument in behalf of
this book; and we need not repeat our answers to the common
ones. Let us, on our side, bring some proofs to shew that the
book is not canonical. First, we may collect that this book is
not canonical from the fact of its having been written in Greek,
upon the principles already explained. The grandfather of Jesus
had written some things in Hebrew, which this Jesus translated
into the Greek language, as we read in the prologue[2]. But the
Hebrew original itself, when it was extant, never possessed a
prophetic credit or authority, and hath now entirely disappeared;
so that now nothing remains but Jesus' Greek version, which is full
of many faults and blemishes. Nor was this Jesus anything more
than a mere translator.

Secondly, how highly this translator thought of himself and
his own version, appears plainly from his own words and confession
in the prologue. He says, that the Hebrew cannot be exactly
rendered into Greek: (why so?) and he asks pardon, if he should

[1 Vide supra, p. 76.]

[2 Ὁ πάππος μου Ἰησοῦς .... προήχθη καὶ αὐτὸς συγγράψαι τι τῶν εἰς παιδείαν
καὶ σοφίαν ἀνηκόντων. Prolog. in Sapient. Jesu fil. Sirach.]

seem in some places to fail of an adequate power of expression[3].
By all which he sufficiently proves that he is neither a prophet
nor endowed with a prophetic spirit. For the Holy Spirit asks
pardon of no one, hesitates not in the choice of words, and ever
reaches the mark he aims at; especially if the writer apply due
diligence, as this author professes that he hath.

Lastly, what is written of Samuel in this book, chap. 49[4], is
taken variously and doubtfully by many, as we see from Augustine (ad Simplicianum, Lib. II. quæst. 3, and de Cura pro mortuis,
cap. 15). For the passage, 1 Sam. 28, is rather to be understood
of a diabolical spectre; since the souls of the saints cannot be
evoked by magical arts or incantations. Wherefore Augustine
(De Doctr. Chr. Lib. II. c. 23[5]) says, "that the image of the dead
Samuel gave a true prediction to Saul." Where he indicates that
it was not Samuel himself, but an image or semblance of Samuel,
that conversed with Saul. The same father, in his book de Octo
Dulcit. Quæst. (quæst. 6), after disputing somewhat on the other
side of this question, at last subjoins: "However there is in this
matter a readier way of escaping difficulty, and more easy view of
the meaning of the passage, if we suppose that it was not really the
spirit of Samuel that was roused from its repose, but some phantom
and imaginary illusion produced by diabolical devices: which the
scripture therefore calls by the name of Samuel, because images
are wont to be called by the names of those things of which they
are images." And so in the sequel he concludes that "the scripture says that Samuel appeared, even though, perchance, it was
the image of Samuel shewn by the devices of him who transforms
himself into an angel of light, and his ministers as the ministers
of righteousness[6]." Likewise in his treatise de Mirabilib. Scripturæ

[3 Παρακέκλησθε .... συγγνώμην ἔχειν ἐφ᾽ οἷς ἂν δοκῶμεν τῶν κατὰ τὴν
ἑρμηνείαν πεφιλοπονημένων τισὶ τῶν λέξεων ἀδυναμεῖν· οὐ γὰρ ἰσοδυναμεῖ αὐτὰ
ἐν ἑαυτοῖς Ἑβραϊστὶ λεγόμενα, καὶ ὅταν μεταχθῇ εἰς ἑτέραν γλῶσσαν. Ibid.]

[4 xlvi. 20. Καὶ μετὰ τὸ ὑπνῶσαι αὐτὸν ἐπροφήτευσεν. The Church of
England omits this verse in reading Ecclus. xlvi. as the evening lesson for
November 16.]

[5 Non enim, quia imago Samuelis mortui Sauli regi vera prænuntiavit,
propterea talia sacrilegia, quibus imago illa præsentata est, minus exsecranda
sunt.]

[6 Quanquam in hoc facto est alius facilior exitus et expeditior intellectus,
ut non vere spiritum Samuelis excitatum a requie sua credamus, sed aliquod
phantasma et imaginariam illusionem diaboli machinationibus factam: quam
propterea scriptura nomine Samuelis appellat, quia solent imagines earum

(Lib. II. c. 11),—if that book deserves to be reckoned a genuine
piece of Augustine's—he writes in this manner : "Whence from the
fact itself we may the more readily understand that this was not
the prophet Samuel, but that the devil, who transforms himself into
an angel of light, is considered in the phantastic form of Samuel.
This appears from his discourse, since he tells Saul, who was an
execrable man, 'Thou and thy sons shall be with me.'   Surely, if
it had been the true Samuel who was here exhibited, he would
never have said that this unjust king would be a participator of his
reward after death[1]."   And most plainly in his book of Questions
on the old and new Testaments, in the seven and twentieth
question, he determines thus : "I deem it a most unworthy act
to repose belief in this narrative in the strict literal sense of it.
For how is it possible that a man holy in his birth and righteous
in his actions when alive should be dragged up by magic arts ? or,
if not dragged up, should have consented to them ? Either alter-
native we can not without absurdity believe of a just man[2]."   To
say that the soul of the holy prophet was troubled by the spells of
witches, even Isidore himself detests as impious, as we see in Gratian (26 quæst. 5. cap. *Nec. Mirum.*); and he says that this was
" a piece of Satan's jugglery[3]."   Augustine too, in his book de
Cura pro Mortuis (c. 15.[4]), bears witness that many thought that it

rerum nominibus appellari quarum imagines sunt .... Non mirum est quod
scriptura dicit Samuelem visum, etiam si forte imago Samuelis apparuit ma-
chinamento ejus qui transfigurat se velut angelum lucis, et ministros suos
velut ministros justitiæ.—The treatise De VIII. Dulcitii quæstionibus is the
fourth piece in T. VI. of the Benedictine edition, Paris, 1679.]

[1 Unde non hunc esse Samuelem illum Prophetam per factum facilius
intelligitur, sed diabolus qui se transfert in angelum lucis, in phantasia
Samuelis consideretur.   Quod ex sermonibus ejus recte dignoscitur, quoniam
funesto Sauli dicebat, Tu et filii tui mecum eritis.   Etenim si verus hic
Samuel ostensus esset, nullo modo iniquum regem consortem sui meriti post
mortem diceret.—This spurious work is to be found in the Appendix to Part
I. of T. III. of the Benedictine edition.   The author is supposed to have been
an Irish monk, named Augustine.]

[2 Indignum facinus æstimo, si secundum verba historiæ commendetur
assensus.   Quomodo enim fieri potuerat, ut arte magica attraheretur vir et
nativitate sanctus et vitæ operibus justus ? aut, si non attractus est, consensit ?
quod utrumque de viro justo credere absurdum est.—This is also a spurious
piece; it is the third in the Appendix referred to in the last note.]

[3 Porro autem hoc est præstigium Satanæ. Decreti Pars Secund. Caus.
26. Quæst. 5. c. 14.]

[4 It is the nineteenth piece in Tom. VI. of the Benedictine edition.]

was not Samuel himself, but an evil spirit. And concerning the book of Ecclesiasticus his expression is[5]: " But if this book be objected to on account of the Hebrew canon which does not give it a place, what shall we say of Moses ?" He concedes therefore that this book is open to objections. So Aquinas (I. p. 89. 4. 8. Art. ad 2[m].) gives three answers to this place : 1. That Samuel appeared by a divine revelation. 2. Or, that the apparition was produced by demons. 3. Or, that the authority of Ecclesiasticus must not be admitted by reason that it is not esteemed by the Hebrews a portion of the canonical scriptures.

CHAPTER XIV.

OF THE BOOKS OF MACCABEES.

BESIDES those common pleas, upon which we have already said enough and answered sufficiently, our opponents adduce two arguments to establish the authority of these books. The first is, that they are placed by Clement in the canon of sacred scripture, as appears in the last of the apostolic canons. The second is the testimony of Augustine, in his City of God, (Lib. XVIII. c. 36), which is to this effect : " These books not the Jews, but the Church hold to be canonical[6]." A similar testimony is found also in his second book against the Epistles of Gaudentius, cap. 23[7]. Hence they conclude that these books are truly and properly canonical. I proceed to return a brief answer to both allegations.

To the former I reply, in the first place, that we have already shewn what should be thought of that book of apostolic canons, and have stripped it of the name and authority of the apostles[8]. In the second place, I am surprised that Bellarmine should choose to avail himself of such a witness, whose evidence he must know

[5 Sed si huic libro ex Hebræorum, quia in eo non est, canone contradicitur, quid de Mose dicturi sumus?—Id. ibid.]

[6 The whole passage upon which Whitaker reasons in his reply is as follows: Ab hoc tempore apud Judæos restituto templo non reges sed principes fuerunt, usque ad Aristobulum: quorum supputatio temporum non in scripturis sanctis, quæ canonicæ appellantur, sed in aliis invenitur; in quibus sunt et Machabeorum libri; *quos non Judæi, sed ecclesia pro canonicis habet* propter quorundam martyrum passiones vehementes atque mirabiles.]

[7 It is the last piece in T. IX. of the Benedictine edition, where this passage stands. Lib. I. § 38. p. 655.]　　　[8 Supra, p. 42.]

very well to make much more against the cause which he defends
than it weighs in favour of these particular books. For, except
these books of Maccabees, that apostolical canon recites none of
all those pieces which our churches hold apocryphal, amongst the
canonical books of the old Testament. If, therefore, this apostolical canon hath made these books canonical, it hath certainly left
the rest in the class of apocryphal and spurious. Let the papists
consider, whether they would choose that these books should be
received on condition that all the others be excluded. Besides, in
this apostolical canon *three* books of Maccabees are recited, whereas
the papists allow only two of them to be canonical[1]. If then
they rely on the authority of these canons to prove the canonicity
of two books, what are they to determine concerning the third?
They must consequently give up the argument derived from these
canons, and Bellarmine hath acted discreetly in omitting it in the
edition published by Sartorius.

I come now to the testimonies of Augustine. And, first, to the
former from the City of God, Lib. XVIII. c. 36. How Augustine
calls these and the other books canonical, by a certain common
use of that term in a loose sense, hath been already explained.
The Jews did not hold these books canonical; for they were of
no account whatever amongst them. But the christian church
may be said to hold them canonical, forasmuch as they are read in
the church, and held in some value, although they are not admitted to an equal authority and credit with the rest. This we
may learn from Augustine himself, who writes thus in that very
same passage: "The calculation of which times is not to be found
in the sacred scriptures which are called canonical, but in others,
amongst which are also the books of Maccabees." Then follow the
words upon which the argument is founded. Now in these words
of Augustine two things present themselves which deserve notice.
The first, that these books are not, in truth and fact, sacred and
canonical. The other, that they are nevertheless held canonical
in the church,—that is, read publicly, set forth, and esteemed of
great value in the church. Augustine subjoins the reason when
he says, "on account of the violent and admirable sufferings of
certain martyrs." Does he not in these words sufficiently shew
that Christians were led to ascribe so much importance to these
books on this account, because in them mention was made of cer-

[1 There is some reason for believing the words Μακκαβαίων τρία to be an
interpolation. See Cosin's Scholast. Hist. p. 30. Beverege's Annotations,
pp. 5, 39, and Gibbings's Roman Forgeries, pp. 113, 114.]

tain martyrs who fell in the cause of religion with the utmost fortitude and constancy? On this account Nazianzen hath pronounced a most beautiful panegyric upon that mother and her seven sons[2]. But in what sense can it be said that a book is held canonical on account of this or that? For a book which is truly canonical is to be received absolutely and entirely, not on account of this or that part or reason. Augustine says, in the City of God, Lib. I. c. 20 : " Nor is it in vain, that nowhere in the sacred canonical scriptures do we find any divine precept or permission to take away our own lives[3]." In these books if not a precept, at least a permission for a man to take his own life, is to be detected. For in 1 Macc. chap. vi. Eleasar is praised for voluntarily rushing upon death. And in 2 Macc. chap. xiv., the fortitude of Razis is commended, who laid violent hands upon himself. Yet Razis deserved no praise for his fortitude. For this was to die cowardly rather than courageously, to put himself voluntarily to death in order to escape from the hands of a tyrant. The Holy Spirit judges not of valour by the same measures as profane men, who extol Cato to the skies for committing suicide lest he should fall into the power and hands of Cæsar : for he either feared, or could not bear to see him, or sought to catch renown by an act of such prodigious horror. Thus he was crushed and extinguished either by despair, or grief, or some other perturbation of mind ; any of which motives are foreign from true fortitude. Rightly, therefore, did Augustine deny those books to be canonical, in which such a crime is narrated with some commendation by the authors.

The second testimony of Augustine occurs Lib. II. c. 23 ; where also Augustine opposes our adversaries more than he favours them. For he requires that " the book should be read and heard with sobriety." Say you so? What, I pray, do these words mean, " not unprofitably, if done soberly?" Is there ground to fear that scripture may be read unprofitably? And what is this sobriety which he demands in the perusal of these books? Every thing, indeed, should be read soberly ; no one doubts that ; and rashness should always be avoided. But if Augustine had meant that sobriety which is everywhere required in all scriptures, he would not have peculiarly prescribed that caution to the readers of this

[2 Inter Opp. Gregorii Nazianzen. T. I. p. 397. *Colon.* 1690.]

[3 Neque enim frustra in sanctis canonicis libris nusquam nobis divinitus præceptum permissumve reperitur, ut nobismet ipsis necem inferamus.]

book. The meaning, therefore, is, that there are some things in
the book which, if they be examined by the strict rule of faith,
cannot be defended, and therefore are not fit models for imitation ;
and that consequently the book requires to be read soberly. This
is moreover to be noted, that Augustine writes in that same place,
that Christ does not bear testimony to these books as his witnesses ;
which sufficiently shews that Augustine did not deem these books
truly canonical.

These matters being thus explained, let us now adduce our arguments against the authority of these books.

First, Jerome, in his catalogue of illustrious men[1], and in his
second book against Pelagius[2], says that Josephus was the author
of these books. Now Josephus was no prophet, and lived after
Christ and beyond the limits of the old Testament; for which
reasons he could not have written any book belonging to the
canon of the old Testament. Others, although they do not think
Josephus the author of these books, yet allow that the chronology
in them was supplied by Josephus; in consequence of which the
books became apocryphal, because the dates in these books do
not agree. So the popish writer Annius[3] delivers his opinion,
upon the Second book of Philo's Chronology.

Secondly, these books are expressly styled apocryphal by
Gregory the Great, who was Pope of Rome, in his Morals, Lib. xix.
c. 16. These are his words : " We shall not transgress the due
bounds of order, if we produce a testimony upon this subject from
books, not indeed canonical, yet set forth for the edification of the
Church[4]." Then he cites a passage from the Maccabees. Therefore, before Gregory, that is, within six hundred years after Christ,
the Church did not esteem the Books of Maccabees canonical.

[1 Alius quoque liber ejus, qui inscribitur περὶ αὐτοκράτορος λογισμοῦ,
valde elegans habetur, in quo et Machabæorum sunt digesta martyria.   Cap.
XIII. Opp. T. II. 837.]

[2 Unde et Josephus, Machabæorum scriptor historiæ, frangi et regi posse
dixit perturbationes animæ, non eradicari. Ibid. 735.—The reader must be
reminded, that neither this, nor the preceding passage, mean anything like
what Whitaker supposes; the piece attributed to Josephus being, not the
books of Maccabees commonly so called, but a discourse or oration on the
Maccabees, which may be found in his works.]

[3 Josephus tempora adjiciens apocryphas reddidit.   Annii Viteberg.
Antiquitt. ap. Ascenscium. 1512. Fol. ci.]

[4 De qua re non inordinate agimus, si ex libris non canonicis, sed tamen
ad ædificationem ecclesiæ editis, testimonium proferamus.]

Hence we see clearly what we should think of pope Innocent and Augustine. They call these books canonical; Gregory denies them to be such. They and he, therefore, without doubt used that term in different senses. The same judgment on these books is passed by Eusebius (Lib. de Temp.)[5], Richard of S. Victor. (Except. Lib. ii. c. 9)[6], and Occam (3 Part. Dial. Tract. i. Lib. iii. c. 16)[7].

Thirdly, in 2 Macc. chap. xii., Judas Maccabæus is praised for offering sacrifice for the dead. Whereas he really deserved no praise on that account, since God had commanded the making of no such sacrifice. Now, whatever is done in religious service without divine precept, is displeasing to God, and deserves not praise, but blame; and all sorts of *will-worship* were ever condemned in scripture. But upon this whole matter and argument we shall have to speak hereafter.

Fourthly, that sacrifice was offered for men who had brought themselves under the guilt and pollution of idolatry and sacrilege, and had perished in that crime, as we read in the twelfth chapter. For the soldiers of Judas had plundered some things consecrated to the Jamnite idols, and had hidden these offerings under their clothes; which, when they were slain, were discovered under their vesture. And this author says it was a clear case that they had fallen on account of that crime. Now the papists themselves allow that no sacrifice should be offered for persons guilty of such idolatry and sacrilege : for this was a mortal sin; and they tell us themselves that for those who are certainly in mortal sin, as the author affirms these men to have been, no sacrifice should be made. For —as to the pretence which Bellarmine has borrowed from Lyra, that Judas piously supposed that they had repented of their sin in the very article of death—not to mention that it rests wholly upon a dim surmise, yet, however probable it may have been that they had grieved in death for their offence, a public sacrifice should never have been offered for persons of this sort, who had polluted themselves with idolatry, unless there were certain proof of their true repentance.

[5 Machabæorum Historia hinc supputat regnum Græcorum. Verum hi libri inter divinas scripturas non recipiuntur. P. 348, ed. Majo. et Zohrab. Mediol. 1818.]

[6 Alii non habentur in canone, tamen leguntur. Hi sunt . . . . . Libri Machabæorum. Deinde sanctorum patrum scripta, &c. Opp. Ven. 1592. p. 331.]

[7 Secundum Hieronymum . . . . Libri . . . . Machabæorum . . . . non sunt recipiendi ad confirmandum aliquid in fide. Dialog. Guil. Ockam. Lugd. 1495. Fol. ccxii. 2.]

7

Fifthly, the Holy Spirit is not accustomed to epitomize the history of a profane author. But the Second Book of Maccabees, as we read in chap. ii., is a contraction of the five volumes of Jason of Cyrene, comprising in one little book what Jason had minutely detailed in five. Who that Jason was is uncertain. A prophet he was not : that no one ever said, or could say. Consequently this synopsis of Jason's history, composed in such a manner, cannot be counted part of the canonical scriptures.

Sixthly, in 2 Macc. chap. ii. we have a long narrative about the sacred fire, the ark, the tabernacle, and the altar, which are said there to have been hidden in a certain mountain and laid up by Jeremiah. Now there is not a word of all this in Jeremiah himself. And this author adds, that God had promised that he would shew them, when he had collected the people. But, after the Babylonian captivity, the Jews neither had nor found that ark, that tabernacle, nor that altar, nor did God, after that event, shew these things to any one. The papists object, that this is not to be understood of the return under Cyrus, when that remnant of the Jews was collected, but of the advent of Christ, when the whole people shall be collected, or of the conversion of the Jews a little before the end of the world. But this is an utterly vain conjecture. For what reason is there why these things should be shewn to the Jews at such a period ? Or who does not feel the absurdity of so ridiculous a figment? However, if we consult the sacred history, we shall find that this which is told of Jeremiah is contrary to the truth of facts. For Jeremiah was in prison until the destruction of the city. Jer. chaps. xxxvii. and xxxviii. : so that he could not take these things away and hide them, while the city and temple stood ; nor would the priests and princes have permitted it. But, after the taking of the city, the Chaldeans fire the temple, plunder all its valuables, whether gold, or silver, or brass, and carry them off with themselves, as we read 2 Kings xxv., and in the last chapter of Jeremiah. Jeremiah, therefore, had no opportunity of taking away the ark of the Lord, and the altar of incense, which were overlaid and covered entirely within and without with pure gold, Exod. xxv. 11. Besides, where are those records of Jeremiah to be found, which are mentioned in the beginning of this chapter ?

Seventhly, there are many things in these books irreconcileable and contradictory, such as the following examples which I shall proceed to specify. In the *first* place, these books are not agreed about the death of Antiochus Epiphanes, who was a most bitter enemy of the Jews. For in 1 Macc. vi. 8 and 16, Antiochus is said to have died of mental anguish upon the receipt of evil tidings, and to have died at Babylon in his bed; at which time also he gave his son in charge to Philip, whom he set over the kingdom. But in 2 Macc. i. 16, he is beheaded and cut in pieces in the temple of Nanæa. So that we have now been told of two deaths of Antiochus, since the manner of dying on these two occasions is different. But this author tells us further of a third death of the same man Antiochus, 2 Macc. chap. ix; where he writes that he died far away in the mountains of an internal pain in the bowels, out of which worms were seen to crawl, and a horrible stench issued through almost the whole army. One man could not have died so many and such different deaths. The papists however set up some pretences. Canus says (Lib. II. cap. 11 ad quartum) that it is not the same Antiochus. But the history itself refutes him at once; and Bellarmine was compelled to allow that the person meant was one and the same. He endeavours to reconcile the accounts thus: Antiochus lost his army in the temple of Nanæa, on the road he fell from his chariot, afterwards he was carried to Babylon and breathed his last. They confess therefore that Antiochus died at Babylon, as is related in the first book: and, indeed, the first book deserves more credit than the second. Now read what is related in the second book concerning the death of Antiochus in the places already cited. In chap. i. we read, that the leader himself was stoned by the priests, and cut in pieces, and his head thrown out to those who were outside. Now this leader is called Antiochus. Antiochus, therefore, perished in this temple, unless a man who hath been stoned, and cut to pieces, and beheaded, can escape alive. Let us now go on to chap. ix. There we shall find that this murderer and blasphemer, whilst in a transport of fury he was marching from Persia towards Jerusalem, in a remote and mountainous region exchanged a miserable life for a deplorable death. If he died at Babylon, he did not die in the country, nor in a mountainous region. Nor can both narratives possibly be true.

In the *next* place, Judas is said, 1 Macc. ix. 3, to have been slain in the year 152 of the reign of the Seleucidæ. But in 2 Macc. i. 10 he writes in the year 188[1] letters to Aristobulus the master of Ptolemy,—that is, 36 years after his death.

[1 In the common text indeed the date stands thus: but one of Mr Parson's MSS. reads τεσσαρακοστοῦ for ὀγδοηκοστοῦ. The difference is very slight between ρωή and ρπή: and the latter doubtless is the true reading.

7—2

In the *third* place, Judas is said, 1 Macc. iv. 36, to have purified the temple before the death of Antiochus, after Lysias had been routed. But in 2 Macc. at the commencement of chap. x. this purification of the temple is said to have been made after the death of Antiochus. For it is the same purification, as our adversaries allow.

In the *fourth* place, according to 2 Macc. x., Antiochus Eupator, the son of Epiphanes, upon his accession to the throne, confided the administration of affairs to Lysias. But, according to 1 Macc. vi., Lysias was long before in charge of that administration, and educated king Antiochus, and gave him the name of Eupator.

Eighthly, the second book shews that it is written by a human spirit. For, in the *first* place, at the end of the book the author begs pardon of his readers, which is altogether alien from the Holy Ghost; since he always writes the truth, and writes it as it ought to be written, erring neither in the matter nor in the manner, and standing in no need of our indulgence.

They object that Paul used a similar excuse, when he confesses himself to have been "rude in speech," 2 Cor. xi. 6. I reply: Paul never excused himself for writing poorly or slenderly, or accomplishing less than he proposed. But this author acknowledges the poorness and slenderness of his composition; and therefore, impelled by the sense of his own weakness, could not help imploring the humane indulgence of his readers. Paul never did this, nor any prophet or apostle. For, as to Paul's calling himself *rude in speech*, (ἰδιώτην λόγῳ), it is spoken in the sense and style of the false apostles, who, puffed up with a certain empty shew of eloquence, despised the apostle as rude and unskilful in discourse. In those words, therefore, he did not describe himself such as he really was, but such as he was represented by certain false apostles. For the apostle was lacking in no commendable part of true, simple, holy and divine eloquence, fit for so great a

For had the letter been written after 170, it would have been dated from the era of Liberty, 1 Macc. xiii. 14. Still the difficulty remains, how an event could be spoken of as passed in 148, which the first book of Maccabees (vi. 14) tells us did not occur till 149. But Basnage (Hist. of the Jews, B. ii. c. 1. § 20) long ago observed, that the years are counted differently in the two books of Maccabees. The first, following the Jewish mode, begins the year in March: the second in September. Thus the first makes Eupator declare war in 150, while the second dates the same event in 149. I wonder that Valckenaer did not remember this. See his dissertation *de Aristobulo Judæo*, pp. 40, 41.]

teacher and apostle : but, because these pretenders called him
ἰδιώτην λόγῳ, he acknowledges that, in their way of thinking, and
judged by their model and standard, he was an ἰδιώτης.   For this
is that eloquence which he calls "wisdom of words" (σοφίαν
λόγου), 1 Cor. i. 17, and "words which man's wisdom teacheth"
(διδακτοὺς ἀνθρωπίνης σοφίας λόγους), 1 Cor. ii. 13, and "excel-
lency of speech" (ὑπεροχὴν λόγου), 1 Cor. ii. 1; and which St Peter
calls "cunningly-devised fables" (σεσοφισμένους μύθους), 2 Pet.
i. 16.   So Œcumenius interprets the apostle : Λόγον λέγει τὸ
ἐγγεγυμνάσθαι τῇ ἑλληνικῇ σοφίᾳ.   "He means by *speech* the
being exercised in the wisdom of the Greeks."   To a similar
purpose Aquinas upon that place : "Because the apostle proposed the faith plainly and openly, therefore they said that he was
rude in speech[1]."   So Lyra : "He says this to refute the saying
of the false apostles, who despised his doctrine, because he spoke
plainly and coarsely.   Therefore he tells them that he did this
not from lack of knowledge, but because, as times then were, it
was not expedient for the Corinthians to have subtle questions
preached to them[2]."   The same is the opinion concerning this
place expressed by Catharinus archbishop of Campsa : "I do
not think," says he, "that Paul confesses himself to have been
really rude in speech, since he was an excellent preacher.   But he
seemed so to those according to whose opinions he is speaking,
because his style had a spiritual simplicity, and was not redolent
of their secular and affected eloquence[3]."   For what Canus says,
(Lib. II. c. 11, on the fourth head,)—"There is no reason why
the Holy Ghost should not assist an author who yet speaks modestly
in a human manner[4],"—is an insult to the Holy Spirit.   The Holy
Spirit ever teaches us modesty ; but meanwhile ever speaks and

[1] Apostolus proposuit eis fidem non in subtilitate sermonis, sed . . . . . .
plane et aperte ; ideo isti dicebant eum imperitum esse sermone.—In 2 Cor. xi.
Lect. 2. Comm. p. 140. Ant. 1569.]

[2] Hoc dicit ad repellendum dictum pseudapostolorum, qui contem-
nebant ejus doctrinam, eo quod plana et grossa dicebat : ideo dicit, quod hoc
non ex defectu scientiæ, sed quod non expediebat Corinthiis pro tunc subtilia
prædicari.—Biblia cum Gloss. Lyr. P. VI. p. 74. Lugd. 1520.]

[3] Non puto Paulum se fateri esse imperitum sermone, cum esset præ-
dicator eximius : sed ita illis videbatur ad quorum opinionem loquitur ; quia
sermo ejus habebat simplicitatem spiritualem, et non secularem illam affec-
tatam redolebat eloquentiam.—Comm. in Paul. Epp. p. 232. Paris. 1566.]

[4] Nihil impedit ut Spiritus Sanctus scriptori assistat, qui in quibusdam
tamen, humano more, ex modestia loquitur.]

writes in a way that cannot be excelled by any one possessed of a mere human spirit.

In the *second* place, this author speaks of the labour of making this epitome as troublesome, and full of toil and difficulty, 2 Macc. ii. But nothing is so difficult as to give any trouble to the Holy Spirit : for the Holy Spirit is God, and labours under no human weakness, and possesses infinite wisdom and power. Bellarmine, indeed, objects, that, although God ever assists all the sacred writers, yet the mode is different in the case of the historians from what it is in the case of the prophets. The prophets had no other trouble than that of dictating or writing, since God inspired them with a knowledge of all that they were to write or dictate ; as we read of Baruch writing things down from the lips of Jeremiah. But the historians underwent much labour in searching and thoroughly examining their subject, as Luke declares of himself, chap. i. 3. I confess, in reply to this, that those who published histories used diligence and industry : for the Holy Spirit does not make men lazy, or slothful, or negligent. So Luke thoroughly investigated, and knew accurately, and wrote most truly, all things pertaining to his subject. But I absolutely deny that this writing was troublesome or difficult to Luke, because nothing can be troublesome to the Holy Spirit ; and Luke, when he wrote his narrative, had the Holy Spirit as much as John when he wrote the Apocalypse. "The Holy Ghost," as Ambrose says, "knows nothing of slow efforts[1]." Besides, how could the task of making a short epitome of five books by Jason of Cyrene have been so troublesome to the writers of the Maccabæan history ? Certainly it is very easy to take out of another work what we choose, and to omit what we choose not. The mind, the spirit, the genius, the confession, the history are here all human.

CHAPTER XV.

OF THE BOOKS ALLOWED BY THE PAPISTS TO BE APOCRYPHAL.

WE have now spoken of those apocryphal books of the old Testament, which the papists maintain to be canonical, and have shewn them to be truly apocryphal. It remains now that we

[1 Vide supra, p. 38.]

come to those apocryphal pieces of the old Testament which are judged apocryphal by the papists themselves. Concerning these there is no dispute between us and them. Nevertheless, I will give a brief enumeration of them, so as to let you understand what and of what sort they are. They are these : The third and fourth books of Esdras : the third and fourth of Maccabees ; whereof the third is found in some copies of the Bible, and the fourth is mentioned by Athanasius in his Synopsis. To these must be added the prayer of Manasseh, which is set after the books of Chronicles: the 151st Psalm : the Appendix to the book of Job in the Greek copies. There is also a little preface to the Lamentations of Jeremiah, which is apocryphal. All these are conceded to be apocryphal parts of the old Testament, because not found in the Hebrew text, nor reckoned in the canon by any council or pope. The third book of Maccabees, however, is counted in the canon by Clement[2], whom some suppose to have collected the canons of the apostles, and who was a sovereign pontiff; upon which difficulty they know not what to say.

The fourth book of Esdras, chap. vi., contains some fables about the two fishes, *Enoch* and *Leviathan,* which are pretended to be of such vast and prodigious magnitude, that no waters can contain them. There are many things of the like stamp in these books, fit to please and feed human curiosity, but discordant from all sound and solid instruction. Such is the fiction in chap. iv., that the souls of the righteous are kept in certain subterranean cells until the number of the righteous shall be complete, and that then they will no longer be able to retain them, even as the womb cannot hold the fœtus beyond the ninth month. Such also is the story, chap. xiv, that the sacred books were lost in the captivity, and restored to their integrity by Ezra, after a retirement of forty days. For if these books had been lost, and written anew by Ezra, their language would be Chaldee, and not Hebrew ; upon which point we shall speak hereafter. But these are false and incredible figments, rejected even by the papists, who yet generally are wont to entertain such fables with wonder and veneration. Indeed Genebrard, in his Chronology (anno mundi 3749), calls both these books canonical ; which may well excite astonishment, as being not only repugnant to right reason and the common opinion of the doctors, but also made in contradiction to the authority of the council of Trent. Genebrard, however, builds his cause upon the

[2 Vide supra, p. 94.]

same reasons by which Bellarmine, as noticed above, seeks to prove
the canonicity of Tobit, Wisdom, and the rest. Genebrard shews
that these books are cited by ancient fathers, and that the Church
is wont to read portions of them upon her sacred anniversaries.
All this is perfectly true, since in the third week of Pentecost, and
the commemorations of Martyrs, lessons are taken from the fourth
of Esdras. Therefore either this argument, which Bellarmine hath
hitherto used so often, does not prove the matter proposed, or these
books of Esdras must come in as canonical on the same plea : which
yet the Jesuits would be so far from granting, that they would
oppose it as grossly erroneous. However Genebrard does not
stand alone in this mistake. For John Benedictus also, in the beginning of his bible, places the third and fourth of Esdras in the
number of those books which, although not contained in the Hebrew
canon, are yet received by the christian Church. In like manner
Renatus Benedictus in his Stromata Biblica, Lib. I. c. 9, counts
the third and fourth of Esdras among the canonical books.

The prayer of Manasseh is extant neither in Hebrew, nor in
Greek ; and although it seems pious, yet I cannot understand how
that passage can be defended where he says, "Thou hast not appointed repentance to the just, as to Abraham, and Isaac, and
Jacob, which have not sinned against thee ;" unless we suppose,
indeed, that this is only said comparatively. For they too had
sinned, and stood in need of repentance.

Psalm cli. is found in the Greek, but not in the Hebrew copies.
It contains thanks to God for the victory over Goliah, and was
translated by Apollinarius in his Metaphrase[1]. However it was
always esteemed apocryphal. The appendix to the Book of Job[2]
is condemned by Jerome, as translated only out of the Syriac
tongue, and not found in the Hebrew, and because Job is there
said to have been the fourth from Esau, whereas he was of the
race of Uz, who was the son of Nahor. So Jerome in his Questions
and traditions upon Genesis[3]. In his Epistle to Evagrius, however,
(Quæst. 126) he says that Job was more probably descended from
Esau, yet affirms that the Hebrews think otherwise.

All these the papists allow to be apocryphal; and they may as
well add to them what we esteem apocryphal also. For the arguments, as you have already seen, are no less valid against the latter
than against the former. Hence too it appears evidently, that it is

[1 Fabricius, Cod. Pseud. V. T. T. II. p. 907.]
[2 Ibid. p. 793.]   [3 Hieronym. Opp. T. III. p. 339.]

not everything that is read in the Latin bibles that can claim canonical authority, since many apocryphal pieces are found there. But
from this it arose that the apocrypha, being bound into one volume
with the canonical scriptures, obtained by degrees more and more
credit and authority, and at last were esteemed even canonical
themselves.

CHAPTER XVI.

OF THE BOOKS OF THE NEW TESTAMENT.

It follows that, in the next place, we should speak of the books
of the new Testament. But I will omit this portion of the subject,
inasmuch as it involves no controversy between us and the papists.
For we acknowledge without any exception those same books as
they judge to be canonical. Those books of the new Testament
which the council of Trent hath enumerated, those all, and those
only, our church receives. If Luther, or some of Luther's followers,
have thought or written otherwise concerning some of them, as the
Epistle of James or that of Jude, or some other pieces, they must
answer for themselves : their opinions are no concern of ours, nor
is it incumbent upon us to defend them, since we are, in this
respect, no followers of Luther, and submit to the direction of
better reason. However the persons just mentioned can produce
in their behalf the judgment and example of the ancient christian
Church and of certain fathers. For it is sufficiently known, that in
old times some christian churches and fathers, distinguished for their
piety and their learning, removed from the canon all those books
which Luther called in question. There is, therefore, no just cause
why our adversaries should inveigh so vehemently and with such
acrimony against Luther on this account, since he hath erred no
more in this respect than several catholic churches and some holy
fathers formerly, and even some very distinguished papists at the
present day. Cajetan openly rejects all the following :—the
Epistle of James, the second of Peter, the second and third of
John, the Epistle of Jude, the Epistle to the Hebrews (which
Luther certainly never disputed), the history of the woman taken
in adultery, John viii., the last chapter of Mark, and throughout
the gospels and other books several passages about which it never
entered into the mind of Luther to entertain a doubt. However

all who doubted about some canonical book were not, in former times, therefore reputed heretics. But I will not pursue this subject farther, since it hath no connexion with our cause. Let them attack others, but not from henceforth molest us.

Thus, then, we doubt not of the authority of any book of the new Testament, nor indeed of the author of any, save only the Epistle to the Hebrews. That this epistle is canonical, we all concede in the fullest sense; but it is not equally clear that it was written by the apostle Paul. Some judge it to be Paul's, others think otherwise. This was a questionable point in the earliest period of the Church. Eusebius (Lib. III. c. 3) writes[1] that the church of Rome denied this Epistle to be Paul's; but now that church hath changed its opinion, and attributes the authorship to Paul. Jerome, in his Catalogue under the Article PAUL, hath these words: "The Epistle called that to the Hebrews is not thought to be his, on account of the difference of the style and diction[2]." He writes to the same effect in his Epistle to Paulinus, and upon the 13th chapter of Jeremiah. Tertullian ascribes it to Barnabas[3]. Some to Luke the Evangelist, as Jerome testifies. So Caius, an ancient and learned writer, enumerates no more than thirteen epistles of Paul, as Jerome tells us in the Catalogue. "In the same volume," says he, "enumerating only thirteen epistles of Paul, he says that the fourteenth, which is inscribed to the Hebrews, is not his. Yea, and amongst the Romans, even to this day, it is not looked upon as the work of the Apostle Paul[4]." Eusebius also hath mentioned this Caius, Lib. VI. c. 16. Hence it appears clearly, that many in former times thought this epistle not to have been written by Paul.

But now, if I were to seek to mention all who attribute this epistle to the apostle Paul, I should never find an end. Jerome, in his epistle to Dardanus, says, that almost all the Greek authors affirm it to be Paul's[5]; and of this mind is Origen (in Eusebius, Lib. VI. c. 18),—Clemens Alexandrinus (in Eusebius, Lib. VI. c. 11),

[1 ὅτι γε μὴν τινὲς ἠθετήκασι τὴν πρὸς Ἑβραίους, πρὸς τῆς Ῥωμαίων ἐκκλησίας ὡς μὴ Παύλου οὖσαν αὐτὴν ἀντιλέγεσθαι φήσαντες, οὐ δίκαιον ἀγνοεῖν.— Eccl. Hist. T. I. pp. 189, 190. ed. Heinrich.]

[2 Epistola quæ fertur ad Hebræos non ejus creditur, propter styli sermonisque dissonantiam.—Opp. T. II. p. 823.]

[3 De Pudicitia. c. 20. Extat enim et Barnabæ titulus ad Hebræos.]

[4 Et in eodem volumine epistolas quoque Pauli tredecim tantum enumerans, decimam quartam, quæ fertur ad Hebræos, dicit ejus non esse. Sed et apud Romanos usque hodie quasi Pauli Apostoli non habetur.—c. 59. T. II. p. 886.]   [5 T. II. p. 608, alias Ep. 129.]

—Eusebius himself (Lib. ii. c. 3),—the council of Laodicea (c. 59)[6], —Athanasius, in the Synopsis and elsewhere,—Irenæus[7], Cyril (Thesaur. Lib. xii. c. 9),—Chrysostom upon the epistle, and Nazianzen in many places. Theophylact wonders at the impudence of those who deny it. Damascene cites a testimony from it as a work of Paul's[8]. Even the more celebrated of the Latins hold the same language. Augustine, de Doctr. Christ. Lib. ii. c. 8, and many other places. Ambrose wrote commentaries upon this, as one of Paul's epistles, and calls it a work of Paul's, in commenting upon Psalm cxix.[9] So also Gregory the Great, Moral. Lib. v. cap. 3. And the apostle Peter seems to testify that this is an epistle of Paul's, in these words, 2 Pet. iii. 15,—"As our brother Paul hath written to you." Now they were Hebrews: for it was to Hebrews that Peter wrote, as is plain from the inscription of his first epistle; and it was to the same persons that the second also was sent, since he says, "This second epistle I now write unto you." ch. iii. 1.

This, however, I leave to the judgment of the reader, without determining anything absolutely one way or other. I know that some allege reasons to shew that this cannot possibly be an epistle of Paul's. But I perceive that these have been opposed and refuted by others, as Illyricus, Hyperius, &c. We need not be very earnest in this debate. It is not a matter of necessity, and the question may well be left in doubt, provided that, in the meanwhile, the authority of the epistle be allowed to remain clear and uncontested. Jerome, in his epistle to Dardanus, hath sagely reminded us, that it makes no great matter whose it is, "since it is certainly the work of an ecclesiastical man, and is continually used every day in the reading of the churches[10]." Gregory, in like manner, wrote excellently well of the author of the book of Job, when, in the preface to his commentary upon that book, cap. 10, he answers the inquiries put to him upon that subject: "Who wrote these things, it is superfluous to ask, if only we believe faithfully that the Holy Spirit was the author of the book. He himself, therefore, wrote these things, since he dictated them to be

[6 Mansi, T. ii. p. 574.]

[7 It seems a mistake to say that Irenæus cites this epistle as Paul's. Stephen Gobar (apud Photium cod. ccxxii. p. 904) affirms the contrary.]

[8 De fide Orthodox. Lib. iv. c. 17. T. i. p. 283.]

[9 See also in Job. Lib. xvii. c. 23, p. 546, e.]

[10 Et nihil interesse cujus sit, quum ecclesiastici viri sit, et quotidie ecclesiarum lectione celebretur. ut supra, p. 106. n. 5.]

written. If we read the words in some letter which we had gotten
from some great man, and raised the question, what pen they were
written with ; it would surely be thought ridiculous that we should
be curious not to know the author and understand his meaning, but
discover what sort of pen it was with which their characters were
traced[1]." Since, then, we perceive that the Holy Ghost is the
author of this epistle, it is superfluous to inquire so anxiously
and curiously about the pen, and rash to affirm anything without
certain evidence.

Apocryphal, by the confession and in the opinion of all, are
those numerous spurious gospels under the names of Thomas,
Andrew, Nicodemus, the Nazarenes, &c., whereof we read in Gratian, Dist. 15. c. *Sancta Romana.* These are not now extant,
although they were formerly read and highly esteemed by many.
But the Lord provided for his church that, while the true gospels
were constantly preserved, those fictitious ones should perish utterly.
Besides, that piece which goes about under the title of the Epistle
to the Laodiceans, is likewise apocryphal ; of which Jerome writes
in the catalogue under the article PAUL : " Some read the epistle to
the Laodiceans, but it is universally exploded[2]." And the fathers of
the second Nicene council, Act. 6, say : " Amongst the epistles of
the apostle there is one which goes under the title of that to the
Laodiceans, which our fathers have rejected as spurious[3]." I know
not whence the notion of such an epistle originated, if it were not
from the error and fault of the Latin version, Coloss. iv. 16. For
the Vulgate reads there, *et illa quæ est Laodicensium,* as if there
had been some epistle written to the Laodiceans by Paul. The
Latin words are ambiguous, and may be understood in such a sense.
But the Greek text immediately removes this suspicion, καὶ τὴν ἐκ
Λαοδικείας. Therefore this epistle which Paul here mentions,
whatever it was, was not written to the Laodiceans, but from the
Laodiceans ; which all the Greek expositors have observed.

[1 Quis hoc scripserit supervacanee quæritur, cum tamen auctor libri
Spiritus Sanctus fideliter credatur. Ipse igitur hæc scripsit, qui hæc scri-
benda dictavit. Si magni cujusdam viri susceptis epistolis legeremus verba,
eaque quo calamo essent scripta quæreremus ; ridiculum profecto esset, si
non epistolarum auctoritatem scire, sensumque cognoscere, sed quali calamo
earum verba impressa fuerint, indagare studeremus.—Opp. T. I. p. 7. Paris.
1701.]

[2 Legunt quidam ad Laodicenos, sed ab omnibus exploditur. T. II. p. 823.]

[3 Καὶ γὰρ τοῦ θείου Ἀποστόλου πρὸς Λαοδικεῖς φέρεται πλαστὴ ἐπιστολὴ . . .
ἣν οἱ πατέρες ἡμῶν ἀπεδοκίμασαν.—Concil. Labb. et Cossart. T. VII. p. 475.]

There is also a book of Hermas, called *the Shepherd*, which Jerome speaks of in the catalogue, under the article HERMAS. The papists concede this also to be apocryphal, yet so as to be capable of being made and adjudged to be canonical by the church. For so Stapleton writes of this book, Doctrinal. Princip. Lib. IX. cap. 14, and he says as much of the Clementine Constitutions. Nor should this surprise us, since Gratian, upon the foot of a passage from Augustine (which, however, he hath most shamefully and foully corrupted), asserts that the decretal epistles are to be reckoned a part of the canonical scriptures, Dist. 19[4]. Which intolerable falsification of this compiler Alphonsus de Castro (contra Hær. Lib. I. c. 2), and Andradius (Def. Trident. Lib. III.) acknowledge and condemn. Yet there are still some papists who persist in the same impudent blasphemy. For one Alphonsus de Guerero adduces the evidence of this place to prove that the decretal epistles of the Roman pontiffs are equal to the sacred scriptures; whose words stand as follows in the *Thesaurus Christianæ Religionis*, cap. 3. Num. 5 : " Also decretal epistles have the force of authority, and decretal epistles are reckoned part of the canonical scriptures[5]." Also John Turrecremata, (de Ecclesia. Lib. IV. p. 2. c. 9), and Cajetan, in his book *de Primatu Papæ*, make use of this corrupt place in Gratian to prove the authority and primacy of the Roman pontiffs. Thus the volume of the new Testament will be augmented by a glorious accession, if all the decretal letters of the popes are to be counted amongst the sacred scriptures. But look yourselves at the passage in Augustine, de Doctr. Christ. Lib. II. c. 8, and see there the manifest ignorance or manifest fraud of Gratian. For Augustine says not a word of decretal epistles, or Roman pontiffs, and the scope of the whole place is directed quite another way.

But we have now finished the first question which we proposed concerning the canonical books.

[4 c. vi. *In Canonicis.* Where the Roman editors, having cited the passage as it really stands in Augustine, very fairly add : " Quæ quidem B. Augustini sententia non ad decretales Romanorum pontificias, sed ad canonicas et sacras scripturas referenda est."]

[5 Et decretales epistolæ vim auctoritatis habent, et in canonicis scripturis decretales epistolæ connumerantur. Ap. Roccaberti, Bibl. Max. Pontif. T. II. p. 15. Romæ, 1698.]

THE FIRST CONTROVERSY.

QUESTION II.

OF THE AUTHENTIC EDITION OF THE SCRIPTURES.

CHAPTER I.

THE STATE OF THE QUESTION.

THE first point raised in our inquiry concerning the duty of searching the scriptures, as between us and the papists, hath now been sufficiently explained. For we have found what are the books of holy scripture which we are commanded to search, and have rejected the error of our adversaries, who seek to introduce certain apocryphal books into the canon. Wherein, indeed, no one can fail to perceive their manifest unreasonableness, and the utter hopelessness of their cause. For, in the first place, not content with those books which are truly canonical and inspired, those books in which the Lord hath desired us to seek his will, they add to this list of sacred pieces many others of a foreign and wholly heterogeneous character. Farther still, they cannot think that even with all this they have enough, but join to these scriptures even unwritten traditions also; that so they may be enabled to prove by their spurious scriptures and traditions those dogmas of which they can find no vestige in the genuine scriptures. On the other hand, we have already shewn these books to be apocryphal, and I shall presently speak of their traditions in the proper place. Order requires that we should now proceed to the second question of our controversy, which contains two divisions. The first is concerning the authentic edition of the scriptures: the second, concerning the versions of scripture and sacred rites in the vulgar tongue. We shall handle each in its proper order.

Rightly to understand the state of this question, we must remember what the council of Trent hath enjoined upon this subject; which synod we read prescribing in the second decree of its fourth session, that "the old Latin vulgate edition should be held for authentic in public lectures, disputations, preachings, and expositions, and that no man shall dare or presume to reject it under any pretext whatsoever[1]." Consequently, the point to be decided in this question is, whether this Latin version, commonly styled the vulgate, is the authentic edition of scripture, or not rather the Hebrew text in the old Testament, and the Greek in the new. Our opponents determine the Latin to be authentic, and so the council of Trent hath defined it. So Melchior Canus (Lib. ii. c. 13) interprets this decree, and deduces from it four conclusions. The first is, that the old vulgate edition must be retained by the faithful in all points which pertain to faith and morals: the second, that all questions concerning faith or morals must be determined by this Latin edition: the third, that we must not in a disputation appeal to the Hebrew or Greek copies: the fourth, that, in matters of faith or morals, the Latin copies are not to be corrected from the Hebrew or Greek. In like manner our countrymen the Rhemists, in the preface to their version of the new Testament, run out into a long panegyric upon this Latin edition, and contend for its superiority not only to all other Latin versions, but even to the Greek itself which is the original and prototype. Lindanus, in the first book of his treatise *de optimo genere interpretandi*, prefers the Latin edition to the Hebrew and Greek; and Andradius (Defens. Trident. Lib. iv.) declares it intolerable that any one should be permitted to despise the authority of that edition which is used by the church, or to appeal freely to the Hebrew and Greek.

Although, therefore, our adversaries do not condemn the Hebrew and Greek originals, yet they conclude that not these originals, but the vulgate Latin edition is the authentic text of scripture. Our churches, on the contrary, determine that this Latin edition is very generally and miserably corrupt, is false and not authentic; and that the Hebrew of the old Testament, and the Greek of the new, is the sincere and authentic scripture of God; and that, consequently, all questions are to be determined by these originals, and versions only so far approved as they agree with these originals. Consequently, we and our adversaries maintain opinions manifestly contradictory.

[1 Sancrosancta synodus . . . . . statuit et declarat, ut hæc ipsa vetus Vulgata editio, quæ longo tot seculorum usu in ipsa ecclesia probata est, in publicis lectionibus, disputationibus, prædicationibus, et expositionibus pro authentica habeatur, et ut nemo illam rejicere quovis prætextu audeat vel præsumat. p. 20. Lips. 1837.]

It behoves me to proceed in this question in such a course
as to say something,—first, of the Hebrew edition of the old
Testament; secondly, of the Greek of the new; thirdly, of this
Latin vulgate itself. Upon this last point I shall shew that it
is corrupt, and therefore to be corrected and judged of by the
standard of the original text, which is, indeed, the grand hinge
upon which this whole controversy turns. The former matters
therefore I shall dispatch briefly, so as to come without delay
to the main subject.

CHAPTER II.

OF THE HEBREW EDITION.

THE Hebrew is the most ancient of all languages, and was that
which alone prevailed in the world before the deluge and the erec-
tion of the Tower of Babel. For it was this that Adam used, and
all men before the flood, as is manifest from the scriptures, and as
the Fathers testify. So Augustine in his book *de Mirabilibus
Scripturæ* (cap. 9): "Whereas, up to that time, the whole race of
all men were of one language, he divided their tongues into different
terms[1]." And, in his City of God (Lib. xvi. c. 4): "Time was
when all had one and the same language[2]." This is likewise confirmed by that testimony of the Sybil, which Josephus hath set
down, Antiquit. Lib. i. c. 6: "When all men were of one language, some of them built a high tower, as if they would thereby
ascend to heaven; but the gods sent storms of wind, and overthrew
the tower, and gave every one his peculiar language[3]." Which

[1 Cum ad illud tempus esset unius linguæ cunctus populus, universorum
lingulas in diversa verba divisit.]
[2 Cum ergo in suis linguis istæ gentes fuisse referantur, redit tamen ad
illud tempus narrator, quando una lingua omnium fuit.]
[3 Πάντων ὁμοφώνων ὄντων ἀνθρώπων, πύργον ᾠκοδόμησάν τινες ὑψηλό-
τατον, ὡς ἐπὶ τὸν οὐρανὸν ἀναβησόμενοι δι' αὐτοῦ· οἱ δὲ θεοὶ ἀνέμους ἐπιπέμ-
ψαντες ἀνέτρεψαν τὸν πύργον, καὶ ἰδίαν ἑκάστῳ φωνὴν ἔδωκαν. Lib. I. c. 4.
§. 3. ed. Richter. Lips. 1826. The lines, as given by Opsopæus, are these:
ὁμόφωνοι δ' ἦσαν ἅπαντες,
Καὶ βούλοντ' ἀναβῆν' εἰς οὐρανὸν ἀστεροέντα,
Αὐτίκα ἀθάνατοι. . . . . . ,
Πνεύμασιν.
Sibyll. Orac. Lib. III. p. 223. edit. Opsop. Paris. 1599.]

testimony of that aged prophetess is not to be rejected, since it agrees with the scriptures. It was, therefore, no slight error of Philastrius (Hæret. c. 106) to contend that there were many languages from the beginning, and to stigmatize as heretical the opinion that there was but one language before the building of Babel. For so the scripture tells us plainly, Gen. xi. 1 : " The whole earth was of one language and one speech." Now Augustine, in his City of God (Lib. xvi. c. 11) tells us, that this common language remained in the family of Heber[4], and was thence called Hebrew; which is also expressly affirmed by Eucherius upon Genesis (Lib. II. c. 2) : " At that time, wherein a diversity of languages was produced, the former tongue retained its place in the family of Heber alone[5]." Thus, whilst all other races were punished with a sudden change of dialect, Heber preserved his ancient language, and transmitted it to his posterity, not all of them indeed, but that line from which Abraham descended. And, along with the language, the pure religion also was propagated in the family of Abraham. Furthermore, in that perturbation and confusion of tongues which took place at Babel, the Hebrew was the mother of the rest. For the others are generally but dialects and varieties of this, some more closely allied and bearing a greater resemblance to their parent, while others have deflected farther from the primitive stock : but all the rest are derived from it. " We may perceive," says Jerome, on Zephaniah, chap. iii. " that the Hebrew language is the mother of all languages[6]." He gives there one example in proof, the identity of the Hebrew *Nugei* with the Latin *Nugæ*.

In this language, which the faithful after that time preserved incorrupt in one family, the old Testament was published, as all unanimously agree. Upon this subject Jerome thus writes in his

[4 Non defuit domus Heber, ubi ea quæ antea fuit omnium lingua remaneret.]

[5 Eo tempore quando linguarum facta est varietas, in sola domo Heber quæ antea fuit lingua commansit.—c. 7. p. 61. These commentaries are falsely attributed to Eucherius of Lyons, who flourished A. D. 434, as they make citations from Gregory I. and Cassiodorus. They were published among his works, Basil. 1531.]

[6 Ut nosse possimus, esse Hebraicam linguam omnium matricem. T. VI. p. 730. The verse referred to is 18. But in נוגי, which Jerome translates *nugas* in its obsolete sense of *mourners*, the נ is not radical but servile,— the mark of the Niphal participle from יגה corresponding to the Sanscrit *wig*.]

142nd Epistle: "All antiquity agrees to witness that the beginning of speech and common discourse, and the whole substance of human language, is the Hebrew tongue, in which the old Testament is written[1]." It is also certain that Moses is the earliest writer, although some persons think otherwise, and allege certain names of books which are found in the scriptures. These objections may be easily answered; but I shall not enter upon that subject as not pertaining to the matter in hand. God himself shewed the model and method of writing, when he delivered the law, inscribed by his own finger, to Moses. This is the opinion of Chrysostom (Opp. T. II. p. 1. Eton. 1612), and Theophylact (upon Matth. i.); and it is also embraced by the Papists, as Hosius, in his Confessio Petrocoviensis, cap. 15, and the Jesuit Schröck, in his 13 Thesis de Verbo Dei. Augustine, indeed, (Civit. Dei. Lib. xv. c. 23,)[2] affirms it to be certain that Enoch committed some things to writing, since Jude asserts as much in his Epistle. But it does not appear that this is a fair inference from Jude's expression: for Jude does not say, " Well wrote Enoch;" but, "well prophesied," προεφήτευσε. The passage cited, therefore, is either some oral speech of Enoch's, or else written by some other person. But we must not say that any book written by Enoch was extant at the time when this epistle was written: for if so, it would have been canonical. But the Jews had no such book in their canon. It was Moses, therefore, the greatest of the prophets, who wrote the first canonical book of scripture; after whom other prophets published several volumes. Some wrote before the captivity, as Samuel, Nathan, Isaiah, Hosea, and many more: some in the captivity, as Ezekiel and Daniel: some for a space after the captivity, as Ezra, Haggai, Zechariah, Malachi. These all wrote in Hebrew, except a few pieces which we find composed by Daniel and Ezra in Chaldee. But the Chaldee tongue is near akin to the Hebrew, and was then a language known to the church. Nor is this exception a matter of sufficient moment to prevent Jerome from saying that the old Testament is entirely written in Hebrew.

There are some, however, who imagine that the whole old Testament perished in the captivity. This suspicion, perhaps, arose

[1 Initium oris et communis eloquii, et hoc omne quod loquimur, Hebræam linguam, qua vetus Testamentum scriptum est, universa antiquitas tradidit.—Ep. 18. T. I. p. 49.]

[2 Scripsisse quidem nonnulla divina Enoch, illum septimum ab Adam, negare non possumus, cum hoc in epistola canonica Judas Apostolus dicat.]

from considering that, when the temple was burnt, all that was in it must have been consumed in the same conflagration. Hence they believe that the sacred volumes of scripture must have been destroyed in the flames; but that, after the captivity, Ezra, instructed by the Holy Spirit, published these afresh, as it were again recovered. In this opinion was Clemens Alexandrinus (Strom. Lib. I.)[3] and Irenæus (Lib. III. c. 25), who writes thus : " In that captivity of the people which took place under Nebuchadnezzar, the scriptures being impaired, when, after the expiration of seventy years, the Jews returned to their own land, and after that again in the times of Artaxerxes, king of the Persians, God inspired Ezra, who was of the tribe of Levi, to renew all the discourses of the prophets, and restore to the people the law which had been given them by Moses[4]." Similar are the words of Leontius (de Sectis. Act. 2): " Ezra, coming to Jerusalem, and finding that all the books had been burnt when the people were taken captive, is said to have written down from memory those two and twenty books of which we have given a list in the foregoing place[5]." Isidorus (de officiis), and Rabanus Maurus (de Inst. Cleric. c. 54) write to the same effect. They affirm, therefore, two things : one, that the whole sacred and canonical scripture perished in the Babylonian captivity : the other, that it was restored to its integrity by Ezra, instructed and inspired in a wonderful manner by the direct agency of God.

But the falsehood of this opinion is manifest. For the pious Jews had, no doubt, many copies of the scripture in their possession, and could easily save them from that calamity. What man in his senses will say that there was no copy of the scriptures beside that in the temple? Besides, if these books had been deposited in the temple, would not either the priests or somebody else have been

[3 δι' ὅν γίνεται . . . . . ὁ τῶν θεοπνεύστων ἀναγνωρισμὸς καὶ ἀνακαινισμὸς λογίων. P. 329, D. Morell. Paris. 1629. Compare also 342, B.]

[4 ἐν τῇ ἐπὶ Ναβουχοδονόσορ αἰχμαλωσίᾳ τοῦ λαοῦ διαφθαρεισῶν τῶν γραφῶν, καὶ μετὰ ἑβδομήκοντα ἔτη τῶν Ἰουδαίων ἀνελθόντων εἰς τὴν χώραν αὐτῶν, ἔπειτα ἐν τοῖς χρόνοις Ἀρταξέρξου τοῦ Περσῶν βασιλέως ἐνέπνευσεν Ἔσδρα τῷ ἱερεῖ ἐκ τῆς φυλῆς Λευὶ, τοὺς τῶν προγεγονότων προφητῶν πάντας ἀνατάξασθαι λόγους, καὶ ἀποκαταστῆσαι τῷ λαῷ τὴν διὰ Μωσέως νομοθεσίαν. P. 293. ed. Fevard. Par. 1675. The Greek is given by Eusebius, H. E. v. 8.]

[5 Ὁ δὲ Ἔσδρας ἐλθὼν εἰς τὰ Ἱεροσόλυμα, καὶ εὑρὼν ὅτι πάντα βιβλία ἦσαν καυθέντα, ἡνίκα ἠχμαλωτίσθησαν, ἀπὸ μνήμης λέγεται συγγράψασθαι τὰ κβ′ βιβλία, ἅπερ ἐν τοῖς ἄνω ἀπηριθμησάμεθα. §. 8. p. 632. ap. Gallandi Bibl. V. P. T. XII. Venet. 1788.]

able to rescue them from the flames? It is incredible that the
religious Jews should have been so unmindful of piety and religion
as to keep no copies whatever of the scriptures, whilst they lived
in Babylon, especially while they had such men among them as
Ezekiel and Daniel. But it is certain that they had many copies.
For even Antiochus himself could not utterly destroy them all,
though he set himself to do so with the utmost zeal and sedulity.
Hence it appears that there were everywhere a very great number
of copies; and now the Babylonians made no such fierce assault upon
the sacred books. In accordance with what we might expect from
such premises, Ezra is simply said, Nehem. viii., to have brought
the book of Moses and read it. The books of Moses therefore,
and, in like manner, the other books of scripture, were preserved
safe in the captivity; and we have now no other, but the very
same books of scripture of the old Testament as those which were
written by Moses and the rest of the prophets.

However, it is very possible that the books, which may have
been previously in some disorder, were corrected by Ezra, restored
to their proper places, and disposed according to some fixed plan,
as Hilary in his prologue affirms particularly of the Psalms. Perhaps, too, Ezra either changed or reformed the shapes and
figures of the letters. Jerome indeed, in his epistle to Paulinus,
maintains that "Ezra invented new forms for the letters after the
return from the captivity; for that previously the Jews had used
the same characters as the Samaritans[1]." Hence, if we credit Jerome,
Ezra introduced new forms of the letters, more elegant and easy
than those which were before in use, copied out the law in these
new characters, and left the old ones to the Samaritans. In conformity with this statement, Jerome further tells us, upon Ezekiel
ix.[2], that the last letter of the alphabet was formerly similar to the
Greek Ταῦ, and that it still, in his time, retained that figure in the
Samaritan character; while the last letter of the Hebrew alphabet
has now quite another and different shape.

[1 Certum est, Esdram scribam Legisque doctorem, post captam Hiero-
solymam . . . . alias literas repperisse, quibus nunc utimur: cum ad illud
usque tempus iidem Samaritanorum et Hebræorum characteres fuerint.]

[2 Antiquis Hebræorum literis, quibus usque hodie utuntur Samaritani,
extrema Thau litera, crucis habet similitudinem.—T. v. p. 96. The remark
was made by Origen before him: τὰ ἀρχαῖα στοιχεῖα ἐμφερὲς ἔχειν τὸ Ταῦ τῷ
τοῦ σταυροῦ χαρακτῆρι. Coins are still found which preserve the old cruciform
Phœnician Tau, though the Samaritan has ceased to bear that shape.]

But, though Jerome affirms that Ezra invented new characters, he never says that he made everything new. He might very easily copy and set forth the same ancient text in the new letters. We must hold, therefore, that we have now those very ancient scriptures which Moses and the other prophets published, although we have not, perhaps, precisely the same forms and shapes of the letters.

CHAPTER III.

OF THE GREEK VERSION BY THE SEVENTY TRANSLATORS OF THE HEBREW BOOKS.

THESE Hebrew books of sacred scripture were, of old, translated into various languages, particularly into Chaldee and Greek. The Chaldee paraphrase is generally allowed great credit and authority, especially that of the Pentateuch which was made by Onkelos[3]. The rest were turned into Chaldee by Jonathan and Joseph, who lived a little before, or about the time of Christ[4]. There were many Greek translations of scripture published by various authors. But, without question, the noblest and most famous of them all was that which was composed by the seventy-two interpreters in Egypt, in compliance with the pious wishes of Ptolemy Philadelphus. We may read large accounts of this Greek version in Epiphanius (de Mensur. et Ponder.[5]), Eusebius (Præparat. Evangel. Lib. VIII.[6]), Justin Martyr (Dial. c. Tryph.[7]), besides many others. Nay, there is still extant a book of Aristæus, who pretends to have been one of Ptolemy's body-guards, and gives a narrative of the whole transaction. But Ludovicus Vives[8] (in Lib. XVIII.

[3] It is printed in Buxtorf's Rabbinical Bible, Basil, 1719, and in the Paris and London Polyglotts. Onkelos's history is involved in great obscurity. The best book on the subject is perhaps Luzzato's Philoxeaus, Vienna, 1830.]

[4] Jonathan Ben Uzziel lived probably a little before the time of Christ; but Joseph the Blind presided over the school at Sora about A.D. 322. A great part of the Targum, which goes under his name, was probably written much later.]

[5] c. 3, 6, 9—11.]

[6] pp. 206—209. ed. Steph. Par. 1544.]

[7] p. 294. Opp. Just. Mart. Par. 1636.]

[8] Circumfertur libellus ejus nomine de LXX. interpretibus, confictus ut

c. 43. August. de Civit. Dei,) supposes this book to be the fiction of a more modern writer. That the scriptures were translated into Greek, there can be no doubt, since all antiquity attests the fact. But the other parts of the story are not equally certain. This version I suppose to have been the first and earliest of all the Greek versions; although Clemens Alexandrinus (Stromat. Lib. i.[1]) seems to say that the scripture was translated into Greek long before this period, and read by Plato; and the question of Numenius, a Pythagorean philosopher, is alleged by him, τί γάρ ἐστι Πλάτων ἢ Μωσῆς ἀττικίζων; *What else is Plato but an Attic Moses?* But if the sacred books of scripture had been translated into the Greek tongue previously, then Demetrius, who collected the library for king Ptolemy, would not have been ignorant of that version or desired a new one. Plato, indeed, and the Pythagoreans might have known something of these books from the common discourse of men and intimacy with those who were acquainted with them; but I hardly think that they ever read the books in Greek. For this was the first Greek translation, published about three hundred years before Christ, as Theodoret writes in these words: "This first edition was published three hundred and one years before God the Word, our Lord Jesus Christ, came to sojourn with us in the flesh[2]."

Some there are who think that the seventy interpreters did not translate the whole scripture of the old Testament, but only the law into the Greek language, understanding under the name of the law not the entire ancient scripture, but merely the Pentateuch. Such was the opinion of Josephus, as we find in the Proem to his antiquities, where he hath these words: "For Ptolemy did not

puto ab aliquo recentiore.—P. 620. ed. Froben. Basil. 1512. The spuriousness of this piece was finally demonstrated by Hody, in a treatise which forms the first part of his great work, De Bibliorum Textibus, &c. Oxon. 1705.]

[1 διηρμήνευται δὲ καὶ πρὸ Δημητρίου. . . . . τά τε κατὰ τὴν ἐξ Αἰγύπτου ἐξαγωγὴν τῶν Ἑβραίων τῶν ἡμετέρων πολιτῶν, καὶ ἡ τῶν γεγονότων ἁπάντων αὐτοῖς ἐπιφάνεια, καὶ κράτησις τῆς χώρας, καὶ τῆς ὅλης νομοθεσίας ἐπεξήγησις· ὥστε εὔδηλον εἶναι τὸν προειρημένον φιλόσοφον εἰληφέναι πολλά. γέγονε γὰρ πολυμαθής.—P. 342. B.C. The passage is quoted from Aristobulus, upon whom see Valckenaer, de Aristobulo Judæo Diatribe. It appears to me, however, that Aristobulus is there not speaking of any regular translation, but of such pieces as those of Ezekiel Tragœdus, in which the greater part of the Mosaic history was paraphrased in Greek verse or prose.]

[2 πρώτη δὲ αὕτη ἡ ἔκδοσις ἐγένετο πρὸ τριακοστοῦ πρώτου ἔτους τῆς μετὰ σαρκὸς πρὸς ἡμᾶς ἐπιδημίας τοῦ Θεοῦ Λόγου καὶ Κυρίου ἡμῶν Ἰησοῦ Χριστοῦ.]

obtain the whole scripture; but the interpreters only delivered to him the law[3]." Which, he says, was the circumstance that led him to introduce the whole scripture to Grecian readers. That this was Josephus' opinion is confirmed also by the testimony of Jerome. But others hold that all the books were translated; and theirs seems the more probable view. For the reason which led them to make any version at all is sufficient to persuade one that they made a complete one; nor would the king have been satisfied with only a part. The wonder, too, which some relate of the incredible celerity with which the task was performed would have no place, if they translated so small a piece only. Chrysostom, in his discourse against the Jews, affirms that the scriptures translated by them were reposited in the temple of Serapis, and the version of the prophetic books might be found there even still: μέχρι νῦν ἐκεῖ τῶν Προφητῶν αἱ ἑρμηνευθεῖσαι βίβλοι μένουσιν[4]. And Theodoret says that the Jews sent to king Ptolemy not a part only of the scripture, but the whole written in golden characters, χρυσοῖς γράμμασι τὴν πᾶσαν γραφὴν εὐσημηνάμενοι. Now, if the books of the prophets translated into Greek by them remained in the royal library to the time of Chrysostom, and if the Jews sent the whole scripture along with the interpreters to the king, there is no room left to doubt that the whole scripture was translated by them into the Grecian language.

What authority, however, this version should command is uncertain. The ancients used to hold it in the highest estimation, and looked upon it as unique and divine. Epiphanius, in his book of Weights and Measures, says that the translators were not mere interpreters, but, in some sort, prophets also[5]. And Augustine (de Doct. Christ. Lib. II. c. 15) says, that this version was made by a divine dispensation, and was held in greatest repute among the best learned churches, since the translators were said to have been "aided by such a presence of the Holy Spirit in their interpretation as that they all had but one mouth[6]." Upon this subject he

[3 οὐδὲ γὰρ πᾶσαν ἐκεῖνος ἔφθη λαβεῖν τὴν ἀναγραφήν, ἀλλ' αὐτα μόνα τὰ τοῦ νόμου παρέδοσαν οἱ πεμφθέντες ἐπὶ τὴν ἐξήγησιν εἰς τὴν Ἀλεξανδρείαν. Prooem. § 3. p. 6.]

[4 Tom. VI. p. 37. ed. Savil.]

[5 οὐ μόνον ἑρμηνευταὶ ἐκεῖνοι γεγόνασιν, ἀλλα καὶ ἀπὸ μέρους προφῆται. De Pond. et Mens. § 17. Opp. T. II. p. 173. c. ed. Petav. Coloniæ. 1682.]

[6 Septuaginta interpretum, quod ad vetus Testamentum attinet, excellit

hath also written largely in his City of God, Lib. xviii. c. 42 and
43. In like manner, Irenæus (Lib. iii. c. 25) writes that, though
each made his translation apart, yet in the end, when they all
met together and compared their several versions, "they all recited
the same thing and in the very same words and terms from
beginning to the end; so as that the gentiles who stood by might
easily perceive, that it was by the inspiration of God that the
scriptures were translated[1]." So Augustine, in the City of God,
Lib. xviii. c. 42: "The tradition is that there was so wonderful,
stupendous, and absolutely divine agreement in their expressions,
that although each sat down separately to this task (for so Ptolemy
chose to try their fidelity), yet none differed from another even in
a single word, though it were synonymous and equivalent, or in
the order and placing of the words. But, as if there had been
but one translator, so the translation was one; as, indeed, it was
one and the same Holy Spirit which was in them all[2]." Now,
while I doubt not that this version was held in high authority,
and that deservedly too, I cannot think that the miracles which
are told to magnify its authority deserve credit; and, indeed, we
find that they are treated as fables by Jerome in the Preface to
the Pentateuch[3]. However great may have been the authority
of this version, it could not have been greater than that of our
version. They, therefore, attribute too much to it, who make it
inspired, and equal to the authentic scriptures themselves. For
the authority of those interpreters was not so illustrious and certain as that of the prophets: nor is it the same thing to be an

auctoritas: qui jam per omnes peritiores ecclesias tanta præsentia Sancti
Spiritus interpretati esse dicuntur, ut os unum tot hominum fuerit.]

[1 τῶν πάντων τὰ αὐτὰ ταῖς αὐταῖς λέξεσι καὶ τοῖς αὐτοῖς ὀνόμασιν ἀναγορευ-
σάντων ἀπ' ἀρχῆς μέχρι τέλους, ὥστε καὶ τὰ παρόντα ἔθνη γνῶναι ὅτι κατ' ἐπίπνοιαν
τοῦ Θεοῦ εἰσὶν ἡρμηνευμέναι αἱ γραφαί.—P. 293. ut supra.]

[2 Traditur sane tam mirabilem ac stupendum planeque divinum in eorum
verbis fuisse consensum, ut cum ad hoc opus separatim singuli sederint, (ita
enim eorum fidem Ptolemæo regi placuit explorasse,) in nullo verbo, quod
idem significaret et tantundem valeret, vel in verborum ordine, alter ab altero
discreparet, sed tanquam si unus esset interpres, ita quod omnes interpretati
sunt, unum erat, quoniam revera Spiritus erat unus in omnibus.]

[3 Nescio quis primus auctor septuaginta cellulas Alexandriæ mendacio
suo extruxerit, quibus divisi eadem scriptitarint, cum Aristæus ejusdem
Ptolemæi ὑπερασπιστὴς, et multo post tempore Josephus nihil tale retu-
lerint, sed in una basilica congregatos contulisse scribant, non prophetasse.
T. ix. p. 3.]

interpreter and to be a prophet. Rightly, therefore, does Jerome[4], in the Preface to the Pentateuch, call the seventy interpreters, not prophets. In his Commentaries also he frequently blames the Greek version of the seventy translators, not only as depraved by the scribes, but even as faulty in itself; which he surely would not have done, if he had deemed that translation to be possessed of such divine and supereminent authority.

Learned men question, whether the Greek version of the scriptures now extant be or be not the version of the seventy elders. The sounder opinion seems to be that of those who determine that the true Septuagint is wholly lost[5], and that the Greek text, as we have it, is a mixed and miserably corrupted document. Aristæus says that the Septuagint version was exactly conformable to the Hebrew originals, so that, when read and diligently examined by skilful judges, it was highly approved by the general suffrage of them all. But this of ours differs amazingly from the Hebrew copies, as well in other places and books, as specially in the Psalms of David. Nor is there room for any one to reply that the Hebrew is corrupt. For even the papists will not venture to maintain that the Greek is purer than the Hebrew. If they did, they would be obliged to condemn their own Latin version, which agrees much more closely with the Hebrew than with the Greek. Nay, the faults of the Greek translation are so manifest, that it is impossible to find any way of excusing them. There is the greatest difference between the Hebrew and Greek books in the account of times and years. The Greek books reckon 2242 years from Adam and the beginning of the world to the flood, as we read in Augustine, Eusebius, and Nicephorus' Chronology. But in the Hebrew books we see that there were no more than 1656. Thus the Greek calculation exceeds the Hebrew by 586 years. Again, from the deluge to Abraham there is, according to the LXX., an interval of 1082 years. But if you consult the Hebrew verity, you will not find more than 292[6]. Thus the Greek books exhibit

[4 Aliud est enim esse vatem, aliud esse interpretem. Ibi Spiritus ventura prædicit: hic eruditio et verborum copia ea quæ intelligit profert. Ibid.]

[5 This opinion is most learnedly, but in my opinion most hopelessly maintained by Ussher, in his Syntagma De LXX. Interprett. See Walton Proleg. IX. pp. 125—159. (Vol. II. ed. Wrangham.)]

[6 See some admirable remarks upon the comparative merits of the Hebrew, Samaritan, and Greek chronologies in Gesenius, De Pentateuchi Samar. Orig. &c. Halæ. 1815.]

790 years more than the Hebrew: and all concede the Hebrew numbers to be much truer than the Greek. Gen. v., in the Greek books, Adam is said to have lived 230 years, or, according to some copies, 330, when he begat Seth. But the Hebrew text shews that Seth was born when Adam was 130 years old. In the rest there is a similar discordance of reckoning times, so as to prove that it was not without reason that Jerome wrote that the LXX. sometimes erred in their numbers. It is even a laughable mistake in the Greek by which Methusalem is made to survive the flood fourteen years[1]. Where did he remain during the deluge? or how was he preserved? Certainly he was not in the ark; in which the scripture testifies that there were no more than eight persons. This, therefore, is a manifest falsity in the Greek edition. But the Hebrew text speaks much more truly of the years and age of Methusalem; and we collect from it that he died in that same year in which the world was overwhelmed by the deluge. Augustine treats of this matter in his City of God, Lib. xv. c. 11. So Jonah iii., according to the Hebrew reading, destruction is denounced against the Ninevites after 40 days. But in the Greek we read otherwise, " Yet three days, and Nineve shall be destroyed:" which is manifestly a false reading; for he could scarcely have traversed the whole city in three days. Augustine (Civit. Dei. Lib. xviii. c. 44) invents I know not what mystery in this change of numbers to preserve the authority of the Septuagint, which, nevertheless, in the former place about Methusalem he is unable to defend.

From these and innumerable examples of the like sort we may conclude, either that this Greek version which hath come down to our times is not the same as that published by the seventy Jewish elders, or that it hath suffered such infinite and shameful corruptions as to be now of very slight authority. Even Jerome had not the Greek translation of the seventy interpreters in its purity; since he often complains in his commentaries that what he had was faulty and corrupt.

[1 Whitaker might have remembered, that Augustine (Civit. Dei, xv. 13), and the author under his name of the Questions on Genesis, Q. ii. appeal to ancient MSS. of the LXX. which are free from this fault. Walton (Proleg. ix. T. ii. p. 168. edit. Wrangham) observes, that Methusalem's age at the birth of Lamech is made 187 instead of 167 in the Cotton MS., the octateuch of J. Clemens, and the Aldine edition.]

CHAPTER IV.

OF OTHER GREEK TRANSLATIONS OF THE OLD TESTAMENT.

BESIDES this first and most famous translation, which was made by the seventy interpreters, there were formerly other Greek versions also of the old Testament, composed by various authors after the gospel of Christ had been spread far and wide over the world. The first of these was Aquila of Sinope, whom the emperor Hadrian employed as præfect and curator of the works when he repaired Jerusalem. Epiphanius, in his book of Weights and Measures, relates that this Aquila, having originally been a Greek, received baptism and was admitted into the christian society; but, on account of his assiduous devotion to astrology, was first censured by the Christians, and finally, when he disregarded their censures and admonitions, ejected from the Church ; that, stung by such a disgrace, this impious man revolted from the Christians to the Jews, had himself circumcised, learned the Hebrew language and literature, and translated the scriptures of the old Testament into Greek, but not with faithfulness or sincerity, but with a depraved and perverse intention (καμπύλῳ καὶ διεστραμμένῳ λογισμῷ, as Theodoret says,) of obscuring the testimonies which confirm the doctrine of Christ, and giving a plausible colour to his apostasy.

He was followed by Symmachus, whom Epiphanius testifies to have lived in the time of Aurelius Verus[2], and who was a Samaritan according to Theodoret. Being ambitious of power and dignity, and unable to obtain from his countrymen that authority and honour which he desired, he betook himself to the Jews, and translated the scriptures from Hebrew into Greek (πρὸς διαστροφὴν) *for the confutation* of the Samaritans. Epiphanius relates that this Symmachus was twice circumcised; καὶ περιτέμνεται, says he, δευτέραν τὴν περιτομήν· which he shews to be possible by adducing those words of the apostle, περιτετμημένος τις ἐκλήθη; μὴ ἐπισπάσθω, and ascribes the device there meant to Esau as the inventor.

Next came[3] one Theodotion of Pontus, of the party and sect of Marcion. He, having not only rejected the Marcionite opinions,

[2 Ut supra, c. 16.]

[3 Whitaker has fallen into a mistake in placing Theodotion after Symmachus. See Hody, p. 179.]

but also utterly abjured Christianity, went over to the Jews ; and, having learned their language, translated the scriptures into the Greek tongue, "for the confutation," as Theodoret says, "of his own sect" (πρὸς διαστροφὴν τῆς αὐτοῦ αἱρέσεως). These three interpreters were enemies of the christian faith, and did not translate the scriptures honestly. Yet Jerome and other ancient writers often cite their translations in commenting upon the bible. Those versions have now perished, save that the papists retain some parts of Theodotion's version, and obtrude them on the world as canonical. For they have the apocryphal 13th and 14th of Daniel not from the pure Hebrew originals, but from the Greek translation of Theodotion, an impious heretic or apostate.

There was also another Greek translation by Lucian[1], a presbyter of the church of Antioch, and a martyr about the time of Diocletian, which is mentioned by Theodoret, in the Synopsis of Athanasius, and elsewhere[2]. They say that this was found written by the martyr's own hand, at Nicomedia, in a marble tower. And Jerome, in the catalogue, says that in his time some copies were called *Lucianea*. There were also two other editions by unknown authors. The first was found at Jericho in a pitcher[3], in the reign of Caracalla ; the other in a similar vessel, at the northern Nicopolis, in the reign of Alexander the son of Mammæa, as Epiphanius and Theodoret testify.

I come now to Origen, who, according to the narrative of Epiphanius and others, being assisted by the resources of Ambrosius, a rich and pious person, bestowed incredible pains upon collecting and comparing the various editions of the scriptures[4]. He brought together the Greek versions of Aquila, Symmachus, the seventy-two, and Theodotion, into one volume, arranged in four distinct columns. This formed what is called Origen's Tetrapla (τετραπλᾶ βιβλία). Afterwards he added the Hebrew text in two columns, expressing in one in Hebrew, in the other in Greek characters. This was the Hexapla. Lastly, he appended the two anonymous versions found in jars, and so constructed the Octapla, a laborious and super-human

[1 Lucian made no new translation, but only revised the text of the LXX. See Hody, p. 627.]

[2 Synopsis Script. inter Opp. Athanasii. T. II. pp. 203, 204. cf. Suidas, voc. Λουκιανός.]

[3 Epiphan. de Mens. et Pond. c. 17.]

[4 See what is still the fullest and best account of Origen's labours in Hody, Lib. IV. c. 11.]

work, which is now lost, to the irreparable injury of the Church. Origen marked these texts with various asterisks and obeli, lemnisci and hypolemnisci, according as the various and manifold characters of those editions required. This was a work the loss of which we may deplore, but cannot compensate.

CHAPTER V.

OF THE GREEK EDITION OF THE NEW TESTAMENT.

WE have next, in the second place, to speak of the Greek edition of the new Testament. It is certain that the whole new Testament was written in Greek, unless, perhaps, we are to except the Gospel of Matthew and the Epistle to the Hebrews. Hosius of Esmeland (in his book de Sacro Vernac.) says, that it was only the Gospel of Matthew which was written in Hebrew. Jerome affirms the same thing in these words of his Preface to the four evangelists addressed to Damasus : " The new Testament is undoubtedly Greek, with the exception of the Apostle Matthew, who first published the gospel in Judæa in Hebrew letters[5]." Nevertheless in the catalogue, under the article *Paul*, he says that the Epistle to the Hebrews was written in Hebrew. Thus he writes : " He wrote most eloquently as a Hebrew to the Hebrews, in the Hebrew, that is, in his own language[6]." The translation of this epistle into Greek some ascribe to Barnabas, as Theodorus Lector[7] in his second book of Collectanea, some to Luke[8], and some to Clemens[9]. But, however that may be, the Greek edition both of the Gospel according to Matthew and of the Epistle to the Hebrews is authentic. For the Hebrew originals (if any such there were) are now nowhere extant, and the Greek was published in the life-time of the apostles,

[5 De novo nunc loquor Testamento, quod Græcum esse non dubium est, excepto apostolo Matthæo, qui primus in Judæa evangelium Christi Hebraicis literis edidit.—Opp. T. I. p. 1426.]

[6 Scripserat, ut Hebræus Hebræis, Hebraice, id est suo eloquio, disertissime.]

[7 I think this is a mistake. At least I can find no such statements in Theodorus.]

[8 So Clemens Alex. ap. Euseb. H. Eccl. L. VI. c. 14.]

[9 Euseb. H. E. Lib. III. c. 38. οἱ μὲν τὸν εὐαγγελιστὴν Λουκᾶν, οἱ δὲ τὸν Κλήμεντα τοῦτον αὐτὸν ἑρμηνεῦσαι λέγουσι τὴν γραφήν.]

received in the church, and approved by the apostles themselves.
Jerome in the Catalogue (Article MATTHÆUS), tells us : " He first
composed a gospel in the Hebrew character and language, in Judæa,
for the sake of those of the circumcision who had believed ; but it is
not certainly known who translated it into Greek." He adds, that
" the Hebrew text itself was preserved in his time in the library of
Cæsaræa which was built by the martyr Pamphilus[1]." So Nazianzene in his version upon the genuine books[2] :

$$\text{Ματθαῖος μὲν ἔγραψεν Ἑβραίοις θαύματα Χριστοῦ·}$$

where, when he says that Matthew wrote the miracles of Christ for
the Hebrew, it is implied that he wrote his gospel in Hebrew. So
Irenæus, Lib. III. c. 1, relates, that "Matthew published the scripture
of the gospel amongst the Hebrews in their own language[3]." These
fathers then suppose that Matthew wrote his gospel in Hebrew, and
that it was translated by an unknown hand. Athanasius, however,
in his Synopsis[4], writes that the Hebrew gospel of Matthew was
translated into Greek by the apostle James, but brings no argument
to command our credence.

Nor is the opinion of a Hebrew original of the gospel of
Matthew supported by any proofs of sufficient strength. For
at the time when Christ was upon earth the Jews did not speak
Hebrew, but Syriac. Matthew, therefore, would rather have
written in Syriac than in Hebrew; as indeed it is the opinion
of Widmanstadt and Guido Fabricius, to which our jesuit also
subscribes, that Matthew wrote his gospel not in the Hebrew, but
in the Syriac language. And they allege that, when the fathers
say that Matthew wrote in Hebrew, we must understand them to
mean that Hebrew dialect which the Jews then used, and which was

[1 Primus in Judæa, propter eos qui ex circumcisione crediderant, evangelium Christi Hebraicis literis verbisque composuit: quod quis postea in Græcum transtulerit non satis certum est. Porro ipsum Hebraicum habetur
usque hodie Cæsariensi Bibliotheca, quam Pamphilus Martyr studiosissime
confecit. c. 3. It seems to be certain, nevertheless, that Jerome believed
this Gospel to have been written in Syriac. Compare Adv. Pelag. Lib. III.
c. 1. In evangelio juxta Hebræos, quod *Chaldaico quidem Syroque sermone,*
sed Hebraicis literis scriptum est, quo utuntur usque hodie Nazareni, secundum apostolos, sive (ut plerique autumant) juxta Matthæum, *quod et in Cæsariensi habetur Bibliotheca,* &c.]

[2 Poem. XXXIII. 31. Opp. T. II. p. 99. Lips. 1690.]

[3 ὁ μὲν Ματθαῖος ἐν τοῖς Ἑβραίοις τῇ ἰδίᾳ διαλέκτῳ αὐτῶν καὶ γραφὴν ἐξήνεγκεν εὐαγγελίου. P. 220. et ap. Euseb. H. E. Lib. v. c. 8.]

[4 Inter Opp. Athan. T. II. p. 177.]

not pure Hebrew, but Syriac, or a mixture of Hebrew and Chaldee.
Yet Jerome thought that the gospel of Matthew was written in pure
Hebrew: for, in the catalogue under the article MATTHÆUS, he writes
that there was a MS. remaining of this Hebrew gospel in the
library of Nicomedia[5], and that he was permitted to make a copy
of it. On the whole, therefore, it seems uncertain that Matthew
wrote his gospel either in Hebrew or in Syriac; and it is rather to
be thought that both Matthew and the author of the epistle to the
Hebrews wrote in Greek, since the Greek language was then not
unknown to the Jews themselves, and the other apostles used the
Greek language not only in those pieces which they wrote for all
promiscuously, but also in those which were inscribed peculiarly to
the Jews, as we see in the case of James and Peter. However,
the learned are agreed that those Hebrew copies of this gospel and
epistle which are now extant are not genuine.

The Lord willed the new Testament to be written in Greek,
because he had determined to bring forth the gospel from the
narrow bounds of Judæa into a broader field, and publish it to
all people and nations. On this account the Lord selected the
Greek language, than which no other was more commonly known
by all men, wherein to communicate his gospel to as many countries and persons as possible. He willed also that the heavenly
truth of the gospel should be written in Greek in order to provide a confutation of the Gentiles' idolatry and of the philosophy
and wisdom of the Grecians. And, although at that time the
Romans had the widest empire, yet Cicero himself, in his oration for the poet Archias, bears witness that the language of the
Greeks was more widely extended than that of the Romans[6]. As,
therefore, before Christ the holy doctrine was written in that language which was the peculiar and native tongue of the Church; so
after Christ all was written in Greek, that they might more easily
reach and be propagated to the Church now about to be gathered
out of all nations.

[5 Mihi quoque a Nazaræis, qui in Beræa urbe Syriæ hoc volumine utuntur, describendi facultas fuit. Vide supra.]

[6 Græca leguntur in omnibus fere gentibus: Latina suis finibus, exiguis
sane, continentur. Cic. Opp. T. v. p. 445, ed. Lallemand. Paris. 1768.]

CHAPTER VI.

OF THE LATIN VULGATE EDITION.

I COME now, as was proposed in the third place, to the Latin edition, which is commonly called the Vulgate. That there were formerly in the church very many Latin versions of the scriptures, we have the testimony of Augustine (de Doctr. Christ. Lib. II. c. 11) to assure us. His words are: "Those who have translated the scriptures into Greek out of the Hebrew language may be counted, but the Latin translators cannot[1]." Augustine expresses an opinion, that a theologian may derive some assistance from this multitude of versions; but shews plainly that he did not consider any one in particular authentic, but thought that whatever in each was most useful for the reader's purpose, should be employed as a means for the right understanding of scripture. But Jerome, in the preface to Joshua, complains of this so great variety of the Latin texts: for he says that "there were as many texts as copies, since every one, at his own caprice, added or subtracted what he pleased[2]." But among the rest there was one more famous, which was called *Itala*[3]; and which Augustine (Doctr. Christ. Lib. II. c. 15) prefers to the others, for keeping closer to the words and expressing the sense more clearly and intelligibly. This was not, however, that version which Jerome published. Who the author of this version was is not known, but it was certainly more ancient than the Hieronymian: for Gregory, in his epistle to Leander[4], says that the Roman

[1 Qui ex Hebræa lingua scripturas in Græcam verterunt numerari possunt, Latini autem nullo modo.]

[2 Maxime cum apud Latinos *tot sint exemplaria*, quot codices, et unusquisque pro arbitrio suo vel addiderit vel subtraxerit quod ei visum est.]

[3 As this is the only passage in which any ancient Latin father speaks of a *versio Itala*, various critical efforts have been made to alter the text; the most ingenious being that of Archbp. Potter: "In ipsis autem interpretationibus USITATA ceteris præferatur; nam est verborum tenacior cum perspicuitate sententiæ." He supposes the present reading to have originated by the absorption of the Us in the last syllable of the preceding word, after which *Itata* was easily changed into *Itala*. But see, in defence of the old reading, Hug. Einl. 115.]

[4 Novam vero translationem dissero; sed ut comprobationis causa exigit, nunc novam, nunc veterem, per testimonia assumo: ut quia sedes apostolica (cui auctore Deo præsideo) utraque utitur, mei quoque labor studii ex utraque fulciatur. T. I. p. 6. Opp. Paris. 1705.]

church made use of two versions, one of which he calls the old, and the other the new. The old was most probably that same *Italic*; the new the Hieronymian, which presently after its publication began to be read in some churches, as we may collect from Augustine's 10th epistle to Jerome, where he writes that some Christians were offended by a new word occurring in it: for in the fourth chapter of Jonah the old Latin edition had *cucurbita* (a gourd); but Jerome in his version made it *hedera* (ivy)[5]. Perhaps the Hebrew term does not really denote either, but a quite different plant called *Ricinus* (or Palma Christi). Now, although there were formerly many and almost infinite Latin versions in the Latin Church, yet these two were undoubtedly the most celebrated and used in the greatest number of churches, since we find Gregory attesting the use of them both in the Church of Rome.

At length, however, not only the rest, which were more obscure, but even the Italic too fell altogether out of use, and the Hieronymian alone prevailed everywhere throughout the Latin churches,—if indeed it hath any just claims to be called the Hieronymian. For I am well aware that there are learned men who entertain great doubts upon that subject: and, although most of the Papists, and the Jesuits especially, maintain the present Latin edition to be the pure Hieronymian, there are, nevertheless, amongst them theologians of great erudition and judgment, who determine quite the other way, and that upon very weighty grounds. Xantes Pagninus, in the Preface to his Translation, which he inscribed to Clement VII., declares himself of opinion that it is not Jerome's, and wishes earnestly that Jerome's own version were remaining. In like manner Paul of Forossombrone, *De Die Passion. Domin.* Lib. ii. c. 1; not to mention Erasmus, Munster, and the rest of that sort. Others, though they allow it to be partly the Hieronymian, yet think it not throughout that same version which Jerome composed with so much care and fidelity, but a mixture of the Hieronymian and some other ancient version. So John Driedo, *de Catalog. Script.* Lib. ii. c. 1: "There are some who say that this Latin translation, which the whole church of the Latins commonly makes use of, is neither the work of St Jerome, nor in all points perfectly consonant

[5 In hoc loco quidam Cantherius . . . . . dudum Romæ dicitur me accusasse sacrilegii, quod pro cucurbita hederam transtulerim: timens videlicet, ne si pro cucurbitis hederæ nascerentur, unde occulte et tenebrose biberet non haberet.—Hieron. Comment. in Jon. iv. Opp. vi. 425. Compare also his Epistle to Augustine. Ep. 112.]

[WHITAKER.]

9

to the sacred original of scripture[1]:" and he adds that it is blamed
and corrected, not only by Armachanus and Lyra, but also by other
persons of the present time well skilled in both languages. Afterwards, in his first proposition, he determines that this Latin translation,
as well of the old as of the new Testament, is neither an altogether
different translation from Jerome's, nor yet altogether the same with
it. Sixtus Senensis (Bibliotheca, Lib. viii) is of the same opinion,
and confesses that he has been brought to that opinion by demonstrative arguments. Bellarmine (Lib. ii. c. 9) lays down the three
following propositions. *First*, that the Books of Wisdom, Ecclesiasticus, Maccabees, and the Psalms, as they have them, are not
part of Jerome's version. The former three he did not translate,
because he judged them apocryphal. The Psalms he translated with
the utmost care and religious scrupulousness from the Hebrew: but
this Vulgate version (as they call it) of the Psalms was made from
the Greek, as appears on the face of it, and as our adversaries themselves allow. It is even good sport to see how Genebrard, in his
Scholia, tries to reconcile the Latin version with the Hebrew. *Secondly*, that the Latin edition of the new Testament was not made,
but only amended, by Jerome: for Jerome, at the request of Damasus,
corrected the old version, but did not make a new one; as he himself testifies in several places, and specially in the catalogue towards
the end. "The new Testament," says he, "I restored to the Greek
fidelity; the old I translated according to the Hebrew[2]." *Thirdly*,
that all the other parts of the old Testament are exhibited in the
Vulgate according to Jerome's version.

The reasons which he alleges shew, that this is not the sincere
Hieronymian edition of either the old or the new Testament,
but that it may perhaps be not altogether a different version
from the Hieronymian, as Driedo and Sixtus Senensis suppose.
Much might be said upon this subject, but we must not spend too
much time upon such matters. I shall, therefore, in a few words
make it as plain as the light, that this is not the version which
Jerome either made himself or published in an amended form.
For, first of all, Jerome translated the old Testament accurately
from the Hebrew, as he hath himself frequently professed and

[1 Sunt qui dicunt translationem hanc Latinam, qua communiter utitur
tota Latinorum ecclesia, neque esse divi Hieronymi, neque in omnibus con-
sonam scripturæ sacræ originali.—Opp. Lovan. 1550. T. i. p. 24.]

[2 Novum Testamentum Græcæ fidei reddidi. Vetus juxta Hebraicam transtuli. c. 135. Opp. ii. 941. The latter clause, *Vetus*, &c. is wanting in one MS.]

testified. In the Preface of the Psalter to Sophronius (which is the Epistle 133) he writes thus of his translation: " Certainly I will say it boldly, and can cite many witnesses of my work, that I have changed nothing of the sense, at least from the Hebrew verity. Wherever, therefore, my edition clashes with the old ones, ask any Hebrew, and you will see clearly that I am unreasonably attacked by my rivals, who choose rather to seem despisers of what is excellent than to become learners[3]." Again, in the Preface to the five books of Moses : " Wherever you think I go wrong in my translation, ask the Jews, consult the masters in various cities, &c.[4]" And in the preface to Kings he declares that he hath nowhere departed from the Hebrew verity[5]. So that Jerome everywhere most carefully compared and adjusted his version by the standard of the Hebrew books. This Augustine also (Civit. Dei, Lib. XVIII. c. 43) testifies concerning him : " We have had in our own time the presbyter Jerome, a very learned man and one exquisitely skilled in the three languages, who hath translated the divine scriptures not from the Greek, but from the Hebrew, into Latin ; whose stupendous literary work the Hebrews acknowledge to be faithful to the original[6]." So Isidorus of Seville, in his Etymologicon, Lib. VI. c. 5, prefers the version of Jerome to all others, as adhering more closely to the words and expressing the sense with greater perspicuity. That such was the character of the Hieronymian version no man can reasonably doubt, since Jerome himself affirms it so often, and others agree in the same testimony.

But now this Vulgate, which we now have, exhibits in the several books considerable variations from the Hebrew text, as Jerome himself, if he returned to life, would not be able to deny. Nor can they answer that the Hebrew is corrupt. For, although

[3 Certe confidenter dicam, et multos hujus operis testes citabo, me nihil duntaxat scientem de Hebraica veritate mutasse. Sicubi ergo editio mea a veteribus discreparit, interroga quemlibet Hebræorum, et liquido pervidebis, me ab æmulis frustra lacerari, qui malunt contemnere videri præclara, quam discere. Opp. T. IX. 1156.]

[4 Sicubi in translatione tibi videor errare, interroga Hebræos, diversarum urbium magistros consule. Ibid. 6.]

[5 Quanquam mihi omnino conscius non sim, mutasse me quidpiam de Hebraica veritate. Ibid. 459.]

[6 Non defuit temporibus nostris presbyter Hieronymus, homo doctissimus et trium linguarum peritissimus, qui non ex Græco, sed ex Hebræo in Latinum divinas scripturas converteret: cujus tantum literarum laborem Hebræi fatentur esse veracem.]

some papists do indeed say this, yet they are refuted by plain
reason and by the authority of their own party.   Bellarmine, Lib.
II. c. 2, defends, against Jacobus Christopolitanus and Melchior
Canus, the integrity of the Hebrew copies, and proves by some
arguments that they could not have been corrupted by the Jews,
as those writers supposed.   How were they corrupted?   By the
copyists?   This cannot be said, since all the MSS. agree; and,
besides, might just as well be said of the Latin as of the Hebrew
books.   Since, then, the Vulgate edition differs so greatly from the
Hebrew, they must either pronounce the Hebrew grievously corrupt (which their more prudent champions will not venture to say),
or concede that the present Latin text is not the Hieronymian.
Besides, Jerome in his Questions upon Genesis, his Commentaries
on the Prophets, and his book *De Optimo Genere Interpretandi*,
hath judged that many passages ought to be translated otherwise
than we find them translated in this version.   How then can that
be called Jerome's version, which Jerome himself condemns?   Now
we could shew by many examples that many things in this version
are censured by Jerome.   But it will suffice to give a specimen in
a few, which will be enough to establish our desired conclusion.

Whereas we read, Gen. i., in the Vulgate edition, *Spiritus Dei
ferebatur super aquas*, there is, says Jerome, in the Hebrew a term
which means "brooded, or cherished, as a bird warms its eggs with
animal heat[1]."   In Gen. iv. the Vulgate has, *Et respexit Dominus
ad Abel et ad munera ejus; ad Cain autem et ad munera ejus non
respexit*.   Jerome thinks that the place should rather be translated,
as Theodotion hath translated it, "And the Lord sent fire upon
Abel and his sacrifice : but upon Cain and his sacrifice he did not
send fire;" which translation he pronounceth to be most exact[2].

In the same chapter he pronounces that clause, "Let us pass
into the field," to be superfluous[3], though it appears both in the
Greek and Samaritan editions.   Yet this is the same thing as the
Vulgate exhibits in the words, *Egrediamur foras*.

[1 In Hebræo habet MEREFETH, quod nos appellare possumus *incubabat*,
sive *confovebat*, in similitudinem volucris ova calore animantis. Quæst. Hebr.
in Genes. Opp. T. III. 306.]

[2 Unde scire poterat Cain, quod fratris munera suscepisset Deus, et sua
repudiasset; nisi illa interpretatio vera est, quam Theodotion posuit, *Et
inflammavit Dominus super Abel, &c.* ib. 310.]

[3 Superfluum ergo est, quod in Samaritanorum et nostro volumine repo-
ritur, *Transeamus in campum*. ib. 312.]

In Gen. xxx. 32, where we read *cunctum gregem unicolorem,*
Jerome observes that we ought to read *non unicolorem*[4]; and so
reason and the context require. Likewise in the first chapter of
Isaiah, where the Vulgate hath, *ut ambularetis in atriis meis,* Jerome translates, "No longer tread my court[5];" and so the version,
which we find in his works along with his Commentaries, still reads
it. So where the Vulgate hath, *facti estis mihi molesti,* Jerome
reads, *facti estis mihi in satietatem.* And, in the end of the chapter,
that passage, which the Vulgate represents by *cum fueritis velut
quercus,* Jerome translates, "They shall be like a terebinth[6]."
Examples of this kind are almost innumerable.

Nor does this occur only in the old Testament, but in the new
also. In the first chapter of the Galatians, the passage, *Non ac-
quievi carni et sanguini,* Jerome in his Commentary says should
be translated, "I conferred not with flesh and blood[7]." In the
same Epistle, chap. iii. 1, Jerome omits in his version these words,
non credere veritati[8], which appear in the Vulgate; whence Erasmus in his Annotations writes, that this is one place out of many,
which prove that the present edition is not altogether the same as
Jerome's[9]. And in Eph. chap. i., Jerome blames the interpreter for
putting *pignus* for *arrhabo,* and proves, by excellent reasons, that
this is a false translation[10]: yet in all the books of the Vulgate
edition we have still not *arrhabo* but *pignus,* contrary to Jerome's
determination. Upon Eph. iv., where the vulgar copies have, *qui*

[4 Ibid. 352.]

[5 Calcare atrium meum non apponetis. Opp. T. IV. 2, 1.]

[6 Jerome gives both translations: Usque hodie Judæi legentes scripturas
sanctus *terebinthus* sunt, sive *quercus,* ut interpretatus est Symmachus. T. IV.
39.]

[7 Sive, ut in Græco melius habet: *Non contuli cum carne et sanguine.*
T. VII. 391.]

[8 Legitur in quibusdam codicibus: *Quis vos fascinavit non credere veritati?* Sed hoc, quia in exemplaribus Adamantii non habetur, omisimus.
Ibid. 418.]

[9 Hic est unus locus e multis, quo coarguitur hæc editio non esse tota
Hieronymi. Etenim quum ille testetur se hanc particulam omisisse, quod in
Adamantii codicibus non inveniretur, in nostris codicibus constanter habetur.
—Erasmi Annot. in N. T. p. 576. Basil. 1535.]

[10 *Pignus* Latinus interpres pro *arrhabone* posuit. Non idipsum autem
arrhabo quod *pignus* sonat. Arrhabo enim futuræ emtioni quasi quoddam
testimonium et obligamentum datur. Pignus vero, hoc est, ἐνέχυρον, pro
mutua pecunia opponitur; ut quum illa reddita fuerit, reddenti debitum pignus a creditore reddatur.—Hieron. Opp. T. VII. 560, 561.]

desperantes semetipsos tradiderunt impudicitiœ, "it is otherwise," says Jerome, " in the Greek. For the Gentiles do not despair, since they have no sense of their ruin, but live like brute beasts according to the flesh." And he subjoins that instead of " being in despair," we may read, " being without feeling[1]." Why should I endeavour to go through all the rest ? It will be easier to find a beginning than an end.

What Bellarmine adduces to obscure this light of truth, may be dispelled without difficulty. For, first, in these and innumerable other passages there is no error of the copyists ; for all the books, whether ancient or modern, agree in the reading. Next, as to the various signification of words, it is the duty of a good interpreter to consider well what signification is most suitable, and to choose it. But when Jerome says plainly, that he thinks a certain place or word should be translated otherwise than it is translated in the Vulgate, it is manifest that that version cannot be Jerome's. For, as to his third pretence—that Jerome changed his opinion,—although it might be allowed in the case of a few passages, yet in the case of so many it is incredible. If he had made so many changes, he would have impaired, in no slight degre, the authority of his judgment. Besides, in most of the instances he had no reason for changing. For in Gal. i. προσανεθέμην is more correctly rendered " conferred," than " acquiesced." Eph. i., ἀρραβών is not the same as *pignus*, as Jerome himself hath taught us in his Commentaries. " A pledge," says he, " is given for money borrowed ; but an earnest is given as a sort of evidence and security of a future purchase[2]." And Eph. iv., ἀπηλγηκότες does not mean " despairing," but " being past or without feeling," as Jerome says. Who that reads Jerome, disputing and proving by arguments, that these places should have been thus translated, can doubt that he translated them thus himself ? Nay, it is not only clear that this is not Jerome's version, but manifest also that it is a version condemned by Jerome.

As to Bellarmine's last excuse,—that the church hath interposed its authority, and judged the first version to be the truer—I ask, when, or how the church declared that judgment ? or what church it is that he means ? or what right any church had to

[1 Multo aliud in Græco significat quam in Latino . . . . exprimamus si possimus verbum de verbo, et dicamus, ἀπηλγηκότες *indolentes*, sive *indolorios*. Ibid. 621.]

[2 See preceding page, note 10.]

determine a false or improper version to be truer than a true[3] and proper one ?

These, to omit the rest, are sufficiently plain reasons to prove, that the Latin Vulgate is not that pure version which Jerome so diligently composed and published. Since, however, so many things are found in it which were in the Hieronymian, the opinion of those who think it made up of Jerome's and some other ancient version appears to commend itself to our approval.

CHAPTER VII.

WHEREIN AN ANSWER IS GIVEN TO THE ARGUMENTS OF OUR OPPONENTS, WHEREBY THEY ENDEAVOUR TO PROVE THAT THE LATIN VULGATE EDITION IS AUTHENTIC.

WE have next to discourse of the authority of this Vulgate edition, which point is the hinge whereupon this controversy particularly turns. Our adversaries determine that the authentic scripture consists not in the Hebrew and Greek originals, but in the Vulgate Latin version. We, on the contrary side, say that the authentic and divinely-inspired scripture is not this Latin, but the Hebrew edition of the old Testament, and the Greek of the new. We shall first obviate the arguments of the adversaries, and then produce our own. Upon this question many papists have written, and published works, both great and numerous; whose diligence Bellarmine has sought to imitate, and endeavours to prove this same conclusion by the following arguments.

He proposes his FIRST argument in this form : For nearly a thousand years, that is, from the time of Gregory the Great, the whole Latin church hath made use of this Latin edition alone. Now it is absurd to say, that for eight or nine hundred years together the church was without the true interpretation of scripture, or respected as the word of God, in matters pertaining to faith and religion, the errors of an uncertain translator, since the apostle, 1 Tim. iii., declares the church to be the pillar and ground of truth.

[3 In the original, " aut quo jure potuit ulla ecclesia judicare versionem aut falsam aut impropriam esse *falsa* propriaque veriorem ?" Where *falsa* is plainly a mistake, though not marked in the errata.]

Bellarmine says that this is the argument of the council of Trent, and it is the same which Canus uses, Lib. II. c. 13.

I answer, in the first place, that the Latin was not at that time the whole church; for there were many and very populous churches of the Greeks and others. Although, therefore, the Latin church had erred, yet it would not follow that the whole church of Christ had remained for such a length of time subject to that error.

Secondly, that the church may be deceived in the translation of some passages without, in the meanwhile, ceasing to be the church. For the church is not subverted by the circumstance, that some place of scripture happens to be improperly rendered; and the Roman church, if it had no other errors except this faulty version, and if it put a sound and pious meaning upon this Latin scripture which it receives, might still be the church of Christ. The fundamental points of the faith are preserved intact in this Latin edition, if not everywhere, yet in very many places. But that church not only receives and defends this faulty version as the authentic scripture, but also pollutes by its expositions those places in it, which are well or tolerably rendered.

Thirdly, if it were so necessary that the Latin church should have an authentic Latin version, which might claim equal credence with the originals, it would have prevailed always in the Latin church, not only after Gregory, but also before Gregory's time. But we have shewn that there were many Latin versions in the Latin church before Gregory, and no one in particular authentic: and after Gregory there was no provision made by any decree of the church that this Latin version should be authentic, until the publication of this very decree of the council of Trent.

Fourthly, Bellarmine does not prove that the Latin church from the time of Gregory used this edition only. For Isidore, who lived after Gregory, says, Etymol. Lib. VI. c. 4, "that Jerome's version is deservedly preferred to all the rest[1]." There were, therefore, other versions besides this of Jerome, though he confesses it to be the purest and best. Besides, interpreters and expositors, even after Gregory, do not always use to recite the

[1 Presbyter quoque Hieronymus, trium linguarum peritus, ex Hebræo in Latinum eloquium easdem scripturas convertit . . . cujus interpretatio merito ceteris antefertur. Nam est et verborum tenacior et perspicuitate sententiæ clarior. Madrit. 1599. p. 103. Which last are almost the very words in which Augustine commends the old Italic, De Doctr Christ. II. 15.]

VII.]   QUESTION THE SECOND.   137

words of scripture as they are now read in this edition, as is plain
from Bede and Gildas, and other writers, who flourished in the
church after Gregory.

Fifthly, as to the passage of St Paul, we shall explain it hereafter in the proper place.

Bellarmine draws his SECOND argument from the testimonies of
the ancients. This version is either the Italic, which Augustine
praises, or that of Jerome, which Damasus, and Augustine, and
Isidore, and Rabanus, and Bernard, and others, commend and
follow. Nor is it the Latins only who give this approbation, but
the Greeks also, who turned out of Latin into Greek some books
which had been translated by Jerome out of Hebrew into Latin,
as Jerome himself testifies in his second book against Ruffinus, and
in his Catalogue under the article SOPHRONIUS[2].

I answer, first, that this argument is wholly inconclusive. For
what if those authors praise and commend this version? Will it
therefore follow that this alone is authentic, or preferable to the
originals themselves? Nothing less. They praise it, and deservedly : but yet they always prefer the originals to it. Jerome
himself adjusted his version by the standard of the originals, and
wished it to be judged of by that same standard. Augustine, as
we have previously shewn, passes a long encomium upon that
translation which the Seventy published. Will our adversaries
thence conclude that that translation is authentic? On the contrary, they now esteem it very slightly. With what pertinency
then do they allege that Jerome's version is approved by Augustine and other Fathers? Which yet was certainly never praised
in such a manner as not to imply, that not only the originals were
considered preferable, but even that higher praise might be deservedly challenged by the translation of the Seventy elders. In a
word, it is praised as a carefully executed translation, and is preferred to other Latin versions, but not required to be received
as authentic scripture. Isidore, Etymol., Lib. VI. cap. 5, has these
words: "His [Jerome's] version is deservedly preferred to the
others[3];" that is, to the other versions, not to the originals themselves.

Secondly, his assumption that this is either the Italic or the

[2 Sophronius .... opuscula mea in Græcum eleganti sermone transtulit,
Psalterium quoque et Prophetas, quos nos de Hebræo in Latinum transtuli-
mus. Catalog. Scriptt. c. 134.]
[3 Vide supra, pp. 131, 136.]

Hieronymian, rests upon no certain basis. Some think it a Latin version of Aquila's, or Symmachus's, or Theodotion's, Greek. That it is not the pure text of Jerome's translation, the reasons which we have previously adduced establish. The argument is, therefore, faulty every way.

The THIRD argument is this : The Hebrews had the authentic scripture in their own language, and the Greeks in theirs ; that is, the old Testament in the Septuagint version, and the new Testament in the original. Therefore it is fit that the Latin church also should have the authentic scripture in its own language.

I answer, first, by requiring to know in what sense it is that he makes the Septuagint version authentic. Is it in the same sense in which they make their Latin text authentic? If so, I deny its authenticity. For Augustine, who allowed most to the authority of the Septuagint version, yet thought that it should be corrected by the originals. But the papists contend that their Latin text is authentic of itself, and ought not to be tried by the text of the originals. Now in this sense no translation ever was, or could be, authentic. For translations of scripture are always to be brought back to the originals of scripture, received if they agree with those originals, and corrected if they do not. That scripture only, which the prophets, apostles, and evangelists wrote by inspiration of God, is in every way credible on its own account and authentic. Besides, if the Septuagint was formerly authentic, how did it become not authentic? At least in the Psalms it must continue authentic still, since they derive their Latin version of that book from no other source than the Greek of the Septuagint. Even in the other books too it must still be authentic, since it is plain from the commentaries of the Greek writers that it is the same now as it was formerly.

Secondly, I would fain know how this argument is consequential,—God willed his word and authentic scripture to be written in Hebrew and Greek ; therefore also in Latin. The authentic originals of the scripture of the old Testament are extant in Hebrew, of the new in Greek. It no more follows from this that the Latin church ought to esteem its Latin version authentic, than that the French, or Italian, or Armenian churches should esteem their vernacular versions authentic. If he grant that each church should necessarily have authentic versions of its own, what are we to do if these versions should (as they easily may) disagree ? Can they be all authentic, and yet disagree amongst themselves ? But if he will not assign authentic versions to all churches, upon what grounds will he determine that a necessity, which he grants to exist in the Latin church, hath no place in others? Cannot the churches of the Greeks at the present day claim their version likewise as authentic?

Thirdly, I know not with what truth they call theirs the Latin church. For it does not now speak Latin, nor does any one among them understand Latin without learning that language from a master. Formerly it was, and was called, the Latin church. Now it is not Latin, and therefore cannot truly be so called, except upon the plea that, though not Latin, it absurdly uses a Latin religious service.

The FOURTH argument is: It may happen that in general councils either very few persons, or none at all, may understand Hebrew or Greek. So Ruffinus, in his Ecclesiastical History, (Lib. x. c. 21), writes that no bishop was found in the council of Rimini who knew the meaning of the term ὁμοούσιος. Now in such cases the Church's interest would be badly provided for, if it did not understand the authentic scripture.

I answer, in the first place, That it is absurd to draw an argument against the authority or necessity of the originals from the ignorance of prelates and bishops.

Secondly, There never was any general council in which some persons could not be found who understood the scriptures in the original. But it is not necessary that all who understand the scriptures should be masters of those languages in which they were first written. The true Church, indeed, hath always had, and still possesses, many persons well skilled in those languages. What sort of persons come to their councils, is no concern of ours. But we grant that many come who know nothing of the Hebrew, or Greek, or perhaps even the Latin, tongue.

Thirdly, It is false, that no one was found in the council of Rimini capable of understanding the term ὁμοούσιος. For there were present many bishops from Greece, who were well acquainted with the Greek language: but perhaps there were not many among them who exactly perceived the whole force of that term. Hence, suspecting that something wrong lay hid under the word, they rashly rejected and condemned the ὁμοούσιον. But this may happen to persons who are ever so well acquainted with the languages.

The FIFTH argument. It would follow that all men, who are not skilled in the Hebrew and Greek tongues, should always be in

doubt whether it is the true scripture which they read. This
argument Bellarmine hath omitted in the Sartorian edition; having,
perhaps, upon reflection disapproved of it. Indeed it really contributes
nothing towards confirming the authority of the Latin version.

However I answer, in the first place, that the Church would
act wisely in not permitting every one to publish a new version
at his own caprice, and taking care that all versions should be as
pure and faithful as possible.

Secondly, men unskilled in the tongues, although they cannot
judge of the sense of each separate passage, whether all be correctly rendered, can yet, being instructed by the Holy Spirit,
acknowledge and approve the doctrine.

Thirdly, this argument no more proves the Latin to be authentic than any other version. For they themselves allow vernacular
versions to the people under certain conditions. How then do
those who are unlearned and illiterate understand that they are
reading the true scripture? The unlearned in our country who
read the English version of the Rhemists could never, if this
argument have any weight, be certain that they read the true
scripture. But Bellarmine hath himself renounced this argument.

The LAST argument is: The heretics, who despise the ancient
editions, make various and mutually discordant editions of their
own; so that Luther, in his book against Zwingle, was moved to
say, that, if the world lasted long, it would again be necessary to
receive the decrees of councils, on account of these diverse interpretations of scripture. I answer, in the first place, what sort of
an argument is this? The editions of the heretics are various
and discordant; therefore the old Latin edition is authentic.
Secondly, we do not approve discordant editions and versions.
Thirdly, we make no edition authentic, save the Hebrew in the old,
and the Greek in the new, Testament. We approve translations,
if they agree with these standards: we reject them if they do
not. Fourthly, as to Luther, I do not know whether he said this
or not. The slanderous Cochlæus hath affirmed it of him. It is a
matter of no moment. Such then are Bellarmine's arguments.

But Melchior Canus (Lib. II. c. 13) hath made use of some others
in this cause, but such as perhaps the Jesuit considered too futile.
Of this kind is this (which Canus, however, thinks a noble argument), that the scholastic theologians have followed this alone, and
that the inquisitors of heretical pravity are wont to convince and
condemn heretics out of it. I answer, in the first place, that those
divines, whom they call scholastic, have drawn some most absurd

conclusions from the Latin Vulgate edition, as appears plainly from their books and disputations. I could produce a great many examples. In Canticles, II. 4, the old interpreter hath translated thus: *Ordinavit in me caritatem.* Hence Thomas (I believe a thousand times) proves that there is a certain order and certain degrees in charity. That all this is true and accordant with the scriptures, I allow: but it is supported by no authority from this place and testimony; for the words should be translated otherwise: " His banner towards me is charity." Again, Rom. xiii. 2 is read thus in the Vulgate: *Quæ a Deo sunt, ordinata sunt.* Hence this same Thomas, undoubtedly the chief of all the schoolmen, collects in many places that all things are well and rightly constituted by God; and specially in *Prima Secundæ,* q. 102, art. 1, he proves from these words, that ceremonial precepts have a reason. A question, verily, both proposed and concluded with singular wisdom! For the place is most perversely rendered by that translator; who first omits altogether the word ἐξουσίαι, "powers," and then sets a comma after *a Deo,* when it should have been set before it: not to mention that the reading is *ordinata,* when it should be *ordinatæ.* Thus those theologians frequently abuse the errors of the Vulgate version, to confirm their own inventions.

CHAPTER VIII.

IN WHICH AN ANSWER IS GIVEN TO THE TEN REASONS OF THE ANGLO-RHEMIST TRANSLATORS, WHEREBY THEY ENDEAVOUR TO PROVE THE AUTHORITY OF THE VULGATE VERSION IN THE NEW TESTAMENT.

CERTAIN English popish divines, who have taken up their abode in the seminary of Rheims, some years since translated the new Testament into the English tongue, not from the Greek text, but from the old Latin Vulgate[1]. In order to persuade us of the wisdom and prudence of this proceeding, they produce in their preface ten reasons to prove that this Latin Vulgate edition is to be followed in all things rather than the Greek. We shall now briefly report and refute those reasons.

[1 It was first printed at Rheims in 4to in 1582. The principal translators appear to have been Allen, Martin, and Bristow.]

I. This edition is so ancient that it hath been received in the church by the space of 1300 years, as appears from the fathers of those times.

I answer : However ancient they make it out, yet they must needs confess that it is younger than the Greek edition. For the Greek was not only older than the Latin, but than all other versions, which are but streams derived from the fountain of the Greek edition. If, then, an antiquity of 1300 years commends the Latin version, the Greek text should be yet more strongly commended to us, which we gather from the genuine monuments of those times to have been publicly received 1500 years ago in the churches of Christians. And it is marvellous that these noble translators did not bethink themselves, when they vaunted the antiquity of their version, that by this plea of antiquity more was gained for the Greek edition, which was undoubtedly the first and most ancient of all, than for this Latin Vulgate, and that by their own shewing.

II. This is (as is commonly thought and most probable) that very same version which Jerome afterwards corrected from the Greek, by order of Damasus, as he writes in the preface to the Evangelists, in the catalogue at the end, and in the 102nd Epistle.

I answer : First, they confess it to be by no means certain and clear, that this Vulgate Latin edition of the new Testament is altogether the same as that which Jerome corrected, since they say that the fact rests upon common opinion and probability alone. Now we, not doubtfully or only with some probable shew, but most certainly, know that this Greek edition of the new Testament is no other than the inspired and archetypal scripture of the new Testament, commended by the apostles and evangelists to the christian church.

Secondly, Jerome's correcting the Latin edition from the Greek originals sufficiently shews, that the authority of the Greek is greater than that of the Latin edition. Jerome corrected the Latin from the Greek ; but our Rhemists, on the contrary, determine that the Greek should be corrected from the Latin.

III. Consequently, it is the same which Augustine so highly praises and approves in a certain letter to Jerome, Ep. 10.

I answer : In the first place, this plea depends upon the same opinion and conjecture as the preceding. Secondly, Augustine's praise is not weighty enough to constitute an edition authentic. He praised also the Italic and many others, but preferred the Greek to all, and would have them all corrected and estimated by the Greek. Thirdly, Augustine praised that edition, not as absolutely authentic, but as more faithful than the rest.

IV. This is that same edition which thenceforth was almost always used in the church-offices, in sermons, in commentaries, in the writings of the ancient fathers of the Latin church.

I answer: In the first place, for two hundred years after Jerome, and more, it never obtained any singular prerogative and authority, as we have already shewn. Secondly, I ask, Is it any consequence, that, because the Latin fathers and writers have made special use of this, it is therefore absolutely authentic and preferable to the Greek? Thirdly, Much more ought the Greek to be concluded authentic, which the churches of the Greeks have always used from the apostles' times in their public liturgies, homilies, commentaries, and books.

V. The sacred council of Trent, for these and many other very weighty reasons, hath defined this alone of all Latin translations to be authentic.

I answer: In the first place, that Tridentine Synod hath no authority with us. Secondly, What right had it to define this? Thirdly, It hath proposed no grounds of this decree, except this only,—that that edition had been for a long time received in the church; which reason, at least, every one must perceive to be unworthy of such great divines. Fourthly, I desire to know whether the council of Trent only commanded this Latin edition to be considered the authentic one amongst Latin editions, or determined it to be absolutely authentic? For if it only preferred this one to other Latin translations, that could be no reason to justify the Rhemists in not making their version of the new Testament from the Greek; since the council of Trent prefers this, not to the Greek edition, but to other Latin translations. Do they, then, make both this Latin and that Greek edition authentic, or this Latin only? Indeed, they express themselves in such a manner as not to deny the authenticity of the Greek, while nevertheless they really hold no edition of either old or new Testament authentic, save this Latin Vulgate only. This is the judgment of these Rhemists who have translated the new Testament from the Latin; and this the Jesuits defend most strenuously, maintaining that, where the Latin differs from the Greek or Hebrew, we should hold by the Latin rather than the Greek or Hebrew copies. And it is certain that this is now the received opinion of the papists.

VI.   It is, of all others, the weightiest, purest, most venerable and impartial.

I answer : 1. That all these virtues must needs be still greater in the Greek edition, which is that of the apostles and evangelists, and, finally, of the Holy Ghost himself, than in the Latin, which cannot derive the beginning of its credit and dignity higher than from the time and person of Jerome. 2. In many places it is absurd and erroneous, as will hereafter be shewn; and therefore, in such cases, destitute of weight, and majesty, and purity.

VII.   It agrees so exactly and thoroughly with the Greek, in regard both of the phrases and the words, that the fastidious heretics have blamed it on that account as rude and unskilful.

I answer : 1. That it is no great praise to be rude and unskilful. 2. If it deserves commendation for agreeing and corresponding remarkably with the Greek, then it follows that the Greek itself is still more deserving of commendation. 3. It differs from the Greek in many places, as we shall see hereafter.

VIII.   The adversaries themselves, and Beza in particular, prefer this to all the rest. See his Preface to the new Testament, published in the year 1556. And elsewhere he says, that the old interpreter translated very religiously. Annot. in 1 Luc. v. 1.

I answer : Although Beza hath preferred it to other versions in the translation of certain places, and said that the old interpreter seems to have translated the sacred books with religious care ; yet it never came into his mind to prefer that Latin edition to the Greek, or to make it authentic, or pronounce that the Latin translator never erred. Nay, in this very place he blames the old interpreter for not understanding the difference between $\pi\lambda\eta\rho o\phi o\rho\iota a$ and $\pi\epsilon\pi o\iota$-$\theta\eta\sigma\iota\varsigma$. If Beza had thought this as perfect as they would have it, he would never have published a new translation of his own.

IX.   In other translations there is the greatest difference and discordance.

I answer : 1. If it were agreed that this is better than all other translations, what would that be to the purpose ? For it does not therefore follow, either that the Latin is authentic, or that the Rhemists ought to have translated the new Testament from the Latin, and not from the Greek. 2. They cannot find so great a difference between our versions, as there is between their Latin Vulgate and the Greek edition. 3. Although some of our translations differ in some places, yet those places are not numerous, nor is the difference dangerous ; since we do not say that one should stand by these translations as of themselves authentic, but appeal to the originals alone as truly authentic.

X. It is not only better than all other Latin versions, but preferable even unto the Greek edition itself in those places where they differ.

I answer: 1. Hence it appears what value these men set upon the Greek edition, who maintain that the Latin is superior to it in all those places where any discrepancy is found. 2. How false is this assertion we shall hereafter shew, and many other writers have already often and copiously demonstrated.

CHAPTER IX.

WHEREIN THE ARGUMENTS ARE EXPLAINED WHEREBY THE LATIN VULGATE EDITION IS PROVED NOT TO BE THE AUTHENTIC SCRIPTURE.

IT remains that we should shew by good and solid reasons, that this Latin Vulgate edition is not to be esteemed authentic scripture. Upon which subject I might use many words, and adduce many arguments; but I shall endeavour to cut off all matters of inferior importance, and concern myself only with those things which are fitted to the immediate cause and question.

The first argument. Jerome, who either made or amended this edition, did not himself deem it authentic, although it was then in a much purer state than it is at present. Nay, he left it to his readers to choose in many places between different interpretations, being doubtful whether they were rightly understood and rendered by himself. Sometimes he even ingenuously confesses that he hath translated otherwise than the Hebrew verity required. So Jonah iv. he translates "ivy," following Aquila, not "a gourd" with the Septuagint; whereas in his Commentary on Jonah he teaches us that neither ivy nor gourd can be really denoted by the word. "For," says he, "gourds and ivy are naturally prone to creep upon the earth, and cannot gain any height without props and stays to support them[1]." But he testifies that the shrub which the Lord prepared for Jonah supports itself by its own

[1 Cucurbita et hedera hujus naturæ sunt ut per terram reptent, et absque furcis vel adminiculis quibus innituntur altiora non appetant.—T. VI. p. 426.]

stem, and grows commonly in Palestine. If, therefore, Jerome hath not ventured to defend that edition everywhere, and in some places owns that it is very wide of the true sense of the Hebrew, it follows that it is not to be taken for authentic. Assuredly Jerome never even so much as dreamed, that a time would come when the church would receive his translation for authentic scripture. Since, therefore, our opponents ascribe this version to Jerome, and deem it to be commended by his authority, it is fair that in this question they should be ruled by the testimony and judgment of Jerome, and learn from Jerome himself that it is not authentic.

The second argument. If this Latin edition were authentic, then the Latin church would have presently received it as authentic. The validity of the consequence may be perceived from the following consideration:—Jerome, as they say, translated the old Testament, and corrected the new, at the request of Damasus. Wherefore, if he had made this Latin edition, and delivered it to the church with the intention that it should everywhere be esteemed authentic scripture in the Latin churches; then it would have been forthwith received and approved by the judgment of the church and the order of the pontiff. But such was not the case. For in the time of pope Gregory, who lived in the Latin church more than two hundred years after Jerome, that version could not maintain exclusive sway, even in the Roman church, or be esteemed authentic, as is evident from Gregory's Preface to Job, c. v. If then it was neither published to serve as authentic, nor then held authentic when it was sounder and purer than it is at present, no one can, without extreme injustice, require us to reverence and follow it as authentic.

The third argument. Jerome himself, whom these men make either the author or corrector of this edition, blames many things in it. Therefore he by no means deemed it authentic. The antecedent hath been proved by many previous testimonies; and the consequent needs no proof. For, if Jerome found and remarked many errors in this edition, it is certain that it could not have been regarded by him as either authentic or true. Now Jerome, in his Traditions upon Genesis and other books, shews many faults of this edition, which are still found in it. And, as to the answer of our adversaries,—that Jerome in his Commentaries judged some things to be wrongly translated, which afterwards, when he came to publish that Latin edition, he perceived to be quite correctly rendered, and therefore did not change; this pretence, I say, may be easily refuted, if we will only remember that those Commentaries upon the Prophets, in which he often blames this Vulgate version, are later than that edition, as manifestly appears from Jerome's own words at the end of the Catalogue[1].

The fourth argument. Jerome was neither a prophet, nor endowed with a prophetic spirit. It is one thing to be a prophet, and another to be an interpreter of prophetic writings. So Jerome himself, in the Preface to the Pentateuch: " It is one thing to be a prophet, and another to be an interpreter. In the former case, the Spirit predicted future events; in the latter, learning and copious command of words translates what it understands[2]." Hence a conclusive argument may be formed. Since the Vulgate edition is nothing more than a version, it is not of itself authentic or inspired scripture. For it is the function of an interpreter to translate the authentic scripture, not to make his own translation authentic scripture. Now Jerome both might, and did err in translating. That he might have erred no one doubts, and Augustine in his 8th Epistle to Jerome takes it for granted. That he did err, Jerome himself ingenuously acknowledges in many places. Nay, though we were to suppose that Jerome never erred in translating, yet what answer can our adversaries give as to the Vulgate Latin version of the Psalms, which is widely different from the Hieronymian version? Finally, what account can they give of those parts of the Latin edition which are read in the Latin Bibles from the Greek version of Theodotion, a man most averse from the christian faith? Will they affirm that Theodotion too, from whom they have received some of the fragmentary pieces in their collection, as either interpreter or author, was endowed with a prophetic spirit? I trow not. Wherefore this Latin edition, being put together by persons who both could and did err, cannot possibly be the authentic word of God and inspired scripture.

And, whereas our adversaries object that, although Jerome was himself obnoxious to error, yet his version was approved by the church;—I answer first, that our assertion is not only that Jerome might have erred, but also that he hath committed

[1 (Vetus Testamentum) juxta Hebraicam transtuli .... multaque alia de opere prophetali, quæ nunc habeo in manibus.—T. II. p. 941.]

[2 Aliud est esse vatem, aliud esse interpretem. Ibi Spiritus ventura prædixit; hic eruditio et verborum copia ea quæ intelligit transfert.]

great errors in this version, if it be his version; and this assertion
we shall presently prove. Therefore if the church approved this
version, it approved very many errors of translation. Secondly,
the church hath not power of approving any man's translation,
however accurate, in such a manner as to pronounce it alone to be
authentic scripture, and preferable to the sacred originals themselves. For authentic scripture must proceed immediately from
the Holy Ghost himself; and therefore Paul says that all scripture
is divinely inspired, 2 Tim. iii. 16. Now Jerome's translation is
not divinely inspired; therefore it is not authentic scripture.
Thirdly, the church hath never approved nor received as authentic
this Latin edition before the very recent council of Trent. For
if the church had ever approved it before, so many learned and
catholic men would not have blamed this Latin version, as Lyra,
Paul of Bruges, Richard of Armagh, Valla, Eugubinus, Isidore
Clarius, John Isaac, Cajetan, Erasmus, Jacques De-Ferre, Ludovicus Vives, Lucas of Bruges, and many more. The Latin church
did indeed use this version, because it was needful that Latin
churches should have some Latin edition of the scriptures; but it
never before made it authentic or canonical. Now first, in the
Tridentine synod, we are commanded to receive the old Latin
version as our authentic scripture. Whence we perceive that their
authentic scripture is only the version, such as it is, of Jerome and
others, one knows not whom. Their Moses, their prophets, their
apostles, their evangelists, yea, their Christ, is Jerome: for, in
receiving his writings as authentic, they attribute to him what
truly appertains to Moses, the prophets, the apostles, the evangelists, and Christ.

The fifth argument. If God had permitted the scripture to
perish in the Hebrew and Greek originals, in which it was first
published by men divinely inspired, he would not have provided
sufficiently for his church and for our faith. From the prophetic
and apostolic scripture the church takes its origin, and the faith
derives its source. But whence can it be ascertained that these
are in all respects prophetic and apostolic scriptures, if the very
writings of the prophets and apostles are not those which we consult? What reason can be alleged, why the authentic word of
God should perish in those languages in which it was first published, and become authentic in a new tongue, into which it was
translated by a man who was no prophet? or why in the Latin,
rather than in any other language?

The sixth argument. The ancient fathers of the Latin church
did not all follow one edition, namely, Tertullian, Cyprian, Arno-
bius, Lactantius, Victorius, Hilary, Ambrose, Augustine, Jerome
himself, Leo, Gregory, Bede. Therefore there was not then one
authentic edition through so many ages of the church. Which
since experience shews to be a certain fact, why now must Latins
have one authentic Latin edition ? It might rather seem to have
been more necessary then that there should have been one
authentic edition, because there were then more Latin versions
than there are now : for Augustine says that in his time they
were innumerable (Doct. Christ. Lib. II. c. 11) ; but those which
are now extant may be easily counted. Yet the council of Trent
willed that one out of many should be held authentic; and Andradius (Defen. Trid. Lib. IV.) says that the synod acted wisely in
determining that, out of the many which are now in men's hands,
one should become and be esteemed authentic. If this be a good
reason—an adequate cause—it was much more fit that there
should have been one authentic edition in those times in which
many more versions than now were everywhere in the hands of
men.

The seventh argument. I ask whether the council of Trent
made this Latin edition authentic, or only declared it to be so ?
The reason of this question is, because they say that they receive
the books of scripture from the church, not that they may become canonical and most holy, but that they may be so esteemed,
as we shall hear afterwards. Is this Latin edition therefore now
made by them authentic, or is it only declared to be authentic ?
If they say that it is now made authentic, it will follow that it was
not authentic before. Then by what right could they make a
non-authentic edition become authentic ? In the same way it will
be lawful for them to convert a book, which is not sacred, into
sacred and canonical : which yet they profess not to arrogate to
themselves the power of effecting, But if they only declared this
edition authentic, let them tell us when it first began to be authentic.
For at first, as we have shewn, it was not authentic. It behoves
them therefore to let us know when, and from whom, it received
the privilege of authenticity, if they will not profess that it was
made authentic by themselves.

The eighth argument. The Latin Vulgate edition is in many
places utterly barbarous and full of solecisms : whence we collect
that its author was very careless. I readily acknowledge that the
style of scripture is simple and unadorned ; and am so far from

blaming it, that I admire it rather as divine. But in the authentic original scriptures you shall never find such barbarity and
disgraceful solecisms as are everywhere occurring in the Latin
Vulgate. Gen. xxi. 26 : *Non audivi præter hodie.* Gen. xlii. 13 :
Alius non est super,—for *superest.* Ps. lxvii. 20 : *Benedictus
Dominus die quotidie.* Ps. cxxv. 1 : *In convertendo Dominus
captivitatem Sion facti sumus sicut consolati.* Matt. xxii. : *Neque
nubent neque nubentur.* Matt. vi. : *Nonne vos magis pluris estis
illis ?* Matt. xx. : *Filius hominis non venit ministrari.* Luc. vii. :
Lamentavimus vobis. Luc. xxi. : *Omnis populus manicabat ad
eum.* John xv. : *Ut fructum plus afferat.* Acts iii. : *Pœnitemini.*
James i. : *Deus intentator est malorum.* These are expressed in
the original quite otherwise, and with sufficient purity and elegance.
Matt. xxii. 30 : οὔτε γαμοῦσιν οὔτε ἐκγαμίζονται. Matt. vi. 26 :
οὐχ ὑμεῖς μᾶλλον διαφέρετε αὐτῶν; Matt. xx. 28 : ὁ υἱὸς τοῦ
ἀνθρώπου οὐκ ἦλθε διακονηθῆναι ἀλλὰ διακονῆσαι. Luke vii. 32 :
ἐθρηνήσαμεν ὑμῖν. Luke xxi. 38 : πᾶς ὁ λαὸς ὤρθριζε πρὸς
αὐτόν. John xv. 2 : ἵνα πλείονα καρπὸν φέρῃ. Acts iii. 19 :
μετανοήσατε. James i. 13 : ὁ Θεὸς ἀπείραστός ἐστι τῶν κακῶν.
In these Greek expressions there is no lack either of purity or of
elegance. But the Latin are such that nothing can be conceived
more barbarous or absurd. Assuredly the Holy Spirit is never
wont to speak so barbarously and foolishly. For though there be in
the holy scriptures some pendent sentences, and inversions, and apparent solecisms, and other things of that kind, yet the same may be
found in the most eloquent and approved authors ; so that nothing
occurs in the originals, as far as the style and diction are concerned, for which one cannot find a parallel in some approved
writer. But those Latin expressions are strange and unparalleled ;
nor did ever any man speak in this style, who knew or cared how
to speak. Jerome, in his letter to Paulinus, says that this
rudeness, which is found in versions of the scriptures, hath occurred
partly through the fault of the translators. It is a fault therefore
to translate foolishly and awkwardly what is capable of being
neatly rendered ; and the examples adduced shew it to be a fault
into which this interpreter hath fallen. It is true indeed that
every thing, especially in sacred writings, must not be brought
strictly to the rules of Donatus¹, as Gregory reminds us in his
preface to Job : but the scriptures, though never superstitiously
exact, are everywhere clear and pure, and, I will add too, eloquent. So writes Augustine (Doct. Christ. Lib. iv. c. 6) excel-

[¹ A famous grammarian.]

lently well: "Here perhaps some one may ask whether our writers are only to be styled wise, or to be called eloquent also?" Which question Augustine answers thus: "Where I understand them, nothing can seem not only wiser but more eloquent than they are. And I venture to say, that all who rightly understand what they say, understand at the same time that they ought to have said it in no other manner[2]." He observes that there is one kind of eloquence which becomes youth, and another which is suitable to age; and that nothing, which is not suited to the person of the speaker, can deserve to be called eloquence: in a word, that there is a certain kind of eloquence suitable to divine writings, and that the sacred writers possess this kind of eloquence. Any other would not have become them, nor this any other writers.

The ninth argument. The Papists themselves maintain that the originals are useful; but the points of utility which they enumerate prove the originals to be even necessary, and that the original scripture in both testaments is more authentic than the Latin edition. Bellarmine tells us of four occasions upon which we may recur to the Hebrew and Greek originals. 1. Where there seems to be a mistake of the transcribers in the Latin copies; of which he produces some examples, and of which very many might be produced. 1 Sam xix. 24, the Vulgate had for many ages, *Cecinit nudus tota illa die.* If you look at the Hebrew original, you will see that one should read *cecidit*, not *cecinit.* Yet they persist in retaining the latter (*cecinit*) in the text, and write *cecidit* in the margin. Ecclus. xxiv. 30, the old edition hath, and hath had this long time back, *Ego quasi fluvius Dorix.* If you ask what river that is, Rabanus tells you in his commentary upon this place, that there is a river in Armenia which is called the Dorix. But the Louvain editors have noted that we should read *vorax;* and Bellarmine corrects it from the Greek, *Ego quasi fluvius Dioryx.* For "διῶρυξ," says he, "signifies a trench dug from a river to irrigate the ground." Be it so: but what Latin writer ever used this term? or what are we to think of

[2 Hic aliquis forsitan quærit, utrum auctores nostri . . . . . . sapientes tantummodo, an eloquentes etiam nuncupandi sunt. Quæ quidem quæstio apud meipsum, et apud eos qui mecum quod dico sentiunt, facillime solvitur. Nam ubi eos intelligo, non solum nihil eis sapientius, verumetiam nihil eloquentius mihi videri potest. Et audeo dicere omnes, qui recte intelligunt quod illi loquuntur, simul intelligere non eos aliter loqui debuisse.—T. III. p. 88. Bassan. 1797.]

such a Latin version? or, if this be the true reading, why is not the old one corrected, but even still, when the error hath been detected, left to remain in their books? Ecclus. xlv. 6 : it is read in the Vulgate, and so in the old missals, *Dedit ei cor ad præcepta.* But the Louvain editors have corrected the place thus, *coram præcepta;* and Bellarmine approves that emendation, since the Greek exhibits κατὰ πρόσωπον[1], and says that it is now so corrected in the new missals. But why is it not amended in the Bibles? Is this your solicitude, to have your missals more correct than your Bibles? So again the old books exhibit that place in Psal. xli., *ad Deum fontem vivum*[2]: but Bellarmine thinks it might safely be changed to *ad Deum fortem vivum,* as is plainly required by the evidence of the Hebrew and Greek copies. Yet, though this be certainly the case, they still retain *fontem* in the text, and only set *fortem* in the margin. Again, Deut. iv. 23[3], the old Latin books have *sulphure et solis ardore comburens;* whereas the Hebrew text shews that the true reading is *salis,* not *solis :* which error I am surprised that the Louvain editors did not perceive, and correct at least in the margin. An infinite number of other like examples might be given; and Canus (Lib. ii. c. 15) hath adduced many in which it is obviously evident that the Latin edition is corrupt, and requires to be corrected from the Hebrew and Greek originals. Do we not hence see that the original edition possesses greater purity and authority than this Vulgate Latin? The Latin books must be corrected from the originals, not the originals from the Latin edition : therefore the Latin edition is less authentic than the original scripture.

Bellarmine's second occasion is, when the Latin copies present such various readings as to make it impossible to determine which is the true. For example, in Joshua v. some copies of the Vulgate edition have[4], *Quibus juravit ut ostenderet eis terram;* others, *ut non ostenderet,* with a directly contrary sense. The latter, says Bellarmine, is said to be the truer, because in the

---

[1] καὶ ἔδωκεν αὐτῷ κατὰ πρόσωπον ἐντολὰς, νόμον ζωῆς καὶ ἐπιστήμης. Ecclus. xlv. 5, ed. Grabe.]

[2] Ps. xlii. 2, in the Hebrew, לְאֵל חָי. In the Greek, πρὸς τὸν Θεὸν τὸν ζῶντα.]

[3] This is a mistake. The true reference is Deut. xxix. 22, where the Hebrew is, גׇּפְרִית וׇמֶלַח שְׂרֵפׇה.]

[4] ver. 6. נִשְׁבַּע יְהוׇה לׇהֶם לְבִלְתִּי הַרְאוֹתׇם.]

Hebrew text the negative is constantly added. Why then do their books retain the former, which they themselves know and confess to be false ? So again, Josh. xi.[5], some copies have, *Non fuit civitas quæ non se traderet;* some, on the contrary, *quæ se traderet.* And this is affirmed to be the truer reading, because it agrees with the Hebrew and is required by the context. So Luke i.[6] in the common books we read, *Redemptionem plebis suæ :* but it is evident that we should read *plebi suæ,* because the Greek is τῷ λαῷ αὐτοῦ. Thus they allow that their Latin edition, which they determine to be alone authentic, hath in it many things not only futile, but even utterly wrong, and that it may be judged of and corrected by the originals. Meanwhile, however, errors of this kind are not removed, but preserved in their Bibles. Who, then, will not much rather trust the originals than this Vulgate edition ?

The third occasion is, when the Latin copies have something ambiguous, either in the expression or in the sense. Bellarmine gives some examples : one is taken from Luke ii.[7], *Hominibus bonæ voluntatis.* The words, *bonæ voluntatis,* may be referred, he thinks, either to *homines,* or to *pax,* but more correctly to the latter ; so that the sense shall be, " on earth peace to men, peace (I say) of the good-will of God towards men." For εὐδοκία is the good-will of God towards men. If this be true, as Bellarmine justly deems, our Rhemists have erred grossly, in gathering from this place a proof of the freedom of the human will.

Fourthly, we may recur to the original, in order to discover the full energy and propriety of the terms : which opens to us a very wide door. For in the well-spring every thing is more emphatic than in the streams of the translations ; which not a little illustrates their inferior excellence and dignity.

Melchior Canus, Lib. II. c. 15, sets forth many advantages which attend a knowledge of the originals. First, when we dispute with infidels. Secondly, when we wish to explain the peculiar emphasis of terms. Thirdly, to help us to a number of meanings. Fourthly, to give us an acquaintance with the idioms, phrases, and proverbs, of a foreign tongue. Fifthly, to correct errors. Sixthly, to shew us the meaning of some places which cannot be explained without a knowledge of languages. Seventhly, to escape the doubtfulness

[5 ver. 19.]
[6 v. 68, ἐποίησε λύτρωσιν τῷ λαῷ αὐτοῦ.]
[7 v. 14, where the Vulgate reads εὐδοκίας.]

and ambiguity of the Latin. Eighthly, to give us right interpretations of some terms in common use, as Anathema, Maranatha, and
the like. That all these advantages may be obtained from the
originals, they allow. Consequently, I may argue thus from their
own confession : That edition which is corrupt, faulty, ambiguous,
futile, and neither explains the meaning nor teaches the majesty of
the Holy Spirit, nor hath light enough in itself to illustrate the
diction and sense of scripture, is not authentic. Now the Latin
Vulgate edition is such, by the ingenuous confession of our adversaries themselves. Therefore it is not authentic : and consequently
the Hebrew and Greek are authentic ; because not only are they
free from those faults and disadvantages with which the Latin is
replete, and adorned with all those privileges which are by no
means conceded to the Latin, but even they, who press the Latin
edition upon us as authentic, are compelled to have recourse to the
Hebrew and Greek, and appeal to them as to a superior judge.

And now I would desire to put this question to them : Since
the Louvain divines have found many mistakes and faults in their
Latin Bibles, and have indicated them in the margin, what reading
is it which they determine to be authentic—the old one of the text,
or the new one of the margin ? If the old, why have they branded
it, and changed it in their missals ? If the new, why do they not
receive it into the text, but leave it to stand, as it were, without
upon the threshold ? I will make the matter plain by a single
example. In Proverbs xvi. 11, the old copies of the Latin edition
have this reading; " Pondus et statera judicia Dei sunt, et opera
ejus omnes lapides seculi." They now perceive that it should be
read, " et opera ejus omnes lapides sacculi ;" for the Hebrew word
denotes a scrip, or purse, or little bag[1]. Here there is no doubt
that the reading *seculi* is erroneous. Yet the author of the Commentary upon Proverbs, which appears amongst the works of
Jerome, reads *seculi*, and explains " the stones of eternity" to
mean just men and strong in faith. No doubt a most brave exposition ! Innumerable similar instances might be found in Latin
authors, who, for the last thousand years, and from the time that
this version began to prevail in the Latin churches, deluded by
the mistakes and faults of this edition, have invented absurd opinions and interpretations in consequence. So that passage in Wisdom, xii. 15, which the Louvain editors now read thus in their

[¹ כִּיס.]

Bibles, " Qui non debet puniri, condemnare exterum æstimas a virtute tua[2]," was formerly read thus : " Qui non debet puniri, condemnas, et exterum æstimas a tua virtute." For Gregory upon Job (Lib. III. c. 11) understands it of God the Father, who delivered up to death Christ, the most righteous of all men, and deserving of no punishment. Thus this fault hath remained more than a thousand years in the Latin books. Wherefore, if that reading be false (as it certainly is), then the Latin church hath followed a false, and consequently by no means authentic, reading, in an infinite number of places,—for of such places the number is infinite. So Canticles ii. at the end, the old books have " Super montes Bethel." But the Louvain critics bid us read *Bether* for *Bethel;* which is confirmed also by the Hebrew verity. Yet Gregory, a thousand years ago, read the text just as it used to be read in their corrupt copies ; from which circumstance we may perceive the great antiquity of that corruption. For, in his Commentary upon the Canticles, he interprets *Bethel* in this place to mean the church, as that in which God dwells. Thus almost all the Latin expositors read and expound that place, in which, nevertheless, unless by means of a corruption, no mention of Bethel can be found.

The tenth argument. That scripture which was authentic for the old Testament before Christ, and for both old and new six hundred years after Christ, should now also be deemed authentic by us. Now the Hebrew edition of the old, and the Greek of the new Testament, was always held the authentic scripture of God in the christian churches for six hundred years after Christ. This, therefore, ought to be received by us also as authentic scripture. If they doubt the major, we must ask them, Whether the church hath changed its authentic scripture, or hath not rather preserved, and commended to all succeeding generations, that which was in truth authentic from the very first ? If it lost that which was published by the prophets and apostles, who can defend that negligence, who excuse so enormous a sacrilege ? If it lost it not, then let it deliver to us the writings of the prophets and apostles, and approve them by its testimony as the authentic word of God ; not substitute for this divinely-promulgated scripture a mere translation of it into Latin, not made by either prophets or apostles ; nor persuade us that such a document as this is the authentic word

[2 In the Greek, τὸν μὴ ὀφείλοντα κολασθῆναι καταδικάσαι ἀλλότριον ἡγού-μενος τῆς σῆς δυνάμεως.]

of God.   In which proceeding they really assume to themselves
the privilege of doing that which they allow themselves incompe-
tent to do.   For those who make scripture authentic, make it
canonical; since it is only authentic scripture that is canonical, and
it is canonical, because it is authentic.   Now they have made their
scripture authentic, forasmuch as it was not authentic previously.
Therefore they make scripture canonical; which yet they confess
not to be placed in the power and judgment of the church.

  To return to the argument. I suppose that no one doubts the authenticity of the Hebrew edition of the old Testament in Christ's time.
But now it may be demonstrated by many testimonies of the fathers,
that the Hebrew edition of the old, and the Greek of the new
Testament, was held authentic in the church for many ages after
Christ. Jerome, in his book against Helvidius, writes thus : " We
must suppose that the water of the fountain ran much clearer than
that of the stream[1]." The same author, in his letter to Sunnia and
Fretella, observes : " As in the new Testament we recur to the
fountain of the Greek language, in which the new Testament is
written, so in the old Testament we recur to the Hebrew verity[2]."
So, in his letter to Marcella, at the end of the second volume : " I
wish to recal the corruption of the Latin copies to the Greek original[3]." And in his Preface to the Pentateuch he rejects as absurd
the opinion of those persons, who said that the Latin copies were
more correct than the Greek, and the Greek than the Hebrew.

  To the same effect in his Commentary on Zechariah, chap. viii.:
" We are compelled to have recourse to the Hebrews, and to seek
certain knowledge of the truth from the fountain rather than from
the streamlets[4]." Yea, in his Epistle to Vitalis he writes that he
was wont to betake himself to the Hebrew verity, as a sort of
citadel and fortress[5]. To this we may add the consideration, that

[1 Multo purior manare credenda est fontis unda quam rivi.]

[2 Sicut in novo Testamento . . . . recurrimus ad fontem Græci sermonis,
quo novum scriptum est instrumentum; ita in veteri Testamento ad Hebraicam
veritatem confugimus.—T. i. p. 637.]

[3 Latinorum codicum vitiositatem ad Græcam originem volui revocare.—
T. i. p. 132.]

[4 Cogimur ad Hebræas recurrere, et scientiæ veritatem de fonte magis
quam de rivulis quærere.—T. vi. p. 851.]

[5 Si quidem in historiis aliter haberent lxx. interpretes, aliter Hebraica
veritas; confugere poteramus ad solita præsidia, et arcem linguæ tenere ver-
naculæ.—T. i. p. 434.]

Damasus urged Jerome to the task of correcting the new Testament from the Greek; that prelate being sufficiently aware that the Greek deserved to be preferred by a great deal to all the Latin copies. Much to the same purpose may be found in Ambrose, de Spiritu Sancto, Lib. II. c. 6[6], and in his book, de Incarn. Domin. Sacram. c. 8[7]: also in Augustine de Doctr. Christ. Lib. II. c. 7[8], and elsewhere. From Augustine, Gratian hath transcribed in his Decree what we read Dist. 9, cap. *Ut veterum:* " As the correctness of the old books is to be estimated by the Hebrew volumes, so the truth of the new requires the standard of the Greek text[9]." Also, in his City of God (Lib. xv. c. 13), Augustine makes a large defence of the Jews, and reminds us, that " we must not trust a translation so implicitly as the language from which interpreters made that translation into a different one[10]." Ludovicus Vives thus comments upon that chapter : " The same answer may be given to those who object that the MSS. of the old Testament have been falsified and corrupted by the Jews, and those of the new by the Greeks, to prevent us from seeking the true sense of the sacred books from those originals[11]."

But our adversaries allow that what the fathers write of the authority of the originals was true indeed formerly; and they would not deny that we ought to do the same, if the Hebrew and Greek originals were still uncontaminated. But they maintain that those originals are now corrupted, and that therefore the Latin streamlet is deserving of more regard than the ancient wellspring. Hence it is now the earnest effort of the popish theologians, and the champions of the council of Trent, to persuade us of the depravation of the original scriptures. In the conduct of which argument, however, some are more keen and impudent than

[6] Lib. II. c. 5. § 42. T. VI. Paris. 1839. p. 341.]

[7] § 82. p. 475, ut supra.   Ita enim et in Græcis codicibus invenimus, quorum potior auctoritas est.]

[8] c. 13. ed. Bruder. Lipsiæ, 1838.]

[9] *Ut veterum* librorum fides de Hebræis voluminibus examinanda est, ita novorum Græci sermonis normam desiderat.—Decret. p. 1. Dist. ix. c. vi. The title does indeed ascribe these words to Augustine, but the note, more correctly, to Jerome, Epist. 28. ad Lucinium Bæticum.]

[10] Ei linguæ potius credatur, unde est in aliam per interpretes facta translatio.]

[11] Hoc idem responderi potest his qui falsatos corruptosque et ab Hebræis codices veteris instrumenti, et a Græcis novi objiciunt, ne veritas sacrorum librorum ex illis fontibus petatur.—Ludov. Vives, Annot. p. 459. ed. Froben.]

others. For Lindanus, *De optimo Genere Inter.*, Lib. I. c. 11, and
Canus, Lib. II. c. 13, pretend most slanderously that the originals
are utterly corrupted. But others come to much more moderate
and equitable conclusions. Neither party, however, can do anything really serviceable to the cause of the authentic authority
of the Latin edition, until they can shew us that not only the
originals are corrupt in some places, but even generally more
corrupt than the Latin copies; which is beyond what any papist
hitherto hath hoped to demonstrate. Bellarmine is of the number
of those who treat the originals with some respect; and consequently he refutes the opinion of Lindanus and Canus. Nevertheless, lest he should seem not to approve the Tridentine Decree, he
maintains that there are some corruptions in the original text. Let
us see what sort of corruptions he speaks of.

In order, then, to shew that the Hebrew originals are not
absolutely pure, Bellarmine proposes five places, which he thinks
undoubtedly corrupt. The first place is Is. ix. 6, where he says
that we should read, " He shall be called Wonderful;" as Calvin
also contends. But the Hebrew text not only does not exhibit
jikkare, [יִקָּרֵא] "he shall be called," but does exhibit *jikra,* [יִקְרָא]
"he shall call." I answer;—first, as to the sense, it makes no difference whether we read, " His name shall be called Wonderful," or
" He shall call (i. e. God the Father shall call) his name Wonderful."
So Junius and Tremellius have rendered it, in conformity with the
present Hebrew reading, " vocat;" which they would not have
done, if they had supposed that there was any important difference
in the sense. Secondly, the opinion of some, that we should rather
read in the passive than in the active, does not prove the originals
to be corrupted. The points indeed require the latter reading,
but the letters will bear either. Thirdly, the Hebrew doctors tell
us, as Vatablus observes upon this place[1], that verbs of the third
person are often used impersonally by the Hebrews, as " he shall
call " [one shall call], for " he shall be called."

The second place is Jerem. xxiii. 6, in which we should read,
as Calvin thinks also, " This is his Name, whereby they shall call

[1 So Buxtorf, Thes. Gramm. Lib. II. c. 10. "Tertiæ personæ verba
sæpissime quoque usurpantur indefinite et quasi impersonaliter, nullo nomi-
nativo expresso." He cites Is. ix. 6, Jerem. xxiii. 6, as instances. There are
some remarks upon this idiom, both very curious and very valuable, in
Gataker, de Stylo N. T. pp. 66—72. London, 1648. Cf. Nordheimer's
Hebrew Syntax, § 763, New York, 1841.]

him, The Lord our Righteousness." But the Hebrew text reads
constantly in the singular, " he shall call," not " they shall call." I
answer, in the first place, That we plainly perceive this place not
to be corrupt from the circumstance, that of old in Jerome's time
it was read exactly as it is read at present. For Jerome left it
optional with us to read it either in the singular or the plural;
and the Seventy, before Jerome, rendered the word καλέσει,
" he shall call." Secondly, the Hebrew word may be rendered,
" they shall call," as Vatablus, Pagninus, and Arias Montanus
have translated it. Thirdly, if we read " He shall call," as
our Hebrew text invites us, the sense will be neither impious
nor unsuitable, as is plain from the annotations of Junius and
Tremellius.

The third place is Ps. xxii. 17. All Christians read, " They
pierced my hands and my feet." But the Hebrew MSS. have not
Caru, [כָּרוּ] " they pierced," but *Caari*, [כָּאֲרִי] " as a Lion." I
answer, that this is the only specious indication of corruption in
the Hebrew original; yet it is easy to protect this place also
from their reproaches. For, first, learned men testify that
many Hebrew copies are found in which the reading in *Caru*;
Andradius, Defens. Trid. Lib. IV., and Galatinus, Lib. VIII. c. 17.
And John Isaac writes that he had himself seen such a copy,
in his book against Lindanus, Lib. II.; and the Masorites themselves affirm that it was so written in some corrected copies[2].
Secondly, in those books which have this reading, the Masorites[3]
tell us that it is not to be taken in the common acceptation:
whence it plainly appears that nothing was farther from their minds
than a design to corrupt the passage. Thirdly, the place is now
no otherwise read than it was formerly before Jerome's time.
For the Chaldee Paraphrast hath conjoined both readings[4], and
the Masorites testify that there is a twofold reading of this place.
Jerome, too, in his Psalter read in the Hebrew *Caari*, as our
books have it, though he rendered it " fixerunt." So that it
can never be proved, at least from this place, that the Hebrew
originals were corrupted after the time of Jerome.

The fourth place is Ps. xix. 5, where the Hebrew copies have,

[2 In the textual Masora on Numb. xxiv. 9, כארי ידי ורגלי כארו
כתיב.]

[3 The smaller Masora on Ps. xxii. 17, ב. קמצין בתרי לישכי.]

[4 נכתין היך כאריה אידי ורגלי.   " They pierced, like a lion, my
hands and my feet."]

" their line¹ went into all the earth ;" whereas the Septuagint render it, φθόγγος αὐτῶν, "their sound;" and Paul hath approved that reading, Rom. x. 18. I answer with Genebrard, in his Scholia upon the passage, that the Hebrew term does indeed denote a line, but the Septuagint regarded the general sense, and were followed by the apostle. For that line, or (as Tremellius translates it) *delineation* of the heavens,—that is, that frame and structure of the heavenly orbs, smoothed as it were by the rule, proclaims the infinite power and wisdom of the divine artist.

The fifth place is Exod. chap. ii., in which this whole sentence is wanting : "He begat another also, and called his name Eliezer, saying, The God of my father hath helped me, and delivered me from the hand of Pharaoh²." I answer, that in this place it is the Latin rather than the Hebrew copies that are corrupt. For the asterisk which the Latin editions, even that of Louvain, prefix to these words, is a brand which shews that the whole sentence should be removed from the Latin books; and this the more learned and candid of the papists themselves confess. For so Cajetan writes in his commentary upon that place : "This whole paragraph about the second son is superfluous³."

These then are the passages which Bellarmine was able to find fault with in the originals; and yet in these there is really nothing to require either blame or correction. But, even though we should allow (which we are so far from doing, that we have proved the contrary), that these were faulty in the original, what could our adversaries conclude from such an admission? Would it follow that the Hebrew fountain was more corrupt than the Latin streamlets, or that the Latin edition was authentic? Not, surely, unless it were previously assumed, either that canonical books of scripture cannot be erroneously copied sometimes by transcribers, or that it is not very easy for us to discover many more errors in the Latin edition which ought not, and cannot be defended, as we shall hear presently.

Here indeed the Jesuit hath betrayed the papal cause. For, to maintain the reasonableness of the Tridentine decree, we must

[¹ קָוָם. See Pococke in his Appendix to Maimonidis Porta Mosis, c. iv. pp. 47—51.]

[² Alium quoque genuit, et vocavit nomen ejus Eliezer, dicens, Deus patris mei auxiliatus est mihi, et liberavit me e manu Pharaonis.—Exod. ii. 22.]

[³ Tota ista particula de secundo filio superflua est.—Cajet. in Pentateuch. p. 82. 2. Romæ. 1531.]

assert that the Hebrew text is utterly corrupt, and the Latin uncorrupted; which Lindanus and Canus endeavour to do; and that, constrained by the authority of this Tridentine decree : but Bellarmine is so far from doing this, that he censures Lindanus and Canus for saying that the Hebrew originals have been corrupted by the Jews; which thesis, although these men assert it with strenuous earnestness, hath been long since exploded by the senate (so to speak) of more learned and sound-minded papists.   Sixtus Senensis, Lib. VIII. c. 2, delivers his opinion thus : " It cannot be said that the divine scriptures of the old Testament have been falsified by the malice either of Jews or Christians[4] :" which he presently demonstrates by many arguments.   We might adduce similar passages from other popish authors.   Now then, if the originals of sacred scripture have not been so disgracefully corrupted by any malice of Jews or adversaries, as some persons have ignorantly suspected ; and if no mistakes have crept into the originals, but such as may casually be introduced into any book, (which our opponents expressly allow ;) why, I pray, did not the Tridentine fathers rather command that the originals should be purified with the greatest care and diligence than that the muddy stream of the Latin edition should be preferred to the fountain, and become authentic ?   For they who assert the Latin to be authentic scripture, close up the Hebrew and Greek fountains.   Indeed these men are unwilling to seem to do this ; and yet they do it nevertheless, when they determine the originals not to be authentic.   Thus, therefore, I frame my argument : If the originals are not authentic, it must be because they are corrupt.   But they are not corrupt : therefore they are authentic.   Upon the major we shall have no dispute.   For what other reason can be assigned for denying, that books which were authentic once, should still be so, and be so esteemed at present ?   As to the minor, if they answer that they are corrupt ; I demand, whether by the deliberate malice of adversaries, or by chance ?   If they say the former,—what adversaries do they mean ?   In the case of the old Testament they can dream of none except the Jews.   Now the Jews are, as you have heard, acquitted by the very papists, and by Bellarmine himself, and are indeed wholly free from blame.   For when could they have made these corruptions ?   Neither before Christ, nor for 400 years after Christ.   For then Christ and the doctors of the church would have

[4 Dici non potest divinas veteris Testamenti scripturas aut Judæorum aut Christianorum malignitate falsatas. p. 613. Paris. 1610.]

[WHITAKER.]

11

blamed them upon that score ; whereas, on the contrary, they praise
their fidelity and diligence in preserving the originals, and call them
the *book-keepers* (capsarii) of the scriptures[1]. Besides, if the Jews had
wished to corrupt the original scriptures, they would have laid their
sacrilegious hands specially upon those places which concern Christ
and confirm the faith. But in those places these fountains run so clear
that one feels no lack : nay, they sometimes run far clearer than the
Latin streams. For instance, in Psalm ii. the Latin copies have, *Am-
plectimini disciplinam;* which reading says nothing emphatical of
Christ. But the Hebrew original leads us at once to the Son of
God, and celebrates his far-extended sway over all: " Kiss the
Son." The same may be affirmed of many other passages. John
Isaac, the Jew, in his second book against Lindanus, writes that
more than two hundred arguments against Jewish opinions may be
drawn more strongly from the Hebrew text than from the Latin
translation. To the same effect Andradius (Defens. Lib. IV.):
" Those who handle the Hebrew text with piety and religious care,
meet in it with much larger testimonies to Christ than in the Latin
and Greek[2]." This was testified long ago also by Jerome, in his
74th Epistle to Marcella[3]. But if they say that the originals are
only corrupted by some accident, we too may affirm the same, and
with much more justice, of their own Latin version : for such
accidental causes extend no less to the Latin than to the Hebrew
and Greek books.

The eleventh argument. The Latin Vulgate edition is most
certainly and most plainly corrupt. And the corruptions I speak of
are not casual, or slight, or common errors, such as the carelessness of copyists often produces in books ; but errors deeply rooted
in the text itself, important and intolerable. Hence is drawn the
weightiest argument against the authority of this edition. Upon
this subject many excellently learned men, even of the popish party,
have written,—Valla, Isaac, Erasmus (if indeed they rank him in
their number at all), and Clarius, whom Canus censures most
severely upon this account : but the thing is certain and manifest.
Yet here the Jesuit, who hitherto did not dare to accuse the
Hebrew originals, toils hard to save the credit of the Latin edition,

[1 E. g. Augustine, Enarr. in Ps. xli. n. 14. T. IV. Contr. Faust. L. XII.
c. 23. T. VIII. &c.]

[2 Qui Hebræa pie et religiose tractant, multo in illis ampliora de Christo
testimonia quam in Latinis Græcisque offendunt.]

[3 T. I. p. 150. Ep. 32.]

and is large in his replies to Chemnitz, Calvin, and others. In which task he has no more formidable adversary than himself. For, unless the Hebrew and Greek originals be most foully corrupt, it follows that this Latin edition is most foully corrupt, inasmuch as it differs widely in all the books from those originals. Who does not see from this that either the originals are corrupted, or the Latin Vulgate edition is full of innumerable errors? For, where the difference and opposition of the readings is so great as is actually found between the originals and the Latin edition, it cannot be said or conceived that every thing is sound and uncorrupted. Bellarmine therefore cannot possibly defend them both together; and he must necessarily confess either the Hebrew original of the old, and the Greek of the new Testament, or else the Latin edition in both Testaments, to labour under most wretched depravation. For whoever will compare the Latin with the originals, shall find almost everywhere a remarkable discordance. Were I to go in detail through all the errors of this edition, I should never make an end, and should weary your attention with a vain prolixity. You may spend your leisure in reading what others have written upon the subject. It shall suffice for me to discharge what my duty requires, and to lay before you some faults of this edition, from which it will plainly appear that it is really corrupt and erroneous. And, though I might bring forward many passages, and follow the regular order of the several books and chapters, I shall prefer to tread in the steps of Bellarmine, and examine his defence of certain places. He first proposes severally and defends the faults of the Vulgate edition of the old Testament which had been censured by Chemnitz, then those by Calvin in the Psalms, lastly those by others in the Latin edition of the new Testament. These let us now examine, and, as occasion offers, interpose a few remarks.

CHAPTER X.

WHEREIN CERTAIN CORRUPT PLACES IN THE VULGATE EDITION OF
THE OLD TESTAMENT ARE SET FORTH.

THE first place is Gen. iii.[4]: *Ipsa conteret caput tuum.* So it is wrongly and corruptly read in the Vulgate. For the reading

[4 ver. 15. הוּא יְשׁוּפְךָ רֹאשׁ.]

11—2

ought to be *Ipse* or *Ipsum*, so as to make the reference to the Seed
of the woman, not to the woman herself.   Bellarmine affirms that
it is not improbable that the true reading is *Ipsa*, and that many
of the ancients read so; and that, as to the verb, which is in the
Hebrew of the masculine gender, being coupled with a noun in the
feminine, we must consider that there is a great mystery contained
in that construction—namely, that the woman crushes the serpent's
head, not by herself but by her Son.   However, he hath omitted
to notice this mystery in the Sartorian edition.

I answer.   Though all the fathers were to say that we should
read *Ipsa,* yet it should by no means be admitted or approved.
For the Hebrew copies constantly read *Hu;* the Septuagint exhibits
αὐτός; the Chaldee Paraphrase confirms the same reading; and
lastly, some copies of the Vulgate edition retain *Ipse,* some *Ipsum.*
Finally, the very drift of the sentence requires that we should
understand it of the Seed of the woman, not of the woman.
What woman could crush the serpent's head?   Was it Mary?   I
am well aware that this is what is said by them.   But how?   When
she bore Christ?   But to bear Christ is not to crush the head of
the serpent: to give birth to him by whom the serpent's head is
crushed is one thing, and to crush the head of the serpent is another.
Was it when she believed in Christ[1]?   But this applies to all believers.   Christ therefore, and Christ only, is he who by his power
could crush and destroy the head of the infernal serpent, and rescue
and deliver us out of his jaws.   Indeed it is wonderful that this first
promise of our redemption, upon which the whole safety of the
human race depends, should not have been more diligently cared
for by these men.   If they had been as solicitous as they ought for
the salvation of men, they would never have permitted its foundation to have been so perilously and impiously shaken.   Augustine
indeed, *De Gen. ad Liter.* Lib. II. c. 36[2], reads the whole passage
corruptly, *Ipsa tibi servabit caput:* but Cyprian reads *Ipse* in
his Second Book to Quirinus[3]; and before him Irenæus, Lib. III.

[1 Salmeron however determines, "Christum Matrem suam prope crucem
vocasse, ut ipsa Mater Filium suum in sacrificium Patri æterno pro toto
mundo offerret, ut Abraham filium suum Isaac ex obedientia offerre voluit."—
Opp. T. x. Tract. 41. p. 933. cited by Glass. Philol. S. p. 693. (Amstel. 1694.)]

[2 So also Enarr. in Ps. ciii. T. IV. pp. 1668—9, and elsewhere.   The
reading *servabit* is from the Septuagint τηρήσει.   See Gesenius in voc. שׁוּף.]

[3 Testim. adv. Judæos, II. 9. p. 37.   Hoc semen prædixerat Deus de
muliere procedere, quod calcaret caput Diaboli .... ipse tuum observabit
caput.]

c. 77[4]; and Leo the pope of Rome interprets this place of the Seed
of the woman, Serm. 2 De Nativitate Domini[5]. And that this is
the true reading, Jerome teaches us in his Questions upon Genesis:
so that either the Vulgate edition is not Jerome's, or Jerome hath
contradicted himself. Chrysostom sometimes seems to read *Ipsa;*
but Philip Montanus hath shewn that this is the fault of his
translator. Canus, Lib. II. c. 15, acknowledges that there is a
manifest error in this place. To the same effect Andradius, Defens.
Lib. IV., and Cajetan[6], upon the three Chapters of Genesis, writes
plainly that this is not spoken of the woman, but of the Seed of the
woman. Isidore Clarius hath restored *Ipsum* in his Bible; and
John Benedictus, in his Scholia upon this place, says that we should
not read *Ipsa* but *Ipsum,* so as to understand it of the Seed.
Wherefore to defend this reading of the Vulgate edition is to excuse
a manifest error, and to contradict a plain truth.

The second place is Gen. vi., which is read thus in the Vulgate
edition: *Cuncta cogitatio cordis est intenta ad malum.* The
Hebrew would require: *Figmentum cordis ejus tantummodo
malum omni die*[7]. Bellarmine says, in the first place, that the sense
is the same.

I answer. Although this were true, it would not amount to a
just defence. For it behoves a translator of scripture not merely
to take care that he do not corrupt the meaning, but also, as far
as it is at all possible, not to depart a hand's breadth from the
words; since many things may lie under cover in the words of the
Holy Spirit, which are not immediately perceived, and yet contain
important instruction. But in this place the sense *is* changed.
For it is one thing to be *intent on evil*, and another *to be evil*, and
only evil. For it is a lighter thing to be propense towards evil, than
to be already actually evil. Besides the Vulgar translator says that
"every thought of man's heart is intent on evil:" as if the Holy
Spirit only blamed the thoughts; whereas he condemns both the
thoughts and the principle and source of all the thoughts. The
faults of this passage, then, are these. First, there is nothing in
the Hebrew to answer to the word *Intenta*. Secondly, "every

[4 Lib. III. c. 38. p. 309, A. (ed. Fevard. Par. 1675) Lib. IV. c. 78. p.
425, c. The reference in the text is a mistake, since there are not seventy-
seven chapters in the third book in any edition that Whitaker could have used.]

[5 Denuntians serpenti futurum semen mulieris, quod noxii capitis elatio-
nem sua virtute contereret. pp. 13, 14. Opp. Lugd. 1623.]

[6 Opp. Lugd. 1639. T. I. p. 29.]

[7 וְכָל־יֵצֶר מַחְשְׁבֹת לִבּוֹ רַק רַע כָּל־הַיּוֹם. Gen. vi. 5.]

thought of the heart" is substituted for the whole figment of the thoughts of man's heart. Thirdly, the particle *only* is omitted, which hath the greatest possible weight in the expression.

Bellarmine's second observation is, that it does not follow from this that, as the Lutherans suppose, all the works of men are evi ; since this is a hyperbole, similar to that which is said in the same chapter, "All flesh had corrupted its way," while yet Noah is called in the very same place a righteous man and a perfect.

I answer. In the first place, the Lutherans do not say that all man's works are evil, but only the works of men not yet regenerate. Now, that these latter are all evil, is most manifestly plain from other testimonies of scripture, and specially from this place. Secondly, there is no hyperbole in this passage; for in reality the desires of such men are nothing but evil. This even Andradius acknowledges, Orthodox. Explic. Lib. III. and Defens. Lib. V. For he says that that is evil, "which the human heart itself begins the effort to frame and form." If the first movements of the heart be so vicious and impure, what remains at all sound in the human breast? For we do not speak of the substance of the heart, but of the qualities. Thirdly, there is nothing whatever hyperbolical in the assertion, that all flesh had corrupted its way. Noah was, indeed, a just man and a perfect; yet so as that his justice was not innate in his nature, but received as a gift from God: for Noah was not entirely pure from all that corruption which had pervaded all flesh. See what hyperboles these men have found in scripture! Concerning Noah, Jerome writes thus in his Questions on Genesis: "It is emphatically said, 'in his generation,' to shew us that he was righteous not according to the measure of absolute righteousness, but according to the righteousness of his generation[1]."

The third place is in Gen. ix., where they read thus: *Qui fuderit sanguinem hominis, fundetur sanguis illius.* Here the words "by man[2]" are omitted. Bellarmine says that this omission does not render the sense imperfect, since the sense is the same in the Hebrew and in the Latin: "He who shall slay man shall be slain himself."

I answer. The sense is not so full in the Latin as in the Hebrew. For the clause " by man," or, as others render it, " in man," is emphatic, as Cajetan in his Commentaries and others also inform us, and is variously explained by many expositors; all

[1 Ut ostenderet non juxta justitiam consummatam, sed juxta generationis suæ justitiam, fuisse eum justum.   T. III. p. 316.]

[2 שֹׁפֵךְ דַּם הָאָדָם בָּאָדָם דָּמוֹ יִשָּׁפֵךְ.   Gen. ix. 6.]

which explanations are taken from us, if these words be removed from the text. It is false, therefore, that the sense is not impaired by this omission. The truest explanation seems to be that given by those who think that the authority of the magistrate and the judge is sanctioned in these words, and that a murderer is not to be merely left to the divine vengeance, but searched out and punished by those to whom the sword hath been delivered by God. For it is not the same thing for one to say merely, " he who slays man shall be himself slain," as it is when one adds "by man." For the former might be understood only to mean that he should be slain by God; but the latter implies that he is to be consigned to death by man.

The fourth place is Gen. xiv. 18, where in the Hebrew neither is there any trace of the word "offering," nor of a causative conjunction.

Bellarmine objects, in the first place, that the Vulgate edition does not read *obtulit*, but *protulit panem et vinum*.

I answer. Nevertheless in some copies we do find *obtulit ;* nor does Andradius deny it in the fourth book of his Defence. But most of the Latin copies do indeed now read *proferens panem et vinum*, not *offerens*. Which shews that our adversaries do the more grossly abuse this place, when they apply it to support the sacrifice of the mass.

Secondly, he objects that the particle *Ve* is in Hebrew often taken for *Chi, because*[3].

I answer. This is not denied; nor was there any occasion to prove it by the citation of so many instances. However, it hath not that force in this passage. For Melchisedek brought forth the bread and wine, not to offer sacrifice or discharge any priestly

[3 The clause in question is : הוֹצִיא לֶחֶם וָיַיִן וְהוּא כֹהֵן לְאֵל עֶלְיוֹן,
and the question seems to be whether his being priest of the Most High be mentioned in connexion with the bringing forth of the bread and wine, or with his blessing Abraham. If with the former, then the ו may be *causative*. For when the sense of a clause in Hebrew is such as to leave the reader's mind searching for a reason of the thing stated in it, then the conjunctive particle is often used to carry on the train of thought thus implied rather than expressed :—i. e. it becomes causative. But there seems no reason here for any such connexion; because there was nothing for which the reader would naturally seek any reason, not to be found amongst the other circumstances, in the act of Melchisedech bringing refreshment for Abraham and his followers : whereas the clause is perfectly fitted to introduce the circumstance of the benediction.]

function, but rather to do as became a king,—that is, refresh with
provisions Abraham and his comrades in the battle.   This answer
you will not perhaps approve when given by me.   Listen, therefore,
to the reply of your own fellows.   Cajetan speaks thus in his
Commentary upon this place: "That which in the Vulgate edition
is subjoined as the cause of the oblation ('for he was priest of the
most high God') is not given in the Hebrew as a reason, but as a
separate clause: ' Also he was priest to the high God.'   It adds
his priestly dignity, to his royal honour and bounty[1]."   Thus
Cajetan refers his production of the bread and wine to his royal
bounty, his benediction of Abraham to his sacerdotal dignity, and
that with perfect justice.   So Andradius, Defens. Trid. Lib. IV.:
" I agree with those who say that Melchisedek refreshed with bread
and wine the soldiers of Abraham, wearied and broken with the
long battle[2]."   You have, therefore, Andradius and Cajetan, and
many more, differing from your notion, that the bread and wine
were produced by Melchisedek to offer them as a sacrifice to God.
As to the judgment of the fathers, there will be another place for
answering that argument.

Bellarmine objects thirdly, that in Ps. cix. it is said of Christ:
" Thou art a priest for ever after the order of Melchizedek!"
Why is Christ a priest after the order of Melchizedek, unless
because the one offered bread and wine, the other himself in the
forms of bread and wine ?

I answer.   The apostle plainly teaches us in the Epistle to the
Hebrews, chap. v. vii. how Christ is a priest after the order of Melchizedek; so that there is no necessity for inventing this new
analogy.   But if Melchizedek was no otherwise a type of Christ
but because he offered bread and wine, the apostle hath compared
Christ with Melchizedek in vain, and said not one word to the
purpose; for he hath made no mention of this sacrifice in the comparison.   If then it was by reason of this sacrifice alone that
Christ was a priest after the order of Melchizedek, then the apostle,
in drawing this comparison of Christ with Melchizedek, hath
omitted that altogether which was the only thing worth mention-

---

[1 Quod in vulgata editione subditur, ut causa oblationis (erat enim
sacerdos Dei altissimi), in Hebræo non habetur ut causa, sed separata clausula, ' et ipse erat sacerdos El excelso.'   Adjungit siquidem regiæ dignitati
et liberalitati dignitatem sacerdotalem.   T. I. p. 66.]

[2 Ego cum illis sentio, qui lassos Abrahæ milites et diuturna pugna frac-
tos Melchisedechum pane vinoque refecisse aiunt.]

ing, and hath not proved with any sufficient care and pertinency the very thing which was to have been proved. What else is this, but to offer an open insult to the Holy Spirit? Which is, indeed, what these men do, when they say that Christ is a priest after the order of Melchizedek, upon no other grounds than because the one offered bread and wine, the other himself in the forms of bread and wine. But we shall have an occasion elsewhere of speaking of this whole matter.

The fifth place is in the last chapter of Numbers, where the Vulgate copies exhibit the following reading : *Omnes viri ducent uxores de tribu et cognatione sua, et cunctæ fœminæ de eadem tribu maritos accipient*[3]. That this is an erroneous interpretation, any one may readily understand in many ways, who shall compare it with the Hebrew text. In these words it is absolutely forbidden that any man should take a wife, or any woman marry a husband, out of their own tribes respectively. But many examples occur in scripture of marriages contracted between persons of different tribes. It was not, therefore, the meaning of the law, that every man and woman should marry only into their own tribes; but the command extended only to heritors, to prevent the possessions and estates of the several tribes from being confounded, or passing into other tribes. Whatever, then, Bellarmine may say to excuse the fault of this version, whoever will give the place even the slightest inspection, will immediately detect its erroneousness. And whereas Bellarmine affirms that the words run just the same way in the Hebrew as in the Latin, (which I marvel how he could assert so confidently and yet so falsely,) I will confute him with no other testimony than that of Cajetan. This is Cajetan's remark upon the place : "This clause is not contained in the Hebrew[4]." That cardinal denies that to be contained in the Hebrew, which Bellarmine affirms to be contained in it : but the cardinal is Bellarmine's superior both in authority and in truth. Afterwards the same cardinal presently subjoins : "See how many and how important additions to the law the translator hath passed over in silence. The law is not delivered concerning every daughter, but of a daughter that is an heiress[5]," &c. Thus there are many faults of the Vulgate edition in this place, if we believe Cajetan ;

[3 Numbers xxxvi. 7, 8.]
[4 Non habetur hæc clausula in textu Hebraico. T. I. p. 428.]
[5 Vide quot et quales additiones legis siluit interpres. Non traditur lex de qualibet filia, sed de filia hærede.]

and yet Bellarmine could see none, lest perchance he should be
forced to acknowledge some error in the Vulgate edition, which, no
doubt, would be a most deplorable catastrophe!

The sixth place is Ezra ix. 8, where the reading is *pax illius*,
whereas we should read *paxillus*[1]. Here Bellarmine acknowledges
an error of the transcribers; for the Hebrew word denotes a
stake, so that there is no room to doubt that this is the true reading. As to Bellarmine's assertion that many Latin copies exhibit
paxillus, I think it by no means probable, since the Louvain correctors of the Bible retain the old and wrong reading in the text;
which surely they would not have done, if they had felt that the
authority of copies would have supported them in amending the
passage. Indeed, we may well ask why they did not amend it?
Is the matter doubtful or obscure? Bellarmine confesses that to
be the true reading which they have excluded from the text, that
false which they retain in the text. Yet the divines of Louvain,
who profess themselves to be desirous of correcting the errors of
the Vulgate edition, have marked indeed, but not removed, this
error, certain and shameful as it is. And with other such mistakes
of the transcribers, known, manifest and acknowledged, does that
edition abound. Should we receive that for authentic scripture,
which its very correctors have left so full of blemishes?

The seventh place is Job v. 1: *Voca si quis est qui tibi re-
spondeat, et ad aliquem sanctorum convertere.* Bellarmine says
that Chemnitz pretends that this place was corrupted to support
the invocation of saints; and thereupon, with sufficient impudence,
pronounces him *drunk*. But Chemnitz blames not the version of
the passage, but the reasoning of the papists from that version;
that the saints are to be invoked, because we are bidden to betake
ourselves to some of the saints: whereas those are called saints
in scripture, who cultivate holiness during their lives. And thus
these men often abuse the Latin version to the support of their
doctrines in a way that can hardly be called *sober* argumentation.

The eighth place is Prov. xvi. 11, where they read *lapides
seculi*[2], instead of *lapides sacculi;* which passage we have mentioned before. And Bellarmine confesses that the reading which

---

[1 The word in the Hebrew is יָתֵד, upon which Gesenius observes, "*pan-
gere paxillum.* Hebræis (et Arabicus, v. vit. Tom. I. p. 134, 228. ed. Mauger)
imago est sedis firmæ et stabilis Jer. xxii. 23, de qua יָתֵד dicitur, Esr. ix. 8."]

[2 אַבְנֵי כִיס.]

exhibits *sacculi* is the true one, but the Vulgate, even in its latest Louvain edition, false, which exhibits *seculi*.

The ninth place is Eccles. ix. 2 : *Nescit homo, utrum odio ve¹ amore dignus sit, sed omnia in futurum servantur incerta*³. Bellarmine says that the Vulgate interpreter hath rendered the passage excellently well, not counting, indeed, the Hebrew words, but weighing them and expressing their sense.

I answer. The Vulgate interpreter in this place hath neither counted the words, nor weighed them, nor expressed the sense, but rendered them most falsely ; which will readily appear evident, if the Hebrew words be compared with this translation. For those interpreters who have translated the scriptures from the Hebrew, with the greatest care and fidelity, have perceived that these words required a totally different interpretation. Vatablus hath translated the passage thus : " And that man is ignorant alike of love and hatred, but to him (God) all things are set open⁴." Pagninus thus : " Both love and hatred man knows not; all which are before them⁵." Cajetan thus : " Both love and hatred man knows not ; all in their face⁶." Jerome himself translated this passage far otherwise, as appears from that other interpretation of this book, which is extant amongst his works, where we read : *Et quidem caritatem, et quidem odium non est cognoscens homo : omnia in facie eorum.* This differs, both in words and in sense, from yours, which yet ye call Jerome's. As to the sense, it is not what you suppose ; that all things here are doubtful and uncertain, so that no man, while he remains in this life, knows whether he enjoys the love of God or labours under his hatred. This is an utterly false assertion, and contrary to the whole teaching of the scriptures : for the scriptures every where teach, that those who believe are certain of the favour of God and their own salvation ; which most true and sacred doctrine should not be rejected for the sake of the error of your version. We shall speak of the matter itself elsewhere : for the present, let cardinal Cajetan teach Bellarmine that this is not the sense of the place in hand. " Before us are those things which are carried on about us, whether prosperous or adverse:

[³ גַּם־אַהֲבָה גַם־שִׂנְאָה אֵין יוֹדֵעַ הָאָדָם הַכֹּל לִפְנֵיהֶם.]

[⁴ Quodque pariter amorem et odium ignorat homo, ipsi autem (Deo) sunt omnia proposita.]

[⁵ Etiam amorem, etiam odium nescit homo : quæ omnia ante eos sunt.]

[⁶ Etiam amorem etiam odium non sciens homo : omnia enim in facie eorum.]

at the same time we know not the cause of adversity or prosperity, whether it be the love or hatred of God, that is, whether
God out of his love to a man governs him by adverse circumstances, and in like manner, out of his hatred to a man governs
him by adversity; and the same may be said of prosperity [1]."
Mercer, a man exquisitely skilled in the Hebrew tongue and scripture, interprets and explains the passage to the like effect; nor
does he think that your own translator meant any thing more than
this, that it cannot be judged and certainly determined by external
circumstances, whether any one is loved by God or not, since all
happen alike to all, to the just and the impious, the pure and the
impure, the good and the unrighteous, those who sacrifice and
those who sacrifice not, those who swear and those who reverence
an oath, as it follows in the succeeding sentences.

The tenth place is Ecclus. v. 5 : *De propitiato peccato noli
esse sine metu.* The place is badly translated, since the Greek is
περὶ ἐξιλασμοῦ μὴ ἄφοβος γίνου. Which words warn men not to
sin presumptuously through confidence of obtaining remission of
their sins : for it follows, " nor add sin to sin." For many heap
sin upon sin, because they promise themselves certain remission;
whom Ecclesiasticus deters by this most solemn admonition.
As to Bellarmine's pretence, that we say that a man should be
secure of obtaining pardon, and therefore that our opinion is confuted by these words, he seems to understand our doctrine but
badly. For we do not approve security in any man, as he slanderously lays to our charge.

The eleventh place is Ecclus. xvi. 15 : *Misericordia faciet
locum unicuique secundum meritum operum suorum.* Here in a
few words are many errors. For thus stands the Greek text :
πασῇ ἐλεημοσύνῃ ποίησον τόπον · ἕκαστος γὰρ κατὰ τὰ ἔργα
αὐτοῦ εὑρήσει · " Make way for every work of mercy : for every
man shall find according to his works." The words are not the
same, and the sense different. That word *merit*, whence did the
Vulgate translator get it ? Certainly he did not find it in the
Greek. For as to Bellarmine's pretence that κατὰ ἔργα is the
same as " according to the merit of one's works," which he says

[1 Coram nobis sunt ea quæ circa nos geruntur, sive prospera, sive adversa; et cum hoc nescimus causam adversitatis vel prosperitatis, an sit
odium vel amor Dei, hoc est, an Deus tanquam amans aliquem gubernet
eum per adversa : et similiter an tanquam odio habens aliquem gubernet eum
per adversa : idemque dicito de prosperis. p. 165. sine loco. 1545.]

that every one knows who is ever so slightly skilled in the Greek
language; I would fain know from him who is so skilful in the
Greek tongue, in what Lexicon or other book he ever found that
κατὰ ἔργα means any thing else but "according to works?" And if
Bellarmine can make no distinction between works and the merit of
works, he hath no reason to attribute to himself any great skill and
expertness in either the Greek language or theology. To works there
is a reward promised in scripture; to the merits of works none, but
that of death.

The twelfth place is Joel ii. 13: *Præstabilis super malitia*². What is this? Let us hear Bellarmine's explanation:
"*Præstabilis super malitia*," saith he, "means excelling in compassion." As if *præstabilis super* were all one with excelling, or
malitia the same thing as compassion. Or otherwise: "*Præstabilis
super malitia* is as much as to say, so good as not to be overcome
of evil." But that is not the meaning of the prophet. The prophet extols the clemency and goodness of God, and says that it is
so great that God repents him of the evil with which he had
determined to afflict the people. This may easily be understood.
The other is not only obscure, but absolutely barbarous.

The thirteenth place is Micah v. 2, which Osiander says is
wrongly rendered by the old translator. For it should not be
translated, *parvula es in millibus Judah*³, but, "it is too slight a
thing that thou shouldst be in the thousands of Judah." I have
no business to answer in behalf of Osiander. His correction seems
to deserve some regard, since Matthew in reciting this place, chap.
ii. 6, does not read "art little," but οὐδαμῶς ἐλαχίστη εἶ, "art by
no means least:" and the place might undoubtedly be rendered
better than it is rendered by the Vulgate interpreter.

Thus then hath Bellarmine excused some faults of the old
Latin version; with what skill, learning, or truth, let others judge.
I believe that no one who is not under an immoderate influence of
party spirit will say that the Vulgate translation is nobly vindicated by Bellarmine. If there were no other error in that version,
yet it might be sufficiently understood and perceived by those now
adduced, that it is by no means so pure and perfect as to merit to
be esteemed the authentic scripture of God. But besides these there
are others also, and those so many that they cannot be detailed

[² נִחָם עַל־הָרָעָה.]

[³ צָעִיר לִהְיוֹת בְּאַלְפֵי יְהוּדָה. Osiand. Bibl. P. II. p. 482. Tubing.
1597. He translates, Parum est ut sis in millibus Judæ.]

and enumerated. And lest any one should think that I say this rashly, I will exhibit yet more clearly by fresh instances the infinite perversity of that version.

I shall commence with Genesis, wherein at the 30th verse of the first chapter these words, " all green herbs," are wanting in your Vulgate edition. Nor ought they to be deemed superfluous. The Lord in this place plainly distinguishes the food of man from that of cattle : to man God gave the herbs and trees which yield fruit ; to the beasts all green herbs for food. The Vulgate translator, omitting these words, says that the same provision is given by God to the brutes and to man.

Gen. ii. 8, the Vulgate hath, *Plantaverat Deus Paradisum voluptatis a principio*, instead of, " God had planted a garden in Eden eastward." For *Heden* indicates the proper name of a place, as appears from Gen. iv. 16, where we read that Cain settled on the east side of this place : and God had not planted that garden " from the beginning[1]," since it was only on the third day that he created the herbs and fruitful trees, as is manifest from chap. i. 12. More correct is the rendering of the Seventy, κατὰ ἀνατολάς : and so Vatablus, Pagninus, and Tremellius, *ab oriente*.

Gen. ii. 23, *Hoc nunc os ex ossibus meis*, instead of[2], " for this turn bone of my bone ;" and Cajetan tells us that there is in these words an emphasis usual with the Hebrews.

Gen. iii. 6, *Aspectuque delectabile*, instead of, " desirable to make one wise." Verse 8, *in medio ligni Paradisi*, for, "amongst the trees of Paradise." Verse 17, *maledicta terra in opere tuo*[3], for, " cursed be the earth on thine account." Gen. iv. 13, *Major est iniquitas mea quam ut veniam merear.* In the Hebrew there is not even the shadow of any word denoting merit. It should be rendered "than I can bear," or "sustain[4];" or, " than that I should obtain forgiveness," as the Septuagint translates it, τοῦ ἀφεθῆναί με. At verse 15, *Nequaquam ita fiet*, is redundant. For the Lord does not promise Cain that no one should slay him. Verse 16, *Profugus in terra*, for, "in the land of Nod," or *Naid* as the Septuagint read it, or " the land of wandering." Verse 26, *Iste*

[1 The word is מִקֶּדֶם, which is ambiguous: cf. Ps. lxxiv. 12; lxxvii. 6.]

[2 זֹאת הַפַּעַם.   I cannot see the fault of the Vulgate here.]

[3 The translator mistook the word בַּעֲבוּרְךָ, reading it with a Daleth ד instead of a Resh ר, and so making an unauthorised derivative from עָבַד ʝuivalent to עֲבֹדָה.]

[4 מַנְשׂוֹא.]

cœpit invocare, for, "then began men[5] :" for it is not the person but the time which Moses particularises. Gen. v. 22, those words, *et vixit Enoch*, are superfluous.

Gen. vi. 3, *Non permanebit Spiritus meus in homine in æternum*, instead of, " My Spirit shall not strive[6]." Verse 6, *et præcavens in futurum*, should be struck out.

Gen. viii. 4, *Vicesimo septimo die mensis*, instead of, " upon the seventeenth day of the month;" where the Vulgate edition follows not the Hebrew original, but the seventy interpreters : which is also the case verse 7, where it translates, *qui egrediebatur et non revertebatur*. For the raven went and returned into the ark, as is plain from the Hebrew, until the waters dried up. Hence Eugubinus, though a papist, deservedly blames in his Scholia the Vulgate version of this verse.

Gen. xi. 12. Arphaxad is said in the Vulgate edition to have lived, after he had begotten Saleth, three hundred and three years. But the Hebrew text proves him to have lived four hundred and three years.

Gen. xiii. 2, *Dives valde in possessione[7] auri et argenti*, instead of, " very rich in flocks, in silver, and in gold." And verse 11, *Divisique sunt alterutrum a fratre suo*, which is absolutely unintelligible. The Hebrew text is plain, that they separated the one from the other.

Gen. xiv. 3. That is called *vallis sylvestris*, which should have been called *Siddim*, or a plain. For, unless it be a proper name, it denotes arable, and not woody ground[8]. Gen. xvii. 16, *Orientur ex eo*, for, "from her." Gen. xix. 18, *Quæso, Domine mi*, for, " No, I pray thee, my Lord."

Gen. xxi. 9. The expression of the Vulgate is too gentle, when it says that Ishmael *played with*[9] (*lusisse*) Isaac. He rather

[5] אָז הוּחַל לִקְרֹא בְּשֵׁם יְהֹוָה. The verb, being in the passive, must be taken impersonally.]

[6] לֹא יָדוֹן. Gesenius translates, "Non in perpetuum Spiritus meus in hominibus humiliabitur;" making the radical idea of דּוֹן to be, like that of the Arabic دَانَ *depression;* in which case it is cognate with the Anglo-Saxon *down.*]

[7] בְּמִקְנֶה. However, the word does denote *possession* in general, as well as the particular possession of cattle.]

[8] עֵמֶק הַשִּׂדִּים from שָׂדָה *to level.*]

[9] מְצַחֵק.]

played *upon* Isaac, than *with* him. And that it should be so rendered, appears from the apostle to the Galatians, iv. 29, who interprets this version to mean nothing slighter than a hostile persecution. But now, if Ishmael had done nothing more than play with his brother, neither would Sarah have taken it so unkindly, nor would the apostle on that account have charged Ishmael with so great a crime.

Gen. xxiv. 22, we have *duo sicli*, instead of, "the half of a shekel." And at verse 32, what is the meaning of *distravit camelos ?* He should have said that he loosed, or took their burdens off the camels; which, as I take it, is not the sense of *distravit*. In this verse too water is said to have been brought to wash the camels' feet, which, however, was really prepared for washing the feet, not of the camels, but of the servant. And at verse 6, the Vulgate hath, *qui festinus revertebatur ad Dominum suum*, instead of, "and that servant took Rebecca, and departed." In the last verse of Gen. xxviii., Esau is said in the Vulgate to have "counted it a slight thing that he had sold his birthright." But the Hebrew text says that he despised the birthright itself. For Esau might have thought slightly of the sale of the birthright, and yet might have prized highly the birthright itself. So that the Vulgate translator hath by no means come up to the sense of the words or the enormity of the sin intended. Gen. xxvii. 5, *ut jussionem patris impleret*, instead of, "to take the prey which he should bring." At verse 33, those words, *ultra quam credi potest admirans*, are redundant. Likewise Gen. xxxi. 32, these, *quod autem furti me arguis*.

Gen. xxxiv. 29, the clause, "and they plundered finally whatsoever was in any house," is omitted, while *quibus perpetratis audacter* is added superfluously. Gen. xxxvi. 24, the Vulgate interpreter says that Anan found "warm waters" in the desert; which version all who know any thing of Hebrew know to be false[1]; for Anan found not hot springs, of which there is no mention made in this place, but *mules*. This place, therefore, the Septuagint translated ill[2], and the Vulgate interpreter in following them hath erred from the Hebrew verity.

[1 Gesenius (Lex. voc. יֵמִם) observes, "Quod Hieronymus scribit in Quæst. ad l. c., 'nonnulli putant aquas calidas *juxta Punicæ linguæ* viciniam, quæ Hebrææ contermina est, hoc vocabulo significari,' non contemnendum ...... Conjectura sat infelici ex contextu facta *mulos* intelligunt nonnulli Hebræi et Lutherus."]

[2 This seems to be an oversight of Whitaker's: for the Septuagint have

Gen. xxxvii. 2. Joseph is said in the Vulgate to have been *sixteen* years of age, when he fed his father's sheep along with his brothers. But in the Hebrew text it is *seventeen.* In the same verse the Vulgate interpreter says that Joseph accused his brethren to his father with a very grievous accusation, as if some fixed and foul crime were intended ; but the Hebrew text runs thus : " And Joseph reported the ill report of them to their father,"—i. e. he related their ill behaviour to their father, and informed him of all their faults.

Gen. xxxviii. 5, the Vulgate translator reads : *Quo nato, parere ultra cessavit ;* which is foreign from the meaning of the Hebrew text. It ought to have been rendered, " And she was in Chezib when she bore him³;" for Chezib is the name of a city of the Philistines. And, verse 12, Hirah is called *opilio gregis* by the Vulgate interpreter, as by the Septuagint ὁ ποιμὴν αὐτοῦ. But Jerome blames this version, and teaches us that the Hebrew word denotes not a *shepherd,* but a *friend*⁴: so that this Hirah, who went to the town with Judah, was his friend, and not his shepherd. At verse 23, the old version hath, *Certi mendacii arguere nos non potest.* But the true sense of the Hebrew is, " that we be not despised⁵."

Gen. xxxix. 6, these words, " Wherefore he left all his goods in the hand of Joseph," are omitted. At verse 10, something is wanted to make the sense complete : for thus we read in the Vulgate, *Hujusmodi verbis per singulos dies.* It should have been filled up from the Hebrew original, " with such words every day *did she address Joseph.*" But the words which follow are superfluous, *Et mulier molesta erat adolescenti.*

Gen. xl. 5, this whole clause is left out, " The butler and the baker of the king of Egypt who were bound in the tower of the prison." At verse 16 we have *tria canistra farinœ,* for " three white (or osier) baskets⁶." But here the Vulgate interpreter followed the Septuagint, not the Hebrew original itself.

not translated it at all, but retained the original word, ὃς εὗρεν τὸν Ἰαμεὶν ἐν τῇ ἐρήμῳ.]

[³ וְהָיָה בְכִיב בְּלִדְתָּהּ אֹתוֹ.]

[⁴ רֵעֵהוּ. The difference is in the points ; רֵעֶה *a friend,* רֹעֶה *a shepherd.*]

[⁵ פֶּן נִהְיֶה לָבוּן.]

[⁶ סַלֵּי חֹרִי. Gesenius translates חֹרִי *panis albus.* LXX. κανᾶ χονδριτῶν. I think the Vulgate is not here to be blamed.]

12

[WHITAKER.]

Gen. xli. 45, the Vulgate interpreter, in explaining the name
which Pharaoh gave to Joseph, hath followed conjecture rather
than 'any certain reason.   For he first says that those words are
Egyptian ; and then he explains them to mean *the Saviour of the
world*[1] : for thus we read in the text of the Vulgate edition,
Et vocabit eum lingua Ægyptiaca Salvatorem mundi.   The
Septuagint have set down these two words without any explanation ;
and the Hebrews doubt whether they are Egyptian or Chaldee.
Josephus interprets them, " the discoverer of secrets[2];" and with
him agree the later Jews and the Chaldee Paraphrast.   It may
seem strange whence Jerome learnt that these were Egyptian
terms, and that they denoted " the Saviour of the world."

Gen. xlix. 10, Jacob says of Judah, " binding the foal of his
ass to the vine."   But the Vulgate translator hath rendered those
words thus ; *Ligans ad vitem, O fili mi, asinam suam.*   And,
at verse 22, Joseph is compared to a fruitful branch beside a well ;
which words the Vulgate translates thus, *accrescens et decorus
aspectus*[3].   At verse 24, Jacob says of Joseph, " and the arms of
his hands were strengthened ;" which, in your edition, is turned to
a quite contrary sense, *dissoluta sunt vincula brachiorum et
manuum ejus.*   In this place the translator followed the version of
the Septuagint, and not the Hebrew text.

At the end of that chapter, after the 32nd verse, this whole
clause is omitted : " Now that piece of ground was bought, and also
the cave which is therein, from the sons of Heth."   Thus that
chapter is, in the Vulgate edition, too short by one entire verse.

Hitherto we have run over a single book ; in which review we
have not been at all so curious or malicious as to let nothing which

[1 פַּעְנֵחַ צָפְנַת. Gesenius, after Bernard and Jablonski, thinks the
Vulgate interpretation right, deriving the word from the Egyptian article
p—sot—Saviour, and *phenec αἰών.* This explanation regards the form given
by the LXX. Ψονθομφάνηχ as correct; for the above words, when compounded, would in Coptic be *Psotmphenec*: the interposed *m* being sounded
om in the dialect of upper Egypt.   See Scholtz, *Expos. Voc. Copt.* in Repert.
Litt. Bibl. et Orient. T. XIII. p. 19.]

[2 Σημαίνει γὰρ τὸ ὄνομα κρυπτῶν εὑρετήν.   Joseph. Antiq. L. II. c. vi. 1.]

[3 עַיִן עֲלֵי. The Vulgate took עַיִן in the sense of *mien.*   The LXX.
give a different turn, but still understand עַיִן in the sense of an *eye*, not a *well*.
Indeed we have two different versions in the present text of the LXX.
Μου ζηλωτής (who has his eye on me), and Πρός με ἀνάστρεψον (turn back
thine eye on me.)]

might justly deserve blame escape our hands. Many things I have knowingly and deliberately passed over, which nevertheless ought certainly to be accounted errors, because repugnant to the truth of the originals.

Were I to examine in the same way the remaining books of the old Testament, I should find an abundant crop of errors, and fill many pages with the enumeration of them. For your version is not a whit more exact in the other books than we have seen it to be in this; whence we may easily form an estimate of the grossness of its faults throughout. Indeed, since many have translated the scriptures from the original into various languages, and corrected in their versions the errors of this Vulgate edition, whoever would compile a separate book, diligently and accurately executed, upon the errors of this edition, would, in my opinion, undertake and perform a work of very great utility. For from such a work all would reap the benefit of seeing and understanding the great difference there is between the pure springs of the Hebrew verity, and the muddy and turbid streams of this version which they call the Vulgate. Were I to enter on the remaining books, I should engage in a task not at all required by the plan of my undertaking, and be drawn into a digression which would interrupt the course of our disputation. I have, I hope, sufficiently proved to you that this Latin edition is full of many errors and mistakes, such as our adversaries have never hitherto found even a single instance of in the originals. This it is not we alone that affirm: even some leaders of the popish sect maintain the same thing. No reason then can be adduced, why the Hebrew edition in the old Testament, and the Greek in the new, should not command a great and deserved preference to the Latin Vulgate. I shall now return to Bellarmine, and sift the remainder of his defence.

CHAPTER XI.

OF THE LATIN EDITION OF THE PSALMS AND ITS MANIFOLD CORRUPTIONS.

BELLARMINE next inveighs against Calvin, and pleads in defence of the Latin edition of the Psalms, which Calvin, in his Antidote to the council of Trent, had most truly declared, and proved by some

12—2

instances, to be corrupt and vicious. And who is there, but the
patron of a desperate cause, who can maintain the claims of this
edition to the character of an authentic and uncorrupted document?
For it is absolutely certain that it is rendered into Latin, not from
the Hebrew, but from the Greek; not by Jerome, but by some
unknown and uncertain author. Would it not be more conformable
to reason for these men to make the Greek, from which that version
is derived, authentic? since the latter is only the daughter, or
image rather, of the former. Why do they, in the case of the
other books, receive what they think to be the Hieronymian
version, and yet reject it here? Jerome expended as much labour
upon translating the Book of Psalms into Latin as upon the other
books; and that Latin edition, which was in most general use
before Jerome, was no less faulty in the Psalms than in the other
parts: but on account of the constant and customary use of the
Psalms, which had everywhere propagated that old Latin version
in the churches, and made it familiar to men's ears, the Hieronymian
Latin translation was not publicly received. Is this, then, to be
held superior to Jerome's version in the Psalms? By no means.
For it was not retained because it was better, but because it was
more common, and could not easily be changed. Upon the same
grounds, if use had confirmed that old version in the case of the
other books also, it would not be now the Hieronymian, but it,
however corrupted, that would, in spite of all its faults, be esteemed
authentic. For thus the case stands with respect to the Psalms.
The Latin edition is ratified as authentic. Why? We have the
Hebrew and the Greek: whereof the Hebrew proceeds directly
from the Prophets, David, Moses, Asaph, Solomon, and others who
wrote the Psalms; and the Greek was made, as most people suppose, by the seventy Interpreters. This latter, though it must not
absolutely be despised, hath yet most foully corrupted in many
places the pure fountains of the Hebrew verity. Now the Latin is
still more corrupt than this, as being still farther removed from the
fountain head, and derived from the stream and not from the
spring. Yet it is not the Hebrew, nor the Greek, but this Latin
edition, such as I have described it, that the Tridentine fathers
have made the authentic scripture of the Psalms. And although all
can see the enormous impudence of this proceeding, yet their
most reckless rashness and temerity will appear yet more plainly
when some errors of this edition are set before your eyes. Since
then Bellarmine hath endeavoured to excuse those which Calvin

had remarked, let us see with what shew of success or probability
he hath performed his task.

The first place is Psalm ii. 12 : *Apprehendite disciplinam*[1].
Bellarmine says that in the Hebrew it is, "kiss," or "adore the
Son;" but that the sense is excellently well expressed by *apprehendite disciplinam*, since we can no otherwise acknowledge the
Son to be the Messiah than by receiving his faith and doctrine.
I answer, in the first place, that a translator of scripture hath
no right, first to change the words, and then to plead this excuse,
that the sense hath been rendered by him. For we are not
to consider the sense which he renders, but what the inspired
words require. Secondly, the sense is not the same. For
who will say, that to apprehend discipline is the same thing as
to kiss the Son? For it does not follow that, because we must
needs embrace Christ's discipline, if we acknowledge him as Messiah and our King, therefore the sense of these two expressions is
the same. In this way all propositions, which agreed with each
other, might be made out absolutely identical. Thirdly, a most
noble testimony to Christ, for the refutation of Christ's enemies, is
by this version wrested from us. For discipline may be understood in such a sense as to have nothing to do with Christ; but
the command to kiss the Son commends to us both his divine
nature and his royal sway.

The second place is Psalm iv. 3 : *Usque quo gravi corde*[2]? In
the Hebrew it is, "how long my glory into shame?" Bellarmine
says, first, that the Hebrew text is probably corrupt; secondly,
that the sense is the same.

I answer to the first plea : The Hebrew text is now precisely
the same as it was in Jerome's time, as appears from his Psalter.
The Septuagint read and translated the passage erroneously, and
this interpreter followed them. The cavils and calumnies of Lindanus upon this place are sufficiently refuted by his master, Isaac.
Then as to the sense, who does not see that there is a great diversity,
especially if we follow Bellarmine's exposition? For he says,
that God here complains concerning men. But that is a mistake :

[1 נַשְּׁקוּ־בַר. LXX. δράξασθε παιδείας. Jerome, *Adorate pure*. Ewald,
however, (Poetischen Bücher. III. p. 66) prefers the LXX. and Vulgate. He
translates "nehme Rath an."]

[2 כְּבוֹדִי לִכְלִמָּה. The Vulgate follows the LXX. βαρυκάρδιοι; they
read, כְּבוּדֵי לֵב לָמֶה.]

the speech is not God's, but David's, complaining of the boldness
and wickedness of his enemies. " O sons of men, ye insolent
foes of mine, who, buoyed up with arrogance and fury, despise all
others, how long will ye treat my glory with ignominy ?" But
Bellarmine pretends that God speaks and complains of men for
neglecting eternal things, and loving temporal ; which kind of men
are heavy of heart by reason of their own fault, yet the glory of
God by reason of the divine goodness. Who now will not confess
that Bellarmine is a notable interpreter of the Psalms ? Does God
then call those who are heavy of heart his glory ? Does God
call those men his glory, who despise the things of heaven and
pursue the things of earth ? Who must not laugh at such an
exposition ? Genebrard, however, hath explained the meaning
better, who by the glory of David understands God himself, towards whom these men were disrespectful.

The third place is Psalm xxxi. 4 : *Conversus sum in ærumna
mea, dum configitur spina*[1]. These ought to be translated, as
Bellarmine himself translates them from the Hebrew : " My juice
is without moisture, and my freshness is turned into the summer
droughts." These versions are sufficiently different. Yet Bellarmine says that the Vulgate interpreter cannot be blamed in this
place. He alleges two pleas in defence of him. One is, that he
translated not from the Hebrew, but from the Greek into Latin ;
the other, that there is an error of the transcribers in the
Hebrew. To the first I answer, that the fact of his translating
from the Greek, and not the Hebrew, makes more for the blame
than for the excuse of that interpretation : for in proportion as
the Greek yields to the Hebrew text in fidelity and authority, in
the same proportion must the value be depreciated of a version
made not from the Hebrew but from the Greek. Then, as to his
suspicion that the Hebrew text hath been here corrupted by the
scribes, it is an assertion which Genebrard hath not ventured to
make, nor would any one but Bellarmine, unless he were extrava-
gantly prejudiced against the Hebrew originals, think of saying
it ; nor indeed would Bellarmine himself, most probably, have
raised such a suspicion, if he had been able to excuse this error in
any other way. The Hebrew words afford a certain and easy
sense. The Latin will scarcely bear any tolerable explanation.
For what is the meaning of *dum configitur spina ?* The ancients

[1 בְּחַרְבֹנֵי קַיִץ. In the Hebrew, Ps. xxxii. 4.]

expounded the thorn to denote sin : Bellarmine says that we should understand the thorn of calamity. Be it so. But what then will be meant by *dum configitur spina?* The Greek reading, though not deserving much commendation, is yet intelligible, ἐν τῷ ἐμπαγῆναί μοι ἄκανθαν—" while the thorn is driven into me." I see what this means ; but I wish that Bellarmine would give some interpretation, consistent with the laws of grammar, of the other, *dum configitur spina.*

Bellarmine's explanation of the former clause of this verse, *Conversus sum in ærumna,* which he makes to mean, " I am turned to repentance in the time of trouble," is neither admitted by Jerome's version, nor approved by Genebrard, who observes that the word *Haphac* is scarce ever spoken of *repentance*[2].

The fourth place is in the same Psalm, verse 9 : *In chamo et fræno maxillas eorum astringe, qui non approximant ad te.* The place should have been rendered thus : " Their mouth must be held in with bit and bridle, lest they come nigh to thee[3]." Bellarmine says that Calvin here exhibits amazing impudence. Why? Because, says he, the Septuagint[4] and Saint Jerome, and all the fathers, always read this passage as it is read now.

I answer, first, that the Seventy have varied in many places very widely from the Hebrew, and Jerome gives large testimony to the fact. Secondly, Jerome in this place abstained from changing the old version, not because he deemed it incapable of amendment, but because he thought it was tolerable as it stood. Thirdly, the fathers' reading according to the present text is nothing to the purpose : they follow the version in common use, which from an indifferent Greek text was made a worse Latin. But further, in reply to Bellarmine's assertion that the Hebrew words, even as they are now read, may very well bear this interpretation, I must say that it would have been better to have proved this, than merely to have said it. Certainly Pagninus, Vatablus, Montanus, and Tremellius were of a different opinion ; and Genebrard owns that the sentence was indeed broken up by the Septuagint, but

---

[2 I can find no instance of such a use of הָפַךְ.]

[3 The Hebrew is בְּמֶתֶג־וָרֶסֶן עֶדְיוֹ לִבְלוֹם בַּל קְרֹב אֵלֶיךָ, thus rendered by Ewald : Zaum und zügel müssen dessen Bachen Schliessen, der sich dir nicht freundlich naht, p. 35, ut supra.]

[4 ἐν χαλινῷ καὶ κημῷ τὰς σταγόνας αὐτῶν ἄγξαι τῶν μὴ ἐγγιζόντων πρὸς σέ. Jerome : In camo et freno maxillas ejus constringis, ut non appropinquet ad te.]

for the sake of making it more easy. In fact, however, they have made it more intricate and difficult by this plan of breaking it up. For the prophet warns us not to be devoid of reason and discretion, "like the horse and the mule, whose mouths must be held in with bit and bridle, lest they fall upon us." The old translator hath set forth a totally different sense of the words, as if God had commanded David to bind with bit and bridle the throats of all those who (in Genebrard's words) do not approach "thy nature, which is that of a man, reason and virtue." Nothing could possibly be alleged more remote from the prophet's meaning than such an exposition.

The fifth place is in Psalm xxxvii. 8: *Quoniam lumbi mei repleti sunt illusionibus*[1]. Calvin asks, how we are to understand that his reins were filled with illusions? Bellarmine says that the Hebrew word denotes not only shame, but heat[2]. I answer, that this is indeed true; but how then does he interpret his loins being "filled with illusions?" Forsooth, by putting the effect for the cause; since David speaks of the heat and titillation of lust, which produces illusions in the mind. Away with this. Nothing was farther from the Psalmist's meaning. Genebrard hath made a much better attempt, who by these "illusions" understands diseases on account of which he was mocked and insulted by his enemies. For David's meaning is, that his loins or reins were filled with a sore and sharp disorder.

The sixth place is Psal. lxvii. 7[3]: *Qui inhabitare facit unius moris in domo.* The place should be rendered thus: "Who setteth the single, or solitary, persons in a family." Bellarmine says that the Hebrew words may very well receive several senses. I answer: The words will bear but one true sense, and that an easy and ready one. Amongst the praises of God, the prophet mentions this, that *those who are by themselves*, that is, the desolate and solitary, without kindred, friends or wealth, are so increased, enriched, and adorned by him, as now to have families, in which are contained both children and servants. Thus Pagninus renders the words, and Vatablus and Montanus, and, in the old times, Jerome. The Hebrew word does not denote μονοτρόπους (as the Seventy render it[4]),

[1 In the Hebrew, xxxviii. 7.]

[2 נִקְלָה. The Radical of קלה, in the sense of *heat*, seems the same as appears in *cal*-eo, *cal* or.]

[3 Heb. Ps. lxviii. 6.]

[4 The Seventy seem unjustly blamed here. They used μονότροπος, in the sense recognised by good authors, to express the notion of solitariness.

that is *of one manner*, but solitary or lone persons. So that all
the common disquisitions upon this place concerning similitude of
manners and the identity of tastes, however true in themselves, are
foreign to the subject and impertinent to the matter in hand.

The seventh place is in the next verse of the same Psalm : *Qui
habitant in sepulchris.* Calvin contends that we should read, " in
a dry place[5]." By this expression, says Bellarmine, the translator
wished to declare the horrors of that desert from which God brought
his people forth.

I answer : This man imagines that the Latin version of the
Psalms, in its present state, is nobly defended, and his duty as its
champion sufficiently discharged, when he is able to assign any
sense at all to the words, no matter what, provided it be not impious
and heretical. As if nothing else were required of a translator of
scripture, but only to express some sense or other not absolutely
absurd, however remote from the real meaning of the Holy Spirit.
For what can be more foreign to the mind of David than this
meaning which our opponent ascribes to these words ? The prophet is not, as Bellarmine supposes him to be, speaking of that
desert out of which God had brought his people, which might, for
its horridness, be compared to the tombs ; but is saying that those
who prove rebellious are thrust by God into dry and thirsty regions.
What hath this to do with the desert through which God led his
people into the land of Canaan ? But this is not all that Calvin
finds fault with in the verse before us. For the words sound thus
in the Hebrew : " He bringeth forth those that are bound with
chains, but the rebels dwell in a very dry place." The Latin
interpreter translates them thus, falsely and foolishly : *Qui educit
vinctos in fortitudine, similiter eos qui exasperant, qui habitant
in sepulchris.* What could possibly be expressed with greater confusion ? Yet Genebrard applies to this place some medicine in his
scholium, to cure the disorder of the Latin version. The words,
according to him, are to be thus explained ; that the rebels, who
dwell in the sepulchres, or the dry places, are brought forth and
delivered from death and the devil, or from dangers and evils.
Thus this man by his exposition changes a most gloomy punishment

It is so used by Josephus, B. J. II. xxi. 1, where he speaks of John of Giscala,
λῃστὴς γὰρ ἦν μονότροπος, ἔπειτα καὶ συνοδίαν εὗρε τῆς τόλμης ; and by Plutarch
in Pelopid. c. 3., μονότροπον βίον ἀπ᾽ ἀρχῆς ἑλόμενος.   Compare Bochart.
Hierozoic. P. I. Lib. II. c. 45. col. 491.]

[5 צִחְיָה. LXX. ἐν τάφοις.]

into a most joyous and delightful benefit. If this be interpreting
scripture, it certainly will be easy enough to make scripture say
any thing we please.

The eighth place is in the same Psalm, verse 12, &c. *Dominus
dabit verbum evangelizantibus virtute multa. Rex virtutum
dilecti, dilecti, et speciei domus divide spolia. Si dormiatis inter
medios cleros, pennæ columbæ deargentatæ, et posteriora dorsi ejus
in pallore auri*[1]. These are not the oracles of the Holy Spirit, but
rather, as Calvin truly says of them, ænigmas which Œdipus himself
could never solve. It is not only difficult to elicit and educe any
consistent meaning at all from these words, utterly incoherent as they
are ; but to torture them into any thing which approaches the meaning of the prophet exceeds all the powers of art. Yet, if you please, let
us have the explanation of Bellarmine. *Rex virtutum dilecti
dilecti :* that is, the King most mighty, and Father of Messiah his
entirely beloved Son. *Speciei domus divide spolia :* that is, he
will give to the preachers to divide the spoils of nations, for the
beauty of the house, that is, the adornment of the church : for
that *speciei* is in the dative case, and is equivalent to *ad speciem.*
Wondrous well! First let me ask him whence he gets those two
words, " he will give," and " to the preachers," which are not contained in this verse through the whole compass of its words ? For
the preceding verse is divided from it in the Hebrew and the Greek,
and the version of Jerome; and those words can by no means be
carried over into it. Next, it is absolutely intolerable to make
speciei the same as *ad speciem*, so as that *dividere spolia speciei
domus* shall mean, " to divide spoils to the beauty," that is, to
the grace and adornment " of the house," which is the church.
Who speaks Latin after this fashion ?

Genebrard hath excogitated another interpretation, more tolerable indeed, but still alien from the prophet's meaning. He denies
that *Rex virtutum* here means God, but supposes it to denote
any very brave and powerful prince. The sense therefore will be

[1 In the Greek, Ὁ Θεὸς Κύριος δώσει ῥῆμα τοῖς εὐαγγελιζομένοις δυνάμει
πολλῇ. Ὁ βασιλεὺς τῶν δυνάμεων τοῦ ἀγαπητοῦ, τοῦ ἀγαπητοῦ, καὶ ὡραιότητι
τοῦ οἴκου διελέσθαι σκῦλα. They took מַלְכֵי צְבָאוֹת as one word, regarding
the י as merely a vowel of composition, as it is in מַלְכִּיצֶדֶק, and other
proper names. יְדִדוּן they derived from יָדַד *dilexit*, taking the termination
וּן for a diminutive; and gave to נָוֶה a meaning of which its radical shews
traces in the Hiphil voice, Exod. xv. 2.]

this : The most powerful princes shall be the Beloved's, that is,
shall yield to the Beloved of God, or the Son of God: and *speciei*
he makes not the dative, but the genitive, (although in spite of the
authority of the Greek text which exhibits τῇ ὡραιότητι,) and
explains thus; "it is of the beauty of the house to divide the spoil,"
—that is, it pertains to the glory of the house of God to divide
the spoils of conquered kings, that is, demons. Is not this now a
neat interpretation? The remainder is thus explained by Bellarmine. *Si dormiatis inter medios cleros :* that is, if you, O
preachers, remain between two lots, the heavenly and the earthly,
that is, be not wholly engaged in action nor wholly in contemplation, but in a mean between both, then shall the church be like
a most beautiful dove, &c. But ought the preachers to be in the
middle between action and contemplation? What else can this
mean but to keep clear of either action or contemplation; in other
words, to be wholly useless? *Dormire inter medios cleros,* is, in
an unexampled manner, translated, "to sleep between the two lots ;"
and then these two lots are most absurdly understood of action and
contemplation. But everything hath its proper counterpart [2], and
the exposition suits the version. Genebrard confesses that the wits
of all expositors have been, as it were, crucified in seeking an explanation of this passage : undoubtedly it tortured Bellarmine. But
how hath Genebrard himself taken away this cross? *Dormire
inter medios cleros* is, if we believe Genebrard, to be in the most
certain and imminent perils. Our translators generally explain the
word, which the Latin version represents by *cleros,* to mean "the
pots [3]." But Bellarmine says that it cannot possibly bear that signification. The contrary, however, is the opinion of Genebrard, the
king's professor of Hebrew in the university of Paris, who tells us
that the Hebrew term denotes cauldrons, tripods, or pots.

You have now heard how perplexed, confused, and tortured are

[2 Whitaker's words are, " Similes habent labra lactucas." The proverb
occurs in Jerome, and is thus explained by Erasmus : " Usurpat, simulque
interpretatur, hoc proverbium Divus Hieronymus, scribens ad Chromatium
in hunc modum : Secundum illud quoque, de quo semel in vita Crassum
ait risisse Lucilius ; similem habent labra lactucam, asino carduos come-
dente : videlicet ut perforatam navim debilis gubernator regat, et cæci cæcos
ducant in foveam, et talis sit rector quales illi qui reguntur." Adagia. p. 644.
Hanov. 1617.]

[3 שְׁפַתָּיִם, the meaning of which is much disputed. Gesenius renders
it, " stabula, caulæ." So Ewald, " So ofs ihr zwischen Hürden ruhet."]

all these explications. But the Hebrew text hath no similar difficulty in it; which Pagninus and Montanus translate thus: "Kings
of armies fled, they fled; and she that dwelt at home divided the
spoil. If ye have lain in the midst of the pots, ye shall be as the
plumage of a dove, which is covered with silver, and her wings
with yellow gold." This text hath given the interpreters no such
torture, as, according to Genebrard, hath, in the case of the Latin,
set them on the rack.

The ninth place is in the same Psalm at verse 17 : *Ut quid
suspicamini montes coagulatos?* Calvin says that we should read,
"Why do ye envy the fat mountains?" In regard of this place
Bellarmine hath no other answer to give but this, that the Hebrew
word[1] is found nowhere else but here; and therefore, since we
must abide by the judgment of some interpreters, the Seventy
should be preferred to all the rest. If this be so, how comes it
that Jerome and Vatablus and Pagninus and Montanus, and all
who have translated the Psalter from the Hebrew, have put a different sense upon that word? If we must abide by the judgment
of the Seventy, on account either of their own or the church's
authority, they who have assigned another meaning to this word
cannot be defended. But let us follow the seventy interpreters,
and inquire into the meaning of the word. The words stand
thus in the Greek Psalter, ἵνα τί ὑπολαμβάνετε ὄρη τετυρω-
μένα; which the Latin translator renders thus; *Ut quid suspicamini montes coagulatos?* Why hath Bellarmine concealed
from us the meaning of these words? What is it *to suspect co-
agulated mountains?* Bellarmine would do us a favour if he would
inform us.

The tenth place is in the same Psalm also, at verse 19, *Etenim
non credentes inhabitare Dominum Deum;* which translation agrees
neither with the Hebrew[2], nor with the Greek. That it does not
agree with the Hebrew, is no way surprising, since it is not derived
from it. But, at least, it should not depart from the Greek, from
which it hath been taken. Yet depart it does, and very widely.
For the Greek edition reads the passage thus : καὶ γὰρ ἀπειθοῦντας
τοῦ κατασκηνῶσαι. Here there is a full stop; and then a new
sentence begins, Κύριος ὁ Θεὸς εὐλογητός. If the Latin had no

[1] גִּבְנֻנִּים rendered by Jerome, *excelsi;* by Ewald, *gipfeligen;* by Gesenius,
cacumina; substantially to the same sense.]

[2] וְאַף סוֹרְרִים יָהּ לִשְׁכֹּן אֱלֹהִים :]

other fault save that of its ambiguity and obscurity, it ought not to be defended.

The eleventh is also in the same Psalm, verse 23: *Convertam in profundum maris.* The Hebrew words denote the very opposite: "I will bring back from the depths of the sea[3]." Here Bellarmine acknowledges a mistake, and says that some copies of the Vulgate have not *in profundum,* but *in profundis ;* and he explains *convertere in profundis maris* to mean, drawing out those who are in the depths of the sea. But if this reading and interpretation be the true, as Bellarmine confesses, why have not the Louvain critics preferred it to the other which is false? Although perhaps the grammarians will not concede to Bellarmine that to convert in the deep of the sea, is the same as to bring forth from the depths of the sea.

The twelfth place is in the same Psalm, verse 28: *Ibi Benjamin adolescentulus in mentis excessu.* Which translation Bellarmine defends warmly, and maintains that these words are to be understood of the apostle Paul, who was of the tribe of Benjamin; and who, in the transport of his mind, is related to have slept so soundly that he did not know whether he were in the body or out of the body. And because the Hebrew word, which the old interpreter hath rendered, *In mentis excessu,* signifies a prince or governor, he combines this interpretation with the former, because Paul was the chief ruler and spiritual prince of the church of the Gentiles. Thus there is nothing with which Bellarmine cannot bravely reconcile his interpretations. But who can believe that David is here speaking of Paul? or that the Hebrew word[4] is capable of the meaning which the old interpreter hath put upon it? Jerome gives a different rendering, *Continens eos :* Aquila, "their commander: " Theodotion, "the teacher of them," as we learn from Theodoret in his Commentaries upon the Psalms. All the later translators too differ from the Vulgate, giving *Lord, Ruler, Prince,* and never "in a trance." But, at any rate, Bellarmine's device of combining both translations is a stroke of excessive subtilty ; for the Hebrew cannot possibly mean both, but at least one or other. There must needs therefore be an error here either in our editions or in the old Latin.

[3 אָשִׁיב מִמְּצֻלוֹת יָם : In the LXX. ἐπιστρέψω ἐν βυθοῖς θαλάσσης.]

[4 רֹדֵם, LXX. ἐν ἐκστάσει, deriving it from רָדַם, which is used, in Niphal, to denote deep slumber and prostration of sense.]

The thirteenth place is Psalm cxxxi. [cxxxii.] 15 : *Viduam ejus benedicens benedicam.* It is in the Hebrew, " her victuals." There cannot possibly be a more shameful mistake than this. For what hath the Lord's promise to supply us abundantly with victuals, and, as it were, to care for our necessary provisions; what hath this, I say, to do with "a widow ? " Here, though Bellarmine cannot avoid acknowledging a manifest error, yet he does not think that the place should be altered, because *viduam* hath been ever read and chanted in the church. Is it thus that errors are defended by their antiquity ? Could the church thus perversely interpret scripture ? Is it so, that false interpretations should not be corrected when once confirmed by long usage in the church ? That we should read *victum* and not *viduam*, the Hebrew word itself cries out to us, Jerome testifies in his Psalter and his Questions on Genesis, Symmachus, cited by Theodoret, on the Psalms, Chrysostom and Theodoret himself. The fact that some Latin copies of the Vulgate edition have *viduam*, hath arisen from an error of certain Greek MSS., in which χήραν was read instead of θήραν. Yet so obstinate are our adversaries in the defence of all errors that, let the mistake be never so notorious and the cause of it never so manifest, they will nevertheless endure no change, no correction.

Hitherto then Bellarmine hath fought his best for the old Latin edition of the Psalms, and yet hath no great reason to suppose that he hath fully acquitted himself of his task. For these which Calvin hath touched are but a few errors, if compared with that multitude which are to be found in that old Latin edition of the Psalms. To enable you the more readily to perceive this, I will adduce the testimony of a single Psalm ; and that shall be the ninetieth (or, as they reckon, the eighty-ninth), which was composed by Moses the man of God. Let us briefly run over some verses of this Psalm, and compare their old Latin version with the Hebrew text. In the third verse the Latin copies read, following the version of the seventy translators : *Ne convertas hominem in humilitatem : et dixisti, convertimini filii hominum.* The Hebrew original yields a far different sense : " Thou convertest man to contrition, and sayest, Return, ye children of men." How different are these two sentences ! In the fifth verse the old Latin hath : *Quæ pro nihilo habentur, eorum anni erunt ;* of which words I am not sure that any sense can be given. In the Hebrew it is thus : " Thou takest them off with a flood : they are asleep." In the eighth verse the Vulgate reads ; *Posuisti seculum nostrum in illuminationem vul-*

tus tui. In the Hebrew text it is: " Thou hast set our secrets in the light of thy countenance." In the nineteenth verse it is thus in the Vulgate : *Quoniam omnes dies nostri defecerunt, et in ira tua defecimus. Anni nostri sicut aranea meditabantur : dies annorum nostrorum in ipsis septuaginta anni : si autem in potentatibus, octoginta anni : et amplius eorum labor et dolor; quoniam supervenit mansuetudo, et corripiemur.* What is the meaning of these words? or what interpreter is there learned enough (always excepting Genebrard) to undertake to give a suitable explanation of them? The Hebrew is quite otherwise, both in expression and in sense : " For all our days have declined in thine anger, we have spent our years like a tale. The days of our years, there are seventy years in them, or, at most, eighty years. Even the best of them is labour and trouble : when it is past, forthwith we flee away."

In the eleventh and twelfth verses the Vulgate reads thus : *Et præ timore tuo iram tuam dinumerare. Dextram tuam sic notum fac, et eruditos corde in sapientia.* In the Hebrew it is : " And as thy fear, is thy wrath: so teach us to number our days, and we shall bring our heart to wisdom." In the sixteenth verse, the Vulgate hath : *Respice in servos tuos, et in opera tua, et dirige filios eorum.* But the Hebrew : " Let thy work be clear to thy servants, and thy beauty in their children."

This is sufficient to shew us how remarkable is the agreement between the Hebrew original and the Latin edition. There are seventeen verses in this Psalm ; and I will venture to say that there are more errors in the old version of it than there are verses in the Psalm. But should any one suspect that the Hebrew text which is now in our hands is corrupt, let him consult Jerome's version in his Psalter and in his 139th Epistle to Cyprian[1], where he will find the same Hebrew text of this Psalm as we have at present. The same is the case of the other Psalms also ; so that it may be said with truth, that these which they read and chant in their sacred offices, are not the Psalms of David, but the blunders of the Greek and Latin translators. And since Bellarmine, at the close of his Defence, presses us strongly with the testimony of Pellican, I will pay him back with two for his one, and return him his own with interest.

The first is that of Bruno Amerbach, in the Preface to his readers, which he has prefixed to his Psalter of Jerome ; where, speaking of the old Greek and Latin editions of the Psalms, he

[1] Ep. cxl. ed. Vallars. T. I. p. 1042.]

says : " I have added the Greek, with which corresponds the next column, that common translation which is every where in use, which is the work of an uncertain author, and, to tell the truth, is sometimes utterly at variance with the Greek copy. Whether we are to blame for this the negligence of the translator, or the carelessness of the transcribers, or, which is more probable, the presumptuous ignorance of some meddling coxcomb, is a question which I shall not now examine[1]." The second is that of Lindanus a follower of the popish cause, who, in his third book *de Optimo Gen. Interpr.* c. 6, expresses his opinion that the Greek edition of the Psalms is not the version of the seventy interpreters, but of the apostate Symmachus, and that this old Latin translation is the work of some obscure Greek. His words are these : " After frequent and deep reflection upon the translator of our Latin edition, I seem to perceive many indications which suggest to me a suspicion that the man was not a Latin, but some petty Grecian. Surely the ancient Church 1500 years ago, which used this version, could not have degenerated so much in so short a time from the purity of the Latin tongue. For the strange renderings which occur both in the Psalms and the new Testament are more numerous than we can possibly suppose the blunders of any man conversant with the Latin tongue, even learned from common talk and not from reading[2]." And then he goes on to prove, that the Greek edition of the Psalms now extant is not that ancient one which was composed by the seventy interpreters[3]. Hence we may learn what to think of Genebrard, who, in his Epistle to Castellinus, bishop of Rimini, maintains that this Greek edition is not only catholic, but either apostolical or the Septuagint. So far of the book of Psalms.

[1. Græcum item adjecimus, cui respondet e regione translatio, quæ passim legitur, ἄδηλος, hoc est, auctore incerto, nonnunquam, ut dicam id quod res est, δὶς διὰ πασῶν ab exemplari Græco dissidens. Cujus rei culpa in interpretis oscitantiam, aut in librariorum incuriam, aut, quod verisimilius sit, alicujus nebulonis audacem imperitiam rejici debeat, nolo excutere in præsentia.]

[2 Sæpe multumque de nostræ Latinæ editionis interprete cogitans, plurima videre videor quæ ad suspicandum me invitant, ut non Latinum hominem sed Græculum quempiam fuisse existimem. Siquidem illa prisca ecclesia, ante annos 1500 hoc versione usa, haud ita potuit a Romanæ linguæ puritate intra tantillum temporis degenerare. Nam quæ cum in Psalmis, tum in Novo Testamento occurrunt versionis offendicula, majora sunt quam ut ab homine Latinæ linguæ, etiam quæ non jam ex lectione, sed ex sermone discitur, potuerint peccari.—p. 106. Colon. 1558.]

[3 Compare Hody, Lib. IV. p. 588.]

CHAPTER XII.

OF CORRUPTIONS IN THE LATIN EDITION OF THE NEW TESTAMENT.

FINALLY, Bellarmine now undertakes the defence of the old Latin edition of the new Testament, and answers the objections of Chemnitz and Calvin to those places which they have asserted to be corrupted by the Latin translator. We proceed to break the force of this portion also of Bellarmine's defence, and to shew that the Greek original in the new Testament is purer than the Latin edition.

The first place is Matth. ix. 13 : *Non veni vocare justos, sed peccatores.* Chemnitz asserts that a most noble passage is here mutilated, because the Latin hath nothing to represent " to repentance[4]." Bellarmine's defence consists of three heads. First, he says that that clause is found in some Latin copies. I answer, that, however, it is not found in those which they use as the most correct and authentic, that is, the copies of that edition which the Louvain divines have published. And in their latest missal, when this part of the gospel is repeated upon the Feast of St. Matthew, the clause in question is omitted.

Secondly, he pretends that it is most likely that this clause is superfluous in the Greek, and did not appear in the more accurate MSS.

I answer, that this is by no means likely, since Chrysostom read that clause, as appears from his commentaries ; and it is likely that Chrysostom had access to the most correct MSS. Theophylact too found the same clause in his copies ; and Robert Stephens in those numerous and very faithful ones (one of which was the Complutensian) by the help of which he corrected his edition of the new Testament.

Thirdly, he says that this clause is not necessary, since to call sinners and not the righteous, is the same thing as to exhort to repentance those who need it.

I answer, that it is plainly necessary, because Luke, without all controversy, adds these words, chap. v. 32. For thus, by the unanimous suffrage of all the copies, we read in Luke, οὐκ ἐλήλυθα καλέσαι δικαίους, ἀλλ᾽ ἁμαρτωλοὺς εἰς μετάνοιαν. Besides, the

[4 εἰς μετάνοιαν is wanting in the Vatican, Cambridge, and other ancient MSS. ; in the Persian, Syriac, Ethiopic, and Armenian versions, as well as in the Vulgate.]

13

[WHITAKER.]

reason of the thing leads us to the same conclusion. For it is one thing to call sinners, and another to call sinners to repentance; as Theophylact writes, with great truth, upon this place in Matthew : οὐχ ἵνα μείνωσιν ἁμαρτωλοὶ, ἀλλ᾽ ἵνα μετανοήσωσιν· "not that they should remain sinners, but that they should repent."

The second place is John xiv. 26 : *Spiritus Sanctus suggeret vobis omnia, quæcunque dixero vobis.* The papists abuse this passage to prove, that whatever is defined in councils should be received as the oracles of the Holy Spirit. But in the Greek it is not "I shall say," but, "I have said," ἃ εἶπον ὑμῖν. Bellarmine says that the sense is the same as in the Greek ; since we are to understand it to mean, not "what I shall *then* say," but "what I shall *now* say."

I answer. The papists seize greedily upon all occasions, however futile and absurd, to gain proof for their dogmas, and not seldom use arguments which are founded only in the errors of a translation. Thus from this place they gather that the Holy Ghost is the author of all the dogmas which they have invented and confirmed in their councils, although they cannot be supported by any scripture evidence. But Christ did not promise that he would hereafter say something which the Holy Ghost should teach them, but that what he had already said to them should be recalled to their mind and memory by the Holy Ghost. For Christ says not, πάντα ἃ ἂν εἴπω ὑμῖν, but ἃ εἶπον ὑμῖν. Christ, therefore, had already told them all; but they had not yet learned it accurately enough, nor committed it to memory. Whence the falsehood of Bellarmine's exposition sufficiently appears ; since Christ does not say, as he supposes, "The Spirit shall suggest to you whatever I shall now say," but "whatever I have already said to you :" for ἃ εἶπον does not mean "what I shall say," but "what I have said." Thus the Latin version of this place is false, and even Bellarmine's own exposition proves it false.

The third place is Rom. i. 4 : *Qui prædestinatus est filius Dei.* In the Greek it is ὁρισθέντος, i. e. who was declared or manifested. Bellarmine tells us that ὁρίζειν never in the scriptures means to declare, and that all the Latins read thus, *Qui prædestinatus est.*

I answer. Firstly, that ὁρίζειν in this place does denote " to declare," as Chrysostom interprets it, who cannot be supposed ignorant of the just force and significance of the word. For having, in his first Homily upon the Romans, put the question, τί

οὖν ἔστιν ὁρισθέντος ; he subjoins as synonymous terms, δειχθέν-
τος, ἀποφανθέντος, κριθέντος· where he teaches us that ὁρίζειν
in this passage means nothing else but to *declare, shew,* or *judge.*
In the same way Œcumenius asserts that τοῦ ὁρισθέντος is equivalent to τοῦ ἀποδειχθέντος or ἐπιγνωσθέντος. Nor do Theodoret
or Theophylact vary from this explanation : so that Bellarmine's
confident assertion is manifestly destitute of all truth. What may
be said with truth is, that neither in the scriptures nor anywhere
else does ὁρίζειν mean the same thing as to predestinate.

Secondly, the Latin fathers followed the Vulgate translator,
by whom this word is unskilfully and absurdly rendered, as Erasmus and Faber and Cajetan tell us, and as every one who knows
any thing of Greek must needs confess. As to Bellarmine's
assertion, that *defined* and *predestinated* are perfectly equivalent
terms, I leave it without hesitation to the general judgment of all
learned men.

The fourth place is Rom. i. at the end, where we have in the
Vulgate edition, *Qui cum justitiam Dei cognovissent, non intellexerunt, quoniam qui talia agunt digni sunt morte; non solum qui
ea faciunt, sed etiam qui consentiunt facientibus*[1]. Chemnitz,
Valla, Erasmus, and others, agree that this place is corrupt. For
in the Greek text it runs thus : οἵτινες τὸ δικαίωμα τοῦ Θεοῦ
ἐπιγνόντες (ὅτι οἱ τὰ τοιαῦτα πράσσοντες ἄξιοι θανάτου εἰσὶν)
οὐ μόνον αὐτὰ ποιοῦσιν, ἀλλὰ καὶ συνευδοκοῦσι τοῖς πράσσουσι.
Yet Bellarmine is not ashamed to say that the Latin reading is the
truer. For, says he, according to the Greek the sense is, that it
is worse to consent to an evildoer than to do ill oneself; whereas,
taken absolutely, it is worse to do ill than to consent to another
doing ill.

I answer : Bellarmine is not very accurate in his estimate of
the magnitude of sins. For to have pleasure in the wicked is one
of those gravest sins, which are not committed but by the most
abandoned men. To sin at all is of itself impious, and deserves
eternal punishment, however much it be done against our better conscience and with internal struggles; but to approve our sins and
those of other men, to deem them well done, to applaud them in
our feelings and judgment, and to take pleasure in sins (which is

---

[1] This reading of the Vulgate is however strongly supported by the
Clermont MS., and the apparent citation in Clement's 1 Ep. ad Cor. c. 35
(pp. 120, 122, ed. Jacobson). Mill and Wetstein declare in its favour; but see
on the other side Whitby, Examen Var. Lect. II. 1. § 1. n. 16.]

what the apostle means by συνευδοκεῖν), is almost the very height and climax of iniquity. This is the assent which Paul condemns in this place, and which is indeed almost the last step in sin. The sense of the Greek therefore is very true; and is what is given by the Greek interpreters, Chrysostom, Theodoret, Œcumenius and Theophylact. And in all the Greek copies which Stephens followed, that is, all which he could by any means procure, there was no variety of reading in this place. That the Latin fathers read it otherwise, need not surprise us; since they did not consult the originals, but drew from the streams of this Vulgate translator. And though Bellarmine affirms the Latin text to be altogether preferable to the Greek, yet other papists entertain an altogether different opinion. "To speak my mind freely," says Catharinus, upon the first chapter of the Epistle to the Romans, "the Greek reading pleases me far better. The construction runs on easily and without any rubs[1]."

The fifth place is Rom. iv. 2; where Abraham is said not to have been justified by works. In their Latin edition it is added "of the law," as if the apostle were speaking of the ceremonies of the law. But Bellarmine says that all, or almost all, the Latin copies omit the word *legis*. This I admit, if he speak of the copies at present generally in men's hands: for some centuries ago all, or almost all, the copies had *legis*, as is plain from some ancient fathers, the scholastic divines, Lyra, Aquinas, Carthusianus, and others. How the passage ought to be understood, and what kinds of works the Apostle excludes from justification, shall be explained hereafter in its proper place.

The sixth place is Rom. xi. 6; where these words are omitted, "But if it be of works, then is it not of grace: otherwise work is no more work[2]." Bellarmine confesses that this sentence is in the Greek, but says that it is recognised by none of the commentators upon this place except Theophylact. Which assertion is wholly untrue; since Œcumenius exhibits and explains this same sentence, as also Theodoret and Chrysostom: which latter he nevertheless affirms, naming him expressly, not to have made any mention of this sentence. Bellarmine did not examine Chrysostom in this

[1 Ne quid autem dissimulem, longe magis mî placet Græca lectio:..... facile procedit litera et sine ullo scrupulo. Comm. in Epp. Paul. p. 21. Paris. 1566.]

[2 This clause is omitted in the Alexandrian, and several other ancient MSS.]

place, but gave too much credit to Erasmus, who falsely denies that it is to be found in Chrysostom[3]. For Chrysostom reads it thus: εἰ δὲ ἐξ ἔργων οὐκ ἔτι ἐστὶ χάρις· ἐπεὶ τὸ ἔργον οὐκ ἔτι ἐστὶ ἔργον. But what if the clause were not to be found in the commentaries of these writers? Must we, therefore, deem it spurious? By no means. For the Greek copies, and very numerous MSS. of the greatest fidelity, and the most ancient Syrian translator, will suffice to prove that this sentence came from the apostle's pen; whose evidence is still more confirmed by the very antithesis of the context and the sequence of the reasoning. For, as the apostle says, "If it be of grace, then it is not of works; for then grace would not be grace;" so to balance the antithesis he must say, "If it be of works, it is not of grace; for then work would not be work."

The seventh place is Eph. v. 32: *Sacramentum hoc magnum est.* Where our divines have no other complaint to make, but that the papists abuse the ambiguity of the term to prove that matrimony is a sacrament. For the word in the Greek is μυστήριον, which is never in scripture used to denote what we properly call a sacrament. It is absurd, therefore, for the schoolmen to conclude from this place that matrimony is a sacrament. Cajetan's words are these[4]: "A prudent reader will not gather from this place that Paul teaches that marriage is a sacrament. For he does not say, This is a sacrament, but a great mystery." For which true speech of his the cardinal receives hard usage from Ambrose Catharinus in the fourth book of his Annotations.

The eighth place is Eph. vi. 13: *Ut possitis resistere in die malo, et in omnibus perfecti stare.* In the Greek it is ἅπαντα κατεργασάμενοι, which does not mean *perfect in all things.* Some explain the passage as if it were *omnibus perfectis,* "all things being complete," that is, when ye have procured and put on all the arms which are needful to you for this warfare. But Chrysostom (followed here by Œcumenius) hath better understood the force of the verb κατεργάσασθαι. For κατεργάσασθαι denotes to conquer completely, to subdue and quell all the powers of an adversary. The panoply here spoken of enables us not only to resist in the evil day, but also ἅπαντα κατεργασάμενοι, that is,

[3 It is indeed in the Text, but not in the Commentary.]
[4 Non habet ex hoc loco prudens lector a Paulo, conjugium esse sacramentum. Non enim dicit sacramentum, sed, Mysterium hoc magnum est. p. 278. 2. Paris. 1571.]

having quelled and taken out of the way (for so Chrysostom and
Œcumenius explain the apostle's expression) whatever opposes us,
to stand firm ourselves and unconquered.

But this is quite a different thing from the reading in the old
books, *in omnibus perfecti*; from which false rendering false explanations also have arisen. Thomas explains the words "in all
things" to mean in prosperity and in adversity; and here he makes
out a twofold perfection[1], one of the way, the other of the home;
which, although they are true in themselves, are things wholly
impertinent to the passage before us.

The ninth place is Heb. ix. 28 : *Ad multorum exhaurienda
peccata.* In the Greek it is, εἰς τὸ πολλῶν ἀνενεγκεῖν ἁμαρτίας·
which means, "to bear away the sins of many." Now sins are
borne away when they are remitted, which takes place in this
life; but they are exhausted or drained off, when we are wholly
purified and no remains of sin left in us, which does not take place
in this life. For, since our adversaries seize on the most slender
occasions to sophisticate the truth, the Holy Spirit must be everywhere vindicated from their calumnies. Now whereas Bellarmine says
that the translator hath rendered this place with great propriety, I
would desire him to produce an example where ἀνενεγκεῖν means
to exhaust. For, although ἀναφέρω means "to bear upward," yet
bearing up and drawing are not the same thing as exhausting or
draining. He who draws from a fountain, does not consequently
exhaust the fountain itself. But ἀναφέρειν more frequently denotes
"to take away or bear;" as, both in this place and another similar
one, 1 Peter ii. 24, Christ is said ἀνενεγκεῖν εἰς τὸ ξύλον our
sins, that is, "to have borne them on the tree," as there even the
old translator hath rendered it.

The tenth place is Heb. xiii. 16: *Talibus hostiis promeretur
Deus.* In the Greek it is, τοιαύταις θυσίαις εὐαρεστεῖται ὁ Θεός·
"with such sacrifices God is well pleased." Bellarmine is not
ashamed to produce a defence of his own, such as it is, for this
place also. In Latin, says he, one is correctly said to deserve
well of the person whom he gratifies by his actions.

I answer in the first place, that I grant that amongst men
there is room for merit, since all things are not due to all. It
may therefore be correctly said, that we deserve well of those

[1 P. 171. Antverp. 1591. The Schoolmen were fond of the distinction
of *Via* and *Domus;* meaning by the former, the present, and by the latter,
the eternal life.]

upon whom we have bestowed any benefit which hath flowed merely from our own free choice. But when the matter is between us and God, farewell all merit; since whatever we do pleasant to him, we yet do no more than we already owed to him. Wherefore when we have done all that we can do in any way, we are nevertheless still, as Christ expresses it, ἀχρεῖοι δοῦλοι. Besides, I ask Bellarmine whether, in their theology, to deserve well of God means nothing more than to do what is pleasing to him. I would it were so : for then they would not err so much upon the merit of works. We ourselves say that the good works of the saints are grateful and pleasant to God; but the whole dispute is about the merit of works. Lastly, how senseless is this expression, *Talibus hostiis promeretur Deus!*

The eleventh place is James v. 15: *Et alleviabit eum Dominus.* In the Greek it is, καὶ ἐγερεῖ αὐτὸν ὁ Κύριος. "And the Lord shall raise him up." Here Bellarmine disputes, by the way, upon the effects of extreme unction against Chemnitz. Although there is no capital fault in the translation, yet the place might be more correctly rendered than it is by the Latin interpreter. As to their popish unction, James makes no mention of it here; as Cajetan himself abundantly teaches us in his commentary upon the passage. His words are: "Neither in terms, nor in substance, do these words speak of the sacramental anointing of extreme unction[2];" which he proves by three very solid arguments drawn from the passage itself. But this is not the place for disputing concerning the sacramental unction.

The last place is 1 John v. 13 : *Hæc scribo vobis, ut sciatis quoniam vitam habetis æternam, qui creditis in nomine Filii Dei.* And so indeed the text is exhibited in some Greek copies, as Robert Stephens informs us in his Greek Testament. But the majority, even the Complutensian, otherwise, thus: ταῦτα ἔγραψα ὑμῖν τοῖς πιστεύουσιν εἰς τὸ ὄνομα τοῦ Υἱοῦ τοῦ Θεοῦ, ἵνα εἰδῆτε ὅτι ζωὴν αἰώνιον ἔχετε, καὶ ἵνα πιστεύητε εἰς τὸ ὄνομα τοῦ Υἱοῦ τοῦ Θεοῦ. But we do not choose to raise any great contention with our opponent upon the reading of this passage, since there is no difference in the sense. For Bellarmine's attempt to shew that it is better in the Latin than in the Greek, because there was no need to admonish them to do what they had done already, is a mode of reasoning unworthy of so great a theologian.

[2 Nec ex verbis, nec ex effectu, verba hæc loquuntur de sacramentali unctione extremæ unctionis. p. 419.]

For we too often admonish men to do what they are doing, according to that saying, *Qui monet ut facias quod jam facis;* and this is a thing of constant occurrence in the scriptures. Thus those who believe in Christ are to be perpetually admonished to increase and remain constant in that faith.

And now Bellarmine thinks that he hath satisfactorily answered all our charges against the old translation of the new Testament. But how small a portion is this of the errors which may be found and censured in that version! I am disposed therefore to bestow a little more time upon examining it, and producing some more of its faults, not all indeed (for that would be a tedious and difficult task), but still too many, so as to enable you the better to judge how very far it is from being pure and authentic.

Matth. iii. 2, the old version hath, *appropinquabit regnum cœlorum.* In the Greek it is ἤγγικε, " *hath* drawn nigh." So also in chap. iv. 17. In Matth. iv. 4, the word " openly" is omitted in the old version, though the Greek text is, ἀποδώσει σοι ἐν τῷ φανερῷ. And v. 7, the old translator renders μὴ βαττο-λογήσητε by *nolite multum loqui.* But βαττολογεῖν means something different from much speaking. For Christ does not prohibit long prayers, but the tedious and hypocritical repetition of the same words. At v. 11, he hath rendered ἄρτον ἐπιούσιον by *panem supersubstantialem.* And v. 25 in the Latin runs thus: *Ne solliciti sitis animæ vestræ quid manducetis.* In the Greek, τί φάγητε καὶ τί πίητε· " What ye shall eat and what ye shall drink." At v. 32, in the Latin, *Scit Pater vester :* in the Greek, ὁ Πατὴρ ὑμῶν ὁ οὐράνιος. Chap. vii. 14, in the Latin, *Quam angusta porta!* In the Greek, ὅτι στενὴ ἡ πύλη· " For strait is the gate." Chap. ix. 8, *timuerunt* occurs in the Latin, instead of " they wondered," since the Greek hath ἐθαύμασαν. Chap. ix. 15, *Filii sponsi* for the " children of the bride-chamber," the Greek being οἱ υἱοὶ τοῦ νυμφῶνος. The same mistake recurs Luke v. 34. Chap. xiv. 3, the name of Philip is omitted in the Latin, though exhibited by the Greek copies. He was the brother of Herod, whose wife the impious Herod had united to himself in an incestuous union. Verse 21, the Latin reads, *quinque millia;* in the Greek it is, ὡσεὶ πεντακισχίλιοι, " about five thousand." Verse 26, the word, " the disciples," is omitted : for in the Greek we have ἰδόντες αὐτὸν οἱ μαθηταί, where the Latin gives only *videntes eum.* Chap. xv. 8, in the Latin, *Populus hic labiis me honorat;* but in the Greek, ἐγγίζει μοι ὁ λαὸς οὗτος τῷ στόματι αὐτῶν, καὶ τοῖς χείλεσί με τιμᾷ· "This people draweth nigh unto me with their mouth, and honoureth me with their lips." At v. 31 there is nothing to express "the maimed to be whole," though the Greek hath κυλλοὺς ὑγιεῖς. Chap. xvii. 19 : in the Latin, *Quare nos non potuimus ejicere illum?* instead of *illud* "it," that is, the demon ; for the Greek is, ἐκβαλεῖν αὐτό. Chap. xviii., in the last verse, there is nothing in the Latin corresponding to τὰ παραπτώματα αὐτῶν, "their offences," in the Greek. Chap. xix. 7 stands thus in the Latin : *Quid me interrogas de bono?* *unus est bonus, Deus.* But in most, and the most correct, Greek copies, we read, τί με λέγεις ἀγαθόν; οὐδεὶς ἀγαθός, εἰ μὴ εἷς, ὁ Θεός· that is, "Why callest thou me good? There is none good but one, God." Chap. xx. 9 : in the Latin, *acceperunt singulos denarios,* instead of "every man a penny;" for the Greek hath ἔλαβον ἀνὰ δηνάριον. And the like mistake is made again in the next verse. At verse 15, we have in the Latin, *aut non licet mî quod volo facere?* instead of, "is it not lawful for me to do what I will with mine own?" In the Greek, ἢ οὐκ ἔξεστί μοι ποιῆσαι ὃ θέλω ἐν τοῖς ἐμοῖς ; Chap. xxi. 30 : *Eo, domine,* is in the Latin instead of, "I, Sir," ἐγὼ, κύριε. Chap. xxiv. 6 : *Opiniones præliorum,* in the Latin, for "rumours of wars," ἀκοὰς πολέμων. Chap. xxvi. 61 : διὰ τρίων ἡμερῶν, which means, "in three days," is rendered in the old version *post triduum ;* and v. 71, the Latin hath *exeunte illo januam,* instead of, "when he went out into the vestibule," since the Greek is ἐξελθόντα εἰς τὸν πυλῶνα. Chap. xxviii. 2, in the Latin, after the words *revolvit lapidem,* there is an omission of "from the door," ἀπὸ θύρας.

Mark ii. 7, the Latin reads : *Quid hic sic loquitur?* *blasphemat;* instead of, "Why doth this man thus speak blasphemies?" τί οὗτος οὕτω λαλεῖ βλασφημίας ;

Mark iii. 39, in the Latin, *Reus erit æterni delicti,* instead of "eternal judgment," αἰωνίου κρίσεως. Mark xiv. 14, in the Latin there is, *Ubi est refectio mea?* instead of, "Where is the guest-chamber?" ποῦ ἐστὶ τὸ κατάλυμα ;

Luke i. 28 in the Latin runs thus, *Ave, gratia plena ;* but κεχαριτωμένη is "highly favoured" or "freely loved," not "full of grace." Luke ii. 40, the Latin hath, *puer crescebat et confortabatur,* wherein "in spirit" is left out[1]. Luke iii. 13, in the Latin, *nihil amplius, quam quod constitutum est vobis, faciatis.*

[1 πνεύματι is omitted in some Greek MSS. also.   See Grotius in loc.]

But in this place πράσσειν does not mean "to do," but "to exact;" for it is the publicans that the Baptist here addresses. Luke vi. 11, in the Latin, *ipsi repleti sunt insipientia*, instead of, "with madness ;" ἐπλήσθησαν ἀνοίας. Luke xi. 53, the old translator renders, ἀποστοματίζειν αὐτὸν ἐπὶ πλειόνων by, *os ejus opprimere de multis;* absurdly, since it means that they pressed him to speak of many things[1]. Luke xiii. 3, 4, runs thus in the Latin, *nisi pœnitentiam habueritis, omnes similiter peribitis : sicut illi decem et octo*, instead of, "or those eighteen," &c. Luke xv. 8, *Evertit domum*, instead of *everrit*, "she sweeps ;" σαροῖ τὴν οἰκίαν. A shameful and manifest error, which the Louvain editors perceived, but would not correct; I suppose on account of its antiquity, for thus hath the place been constantly read in their churches for many ages. The Ordinary Gloss interprets this woman to mean the church, who then turns her house upside down when she disturbs men's consciences with the conviction of their guilt. But Dionysius Carthusianus hath a somewhat better explanation of the way in which the house is turned upside down, that is, when the contents of the house are carried about from one place to another, as people are wont to do when they search diligently for any thing. Nay, what surprises one still more, Gregory of Rome, a thousand years ago, read and expounded *evertit domum*, Hom. 34 in Evangel. : so ancient are many of the errors of this translation. In the same chapter, verse 14, we have *postquam omnia consummasset*, instead of *consumpsisset*, δαπανήσαντος. Chap. xvi. 22 is read thus in the Latin, *Sepultus est in inferno. Elevans autem oculos, &c.* Whereupon some Latin doctors and interpreters run out into many philosophical speculations concerning the burial of the rich man in hell, which are all derived from the erroneous version of the place. For it ought to have been read, as it is read with great unanimity by the Greek copies, " The rich man also died, and was buried :" where Euthymius justly observes, that mention of the burial was made in the case of the rich, and not of the poor man ; because the poor man had a mean grave, whereas the funeral of the rich man was performed with splendour and magnificence. Then in the text a new sentence begins, " And in hell raising up his eyes," &c. Chap. xix. last verse, *Omnis*

---

[1] ἀποστοματίζειν rather means to require one to speak off-hand and without premeditation. The reader will find all the learning of the question, as to the sense of this word, in Grotius upon Luke xi. 53, and Runkhen's note upon the word in Timæus Lex. Platon.]

populus suspensus erat, audiens illum, instead of, "All the people hung upon him while they heard him." ὁ λαὸς ἅπας ἐξεκρέματο αὐτοῦ ἀκούων. John, chap. v. 16, after the words, *persequebantur Judæi Jesum*, the clause, "and desired to slay him," καὶ ἐζήτουν αὐτὸν ἀποκτεῖναι, is left out. Chap. xii. 35 : *Adhuc modicum lumen in vobis*, for, "yet a little while is the light with you," ἔτι μικρὸν χρόνον τὸ φῶς μεθ' ὑμῶν ἐστί. Chap. xxi. 22: *Sic eum volo manere donec veniam. Quid ad te?* Whence some, deceived by the error of this version, have supposed John to be still alive. But we ought to read, "If I will that he tarry till I come, what is that to thee?" In the Greek, ἐὰν αὐτὸν θέλω μένειν ἕως ἔρχομαι, τί πρός σε;

Acts ii. 42 : *Et communicatione fractionis panis*, for, "in communion and breaking of bread," καὶ τῇ κοινωνίᾳ καὶ τῇ κλάσει τοῦ ἄρτου. And at the last verse, *in idipsum²*, for, "the church," τῇ ἐκκλησίᾳ. Chap. iii. 18 : *Qui prænunciavit*, for, "which things he foretold," ἃ προκατήγγειλε. Chap. x. 30 : *Usque ad hanc horam, orans eram hora nona*, instead of, "I was fasting until this hour, and at the ninth hour I was praying:" μέχρι ταύτης τῆς ὥρας ἤμην νηστεύων³, καὶ τὴν ἐννάτην ὥραν προσευχόμενος. Also at the close of verse 32, these words, "who when he is come shall speak to thee," ὃς παραγενόμενος λαλήσει σοι, are omitted. Chap. xii. 8 : *Calcea te caligas tuas*, for, "bind on thy sandals," ὑπόδησαι τὰ σανδάλιά σου. Chap. xvi. 13 : *Ubi videbatur oratio esse*, for, "where prayer was wont to be made," οὗ ἐνομίζετο προσευχὴ εἶναι. Chap. xviii. 5 : *Instabat verbo Paulus*, for, "Paul was bound in the spirit," συνείχετο τῷ πνεύματι. In the same chapter at verse 16, *Minavit eos a tribunali*, for, "he drave them from the judgment-seat," ἀπήλασεν. And at verse 21, this clause is omitted, "I must by all means keep this feast which cometh on in Jerusalem⁴:" Δεῖ με πάντως τὴν ἑορτὴν τὴν ἐρχομένην ποιῆσαι εἰς Ἱεροσόλυμα. Chap. xix., in the last verse : *Cum nullus obnoxius sit*, for, "since there is no cause," μηδενὸς αἰτίου ὑπάρχοντος. Chap. xxii. 12 : *Vir secundum legem*, for, "a pious man according to

[2 The mistake arose from connecting the words ἐπὶ τὸ αὐτὸ, which form the commencement of the next chapter, with the close of this one. The Ethiopic agrees with the Vulgate in omitting τῇ ἐκκλησίᾳ.]
[3 Some MSS. agree with the Vulgate in omitting νηστεύων.]
[4 It is omitted in the Alex. and several other MSS.]

the law," ἀνὴρ εὐσεβής. Chap. xxiv. 14 : *Quod secundum sectam, quam dicunt hæresin, sic deservio Patri Deo meo,* instead of, " that according to the way which they call heresy, so worship I the God of my fathers :" ὅτι κατὰ τὴν ὁδὸν, ἣν λέγουσιν αἵρεσιν, οὕτω λατρεύω τῷ πατρώῳ Θεῷ. Chap. xxvii. 42 : *Ut custodias occiderent,* for, " that they should slay the prisoners[1]," ἵνα τοὺς δεσμώτας ἀποκτείνωσι.

Rom. ii. 3 : *Quod judicas,* instead of, " thou that judgest," ὁ κρίνων. Chap. v. 6 : *Ut quid enim Christus, cum adhuc infirmi essemus, &c.,* instead of, " for Christ, when we were yet without strength," ἔτι γὰρ Χριστὸς ὄντων ἡμῶν ἀσθενῶν. And verse 13 : *Peccatum non imputabatur, cum lex non esset,* for, " sin is not imputed where there is no law," ἁμαρτία οὐκ ἐλλογεῖται μὴ ὄντος νόμου. Chap. vii. 25 : *Quis me liberabit de corpore mortis hujus?* *Gratia Dei per Jesum Christum,* for, " I thank God through Jesus Christ," εὐχαριστῶ τῷ Θεῷ διὰ Ἰησοῦ Χριστοῦ. Chap. viii. 18 : *Existimo quod non sunt dignæ passiones, &c.,* for, " I reckon for certain," λογίζομαι. Chap. xii. 19 : *Non vosmet ipsos defendentes,* instead of, " avenging," ἐκδικοῦντες. Chap. xiii. 1 : *Quæ autem sunt a Deo, ordinata sunt[2],* for, " the powers that be, are ordained of God," αἱ δὲ οὖσαι ἐξουσίαι, ὑπὸ τοῦ Θεοῦ τεταγμέναι εἰσιν. Chap. xiv. 5 : *Unusquisque in suo sensu abundet,* for, " let each be fully persuaded in his own mind," ἕκαστος ἐν τῷ ἰδίῳ νοὶ πληροφορείσθω. And at verse 6 is omitted, " and he that regardeth not the day, to the Lord he doth not regard it," καὶ ὁ μὴ φρονῶν τὴν ἡμέραν Κυρίῳ οὐ φρονεῖ. Chap. xvi. 23 : *Salutat vos Gaius hospes meus, et universa ecclesia,* for, " and of the whole church," καὶ τῆς ἐκκλησίας ὅλης.

1 Cor. iii. 5 : *Ministri ejus cui credidistis,* for, " ministers by whom ye believed," διάκονοι δι' ὧν ἐπιστεύσατε. Verse 9 : *Dei adjutores,* instead of, " administrators or co-operators, σύνεργοι. Chapter vi. last verse : *In corpore vestro,* omitting[3], " and in your spirit, which are God's," καὶ ἐν τῷ πνεύματι ὑμῶν, ἅτινα ἐστὶ τοῦ Θεοῦ. Chapter ix. 22 : *Ut omnes salvos faciam,* for, " that

[1 Instances however are found in good authors of *Custodia* meaning a prisoner as well as a guard. I need not cite instances of a meaning given in every common dictionary.]

[2 The fault is in the stopping. It should be, " Quæ autem sunt, a Deo ordinatæ sunt."]

[3 This clause is omitted also in the Alexandrian and several other MSS.]

I may by all means save some," ἵνα πάντωςτινὰς σώσω⁴. Chap. xv. 23: *Deinde ii qui sunt Christi, qui in adventum ejus crediderunt*, for, "then those who are Christ's at his coming," ἔπειτα οἱ Χριστοῦ ἐν τῇ παρουσίᾳ αὐτοῦ. Verse 34: *Ad reverentiam vobis loquor*, for, "I speak to inspire you with shame," πρὸς ἐντροπὴν ὑμῖν λέγω. Verse 51: *Omnes quidem resurgemus, sed non omnes immutabimur*, instead of, "We shall not indeed all sleep, but we shall all be changed," πάντες μὲν οὐ κοιμηθησόμεθα, πάντες δὲ ἀλλαγησόμεθα⁵. Verse 54, there is omitted, "when this corruptible shall have put on incorruption," ὅταν τὸ φθαρτὸν τοῦτο ἐνδύσηται ἀφθαρσίαν. Verse 55: *Ubi est mors stimulus tuus?* for, "Where is thy victory, O grave or hell?" ποῦ σοῦ ᾄδη τὸ νῖκος;

2 Cor. i. 11: *Ut ex multarum personis facierum ejus quœ in nobis donationis, per multos gratiœ agantur pro nobis*. The words in the Greek are, ἵνα ἐκ πολλῶν προσώπων τὸ εἰς ἡμᾶς χάρισμα διὰ πολλῶν εὐχαριστηθῇ ὑπὲρ ἡμῶν· that is, "that the gift conferred upon us by many persons may be celebrated by many in returning thanks on our account." Chapter vii. 8: *Non me pœnitet etsi pœniteret*, instead of, "I do not repent, though I did repent," οὐ μεταμέλομαι, εἰ καὶ μετεμελόμην. Chapter ix. 1: *Ex abundanti est mi scribere*, for, "it is superfluous," περισσόν μοι ἐστί. Chap. xii. 11: *Factus sum insipiens*, omitting the next word "in boasting," καυχώμενος.

Gal. iii. 24; *Lex pœdagogus noster fuit in Christo*, for "to Christ," εἰς Χριστόν. Chap. iv. 18: *Bonum œmulamini in bono semper*, for, "it is good to be zealously affected always in a good thing;" καλὸν τὸ ζηλοῦσθαι ἐν καλῷ πάντοτε. At the end of this chapter the words, *Qua libertate Christus nos liberavit*, should be joined with the commencement of the next chapter. "In the liberty, wherewith Christ hath made us free, stand fast:" τῇ ἐλευθερίᾳ ᾗ Χριστὸς ἡμᾶς ἠλευθέρωσε στήκετε.

Eph. i. 22, *Super omnem ecclesiam*, instead of, "over all things to the church," ὑπὲρ πάντα τῇ ἐκκλησίᾳ. Chap. ii. 10: *Creati in Christo Jesu in operibus bonis*, for, "to good works, ἐπὶ

[⁴ Several MSS. read πάντας for πάντως τινὰς, and Mill was disposed to think it the true reading.]

[⁵ There is here considerable difference in the MSS. The Clermont reads with the Vulgate. Lachmann's text gives πάντες [μὲν] κοιμηθησόμεθα, οὐ πάντες δὲ ἀλλαγησόμεθα, following the Alexandrian MS. though not exactly.]

ἔργοις ἀγαθοῖς. Chap. v. 4, *Quæ ad rem non pertinent*, for, " which are not convenient :" τὰ μὴ ἀνήκοντα.

Col. ii. 14 : *Chirographum decreti*, for, " contained in ordinances," τοῖς δόγμασιν.

2 Thess. ii. 13 : *Elegit nos Dominus primitias*[1] *in salutem*, instead of, " from the beginning," ἀπ' ἀρχῆς.

1 Tim. vi. 5 : It omits, " withdraw from those that are such[2]," ἀφίστασο ἀπὸ τῶν τοιούτων. 2 Tim. ii. 4 : *Ut ei placeat, cui se probavit*, for, " that he may please him who hath chosen him to be a soldier :" ἵνα τῷ στρατολογήσαντι ἀρέσῃ.

Philem. 9 : *Cum sis talis ut Paulus senex*, instead of, " since I am such an one as Paul the aged."

Heb. i. 3 : *Purgationem peccatorum faciens*, omitting the words, " by himself," δι' ἑαυτοῦ[3]. Heb. iii. 3 : *Quanto ampliorem honorem habet domus*[4], for, " as he that built it hath more honour than the house," &c. Heb. xii. 8 : *Ergo adulteri*[5] *et non filii estis*, for "bastards and spurious, not sons :" ἄρα νόθοι ἐστὲ, καὶ οὐχ υἱοί. In the same chapter, verse 18, *accessibilem*[6] *ignem*, for, "inflamed with fire," κεκαυμένῳ πυρί.

James i. 19 : *Scitis, fratres mei dilectissimi*, instead of, "Wherefore, my beloved brethren," ὥστε[7], ἀδελφοί μου ἀγαπητοί.

1 Pet. ii. 5 : *Superædificamini domos spirituales*, for, " a spiritual house," οἶκος πνευματικός. Ibid. verse 23 : *Tradebat autem judicanti se injuste*, for, " that judgeth righteously," τῷ κρίνοντι δικαίως. 1 Pet. iv. 14, it leaves out, " on their part he is blasphemed, but on your part he is glorified[8] :" κατὰ μὲν αὐτοὺς βλασφημεῖται, κατὰ δὲ ὑμᾶς δοξάζεται.

2 Pet. i. 3 : *Quomodo omnia nobis divinæ virtutis suæ, quæ*

[1 The Vulgate translator seems to have read ἀπαρχήν, (which is still exhibited by some Greek MSS.) unless, indeed, *primitias* be itself a corruption of *primitus*.]

[2 The clause is also omitted by the Alexandrian, Clermont, and other ancient MSS., and by the Ethiopic and Coptic versions.]

[3 They are omitted in the Alex. and Vatican MSS., and several others.]

[4 But *domus* is here in the genitive, being governed of *ampliorem*, to correspond, barbarously enough, with the Greek construction.]

[5 But *adulter* is used adjectively in the sense of *adulterinus*, by Pliny, N. H. L. 33. c. 7.]

[6 Here we should read " accensibilem," the translator taking κεκαυμένῳ to agree with πυρὶ, as ψηλαφωμένῳ does with ὄρει. See Grotius in loc.]

[7 The Alex., Vatican, and some other MSS. read ἴστε.]

[8 It is omitted in the Alex. and some other MSS.]

ad vitam et pietatem, donata sunt, for, "forasmuch as his divine
power hath given us all things that are needful for life and
godliness:" ὡς πάντα ἡμῖν τῆς θείας δυνάμεως αὐτοῦ τὰ πρὸς
ζωὴν καὶ εὐσεβείαν δεδωρημένης⁹ : verse 16, *indoctas fabulas se-
quuti,* for "learned," σεσοφισμένοις μύθοις ἐξακολουθήσαντες, and
in the same verse, *Christi virtutem et præscientiam* for, "the
power and presence," δύναμιν καὶ παρουσίαν. 2 Pet. ii. 8 : *Aspectu
enim et auditu justus erat, habitans apud eos, qui de die in diem
animam justam iniquis operibus excruciabant;* instead of, "for in
seeing and hearing that righteous man, dwelling amongst them,
vexed his righteous soul from day to day with their unrighteous
deeds:" βλέμματι γὰρ καὶ ἀκοῇ ὁ δίκαιος, ἐγκατοικῶν ἐν αὐτοῖς,
ἡμέραν ἐξ ἡμέρας ψυχὴν δικαίαν ἀνόμοις ἔργοις ἐβασάνιζεν.

1 John v. 17 : *Et est peccatum ad mortem,* for, "and there is
a sin *not* unto death;" καὶ ἔστιν ἁμαρτία οὐ πρὸς θάνατον¹⁰.
3 John, 4. *Majorem horum non habeo gratiam,* for, "I have
no joy greater than these," μειζοτέραν τούτων οὐκ ἔχω χαράν¹¹.

Jude, 5 : *Scientes semel omnia,* for, "since ye know this once,"
εἰδότας ἅπαξ τοῦτο¹². Rev. ii. 14 : *edere et fornicari,* for, "to eat
those things which are sacrificed to idols, and to commit whore-
dom :" φαγεῖν εἰδωλόθυτα, καὶ πορνεῦσαι.

I have selected a few instances from many. Were I to pursue
them all, I should make a volume. But these sufficiently prove the
infinite and inveterate faultiness of the old Latin Version in the new
Testament. Erasmus, therefore, when he desired a review of the
new Testament, preferred translating it anew according to the Greek
verity to spending his pains in correcting this old Latin edition.
In like manner, Isidore Clarius of Brescia¹³ bemoans the wretched
and squalid plight of this edition in both Testaments, and wonders
at the negligence of learned men, who have never attempted to
remove the innumerable errors, under which he affirms it to labour,
adding that he hath himself noted and amended eight thousand
passages¹⁴.

Such is that edition, even by their own confession, which we

[⁹ A couple of unimportant MSS. read here δεδωρημένα with the Vulgate.]
[¹⁰ The οὐ is also omitted in the Ethiopic.]
[¹¹ Some MSS. here read χάριν with the Vulgate.]
[¹² The Alex. and other most ancient MSS. here read πάντα with the Vulgate. The Syriac appears to have read πάντες.]
[¹³ In the preface to his edition of the Vulgate, Venice 1542.]
[¹⁴ Etsi ea quam diximus usi fuerimus moderatione, loca tamen ad octo

are now forsooth, at the pleasure of the Tridentine Fathers, commanded to receive as authentic scripture. But let them take to
themselves this old edition of theirs, while we, as the course to
which reason constrains us, and Augustine, Jerome, and other illustrious divines persuade us, and even the ancient decrees of the
Roman pontiffs themselves admonish us, return to the sacred originals of scripture.

CHAPTER XIII.

WHEREIN THE STATE OF THE QUESTION CONCERNING VERNACULAR VERSIONS IS EXPLAINED.

WE have now completed the first part of this second question,
wherein we have proved that the authentic scripture lies not in the
Latin version of the old translator, as the Tridentine fathers and
the Jesuits would have it, but in the Hebrew and Greek originals.
We have obviated the arguments of our opponents, and confirmed
our own opinion. Now follows the second part of this question,
which hath two principal divisions. For we must, in the first place,
discuss vernacular versions of the scripture; and, in the second
place, the performance of divine service in the vulgar tongue.
Upon both subjects there are controversies between us.

Now, as to vernacular versions of scripture, we must first of all
inquire what is the certain and fixed opinion of the papists thereupon. Concerning vernacular versions of scripture there are at the
present day three opinions entertained by men. The first, of those
who absolutely deny that the scriptures should be translated into
the vulgar tongue.

The second, the opposite of the former, is the opinion of those
who think that the holy scriptures should by all means be translated
into the vulgar tongues of all people.

The third is the opinion of those who neither absolutely condemn, nor absolutely permit, vernacular versions of the scriptures,
but wish that in this matter certain exceptions should be made,
and regard had to times, places, and persons. This last is the

millia annotata atque emendata a nobis sunt. Of these " octo millia," Walton,
by what Hody calls "ingens memoriæ lapsus," has made *octoginta* millia erro-
rum.—Proleg. §. 10. (T. II. p. 250. Wrangham.)]

opinion held by the papists, and the judgment ratified at Trent. They do not then seem to affirm that it is simply impious or unlawful to translate the scriptures, or read them in the vulgar tongue; but they do not choose that this should be done commonly or promiscuously by all, or under any other conditions than those which the council hath prescribed.

There is extant concerning this matter a decree, in the fourth rule of the index of prohibited books published by Pius IV., and approved by the council of Trent; which determination contains four parts: first, that no man may read the scriptures in the vulgar tongue, unless he have obtained permission from the bishops and inquisitors: secondly, that the bishops should consult with the parish priest and confessor: thirdly, that the bishops themselves must not permit every kind of vernacular versions, but only those published by some catholic author: fourthly, that the reading even of these must not be permitted to every one, but only to those who, in the judgment of their curates and confessors, are likely to receive no damage therefrom, but rather an augmentation of faith, —those, that is, and those only, who they hope will be rendered thereby still more perverse and obstinate. Such are the subtle cautions of that decree; whence it is evident that the reading of the scriptures in the vulgar tongue is allowed to as small a number of persons as possible. They subjoin to this a reason which looks plausible at first sight;—that it hath appeared by experience that, if the Bible were allowed to be read by all, without distinction, more injury than advantage would result, on account of the rashness of mankind. The force of this argument we shall examine in its proper place.

Our Rhemish brethren are profuse of words in praising this decree, in the preface to their English version of the new Testament. "Holy church," they say, "knowing by her divine and most sincere wisdom, how, where, when, and to whom, these her maisters and spouses gifts are to be bestowed to the most good of the faithful; and therefore, neither generally permitteth that which must needs doe hurt to the unworthy, nor absolutely condemneth that which may do much good to the worthie[1]:"—and so they conclude that the scriptures, although translated truly and in accordance with the catholic faith, must not be read by every one who has a mind to read them, but only by those who are specially and by name licensed by their ordinaries, and whom their curates

[1] Preface to the Reader, p. 4. Rhemes. 1582.]

[WHITAKER.]

14

and confessors have testified and declared to be fit and proper
readers of the same. Now then, you sufficiently perceive that all
men are excluded from the perusal of the scriptures in the vulgar
tongues, save those who shall have procured a licence to read them;
and such a licence none can procure, but those who are certainly
known, by confession, and the whole course of their lives, to be
obstinate papists. Those, therefore, who might desire to read the
scriptures in order that they might learn from the scriptures the
true faith and religion, these, unless they first swear an absolute
obedience to the Roman pontiff, are by no means permitted to get
a glimpse of the sacred books of scripture. Who does not see that
the scriptures are taken from the people, in order that they may
be kept in darkness and ignorance, and that so provision may be
made for the safety of the Roman church and the papal sovereignty,
which could never hold its ground if the people were permitted to
read the scriptures? Wretched indeed is that religion, and
desperate that state of things, where they are compelled to withdraw the scriptures from the eyes of men, and take off the people
from the reading of the scriptures; which is the course pursued
by our adversaries, as is manifest from the decree of the Tridentine
council, and from the versions of the Rhemists. Such is also the
opinion of Bellarmine, Lib. II. c. 15. To which let me subjoin the
testimony of Johannes Molanus, a divine of Louvain, and censor of
books to both the pope and the king; who hath these words, in
his book of Practical Theology, Tract. III. c. 27: " Yet we deny
that the study of the scriptures is required of them [laymen]; yea,
we affirm that they are safely debarred the reading of the scriptures, and that it is sufficient for them to govern the tenor of their
life by the directions of the pastors and doctors of the church[1];"—
than which nothing could be said more shocking to common sense
and decency. Similar to this is the opinion of Hosius, in his small
piece upon divine service in the vulgar tongue, and that of the
censors of Cologne against the preface of Monhemius. Sanders
too, in the seventh book of his *Monarchia visibilis*, says that it
is heretical to affirm that the scriptures ought necessarily to be
translated into the vulgar languages.

Such then is the determination of our adversaries. We, on the

[1] Negamus tamen ab eis requiri studium scripturarum : imo salubriter
dicimus eos a lectione scripturarum arceri, sufficereque eis, ut ex præscripto
pastorum et doctorum ecclesiæ vitæ cursum moderentur. p. 105. 2. Colon.
1585.]

contrary, affirm that the reading of the scriptures should be common to all men, and that none, however unlearned, should be debarred or deterred from reading them, but rather that all should be stirred up to the frequent and diligent perusal of them; and that, not only when the privilege of reading them is permitted by their prelates, but also although their ordinaries and confessors should prohibit it never so much.

Accordingly we say that the scriptures should be translated into all the languages of Christendom, that all men may be enabled to read them in their own tongue. This is declared by the confession of all the churches. This is true; and this we shall shew to be agreeable to the scriptures. The state of the question, therefore, is,—whether or not vernacular versions of the scriptures are to be set forth and permitted to all promiscuously. They hold the negative, we the affirmative; and we must first examine and refute their arguments, and then apply ourselves to the support of our own cause. Our attention shall be principally directed to our Jesuit Bellarmine.

CHAPTER XIV.

WHEREIN THE ARGUMENTS OF OUR ADVERSARIES AGAINST VERNACULAR VERSIONS ARE REFUTED.

THE first argument of the Jesuit, whereby he proves vernacular versions by no means necessary, is drawn from the practice of the church under the old Testament, from the time of Ezra until Christ. He affirms, that from the times of Ezra the Hebrew language ceased to be the vulgar tongue amongst the people of God, and yet that the scriptures were in the church in Hebrew after those times. But how does he prove that the Hebrew language was then unknown to the people? Because, says he, the Jews who dwelt in Babylon forgot their own language, and learned the Chaldee, and thenceforward the Chaldee or Syriac became their mother tongue. It remains that we listen to the testimonies by which all these statements are substantiated.

The first is taken from the old Testament, Nehem. viii.: where we read that Nehemiah, and Ezra, and the Levites read the book of the law to the people, and gave the interpretation, because the people understood nothing of what was read to them; but upon Ezra's supplying the interpretation the people were greatly rejoiced, because they then understood the words of the law.

I answer, in the first place, that the Jesuit hath grossly abused that place in Nehemiah. For it is clear from the passage itself, that the people did understand correctly enough the words which were read to them; whence it follows that the language was not unknown to them. At verse 3, Ezra is said to have brought the book of the law, and to have read in the presence of a multitude of men and women, and as many as were capable of understanding, that is, who were old enough to understand anything, or, as the Hebrew expression is, who *heard intelligently*[1]. Therefore they not only heard, but heard intelligently, that is, understood what they heard. Hence, in verse 4, Ezra is said to have read before the men and women, and those who understood; and the people to have had their ears attentive to the book of the law. Now, why should the people have listened so attentively, if they did not understand what they heard? In the same place, Ezra is related to have read out of the book from morning until evening; and, in verse 19, every day for seven days, from the first day until the last. Assuredly, he would not have taken so much trouble in reading, unless he had auditors who could understand him; and it was certainly very far from a prophet's wisdom to assemble a multitude of persons, then come forth into the midst of them, open the book, and read so earnestly, and for the space of so many hours, what the people could not at all understand. Besides, what was the reason of his reading (v. 9[2]) *plainly*, as Tremellius, or *distinctly*, as the old translator renders it, but that, by that plain reading of the scripture, the whole people might the better understand what was being read to them? For it is no matter whether you read well or ill to those who understand nothing of what is read.

But Bellarmine objects that great joy was excited in the people, when by Ezra's interpretation they came to understand the words of the law. What a subtle Jesuit! He feigns that Ezra first read to the people words which they did not understand, and afterwards rendered or translated them into other words, and that language with which the people were acquainted; which is alto-

[1] הַמְּבִינִים.]

[2] ver. 8. in the Hebrew. The word is מְפֹרָשׁ.]

gether absurd. For Ezra read the words of the law openly and publicly from a pulpit, and continued that reading through the space of some hours, then expounded the scripture which had been read, and opened up the sense and meaning of the words to the people. For so at verse 9, the Levites are said "to have expounded the sense, and given the meaning by the scripture itself," as Tremellius hath most correctly interpreted the passage. Vatablus hath translated it thus, "explaining the sense, and teaching as they read[3];" which is not very different. And the old translator thus, "Plainly that it might be understood; and they understood when it was read[4];" which sufficiently proves that the people understood what was read to them. Ezra was therefore said to be skilful in the law, not because he could read and understand the words and text of the law, but because he explained the sense and meaning of the law, so as to enable the people to understand it. And hence sprang that gladness, which the scripture tells us that the people felt when they heard the law expounded by Ezra. The thing is plain and certain, nor do we need the aid of commentaries.

The other testimony which the Jesuit uses in this matter, to prove that Hebrew was not the vulgar tongue of the Jews after Ezra, is drawn from the new Testament, from which it appears that the people used the Syriac language. For *Talitha cumi*, Mark v., *Abba*, Mark xiv., *Aceldama*, Acts i., and Matth xxvii. *Golgotha* and *Pascha*, are neither Greek nor Hebrew. More examples are given by Jerome in his book, de Nominib. Hebr. The same fact is indicated by the saying, John vii., "This multitude which knoweth not the law." Hence it is manifest that the Hebrew was not at that time the mother tongue of the Jews.

I answer, in the first place, that this may, to some extent, be allowed true, but that, in the sense in which Bellarmine affirms it, it is altogether false. I acknowledge that the language was not pure Hebrew, but corrupted with many alien and foreign terms, so as to become, as it were, a new dialect compounded of Hebrew and Chaldee. Yet, in the meanwhile, the people had not forgotten the Hebrew language, neither immediately after the captivity, nor in the succeeding times. For, Nehem. xiii., certain Jews are said to have married wives of Ashdod, whose children spake in the language of Ashdod, and not in Hebrew. The people in general

[3 Explicantes sententiam et erudientes inter legendum.]
[4 Aperte ad intelligendum; et intellexerunt cum legeretur.]

therefore spoke Hebrew.   Indeed it is impossible that, in the space
of seventy or even one hundred years, the people should so wholly
lose their native language as not even to understand it.   If this
had been the case, Haggai, Zechariah, and Malachi,—prophets
who lived after the return—would not have published their discourses in Hebrew, but in the vulgar tongue.   It is, therefore,
absolutely certain, that the Jews understood Hebrew after the times
of Ezra.

Secondly, as to the terms which are not pure Hebrew in the
new Testament, the thing proved comes merely to what I have
observed already, that the language of the people had, at that
time, greatly degenerated from its native integrity ; yet not to
such a degree as would be inconsistent with supposing that Hebrew
was spoken by the better educated, and understood by all ; so as
that the scriptures, when publicly read in Hebrew, might be
understood by the people.   Christ, therefore, John v. 39, bids
even the laity " search the scriptures."   Greek they did not
understand ; and the Chaldee paraphrase was not then published,
or, if published, was unintelligible to them.   It was the Hebrew
scriptures, therefore, which Christ commanded them to read ; which
command he never would have issued, if the people could not
understand the scriptures in the Hebrew language.   The Jews
of Berea, also, of whom we have an account, Acts xvii. 11, searched
the scriptures diligently.   So Christ read the prophet Isaiah in
the synagogue, as we find in Luke iv. 18 ; and no one doubts
that he read it in Hebrew.   So Acts xv. 21, James says, that
" Moses of old times hath in every city them that preach him,
being read in the synagogues every sabbath-day."   Whence also
it is plain, that ἀναγινώσκειν and κηρύσσειν are different things.
And, Acts xiii. 15, "after the reading of the law and the prophets,"
Paul was desired to address the people if it seemed fit to him.
What end could it serve to read the scriptures so diligently in the
synagogues, and that the people should assemble every sabbath-day
to hear them read, if they were read in an unknown language ?
The title which Pilate affixed to the cross was inscribed with
Hebrew words, and many of the Jews read it, John xix. 20.   And
Paul, Acts xxvi. 14, says that he heard Christ speaking to him " in
the Hebrew tongue."   He himself also addressed the people in the
Hebrew tongue, Acts xxi. 40.   And (chap. xxii. at the commencement) when they heard him speaking to them in the Hebrew
tongue, they kept the rather quiet, and rendered him still greater

attention. Theophylact observes upon that place, ὁρᾷς πῶς αὐτοὺς εἷλε τὸ ὁμοιόφωνον; εἶχον γάρ τινα αἰδῶ πρὸς τὴν γλῶτταν ἐκείνην[1], as much as to say, that they were caught by perceiving his language to be the same as their own, and by a certain reverence which they entertained for that tongue.   I produce these testimonies not to prove this language to have been pure Hebrew ; but to shew that it was not altogether different from the Hebrew, since it is called Hebrew, and was understood by the people. Now it could not be called Hebrew, if those who used it were not even able to understand Hebrew.   Although, therefore, it was full of foreign mixtures, which the people had brought with them from Babylon, or contracted from the neighbouring nations ; yet it retained a great deal of its native genius, enough to enable the people, though they could not speak Hebrew as purely as in former times, to recognise and understand the scriptures when read to them in Hebrew.   The difference is not so great as to prevent this.   For, although the *dialect* of the Scots and English, nay, of the southern and northern English themselves, is not the same ; yet the Scots read the English version of the scriptures in their churches, and the people understand it.   Thus the Jews, though they did not speak pure Hebrew, as the Scots do not speak pure English, could yet understand the scriptures when read to them in Hebrew by their priests and Levites.   Thus the bystanders could sufficiently understand Peter, although they knew him to be a Galilean by his manner of speaking.   Matth. xxvi. 73. Formerly the Greek language had various dialects, the Ionic, the Doric, and the rest ; yet all Greeks were able to understand each other.

Thirdly, the Jesuit hath shamefully perverted the testimony from John vii. 49 : "This multitude which knoweth not the law." For the saying is to be understood not of the language, words, and letters, but of the sense and meaning of the law. The Pharisees arrogated to themselves a most exact knowledge of the law, and, puffed up with that conceit, thus proudly despised the common people.

Now as to the assumption, that the scriptures were at that time read in Hebrew in the synagogues, I acknowledge it to be true.   Why should they not have been read in Hebrew, when the people understood them in that language ?   Bellarmine ought to have proved that the people could not understand the Hebrew language ; and then he would have done something to the purpose. But there are no proofs to demonstrate that assertion, which hath

[1 Opp. T. III. p. 160. Venet. 1758.]

been already refuted by many arguments. For as to the objection urged in the epitome of Bellarmine's lectures,—that when Christ exclaimed, *Eli, Eli, lama sabachthani,* some said that he called for *Elias,* because they did not understand the language in which he spoke,—I reply, that it may be either that they mocked him maliciously, or had not perfectly heard the words, or were soldiers who were generally foreigners and Romans; which latter supposition is rendered probable by the circumstance that, whereas Luke tells us that "the soldiers gave him vinegar to drink," chap. xxiii. 36; Matthew writes, that one of those who said this hastily filled a sponge with vinegar, and presented it to Christ, chap. xxvii. 48. Jerome explains it otherwise, supposing that the Jews, in their usual manner, seized upon the occasion of maligning the Lord, as if he implored the assistance of Elias through inability to defend and deliver himself. Nothing, therefore, can be elicited from this passage, to prove that the people did not understand the Hebrew language.

The second argument is taken from the example and practice of the apostles. For the apostles preached the gospel through the whole world, and founded churches, as is plain from Rom. x., Col. i., Mark xvi., Irenæus, Lib. i. c. 3[1], who says, that in his time churches were founded in the East, in Libya, in Egypt, in Spain, in Germany, in Gaul; and yet the apostles did not write the gospels or their epistles in the languages of those people to which they preached, but only in Hebrew or Greek. This argument is borrowed by Bellarmine from Sanders, *de visibil. Monarch.* Lib. VII.

I answer, in the first place: the church could for some time do without vernacular versions, just as for some time it could do without the scriptures of the new Testament; for everything was not immediately committed to writing. Meanwhile, however, the principal heads of the doctrine of the gospel were explained to all, and set forth in that language which they understood; and then all necessary matters were committed to writing.

Secondly, I confess the apostles and evangelists did not write the gospel in as many various languages as they preached it in, by word of mouth; for that would have been an infinite labour: it was enough that they left this doctrine of the gospel written in one

[1 Οὔτε αἱ ἐν Γερμανίαις ἱδρυμέναι ἐκκλησίαι .... οὔτε ἐν ταῖς Ἰβηρίαις, οὔτε ἐν Κελτοῖς, οὔτε κατὰ τὰς ἀνατολὰς, οὔτε ἐν Αἰγύπτῳ, οὔτε ἐν Λιβύῃ.— p. 52, B.]

language, from which it might easily be drawn and derived into all other tongues.

Thirdly, they wrote in that language which was the most common, and understood by the greatest number of people, and out of which the scriptures might with most facility be rendered and translated into other tongues,—that is, in the Greek; which, although it was not the mother tongue and native language of all, yet was to most by no means an unknown tongue. For all those nations, whom Irenæus enumerates in that book, either spoke or understood Greek. The Oriental churches were composed of Greeks; and that the Egyptians understood Greek, is manifest from their bishops and doctors, Origen, Alexander, Athanasius, Theophilus, Cyril, who were Alexandrians, and published all their works in Greek. Epiphanius had his see in Cyprus, and delivered his instructions to his people in Greek. At Jerusalem Cyril and others imparted the gospel to their flock in Greek, and the Catechetical Discourses of Cyril written in Greek are still extant. In Gaul, Irenæus himself wrote his books in Greek; which shews that the Greek language was not unknown to the Lyonnese and Gauls. In Italy too Greek was understood, and therefore Paul wrote his Epistle to the Romans in that language: for he would not have written it in Greek, if those to whom he wrote could not have understood it. And Irenæus, cited by Eusebius, Lib. v. c. 24, testifies that Anicetus the bishop of Rome gave Polycarp liberty "to administer the eucharist in his church[2];" which he would not have done, if the Romans could not understand Polycarp who was a Grecian. But, however the case may have been, there were persons who could readily interpret, and the scriptures were immediately translated into almost all languages, into Latin, at least, by many hands, since Augustine, as we have already heard, writes, that, in his time there were innumerable Latin versions. And although a knowledge of Greek was not so common in Africa, yet they had versions of their own, as we learn

[2 καὶ ἐν τῇ ἐκκλησίᾳ παρεχώρησεν ὁ Ἀνίκητος τὴν εὐχαριστίαν τῷ Πολυκάρπῳ κατ᾽ ἐντροπὴν δηλονότι.—H. E. Lib. v. c. 24. (Tom. II. p. 128. ed. Heinich. Lipsiæ, 1828.) Valesius understands these words in the same sense as Whitaker. But Le Moyne, Prolegom. in Var. S. p. 28, and Heinichen in loc. contend, that Irenæus only meant to say that Anicetus gave the Eucharist to Polycarp. However the word παρεχώρησε seems in favour of Whitaker's construction. Lowth compares Constitut. Apostol. II. 58, ἐπιτρέψεις δ᾽ αὐτῷ (that is, a foreign bishop visiting another bishop's see) καὶ τὴν εὐχαριστίαν ἀνοῖσαι.]

from Tertullian, Cyprian, and Augustine, within 400, or 300, or 200, years after Christ.

But Bellarmine objects, that Peter wrote to the Jews in Greek, and that James did the same; and John, in like manner, his Epistle to the Parthians, as Augustine tells us[1], Quæst. Evangel. l. II. quæst. 39, and Hyginus in Epist. I., and Pope John II. in his Epistle to Valerius : and yet Greek was the mother tongue, neither of the Jews nor of the Parthians.

I answer, in the first place, that I cannot see what this is meant to prove, unless it be that the apostles deliberately wrote to some persons what they could not possibly understand; which is a course very abhorrent from the apostles' real purpose.

Secondly, the Jews in their dispersion had learned the Greek language, which was then the language most commonly used by all men, sufficiently to understand the epistles which they received written in Greek from the apostles. And the apostles knew that those letters would be still more profitable to others than to the Jews, and therefore wrote them not in the Jewish but in the Greek language.

Thirdly, I do not think that John wrote his Epistle to the Parthians. Whence Augustine derived this account, is uncertain[2]. One might just as well pretend that he wrote to the Indians as to the Parthians. But suppose he did write to these latter,—still the Parthians do not seem to have been wholly unacquainted with Greek, since Plutarch, in his life of Crassus, tells us that the slaughtered Crassus was mocked by the Parthians in Greek verses[3].

[1 Secundum sententiam hanc etiam illud dictum est a Johanne in Epistola ad Parthos : 'Dilectissimi, nunc filii Dei sumus,' &c.—Opp. T. III. p. 2.]

[2 "How Augustine and some Latins call this Epistle *ad Parthos*, we may explain in the following manner. The Second Epistle of John was called by the ancients *Epistola ad Virgines*, and consequently in Greek, πρὸς παρθένους. Clemens expresses himself thus in the Adumbrations : *Secunda Johannis Epistola, quæ ad Virgines scripta est, simplicissima est.*—Tom. II. Op. Clem. Alex. p. 10. 11. edit. Venet. We find in Greek MSS. the subscription πρὸς πάρθους, in the second Epistle; whence Whiston's conjecture in the "Commentary on the three catholic Epistles of St John," London, 1719, p. 6, that πάρθους was an abbreviation of παρθένους, is confirmed."—Hug. Introd. to N. T. *Waits' transl.* Vol. II. p. 255. Dr Wait, in a note, gives Στρώματα as the proper Greek title of the Adumbrations, but this is a mistake. The book meant is the Ὑποτυπώσεις, from which these Latin collections were made by Cassiodorus.]

[3 ᾀδομένων δὲ τῶν ἐφεξῆς ἀμοιβαίων πρὸς τὸν χορὸν,

But to all objections of this sort one answer is sufficient,—that the apostles chose to use one language for writing, which was the best known of all, in order that what they wrote might with the greater facility be understood by all; which design of theirs is most plainly repugnant to the theory of the papists. And although all might not understand that language, yet the apostolic scripture might with the utmost ease and convenience be translated out of it, and transmitted to the tongues of other nations and countries. Nor was it to be expected that the apostles should write to each people in the mother tongue of every several region.

The third argument is drawn from the use of the universal church; and the conclusion is inferred thus: that which the universal church hath held and observed is right: now, the universal church hath ever confined itself to these three languages, Hebrew, Greek, and Latin, in the common and public use of the scriptures; therefore no other versions are necessary. He proves the major by the testimony of Augustine, Epist. 118[1], where he says that it is a piece of the wildest insolence to dispute against that which is practised by the universal church. And the same father, in his fourth book of Baptism against the Donatists, lays it down, that whatever is practised in the universal church, if its beginning cannot be assigned, should be believed to descend from apostolic tradition, and to have been always as it is now. To the same purpose he adduces also the testimony of Leo from his second discourse *De Jejunio Pentecostes*. He subjoins that now, wherever catholics are, use is made only of the Greek and Latin languages in the public reading of the scriptures, and that the commencement of this custom cannot be assigned.

I answer, in the first place, that this is not the proper time for disputing concerning ecclesiastical traditions and customs. We shall, if the Lord permit, handle that whole question hereafter in its appropriate place.

Secondly, we should consider, not so much what hath been done or observed in the Church, as what ought to have been done and observed. For it does not follow, if the public use of the Latin

τίς ἐφόνευσεν ;
ἐμὸν τὸ γέρας.
Plut. Opp. T. I. 565, A. Francof. 1620.
The lines in which Crassus was so barbarously ridiculed were taken from the Bacchæ of Euripides, and Plutarch tells us that both Hyrodes and Artavasdes were familiar with the Greek literature.]
[1 Ep. 54. p. 164. Opp. T. II. Bassan. 1797.]

tongue exclusively hath obtained in Italy, Spain, France, Germany, and the rest of these nations, that therefore such a practice is in no way open to reprehension; but what we must look to is, whether these churches have done right in publicly reading the scriptures in an unknown tongue. And if the church have forbidden the scriptures to be read in any tongue but the Latin, we must not therefore think that the church hath committed no error in such an inhibition.

Thirdly, that is altogether false which he asserts of this having been the unbroken custom and tradition of the universal church, as shall presently appear. Wherefore these opinions of Augustine and Leo are irrelevant to the present subject, and we seem able to concede that whatever the universal church hath always held is apostolic: but nothing which can justly claim that character is popish.

The whole force of this argument depends upon the proof of the assumption; for which many things are adduced, which we must discuss severally. Nor must you think that time is spent in vain upon these; since they are necessary for the refutation of our adversaries.

Now, first, Augustine is said to affirm, Doctr. Christ. Lib. ii. c. 11, that the scripture was wont to to be read in the church only in three languages, the Hebrew, Greek, and Latin. But, if you will consult the place itself, you will perceive that nothing of the kind is said by Augustine. What Augustine says is[1], that to persons whose language is the Latin, the knowledge of two other tongues is needful, namely, of the Hebrew and the Greek: he subjoins as the reason, " in order that they may be able to recur to the previous exemplars,"—that is, the originals. Does it follow that, because the Latins ought to procure for themselves some knowledge of the Hebrew and Greek tongues in order that they may the better understand the sense of scripture, therefore the scriptures were not customarily read in any but these three languages? For it is to the Latins that Augustine delivers these precepts: he says expressly, " men of the Latin language, whom we have now undertaken to instruct." Hence nothing can be concluded against us, but something may be concluded against them. For, if

[1 Et Latinæ quidem linguæ homines, quos nunc instruendos suscepimus, duabus aliis ad scripturarum divinarum cognitionem opus habent, Hebræa scilicet et Græca, ut ad exemplaria præcedentia recurratur, si quam dubitationem attulerit Latinorum interpretum infinita varietas.]

the Latins ought to learn the Hebrew and Greek languages, to
enable them to understand the scriptures aright, and to square
their versions by the rule of the originals; it follows that more
deference should be given to the Hebrew and Greek editions than
to the Latin, and consequently, that the Latin is not, as they would
have it, authentic.

As to the statement which the Jesuit subjoins, that no ancient
author hath mentioned any other version, I am amazed that he
should have brought himself to make such an assertion. For
Jerome, whom they make the author of the Latin Vulgate, translated the scriptures into the Dalmatian, which was his mother
tongue[2]. This is so certain that Hosius, in his book *de Sacro Vernacule Legendo*, writes thus : " It is undoubted that Jerome
translated the sacred books into Dalmatian[3]." And in the same
book he praises the Dalmatian language, and declares it to be
very famous. So Alphonsus de Castro, Lib. I. c. 13 ; " We confess that the sacred books were formerly translated into the vulgar
tongue[4]:" and he cites Erasmus, who writes that Jerome translated
the scriptures into the Dalmatian language. Harding, Art. III.
sect. 38[5], writes that the Armenians, Russians, Ethiopians, Dalmatians and Muscovites read the scriptures in their own vernacular
tongues. Eckius makes the same confession, in his Enchiridion
de Missis Latine Dicendis[6]. Cornelius Agrippa, in his book of the
Vanity of the Sciences (if that author deserve any credit), says
that it was decreed by the council of Nice, that no Christian should
be without a bible in his house[7]. Socrates too testifies, that Ulphi-
lus, a bishop of the Goths, who was present at the council of Nice,
translated the scriptures into the Gothic language, in order that the
people might learn them. His words are, Lib. IV. c. 38[8]: " Having

[2 This is now universally allowed to be a mistake. It is exposed by
Hody, Lib. III. pars II. c. 2. § 8. p. 362.]

[3 Dalmatica lingua sacros libros Hieronymum vertisse constat.—Opp.
Col. 1584. T. I. p. 664.]

[4 Fatemur . . . olim sacros libros in linguam vulgarem fuisse translatos.
—Col. 1539. fol. 28. 2.]

[5 See Jewel, Controversy with Harding, Vol. I. Parker Soc. edit. p.
334.]

[6 I cannot find this admission in c. 34. of the Enchiridion, l. c. 1534.]

[7 Et Nicena Synodus decretis suis cavit ne quis e numero Christianorum
sacris Bibliorum libris careret.—cap. 100. ad fin.]

[8 τὰς θείας γραφὰς εἰς τὴν Γοτθῶν μεταβαλὼν, τοὺς βαρβάρους μανθάνειν
τὰ θεῖα λόγια παρεσκεύασεν.—p. 206. ed. Vales. Par. 1686.]

translated the divine scriptures into the Gothic language, he prepared the barbarians to learn the oracles of God." And Sixtus
Senensis, Bibliothec. Lib. VIII., says that Chrysostom translated
the scriptures into the Armenian language[1]. Jerome, too, in his
Epitaph upon Paula, affirms that the Psalms were chanted by
the Christians of Palestine at Paula's[2] funeral, in the Hebrew,
Greek, Latin and Syriac, tongues; and that not only for three
days, whilst she was a-burying beneath the church, beside the
Lord's cave, but during the whole week. It is manifest, therefore,
that the Psalms were translated into Syriac. Stapleton, however,
in his English book against bishop Jewel, of sacred memory, Art.
III., says that these were extraordinary hymns, and not the Psalms
of David; which figment rests upon no proof, and offends even
other papists: for Jerome plainly speaks of the Psalms, when he
says, "they chanted them out in order." Our Jesuit, therefore,
pronounces the place corrupt; pretending that some of the books
do not exhibit the word "Hebræo," and that the Syriac is here
used for the Hebrew.

Thus do they turn themselves in every direction to escape that
light. This was the ingenious conjecture of Marianus Victorius,
who hath done noble service in corrupting Jerome. But, in the
first place, Erasmus, who laboured quite as diligently, and far more
faithfully than Victorius, as editor of Jerome, and who had seen as
many copies as he, could discover nothing of the kind in that
place. Furthermore, if the Syriac language here meant the
Hebrew, it ought certainly to have been enumerated in the first
place: for when authors, and especially Jerome, enumerate languages, the Hebrew is usually allowed the first place.

But to proceed. In our own histories we read that the scriptures were translated into the British language, by order of king
Athelstan, nine hundred years ago. And John of Trevisa writes,
that our countryman Bede translated the gospel of John into
English, Lib. V. c. 24; and that the Psalms were translated by
order of Alfred, Lib. VI. c. 1. And Bede tells us, Lib. I. c. 1,
that, in his time, the scriptures were read in five British languages.
His words in that passage are as follows: "This island at present,
according to the number of the books wherein the divine law was

[1 See Hug. Introd. to N. T. §. 86.]
[2 Tota ad funus ejus Palæstinarum urbium turba convenit. . . . Hebræo,
Græco, Latino, Syroque sermone, Psalmi in ordine personabant.—Epist.
xxxvi. T. IV. part. II. 687, 8.]

written, searches and confesses one and the same knowledge of the sublimest truth and truest sublimity in the languages of five people, that is, of the English, the Britons, the Scots, the Picts, and the Latins; which by meditation of the scripture hath become common to all[3]." It is therefore manifest, that the statement that there are no vernacular version mentioned by any ancient author is eminently and most plainly false.

But the Jesuit goes on to mention particular churches; and first he discourses thus concerning the African church. All the Africans did not understand Latin. But the scriptures were in Africa read only in Latin. Now, that the Latin was not the vulgar tongue of all the Carthaginians, we have the testimony of Augustine, in the beginning of his Exposition of the Epistle to the Romans; who affirms that some of the Carthaginians understood both Latin and Punic, some Punic only, and that almost all the rustics were of this latter class. Also, Serm. 35. de Verbis Domini, he says that the Punic language is a-kin to the Hebrew[4]. And Jerome, in the Preface to his Second book upon the Epistle to the Galatians[5], writes that the language of the Africans is the same as the Phœnician, with only a little alteration.

I answer, in the first place: No one says that the Punic language was the same as the Latin. The contrary may be seen even from the Pænulus of Plautus[6]; nor did any one ever entertain a doubt upon that subject. However it is quite uncertain whether there were any Punic version of the scriptures. How will our adversaries prove that there was none, by the testimony of Augustine or of any other writer? Augustine no where denies it; and although no monuments of such a thing be now extant, yet it does not follow thence that there was no version. For in old times the scriptures were translated into our own tongue, and yet scarcely any traces of those versions are now apparent. There were certainly pious bishops in all those parts of Africa, Numidia, Mauritania, who cherished a tender solicitude for the salvation of their people. It

[3 Hæc insula in præsenti, juxta numerum librorum, quibus lex divina scripta est, quinque gentium linguis unam eandemque summæ veritatis et veræ sublimitatis scientiam scrutatur et confitetur, Anglorum videlicet, Britonum, Scotorum, Pictorum et Latinorum, quæ meditatione scripturarum omnibus est facta communis.—Opp. T. i. p. 9. ed. Stevens. Lond. 1841.]

[4 Serm. cxiii. 2. Tom. v. col. 568. Opp. Par. 1679. 1700.]

[5 Quum et Afri Phœnicum linguam non nulla ex parte mutaverint.— T. iv. 255, 6.]

[6 Plauti Pænulus. V. i. &c.]

seems incredible that there should have been no one found amongst them to do that for the Carthaginians, which we read that Jerome did for the Dalmatians,—translate the scriptures into the language of the people.

Secondly, in the more frequented and civilized places, and considerable cities, the Africans understood Latin, and could speak it; so that we are not to wonder that the scriptures were read in Latin at Carthage, as appears from Cyprian; at Milevi, as we find from Optatus; at Hippo, as appears from Augustine. For these fathers read and expounded the scriptures in Latin in their churches: nor would they have used the Latin tongue in their homilies and harangues, if the people could not have understood that language. Augustine upon Psalm xviii. hath these words: "Most dearly beloved, that which we have sung with harmonious voice, we ought also to know and hold in an unclouded breast[1]." In his book de Catechiz. Rudibus, cap. 9[2], he warns the people not to ridicule their pastors, if they shall happen to express themselves ungrammatically in their prayers and sermons. Whence it is plain that some of the common people were often better skilled in Latin than the ministers themselves. In his Retractations, Lib. I. c. 20, he says that he had composed a certain Psalm in Latin letters against the Donatists, with the express object that it should reach the knowledge of the very lowest of the people, the unskilful and illiterate[3]. In his Serm. 24, de Verbis Apost. he speaks thus: "The Punic proverb is well known, which I will tell you in Latin, because all of you do not understand Punic[4]." Therefore the common people understood Latin better than Punic. Upon Psalm l.: "We all know," says he, "that in Latin one cannot say sanguines, or sanguina, but sanguinem[5]." And when he addressed the people, he was much more careful to be intelligible, than to express himself with purity. So on Psalm cxxviii.[6]:

[1 Carissimi, quod consona voce cantavimus, sereno etiam corde nosse et tenere [ac videre] debemus.—T. IV. 81, 2.]

[2 § 13. Tom. VI. col. 272.]

[3 Tom. I. col. 31. Volens etiam causam Donatistarum ad ipsius humillimi vulgi et omnino imperitorum atque idiotarum notitiam pervenire . . . . psalmum, qui eis cantaretur, per Latinas literas feci.]

[4 Proverbium notum est Punicum: quod quidem Latine vobis dicam, quia Punice non omnes nostis.—T. V. 804. (Serm. clxvii. 4.)]

[5 Omnes novimus Latine non dici sanguines nec sanguina, sed sanguinem. —T. IV. 472.]

[6 Ego dicam ossum: sic enim potius loquamur: melius est ut nos reprehendant grammatici, quam non intelligant populi.—T. IV. col. 1545.]

"I will say *ossum*: for so we should rather speak. It is better that the grammarians should blame, than that the people should not understand us." And upon John, Tract. 7, "Lend me your kind attention. It is *dolus*, not *dolor*. I mention this because many brethren, who are not very skilful in the Latin tongue, are in the habit of using such phrases as, *Dolus illum torquet*, when they mean what is denoted by *Dolor*[7]." And Augustine, Confess. Lib. I. c. 14, says that he learned the Latin language, "amidst the caresses of the nursery, the jokes of those that laughed, and the smiles of those that played with him[8]." Now Augustine was born and bred at Tagasta, in Africa, as appears from the Confessions, Lib. IV. c. 7. From these circumstances it is clear that the people of Africa, especially in the cities and more populous places, not only understood Latin, but could speak it too, although perhaps not always with that purity which an exact Latinity would have required.

The Jesuit goes on to enumerate the Spanish, English, French, German, and Italian churches; with respect to which it is not necessary that I should answer him upon each case severally. I am aware that, in these later times, the people were plunged in the densest darkness, and that even in the centre of Italy and Rome every thing was read in a foreign language. But before this ignorance and antichristian tyranny, in the older and purer times of the church, I affirm that the scriptures were never, in any country, read publicly to the people in any other language but that which the people understood. Our adversary will never be able to prove the contrary. The Latin tongue certainly of old prevailed widely in the western part of the world, so that the scriptures may have been read in Latin in those countries which Bellarmine mentions, and yet have been understood by the people. Augustine tells us, in his City of God, Lib. XIX. c. 7, "Care was taken that the imperial city should impose not only her yoke, but her language also, upon the vanquished nations[9]." Plutarch, in his Platonic Questions[10],

[7] Intendat caritas vestra; *dolus*, non *dolor* est. Hoc propterea dico quia multi fratres imperitiores Latinitatis loquuntur sic ut dicant, Dolus illum torquet, pro eo quod est Dolor.—T. III. P. II. 349.]

[8] Inter blandimenta nutricum, et joca arridentium, et lætitias alludentium.]

[9] Data opera est ut civitas imperiosa non solum jugum, verum etiam linguam suam, domitis gentibus imponeret.]

[10] ὡς δοκεῖ μοι περὶ Ρωμαίων λέγειν, ὧν μὲν λόγῳ νῦν ὁμοῦ τι πάντες ἄνθρωποι χρῶνται.—p. 1010. c. T. II. Opp. Francofurt. 1620.]

affirms that almost all men use the Latin language. And Strabo says this expressly of the Gauls and Spaniards. Besides, there may have been versions of the scriptures in those churches, which are unknown, and unheard of, by us. It is quite certain that the reading of the scriptures was everywhere understood in those churches. Isidore, in his book De Offic. Eccles. c. 10, writes thus of the Spanish and all other churches: "It behoves that when the Psalms are sung, all should sing; and when the prayers are said, they should be said by all; and that when the lesson is read, silence should be kept that it may be heard equally by all[1]." Where the language is a strange one, men can neither sing together, nor pray together, nor hear anything together: for not to understand what another reads or says, comes to the same thing as not to hear it. It is therefore sufficiently evident from Isidore, that in Spain the Latin language was known to those who used it in the reading of the scriptures. And this is likewise manifest of Gaul. For Sulpitius Severus, in his Life of Martin, informs us, that, when the people had assembled to choose Martin bishop, upon the reader not appearing, one of the by-standers seized the book, and read the eighth Psalm; at the reading of which a general shout was raised by the people, and the opposite party were reduced to silence[2]. From this testimony we collect that the people understood very well what was read to them; for otherwise no occasion would have been afforded them of raising this acclamation. Whence it follows, either that this people were not unacquainted with the Latin tongue, or that there was then extant some vernacular version of the scripture. Now then we have sufficiently answered this argument; but there will be something to be answered again in the other part upon this subject.

The fourth argument is drawn from the reason of the thing itself. It is requisite that the public use of scripture should be in some language most common to all men, for the sake of preserving the unity of the church. But at present there is no language more common than the Latin. He proves the major by the consideration that otherwise the communion between churches would be destroyed, and it would be impossible that general councils should be celebrated; for all the fathers have not the gift of tongues.

[1 Oportet ut quando psallitur, ab omnibus psallatur: et cum oratur, ut oretur ab omnibus; quando lectio legitur, ut facto silentio æque audiatur a cunctis.—Isid. Opp. Col. Agripp. 1617, p. 393.]

[2 Sulpitii Severi. Opp. Amstel. 1665, p. 452.]

I answer : All the parts of this argument are weak. For, in the first place, it is false that no language is more common than the Latin, even in the West. In truth there is hardly any less common. For at the present day none understand Latin, but those who have learned it from a master. Formerly, indeed, this was the native and common language of many people ; but now, in the greatest multitude that can be collected, how few will you find that are acquainted with Latin !

Secondly, if, as Bellarmine himself confesses, the very reason why the apostles at first wrote almost everything in Greek, was because that language was the most common of all, and the scriptures were afterwards translated into Latin, because afterwards the Latin became more common ; it follows that now also the scriptures should be rendered into other languages which are now more common than either Latin or Greek. Such are now the Dalmatian, Italian, French, German, Polish. For these are the mother-tongues of great nations ; whereas the Latin is the mother-tongue of no nation whatever. At this day the Latin is a stranger in Latium itself, is the vernacular language of no people, but peculiar to learned men and those who have attended the lessons of some master in the schools.

Thirdly, his pretence that the inter-communion of churches would be destroyed, and the celebration of general councils rendered impossible, unless the scriptures were everywhere read in some one most common language, is absurd and repugnant to all reason and experience. For formerly, when the scriptures were read in Hebrew by the Hebrews, in Greek by the Grecians, and in Latin by the Latins, there was nevertheless the greatest friendship amongst Christians and the closest union in the church, nor was there any impediment to the holding of general councils. In the Nicene council there were Greek and Latin fathers, who all, though they did not use one and the same language, yet defended the same faith with the most zealous unanimity. If it be a thing so conducive to the conservation of the church's unity, that the scriptures should everywhere be read in the same language, why were not measures taken to insure it from the beginning ? Or why ought the Latin language to be deemed fitter for such a purpose than any other ? These dreams are only meet subjects for laughter ; and therefore this argument hath been omitted by the editor of the epitome.

The fifth argument. If there be no cause why the scriptures

15—2

should be translated vernacularly, then they ought not to be translated. But there is no cause why they should be translated;
which is thus proved. If they are translated in order that the
people may understand them, this is no good cause, since the
people cannot understand them even when they are translated.
For the people would not understand the prophets and Psalms,
and other pieces which are read in the churches, even if they
were read in the vernacular language. For these things even the
learned do not understand, unless they read and hear expositors.

I answer, in the first place, by confessing that all things are
not immediately understood upon the reading even by the learned,
especially in the prophets and the Psalms. For to enable us to
understand the scriptures, there is need not only of reading, but
of study, meditation and prayer. But if, for this reason, the
people ought not to read the scriptures in their own tongue, then
even the learned ought not to be permitted to read them. However there are many things which can be understood, though not
all: and assuredly, all things which are necessary to salvation are
plainly delivered in scripture, so as that they can be easily understood by any one if he will. And men would know more than
they do, if they would read and hear the scriptures with that
attention which they ought to bestow. For the reason why most
men understand so little, and gain such slender advantage from the
reading of the scriptures, is to be found in their own negligence,
because they neither give a religious attention to the perusal of
them, nor approach it with the proper dispositions.

Secondly, although the whole sense be not immediately perceived, yet the words are understood when they are recited in the
mother-tongue; and this greatly conduces towards gaining a
knowledge of the sense. The eunuch, Acts viii., was reading the
prophet Isaiah, which yet he did not thoroughly understand.
Nevertheless, he was to be praised for reading it, and hath deservedly been praised by many of the fathers. He understood the
words indeed, but knew not that the prophet spoke of Christ, and
was ignorant of the true sense. But these men do not allow the
people to understand even so much as the words. However, as
that reading of the scripture was useful to the eunuch, so it will be
useful to the people to be diligent in reading the scriptures, so as
that, from understanding the words, they may come to understand
the sense of the whole. For the first step is to know the words,
the second to perceive the drift of the discourse. But the papists

are so far from wishing the people to comprehend the sense of scripture, that they prevent them from even reading the words.

The sixth argument. It is dangerous for the people to read the scriptures; since they would not derive benefit from the scriptures, but injury. All heresies have sprung from misunderstanding of scripture, as Hilary observes at the end of his book *de synodis*[1] ; and Luther calls the scriptures the book of heretics: and this is further proved by experience. Hence have sprung the heresies of the Anthropomorphites, the Adamites[2], and of David George[3], who understood no language but his mother-tongue. If the people were to hear the Song of songs read, the adultery of David, the incest of Tamar, the story of Leah and Rachel, the falsehoods of Judith, they would either despise the holy patriarchs, or argue that similar things were lawful to themselves, or believe these to be false. Bellarmine further subjoins, that he heard from a credible witness, that once when in England the twenty-fifth chapter of Ecclesiasticus was being read in the vulgar tongue, wherein many things are spoken of the wickedness of women, a certain woman rose up and exclaimed: "Is this the word of God?— nay, rather it is the word of the devil." And the Rhemists, in their note upon 1 Cor. xiv., say that the translation of holy offices often breeds manifold perils and contempt in the vulgar sort, leading them to suppose that God is the author of sin, when they read, " Lead us not into temptation:" although they seem here to have forgotten what they have observed elsewhere, that the Lord's prayer should be allowed in the vernacular language. The censors of Cologne, too, in their book against Monhemius, p. 20, tell us, " No heresy was ever found which did not make use of scripture ;

[1 The reference meant is most probably ad Constant. August. II. 9. Sed memento tamen neminem hæreticorum esse qui se nunc non secundum scripturas prædicare ea, quibus blasphemat, mentiatur . . . . omnes scripturas sine scripturæ sensu loquuntur.—Col. 1230. Hilarii Opp. Paris. 1693.]

[2 There was an ancient sect of Adamites, said by Theodoret (Hær. Fab. p. 197) to have been founded by Prodicus, (whose tenets are described by Clemens Alex. Strom. I. p. 304. B. and § 3. pp. 438, 439,) and of which the fullest account is given by Epiphanius, (Hæres. 52,) but only upon hearsay, (p. 458, C.) But the persons meant by Bellarmine were probably the Picards, exterminated by Zisca in the 15th century, and the Anabaptists of Amsterdam in the 16th.—See Bayle's Dict. Art. PICARD, and Beausobre's Dissertation at the end of L'Enfant's History of the Hussites, Amsterd. 1731.]

[3 Founder of the Davidists. He died 1556.—See Mosheim, Cent. 16. sect. 3. part. II. c. 3. § 24.]

yea, to speak still more boldly, which did not take its occasion from scripture[1]."

I answer, in the first place: All these suggestions are the product of human ingenuity, and impeach the divine wisdom. For if the reading of these things were so dangerous, why did the Lord will that they should be written, and that in the language which the whole church understood, and afterwards should be translated into the Greek and Latin tongues, which latter our adversary himself affirms to be the most common of all? These things ought rather to have been buried than consigned to writing, if they were so fraught with danger to piety and good morals.

Secondly, there is nothing which the reading of these histories is less fitted to produce than either contempt for the saints, or any kind of petulance and impiety. For though in those histories the adultery of David is narrated, yet so is also, in the same narratives, the penitence of David and his punishment described; the knowledge whereof is useful to the church and all the faithful. For, in the first place, hence we learn that no one can sin with impunity ; but that every one, if he sin, must undergo the penalty of sin, either in the shape of chastisement, as David, or in that of vengeance, as others. We learn farther, that one must not despair though he may have sinned ; but that, however heinous the sin into which he may have fallen, there is hope that God will be merciful for Christ's sake, if the sinner heartily repent. Lastly, that those holy and excellent men were not saved by their own virtues, but by the merits of Christ, and consequently that we ought not to think of them more magnificently than is proper ; as indeed there is less danger of our attributing too little to them than too much : on which account the Holy Spirit did not choose to pass in silence these actions, which were not small delinquencies, but most enormous crimes.

Thirdly, no scandal springs truly and legitimately from scripture. In Rom. xv. 4, the apostle declares why the scriptures were published, and what end they regard ; not to lead men into false opinions, but "they are written for our learning, that we through patience and comfort of the scriptures might have hope." In Psalm cxix. 9, David asks, "Wherewithal shall a young man cleanse his way?" He answers, not by avoiding or remaining ignorant of the scriptures, but, "by taking heed to them." Even young men, therefore, whose age is especially prone to lust, may nevertheless be usefully engaged

[1 Nulla unquam reperta est hæresis, quæ non scripturis fuerit usa: imo ut audentius dicamus, quæ non ex scripturis occasionem acceperit. Colon.1582.]

in the study of the scriptures. In Psalm xii. 7, he says that "the words of the Lord" are "pure words:" but these men are afraid, lest, as the apostle, 1 Cor. xv. 33, reminds us that good manners are corrupted by *evil communication*, so men should be made worse and more estranged from piety by the perusal of the scriptures. Meanwhile, they who remove the scriptures from the eyes of men, as pestilent to all pious behaviour, permit all young men to read Propertius, Martial, Ovid, Plautus, Terence, and forbid not the most shameful comedies and the foulest shews. What can be conceived more impious and antichristian than such conduct?

Fourthly, as to his assertion that heresies spring from the scripture not being understood, I confess its truth. But, as all heresies are wont to spring from not understanding or ill understanding scripture, so all heresies are refuted by the scriptures well and fittingly understood and expounded. Hence the Anthropomorphites, hence the Adamites, hence all the other heretics are convicted of error. Now it is much better that the scriptures should be read, and that, from the scriptures read and understood, heresies should be condemned and overthrown, than that they should not be read at all; and that by such means the rise of heresies should be prevented. For doubtless many more persons perish through ignorance of scripture, than through heresy; and it is from ignorance of scripture, and not from the reading of it, that heresies themselves arise.

Fifthly, whether Luther ever really said that "scripture is the book of the heretics," is neither very certain nor very important. Indeed they are wont to abuse the scriptures, but still may always be convicted and refuted by the same.

Sixthly, the story which he subjoins, as heard from some Englishman, about a certain woman, who, when that chapter of Ecclesiasticus[2] was read in England, rose up in a rage and spoke with little modesty of that scripture, I leave entirely on the credit of the good man from whom Bellarmine heard it. But what if a few persons sometimes abuse the scriptures; does it therefore follow that the scriptures are to be wholly taken away, and never read to the people? In this way of reasoning, even the learned should never read the scriptures, since many even very learned men abuse the scriptures, as is the case with almost all heretics.

[2 It is to be observed that, in our present Calendar, Ecclus. xxv., which is the evening lesson for November 6, is ordered to be read only to ver. 13. No such rule however was made in King Edward's Prayer-book.]

Besides, if the abuse of any thing were sufficient to set aside its use, we should abstain from food and from drink, and even forego the use of clothes, because many people abuse these things to gluttony, drunkenness and pride. This then is the most noted of all fallacies, putting that which is not the cause for the cause, and arguing from accidental circumstances.

In the seventh place, the Jesuit reasons thus: if the scriptures should be read by the people in the vulgar tongue, then new versions should be made in every age, because languages are changed every age; which he proves from Horace's Art of Poetry[1] and from experience. But this would be impossible, because there would be a lack of persons fit to make the versions; and, if it were possible, it would be absurd that the versions should be so often changed. Therefore the scriptures ought not to be read in the vernacular tongue.

I answer, every part of this argument is ridiculous. For, in the first place, it is false that languages change every age; since the primary tongues, the Hebrew, Greek and Latin, have not undergone such frequent alterations. Secondly, there is never in Christian churches a lack of some sufficient interpreters, able to translate the scriptures and render their genuine meaning in the vulgar tongue. Thirdly, no inconvenience will follow if interpretations or versions of scripture, when they have become obsolete and ceased to be easily intelligible, be afterwards changed and corrected. I would assuredly have passed over this argument entirely, if I had not determined not to conceal or dissemble any arguments of our opponents.

The Jesuit's eighth argument is taken from the authority of the fathers. He brings forward the testimonies of two illustrious fathers, to whom we are bound to render the highest deference on account of their consummate and manifold erudition, Basil and Jerome. Basil then, as Theodoret relates, Hist. Lib. IV. cap. 19, when the prefect of the imperial kitchen was prating with intolerable impudence and ignorance concerning the dogmas of theology, answered him thus: "It is your business to mind your sauces, not to cook the divine oracles[2]."

[1   Ut silvæ foliis pronos mutantur in annos,
       Prima cadunt: ita verborum vetus interit ætas
       Et juvenum ritu florent modo nata, vigentque.—v. 60.]

[2 παρῆν δέ τις Δημοσθένης καλούμενος τῶν βασιλικῶν προμηθούμενος ὄψων, ὃς τῷ διδασκάλῳ τῆς οἰκουμένης ἐπιμεμψάμενος ἐβαρβάρισεν, ὁ δὲ θεῖος Βασί-

I answer, This prefect of the imperial kitchen was by name
Demosthenes, and troubled the holy father with exceeding insolence and ignorance; for, being himself a stupid barbarian, he
would yet, as Theodoret tells us, instruct the doctor of the whole
world, τὸν διδάσκαλον τῆς οἰκουμένης,—for so Basil was esteemed.
The courtier imagined, it seems, that he, a person at once wholly
unlearned and very foolish, could maintain a disputation upon the
scriptures with Basil, a man of profound learning, most expert in
scriptures, and a bishop of the church.   This was the reason why
Basil answered him so sharply, Σόν ἐστι τὰς τῶν ζωμῶν καρυκείας
φροντίζειν.   And, indeed, those who are like this man ought to
be treated in like manner, and rebuked with much severity : but
what is this to the purpose ? It is one thing to read the scriptures,
and another thing to suppose ourselves to understand them when
we do not.   Basil did not blame the cook for having read the
scriptures, but for having the conceit that he had obtained such
distinguished knowledge as to be able to dispute with him concerning the scriptures, when he did not understand them.   This
arrogance of his Basil wished to crush, and to shut his impudent
mouth with that answer, not to prevent him from reading the
scriptures.   All should be expected, when they read the scriptures,
to read them with judgment, lest they be like this foolish Demosthenes ; who, because he was altogether illiterate and possessed
with heretical prejudices, seemed to Basil a person unworthy to
discourse upon religious subjects.   For so Basil addresses him :
" Thou canst not hear the divine doctrines, for thine ears are
stuffed against them."

I come now to the testimony of Jerome cited by the Jesuit,
which is contained in the epistle to Paulinus, and runs thus :
" ' Physicians undertake the proper business of physicians, and
workmen handle workmen's tools.'   Skill in the scriptures is the
only art which all claim for themselves.   ' Learned and unlearned,
we all promiscuously write poems.'   This the garrulous crone, this
the doting old man, this the wordy sophist, this all indiscriminately
seize on, tear, teach before they learn.   Some with importance on
their brows, and weighing their pompous words, philosophize upon
the sacred books amongst their female disciples.   Others (O

λειος μειδιάσας, 'Εθεασάμεθα, ἔφη, καὶ Δημοσθένην ἀγράμματον· ἐπειδὴ δὲ πλέον
ἐκεῖνος δυσχεράνας ἠπείλησε, Σόν ἐστιν, ἔφη ὁ μέγας Βασίλειος, τῆς τῶν ζωμῶν
καρυκείας φροντίζειν· δογμάτων γὰρ θείων ἐπαΐειν οὐ δύνασαι, βεβυσμένας ἔχων
τὰς ἀκοάς.—p. 174, c. d. ed. Vales. Paris. 1673.]

shame!) learn from women what they are to teach to men; and,
as if this were not enough, by a certain facility, or rather audacity, of talk discourse to others what they do not understand
themselves[1]." These are the words of Jerome: to which I answer,
that Jerome's complaint is just; since those persons should not treat
of scripture, who are ignorant and unskilful in the subject. But
here it is to be observed, that Jerome does not blame the men and
women of whom he speaks for reading the scriptures, but because,
as soon as ever they had the slightest taste of scriptural knowledge,
they supposed immediately that they understood every thing, that
they could teach others, and could interpret the scriptures to others,
when they did not understand them themselves; and because they
rushed precipitately into the scriptures without that modesty which
is to be preserved in the perusal of them. He blames, therefore,
their impudence, unskilfulness, insolence and arrogance, but does
not prevent them from reading the scriptures; yea, rather, he would
have all to read the scriptures, provided they read with modesty
and reverence.

These are the arguments of the Jesuit; to which, I hope, we
have returned an answer abundantly sufficient. There are others
who handle this question, as Harding, Art. 15. Sect. 3, who distributes this whole controversy under five heads. He proves that
a vernacular translation of the scriptures is, first, unnecessary;
secondly, not fitting; thirdly, not useful; fourthly, unsafe; fifthly,
heretical. But it is not worth while to answer his arguments
also, and obviate the objections which he brings against vernacular
versions of the bible; as well because they are absolutely the
same with those alleged by the Jesuit, as also because they have
been already most copiously and learnedly confuted by that distinguished man, Doctor John Jewel, bishop of Sarum, whom they
may read who desire to see more upon this matter.

[1 *Quod medicorum est promittunt medici, tractant fabrilia fabri.* Sola
scripturarum ars est quam sibi omnes passim vindicant. *Scribimus indocti
doctique poemata passim.* Hanc garrula anus, hanc delirus senex, hanc
sophista verbosus, hanc universi præsumunt, lacerant, docent antequam dis-
cant. Alii adducto supercilio, grandia verba trutinantes, inter mulierculas de
sacris literis philosophantur. Alii discunt (proh pudor!) a feminis quod viros
doceant: et ne parum hoc sit, quadam facilitate verborum, imo audacia, edis-
serunt aliis quod ipsi non intelligunt.—T. IV. p. 571.]

CHAPTER XV.

OUR REASONS FOR VERNACULAR VERSIONS OF THE SCRIPTURES.

I COME now to the defence of our own side, in which I have to prove that the scriptures are to be set forth before all Christians in their vernacular tongues, so as that every individual may be enabled to read them.

Now my first argument shall be to this effect: that which is by God prescribed to all, all should do. But God hath commanded all to read the scriptures: therefore all are bound to read the scriptures. There can be no controversy about the major, unless some one doubt whether we are bound to obey God. The assumption however may perhaps be questioned. We must inquire, therefore, whether God hath prescribed this to all. And this may very easily be made to appear; for God hath chosen that his will should be written, that his word should be committed to writing, that his scriptures should be commended to men, and that in a language known not only to the learned, but to the vulgar also. What could have been his object in this, if it were not that all people should read the scriptures, and recognise the will and word of God? In Deut. xxxi. 11, 12, there is an express command of God concerning the reading of the scriptures before the whole people: "Thou shalt read the words of this law in the presence of all Israel, in their hearing, and to all the people collected together." And lest any of the people should peradventure suppose himself exempted by some special privilege, and discharged from the obligation of this divine command, Moses makes use of a distributive enumeration, naming expressly the women, the children, and the strangers, and subjoining even their posterity. But why does God will his law to be read before the whole people? The reason is added, "that they may hear, and may learn, and fear Jehovah and observe his precepts." Now this is of perpetual obligation: therefore the reading of the scripture is always necessary. For if the end and proximate cause of any law be perpetual, the law itself is to be esteemed perpetual. But the reasons on account of which God willed the scriptures to be read are perpetual. Therefore he wills them to be read to the people perpetually throughout all ages.

In Deut. xvii. 19, 20, it is particularly enjoined upon the king that he should read the scriptures: and the same reasons are added as were given before, and also some peculiar to the king; as that,

lest his soul should be lifted up with pride, and he should despise
his brethren, and depart from this precept, "to the right hand or to
the left." In Deut. vi. 6, 7, 8, 9, this command is proposed to all
Israel, and even urged vehemently upon them, that the words of
the divine law should be graven upon their hearts; that they
should tell them to their sons; that they should speak of them
when they sat at home and when they walked by the way, when
they lay down and when they rose up; that they should have
them, as it were, bound upon their hands, and kept ever before
their eyes; finally, that they should be inscribed upon the posts of
their houses and upon their doors. From all which we understand
that God would have his law most familiarly known to his people.

In Jer. xxxvi. 6, 7, the prophet commands Baruch to read the
book which he had written from Jeremiah's dictation, before the whole
people; and the reason is subjoined, "if peradventure they may
fall down, and make entreaty before Jehovah, and return each man
from his evil way." And in the new Testament Christ, John v.
39, bids men ἐρευνᾶν τὰς γραφὰς, "search the scriptures." In
which place he addresses not only the persons of learning and
erudition, that is, the Scribes and Pharisees, but also the unlearned
people and the illiterate vulgar : for not the learned alone, but
the unlearned also, seek and desire eternal life; yea, salvation and
the kingdom of God pertains to the latter equally with the former
class. Chrysostom observes upon that place, Hom. 40, that Christ
exhorts the Jews in that passage not merely to a bare and simple
reading of the scriptures, but sets them upon a very diligent
investigation, since he bids them not to *read*, but to *search* the
scriptures. John xx. 31, the Evangelist says : "These things are
written that ye may believe that Jesus is the Christ, the Son of
God; and that believing ye may have life through his name."
Now all desire life and salvation; all too desire faith, or, at least,
ought to desire it. Thus then we reason from this passage : without
faith there is no life : without the scriptures there is no faith : the
scriptures therefore should be set forth before all men. Rom. xv.
14, "Whatsoever things were written were written for our learning," says Paul. The Lord therefore willed us to be learned, and
this is saving knowledge. He subjoins, "that we, through patience
and comfort of the scriptures, might have hope." Those therefore
who are without the scriptures are without patience, without
comfort, without hope; for all these things are produced by the
scriptures.

Our second argument stands thus :. The people should not be
deprived of those arms by which they are to be protected against
Satan. Now the scriptures are such arms : therefore the scriptures should not be taken away from the people; for taken away
they are, if the people be prevented from reading them. The
major is self evident. The assumption is proved by the example
of Christ himself, Matt. iv. For when Christ had to deal with
Satan, and was engaged in a close encounter with him, he repressed
and refuted him with no other arms than the scriptures. Thrice
he answered him with, " It is written," and with the third reply
he routed him. If Christ defended himself against Satan with the
scriptures, how much more needful are the scriptures to us against
the same enemy ! And it was for this end that Christ used the
weapons of scripture against Satan, that he might afford us an
example ; for he could have repelled Satan with a single word.
We therefore ought to resist Satan in the same manner. It is
folly to suppose that Satan can be driven away by bare ceremonies,
exorcisms, gesticulations, and outward fopperies. We must fight
with arguments drawn from scripture, and the examples of the
holy fathers : the scriptures are the only arms which can prevail,
or ought to be used against him. Those, therefore, who take the
holy scriptures away from the people, leave them exposed naked
to Satan, and hurl them into most certain destruction. For without the protection of scripture the people must necessarily fall
under all temptations. The apostle Paul, Eph. vi. 16, says that
the shield, θυρεὸν, wherewith the fiery darts of Satan are to be
quenched, is πίστις, *Faith.* Now faith, as the same apostle testifies, Rom. x, 17, is " begotten by hearing, and hearing by the
word of God." And, as we resist Satan by faith, which is produced
by the scriptures, so also is he to be attacked by scripture. For in
the same place that μάχαιρα πνεύματος, *the spiritual sword,*
is said to be the word of God. From the scriptures, therefore, we
must take both what are called *offensive* and *defensive* arms
against Satan, with which furnished upon all sides, we shall undoubtedly obtain a happy victory. All the other arms there
described depend upon faith acquired from the scriptures. Thus
then we conclude this place and our second argument. All who
have to contend with Satan ought to read the scriptures, that
they may use those arms which are supplied by the scriptures
expertly and skilfully against that deadly and most formidable foe.
Now Satan wages war against all men without exception. All there-

fore ought to read the scriptures ; and consequently the scriptures ought to be set forth for all people in their own vernacular languages.

My third argument I form thus : The scriptures are to be read publicly in such a manner as that the people may be able to derive some advantage from them. But they cannot be useful to the people in an unknown tongue : therefore they should be translated into a language known to the people. The major is indubitable ; and, for the minor, it is proved by Paul, 1 Cor. xiv. through almost the whole of which chapter he handles this question : " If I shall come to you," says he, v. 6, " speaking with tongues, what shall I profit you ?" τί ὑμᾶς ὠφελήσω ; as if he had said, " certainly nothing." And, verse 7, he proves by the examples of things without life, as pipe and harp, " which," says he, " unless they give a distinction (διαστολήν) in their tones, how shall it be known what is piped or harped ?" In like manner it behoves our speech to be εὔσημος, or *significant*. So he concludes, verse 19, that he would rather speak five words in the church διὰ νοὸς, with *his understanding*, so as to instruct others, than " ten thousand words in an unknown tongue," ἐν γλώσσῃ. Chrysostom, in his 35th homily upon the first epistle to the Corinthians, exclaims, " What utility can there be in a speech not understood ?" πῶς γάρ ἀπὸ φωνῆς ἧς οὐ συνιέτε[1] ; and in the same homily : " He who speaks with tongues edifies himself: yet he cannot do even so much as this, unless he understand what he says." So that, according to Chrysostom, the reading of what one does not understand, cannot profit either others or even the reader himself : yet the popish priests used to read every thing in Latin, although very many of them were mere illiterate persons. But we shall speak more at large upon this subject in the next part.

The fourth argument. The Lord commands and requires that the people should be instructed, full of wisdom and knowledge, and perfectly acquainted with the mysteries of salvation. He often complains of the ignorance of the people, and commands them to be exercised in his word, that they may thence acquire wisdom and understanding. Therefore the people ought to read the scriptures, since without the reading of the scriptures they cannot acquire such knowledge. Now they cannot read them, unless they be translated : therefore the scriptures ought to be translated. The antecedent is easily proved by many testimonies of scripture. Deut. iv. 6, God wills his people Israel to be so well

[1 T. x. p. 323.]

instructed, so endued with wisdom and knowledge of his law, that foreign nations, when they hear of it, may wonder amd exclaim, " Lo a people wise and understanding, a great nation!" Coloss. iii. 16, the apostle desires that the word of Christ may ἐνοικεῖν, *dwell* abundantly, or *copiously*, πλουσίως, in the Colossians. And, in the same epistle, i. 9, he wishes that they may be filled " with the knowledge of his will, in all wisdom and spiritual understanding." And chap. ii. 2, he requires in them " a full assurance of understanding to the acknowledgment of the mystery of God." And, 2 Cor. viii. 7, he says that the Corinthians περισσεύειν, are abundantly filled " with faith, and utterance, and knowledge." And Numb. ii. 29, Moses wishes that all the people were prophets. And, 1 Cor. xiv. 5, Paul wishes that all might speak with tongues, but rather that they should prophesy. Philip. i. 9, the same apostle prays that the love of the Philippians may abound more and more, " in knowledge and in all judgment." And, 2 Pet. i. 5, Peter admonishes those to whom he writes that they should add virtue to faith, and to virtue and sanctity of life τὴν γνῶσιν, *knowledge*. From these passages we perceive that wisdom, prudence, knowledge and understanding are required in the people of God ; and therefore those who retain them in a stupid and gross ignorance of the scripture inflict a grievous injury upon the people.

Nay, the fathers also confess, that a knowledge of, and acquaintance with, the scriptures is necessary for all Christians. Jerome in his commentary upon the Colossians, iii. 16, says: " Hence we see that the laity ought to have not only a sufficient, but an abundant knowledge of the scriptures, and also to instruct each other[2]." Chrysostom, in his ninth homily upon the Colossians, writing upon the same passage, remarks that the apostle requires the people to know the word of God, *not simply, but in great abundance*, οὐχ ἁπλῶς, ἀλλὰ μετὰ πολλῆς τῆς περιουσίας ; and adds : " Attend, all ye that are secular (κοσμικοὶ), and have wives and families depending upon you, how he (the apostle) specially commands you to read the scripture ; and not merely to read it in a perfunctory manner, but with great diligence," ἀλλὰ μετὰ πολλῆς σπουδῆς. Chrysostom observes in that same place, that the apostle does not say, let the word of God *be* in you ; but, let it *dwell* in you ; and that, πλουσίως, *richly*[3].

[2 Hinc perspicimus non tantum sufficienter, sed etiam abundantur debere laicos scripturarum cognitionem habere, et se invicem docere.—T. xi. 1029. But this Commentary is not Jerome's.]

[3 T. xi. p. 391.]

Œcumenius too observes upon the same passage, that the doctrine of Christ should dwell in us ἐν πολλῇ δαψιλείᾳ, *most abundantly.* Now, how are we to obtain so full a knowledge of it as this implies? Œcumenius informs us by subjoining, διὰ τῆς τῶν γραφῶν ἐρεύνης, *by searching the scriptures.* So Thomas Aquinas in his third lecture upon this chapter : " Some," says he, " are satisfied with a very small portion of the word of God ; but the apostle desires we should have much of it[1]."

Our adversaries urge many objections against such knowledge being diffused amongst the people. In the first place they allege what is found in Luke viii. 10, where Christ says to his disciples : " Unto you it is given to know the mysteries of the kingdom of God, but to the rest I speak in parables." Hence they conclude that the scriptures should only be communicated to the learned and well-instructed, that is, to the ministers, bishops, priests and professors, but refused to the laity and unlearned people.

But I answer, that Christ spoke in that place not of the common people, but of the scribes and Pharisees who proudly resisted him, who " seeing saw not, and hearing did not understand ;" and therefore that those words have no reference to the cause we have in hand. Thus it is that cardinal Hugo (not to mention others) interprets this place ; and so also the ordinary gloss. Thus Hugo : " To you ; that is, who hear willingly, and repose faith in my words[2]." And the ordinary gloss still more plainly in this manner : " Holy things are to be imparted to you who are faithful, not to the incredulous Pharisees[3]." These words of Christ, therefore, are no obstacle to the reading of holy scripture by the laity and unlearned persons.

Against such a knowledge in the people, in the second place, Hosius (in his book de Sacr. Vernac. Legend. Opp. p. 742. Lugd 1563) objects certain testimonies of the fathers ; as namely, Augustine, Contra Epist. Fundament. c. 4, where he says; " It is not the vivacity of their understanding, but the simplicity of belief which best secures the multitude[4]:" and in his 102nd Epistle[5], where he says: "If Christ

[1] Quibusdam sufficit modicum quid de verbo Dei : sed apostolus vult quod habeamus multum, p. 164. 2. T. xvi. Opp. Venet. 1593.]

[2] Vobis, hoc est, qui libenter auditis, et fidem habetis verbis meis.]

[3] Vobis qui fideles estis, non Pharisæis incredulis, sancta sunt danda.]

[4] Turbam non intelligendi vivacitas, sed credendi simplicitas tutam facit. —Tom. x. p. 183. Opp. Bassan. 1797.]

[5] Si propter eos solos Christus mortuus est qui certa intelligentia possunt ista discernere, pene frustra in ecclesia laboramus.—T. ii. p. 786.]

died only for those who can distinguish these matters by a certain intelligence, we labour almost in vain in the church," &c. To the same effect also he produces Gregory Nazianzen, Lib. i. de Theologia, where he says: "It is not the business of all persons to dispute concerning God, and the things of God[6]," &c.

I answer, These testimonies do by no means prohibit the reading of the scriptures, as will better appear upon a particular examination of them. For first, as to Augustine: I allow with him, that an accurate knowledge of mysteries is not required of the common people, but that it is sufficient for them if they hold the foundation of religion sound and whole: for all cannot be quick in understanding, and it is enough if they be simple in believing. But this simplicity is not that sort of brute ignorance which the papists would have in their laity; since such an ignorance, as the papists defend, should rather be styled utter stupidity than simplicity. But the simplicity of Christians should be combined with prudence; for while Christ would have us to be simple as doves, he would have us also to be wise as serpents, Matth. x. 16. Christ died for many, who cannot dispute acutely of the mystery of salvation, or handle and discuss theological questions in a scholastic manner: this I allow to be said, and truly said, by Augustine; but this does not prove that no knowledge is required in the people. I confess that the people do not need to have as much knowledge as the learned, who are wholly occupied in books and literature; but the people ought not to be (as the papists would have them) wholly ignorant of the scriptures and of all knowledge. Gregory the Great hath a somewhat similar maxim: "In the common people it is not knowledge, but a good life that is requisite[7]." And Tertullian, in his Prescriptions against Heretics: "This faith of thine hath saved thee; thy faith, he says, not thy knowledge or expertness in scripture[8]." The same answer will serve for the passage from Nazianzen. He does not say that the scriptures should not be read by the people, but that every body is not competent to determine questions concerning God and abstruse mysteries of religion: οὐ παντὸς τὸ περὶ Θεοῦ φιλοσοφεῖν· which we will-

---

[6 Οὐ παντὸς, ὦ οὗτοι, τὸ περὶ Θεοῦ φιλοσοφεῖν, οὐ παντὸς, οὐχ οὕτω τὸ πρᾶγμα εὔωνον . . . προσθήσω δὲ, οὐδὲ πάντοτε, οὐδὲ πᾶσιν, οὐδὲ πάντα.—Orat. XXXIII. p. 530, c. T. I. Col. 1690.]

[7 Non requiritur in vulgo scientia, sed bona vita.]

[8 Fides, inquit, tua te salvam fecit, non exercitatio scripturarum.—c. 14. p. 10. P. III. Tertull. Opp. Lips. 1841.]

16

[WHITAKER.]

242   THE FIRST CONTROVERSY.   [CH.

ingly allow. "For the matter," says he, "is not so mean and
vile, οὐχ οὕτω τὸ πρᾶγμα εὔωνον, as that every one is able
to philosophize upon it." Then he says a little lower down,
" Neither all subjects indiscriminately should be discoursed of, nor
yet everywhere or to all:" οὔτε πάντοτε, οὔτε πᾶσιν, οὔτε
πάντα. Those, therefore, who have never read or heard anything,
or who are unskilful, and yet venture to discuss divine matters,—
such persons are deservedly obnoxious to blame; and such are the
persons whom Nazianzen means. The unskilful ought, indeed, to
leave such discussions to others. But the same father[1] exhorts all
men to the reading of scripture, from that passage of David,
Psalm i. 2 : " And in the law of the Lord he meditates day and
night;" and from Deut. vi. : " Yea," says he in that same place,
" we should think of God oftener than we breathe : μνημονευτέον
τοῦ Θεοῦ μᾶλλον ἢ ἀναπνευστέον· and, if possible, οὐδὲν ἄλλο
πρακτέον, nothing else should be done." This very learned father
Nazianzen therefore is no patron of the papists.

Our fifth argument is to this effect : Christ taught the people
in their mother-tongue ; so also the apostles and disciples of Christ,
as well when upon the day of Pentecost they published the gospel
in a known tongue, as afterwards when, scattered over the whole
world, they taught all nations in their own native languages.
Hence we draw our conclusion thus : The holy doctrine of the
gospel is not contaminated when preached or taught in the vernacular tongue ; therefore, not when it is written or read in the
vernacular tongue. This is the argument of Chemnitz, which the
Jesuit, in his manuscript lectures, pronounces not worth a farthing.
The question of farthings will give us no concern. The point is to
know, why it is invalid ? " Firstly," says he, " because an
argument from the preaching of the word to the writing of the
word is inconsequential; since in preaching every thing may be
so explained to the people as to make them capable of understanding it; but in writing each matter is propounded nakedly by itself.
Secondly, because the apostles preached in various tongues, but all
wrote in the same language."

Let us examine this reply of the Jesuit's. I allow, indeed, that
the word preached is much more easily understood than when it is

[1 Κἀγὼ τῶν ἐπαινούντων εἰμὶ τὸν λόγον, ὃς μελετᾶν ἡμέρας καὶ νυκτὸς δια-
κελεύεται, καὶ ἑσπέρας καὶ πρωΐ καὶ μεσημβρίας διηγεῖσθαι, καὶ εὐλογεῖν τὸν
Κύριον ἐν παντὶ καιρῷ· εἰ δεῖ καὶ τὸ Μωϋσέως εἰπεῖν, κοιταζόμενον, διανιστά-
μενον, ὁδοιποροῦντα, ὁτιοῦν ἄλλο πράττοντα.—Ut sup. p. 531. B.]

merely read; because, when preached, each several point is explained, and variously accommodated and referred to the use of the
people, which cannot be done when it is merely read. Nevertheless
the same word should be set forth for the people in their mother
tongue, in order that, when it is preached, they may have it in
their hands, and so may see whether that which is propounded to
them be indeed the word of God, as we read of the Berœans, Acts
xvii.; otherwise any one, at his pleasure, might deliver what he
liked to the people, and enjoin it upon them as the word of God.
And the people will derive from this combined preaching and reading of the scripture advantages both solid and abundant. Besides,
although they do not immediately understand all they read, yet
they do understand much, and will understand more every day,
if they persevere in reading. What is to-day obscure, will become
clearer to-morrow; what is now unknown, will afterwards, by use
and exercise, become better understood. Furthermore, I confess,
too, that the apostles wrote only in one language; for it would have
been an infinite task to have written the same things in all the
languages of all nations: but I say that this one tongue was the
commonest and most generally diffused of all, so as to render it the
more easy for the scripture to reach the greatest possible number,
and be the better and more quickly translated into all other languages. Translated, in fact, it was immediately, as we have already
said, and shall presently shew.

But here the Jesuit brings a comparison, of how many farthings' worth it may be well to consider. Nurses, says he, do
not put the food whole into the mouths of infants, but chewed
before-hand; and in the same way, ministers should not deliver
the book of scripture entire to the people. I answer: The people
should not be always like infants, so as always to require chewed
meat; that is, when they hear the scripture in their native language, understand nothing of it unless it be explained by a minister. The minister's voice is indeed required, that the people
may understand obscure passages, and be excited to the practice
and exercise of those duties which they have learned from the
word: yet should they not be so ignorant and childish as not to
recognise and understand the reading of the scriptures. Such a
state of childhood in the people the apostle frequently reprehends,
as in 1 Cor. xiv. 20; Eph. iv. 14; Heb. v. 12; and requires from
them senses exercised in scripture, αἰσθητήρια γεγυμνασμένα. It
is not fit, therefore, that the people should be always infants, but

16—2

in due time they should become men, and "put away childish
things," 1 Cor. xiii. 11.

Our last argument (not to heap up too many) is drawn from
the use and practice of the ancient church. It is evident from
history and the books of the holy fathers, that the scriptures were
translated into all languages, and that the people were always admonished by their pastors to read them with diligence and assiduity.
Hence we draw our conclusion thus : Formerly the scriptures were
extant in vernacular languages, and were also read by the people.
Therefore the same is lawful at the present day.

The antecedent hath been proved already above, where we
shewed that Jerome translated the scriptures into Dalmatian,
Chrysostom into Armenian, Ulphilas, a bishop of the Goths,
into Gothic; and others into other languages. But the Jesuit
replies, that, though the scriptures may lawfully be translated
into vernacular languages, yet, when so translated, they should
not be read publicly in the churches; and that, as to those vernacular versions of Jerome, Chrysostom, and the rest, which
we mentioned above, they were not communicated to all, but
were only written for the consolation of some particular persons.
But the Jesuit cannot thus escape through such a chink as this.
For, since the reason of these versions was a public one, and had
regard to all,—namely, that all might thus be enabled to read the
scriptures, and obtain a knowledge of them,—this fiction of the
Jesuit's is easily confuted. Now the truth of this appears from the
design of all these versions : and specially of the Gothic Socrates,
Lib. iv. c. 33, tells us that its reason and end was that the barbarians might learn and understand "the divine oracles." The scriptures, therefore, were not translated for the sake of a few, but of
all, in order that they might be read by all. For what else could
be the reason of these versions? If they had been unwilling that
the scriptures should be publicly read, they would never have put
them into the vulgar tongue. If it had been unlawful for the
scriptures to be read publicly in the vulgar tongue, as the papists
would persuade us, can we suppose that Jerome, Chrysostom, and
other pious fathers, would ever have rendered them into the proper
and native language of the common people? This is incredible
and absurd. But I shall prove, by many testimonies of the fathers
that the scriptures were read by all. Jerome, upon Ps. lxxxvi.
writes thus[1] : "The Lord hath related in the scriptures of the

[1 T. viii. p. 103.]

people, the holy scriptures; which scriptures," says he, "are read by all people:" whence it appears that none were prevented from reading them. But why were the scriptures read by all people? Jerome answers in the same place, to the end "that all might understand." Not therefore, according to the Jesuit's fiction, that one or a few might understand them. Chrysostom, in his first Homily[2] upon the Gospel of John, writes that the Syrians, Egyptians, Indians, Persians, Ethiopians, and innumerable other nations, had translated the divine doctrines "into their own language, and thus the barbarians had learned philosophy."

If any one desires a still more illustrious testimony, let him read Augustine, *De Doct. Christ.* Lib. ii. c. 5, where these words may be found: "Hence it hath come to pass, that the scripture of God (which is the remedy for such grievous disorders of the human will), proceeding from one language, commodiously fitted for dissemination through the globe, and diffused far and wide by the various tongues of its interpreters, hath become known to all people for their salvation; which when they read, they desire nothing else but to find out the thoughts and will of those by whom it was written, and through them the will of God, according to which we believe that such men as they were spoke[3]." Thus far Augustine, in whose words we may observe these five points : First, that the scripture was published in that language, from which it might most conveniently be transfused into others. Secondly, that in fact it was variously translated. Thirdly, that it thus became known to all for salvation. Fourthly, that it was read by the people ; which is evident from the words, "reading which they desire nothing else." Fifthly, that it was not only read, but understood; which the last words render sufficiently apparent.

Theodoret, in the fifth book of Therapeutic Discourses, establishes the same fact in these words : "The Hebrew books were not only translated into the Greek language, but into the Roman tongue also, into the Egyptian, Persian, Indian, Armenian,

[2 Hom. 2. al. 1. T. viii. p. 10, b.]

[3 Ex quo factum est, ut scriptura divina (qua tantis morbis humanarum voluntatum subvenitur), ab una lingua profecta, quæ opportune potuit per orbem terrarum disseminari, per varias interpretum linguas longe lateque diffusa, innotesceret gentibus ad salutem: quam legentes nihil aliud appetunt, quam cogitationes voluntatemque illorum a quibus conscripta est invenire, et per illas voluntatem Dei, secundum quam tales homines loquutos esse credimus.]

Scythian, and even Sarmatian, or (to say it at once in one
word) into all the languages which nations use up to this day[1]."
Nothing could possibly be written more explicitly.

From what hath been said, it is evident that the scriptures
were formerly translated into the vulgar tongue; not only into
some certain languages, but into all promiscuously. Wherefore now, in like manner, they should be translated and read
vernacularly. Were I now to proceed in detail through all those
sentences of the fathers in which they exhort the people to the
study of the scriptures, I should never come to an end. Chrysostom presses this exhortation most earnestly in many places, and
is so vehement in the matter that we seem actually frigid in comparison of him. In his ninth Homily upon the Epistle to the
Colossians, he uses these expressions: "Hear me, I beseech you,
all men of secular life. Procure for yourselves bibles, the medicines
of the soul. If ye will have nothing else, get yourselves even the
new Testament alone, the Apostolic Epistles, the Acts, the Gospels,
as your constant and perpetual instructors. Should any distress
befall you, apply to this as a dispensary of remedies. Hence draw
your balm, whether it be losses, or death, or domestic bereavement,
that hath befallen you. Nay, not only apply to it, but take it all
in and hold it in your mind. The one great cause of all evils is
ignorance of scripture." In the same place, he addresses fathers
of families thus: "You lay every thing on our shoulders: it were
fitting that you only should need to be instructed by us, and by
you your wives, and by you your children, should be taught[2]."

Hence it appears how absurd is the answer of the Jesuit,
when he endeavours to wrest the testimony of this father out of
our hands. "Chrysostom," says he, "is not to be understood in
the sense which the words seem to bear at first sight; for he
speaks with exaggerated emphasis. He only wishes by these
exhortations to take the people off from the games and spectacles
to which they were at that time wholly given up." To which I
might reply, that now also there are games and spectacles and
many other occasions by which the people are seduced from piety;

[1 Καὶ ἡ Ἑβραίων φωνὴ οὐ μόνον εἰς τὴν τῶν Ἑλλήνων μετεβλήθη, ἀλλὰ
καὶ εἰς τὴν τῶν Ῥωμαίων καὶ Αἰγυπτίων καὶ Περσῶν καὶ Ἰνδῶν καὶ Ἀρμενίων
καὶ Σκυθῶν καὶ Σαυροματῶν, καὶ συλλήβδην εἰπεῖν, εἰς πάσας τὰς γλώττας αἷς
ἅπαντα τα ἔθνη κεχρημένα διατελεῖ.—Græc. Affect. Curat. (ed. Sylburg. 1692.)
Serm. v. p. 81. l. 14.]
[2 T. XI. p. 390.]

and that therefore in these times also they should be exhorted to read the scriptures. But it is manifest that Chrysostom did not merely say these things to deter the people from such trifling and seductive amusements, or take them off from their pursuits, but because he thought the perusal of the scriptures appertained to the duty of the people. In consequence, in his third Homily upon Lazarus, he wishes the people to examine the passage at home which he was about to treat of in the church. His words are as follows : " On this very account we often forewarn you, many days before, of the subject upon which we intend to speak, in order that, in the intervening time, you may take up the book and weigh the whole matter ; and thus, by distinctly understanding what hath been said and what still remains to be said, your minds may be the better prepared to hear what shall afterwards be discoursed to you. And now I constantly exhort you, and shall never cease to exhort you, not merely to attend here to what is said to you, but also, when you are at home, to betake yourselves assiduously to the perusal of the holy scriptures[3]." Then he removes all the excuses which the people used to allege for not reading the sacred scriptures,—not only that about the spectacles, but others much more reasonable, as the following : " I am not a monk, but a layman ; I have a wife, and children, and a family to mind, and am distracted by a multiplicity of avocations ; this appertains to others and not to me." All these he removes, and affirms more than once : " It is impossible, it is, I say, impossible, that any one can obtain salvation, who is not continually employed in spiritual studies." Yea, he removes also the excuse grounded upon the obscurity of scripture, and says that it is nothing but " a pretext and cloak of carelessness." He writes to the same effect, Hom. 29 in Genes. ; Hom. 13 in Joan. ; Hom. 2 in Matt. ; Hom. 3 in 2 Thess. ; and elsewhere ; which testimony I, for the present, omit to cite at length.

　　Other fathers also agree with Chrysostom and us in this matter. Origen, Hom. 12 in Exod.[4], blames the people in many words for not attending to the scripture in church, and meditating upon it at home also. The same author, in his second Homily upon Isaiah, says : " Would that we all did that which is written, ' Search the scriptures[5].' " He says *all*, not merely the learned, or

[3 T. I. p. 737. A. B.]
[4 p. 174. A. ed. Benedict.]
[5 Utinamque omnes faceremus illud quod scriptum est, Scrutamini scripturas.—Opp. T. I. p. 639. Basil. 1536.]

the bishops, or the spiritualty.   Jerome, in his Epistle to Eustochium, exhorts her to the constant reading of the scriptures.   But
here the Jesuit answers, that Eustochium and her mother Paula
understood not only Latin, but Greek and Hebrew also ; and adds
farther, that they were modest women, and that, if all women were
like them, they might without danger be permitted to read the holy
scriptures.   But Jerome invites not only Eustochium, but all pious
women to the reading of the scriptures; and in the epitaph of
Paula he affirms, that not only Eustochium but all the sisters sung
the Psalms of David in course : " None of the sisters," says he,
" was allowed to remain ignorant of the Psalms, or to fail of learning something from the holy scriptures every day [1]."   Writing to
the widow Salvina [2], he exhorts her to be continually occupied with
pious reading.   So also he exhorts a matron named Celancia [3], to
make it " her chief care" to know the law of God.   And he writes
in the same strain to many other females.   Thus of old times all,
both men and women, whose souls were warmed with any zeal for
piety, were occupied in the reading of the scriptures.

Theodoret, in the book already cited, namely, the fifth of his
Therapeutic Discourses, writes thus concerning the present subject:
" You may see everywhere these doctrines of ours understood not
only by those who are masters in the church and teachers of the
people, but by the very cobblers and smiths, weavers and artisans
of every kind, yea, and by women too of all classes; not alone
those, if there be such, who are acquainted with literature, but by
those who work for hire with their needles, by maid-servants and
nursery girls.   Nor is it only the inhabitants of cities who know
these things, but the rustics have almost an equal acquaintance with
them; and you will find men who dig the ground, or tend cattle, or
plant vegetables, who can dispute of the divine Trinity and the creation of all things, and who are better acquainted with human
nature than Plato and the Stagirite were [4]."   Thus Theodoret.   But

[[1] Nec licebat cuiquam sororum ignorare Psalmos, et non quotidie aliquid
de scripturis sanctis discere.—Opp. p. 706. T. I.]
[[2] T. I. p. 493.]
[[3] T. I. p. 1089.]
[[4] Καὶ ἔστιν ἰδεῖν ταῦτα εἰδότας τὰ δόγματα, οὐ μόνους γε τῆς ἐκκλησίας
τοὺς διδασκάλους, ἀλλὰ καὶ σκυτοτόμους, καὶ χαλκοτύπους, καὶ ταλασιουργοὺς,
καὶ τοὺς ἄλλους ἀποχειροβιώτους· καὶ γυναῖκας ὡσαύτως, οὐ μόνον τὰς λόγων
μετεσχηκυίας, ἀλλὰ καὶ χερνήτιδας καὶ ἀκεστρίδας, καὶ μέντοι καὶ θεραπαίνας·
καὶ οὐ μόνον ἀστοὶ, ἀλλὰ καὶ χωριτικοὶ τήνδε τὴν γνῶσιν ἐσχήκασι· καὶ ἔστιν
εὑρεῖν καὶ σκαπανέας καὶ βοηλάτας καὶ φυτουργοὺς περὶ τῆς θείας διαλεγομέ-

the papists now make it a matter of reproach to us, that amongst us women converse about sacred matters, or any men even except the learned. Hosius complains bitterly of this in his book, *De Sacro vernacule Legendo.* " This profanation," says he, " rather than translation of the scripture has brought us not only men belt-makers, porters, bakers, tailors, cobblers; but also female belt-makers, sewers and stitchers, she-apostles, prophetesses, doc-tresses[5]:" as if, forsooth, it were not lawful for women, in what-ever station of life, to understand the mysteries of religion. And Alphonsus de Castro, *de Just. Punit. Hæret.* Lib. III. c. 6, says that the translation of the scriptures into the vulgar tongue is " the cause of all heresies[6] :" of course, because whatever displeases the Roman pontiff is undoubtedly heretical. But Eusebius, Demonstr. Evang. Lib. I. c. 6, passes a much sounder judgment upon this matter, when he says : " The divine doctrines may be learned as well by women as by men, by the poor as by the rich, by servants as by masters[7]." Erasmus, a man of the greatest judgment and extraordinary genius, affirms in many places, that it is necessary that the scriptures should be translated and read by the people ; and, when he was blamed on that account by the divines of Paris, he defended himself against them not only by the precedent of the ancient church, but by the necessity of the thing itself.

And let this suffice upon the first member of the second part of this second question.

νους τριάδος, καὶ περὶ τῆς τῶν ὅλων δημιουργίας, καὶ τὴν ἀνθρωπείαν φύσιν εἰδότας Ἀριστοτέλους πολλῷ μᾶλλον καὶ Πλάτωνος.—p. 81. ed. Sylburg. 1592. I have departed in one word from Sylburgius' orthography, writing ἀποχειρο-βιώτους for ἀποχειροβιότους. There are indeed some instances of ἀβίοτος, but Lobeck I think truly treats them as only a kind of a play upon βίοτος, in connexion with which they occur.—See Lobeck ad Phrynich. p. 713.]

[5 Profanatio hæc scripturæ verius quam translatio non solum zonarios, bovillos, pistores, sartores, sutores, verum etiam zonarias, bovillas, sartrices, sutrices facit nobis apostolas, prophetissas, doctrices.—Opp. p. 745. Lugdun. 1563.]

[6 The title of the chapter is De quinta causa hæresium, quæ est Sacræ Scripturæ translatio in linguam vulgarem. Fol. 208. 2. Salmant. 1547.]

[7 ὥστε τοιαῦτα μανθάνειν καὶ φιλοσοφεῖν μὴ μόνον ἄνδρας ἀλλὰ καὶ γυ-ναῖκας, πλουσίους τε καὶ πένητας, καὶ δούλους ἅμα δεσπόταις. — p. 24. D. ed. Viger. Paris. 1628.]

CHAPTER XVI.

STATE OF THE QUESTION CONCERNING PUBLIC PRAYERS AND
SACRED RITES IN THE VULGAR TONGUE.

WE have now at length come to the second member of the
second part of this question, which concerns the celebration of
divine service, that is, the public prayers and offices of the church,
in the vulgar tongue of all churches. The papists everywhere
make use of the Latin tongue in all their churches throughout all
nations : which practice, impious and absurd as it is, is yet confirmed by the authority of the council of Trent, Sess. XXII. cap.
8 ; where it is said "not to seem good to the fathers, that the mass
should everywhere be celebrated in the vulgar tongue." Now
under the name of the mass they understand the whole liturgy and
all the offices of the church. Nevertheless it is permitted in the
same decree " to pastors and those who have the cure of souls, frequently during the celebration of mass, either themselves or through
others, to expound some parts of what is read in the mass[1]." And
in canon IX. of that session, the council says : " If any affirm that
the mass should only be celebrated in the vulgar tongue, let him be
anathema[2]." Hosius also hath written a book upon this subject,
to which he gives this title, " De Sacro vernacule Legendo ;"
wherein he asserts that the Latin was the only language ever used
in the Western church, and the Greek in the Eastern. We, on
the contrary, maintain that always in all ancient churches of
the Christians the lessons and public prayers were held in that
language which the people understood, and that so it should always

[1 Etsi Missa magnam contineat populi fidelis eruditionem, non tamen
visum est patribus, ut vulgari passim lingua celebretur. Quamobrem, retento
ubique cujusque ecclesiæ antiquo, et a sancta Romana ecclesia, omnium
ecclesiarum matre et magistra, probato ritu, ne oves Christi esuriant, neve
parvuli panem petant, et non sit qui frangat eis, mandat sancta Synodus pastoribus et singulis curam animarum gerentibus, ut frequenter inter missarum
celebrationem, vel per se vel per alios, ex iis quæ in missa leguntur, aliquid
exponant, atque inter cetera sanctissimi hujus sacrificii mysterium aliquod
declarent, diebus præsertim dominicis et festis.—Sess. XXII. c. viii.]

[2 Si quis dixerit, ecclesiæ Romanæ ritum, quo submissa voce pars canonis
et verba consecrationis proferuntur, damnandum esse ; aut lingua tantum vulgari missam celebrari debere ; aut aquam non miscendam esse vino in calice
offerendo, eo quod sit contra Christi institutionem : anathema sit.—Can. IX.
ut supra.]

be. Wherefore the reformed churches have justly banished these Latin services. The state, therefore, of the controversy is this; whether public prayers are only to be held in the Latin tongue, or in the vulgar tongue of every nation? We have already proved that the scriptures should be translated into the vulgar tongue: and since the reason is the same for celebrating prayers and translating scripture vernacularly, the same arguments will serve for confirming this cause as for the former. On this account the Jesuit hath mixed up this question with the previous one, and treated of them both together: yet it seemed to us more prudent to discuss these matters separately.

So much we thought fit to premise upon the state of the question. Let us now proceed to the arguments on both sides.

CHAPTER XVII.

THE ARGUMENTS OF THE PAPISTS FOR SERVICE IN A FOREIGN TONGUE ARE CONFUTED.

IN the first place, as our proposed plan requires, we shall set forth the arguments of the papists, upon which they rely to prove that public prayers and the other offices of the church should only be celebrated in the Latin tongue.

Their first argument is to this effect: The majesty of religious offices requires a language more grand and venerable than the vulgar tongues of every nation. Therefore they should be performed in Latin, not in the vernacular.

I answer: In the first place, What is that peculiar dignity, majesty, or sanctity which the Latin tongue hath more than others? Surely, none. Yea, nothing can be slighter, more futile, or more foolish, than those common Latin services which are used by the Roman church. For my part, I can recognise no greater holiness in one language than in another; nor a greater dignity either; unless, perhaps, they hold the Latin in such high esteem for the sake of its phrases, its antiquity, or the mysteries which are consigned in that language. But gravity, holiness, and majesty are in the things, not in the tongue. The Latin, therefore, cannot contribute any additional dignity to the scripture. Secondly, I deny that the majesty of sacred things can be diminished by any vernacular tongues, however barbarous. Nothing can be more dignified, majestic, or holy than the gospel. Yet, Acts ii., it was expounded

and published by the apostles in all languages, even barbarous
ones : which they certainly never would have done, if they had
supposed that by so doing its majesty would have run the risk of
being in the slightest degree impaired. But the Jesuit urges that
there are many mysteries which must not be imparted to the
people; and that they are profaned when they are translated into
the vulgar tongue, and so commonly published to everybody. This
he proves by the testimonies of certain fathers, as Dionysius the
Areopagite, Basil, and others. Nay, our countrymen the Rhemists,
too, urge the same plea in their Annotations upon 1 Cor. xiv., where
they complain most piteously that the mysteries of the sacraments
are horribly profaned, which should be carefully concealed from the
common people.

I answer : In the first place, neither Christ nor the apostles
ever commanded that those mysteries should be concealed from the
people. Yea, on the contrary, Christ instituted such sacraments in
order to instruct us through our very senses : this was the end of
the institution itself. And, indeed, the whole significance of these
mysteries was of old quite familiarly known by the people; and
therefore the apostle, 1 Cor. x. 15, when about to enter upon a
discourse concerning the sacraments, addresses the Corinthians thus :
" I speak as to wise men ; judge ye what I say." Consequently
they were not ignorant of the sacraments; for he calls them wise
men, and would have them judge of what he was about to say.
Nothing, indeed, could bear a more ludicrous and trifling appearance
than the sacraments, unless their design and reason were known.
For what advantage could a gentile, or any one unacquainted with
that sacrament, suppose to have accrued to an infant by merely
seeing it baptized ? What advantage, in his opinion, would a
Christian receive by taking a morsel of bread and a few drops of
wine ? Surely nothing could seem more foolish to one who was
not acquainted with the reason and object of these ceremonies.
These therefore should not be concealed, but explained to God's
people ; and the hiding of them is an antichristian device to fill the
people with a stupid admiration of they know not what.

I answer, secondly, to the testimonies of the fathers : and, first,
to Dionysius[1], whose words are cited from the book of the Ecclesi-

---

[1 The works of the pseudo-Dionysius were published by Corderius in
Greek, Paris, 1615.   But the last and best edition is that of 1644, printed
also at Paris with the Defensio Areopagitica of Chaumont.   For a full account compare Daillè, de Script. Dion. Areop. Geneva, 1666; and Pearson,
Vindic. Ignat. par. 1. c. 10.]

xvii.] QUESTION THE SECOND.

astical Hierarchy, cap. 1, where he admonishes Timotheus, to whom
he writes, concerning the sacred mysteries, ἀμέθεκτα καὶ ἄχραντα
τοῖς ἀτελέστοις διατηρεῖν, and ἱεροῖς μόνοις τῶν ἱερῶν κοινωνεῖν·
that is, "that they should not be imparted to the uninitiate, because
holy things are only to be given to holy persons, and pearls are
not to be cast to swine." Now, as to this Dionysius, I deny, in the
first place, that he is the Areopagite mentioned Acts xvii. 34. And
this I do, not because I feel uneasy at his testimony (for he says no
more than what Christ himself distinctly enjoins, Matt. vii. 6); but
because I am led to form this opinion by certain arguments, which
it is not, at present, needful for me to touch upon. There will be
another opportunity of speaking about this Dionysius. Secondly,
I say that his opinion is true and pious, and makes, in no respect,
against us, as will readily appear to any one who will consider the
passage. The sense of his words is, that holy things are not to be
exposed or cast before heathen, gentiles, and profane persons :
which, indeed, ought to hold as well in the case of the word, as in
that of the sacraments. But the fathers formerly were much more
cautious with respect to the sacraments than the word; because
heathen and impure men used to deride and despise the sacraments
much more than the preaching of the word. Now that this is the
meaning of Dionysius, his scholiast Maximus informs us; whose
words are as follows: "It is not fit to reveal the holy things to the
profane, nor to fling pearls to swine[2]." But the laity ought not to
be compared to swine, nor treated as profane, or spectators of the
Eleusinian mysteries. If they wish to be pious, holy, and faithful,
they should be acquainted with the design of the mysteries. And
I make the same answer to the testimony of Basil, which is contained in his treatise, de Sp. S., Lib. ii. c. 27[3]. The people certainly are not bound to feel much indebted to those who think of
them so meanly and dishonourably as to regard them as swine and

---

[2] οὐ δεῖ τὰ ἅγια τοῖς βεβήλοις ἐκφαίνειν, οὐδὲ τοὺς μαργαρίτας τοῖς χοίροις
ῥίπτειν. This scholiast was Maximus the Confessor, who flourished about the
year 645.]

[3] ἃ γὰρ οὐδὲ ἐποπτεύειν ἔξεστι τοῖς ἀμυήτοις, τούτων πῶς ἂν ἦν εἰκὸς τὴν
διδασκαλίαν θριαμβεύειν ἐν γράμμασιν.—Basil. Opp. T. ii. p. 211. B. Which,
by the way, is a good instance of θριαμβεύω in the sense of openly displaying.
Cf. Col. ii. 15; 2 Cor. ii. 14. I observe another instance in Cabasilas, as
given in Jahn's *Lerefrüchte byzantinischer Theologie*, in Ullman's *Studien
und Krit.* for 1843, part 3, p. 744, n. 62. δυοῖν ὄντων, ἃ δῆλον καθίστησι καὶ
θριαμβεύει τὸν ἐραστήν.]

dogs. Chrysostom, Hom. 24, in Matt., and Gregory, Dial. Lib. IV. c. 56, contain nothing pertinent to the present question.

The second argument of our adversaries is grounded upon the authority of scripture, namely, Levit. xvi. 17, where the people are commanded to remain without and wait for the priest, whilst he enters the sanctuary, and offers up prayers alone for himself and the people. This is commanded in that passage; and an example of the practice is given Luke i. 10, where we read that the people stood without, while Zacharias offered incense in the temple : whence it is clear that the people not only did not understand the priest, but did not even hear him. Therefore it is considered unnecessary that the people should understand the prayers which are offered by the priest to God.

I answer : That the conclusion does not follow from this precept and example. For, in the first place, there was an express commandment of God that the people should remain without, and the priest alone should offer incense in the sanctuary. Let them, if they can, produce any similar command for their Latin liturgy and foreign services, and we will yield to their opinion. But they cannot; and, in matters of religion, nothing should be attempted without a command. Secondly, this was typical. Therefore the same should not now be done; since all the old types have been done away. The priest was in the place of Christ, and represented him, who thus went up alone into the sanctuary, that is, into heaven, where he now intercedes with God for the church, although we do not now see or hear him. I deny that this should now be imitated by us; for typical observances have now no place. Thirdly, the people were not able even to hear the absent priest speaking, much less to understand what he said : but when the priest spoke in presence of the people, he spoke in such a manner as to be understood by all. But the priests of the papists, even under the eyes and in the audience of the people, perform and celebrate their unholy rites and sacrifices, which are no sacrifices, in a foreign tongue.

Their third argument is that of cardinal Hosius, in his book, *De Sacro vernac. Legendo,* and is to this effect : "Religion and piety have been so far from being increased, that they have been diminished, since some have begun to use the Vulgar tongue in the offices of the church. Therefore they ought rather to be performed and celebrated in the Latin language."

I answer, in the first place, Though we were to concede the

truth of what Hosius affirms, it will not follow thence that the public service should be performed in Latin, and not in the Vulgar tongue. For what if many are made worse? Will it therefore follow that vernacular prayers are to be entirely banished? The doctrine of the gospel renders many more perverse and obstinate; yet it ought not, on that account, to be concealed from the people. When Christ preached and taught the people, the Pharisees were made more obstinate; and the apostle says that the gospel is to some the savour of death unto death: and yet nevertheless the gospel should always be preached. That reason, therefore, is not a just cause why the offices of the church should not be performed in the Vulgar tongue, because many are thereby rendered worse; unless it be proved that the vernacular language is the cause of that ill effect: which they cannot prove. Secondly, I say that what is supposed in the antecedent is untrue. For although there does not appear in the people so much superstition as formerly; yet in the reformed churches at the present day the sincerity of true religion is more flourishing. The people, indeed, are not so superstitious as they were formerly : they then feared everything with a certain stupid superstition, which, it must be allowed, repressed, however, many crimes. Yet they are now much more religious in our churches. For they are deceived, who suppose that there is any piety, or virtue, or religion, in blind ignorance or superstition. And although there be amongst us many profane persons, such as there will never be lacking in the church of God, there are yet many who have a true sense of religion. So much upon the argument of Hosius.

The fourth argument is that adduced by Harding[1] in his third article against Jewel, sect. 8. which stands thus : "A great part of Asia Minor used only the Greek language in their service ; but the whole people did not understand Greek. Therefore it is lawful to use an unknown tongue in the public service."

I answer, firstly, he should prove that all Asia Minor used the Greek language in their service ; which since he fails to do, his syllogism is composed of merely particular propositions, and therefore concludes nothing. Secondly, he should prove his minor. He con-

[1 "The less Asia, being a principal part of the Greek Church, had then the service in the Greek tongue. But the people of sundry regions and countries of the less Asia then understood not the Greek tongue; *ergo*, the people of sundry regions and countries had then their service in an unknown tongue." Apud Jewel, Art. III. §. 8. p. 272. *ut supra*.]

firms it, indeed, by a twofold testimony. The first is taken from Acts xiv. 11, where, when Paul had healed a man who was lame from his mother's womb, the people are said to have lifted up their voice Λυκαονιστὶ, "in the speech of Lycaonia," and to have said, "The gods have come down to us in the likeness of men." Hence he collects that the whole people of Asia Minor did not understand Greek, since the people of Lystra and Derbe, which were two cities of Asia Minor, did not speak in Greek but in Lycaonian. I answer; the Lycaonian tongue was not a different language from the Greek[1], but only a different dialect. For Paul did not preach the gospel to that people in Lycaonian, but in Greek; while yet the people doubtless understood what he said, as is manifest from the instance of the lame man who was cured and converted by Paul. If Paul had spoken in Lycaonian, and not in Greek, why does Luke write particularly that they uttered this exclamation "in the speech of Lycaonia?" This reasoning, therefore, is the same as if he were to say : they spoke Doric, and therefore did not speak Greek. Furthermore, that they both understood and spoke Greek, is evident from the fact that Amphilochius, a bishop of Lycaonia[2], wrote in Greek, some fragments of whom are extant to this day.

The second testimony by which he confirms his minor, is taken from the second chapter of the Acts, where Cappadocia, Pontus, Asia, Phrygia, Pamphylia, &c., are enumerated as sundry regions, and must therefore have used sundry languages. I answer: Some of those tongues which the apostles used, were not altogether different and distinct, but only various dialects. So the speech which the Galileans used was different from that of the Jews; yet not so as to be another language, but only another dialect. For the maid-servant doubtless understood Peter, who was of Galilee, when she said, "Thy speech bewrayeth thee." So a Cappadocian could understand a Phrygian speaking, a Pamphylian

[1 We are left to mere conjecture upon this subject. Grotius supposed the Lycaonian to be the same as the Cappadocian. Jablonsky determines that it was a Greek dialect, but next akin to the Assyrian and thence derived. Guhling published a separate dissertation, *De Lingua Lycaonica a Pelasgis Grœcis orta* Wittenberg, 1726, in which he contends that the Lycaonian was derived from the Greek. See Kuinoel upon Acts xiv. 11.]

[2 i.e. Bishop of Iconium, the capital of Lycaonia. He flourished A.D. 370. The principal fragments that go under his name were published by Combefis, Paris, 1644. But there is an epistle preserved by Cotelerius, in his Monumenta, T. II. p. 99, which is supposed to be the only genuine piece of his now extant.]

a Cretan, an Athenian a Spartan. Now that the people of Asia Minor understood the Greek language is certain : for Paul wrote to the Ephesians, to the Galatians, and to the Colossians in Greek. But Ephesus, Galatia, and Colossæ, were cities of Asia Minor. Therefore either all Asia, or a great part of this Asia, understood Greek : otherwise Paul would never have written to them in Greek. Besides, the same is evident from Polycarp, bishop of Smyrna, Gregory, bishop of Nyssa, Basil, bishop of Cæsarea in Cappadocia ; who all, though bishops of Asia Minor, wrote all their works in Greek. Jerome too, in his second proem to the Epistle to the Galatians, affirms that the whole East spoke Greek[3]. The papists therefore can never prove that Asia Minor did not use the Greek language. Or, if amongst those people some were ignorant of Greek, how will they prove that they had their service in the Greek language? Hence their argument is inconsequential in every possible way of considering it.

The fifth argument, which some at least advance, is of this kind : Three languages were hallowed upon the cross : therefore we ought to use only these languages in the public offices of the church. And Bellarmine says that we should be content with those three languages which Christ honoured upon the cross.

I answer : In the first place, that title was not written in three languages in order that those languages should thereby be consecrated to such a use ; but that the report of Christ's death should so be diffused as widely as possible. Secondly, this is an allegorical argument, and therefore of itself concludes nothing. Thirdly, Cajetan, Jentac. Lib. I. Quæst. 4, says that these three languages " were the representatives of all languages[4]," because the number three denotes perfection. If this be so, then all the languages of all nations can celebrate the death of Christ, and all the services of Christianity.

The other arguments of the adversary in this question have no weight in them whatsoever, and I will not be guilty of seeming to waste time in unnecessary disputes.

[3 Excepto sermone Græco, quo omnis oriens loquitur. T. IV. p. 1. 255.]
[4 Et tribus præcipuis linguis omnium linguarum vices gerentibus, ex ipsius etiam trinarii omnia complectentis perfectione, scribere disposuit. *Jentacula Novi Testamenti.* 27. 2. Paris. 1536.]

17

CHAPTER XVIII.

OUR ARGUMENTS, WHEREBY WE PROVE THAT THE OFFICES OF THE
CHURCH SHOULD BE PERFORMED IN THE VERNACULAR LAN-
GUAGE OF EVERY PEOPLE.

LET us now proceed to the establishment of our own opinion,
whither all those arguments which we used in the former part may
be referred. For if the scriptures should be read in the vulgar
tongue, then certainly the rest of the service should be performed
in the vulgar tongue also. However, we will now use some
peculiar and separate arguments in this question.

Our FIRST argument shall be taken from Paul's first epistle to
the Corinthians, chap. xiv.: in which chapter Paul directs, that
everything should be done for the edification of the people in the
church, that no one should speak in a strange tongue without an
interpreter; and adds, that he would rather speak five words with
his understanding, so as to instruct others also, than ten thousand
words in an unknown tongue. And the whole chapter is spent
upon this subject. Whence it evidently appears that the popish
opinion is repugnant to apostolical teaching. We reason thus from
that chapter against the papists: If prayers in the Latin are
everywhere to be set forth for the people, then the people will
not understand what is said. But the apostle expressly forbids
this in this chapter. Therefore public prayers should not be
everywhere celebrated in the Latin tongue. However, let us
weigh the answer of our opponents to this reasoning; who, in
truth, are wonderfully perplexed at this passage, and have
devised many contrivances to evade it.

Some papists reply, that Paul does not speak in that chapter
of prayers, offices, or stated services, but of exhortations and public
sermons, which they confess should be delivered in the vulgar
tongue. But I deny that the meaning of the apostle was merely
to forbid a strange language in exhortations or sermons. For who
would have been mad enough to deliver an harangue to the people
in an unknown tongue? Who could so much as have hoped that
the people would be sufficiently attentive to hear with patience and
civility a man uttering, by the space of an hour or more, words
which they did not understand? We read that some persons formerly in the church preached in a foreign tongue, but we read also
that there were at the same time interpreters at hand. But this is
quite another matter. I allow, indeed, that the apostle does men-

tion sermons; for it is with such a reference that he says, verse 29, " Let the prophets speak (λαλείτωσαν) by two or three, and the rest judge :" but that this is his whole subject, upon which he is entirely engaged throughout that chapter, I deny. For how are we to understand what is said ver. 14, "If I pray in an unknown tongue, my spirit prayeth, but my understanding is unfruitful ?" Besides he speaks of services to which the people answer *Amen*. Now the people use not to do this to sermons. He mentions also giving of thanks and praising God. Nay, the fathers themselves, Chrysostom, Theophylact, Ambrose, Œcumenius, and all who have well explained this chapter, confess that Paul speaks not only of exhortations and sermons, but also of public prayers. Yea, Harding, Art. iii. Sect. 18 [1], allows that it was needful in the primitive church that prayers should be held in the vulgar and intelligible tongue, but contends that it is now no longer requisite. But now the papists, become more learned, choose another mode of answering. They confess, indeed, that the apostle speaks of public prayers; but they deny it to be requisite that the whole people should understand the prayers which the minister repeats; for they say it is sufficient if one only, whom they commonly call the *clerk*, understand them, who is to answer *Amen* in behalf of the whole congregation. They prove this from those words of the apostle, at verse 16, " If thou shalt bless with the spirit, how (says the old edition) shall he who supplies the place of the unlearned answer *Amen ?*" Thus Stapleton, in his English book against Jewel, Art. iii. Thus a certain papist, who hath made an epitome of Bellarmine's Lectures. So Thomas Aquinas. So Catharinus. So Sixtus Senensis, Bibliothec. Lib. vi. Annot. 263.

I answer : In the first place, the Latin vulgate version is false and foolish, and does not agree with the Greek text. For τόπος never means the person of those represented; and ἀναπληροῦν is to *fill*, not to *supply*. So that the meaning is not, " he who supplies the place of the people," as the old Latin edition renders it ; but, " he who occupies the room, and sits amongst the laity,"— that is, he who is himself a layman and one of the common people. For formerly the minister did not sit promiscuously with the

[[1] 18 is a misprint for 28. Harding's words are: " But St Paul, say they, requireth that the people give assent and conform themselves unto the priest, by answering amen to his prayer made in the congregation. Verily, in the primitive church this was necessary, when the faith was a-learning." Ap. Jewel, p. 317, *ut supra.*]

people, but in a place separate from the people and the rest of
the multitude. This is what is referred to by the phrase, ἀναπληροῦν τὸν τόπον τοῦ ἰδιώτου. And thus it is that Chrysostom,
Theophylact, and Œcumenius interpret this place. Œcumenius
says that he fills the place of the unlearned, who εἰς ἰδιώτην τελεῖ,
is ranked as an unlearned person; and immediately subjoins,
" he calls him unlearned who is ranged in the rank of laymen[1]."
Secondly, I say that there was no such person in the ancient
church as they call a *clerk,* but that the whole congregation together
answered *Amen.* So Jerome, in his second prologue to his commentary on the Galatians : " The whole church," says he, " replies with a thundering Amen[2]." A single clerk, unless he be a
Stentor, cannot answer thus. So Chrysostom, as is manifest from
his liturgy,—if indeed it be his, and not rather the work of some
body else published under his name[3]. So Cyprian, in his discourse
upon the Lord's prayer : " When the minister," says he, " hath
said, ' Lift up your heart,' the whole people answer, ' We lift them
up unto the Lord[4].' " But most plainly of all Justin Martyr, in his
Second Apology for the Christians : πᾶς ὁ λαὸς ἐπευφημεῖ Ἀμήν[5]·
" the whole people reply in token of assent, Amen." These
words, therefore, are not to be understood of such an imaginary
clerk, answering in the name of the whole people, as the papists
would have it.

But the Jesuit Bellarmine, and lately our countrymen, the
Rhemists, following his example, do not venture to trust to this
answer, and therefore have invented another. They say that the
apostle does not speak at all of divine service, or the public reading of the scripture, but of certain spiritual songs, which were
wholly extraordinary, and in which the Christians of those times
used to praise God, and give him thanks, and edify and comfort
one another. These, they say, are mentioned, Ephes. v. 19 and
Coloss. iii. 16, where the apostle bids the Christians to whom he

[1 ἰδιώτην λέγει τὸν ἐν τῷ λαϊκῷ τάγματι τεταγμένον.—T. I. p. 560. Com-
mentt. in N. T. Paris. 1631.]
[2 Tota ecclesia instar tonitrui reboat Amen, *ut supra.*]
[3 See the excellent remarks of "the ever-memorable" Hales, at the end
of the article *Chrysostom,* in Cave's Historia Literaria.]
[4 Ideo et sacerdos ante orationem præfatione præmissa parat fratrum
mentes dicendo, Sursum corda; ut dum respondet plebs, Habemus ad Dominum, &c. p. 152, ed. Fell. Amstel. 1691.]
[5 p. 98. E. Opp. Colon. 1686, or Paris, 1636.]

writes, to speak to each other " in psalms and hymns, and spiritual
songs, singing and making melody in their hearts to the Lord;"
and that such songs are spoken of in this chapter, ver. 26, where
the apostle says, " when ye come together," ἕκαστος ὑμῶν ψαλμὸν
ἔχει, " each of you hath a psalm, hath a doctrine, hath a tongue,
hath a revelation : let all things be done unto edification." Finally,
that Tertullian mentions these in his Apology, c. 39[6], and also
other fathers : and that this cannot be understood of the public
offices and prayers, because the public prayers at Corinth were
then celebrated in the Greek language, which was understood by
all, and no strange tongue ; which Paul must have remembered
very well.

I answer : The apostle, I confess, speaks of those songs, and I
am not unaware of the existence of such hymns formerly amongst
Christians : but the apostle does not speak of them alone. For
he expressly mentions prayers, ver. 14, ἐὰν προσεύχωμαι τῇ
γλώσσῃ, " If I pray in an unknown tongue." And although the
Corinthian church then used the Greek language in the service of
God, it does not therefore follow that these words of the apostle
are not to be understood of the public offices and service. Certainly the whole discourse of the apostle is general. He speaks
generally and in common of all the offices of the church, and
condemns, on general grounds, the use of an unknown tongue in
the church, whether in sermons, or in prayers, or in songs. And
the first ground is this : an unknown tongue is useless ; therefore
it ought not to be used in the church. The antecedent is proved,
verse 2, where he says, " He that speaketh in an unknown tongue
speaketh not to men, but to God ; for no man understandeth him :
howbeit in the Spirit he speaketh mysteries." Ὁ λαλῶν γλώσσῃ,
" he that speaketh in a tongue," that is, an unknown tongue, says
Thomas Aquinas[7]; " for no man heareth," that is, no one understands him. But in the church one should speak so as that not God
alone, but men also may understand him. This he proves also in
the sixth verse, where he says, " If I should come to you speaking
with tongues" (though innumerable), "what shall I profit you?"—as
much as to say, you will derive no advantage whatever from my
discourse. And, verse 9, he says, ἐὰν μὴ εὔσημον λόγον δῶτε,
" unless ye utter with the tongue words easy to be understood, how

[6 Post aquam manualem et lumina, ut quisque de scripturis sanctis vel
de proprio ingenio potest, provocatur in medium Deo canere.—Apolog. c. 39.
p. 112. Opp. Tertull. Part 1. ed. Leopold. Lipsiæ. 1839.]
[7 Comment. in loc.]

shall it be understood what is spoken?" ἔσεσθε γὰρ εἰς ἀέρα
λαλοῦντες, "for ye shall be as if speaking into the air." From
these passages it is manifest that the apostle's meaning is this, that
whatever is spoken in the church in an unknown tongue is spoken
fruitlessly and in vain.

But the Jesuit and the Rhemists, setting themselves in open
opposition to the apostle, affirm that prayers, even when they
are not understood, are very edifying, although perhaps they
may be more edifying when they are understood. But the
apostle's words are clear, and must always be pressed upon
them, "What shall I profit you?"—as if he had said, I cannot be
any way of use to you. So Œcumenius interprets those words,
οὐκ ἔσομαι ὑμῖν ἐπωφελής. And "ye shall be speaking into the
air," that is, fruitlessly and in vain: for so Œcumenius, μάτην
καὶ ἀνωφελῶς. So also Chrysostom, in his 35th Homily upon
this chapter: "Ye depart," says he, "οὐδὲν κερδάναντες, deriving
no advantage from a sound which ye do not understand[1]." But let
us hear how the Jesuit proves that a prayer, though not understood, is useful to the people. Attend to his beautiful reason. The
minister, says he, or priest, does not pray to the people, but to God
for the people. Therefore, it is not necessary that the people
should understand what he says, but it is sufficient that God himself understands him. Now he understands all languages. This
he illustrates by a comparison. As, says he, if one were to inter-
cede with a king for a rustic, it is not necessary that the rustic
should understand what his patron says to the king in his behalf,
nor does he much care, provided only he obtain what he seeks; so
it is not requisite that the people should understand those prayers
which the minister presents to God in their name. Besides, the
church prays even for the infidels and the absent. I answer, this
reasoning of the Jesuit is inconsequential; and it is a bad argument
to say, prayer is not made to the people, but to God for the people;
therefore it is not necessary that the people should understand what
the minister prays. For the minister is, as it were, the people's
mouth. He prays, indeed, to God, but yet for the people; and
although the people remain silent in their lips, while the minister
prays, yet meanwhile they follow him, as he prays, in their hearts,
and respond at the close, Amen; by which expression they shew

[1] Ὁ δὲ λέγει τοῦτό ἐστιν .... γλωττῶν ὧν ἀκουσάντες οὐδὲν κερδάναντες ἀπε-
λεύσεσθε. πῶς γὰρ ἀπὸ φωνῆς, ἧς οὐ συνίετε;—Chrys. Opp. T. x. p. 233. The
Homilies on 1 Cor. are to be found in T. IV. of Saville's ed., and T. x. of the
Paris edition of Fronto Ducæus, 1613.]

that the prayer is their own, and signify that they ask from God whatever the minister himself hath asked. Otherwise, if the people did not pray along with the minister, it would not be necessary for the people to be present, or assemble in the same place with the minister, but the minister alone might pray for the people to God in their absence. But prayers are public, that is, prayers of the whole church. We see, therefore, that it is a foolish comparison which the Jesuit uses. For if the rustic, of whom he speaks, were to hear his advocate pleading his cause before the king in an unknown tongue, and speaking words which he did not understand, he might suspect that he was rather speaking against him than for him. So the people, when they hear the minister pray in an unknown tongue, may doubt whether he prays for them, or for others, or against them. What if even the priest himself do not understand what he is saying? the possibility of which experience hath taught in the case of many priests of the Roman church.

But the apostle, at verse 14, blames altogether all use of an unknown tongue in public prayers: "If I should pray," says he, " in a tongue, my spirit prayeth, but my understanding is unfruitful." And it is plain that he there speaks of public prayers; first, because, verse 19, he says, $\dot{\epsilon}\nu$ $\tau\hat{\eta}$ $\dot{\epsilon}\kappa\kappa\lambda\eta\sigma\dot{\iota}\alpha$, *in the church;* secondly, because he speaks of such prayers as the people said *Amen* to, as a token of their assent, as is plain from verse 16; which is only done when the people are assembled together in one place. Therefore, unless the prayer be understood, the understanding will be $\ddot{\alpha}\kappa\alpha\rho\pi$ος, unfruitful; that is, no advantage will accrue to the church from the conceptions of your understanding. The Jesuit and the papists give a wrong and foolish interpretation of that whole fourteenth verse, to this effect: "If I pray in a tongue, my mind or my understanding is not instructed, because indeed it does not understand what I say: but meanwhile my spirit, that is, my affections," — so they expound it, — "are edified." For example, says Bellarmine, if one were to recite the seven psalms, and not to understand what he was reciting, his understanding is not improved, yet his affections meanwhile are improved. The sum, therefore, of this interpretation is this: if I pray in an unknown tongue, although I do not understand the words, yet my affections are thereby made better.

I answer, in the first place, this is an utterly ridiculous interpretation. For he who recites any prayers or psalms in a language which he does not understand, is no more improved than if he had not recited them at all. His good affection, or desire of praying, is

not assisted by reading he knows not what. But if the affections of
him who prays in an unknown tongue be good, and his reason no
way benefited, because he does not understand his prayer; why
does he not use a language with which he is acquainted, that he
may derive a double advantage, both to his affections and to his understanding? Secondly, the papists themselves confess that prayers
expressed in a language known and understood are more useful and
advantageous. Why then do they not pray in a known tongue?
For prayers should be made in that manner in which they are
likely to be most useful to us. Now that prayers, when understood, are more useful than prayers not understood, the Jesuit concedes; and so does Harding, as may be seen, Art. III. Sect. 29.[1]
And De Lyra also, upon 1 Cor. xiv., says that the people, if they
understand the prayer of the priest, are "better brought to God,
and answer *Amen* with more devotion." If this be, as indeed it is,
most true, we see that there are very just reasons why the people
should understand their prayers: and yet Stapleton was not ashamed
in his English book against the very learned Jewel to say, Art. III.
p. 75, that devotion is not assisted, but impeded, when the language
is known and understood. Thirdly, since it is certain that prayer
is a mode of speech, is it not ridiculous to pray in an unknown
tongue? Who is there so destitute of common sense, as to choose,
especially in the presence of others, to speak in such a language as
either he himself is ignorant of, or the audience do not understand?
Whence Œcumenius upon this chapter distinctly affirms prayer to be
a kind of speech: προσευχὴ, says he, ἔστιν εἶδός τι τοῦ λόγου·
and he interprets verse 14 thus: If I speak anything necessary
and good, and expound it not to my audience, my spirit prays,—
that is, I myself derive some advantage; but my understanding is
unfruitful, that is, the conceptions of my understanding bring no
advantage to others. Hence it is manifest that the sense of these
words is very different from what they suppose. So Chrysostom
expounds this passage; and Basil most expressly and plainly of all,
in his Epitome of Definitions, Def. 278, "My understanding is unfruitful, because no one is benefited:" and he adds, that this is
spoken of them who "pray in an unknown tongue." I will subjoin
the words, because they are very remarkable: τοῦτο περὶ τῶν ἐν
γλώσσῃ ἀγνοουμένῃ τοῖς ἀκούουσι τὰς προσευχὰς ἀναπεμπόντων.
ὅταν γὰρ ἄγνωστα ᾖ τοῖς παροῦσι τὰ ῥήματα τῆς προσευχῆς,

[1 " I grant they cannot say 'Amen' to the blessing or thanksgiving of
the priest so well as if they understood the Latin tongue perfectly." Apud
Jewel, *ut supra*, p. 318.]

ἄκαρπός ἐστιν ὁ νοῦς τοῦ προσευχομένου μηδενὸς ὠφελουμένου[2]. In which words Basil distinctly affirms, that no benefit whatever can redound to the people from prayers which they do not understand. So Augustine, *De Genesi ad Liter.* Lib. XII. c. 8. " No one," says he, " is edified by hearing what he does not understand[3]." Therefore from words not understood no fruit follows; and hence it is manifest, that all their prayers are unfruitful and odious to God.

But here the Jesuit urges us with many allegations to prove that prayers, although not understood, are nevertheless useful to us. These we must examine severally. First, he says, that the figures and ceremonies of the old law were useful to the Jewish people, although they did not understand them. I answer: In the first place, let the Jesuit produce any such express command of God for having prayers in a tongue not understood as the Jews had for those ceremonies. Secondly, although the Jews did not understand the figures and ceremonies of the law so clearly as we now understand them, yet they were not wholly ignorant of them; and there were Levites from whom they could easily learn the whole design of their ceremonies, so as to understand it.

The Jesuit's second objection is taken from Augustine, *de Baptism. contra Donat.* Lib. VI. c. 25[4], where he says that those prayers, which have something heretical mingled with them, may yet be profitable to one who recites them in simplicity, not knowing what he says, and supposing that he prays rightly: whence the Jesuit infers that still more may good and holy prayers be beneficial to the people, although the people do not understand them. I answer: In the first place, we are not obliged to say anything now of those prayers which the church of Rome is wont to use; for many heretical matters might be pointed out in them. Secondly, Augustine does not speak of such prayers as are made in an unknown tongue, but of those in which something heretical is found mixed, which however is not perceived by those who use the prayers. This, he says, will be no way prejudicial to them, provided their intentions be pure; because, as he expresses it, "the affection of the suppliant overcomes the fault of the prayer[5]." But what is this to the present question?

[2 p. 641. B. T. II. Opp. Paris. 1618.]
[3 Nemo ædificatur audiendo quod non intelligit.   T. III. p. 302.]
[4 Augustin. Opp. T. IX. p. 176.]
[5 Quia plerumque precis vitium superat affectus precantis.]

The third objection of the Jesuit is taken from Origen's twentieth Homily upon Joshua: " We often, indeed, do not understand what we utter, yet the Virtues understand it[1]." So, says the Jesuit, though the people do not understand the prayers which the priest utters, yet the Virtues understand them. I answer : Origen, in that place, does not speak of prayers, but of the reading of the scriptures ; where he meets an objection which the laity are accustomed to make : the scriptures are difficult, and transcend our comprehension ; therefore we need not read them. Now, although (says Origen) we often do not understand what we read, yet the Virtues understand it.

The Jesuit's fourth objection is to this effect : If the people should use no prayers which they do not understand, then they should never recite the Psalms and the Prophets. I answer : The case of scripture is different from that of prayer. We must peruse the whole scripture, although we are not masters of its meaning, in order that we may, in the first place, understand the words, and then from the words be able to proceed to the sense. But we should only pray what we know ; because prayer is a colloquy with God, and springs from our understanding. For we ought to know what we say, and not merely, as the Jesuit pretends, know that what we do appertains to the honour of God. Secondly, the reason why we understand so little when we read, is to be found in our own fault, and not in any obscurity of scripture.

The Jesuit's fifth and last objection is taken from St Antony, as reported by Cassian, who says that prayer is then perfect when the mind is so affected, while we pray, as not itself to understand its own words. I answer : I wonder how this, be it what it may, can be made to serve the cause in hand. For Antony does not say that we should pray in an unknown tongue ; but that, when we pray, we should not fix our attention on the words, but have the mind absorbed, as it were, in divine meditation, and occupied in thoughts about the things rather than the words. If the feelings

[1 The Greek is preserved in the Philocalia, c. 12, p. 40, ed. Spencer. Εἰσὶ γάρ τινες δυνάμεις ἐν ἡμῖν, ὧν αἱ μὲν κρείττονες διὰ τούτων τῶν οἱονεὶ ἐπῳδῶν τρέφονται, συγγενεῖς οὖσαι αὐταῖς, καὶ, ἡμῶν μὴ νοούντων, ἐκείνας τὰς δυνάμεις, νοούσας τὰ λεγόμενα, δυνατωτέρας ἐν ἡμῖν γίνεσθαι. The whole chapter is a very curious discourse, in which Origen suggests that the mere words of scripture may have a beneficial effect, after the manner of a spell, upon the man who reads them, through certain spiritual powers which he supposes to be in intimate contact with our souls. The same passage is to be found in Huetius' Origen, T. I. p. 27. C.]

be sincere, we need not doubt but that the Holy Spirit will suggest and dictate words to us, and guide us in our prayers.

Thus then what this argument of the apostle's proves remains unshaken, that all prayers made in an unknown tongue are unfruitful.

The second general argument of the apostle is taken from those words which are contained in ver. 11 : " If I know not the meaning of the voice, I shall be to him that speaketh a barbarian, and he that speaketh shall be a barbarian to me." Therefore, if the minister shall pray in an unknown tongue, he and the congregation shall be barbarians to each other. Now this should not be in the church, that the minister should be a barbarian to the people, or the people to the minister. Therefore, the minister ought not to pray in an unknown tongue. The Jesuit does not touch this argument. The Rhemists pretend that the apostle does not here mean the three learned languages, that is, the Hebrew, Greek, and Latin, but others. They contend, therefore, that not he who speaks Latin, when the people do not understand it, is a barbarian ; but he who speaks English, French, Spanish, or any vulgar tongue which is not understood by the audience. I answer, that the apostle speaks in general of all languages, which the people do not understand. " If I speak in a tongue," says he, that is, in an unknown tongue, whatever it be. For those who speak with the greatest purity and elegance, if they speak not what the people understand, are barbarians to the people. Even Cicero himself or Demosthenes shall be barbarians, if they harangue the people in an unknown tongue which the people do not understand, however sublimely they may discourse. Thus also, if the people know not the Latin tongue, whoever uses it shall be a barbarian to them, since they are not able to judge of it. The poet Ovid, when banished to Pontus, says of himself, Trist. Lib. v. Eleg. 11 [2]:

> Barbarus hic ego sum, quia non intelligor ulli.

Anacharsis, when an Athenian reproachfully called him a barbarian, is said to have replied : " And ye Athenians are barbarians to the Scythians :" ἐμοὶ πάντες Ἕλληνες σκυθίζουσι. So Theodoret, Therapeut. Orat. Lib. v. ; in which same place he observes that this is what St Paul says, " I shall be to him that speaketh a barbarian [3]." Though men were to talk Attic, yet Anacharsis truly pronounces

[2 Trist. Lib. v. Eleg. x. 36.]

[3 Τοῦτο γὰρ ἀτεχνῶς ἔοικε τοῖς εἰρημένοις ὑπὸ τοῦ ἡμετέρου σκυτοτόμου· κ.τ.λ. p. 81. l. 53. ed. Sylburg. 1592.]

them barbarians to the Scythians, because the Scythians knew nothing of the Attic tongue. And Cicero, in the fifth book of his Tusculan Questions says : " In those languages which we understand not, we are just the same as deaf[1]." If deaf, then certainly it is not too much to say barbarians. Chrysostom interprets this passage in precisely the same way, and says that the word barbarian is used "not in reference to the nature of the speech, but with reference to our ignorance[2]." And so also Œcumenius. But, to silence our Rhemists with the testimony of papists, Catharinus writes thus upon the place : " He is here called a barbarian, whose tongue is so diverse that he cannot be understood : for whoever is not understood is a barbarian to the auditor[3]." Then he produces the verse of Ovid which we cited just now. He determines, therefore, that the popish priests are barbarians to the people, however they speak Latin. How well they speak it, makes no difference in this case. Certainly they do not speak better Latin than Ovid, who yet says that he was a barbarian to the people of Pontus. Now we have said enough upon this place of the apostle against the Jesuit and the Rhemists.

Next comes our SECOND argument, which is taken from other words of the apostle in this same chapter. All things, says he, 1 Cor. xiv. 40, should be done in the church " decently and in order," κατὰ τάξιν. Now it is most grossly repugnant to good order, that the minister should pray in an unknown tongue. For so the people, though assembled for public prayer, are compelled to pray, not publicly, but privately : and the custom hath prevailed in the popish churches, that the people recite none but private prayers in the church where public prayer is required. Yea, thus not only the people, but the minister, who ought to offer up the public prayers, utters only private ones : for the people, since they do not understand the liturgy, do not pray publicly ; and, consequently, the minister must needs pray alone by himself. For it does not presently follow that prayers are public, because they are made in a public place ; but those are public, which are made by the united desires and wills of the whole church. Hence the minister should

[1 Omnesque itidem nos in iis linguis quas non intelligimus surdi profecto sumus.—c. xi. 1. Opp. Ciceron. T. VIII. p. 559. ed. Lallemand. Paris. 1768. Barbou.]

[2 Οὐ παρὰ τὴν φύσιν τῆς φωνῆς ἀλλὰ παρὰ τὴν ἡμετέραν ἀγνοίαν. T. VI. p. 477.]

[3 Barbarus hoc in loco is dicitur, qui linguæ differt varietate, ut non intelligatur : quilibet enim qui non intelligitur barbarus est illi qui audit. p. 193. Paris. 1566.]

not pray in the church in an unknown tongue, because he, in so doing, makes that private which ought to have been public, and violates good order.

Our THIRD argument is to this effect : The papists themselves know and concede that the Armenians, Egyptians, Muscovites and Ethiopians perform their services in the vulgar tongue, and hold their prayers in their own native languages. Why then, if they do right, should not other churches do the same? But the Jesuit objects, that they are either heretics or schismatics; and that, therefore, it is no great matter what they do. I answer, that there are, indeed, in those churches many and great errors; yet neither more nor greater than in the church of Rome. These churches are condemned by the papists, because they will not submit to the Roman pontiff, or hold any such communion with him. They are extensive churches, and perhaps more extensive than the popish party, however they boast of their extension. All these are ignorant of the Latin tongue, and use their own language in their services; and in this matter we would rather resemble them than the papists. The same is the case of the Indians, as Eckius testifies in his common places : " We deny not that it is permitted to the southern Indians to perform divine service in their own language; which custom their clergy still observe[4]."

Our FOURTH argument stands thus: Æneas Sylvius, in his book on the origin of the Bohemians, c. XIII., relates, that Cyril and Methodius allowed the Moravians to use their own language in their service[5]. I ask, therefore, why the same might not be allowed to other churches? or why other churches should not do that which they know to be advantageous to them? The Jesuit objects, that Cyril and Methodius converted all the Moravians together to the faith, and that there was just cause then for that permission, because ministers could not be found competent to perform the service in Latin. I answer, if this were needful at first, then it follows that the service may be performed in the

[4 Non negamus Indis australibus permissum ut in lingua sua rem divinam facerent, quod clerus eorum hodie observat. c. xxxiv. Colon. 1532.]

[5 Referunt Cyrillum, cum Romæ ageret, Romano pontifici supplicasse ut Sclavorum lingua ejus gentis hominibus, quam baptizaverat, rem divinam faciens uti posset. De qua re dum in sacro senatu disputaretur, essentque non pauci contradictores, auditam vocem tanquam de cœlo in hæc verba missam: " Omnis spiritus laudet Dominum, et omnis lingua confiteatur ei." Indeque datum Cyrillo indultum. Æn. Sylv. Hist. Bohem. c. xiii. p. 91. Basil. 1571.]

vulgar tongue; which he had before said ought not to be done, because the dignity of the sacred offices requires a more majestic language. If this be a good reason, there can be no just cause for performing them in the vernacular. What he adds about the lack of ministers is an invention of his own.

Our FIFTH argument is taken from the authority of the emperor Justinian; who (Lib. de cap. Eccl. c. 123)[1] orders that the minister in the church should pronounce every thing with a clear voice, in order that the people may hear and answer *Amen*. Harding[2], Art. III. Sect. 14, objects, firstly, that Justinian speaks of a "clear voice," to let us know that it is *vocal*, and not *mental*, prayers that are required. But I answer, the reason subjoined removes all doubt on that score; for he adds, that the people may hear, and be inflamed to *devotion*, and answer *Amen*. Secondly, he objects that this rule was only enjoined upon the Greeks, not on others. I answer: Justinian was not merely emperor of Greece, but of all Europe; and therefore he proposed his laws not only to the prelates of Constantinople, but to those of Rome also, as is manifest from that same chapter: "We order, therefore, the most blessed archbishops and patriarchs, that is to say, of old Rome and of Constantinople[3]:" where expressly and by name he prescribes rules to the bishop of Rome. Thirdly, he objects that these words are not found in ancient copies. I answer, they are, however, found in all the Greek copies, which are more to be trusted than the Latin ones. And Gregory Holoander hath them also in his Latin version, who certainly faithfully translated the Greek text.

Our SIXTH and last argument is founded upon the authority and testimony of the fathers. First, Basil the Great, in Ep. 63, to the clergy of the church of Neocæsaræa, writes thus: "As the day dawns, all together, as with one voice and one heart, offer a Psalm of confession to the Lord, and each in his own words professes repentance." And lest any should suppose that this was spoken only of the Greeks, he subjoins: "These constitutions are observed with one accord by all the churches of God." There follows also in the same place: "If on account of these you fly from us, you must fly also the Egyptians, either Lybia, the Thebeans, the Palestinians, the Arabians, the Phœnicians, the Syrians, and those who dwell

[1 Justinian. Novell. Const. 137 (or 123) pp. 409, 10.   Basil. 1561.]
[2 Ap. Jewel, p. 284, ut supra.]
[3 κελεύομεν τοίνυν τοὺς μακαριωτάτους ἀρχιεπισκόπους καὶ πατριάρχας, τουτέστι τῆς πρεσβυτέρας Ῥώμης καὶ Κωνσταντινουπόλεως.]

upon the Euphrates; in a word, all who have any value for watch-
ing, and prayer, and common psalmody;" παρ᾿ οἷς ἀγρυπνίαι,
καὶ προσευχαί, καὶ αἱ κοιναὶ ψαλμωδίαι τετίμηνται⁴. To the
same effect it is that this same Basil (Hom. 4. in Hexaem. at the
end) compares the church to the sea: for as (says he) the waves
roar when driven upon the coast, so the church "sends forth the
mingled sound of men and women and children in prayer to God⁵."
    We perceive, therefore, that it was the custom of the primitive
church for the whole people to combine their desires and assent
with the prayers of the minister, and not, as is with the papists
(amongst whom the priest alone performs his service in an unknown
tongue), to remain silent, or murmur their own indefinite private
prayers to themselves. Ambrose hath a similar sentence, Hexaem.
Lib. III.⁶ Augustine, in his book *de Magistro*, c. 1, says that we
should pray with the heart, because the sacrifice of righteousness
is offered "in the temple of the mind and in the chambers of the
heart. Wherefore," says he, "there is no need of speech, that is,
of audible words, when we pray, unless, as in the case of the
priests, for the sake of denoting what we mean⁷." But why then
must we speak? Augustine answers, "not that God, but that

[⁴ Ἡμέρας ἤδη ὑπολαμπούσης, πάντες κοινῇ, ὡς ἐξ ἑνὸς στόματος καὶ μιᾶς
καρδίας, τὸν τῆς ἐξομολογήσεως ψαλμὸν ἀναφέρουσι τῷ Κυρίῳ, ἴδια ἑαυτῶν
ἔκαστος τὰ ῥήματα τῆς μετανοίας ποιούμενοι... ἐπὶ τούτοις λοιπὸν εἰ ἡμᾶς ἀπο-
φεύγετε, φεύξεσθε μὲν Αἰγυπτίους, φεύξεσθε δὲ καὶ Λιβύας ἀμφοτέρους, Θηβαίους,
Παλαιστίνους, Ἄραβας, Φοίνικας, Σύρους, καὶ τοὺς πρὸς τῷ Εὐφράτει κατωκι-
σμένους, καὶ πάντας ἁπαξαπλῶς κ.τ.λ.—Basil. Opp. Paris. 1618. T. II. p. 844. A.
The clause, ἴδια ἑαυτῶν, &c., should rather be rendered, "each making the
words of repentance his own:" but in the text the common Latin version
quoted by Whitaker is followed, "Suis quisque verbis resipiscentiam pro-
fitetur."]
    [⁵ εἰ δὲ θάλασσα καλὴ καὶ ἐπαινετὴ τῷ Θεῷ, πῶς οὐχὶ καλλίων ἐκκλησίας
τοιαύτης σύλλογος, ἐν ᾗ συμμιγὴς ἦχος, οἷόν τινος κύματος ἠιόνι προσφερομένου,
ἀνδρῶν καὶ γυναικῶν καὶ νηπίων κατὰ τὰς πρὸς Θεὸν ἡμῶν δεήσεις ἐκπέμπεται;
—Ibid. T. I. p. 53. D.]
    [⁶ Quid aliud ille concentus undarum, nisi quidam concentus est plebis?
Unde bene mari plerumque comparatur ecclesia, quæ primo ingredientis
populi totis vestibulis undas vomit; deinde, in oratione totius plebis tanquam undis refluentibus stridet, cum responsoriis psalmorum, cantus virorum, mulierum, virginum, parvulorum, consonas undarum fragor resultat.
—Hexaem. III. cap. v. § 23. Opp. Ambros. Paris. 1836. Pars I, p. 97.]
    [⁷ Quare non opus est locutione cum oramus, id est, sonantibus verbis,
nisi forte sicut sacerdotes faciunt, significandæ mentis suæ causa.—T. I.
col. 542.]

men may hear us." But why ought men to hear us? "In order," says Augustine, "that they, being moved to consent by our suggestion, may have their minds fixed upon God." But the people cannot be thus fixed upon God by the suggestion of the priest, unless they understand what is suggested by the priest. This consent depends upon the suggestion; but a suggestion without being understood is vain and futile. The same Augustine writes thus, in his second exposition of Psalm xviii.: "Since we have prayed the Lord to cleanse us from our secret faults, and spare his servants from strange ones, we ought to understand what this is, so as to sing with human reason, and not, as it were, with the voice of birds. For blackbirds," says he, "and parrots, and crows and magpies, and such like birds, are frequently taught by men to utter sounds which they do not understand. But to sing with the understanding is granted by the divine will, not to birds, but to men[1]." Thus Augustine; whence we perceive that the people, when they sing or pray what they do not understand (as is the custom everywhere in the church of Rome) are more like blackbirds, or parrots, or crows, or magpies, or such like birds, which are taught to utter sounds which they understand not, than to men. Thus Augustine deems it absurd and repugnant to the common prudence of mankind, that the people should not understand their prayers; which we see taking place everywhere in the popish synagogues. And the same Augustine, upon Psalm lxxxix.: "Blessed is the people which understand the joyful sound. Let us hasten to this blessedness; let us understand the joyful sound, and not pour it forth without understanding."

Chrysostom, in his 35th Hom. upon 1 Corinthians, says, that he who speaks in an unknown tongue is not only "useless (ἄχρηστος) and a barbarian[2]" to others, but even to himself, if he do not understand what he says; and that if he understand it, but others not, small fruit can be gained by the rest from his words.

[1 Deprecati Dominum ut ab occultis mundet nos, et ab alienis parcat servis suis, quid hoc sit intelligere debemus, ut humana ratione, non quasi avium voce, cantemus. Nam et meruli et psittaci et corvi et picæ et hujusmodi volucres sæpe ab hominibus docentur sonare quod nesciunt. Scientes autem cantare non avi, sed homini, divina voluntate concessa est.—T. IV. c. 8. The reference is to the vulgate version of Psal. xix. 12, 13. Ab occultis meis munda me, et ab alienis parce servo tuo: which follows the LXX. ἀπὸ ἀλλοτρίων φεῖσαι τοῦ δούλου σου. They read מְזָרִים for מְזִדִים.]

[2 Tom. x. p. 323.]

Ambrose says upon 1 Cor. xiv.: "If ye come together for the edification of the church, the things spoken should be such as the auditors may understand[3]." Jerome upon 1 Cor. xiv. says: "Every speech is deemed barbarous that is not understood." The Latin, therefore, is barbarous to those who understand it not, that is, to the whole common people of all nations: and when the apostle condemns a barbarous speech in the church, he plainly condemns the use of the Latin tongue in the service. Cassiodorus upon Psalm xlvi.: "When we raise a psalm, we should not only sing, but understand it. For no one can do that wisely which he does not understand[4]." Isidore of Seville, de Eccles. Offic. Lib. i. c. 10: "It is fitting that when the psalms are sung, they should be sung by all; when prayers are made, they should be made by all; when the lesson is read, all keeping silence, it should equally be heard by all[5]." The fathers of the council of Aix, c. 132, say that, of those who sing in the church "the mind should be in concord with the voice;" and, in the following chapter, that such should read, chant, and sing in the church, "as by the sweetness of their reading and melody may both charm the learned and instruct the illiterate[6]." Jacobus Faber, in his Commentary upon 1 Cor. xiv., hath these words: "The greatest part of the world now, when they pray, I know not whether they pray with the spirit, but they certainly do not with the understanding; for they pray in a tongue which they do not understand. Yet Paul approves most that the faithful should pray both with the spirit and the understanding; and those who pray so, as is the general practice, edify themselves but little by the prayer, and cannot edify others at all by their speech[7]." And Cardinal Cajetan, as in many other things

[3] Si utique ad aedificandum ecclesiam convenitis, ea dici debent quae intelligant audientes.—Pseud-Ambros. in 1 Cor. xiv. p. 157. App. Opp. T. ii. Par. 1690.]

[4] Adjecit, Psallite sapienter; ut non solum cantantes, sed intelligentes psallere debeamus. Nemo enim sapienter quicquam facit quod non intelligit.—p. 157. T. ii. Opp. Rothomag. 1679.]

[5] Oportet ut quando psallitur, psallatur ab omnibus; cum oratur, oretur ab omnibus; quando lectio legitur, facto silentio aeque audiatur ab omnibus.—Opp. p. 393. Col. Agr. 1617.]

[6] Labbe, Concill. vii. 966.]

[7] Maxima pars hominum cum nunc orat, nescio si spiritu, tamen mente non orat: nam in lingua orat quam non intelligit. Attamen maxime Paulus probat ut fideles pariter spiritu orent, et mente: et qui sic ut passim

[WHITAKER.]   18

he blames the institutions of the Roman church, so indicates plainly
that he is not pleased with the strange language in the service,
in his Comment upon 1 Cor. xiv. For thus he speaks: "From
what Paul here teaches us we find, that it is more for the edification
of the church that the public prayers, which are said in the audience
of the people, should be said in the common language of the clergy
and people, than that they should be said in Latin[1]." Here Catharinus[2] could not restrain himself from pouring forth many insults
upon his own cardinal; and he maintains that this is an invention of
Luther's, or rather of the devil speaking in Luther[2]: which yet is
plainly a doctrine and precept of the apostles, in spite of the blasphemies of this foul papist. Nicolas de Lyra, in his Postil upon
1 Cor. xiv., writes frankly thus: "But if the people understand
the prayer or benediction of the priest, they are better turned
towards God, and more devoutly answer, Amen." And presently
he subjoins: "What profit does the simple and ignorant folk gain?
As much as to say, nothing or little; because they know not how
to conform themselves to thee, the minister of the church, by answering, Amen. On which account in the primitive church the
benedictions and other common offices were performed in the vulgar
tongue[3]."

And so we have arrived at the conclusion of the Second
Question.

solent orant, parum se oratione ædificant, et alios nequaquam sua sermone
edificare valent.—Fol. 101. Paris. 1517.]

[1 Ex hac Pauli doctrina habetur, quod melius ad ecclesiæ ædificationem
est orationes publicas, quæ audiente populo dicuntur, dici lingua communi
clericis et populo, quam dici Latine.—Fol. 158. 2. Paris. 1571.]

[2 Quæ primo a Luthero, imo a diabolo in Luthero loquente, inventa est.
—p. 57. Catharin. Annotat. in Cajet. Comm. Lugd. 1542.]

[3 Quod si populus intelligit orationem seu benedictionem sacerdotis,
melius reducitur in Deum, et devotius respondet Amen. . . . . Quid proficit
populus simplex et non intelligens? Quasi dicat, nihil, aut modicum;
quod nescit se conformare tibi, qui es minister ecclesiæ, respondendo Amen.
Propter quod in primitiva ecclesia benedictiones et cetera communia fiebant
in vulgari.—p. 55. 2. Biblia cum gloss. ord. et post. Lyr. T. vi. Venet. 1588.]

THE FIRST CONTROVERSY.

QUESTION III.

CONCERNING THE AUTHORITY OF SCRIPTURE.

CHAPTER I.

OF THE STATE OF THE QUESTION.

In commencing this question, we must return to those words of Christ, which are contained in John v. 39, ἐρευνᾶτε τὰς γραφὰς, "Search the scriptures." In these words Christ hath referred and remitted us to the scriptures: whence it follows that they are deserving of the greatest trust, dignity, and authority. The question, therefore, between us and the papists is, whence they have received such great authority, and what it is, and on what this whole weight of such divine dignity and authority depends. The subject is difficult and perplexed; nor do I know whether there is any other controversy between us of greater importance. Though desirous in every question to draw the doctrine of our adversaries from the decrees of the council of Trent, I am unable to do so in the present case; for the council of Trent hath made no decree or definition upon this question. The opinion of the papists must, therefore, be discovered from their books. The Jesuit does not treat this question in this place, but elsewhere in the controversy concerning councils; and even there but briefly and superficially. But, since it appertains to the nature and efficacy of scripture, to know what its authority is, I have judged it proper to be treated here.

It would be too troublesome and laborious to enumerate the opinions of all the papists severally upon this matter, and to inquire what every one may have written upon it. Those who are esteemed the most skilful and the best learned, now deny that they make the scripture inferior to the church; for so Bellarmine and others openly profess, and complain that they are treated injuriously by us in this respect. But, that they make the authority of scripture depend upon the church, and so do in fact make the scripture inferior

to the church, and that we do them no injustice in attributing this
to them, will appear from the words of their own theologians, and
those not the meanest. Eckius, in his *Enchiridion de Authorit.
Eccles.* Respons. 3, says that " the church is more ancient than
the scriptures, and that the scripture is not authentic but by the
authority of the church[1]." And that this answer is wonderfully
acceptable to the papists appears from the marginal note, where
this argument is styled " Achilles pro Catholicis." How well this
reason deserves to be considered *Achillean*, will appear hereafter.
The same author places this assertion amongst heretical propositions, " The authority of scripture is greater than that of the
church," and affirms the contrary proposition to be catholic : which
agrees with the assertion so often repeated in the canon law, " The
church is above the scripture." Pighius, *de Hierarch. Eccles.* Lib.
I. c. 2, disputes against the *scripturarians* (as he calls us), maintaining that the authority of scripture cannot be defended without
the tradition of the church ; and affirms that the whole authority
of scripture, with regard to us, depends upon ecclesiastical tradition,
and that we cannot believe the scriptures upon any other grounds,
but because the church confirms it by its testimony. His express
words are these : " All the authority which the scripture now hath
with us, depends necessarily upon the authority of the church[2]."
So, says he, it happens that the gospel of Mark, who was not an
apostle, is received, while that of Thomas, who was an apostle, is
not received. Hence also, he says, it hath come to pass that the
gospel of Luke, who had not seen Christ, is retained, while the
gospel of Nicodemus, who had seen Christ, is rejected. And he
pursues this discourse to a great length. One Hermann, a most
impudent papist, affirms that the scriptures are of no more avail
than Æsop's fables, apart from the testimony of the church[3]. Assuredly this assertion is at once impudent and blasphemous. Yet,

[1 c. 1. p. 6. Antwerp. 1533.]
[2 Omnis quæ nunc apud nos est scripturarum auctoritas ab ecclesiæ
auctoritate dependet necessario.—Pigh. Hierar. Eccles. Assertio. p. 17. Col.
Agr. 1572.]
[3 Casaubon, Exercit. Baron. I. xxxiii. had, but doubtfully, attributed
this to Pighius : but in a MS. note preserved in Primate Marsh's library, at
St Sepulchre's, Dublin, he corrects himself thus : "Non est hic, sed quidam
Hermannus, ait Wittakerus in Præfat. Controvers. 1. Quæst. 3. p. 314."
If a new edition of those Exercitations be ever printed, let not these MSS.
of that great man, which, with many other valuable records, we owe to the
diligence of Stillingfleet and the munificence of Marsh, be forgotten.]

when it was objected to them by Brentius in the Wittemberg Confession, it was defended as a pious speech by Hosius, *de Authorit.
Script.* Lib. III.: where also he affirms that the scriptures would
have no great weight, except for the testimony of the church.
" In truth," says he, " unless the authority of the church had
taught us that this was canonical scripture, it would have very
slight weight with us[4]." From this every one must see that the
opinion of the papists is, that the authority of the church is really
greater than that of scripture.

But other papists now begin to speak with somewhat greater
caution and accuracy. Cochlæus, in his Reply to Bullinger, chap.
2, avails himself of a distinction. He says that the scriptures
are indeed in themselves firm, clear, perfect, and most worthy
of all credit, as the work of God; but that, with regard to us,
they need the approval and commendation of the church, on account of the depravity of our minds and the weakness of our
understandings. And this he confirms by the authority of Aristotle, who says, in his Metaphysics, that " our understanding is to
divine things as the eyes of owls to the light of the sun[5]." So Canus,
in his Common Places, Lib. II. c. 8, says that we cannot be certain
that the scriptures come from God, but by the testimony of the
church. So our countryman Stapleton explains this controversy
through almost his whole ninth book of Doctrinal Principles. In
the first chapter he examines the state of the question; where he
says that the question is not, whether the scripture be in itself
sacred and divine, but how we come to know that it is sacred and
divine: and therefore he blames Calvin for stating the question
wrongly, when he says that the papists affirm, that it depends
upon the church what reverence is due to scripture. For (says
he) the scriptures are in themselves worthy of all reverence, but,
with regard to us, they would not by themselves have been held in
such honour. This, says he, is a very different thing from making
it depend upon the church, what books should be reckoned in the
canon of scripture. The one (he adds) relates to the reverence due
to scripture in itself; the other to the same reverence in respect to
us. But, I beseech you, what is the difference between these two

[4 Revera nisi nos ecclesiæ doceret auctoritas hanc scripturam esse canonicam, perexiguum apud nos pondus haberet.—p. 269. Opp. Antw. 1571.]

[5 ὥσπερ γὰρ καὶ τὰ τῶν νυκτερίδων ὄμματα πρὸς τὸ φέγγος ἔχει τὸ μεθ᾽
ἡμέραν, οὕτω καὶ τῆς ἡμετέρας ψυχῆς ὁ νοῦς πρὸς τὰ τῇ φύσει φανερώτατα
πάντων.—Metaphys. Lib. II. c. 1. Opp. T. II. p. 856, B. Paris. 1619.]

opinions, It depends upon the judgment of the church what reverence is due to scripture; and, It depends upon the judgment of
the church what books are to be received into the canon; since
that sacred scripture, to which divine reverence is due, is to be
found only in the canonical books? The papists affirm the latter
opinion; therefore, also the first. The same is the opinion of the
Jesuit, *Controv. de Concil.* Quæst. 2; where he says that the scriptures do not need the approbation of the church; and that, when it
is said that the church approves them, it is only meant that it declares these scriptures to be canonical. To the same effect Andradius also writes, *Defens. Trid. Con.* Lib. III., that the church does
not give to scripture its authority, but only declares to us how
great its authority is in itself. This opinion might appear tolerable,
—that scripture is in itself a sacred and divine thing, but is not
recognised as such by us, except upon the testimony of the church.
But in the second book the same author speaks much more perversely: "Nor is there in the books themselves, wherein the sacred
mysteries are written, any divinity to compel us by a sort of religious awe to believe what they contain; but the efficacy and
dignity of the church, which teaches us that those books are sacred,
and commends to us the faith and piety of the ancient fathers, are
such that no one can oppose them without the deepest brand of
impiety[1]." Canisius, in his Catechism, c. 3, sect. 16, says that the
authority of the church is necessary to us, firstly, in order that
"we may certainly distinguish the true and canonical scriptures
from the spurious[2]." They mean, then, that the scripture depends
upon the church, not in itself, but in respect of us.

And now we are well nigh in possession of the true state of
the question, which is itself no slight advantage: for they speak in
so perplexed, obscure, and ambiguous a manner, that one cannot
easily understand what it is they mean. Now these assertions
might seem not to deserve any severe reprehension,—that the
scripture hath authority in itself, but that it cannot be certain to
us except through the church. But we shall presently shew where
the true steps and turning point of the controversy lie.

[1 Neque enim in ipsis libris, quibus sacra mysteria scripta sunt, quicquam inest divinitatis, quæ nos ad credendum quæ illis continentur religione
aliqua constringat: sed ecclesiæ, quæ codices illos sacros esse docet et
antiquorum patrum fidem et pietatem commendat, tanta est vis et am-
plitudo, ut illis nemo sine gravissima impietatis nota possit repugnare.]
[2 Opus Catech. p. 156. Colon. 1577.]

Meanwhile let us see what they mean by this word, the "church." Now, under the name of the church the papists understand not only that church which was in the times of the apostles (for Thomas of Walden is blamed on that account by Canus, Loc. Comm. Lib. II. c. 8, and also by Stapleton, Doctrin. Princip. Lib. IX. c. 12, 13), but the succeeding, and therefore the present church; yet not the whole people, but the pastors only. Canus, when he handles this question, understands by the church sometimes the pastors, sometimes councils, sometimes the Roman pontiff. Stapleton, Lib. IX. c. 1, applies this distinction : The church, as that term denotes the rulers and pastors of the faithful people, not only reveres the scripture, but also by its testimony commends, delivers down, and consigns it, that is to say, with reference to the people subject to them : but, as the church denotes the people or the pastors, as members and private persons, it only reveres the scripture. And when the church consigns the scripture, it "does not make it authentic from being doubtful absolutely, but only in respect of us, nor does it make it authentic absolutely, but only in respect of us." Hence we see what they understand by the term the church, and how they determine that the scripture is consigned and approved by the church.

We will now briefly explain our own opinion upon this matter. It does not appear to be a great controversy, and yet it is the greatest. In the first place, we do not deny that it appertains to the church to approve, acknowledge, receive, promulge, commend the scriptures to all its members ; and we say that this testimony is true, and should be received by all. We do not, therefore, as the papists falsely say of us, refuse the testimony of the church, but embrace it. But we deny that we believe the scriptures solely on account of this commendation of them by the church. For we say that there is a more certain and illustrious testimony, whereby we are persuaded of the sacred character of these books, that is to say, the internal testimony of the Holy Spirit, without which the commendation of the church would have with us no weight or moment. The papists, therefore, are unjust to us, when they affirm that we reject and make no account of the authority of the church. For we gladly receive the testimony of the church, and admit its authority ; but we affirm that there is a far different, more certain, true, and august testimony than that of the church. The sum of our opinion is, that the scripture is αὐτόπιστος, that is, hath all its authority and credit from itself; is to be acknow-

ledged, is to be received, not only because the church hath so determined and commanded, but because it comes from God; and that
we certainly know that it comes from God, not by the church, but by
the Holy Ghost. Now by the church we understand not, as they do,
the pastors, bishops, councils, pope; but the whole multitude of the
faithful. For this whole multitude hath learned from the Holy Spirit
that this scripture is sacred, that these books are divine. This persuasion the Holy Spirit hath sealed in the minds of all the faithful.

The state of the controversy, therefore, is this: Whether we
should believe that these scriptures which we now have are sacred
and canonical merely on account of the church's testimony, or rather
on account of the internal persuasion of the Holy Spirit; which, as
it makes the scripture canonical and authentic in itself, makes it
also to appear such to us, and without which the testimony of the
church is dumb and inefficacious.

CHAPTER II.

HOW MUCH AUTHORITY, WITH RESPECT TO SCRIPTURE, IS AT-
TRIBUTED BY THE PAPISTS AND BY US TO THE CHURCH.

It remains now that we proceed to the arguments of the
papists. But first, we must explain what authority, both in their
opinion and in ours, the church exercises with respect to scripture.

Of all the popish authors, Stapleton hath treated this question
with the greatest acuteness: we shall, therefore, examine him specially
in this debate. He, Doctr. Princip. Lib. IX. cap. 2, makes use of a
distinction which he hath taken from Cochlæus. He says, as we
have touched before, that the scripture must be considered under a
twofold aspect, in itself, and relatively to us. In itself, and of
itself, he says that it is always sacred on account of its author,
" whether it be received by the church, or whether it be not
received." For though, says he, the church can never reject the
scripture, because it comes from God; yet it may sometimes not
receive some part of scripture. But, I pray you, what is the
difference between not receiving and rejecting? Absolutely none.
He who *does not receive* God rejects him; and so the church
plainly rejected those scriptures which formerly it did not receive.
For I would fain know why it did not receive them. Certainly
the reason was, because it judged them spurious, wherein it appears

it might be mistaken. But Stapleton goes on to say, that the church, exercising its just privilege, might sometimes not receive some books; and he shews that some doctrines are now received by the later churches which were not received formerly. These if any one were now to reject, after the church hath received them, he would, says Stapleton, be most justly called and deemed a heretic. But I affirm, that no doctrines have now become matters of faith, which were not received by the ancient church in the times of the apostles; so that all those churches must have erred which formerly did not receive the same. He presses us, however, with particular instances, and produces certain points which he says were not received at first: as for instance, the doctrine of the procession of the Holy Ghost, of the creation of souls immediately by God, of the unlawfulness of repeating heretical baptism: but I affirm once more, that all these doctrines had whatever force they now have at all times, so as that if it be now heretical not to assent to them, it must have been always equally heretical; for the doctrine of scripture never changes in the gospel, but is always equally necessary. Everything that Stapleton adduces, in order to shew that those books which were formerly not received by the church, ought now to be received solely on account of the external testimony of the church, may be reduced to the argument stated above. He subjoins that the authority of the church respects the scriptures only materially; which he explains to mean, that it is fitting we should obey the judgment of the church, and, on account of its judgment, receive the scripture as sacred. But it would not, says he, be fitting that the truth of scripture, or of other objects of faith, should so depend upon the judgment of the church, as that they should only be true on condition of the church's approving them; but now, says he, the church does not make them true in themselves, but only causes them to be believed as true. Mark ye. The scripture is true in itself, and all the doctrines of scripture are true; but they could not appear true to us, we could not believe the scriptures, unless the church approved the scripture and the doctrines of scripture. Although these things be true in themselves, yet they would not have seemed true to us, they would not have been believed, or (to use Stapleton's expression) *received* by us, unless on account of the church's approbation. This is the whole mystery of iniquity.

We determine far otherwise, and with far greater truth: for we resolutely deny that we are indebted to the church for this—that the scriptures are true even in respect to us; but we say that our

belief of their truth is produced by the testimony and suggestion
of the Holy Spirit. It was Cochlæus who taught Stapleton this
blasphemy, in his second book upon the authority of the church
and scripture; where he collects many places of scripture, which
may seem incredible to man, and to which he maintains that human
frailty could not assent, if they were not confirmed by the authority
of the church. Such is the account of David's innumerable army,
which he shews from the smallness of that country to be a thing
which no one would think credible. For he says that the land of
Judæa could never have nourished and supported such a vast
number of men; and demonstrates this from a comparison of that
region with other countries, shewing that so many thousand men
were never enrolled in the whole Roman republic, which was much
larger than Judæa. How, says he, can the human intellect assent
to these things, when nothing of the kind is read in any other
historians, cosmographers, philosophers, orators, nay, even poets?
"For what fable of the poets" (these are his words) "ever ascribed
such a number of warriors to one people, and that not the whole
of the people[1]?" He brings in also the number of talents which
David is said to have left to his son Solomon for the building of
the temple. For this, he maintains, may deservedly seem incredible,
inasmuch as David was very poor; which he endeavours to prove
from the circumstance that he spent so much upon his courtiers,
sons, wives, and concubines which he had in great numbers, and
also in the wars, which lasted almost all through his life. Whence,
he asks, came such wealth to David as neither Crœsus, nor Alexander, nor Augustus, ever possessed? He is profusely prodigal
of words and eloquence upon this subject, and hath produced many
passages of this kind, which shame and weariness alike forbid me
to enumerate. At the close he concludes thus, (and a noble conclusion it is,) that all these things cannot otherwise be believed, but
because the church believes them, and hath required them to be
believed. Certainly I know not what is, if this be not, impudence.
Cannot then these things be believed on any other ground, but
because the church hath delivered them, and would have them to
be believed? What then shall we say of the almost infinite
number of other such things which are contained in scripture; of
the passage of the Israelites through the sea; of the manna; of
the quails by which the people of Israel were fed in the desert so

---

[1] Quæ enim fabula poetarum uni populo nec toti tantum numerum
ascripsit fortium virorum?]

richly; of all Christ's miracles? What of the whole scheme of our redemption, the incarnation, death, resurrection, ascension, of Christ? What must we determine of all these? Can these too be believed as true upon no other reason or testimony, but because the church hath so determined? This is monstrous blasphemy, and worthy of a Cochlæus and a Stapleton! We believe these things, and have no doubt of their truth, not merely because the church hath so determined, but on account of the authority of the word of God and of the Holy Spirit. All therefore that the papists allege tends substantially to make the whole authority of scripture depend upon the authority of the church, which nevertheless they deny: yet that this is the real meaning of their opinion is manifest from what hath been already said. Stapleton subjoins, that it should not appear to us more unbecoming that the church should commend the scripture and bear testimony to it, than it was unbecoming that John the Baptist should bear witness to Christ, and the gospel should be written by men. Now we confess that the church commends the scripture by its testimony, and that this is the illustrious office of the church; but it is a very different matter to say that we could not otherwise believe the scriptures, unless on account of this judgment and testimony of the church. We concede the former; the latter we resolutely deny, and that with the greatest detestation.

You have heard how much these men attribute to the church. It follows now that we consider how much ought really to be attributed to it. We do not indeed ascribe as much to the church as they do (for we could not do so lawfully); but yet we recognise distinguished offices which the church hath to perform in respect of scripture, and which may be reduced to four heads. First, the church is the witness and guardian of the sacred writings, and discharges, in this respect, as it were the function of a notary. In guardians the greatest fidelity is required: but no one would say that records were believed merely on the notary's authority, but on account of their own trustworthiness. So the church ought carefully to guard the scriptures, and yet we do not repose credit in the scriptures merely on account of the testimony and authority of the church. The second office of the church is, to distinguish and discern the true, sincere, and genuine scriptures from the spurious, false, and supposititious. Wherein it discharges the office of a champion; and for the performance of this function it hath the Spirit of Christ to enable it to distinguish the true from the false: it knows the voice of the spouse; it is endued with the highest prudence, and is able to try the spirits. The goldsmith with his scales and touchstone can distinguish gold from copper and other metals; wherein he does not make gold, even in respect of us, but only indicates what is gold, so that we the more easily trust it. Or, if a different illustration be required, another skilful person informs me that a coin, which I do not recognise as such, is good and lawful money: and I, being so instructed, acquiesce; but it is on account of the matter and the form impressed upon the coin that I perceive it to be sterling and royal money. In like manner, the church acknowledges the scriptures, and declares them to be divine: we, admonished and stirred up by the church, perceive the matter to be so indeed.—The third office of the church is to publish, set forth, preach, and promulgate the scriptures; wherein it discharges the function of a herald, who ought to pronounce with a loud voice the decrees and edicts of the king, to omit nothing, to add nothing of his own. Chrysostom, in his first Homily upon the Epistle to Titus, pursues this similitude: "As," says he, "the herald makes his proclamation in the theatre in the presence of all, so also we[1]." Where he shews that the duty of the herald is to publish whatever is consigned to him, to add nothing of his own, and to keep back no part of his commission. Now the people believes and obeys the edict of the magistrates on its own account, not because of the voice of the crier.—The fourth office of the church is to expound and interpret the scriptures; wherein its function is that of an interpreter. Here it should introduce no fictions of its own, but explain the scriptures by the scriptures. Such are the offices, and those surely in the highest degree great and dignified, which we gladly allow to belong to the church: from which, nevertheless, it will by no means follow, that we assent to the scriptures solely on account of the church's authority, which is the point that the papists affirm and maintain.

From what hath been said it is sufficiently evident what are the offices of the church in respect of scripture, both in our opinion and in that of the papists.

[1] ὥσπερ ὁ κῆρυξ πάντων παρόντων ἐν τῷ θε'τρῳ κηρύττει, οὕτω καὶ ἡμεῖς.— Opp. T. IV. p. 383.]

CHAPTER III.

WHEREIN THE FIRST ARGUMENT OF OUR OPPONENTS IS CONFUTED.

WE have drawn the true state of this question from the books of the papists themselves. It follows now that we should approach their arguments, which they themselves deem so exceeding strong as to leave us no capacity to resist them. But we, with God's help, shall easily (as I hope) confute them all. Stapleton hath borrowed much from Canus, and explicated his arguments at greater length. With him therefore we will engage, as well because he is our fellow-countryman, as because he seems to have handled this subject most acutely and accurately of them all. He bestows his whole ninth book upon this question, and in the fourth chapter of that book commences his reasoning against us in this manner: To have a certain canon of scripture is most necessary to faith and religion. But without the authority of the church it is impossible to have a certain canon of scripture; since it cannot be clear and certain to us what book is legitimate, what supposititious, unless the church teach us. Therefore, &c. I answer, as to the major: Firstly, the major is true, if he mean books properly canonical, which have been always received by the church; for these the church ought always to acknowledge for canonical: although it be certain that many flourishing churches formerly in several places had doubts for a time concerning many of the books, as appears from antiquity. Secondly, therefore, it is not absolutely, and in the case of each particular person, necessary for faith and salvation to know what books are canonical. For many can have faith and obtain salvation, who do not hold the full number of the canonical books. Stapleton proves his assumption,—namely, that the canon of scripture can no otherwise be certainly known to us but by the authority of the church,—by three arguments. The first is this: There is no authority more certain than that of the church. But there is need of the most certain authority, that the trustworthiness of scripture may be ascertained, and all doubt removed from the conscience concerning the canon of scripture. Therefore, &c. I answer, that it is false to say, as he does, that no authority is more certain than that of the church: it is a mere begging of the question. For greater and more certain is the authority of God, of the scriptures themselves, and of the Holy Spirit, by whose testimony the truth of scripture is sealed in our minds, and without which all other testimonies are utterly devoid of strength. But God (says he) teaches us through the church, and by no other medium : therefore there is no more certain authority than that of the church. I answer : His own words prove that God's authority is more certain. For the authority of him who teaches is greater than that of him through whom one is taught. God teaches us through the church : therefore the authority of God is greater than that of the church. I am surprised that Stapleton should have been so stupid as not to see that, if it be God who teaches through the church, the authority of God must be greater than that of the church. He confesses that we are taught by God through the church : therefore, since God is the prime and highest teacher, it is evident that his authority and trustworthiness is the chief. For the church is only his minister, subserves him in giving instruction, and expounds his commands. The weakness of his reasoning will easily appear from a parallel instance. A prince publishes his law and edict by a herald, and explains and expounds by his lawyers the meaning of the law and the force of the edict. Does it therefore follow that there is no more certain authority than that of the herald and the lawyers? By no means. For it is manifest that the authority of the law and of the prince is greater than that of the herald or the interpreter. But (says he) nothing is more certain than God's teaching : therefore nothing more certain than the authority of the church, since God teaches through the church. Now where is the consequence of this? We confess indeed that nothing is more certain than God's teaching, and this is the very thing which we maintain, and hence conclude that the authority of the church is not the highest : but his consequence meanwhile is weak, until he prove that God and the church are the same thing. It will more correctly follow from this reasoning, that nothing is more certain than the word of God and the scriptures, because it is God who addresses us in his word, and teaches us through his word; whereas the church discharges merely a ministerial function. Therefore we are not bound absolutely to receive whatever the church may teach us, but only whatever it proves itself to have been commanded by God to teach us, and with divine authority.

The second argument wherewith Stapleton confirms the assumption of the preceding syllogism is this : All other mediums that can be attempted are insufficient without making recourse to the judgment of the church; and then he enumerates the mediums upon which we rely. For as to the style (says he) and phraseology, and other mediums, by which the scripture is usually distinguished,—these the church knows best, and is best able to judge aright. Therefore, &c. I answer: If by the church he understand the pope and the bishops (as the papists always do), I deny that they are best able to distinguish the style and phraseology of scripture; I deny that this is the true church of Christ which knows the voice of Christ. But if he speak of the true church, this fallacy is that called *ignoratio elenchi*, and the state of the question is changed. For before this he had been speaking of the external judgment of scripture, which perhaps may properly belong to the bishops: but here he understands the internal judgment, which is not only proper to the pastors, but common to all Christians: for all Christ's sheep know his voice, and are internally persuaded of the truth of scripture. Secondly, although we should concede all this to him, yet where will be the coherence of his reasoning,— The church knows best the voice of the spouse, and the style and phraseology of scripture; therefore its authority is the most certain? For what though the church know? What is that to me? Are these things therefore known and certain to me? For the real question is, how I can know it best? Although the church know ever so well the voice of its spouse, and the style and phraseology of scripture, it hath that knowledge to itself, not to me; and by whatever means it hath gained that knowledge, why should I be able to gain it also by the same? Thirdly, from what he says, the contrary of his conclusion might much more correctly be inferred, namely, that the authority of scripture is more certain than that of the church. For if the authority of the church be therefore most certain, because it knows best the style of scripture, and judges by the style of scripture, it is plain that the authority of scripture itself is far more certain, since it indicates itself to the church by its style. But I (you will say) should not know that this was the voice of the spouse, that this was the style of scripture, unless the church were to teach me. This, indeed, is untrue, since it can be known that this is the voice of Christ and true and genuine scripture without the judgment of the church, as shall hereafter be shewn more at large. But, although we were to grant him this, that it could not be known otherwise than through the church, that these were the scriptures, yet even so the argument would be inconsequential.

For many would not have known Christ, if John had not taught them, pointed him out, and exclaimed, "Behold the Lamb of God, who taketh away the sin of the world!" Was then the authority of John more certain than that of Christ? By no means. For John brought many to Christ, who afterwards believed much more on account of Christ himself, than on account of the preaching and testimony of John. So many through means of the church believe these to be the scriptures, who afterwards believe still more firmly, being persuaded by the scriptures themselves. Besides, Paul and Peter and the other apostles best knew the voice of Christ; must therefore their authority be rated higher than that of Christ himself? Far from it. It does not therefore follow that because the church knows very well the voice of Christ, the authority of the church is greater than that of Christ. But as to his pretence that because the church delivers the rule of faith, it must therefore be the correctest judge of that rule; we must observe that the terms *deliver* and *judge* are ambiguous. The church does indeed deliver that rule, not as its author, but as a witness, and an admonisher, and a minister: it judges also when instructed by the Holy Spirit. But may I therefore conclude, that I cannot be certain of this rule, but barely by the testimony of the church? It is a mere fallacy of the accident. There is no consequence in this reasoning: I can be led by the church's voice to the rule of faith; therefore I can have no more certain judgment than that of the church.

In the third place, Stapleton proves the fore-mentioned assumption thus: Scripture (says he) cannot be proved by scripture: therefore it must be proved by the church; and consequently the authority of the church is greater than that of scripture. The antecedent is thus established. Should any one, he says, deny Paul's epistles to be canonical, it cannot be proved either from the old Testament, or from the gospel, because there is nowhere any mention there made of them. Then he goes on to say that neither the whole scripture, nor any part of it, can be proved from scripture itself, because all proof is drawn from things better known than the thing to be proved. Therefore (says he) to one who denies or knows not either the whole scripture or any part of it, nothing can be proved from scripture itself. But here, according to him, the church comes to our help in both cases. For, should any one deny a part of scripture, the church persuades him to receive these books upon the same ground as he hath received the others:

he who is ignorant of the whole scripture, it persuades to accept
the scripture in the same way as he hath accepted Christ.

I answer, This is a fine way of persuading a man to receive
these books upon the same grounds as he hath received the others!
But the question is, how he was first induced to receive those
others? Was it by the authority of the church? Why then did
he not receive all upon the faith of the same judgment? For the
church will have us receive the whole scripture as well as certain
parts of it. Stapleton does not meet this scruple. Besides, it is
manifestly absurd to suppose the possibility of a man's believing in
Christ, who denies and rejects the whole scripture: this certainly is
quite impossible. But now let us come to the examination of the
argument itself, to which I return a twofold answer. First, I affirm
that the scripture can be understood, perceived, known and proved
from scripture. Secondly, I say that if it cannot be perceived and
proved in this way, still less can it be proved by the church.

The *first* will be evident from the following considerations.
Scripture hath for its author God himself; from whom it first proceeded and came forth. Therefore, the authority of scripture may
be proved from the author himself, since the authority of God himself shines forth in it. 2 Tim. iii. 16, the whole scripture is called
θεόπνευστος. In 2 Pet. i. 12, we are told, "Prophecy in old
time came not by the will of men, but holy men of God spake as
they were moved by the Holy Ghost," ὑπὸ πνεύματος ἁγίου
φερόμενοι. And, verse 19, the word of prophecy is called βεβαιότερος : Ἔχομεν, says the apostle, βεβαιότερον τὸν προφητικὸν λόγον. That word βεβαιότερος is most pertinent to the matter in hand; for it signifies that the scripture is endued with the
firmest and highest authority. In the same place it is compared to
a lamp shining in a dark place, λύχνῳ φαίνοντι ἐν αὐχμηρῷ τόπῳ.
It hath therefore light in itself, and such light as we may see in
the darkness. But if the opinion of our opponents were correct,
this light should be in the church, not in the scriptures. David
indicates the same thing in the 14th octonary of Psalm cxix., at the
beginning, where he says, "Thy word is a lamp to my feet, and a
light to my path :" therefore the scripture hath the clearest light
in itself. On this account it is frequently styled *the testimony*.
From these and similar passages, we reason thus: There is the
greatest perspicuity and light in the scriptures : therefore the scripture may be understood by the scripture, if one only have eyes to
perceive this light. As the brightest light appears in the sun, so

19

[WHITAKER.]

the greatest splendour of divinity shines forth in the word of God.
The blind cannot perceive even the light of the sun; nor can they
distinguish the splendour of the scriptures, whose minds are not
divinely illuminated. But those who have eyes of faith can behold
this light. Besides, if we recognise men when they speak, why
should we not also hear and recognise God speaking in his word?
For what need is there that another should teach that this is the
voice of somebody, when I recognise it myself; or should inform
me that my friend speaks, when I myself hear and understand him
speaking?

But they object that we cannot recognise the voice of God,
because we do not hear God speaking. This I deny. For those
who have the Holy Spirit, are *taught of God*: these can recognise the voice of God as much as any one can recognise a friend,
with whom he hath long and familiarly lived, by his voice. Nay,
they can even hear God. For so Augustine (Ep. III.), "God addresses us every day. He speaks to the heart of every one of
us[1]." If we do not understand, the reason is because we have not
the Spirit, by which our hearts should be enlightened. With
respect to us, therefore, the authority of the scripture depends
upon, and is made clear by, the internal witness of the Holy Spirit;
without which, though you were to hear a thousand times that this
is the word of God, yet you could never believe in such a manner
as to acquiesce with an entire assent. Besides, the papists should
tell us whether or no this is really the word of God which we possess. Now that it is in itself the word of God, they do not deny,
but they say that we cannot be certain of it without the help of
the church: they confess that the voice of God sounds in our ears;
but they say that we cannot believe it, except upon account of the
church's approbation. But now, if it be the word of God which we
hear, it must needs have a divine authority of itself, and should be
believed by itself and for itself. Otherwise we should ascribe more
to the church than to God, if we did not believe him except for the
sake of the church. God speaks in the prophets, and through the
prophets: whence we find often used by them such phrases as, *the
word of Jehovah*, and, *Thus saith Jehovah*. Now then these men
tell me that I must by no means believe that God really speaks, or
that this is the word of Jehovah, unless the church confirm the
same: in which proceeding every one may perceive that more
credit and authority is ascribed to the church, that is, to men, than

[1] Ep. 137. Opp. T. II. 528. Bassan. 1797.]

to God; which is directly opposite to what should be done: for God ought to be believed before all, since he is the prime and highest verity; while the church is nothing of the kind. If, therefore, God address me, and say that this is his word, I should acquiesce in his authority. Hitherto we have shewn that there is a divine authority in scripture (which we shall do hereafter even still more clearly); and that, consequently, we should believe it by itself and of itself. It now remains that we shew that the scriptures themselves mutually support and confirm each other by their testimony; which is a point easy to be proved.

The old Testament is confirmed by itself, and by the new; the new also by itself, and by the old: so that, as it is certain that there is a God, although the church had never said it, so it is certain that the scripture is the word of God, although the church had been silent upon the subject. But they, perhaps, would not even believe God's existence, except upon the church's word. It is evident that the old Testament is proved by the new. In Luke xxiv. 44, Christ divides the whole old Testament into Moses, the prophets, and the Psalms: therefore he hath declared all these books to be authentic and canonical, and hath besides confirmed his whole doctrine from those books. If, then, we believe Christ, we must believe the whole old Testament to be endued with authentical authority. In Luke xvi. 29, 31, Abraham, when the rich man requests that Lazarus may be sent to his brethren, replies, " They have Moses and the prophets; let them hear them :" as much as to say, those who will not hear them, will hear no man, not even the church. In John x. 35, " the scripture cannot be broken," λυθῆναι, therefore it possesses an eternal and immutable force. In John v. 39, Christ says to the Jews, " Search the scriptures :" where he understands all the books of the old Testament; for the new had not yet been published. Thus we have shewn in general that the old Testament is confirmed by the new; let us now shew the same in detail. Christ himself confirms the books of Moses specially, Matth. v., where he interprets the whole law; Matth. xix., where he explains the law of marriage; Matth. xxii., where he proves the resurrection of the flesh from Moses; and John iii. 14, where he confirms his own death, and its efficacy and benefits, from the figure of the brasen serpent. The historical books of the old Testament are likewise confirmed by the new. Matth. xii. 42, Christ mentions the story of the Queen of Sheba: Luke iv. 26, the story of the widow of Sarepta is repeated, which occurs 2 Kings v. : Acts ii. 25,

30, 34, a testimony is adduced from the Psalms: Acts xiii. 17 and following verses, Paul details a long narrative, drawn from several books of the old Testament: Heb. xi., many examples are produced from the books of Joshua and Judges. Part of the genealogy which Matthew exhibits is derived from the book of Ruth. From the Psalms an almost infinite multitude of testimonies are alleged; very many from Isaiah; many from Ezekiel, and, in a word, from all the prophets, except perhaps one or two of the minor prophets. But Stephen, Acts vii. 42, cites the book of the twelve minor prophets, and thus proves the authority of them all; for all the minor prophets used formerly to make but one book. Now the testimony there cited is taken from the prophet Amos. Thus it is manifest that the confirmation of the old may be drawn from the new Testament. Upon this subject, see further in Augustine, in his book, *contra Adversar. Legis et Prophetarum,* and *contra Faustum Manichæum.*

Now that, in like manner, the books of the new Testament may be confirmed from the old, is sufficiently clear. For the truth of the new Testament is shadowed forth in the figures of the old; and whatever things were predicted in the old, those we read to have been fulfilled in the new. Whatever was said obscurely in the former, is said plainly in the latter. Therefore if one be true, the other must needs be true also. Moses wrote of the Messiah, and so did the prophets. Moses, Deut. xviii. 18, foretold that there should be a prophet like unto himself; and death and destruction is denounced upon any who would not hear him. Peter, Acts iii. 22, and Stephen, Acts vii. 37, teach us that this prediction of a prophet hath been fulfilled. Moses therefore hath sanctioned Christ by his testimony. Peter confirms Paul's epistles by his authority, 2 Pet. iii. 16, and distinctly calls them *scriptures.* "The unlearned," says he, "wrest them, as they do also the other scriptures." Paul confirms his own epistles by his name, and by his judgment. Therefore the old and new Testaments do, by their mutual testimony, establish and consign each other. In other cases, indeed, such a mutual confirmation is of no avail; but in this it should be of the greatest, because no one is so fit a witness of God and his word, as God himself in his word. If then we repose any credit in the old Testament, we must repose as much in the new; if we believe the new, we must believe the old also. But the papists, on the contrary, would have neither Testament believed on its own account, but both on account of the church's authority: the falsehood of which is abundantly evident from what hath been already said.

But human incredulity will still urge, that this may indeed be conceded with respect to some books, but that it cannot be affirmed of every one of the books of the old and new Testament; because we nowhere read that the books of Esther, Nehemiah, and Ezra, were confirmed by the authority of the new Testament: and there are besides many books of the new Testament which cannot be confirmed by the old. Besides, if there were even some one book of the new Testament, in which all the books of the old Testament were severally enumerated, there would yet be need (will the papists say) of the authority of the ancient church, because there may be some who do not acknowledge the authority of any book; and how (they will say) are we to persuade such persons that this scripture is divine?

I answer, in the first place, such men as these, who despise all the sacred books, the church itself will be unable to convince: for with those who hold the authority of scripture in no esteem, the authority of the church will have but little weight. Secondly, if any pious persons have yet doubts concerning the scriptures, much more certain evidences may be gathered from the books themselves, to prove them canonical, than from any authority of the church. I speak not now of the internal testimony of the Spirit, but of certain external testimonies, which may be drawn from the books themselves to prove them divinely inspired writings. Such are mentioned by Calvin, Institut. Lib. I. c. 8[1], and are of the following kind. *First*, the majesty of the doctrine itself, which everywhere shines forth in the sacred and canonical books. Nowhere, assuredly, does such majesty appear in the books of philosophers, orators, or even of all the divines that ever wrote upon theology. There are none of the sacred books which one would be more likely to question than the Epistle of Jude, the second Epistle of Peter, and the second and third of John, since formerly even some churches entertained doubts of them: nevertheless, in these there is contained such a kind of teaching as can be found in no other writer. *Secondly*, the simplicity, purity, and divinity of the style. Never was anything written more chastely, purely, or divinely. Such purity is not to be found in Plato, or in Aristotle, or in Demosthenes, or in Cicero, or in any other writer. *Thirdly*, the antiquity of the books themselves secures them a great authority. For the books of Moses are more ancient than the writings of any other men, and

[1] T. I. pp. 62—69. ed. Tholuck. Berolin. 1834.]

contain the oldest of all histories, deduced from the very creation of the world; which other writers were either wholly ignorant of, or heard of from this source, or contaminated by the admixture of many fables. *Fourthly*, the oracles contained in these books prove their authority to be sacred in the highest sense, by shewing it necessarily divine. For some things are here predicted, which happened many ages afterwards, and names are given to persons some ages before they were born; as to Josiah, 1 Kings xiii. 2, and to Cyrus, Isaiah xliv. 28, and xlv. 1. How could this have been without some divine inspiration? *Fifthly*, miracles, so many and so true, prove God to be the author of these books. *Sixthly*, the enemies themselves prove these books to be sacred; for, while they have endeavoured wholly to destroy them, their fury hath ever been in vain: nay, many of them, by the penalties and torments which befel them, were made to understand that it was the word of God which they opposed. *Seventhly*, the testimonies of martyrs make it evident that the majesty of these books is of no mean character, since they have sealed the doctrine, here delivered down and set forth, by their confession and their blood. *Eighthly*, the authors themselves guarantee, in a great measure, the credit of these books. What sort of men were they before they were raised up to discharge this office by the Holy Ghost? Altogether unfitted for such a function then, though afterwards endowed with the noblest gifts of the Holy Spirit. Who was Moses, before he was called by God? First, a courtier in Egypt, then a shepherd, finally, endued with the richest outpouring of the Spirit, he became a prophet, and the leader of the people of Israel. Who was Jeremiah? A man, incapable, as himself testifies, of any eloquence. Who was David? A youth and a shepherd. Who Peter? A fisherman, an ignorant and illiterate person. Who John? A man of the same low rank. Who was Matthew? A publican, altogether a stranger to holy things. Who was Paul? An enemy and persecutor of that doctrine which he afterwards professed. Who was Luke? A physician. How could such men have written so divinely without the divine inspiration of the Holy Ghost? They were, almost all, illiterate men, learned in no accomplishments, taught in no schools, imbued with no instruction; but afterwards summoned by a divine call, marked out for this office, admitted to the counsels of God: and so they committed all to writing with the exactest fidelity; which writings are now in our hands.

These topics may prove that these books are divine, yet will never be sufficient to bring conviction to our souls so as to make us assent, unless the testimony of the Holy Spirit be added. When this is added, it fills our minds with a wonderful plenitude of assurance, confirms them, and causes us most gladly to embrace the scriptures, giving force to the preceding arguments. Those previous arguments may indeed urge and constrain us; but this (I mean the internal testimony of the Holy Spirit) is the only argument which can persuade us.

Now if the preceding arguments cannot persuade us, how much less the authority of the church, although it were to repeat its affirmation a thousand times! The authority of the church, and its unbroken judgment, may perhaps suffice to keep men in some external obedience, may induce them to render an external consent, and to persevere in an external unity: but the church can of itself by no means persuade us to assent to these oracles as divine. In order, therefore, that we should be internally in our consciences persuaded of the authority of scripture, it is needful that the testimony of the Holy Ghost should be added. And he, as he seals all the doctrines of faith and the whole teaching of salvation in our hearts, and confirms them in our consciences, so also does he give us a certain persuasion that these books, from which are drawn all the doctrines of faith and salvation, are sacred and canonical. But, you will say, this testimony is not taken from the books themselves: it is, therefore, external, and not inherent in the word. I answer: Although the testimony of the Holy Ghost be not, indeed, the same as the books themselves; yet it is not external, nor separate, or alien from the books, because it is perceived in the doctrine delivered in those books; for we do not speak of any enthusiastic influence of the Spirit. But, in like manner as no man can certainly assent to the doctrine of faith except by the Spirit, so can none assent to the scriptures but by the same Spirit.

But here two objections must be removed, which are proposed by Stapleton, of which the former is against this latter reply of ours, and the latter against the former. The first objection is this: If it be by the testimony of the Spirit that we know the scriptures, how comes it that churches, which have this Spirit, agree not amongst themselves? For (so he argues) the Lutherans disagree with you Calvinists, because you receive some books which they reject: therefore, either you or they are without the Spirit. This is an objection urged also by Campian and by others. I answer: In the first place, it does not follow either that they who reject those books, or we who receive them, are without the Holy Spirit. For no saving truth can be known without the Holy Spirit; as for example, that Christ died for us, or any other. This the papists will themselves allow. Yet it does not follow that all who have learned this truth from the Holy Spirit must agree in all other points of faith. Nor does it immediately follow, that all who are in error are without the Holy Spirit, because all errors are not capital. Now the reason why all who have the Holy Spirit do not think exactly alike of all things, is because there is not precisely the same equal measure of the Holy Spirit in all; otherwise there would be the fullest agreement in all points. Secondly, both we who receive some books not received by the Lutherans, have the precedent of some ancient churches, and the Lutherans also, who reject them. For there were some churches who received these books (that is, the epistle of Jude, the second epistle of Peter, and the second and third of John), and also some who rejected them, and yet all meanwhile were churches of God. Thirdly, it does not presently follow that all have the Holy Spirit who say they have it. Although many of the Lutherans (as they call them) reject these books, yet it is not to be concluded that such is the common opinion of that whole church. The papists, indeed, understand and denote by the name of the church only the bishops and doctors; but the sentiments are not to be judged of by merely a few of its members.

The second objection against our former reply is to this effect: The scripture is not the voice of God, but the word of God; that is, it does not proceed immediately from God, but is delivered mediately to us through others. I answer: We confess that God hath not spoken by himself, but by others. Yet this does not diminish the authority of scripture. For God inspired the prophets with what they said, and made use of their mouths, tongues, and hands: the scripture, therefore, is even immediately the voice of God. The prophets and apostles were only the organs of God. It was God who spake to the fathers in the prophets and through the prophets, as is plain from Heb. i. 1. And Peter says, 2 Epist. i. 21, that "holy men of God spake as they were moved, φερομένους, by the Holy Ghost." Therefore the scripture is the voice of the Spirit, and consequently the voice of God. But what though it were not the voice of God immediately, but only the word of God? Therefore (says Stapleton) it requires to be made known by the church like the rest, that is, like other doctrines necessary to salvation. But what? Is it only by the testimony of the church, that we know all other points of religion and doctrines of the faith? Is it not the office of the Holy Spirit to teach us all things necessary to salvation? Mark well how Stapleton affirms that we learn all only from the church, and sets the Spirit and the church asunder. But if the Spirit teach in the church, and it is by the Spirit that we know the other doctrines, then why may we not learn from the Spirit this also, that the scripture is the word of God? Let him speak and tell us, if he can. But this (says he) is a "matter of faith, like the rest." I confess it. But here he strangles himself in his own noose. For if without faith it cannot be understood that the scripture is the word of God, then is there need of some more certain testimony than the external approbation of the church. For the Holy Ghost is the author of faith, and not the church, except as an instrument, an external and ministerial medium. He subjoins: "But this, like the rest, exceeds mere human comprehension." I answer: Therefore men cannot give us this persuasion, but there is need of some higher, greater, more certain testimony than that of man. Now the church is an assembly of men, and is composed of men. "But this (says he further) should not, any more than the rest, be received by immediate revelations." I answer: This is no extraordinary or immediate revelation separate from the teaching of the books themselves; because it springs, derives itself, and is perceived from the word itself through the same Spirit from which that word emanated. But I would gladly know from them, whence it is that the church comes to know that the scripture is the word of God. If they say, by a private revelation; then they concede that extraordinary and private revelations are still employed, and so they establish and confirm enthusiasm; for this authority they attribute even to the present church. If they say, by some ordinary means; then they must acknowledge that the church hath this knowledge by the word itself. Stapleton proceeds: Now it cannot be *discovered by reason* that one book is apocryphal, another canonical; this authentic, and that spurious, any more than the rest. Therefore it must be proved by the church. I answer: The inference does not hold. For it cannot be proved by human reasons that Christ was born of a virgin, rose from the dead, ascended up to heaven with his body. Must then the whole credit of these and other articles depend upon the sole authority and testimony of the church alone? Do we believe these things to be true upon no other grounds but because it pleases the church that we should thus

believe? Assuredly not. But what, though it were conceded that
we came to know through the church, that this is the word of God,
and that this teaching is true and canonical, which we do indeed
gladly concede in a certain sense; yet must this be understood
so as to indicate an external, ministerial means, which God hath
been pleased to use in instructing us, and nothing more. It is
through the ministry of the church, and not on account of the
church's authority. As, therefore, he who receives a message of
great favours promised or bestowed upon him by his sovereign, does
not believe on account of the messenger, or on the messenger's
authority, but on account of the prince's own munificence, or because
he sees the patent or letter signed with the prince's own hand, or
because he recognises some other certain token; nor believes on
account of the servant, although through his ministry; so we receive indeed the scriptures sent to us from God through the church,
and yet do not believe it to be sent from God solely on the church's
authority, but on account of the voice of God, which we recognise
speaking clearly and expressly in the scriptures.

I answer, *secondly*, If scripture cannot be proved by scripture,
as Stapleton says, then certainly much less can it be proved by the
church. For if Stapleton's be a good reason, that scripture cannot
be proved by scripture, because scripture may be unknown or denied, that reason will have still greater force against the church.
For the church is no less liable to be unknown or denied than the
scripture. Stapleton calls this a " weighty question;" and indeed
he must needs find it so. In truth, it is so weighty that he cannot
support himself under it.

But, says he, the case of the church and of the scripture is
not the same. Why? " Because there is no Christian who is
ignorant of the church." In like manner, there is no Christian
who is utterly ignorant of the scripture. The case of both, therefore, is the same. Do you yourself deem him a Christian who
denies the whole scripture? Certainly, he replies; for he affirms that
some Christians deny the scriptures, such as the Schwenkfeldians,
Anabaptists, and in England the Familists[1] and *Superilluminati*.
I answer, our question is about real Christians. These are not
Christians truly but equivocally, as the papists are equivocal
catholics. It may indeed happen that there may be some Christians who are ignorant of the canon of scripture, or have even not
seen some books of it, but yet assent to the doctrine contained in the

[1 Disciples of Henry Nicholas of Amsterdam. See Hooker, Preface to
E. P., Chap. iii. 9, and Mr. Keble's note, p. 184.]

canon of scripture; for otherwise they certainly cannot be called Christians. As to his assertion that there are no Christians who are ignorant of the church, if he mean it of the Roman church, it is certain that many Christians have been, and still are ignorant of it; many have not even so much as heard of it. Will he exclude all these from the hope of salvation? But if he understand any other church, it is nothing to the purpose. However, he proves that no Christians are ignorant of the church, because in the Creed we believe in the church. I confess that in the Creed we do believe in the church, but not in this or that church, but the catholic church; which is no particular assembly of men, much less the Roman synagogue, tied to any one place, but the body of the elect which hath existed from the beginning of the world, and shall exist unto the end. And why do we thus believe? Assuredly by no other argument than the authority of scripture, because the scriptures teach us that there is such a body in the world, as Augustine repeats a thousand times against the Donatists, not because any church attests or professes this proposition. But the church, says he, is "the means of believing all the rest;" therefore it is the means also of believing the existence of the scriptures. I answer, it is indeed the means, not the principal or prime source; and a mean merely external and ministerial. But the principal mean is the word itself, and the prime cause is the Spirit; whereas the church is only an inferior organ.

"But in the Creed," says Stapleton, "we believe in the church, but not in the scriptures." To this I return two answers. First, since Stapleton allows that we believe in the church, I demand how, and on what account? If he say, on account of the church, then we believe a thing on account of the thing itself. But this is no proof even in his own opinion : for every proof (as he says himself elsewhere) proceeds from premises better known than the conclusion. Therefore, we believe the church through some other mean, that is, through the scripture and the church. Secondly, Stapleton thus rejects the scripture from the Creed, since he says that in the Creed we believe in the church, but not in the scriptures. But the scripture is not rejected from the Creed; for the Creed is a compendium and epitome of the whole scripture, and all the articles of the Creed itself are confirmed out of scripture. Besides, in the Creed itself we indicate our belief in scripture : for when I profess that "I believe in God," I profess also that I believe that God speaks truth in his word, and consequently, that I receive and venerate all divine scripture. For the

word " I believe," which occurs at the commencement of the
Creed, is by the fathers expounded in a threefold sense,—that
is, I believe God; I believe that there is a God; and I believe
in God. (*Credo Deo, Credo Deum, Credo in Deum*).

Stapleton goes on to observe, that the whole formal cause of
faith is assent to God revealing something through the church. I
answer, God does, indeed, reveal truth through the church, but so
as through an external ministerial medium. But properly he reveals truth to us through the Spirit and the scripture : for though
" Paul plant and Apollos water," yet these are of no avail unless
" God give the increase." 1 Cor. iii. 6. The church can reveal
nothing to us in a saving way without the Spirit. But nothing can
be hence gathered to make it appear that the authority of the
church and of scripture is not equally doubtful and obscure, nay,
that the authority of the church is not much more so ; since it is
certain that whatever authority the church hath depends entirely
upon the scripture.

So much then in reply to Stapleton's first argument : let us
come now to the rest, which are all, as it were, inferior streams
derived from this first argument, and referred to its confirmation.
However, we will examine them each distinctly and severally, that
a plain answer may be returned on our part to every argument
which he employs.

CHAPTER IV.

WHEREIN STAPLETON'S SECOND ARGUMENT IS PROPOSED AND CONFUTED.

In his ninth Book, chap. 5, he sets forth an egregious piece of
reasoning to this effect : Some writings of the prophets and apostles
have not canonical authority, and some which are not writings of
prophets or apostles are received into the canon. Therefore the
whole canon of scripture rests on, and is defined by, the judgment
of the church. It ought to determine the canon of scripture ; and
consequently the scripture hath its authority from the testimony of
the church.

I have three answers to this. First, it is possible that prophets and apostles may have written some things in an ordinary
way to private persons, as, for instance, David sent private letters to

Joab. These things ought not to be received into the canon. But whatever they wrote as prophets, and inspired by God, for the public instruction of the church, have been received into the canon.

Secondly, I demand of him, whether those writings of which he speaks were in themselves sacred and divine, or not? If they were; then the church ought to admit and approve them by its testimony, as they allow themselves, and the church hath erred in not receiving them: for it is the office of the church to recognise the sacred scriptures and commend them to others. If they were not; then it is certain that they were written by prophets and apostles with some other design than that they should be admitted into the canon of scripture: so that the church neither could nor ought to have admitted them into that canon.

Thirdly, no such public writing of either the prophets or the apostles can be produced, which hath not been received in the canon of the scriptures. Yet Stapleton endeavours to prove that there were many such writings both of prophets and apostles, which the church never chose to sanction. And, in the first place, he enumerates certain writings of the prophets, and then of the apostles which were never admitted into the canon. By Samuel, says he, and Nathan and Gad, the Acts of David were written, as appears from 1 Chron. last chapter, verse 29. But those books are not now canonical. Therefore it is in the discretion of the church, either to receive books of scripture as canonical, or to refuse and reject them as apocryphal. I answer, that in that place the sacred history of the first and second of Samuel is meant, which was drawn up by those three prophets, Samuel, Nathan, and Gad, and which Stapleton rashly denies to be canonical. For it is certain that both these books were not written by Samuel, because Samuel was dead before the end of the first book. Now the church always acknowledged these books to be canonical. But Stapleton supposes that some other history, the work of those distinguished prophets, is referred to; which cannot be established by any proof. Secondly, he says that the Acts of Solomon were consigned to writing by Nathan, Ahijah and Iddo, as appears from 2 Chron. ix. 29. I reply, that the history there meant is that which is contained in the first book of Kings: or, if some other history be indicated, how will he prove that, when it was extant, it had not canonical authority? Thirdly, he proves from 2 Chron. xiii. 22, that the history of Abijah was written by Iddo the prophet, which yet is not now extant in the canon. I answer, that this is the same history of king Abijah which is contained in

1 Kings xv. Fourthly, he says that the history of Jehoshaphat was written by the prophet Jehu; which he proves from 2 Chron. xx. 34. I answer, that the same history is meant which is extant 1 Kings xvi. For it is certain that the histories of Judges, Ruth, Samuel and Kings, were written by many prophets: whence in Matth. ii.[1], at the last verse, a passage is cited from the book of Judges (for it is found nowhere else); and yet Matthew uses the expression, "that it might be fulfilled which was spoken *by the prophets*," τὸ ῥηθὲν διὰ τῶν προφητῶν. Whence we may undertand that that book was written and composed by many prophets. Fifthly, he says that many writings of Solomon's are now not extant in the canon of scripture. I answer, that this is no great wonder, since they have now wholly perished and are not extant anywhere: for I believe that no man doubts that some canonical pieces have perished. But if they were now extant, Stapleton would have to prove that it would depend upon the authority of the church whether they should or should not be in the canon. Next he brings a testimony from Augustine, *de Civit. Dei*, Lib. xvii. cap. ult. where these words occur: "There are writings of theirs" (meaning Zechariah, Malachi, and Haggai,) "as there are of others, who prophesied in great numbers: very few wrote pieces which had canonical authority[2]." I answer, these things which Augustine says have no reference to our question. For he does not say that many things were written by the prophets which had no canonical authority; but that, out of a great many prophets, there were very few who wrote anything: because many prophets left no written compositions whatever. What he says, therefore, is, there were many prophets who taught the church only orally; but few who wrote anything. This is plainly Augustine's sense and meaning: whence, by the way, we may take notice of Stapleton's fidelity in quoting the fathers. These, then, are Stapleton's objections concerning the writings of the prophets. Let us come now to those writings of the apostles which he affirms not to have been received into the canon.

The first specifies the epistle to the Laodiceans, which he proves from Coloss. iv. 16, to have been written by Paul; yet, says he,

---

[1 Whitaker supposes the reference to be to Judges xiii. 5. But a Nazarite is expressed in Greek by Ναζαραῖος, Νάζερ, Νάζιρ, Ναζιραῖος· never, I believe, by Ναζωραῖος.]

[2 Sunt scripta eorum, sicut aliorum qui in magna multitudine prophetarunt: perpauci ea scripserunt quæ auctoritatem canonis haberent. T. ix. p. 640.]

that epistle is not now in the canon.   I answer: No epistle of the
kind is mentioned in that place.   The apostle says, ἐκ Λαοδικείας,
not πρὸς Λαοδικείαν, so that the epistle here referred to was not
written to the Laodiceans, but from Laodicea.   The mistake arose
from the vulgar Latin edition, which reads, *Epistolam Laodicensium*.   Formerly, indeed, there was an epistle which passed
under this name, as Epiphanius (*contra Marcion*.[3]) and others
remark.   Faber Stapulensis counts this amongst Paul's epistles,
but is censured on that account by Erasmus[4].   Those hold a more
reasonable and specious opinion, who think that there was such an
epistle, but that it is now lost.   However, even that cannot be
proved from this passage.   It appears to me, that what is here
indicated is rather that the Laodiceans had written an epistle to
Paul, in which as there were some things which concerned the
Colossians, and which it was important for them to know, Paul
wished it to be read by the Colossians along with this epistle of
his own.   This I judge not incredible, and indeed much the more
probable opinion.   To this effect Œcumenius writes distinctly:
" He does not say, that written *to* Laodicea, but that *from* Laodicea; not that from Paul to the Laodiceans, but that from the
Laodiceans to Paul.   For no doubt there was something in it which
concerned the Colossians[5]."   These remarks Œcumenius took from
Chrysostom.   Catharinus too, a papist, acknowledges in his commentary upon this place, (p. 366,) that it is not an epistle written
by him to the Laodiceans, but one written from that place.   Jerome,
in his catalogue of ecclesiastical writers, under the head of PAUL[6],
makes mention of this epistle, but observes that it is universally
condemned.   The second Council of Nice[7] determines it to be

[3 Whitaker is doubtless mistaken in supposing that the miserable modern
forgery, under this title, is the Epistle to the Laodiceans used by Marcion;
Marcion gave this title to what we call the Epistle to the Ephesians.   See
Tertullian, c. Marc. V. XI. 17.   Epiphanius' loose and inconsistent statements
misled Whitaker.—Hæres. xlii. T. I. pp. 310, 319, 374.]

[4 Etiam Faber, homo doctus sed aliquoties nimium candidus, diligenter
reliquis admiscuit Epistolis.—Erasm. Annot. in Col. iv. 16.]

[5 οὐ γὰρ εἶπε τὴν πρὸς Λαοδικεῖς, ἀλλὰ τὴν ἐκ Λαοδικείας γραφεῖσαν· οὐ τὴν
ἀπὸ Παύλου πρὸς Λαοδικέας, ἀλλὰ τὴν ἀπὸ Λαοδικέων πρὸς Παῦλον.   ῏Ην γάρ τι
πάντως ἐν αὐτῇ ὠφελοῦν Κολοσσαεῖς. p. 146. T. II. Paris. 1631.]

[6 Legunt quidam et ad Laodicenses, sed ab omnibus exploditur.   T. II.
p. 826.]

[7 καὶ γὰρ τοῦ θείου Ἀποστόλου πρὸς Λαοδικεῖς φέρεται πλαστὴ ἐπιστολή.—
Art. 6. p. 5. Concil. Labb. T. VII. p. 475.]

spurious, and rejects it as supposititious. Theophylact[1] thinks that the first epistle to Timothy is meant, because it was written from Laodicea; Tertullian, in his fifth book against Marcion[2], the epistle to the Ephesians.

As to what Stapleton subjoins, that there were some books written by Peter, and a certain book also of the travels of Paul and Thecla[3], which are not in the canon; I answer, that these books were always deemed spurious impostures by the church. Jerome (in Cat. under PETER[4]) rejects them as apocryphal, and not written by Peter. Let me therefore say of these, as we read that Augustine formerly said of some still more ancient (*Civit. Dei*, Lib. XVIII. c. 38): " These writings the chastity of the canon hath not admitted, not because the authority of those men who pleased God is rejected, but because these are not believed to be their works[5]." It rests not therefore with the church's discretion to make the writings of prophets and apostles canonical or not canonical, to reject what is, or to admit what is not, canonical. So far concerning Stapleton's second argument.

CHAPTER V.

WHEREIN THE THIRD ARGUMENT OF OUR OPPONENTS IS EXAMINED AND SET ASIDE.

STAPLETON's third argument is contained in the 6th chapter of his ninth book, and is to this effect. It is owing to the judgment and authority of the church, that apocryphal writings of the first

[1 τίς δὲ ἦν ἡ ἐκ Λαοδικείας; ἡ πρὸς Τιμόθεον πρώτη. αὕτη γὰρ ἐκ Λαοδικείας ἐγράφη.—Theophyl. in Col. iv. 16, p. 676, Lond. 1636.]

[2 Præterea hic et de alia Epistola, quam nos ad Ephesios præscriptam habemus, hæretici vero ad Laodicenos.—V. c. 11.]

[3 Grabe Spicil. i. p. 95, et seqq.]

[4 Libri autem ejus, e quibus unus Actorum ejus inscribitur, alius Evangelii, tertius prædicationis, quartus Apocalypsis, quintus Judicii, inter apocryphas scripturas reputantur. T. ii. p. 814.]

[5 Sed ea castitas Canonis non recepit, non quod eorum hominum qui Deo placuerunt, reprobetur auctoritas, sed quod ista non credantur eorum esse. T. ix. p. 685.]

kind, such as were formerly not certainly canonical but doubtful, were after a while admitted into the canon. Therefore, &c. He calls those books Apocryphal of the first class, concerning which doubts were at first entertained in the church, although they were afterwards ultimately received. Such are those whom this same author and other papists call Deutero-canonical. For those which form the second rank of canonical, are the first rank of apocryphal writings: of which kind, in the old Testament, are Tobit, Judith, Ecclesiasticus, and those other books concerning which we have disputed at large in the first Question; in the new, the Epistle to the Hebrews, the Apocalypse, the second and third Epistles of John, the second of Peter, the story of the woman taken in adultery, the Epistle of Jude, and the Epistle of James. Together with these Stapleton, in the fifth chapter of this book, enumerates the book of the Shepherd, the Epistle of Barnabas, the Acts of Paul, the Gospel according to the Hebrews, and the travels of Paul, styling these also Apocryphal of the first class, although books which neither now nor heretofore were ever received into the canon, which all those other books of the new Testament have long since been. Nevertheless this man tells us that all these pieces are of the same rank, kind, and nature, and that whatever difference is made between them results entirely from the circumstance that the church hath judged some canonical, others not, received the one set, and rejected the other. But there is a wide difference between them besides this: otherwise the church could not make such a difference between writings, all of which were really in the same predicament. For if, as Stapleton says, all these books be of the same kind, rank, and nature, why hath the church received the one part rather than the other? But now let us answer this argument distinctly and in form. The answer shall be fourfold.

Firstly, I say that the church never did receive, by its judgment and approbation, those books of the old Testament which they call Deutero-canonical, or Apocryphal of the first class; which point we have sufficiently established in the first Question of this controversy. If they say the church hath received them, let them tell us when, and in what council? Now whatever councils they are able to produce are merely recent; and no reason can be assigned why canonical books should lie so long unsanctioned by the authority of the church.

Secondly, I say that the church neither could, nor ought to have received them into the canon. For the church cannot make

20

[WHITAKER.]

those books canonical and divine, which are not really in themselves canonical, sacred, and divine. Even the papists themselves do not ascribe so much power to the church, whose office terminates in declaring those books to be canonical, and as such commending them to the people, which are really and in themselves canonical. Now we have already proved that these books possess no such character. The council of Laodicea expressly rejects them as non-canonical writings, βίβλια ἀκανόνιστα. Jerome determines that no religious dogma can be proved by them : whereas, if they were canonical, the doctrines of religion might be established from them just as well as from the rest.

Thirdly, we confess that formerly doubts were entertained concerning certain books of the new Testament, as the Epistle to the Hebrews and others, which books were nevertheless afterwards received into the canon. But we deny that it is merely on the church's authority that these books either are, or are accounted, canonical. For I demand, what reason was it that induced or impelled the church at length to receive them ? Certainly no other cause but this, that it perceived and recognised the doctrine in them to be plainly divine and inspired by God. Why then may not the same reason persuade us also to receive them ? Any other answer which they may give will assign a wholly uncertain criterion.

Fourthly, although in some churches doubts prevailed concerning these books of the new Testament, yet other churches received them. So Eusebius writes concerning these epistles ; as specially of the Epistle of James, Lib. II. c. 23. For although he uses the term νοθεύεσθαι[1], yet he acknowledges that it was publicly received (δεδημοσιευμένην) in many churches : which these men can not say of the Epistle of Barnabas, or the Gospel according to the Hebrews, or other such like spurious or adulterated pieces. But if, as Stapleton says, these books were indeed equal amongst themselves and of the same rank (that is, these canonical books and those spurious ones which he enumerates), and if the church have caused them to be of unequal authority with respect to us, then the church hath fallen into a grievous error : for the church ought not to have caused pieces of equal authority intrinsically to appear otherwise to us. Now Stapleton says that these books are of the same

[1 ἰστέον δὲ ὡς νοθεύεται μὲν . . . . . ὅμως δὲ ἴσμεν καὶ ταύτας [this and the Epistle of Jude] μετὰ τῶν λοιπῶν ἐν πλείσταις δεδημοσιευμένας ἐκκλησίαις.— T. I. p. 175. ed. Heinich. Compare Hug's Einl. I. 119.]

rank in themselves; but in respect of us, he ascribes it to the church's judgment that some are deemed canonical, and not others. But surely the church cannot change the quality of books, but only declare them to us to be such as they really are in themselves. Therefore, if they were all equal, an equal judgment ought to be passed upon them all. That this rests in the arbitrary decision of the church, he will never be able to establish : let us nevertheless attend to the manner in which he attempts to prove it.

Stapleton proceeds to cite many testimonies of the fathers, of which I will only examine the three principal, and pass over what is irrelevant to the question. In the first place, then, he objects to us Eusebius (H. E. Lib. iii. c. 19, or in the Greek, 25), who affirms that the plain mark of the canonical books is *the tradition of the church*. I answer : Eusebius there enumerates all the books of the new Testament, as well those which were always received by all, as those which were rejected by some, and concerning which doubts were then entertained in some churches. Eusebius's own words are as follow : " It was needful that we should draw up such a catalogue of these, distinguishing those pieces which, according to the ecclesiastical tradition, are true and unfeigned and acknowledged scriptures, from those which are not part of the Testament[2]." To which testimony of Eusebius I briefly return a threefold reply. *Firstly*, we should allow no weight in this matter to the authority of Eusebius, because it has no force to establish what Stapleton undertakes to prove. For, while he says that he follows the ecclesiastical tradition, he distinguishes from the canonical books those very pieces which the papists themselves maintain to be canonical, as the Book of Tobit, Judith, &c. the Epistle to the Hebrews, the Epistle of James, the Apocalypse, &c. Therefore, if that tradition which Eusebius follows be true, it will prevail as much against the papists themselves as against us. And if that tradition be so certain a mark of the books, then the authority of some books of the canon is utterly destroyed, as the Epistle of James and other epistles, which this tradition of Eusebius, so much relied on by Stapleton, banishes from the sacred canon. Let him then consider for himself what weight is to be allowed to this testimony. *Secondly*, I deny not that ecclesiastical tradition is a means of proof, whereby it may be shewn what books are canonical and

[² ἀναγκαίως δὲ καὶ τούτων ὅμως τὸν κατάλογον πεποιήμεθα, διακρίναντες τάς τε κατὰ τὴν ἐκκλησιαστικὴν παράδοσιν ἀληθεῖς καὶ ἀπλάστους καὶ ἀνωμολογημένας γραφὰς, καὶ τὰς ἄλλας παρὰ ταύτας, οὐκ ἐνδιαθήκους μὲν, κ. τ. λ.—T. I. p. 247.]

what not canonical; yet I say that it is a merely external means
of proof. Now, in order that we should be thoroughly persuaded
of the authority of the canonical books, there is need besides of the
internal testimony of the Holy Spirit. In like manner, with respect
to God himself and the Trinity, and other articles of our faith, the
church gives us instruction, and this tradition ought to have with
all the force of a great argument: and if any were to deny those
articles, we should press them with the authority of the church as
an external argument, which hath in it all the strength necessary
for convincing and refuting the gainsayers. Yet, unless the internal testimony of the Holy Spirit be added, fortified by the ample
authority of scripture, the human mind will never give a solid
assent with entire acquiescence to those articles. *Thirdly*, Eusebius
writes that he enumerates these books as canonical, not on account
of the ecclesiastical tradition, but *according* to the ecclesiastical
tradition, which is a very different thing. His words are not διὰ
τὴν παράδοσιν, but κατὰ τὴν παράδοσιν. Those who suppose
that there is no difference between these two are greatly deceived.
For it is through the church's ministry that we believe whatever
we believe, but not on account of the church's authority; since our
faith relies upon and is confirmed by an authority much more august,
certain and clear, than that of the church. Let this suffice concerning the testimony of Eusebius.

The second testimony cited by Stapleton is taken from Augustine, *De Doct. Christ.* Lib. II. c. 8, where these words occur: "The
believer will observe this rule with respect to the canonical
scriptures, to prefer those which are received by all churches to
those which some do not receive. In the case of those which are
not received by all, he will prefer those which the more and
more dignified churches receive to those which fewer churches or
churches of less authority admit. But if he should find some
received by the greater number, and others by the more dignified (though indeed such a case cannot easily be found), yet I
think that the two classes should be deemed of equal authority[1]."

[1 Tenebit igitur hunc modum in scripturis canonicis, ut eas quæ ab
omnibus accipiuntur ecclesiis præponat eis quas quædam non accipiunt:
in eis vero quæ non accipiuntur ab omnibus, præponat eas quas plures
gravioresque accipiunt eis quas pauciores minorisque auctoritatis ecclesiæ
tenent. Si autem alias invenerit a pluribus, alias a gravioribus haberi,
(quamquam hoc facile invenire non possit,) æqualis tamen auctoritatis eas
habendas puto.—p. 30. Opp. T. III.]

Thus Augustine ; where (says Stapleton) he shews that this whole truth, and this difference between the books, depends upon the various judgment of the church. I answer, that Stapleton does not consider what he says. For, what ? shall this whole truth and difference between the books depend upon the various judgment of the church ? Must the truth and authority of the canonical scripture be made thus to hang upon the judgment of the church, and that judgment itself a variable one ?—What assertion could possibly be more absurd or more insulting than this ? Churches indeed may judge variously and inconstantly, as was plainly the case in the ancient churches : but the scriptures of God are always the same, consistent with themselves, and admitting of no variety. But Augustine in that place is instructing tyros and novices, and exhorting them in the first place to attend to the church as their mistress and admonisher, and to follow her judgment. Nor will any one deny that this is pious and sound advice. We do not immediately understand everything ourselves ; we must therefore listen to the church which bids us read these books. Afterwards, however, when we either read them ourselves, or hear others read them, and duly weigh what they teach, we believe their canonicity, not only on account of the testimony or authority of the church, but upon the inducement of other and more certain arguments, as the witness of the Holy Spirit, and the majesty of that heavenly doctrine, which shines forth in the books themselves and the whole manner of their teaching. Augustine, therefore, would have us ascribe much, but not all, to the church in this matter. But two points against the papists may be gathered from this place. First, that Augustine never understood or recognised such a public and certain judgment of the church as the papists feign ;—that is, an external judgment, and that passed by the Roman Church, which all Christians should be bound to stand by and obey : for then he would have desired a disciple to follow this judgment, and consult only the Roman Church. Secondly, it may be gathered from this place, that churches may be true churches of Christ, and yet judge variously of certain canonical books. Whence it manifestly appears that all who have the Holy Spirit do not think alike of all the books of scripture. But, to reply briefly and in one word,—I say that the dictate, and voice, and commendation of the church is the occasion and first rudiment of the faith wherewith we believe these books to be divine and given by inspiration of God ; but that the form and full assurance depend

upon the internal witness of the Holy Spirit, which must needs be
added before we can certainly know and hold undoubtingly that
these books are canonical and divine.

The third testimony produced by Stapleton, which I have resolved to answer, is taken from Augustine's eleventh book against
Faustus the Manichean, chap. 5, where Augustine writes to this
effect : " Distinguished from the books of later authors is the excellence of the canonical authority of the old and new Testaments ;
which, having been established in the time of the apostles, hath
through the successions of bishops and propagations of churches
been set as it were in a lofty tribunal, demanding the obedience of
every faithful and pious understanding[1]." Hence it appears, says
Stapleton, that the scripture is set in this high tribunal by the approbation and authority of the church. I answer: Augustine writes
that the canon of the scriptures was established by the apostles,
and is now set in this elevated place through the successions of
bishops and propagations of churches. What does this prove
against us ? Who is so mad as not to perceive that the apostles
established the canonical scripture, and that pious bishops and
churches rendered it the highest reverence ? But does it follow
thence, that we do not know what books are canonical by any
other testimony than that of the church ; or that the scripture hath
no other authority with us than that which the church assigns to
it ? Assuredly not. But from this passage of Augustine we draw
the following observations against the papists. *First,* that the
canon of scripture was settled in the time of the apostles, and consigned in a certain number of books, and that, therefore, those more
recent councils, by means of which the papists prove that certain
apocryphal books of the old Testament are canonical, are of no avail
against us, since the apostles themselves had determined in their own
times what books should be received into the canon of the old Testament. *Secondly,* that the books of the new Testament were
written and confirmed by the apostles themselves, and a definite
number of books marked out. *Thirdly,* that if the canon of scripture were settled by the apostles themselves, it is not now in the
power of the church to add any book to this canon, and so increase

[1 Distincta est a posterioribus libris excellentia canonicæ auctoritatis
veteris et novi Testamenti, quæ, apostolorum confirmata temporibus, per
successiones episcoporum et propagationes ecclesiarum tanquam in sede
quadam sublimiter constituta est, cui serviat omnis fidelis et pius intellectus.
—p. 267. Opp. T. x.]

the number of the canonical books; which yet Stapleton affirms in the 14th chapter of this book. Jerome in his Catalogue, and other authors write that John lived the longest of all the apostles, so as to be able to see all the books and confirm them, and, if any fictitious books were published, to distinguish them from the sacred and truly canonical books. Jerome[2], in his Catalogue, under the article LUKE, relates that a certain book concerning the acts of Paul was presented to John, but that the author was discovered and the book condemned by the authority of the apostle. Tertullian[3] in his Prescriptions says, that the very autographs of the apostles themselves were preserved in his time safe in the churches; and the same writer remarks in the same place, " We determine the document of the gospel to have the apostles for its authors[4]." Augustine, Epist. 19[5], asserts that these scriptures were received to the height of canonical authority by the apostles themselves. The fact that afterwards some persons entertained doubts of certain parts had its origin not in the scriptures themselves, but in our infirmity.

But perhaps some one may object: If the apostles, who were the pastors of the church, had the power of consigning the canon and confirming the canonical scriptures, then the same privilege will belong to the other pastors of the church who succeed them, when assembled together in one place. I answer, the apostles may be considered under a twofold aspect: firstly, as the principal teachers of the church; secondly, as certain immediate organs, chosen by God and designated for the special office of writing and publishing the sacred books. This was so peculiar to themselves, that in this respect they were placed out of the condition of all other men. Now the apostles' consignation of the canon of scripture is to be referred not to the authority of the church, but to that of God. It was not as the ministers of the church that they consigned it, but as the unerring organs of the Holy Ghost, fortified by a divine authority, and commended to the

[2 Opp. T. II. 827. This piece was the story of Thecla, printed by Grabe in the first vol. of his Spicilegium.]

[3 Percurre ecclesias apostolicas, apud quas ipsæ adhuc cathedræ apostolorum suis locis præsidentur, apud quas ipsæ authenticæ literæ eorum recitantur.—c. 36. ed. Leopold. Lips. 1841. P. 3. p. 25.]

[4 This is a mistake. The passage cited occurs in the 4th Book, Adv. Marc. c. 2. (p. 147): Constituimus imprimis evangelicum instrumentum apostolos auctores habere.]

[5 Ep. 82. Opp. T. II. p. 253. Commendata ... ab ipsis apostolis.]

faith of all. For if they had done this as ordinary ministers, then all pastors who succeed the apostles would have the like power. Whence it is manifest that this authority of theirs was of an extraordinary kind. Therefore the apostles consigned the canon of scripture, not as men or ministers, but as the representative of God, the tongue of the Holy Spirit, and, as it were, a divine oracle. Wherefore this act can avail nothing towards establishing the perpetual authority of the church. And so much for Stapleton's third argument.

CHAPTER VI.

WHEREIN THE FOURTH ARGUMENT OF OUR OPPONENTS IS
ANSWERED.

Now follows his fourth argument, which is handled in Lib. ix. c. 7, and is to this effect: The apocryphal books of the second class are therefore not accounted divine, because the church hath never chosen to approve them. Therefore this whole matter (namely, of receiving and rejecting books) depends upon the authority and judgment of the church. He calls those books apocryphal of the second class, which have been published under the name of the apostles, either by heretics, or philosophers, or others: of which kind were, the revelation of Paul, the gospel of Judas Iscariot, the gospel of Thomas, the gospel of Matthias, the gospel of Andrew, and the gospel of Peter, which pope Innocent I. in his third epistle testifies to have been published by philosophers. These books, says Stapleton, the church hath rejected and repudiated. Therefore, it appertains to the church to determine concerning canonical books, and to consign a certain canon of scripture.

I answer, that this argument proves nothing; and that for three reasons. The *first* is, because we have already granted that it appertains to the office, and consequently to the authority, of the church, to distinguish the true and genuine books from spurious. For it possesses the Spirit of God, under whose instruction it hears the voice of its Spouse and recognises his teaching. For that same Spirit, by whom those books were written, still resides in the church, although not always in the same measure. All this, therefore, we allow; but we demand to know how it follows from these premises, that we can judge by no other criterion than the church's determination of their non-canonicity, that these books deserve to be rejected and refused? Would any one draw so loose and inconsequent a conclusion, who trusted to be able to gain his cause by legitimate arguments? For our parts, we affirm that there are other criterions. Let them tell us upon what grounds the church deems these books spurious; and I will answer, that we also may arrive at the same conclusion upon the same inducements. *Secondly*, we concede that against heretics an argument may be taken from the authority and consent of the church, shewing that, since the whole church hath rejected those books, we justly allow them to deserve rejection. For who is there so bold and impudent as not to be greatly moved by the authority of the catholic church? It hath seen and examined these books, and can judge better of them than any private person, because endowed with a greater and more ample abundance of the Holy Spirit and of judgment: since it hath, with so much judgment and deliberation, rejected certain books, we ought not, without any reason, to retain them. This argument, therefore, hath very great weight against heretics, and heretics may be very much pressed and urged by it; nor yet heretics alone, but other opponents also who would either receive supposititious books, or reject really canonical. This argument the fathers frequently used; but, nevertheless, have nowhere said that all this depended upon the authority of the church, or that this was either the sole or the greatest argument, whereby heretics and other adversaries, who held wrong sentiments concerning these books, might be refuted. Nay, some of those very fathers whom Stapleton cites have used other arguments upon this subject, as will appear presently. *Thirdly*, therefore, those fathers who used this argument which is derived from the authority of the church, did not reject these apocryphal books of the second class merely on account of the church's authority, and solely upon the church's external judgment delivered as it were in court; but on account of other proofs which were taken and derived out of the books themselves. For those books had generally open errors and perverse doctrines, from which the church could easily determine that they were fictitious and spurious books, and not truly canonical. This is evident from the testimony of those very fathers, whom Stapleton alleges in his own behalf in this cause, that is, Eusebius and Augustine.

Eusebius, in his third book, chap. xxv. of the Greek copy,

speaking of the gospels of Thomas, Peter, Matthias, and other apocryphal books of the second class, explains at the end of his discourse, why these books were rejected by the church, in the following
words : " The very diction, character, and phraseology, are foreign
from the apostolic. Their drift is widely different from the orthodox religion and doctrine, and therefore they are deservedly
rejected as spurious books and figments of the heretics." It is better
to hear Eusebius's own words : Πόρρω δέ που καὶ ὁ τῆς φράσεως
παρὰ τὸ ἦθος τὸ ἀποστολικὸν ἐναλλάτει χαρακτήρ, ἥ τε γνώμη,
καὶ τῶν ἐν αὐτοῖς φερομένων προαίρεσις, πλεῖστον ὅσον τῆς
ἀληθοῦς ὀρθοδοξίας ἀπᾴδουσα, ὅτι δὲ αἱρετικῶν ἀνδρῶν ἀνα-
πλάσματα τυγχάνει σαφῶς παρίστησιν· ὅθεν οὐδ᾽ ἐν νόθοις
αὐτὰ κατατακτέον, ἀλλ᾽ ὡς ἄτοπα πάντη καὶ δυσσεβῆ παραι-
τητέον[1]. Here we may remark Stapleton's fidelity. He would
fain prove from the testimony of Eusebius, that these books are to
be rejected for no other reason but because the church hath rejected
them ; and he cites a place from this very chapter, and from the
words immediately preceding, where it is said : " None of the ecclesiastical writers hath ever vouchsafed to make mention of these
books in his writings[2]." Here he breaks off the testimony of
Eusebius : whereas the words quoted above follow immediately,
which he hath altogether omitted, because they make against
himself. In those words Eusebius tells us that, besides the testimony of the church, there are two other ways and marks whereby
we may perceive that these books are not canonical : first, τῷ
χαρακτῆρι τῆς φρασέως, from the style and character, because
the apostles never wrote or spoke after such a fashion ; whence it
appears that, in the opinion of Eusebius, the phrase and diction is
a mark of the canonical books : secondly, τῇ γνώμῃ καὶ τῇ
προαιρέσει, from the sentiments and design ; that is, from the
kind of doctrine delivered in these books, which, says Eusebius, is
inexpressibly different from sound doctrine and orthodox religion,
so that they not only should not be received, but should be rejected and abhorred as the impure and wicked productions of the
heretics. Yet Stapleton would fain persuade us that these books
ought to be rejected upon no other account but because the church
hath rejected them. Besides, Eusebius in the same book, chap. 32,[3]

---

[1] T. I. pp. 247—50. ed. Heinichen.]

[2] ὧν οὐδὲν οὐδαμῶς ἐν συγγράμματι τῶν κατὰ διαδοχὰς ἐκκλησιαστικῶν
τις ἀνὴρ εἰς μνήμην ἀγαγεῖν ἠξίωσεν.—Id. ibid.]

[3] Euseb. H. E. III. c. 38. pp. 280, 1. ut supra.]

rejects the dispute of Peter with Apion, on account of its not maintaining the pure unblemished signature of apostolic and orthodox doctrine. Οὐδὲ γὰρ, says he, καθαρὸν ἀποστολικῆς ὀρθοδοξίας ἀποσώζει τὸν χαρακτῆρα : as much as to say, it is manifest that this dispute was not held by an apostle, since it wants the true and genuine mark of apostolical faith and preaching; it does not agree with the doctrine of Peter, and therefore it is falsely ascribed to Peter.

So much for the testimony of Eusebius. I proceed now to Augustine, who certainly never wrote as Stapleton affirms him to have written, but to a far different effect. He does not say that these books were held to be apocryphal solely because they were full of lies, and contained many things impious and false. In his 98th tractate upon John, having mentioned the revelation of Paul, he subjoins, that it is not received by the church: but wherefore? Is it because it was placed in the judgment of the church alone to receive or not receive it? By no means; but because it was "feigned" by certain "vain" men, and because it was "full of fables⁴." Well then, do we reject, upon no other account but the church's testimony, a book "feigned by vain men, and full of fables?" Yea, rather we reject it for being such. The same Augustine, against Faustus the Manichean, Lib. XXII. c. 79, says that the Manichees read certain books written by "stitchers-together of fables⁵." He means the gospels of Matthias, Andrew, Peter, and those other books which Stapleton hath before enumerated. These books therefore were not received by the church, because they were full of fables, not merely because the church chose to reject them. Besides, the same Augustine, in his work *de consensu Evangelistarum*, Lib. I. c. 1,⁶ discusses the question why, since so many had written of the actions and doctrine both of Christ and of the apostles, only four gospels and the Acts of the Apostles were received, and assigns two reasons: first, because the men who wrote those other books were not such as the church deemed worthy of credit, that is, were not endowed with the extraordinary gifts of the Holy Spirit, or so furnished for the task as all those ought to be who write of such sacred and divine matters;

[⁴ Qua occasione vani quidam Apocalypsin Pauli, quam sane non recipit ecclesia, nescio quibus fabulis plenam, stultissima præsumptione finxerunt. —Opp. T. IV. p. 982.]

[⁵ Legunt scripturas apocryphas Manichæi, a nescio quibus *sutoribus fabularum* sub apostolorum nomine scriptas, etc.—T. X. p. 490.]

[⁶ T. IV. p. 1. Bassan. 1797.]

secondly, because they did not write with the same fidelity, but introduced many things which clash and are at variance with the catholic faith and rule of apostolic doctrine. Therefore, the fathers themselves allow that there are other arguments for rejecting these books, besides the sole authority of the church. As to the Acts of the Apostles, Augustine writes in that same place, that no others wrote with the same fidelity as Luke, and therefore that his book only was received. What could possibly be spoken more plainly? These books were at variance with the rule and analogy of faith, and therefore ought not to have been received, neither could the church receive them, nor do otherwise than reject and condemn such books. Now in like manner as the church formerly rejected those books upon this account, so we also would, on the same account, now reject and condemn them, if they were still extant.

So much for the fourth argument brought by Stapleton. It remains now that we address ourselves to his fifth.

CHAPTER VII.

OF THE FIFTH ARGUMENT OF OUR ADVERSARIES.

STAPLETON'S fifth argument is contained in the eighth chapter of his ninth book, and is to this effect: Heretics rejecting any part of scripture, or persons doubting any canonical book, are refuted by the authority and tradition of the church. Therefore it is the privilege of the church to consign the canon of scripture. Here he is very large in his citations of testimonies from Augustine, yet to no advantage of his cause; since they in no way weaken ours, but prove a totally different thing, and therefore might be wholly omitted.

I answer, therefore, that this argument is inconsequential: heretics are refuted by the authority of the church; therefore there is no other stronger argument by which the canon of scripture can be established. This is just as if one were to argue thus: atheists who deny the existence of God are refuted by the authority of the church, which hath ever confessed one God, the maker of all things; therefore there is no other argument whereby either we or others can be convinced of God's existence, no more certain reason whereby either they may be refuted, or we established in the truth. Yea, rather the creatures themselves—the heaven and the earth— cry out that there is a God, as saith the prophet : " The heavens declare the ·glory of God, and the firmament sheweth his handy-work." This is a more certain argument for the confutation and conviction of the atheists than the testimony of the church; but for the most certain argument of all is the testimony of the Spirit, without which it is in vain that all other proofs are applied. It is manifest therefore, that this is a plain fallacy of inconsequence, when our adversary disputes thus : this is an argument, therefore it is the sole argument, or there is no other argument besides. The inconsequence of such reasoning will easily appear from a parallel instance. The philosophers may be so refuted by arguments of their own sort, as to be forced to acknow-· ledge the truth of our religion : are there then no other but philosophical arguments by which they can be refuted ? Far from it.

However, to return a fuller answer: we observe that the fathers have indeed used this argument, and that we also may use it against the heretics; because, since heretics are without the Holy Spirit, and are ignorant of the phraseology and sense of scripture, they will doubtless be more moved by the authority and testimony of men, than either of God or of the scripture. They attribute much to the testimony of men, so as that there is no external argument with which, for the most part, they can be pressed more strongly and effectually. For such reasoning as this hath ever had very great weight and influence with all, even the worst of men : the church hath ever judged these books canonical ; therefore you ought not to reject, or doubt concerning them. A man must be shameless indeed, who will not be moved by this argument. But it is one thing to force men to acknowledge the scriptures, and quite another to convince them of their truth. Heretics may perhaps be forced not only by the authority and testimony of the church, but also by the style of scripture, and the exact harmony between the old and new Testaments; which two points are of no less avail than the testimony of the church for inducing us to confess that these books are canonical : but to persuade our souls thoroughly, it is not these or any other arguments of the same kind that can avail, but only the voice of the Holy Spirit speaking inwardly in our hearts. For in like manner as a man may be compelled by many arguments taken from nature to confess the being of God, and yet will never meanwhile be persuaded of it in his conscience, until the Holy Spirit hath infused this faith and persuasion into his heart; so we may indeed be compelled by the authority of the church to acknowledge the canonicity of the scripture, and yet can never be brought to acquiesce in it as a firm and solid truth, until the internal testimony of the Holy Spirit be added. And this argument persuades not others but ourselves, and prevails not upon others but upon ourselves. We do not therefore endeavour to refute others by the secret testimony of the Spirit, since it is peculiar to the individual, private and internal; but by common arguments taken from the books themselves, and from the judgment of the church, which are of such a nature as to move any one not wholly abandoned, and to leave him nothing to say against them. But it is not sufficient for us that our judgment should be compelled and coerced; the Holy Spirit must excite our whole mind to yield assent. Now although the fathers frequently use this argument [from authority], they do not therefore take away other arguments; so that the papists, Stapleton and the rest, err greatly in leaving us no others. We, for our part, do not take away this argument, as they falsely affirm of us, but allow it to be good, and make use of it; but contend nevertheless that there are some other arguments of a firmer and more certain nature.

It is not necessary that we should reply severally to all those testimonies which Stapleton adduces, since we fully allow that they are all most true. The clearest and strongest testimony which he alleges is taken from Augustine's book *contra Epistol. Fund.* c. 5; where Augustine, being about to cite something from the Acts of the Apostles (which book the Manichees rejected, because, Acts ii., the Holy Ghost is said to have descended upon the apostles, whereas they affirmed that his inspiration belonged solely to themselves), he prefaces the quotation with these words: " I must needs believe this book, if I believe the gospel, since catholic authority commends both books to me alike[1]." Therefore (says Stapleton) we repose faith in the canonical books solely on account of the church's authority. I answer, as I have frequently done already, that we are indeed compelled by the authority of the church to believe these books canonical, but that we do not depend upon this argument alone, since we are supplied with other and stronger evidence. Heretics indeed are coerced by this one argument, and it is specially to be urged against obstinate persons; but those who are not *disturbed by passion*, not *dishonest*, not

[1 Necesse est me credere huic libro, si credo Evangelio, cum utramque scripturam similiter mihi catholica commendat auctoritas.—T. x. p. 185.]

obstinate, but *honest* and *desirous of truth,* may be persuaded by many other arguments. So much may be proved from Augustine himself in his book *de Utilit. Credendi,* cap. 3, where he enumerates several other arguments, such as these : first, the order of the things ; secondly, the causes of the sayings and acts ; thirdly, the exact agreement of the old Testament with the new, " so as that not a tittle is left which is not in unison." These arguments must be allowed to have great force in them ; but, since heretics pay but little care and attention to such matters, they must be pressed with the authority of the church. The same Augustine also, in the 5th chapter of that same book, writes that he can easily persuade any one that this or that book of scripture is canonical, if he be met with a candid mind not obstinate in its prejudices. And in chap. 2, he gives the reason why he makes such frequent use of this argument derived from the authority of the church, and handles it so diligently,— namely, because " the scriptures may be popularly accused, but cannot be popularly defended." For the Manichees rendered the old Testament odious with the people by alleging the adultery of David, Jacob's marriage with two sisters, and many similar things to be found in the old Testament, upon which they declaimed largely to the populace. This is the popular accusation alluded to by Augustine. When therefore the holy father was anxious to defend the old Testament, and the scripture itself supplied no such popular argument ; he recalled his adversaries to the common authority of the church, which was an argument no less popular than their own.

Now we have said enough upon Stapleton's fifth argument.

CHAPTER VIII.

OF THE SIXTH ARGUMENT OF OUR ADVERSARIES.

His sixth argument is contained in the ninth chapter of his ninth book, and is taken from the authority of Augustine, *contra Epist. Fund.* c. 5, where he says: "I would not believe the gospel, if the authority of the catholic church did not move me[2]." These

[2 Ego vero non crederem evangelio, nisi me catholicæ ecclesiæ commoveret auctoritas.—See Laud's Conference, §. 16. n. 19. p. 81. et seqq. Lond. 1639.]

words of Augustine, says Stapleton, have distressed the protestants. Doubtless they have, and no wonder, since, as he confesses in the same place, they have deceived even some of the schoolmen also. They are indeed special favourites, and always in the mouths of the papists generally; so that a papist can scarce exchange three words with you, without presently objecting this testimony of Augustine. This argument is answered by Calvin, Instit. Lib. I. c.7. and by Musculus and Peter Martyr, by alleging that Augustine speaks of himself as a Manichean; that he meant that he, when a Manichean, was moved by the authority of the church to believe the scriptures. Musculus interprets the words so as to take *crederem* for *credidissem*, and *commoveret* for *commovisset;* or, " I, that is, when a Manichean, or if I were a Manichean, would not believe the gospel, &c." And indeed this interpretation is most true : for it is evident from the same chapter that Augustine is speaking of himself as a Manichean. In the words immediately preceding he says : " What would you do with one who said, I do not believe?" Then he subjoins : " But I would not believe the gospel, &c." He speaks, therefore, of himself in an unbelieving state. And in the same chapter, in the words immediately following, he says : " Those whom I obeyed when they said to me, Believe the gospel, why should I not obey when they tell me, Believe not Mani ?" Whence it is plain that he speaks of himself as an unbeliever, and informs us how he first was converted from a Manichean to be a catholic, namely, by listening to the voice of the church.

But Stapleton denies this, and endeavours to prove that he speaks of himself as a catholic by several arguments. His first reason is, because an infidel does not allow anything to the authority of the church. I answer, that Augustine was not altogether an infidel. He was indeed a heretic, but one most desirous of truth, and no obstinate heretic. He was a heretic, not from malice, but from error of opinion. Nor did he doubt, even when he was a heretic, that he ought to agree and communicate with the true church, although he did not judge aright which was the true church. Those who are so disposed are easily moved by the authority of the true church. Stapleton's second reason is, because a heretic is not moved by the authority of the catholic church, which he does not acknowledge. I answer, that Augustine speaks of the church as he thought of it now that he was a catholic, not as he thought of it formerly when he was a Manichean. His third reason is, because infidels do not now believe the preaching ministers, as Augustine in that same chapter affirms that he did. I answer : infidels do not, indeed, while they continue infidels, obey the preaching of the ministers of the church ; but they may be brought to faith by the preaching of the word, and then they will obey. And it was in this very way that Augustine was made a catholic from a Manichean. His fourth reason is, because Augustine in this chapter says of the Acts of the Apostles, "I must needs believe this book." Therefore (says Stapleton) he speaks of himself as he then was, namely, as a catholic. I answer, that this is no reason. For whether he speak of himself as a catholic or as a Manichean, it was needful by all means that he should believe this book, inasmuch as it is the word of God : for all alike must needs either receive or reject the Gospels and the Acts together. His fifth reason is, because Augustine writes in the fourth chapter of this book, that even when he was a bishop, he was kept in the church, on account of the name of the church and the consent of people and nations. I answer, that Augustine does indeed confess this : yet nevertheless, besides these two, he alleges another stronger argument in that same chapter, namely the absolutely constant truth of doctrine ; which if the Manicheans could allege in their behalf, he promises that he would be willing to desert the name of the church and the consent of people and nations, and return to them. Therefore he ascribed more to the truth of doctrine than to the judgment and authority of the church.

Finally, says Stapleton, Augustine everywhere in all the places before alleged attributes to the church the privilege of consigning the canon of scripture to the faithful. I answer, in the first place, it would be repugnant to Augustine himself to make him say that, now that he was a believer and a catholic, he would not believe the gospel, save only upon the authority of the church ; since he himself in the fourteenth chapter of this book says that we, when we believe and are become strong in faith, understand what we believe not now by the help of men, but by God himself internally confirming and illuminating our minds. The faithful, therefore, do not believe merely on account of the church's authority. Secondly, I say that this is also repugnant to reason itself. For all the faithful are endowed with the Holy Spirit. Now his authority is greater than that of the church. Therefore it is not to be doubted that they are kept in the true faith by his rather than by the church's authority. Thirdly, what if we were to acknowledge that the

21

[WHITAKER.]

faithful themselves are moved by the authority of the church to receive the scriptures ?   It does not follow thence, that their intimate inward persuasion is produced by the same way, or that they are induced by no other and stronger reason.   What Christian is there whom the church of Christ, commending the scriptures to him, does not move ?   But to be moved is one thing, and to be persuaded is another.   The Samaritan woman who is mentioned in John iv. moved many of her countrymen by her testimony to Christ, and excited them to flock to Christ and lend his instructions a favourable and willing attention.   But the same persons afterwards, when they had heard Christ, said to the woman, "Now we believe not on account of thy speech (διὰ τὴν σὴν λαλιὰν), but because we have heard him ourselves, and know that this is the Christ, the Saviour of the world."   So the authority of the church may at first move us to acknowledge the scriptures : but afterwards, when we have ourselves read the scriptures, and understand them, then we conceive a true faith, and believe, not because the church judges that we should believe, but, as for many other more certain arguments, so for this specially, because the Holy Spirit persuades us internally that these are the words of God.

But since this testimony of Augustine is urged so vehemently by Stapleton, other papists shall easily either teach or remind him, how little force it hath to establish the perpetual authority of the church.   Driedo, Lib. iv. c. 4, determines that Augustine speaks in these words of the primitive church of the apostles : for if Augustine were now alive, and meant to speak of the church such as it now is, he would rather say, "I would not acknowledge such men to be the church of Christ, unless the authority of the four Gospels taught me so."   Wherefore we do not now believe the gospel on account of the church, but, on the contrary, the church on account of the gospel.   Whence also it follows that the gospel is the truest mark of the church.   Bellarmine himself, in his MSS. Lectures upon the *Secunda Secundæ* of Aquinas, Quæst. I. art. i. Dub. 1, tells us, that Augustine "speaks of the church as the propounding cause, not as the prime foundation of faith."   For we should not believe the gospel unless the catholic church propounded it : which, no doubt, is true.   For, unless the church commended the sacred books to us, and led us, as it were, by the hand, to the very fountains of divine truth, we should never emerge out of the darkest shades of error.   But does it therefore follow that the apocryphal books cannot be distinguished from the canonical otherwise than by the mere authority of the church? By no means. And there is no need that we should say more of this sixth argument.

CHAPTER IX.

OF THE SEVENTH ARGUMENT OF OUR ADVERSARIES.

THE seventh argument is contained in Book IX. chap. 10, where he joins other fathers to Augustine, for the purpose of proving, that the canon of scripture must be consigned by the authority of the church. But what else do all those fathers prove but this, that the scripture should be received because it hath ever been received by the church, and that certain books should be rejected because they have ever been rejected by the church? Now this we most willingly confess. For we concede that the authority of the church is one argument, and a good one too: but it does not immediately follow either that it is the only argument, or that this whole matter depends upon the authority of the church. I might, therefore, disregard all those testimonies, and pass them over as irrelevant; but I prefer to touch upon them briefly, lest I should seem to have omitted anything. Now the testimonies, which Stapleton alleges in this chapter, are five in number: namely, from Theodoret, Tertullian, Irenæus, the first council of Toledo, and Serapion the bishop of Antioch; to each of which severally we shall give a brief reply.

Theodoret, in his argument to the Epistle to the Hebrews, writes thus against the Arians, who denied the authority of that epistle: "If nothing else, they should at least have respected the length of time during which the disciples of the truth have been wont to read this epistle continually in the churches[1]." I answer: What is all this to us? Nothing whatever. We grant that this epistle is to be embraced with all reverence, and that its opponents may be pressed and coerced by the argument drawn

[1 ἔδει δὲ αὐτούς, εἰ καὶ μηδὲν ἕτερον, τοῦ χρόνου γοῦν αἰδεσθῆναι τὸ μῆκος, ἐν ᾧ τήνδε τὴν ἐπιστολὴν ἐν ταῖς ἐκκλησίαις ἀναγινώσκοντες διετέλεσαν τῆς ἐκκλησίας οἱ τρόφιμοι.—Theod. Argum. in Heb.]

21—2

from antiquity. But, I beseech you, hath Theodoret written that nothing else gains authority for this epistle, save this very antiquity of time? By no means, but rather quite the opposite, as is manifest from his words: for he says, "if there were nothing else," they should be moved by the very length of time. Therefore, he intimates that there were other arguments, besides antiquity of time, whereby the authority of this epistle might be confirmed. And amongst these other arguments the principal, no doubt, was the very doctrine itself of the epistle, which the church acknowledges by the assistance of the Holy Spirit. For what else can be adduced? Thus, therefore, this first testimony alleged by Stapleton is answered easily, and almost without any effort.

But peradventure the second is clearer, which we have now, in the next place, to discuss. It is that of Tertullian in his book of Prescriptions against the heretics, where these words are to be found: "I will allege as a prescription, that what the apostles preached should not otherwise be proved, but through those same churches which the apostles themselves founded[1]." What (says Stapleton) could possibly be more plainly said? I answer: I confess indeed that the words are plain, but I affirm that Tertullian speaks not of the apostolic epistles, but of the apostolic doctrine; which is sufficiently manifest from the words immediately preceding. For thus he writes: "We draw up therefore this prescriptive plea: if the Lord Jesus Christ sent apostles to preach, then no other preachers are to be received than those whom Christ instructed; because no man knoweth the Father but the Son, and he to whom the Son hath revealed him, and the Son seems to have revealed him to no others than the apostles, whom he sent to preach, no doubt, that which he had revealed to them[2]." Then he applies this prescription, namely, that the doctrine which the apostles preached should not be proved in any other way but through those churches which they founded. In which words Tertullian does not reject, however, all other testimonies. For if this had

[1 Quid autem prædicaverint, id est, quid illis Christus revelaverit, et hic præscribam non aliter probari debere, nisi per easdem ecclesias quas ipsi Apostoli condiderunt.—c. 21. p. 14.]

[2 Hinc igitur dirigimus præscriptionem, si Dominus Jesus Christus apostolos misit ad prædicandum, alios non esse recipiendos prædicatores quam quos Christus instituit, quia nec alius Patrem novit nisi Filius et cui Filius revelavit; nec aliis videtur revelasse Filius quam apostolis, quos misit ad prædicandum utique quod illis revelavit.—*Ibid.* Whitaker reads *hanc* for *hinc.* I know not on what authority.]

been his meaning, that the evidence of the apostolical epistles to us depended entirely upon the approbation of the apostolical churches, then he would have rejected the testimony of the Holy Spirit; which he certainly never meant to do. Nay, this would not be consistent even with our adversary's own defence. For he, in the last chapter of this his ninth book, will have the canon of scripture to be consigned by the rule of faith. Therefore, besides the approbation of the church, he would have the rule of faith also to be necessary; for the rule of faith is a different thing from the external judgment of the church. But Tertullian's meaning, as appears from the words following, is, that every doctrine is true which agrees and harmonises with that doctrine of the churches, which they received from the apostles, and the apostles from Christ; and that whatever does not so agree is adulterate and false. For thus he subjoins: "If these things be so, it follows thence, that every doctrine which agrees with those apostolical churches, from whose wombs the faith derived its origin, is to be accounted true; and that that is undoubtedly to be held, which the churches received from the apostles, the apostles from Christ, and Christ from God; but all other doctrine is to be judged beforehand to be false[3]." This is so far from taking away the testimony of the Holy Spirit, that it rather establishes it; for the Holy Spirit is the judge of apostolical doctrine. Therefore he attributes nothing to the church, unless it hold this doctrine. Besides, to say, as Tertullian says, that "doctrine should be proved by the church," is a different thing from saying that it should be received only on the authority of the church, which Stapleton means. We concede the former, especially as far as the apostolical churches are concerned, but the latter by no means. For although it be through the church that we know doctrine, yet that it is now upon the authority of the Holy Spirit that we believe, even our adversaries themselves allow, as ye shall hear hereafter. Therefore, when Tertullian speaks of sound and apostolical doctrine, although he says that it should agree with the faith of the apostolic churches, he nevertheless does not, on that account, set aside the testimony of the Holy Spirit.

So much upon the testimony of Tertullian. I come now to

[3 Si hæc ita sunt, constat proinde omnem doctrinam, quæ cum illis ecclesiis apostolicis, matricibus et originalibus fidei, conspiret, veritati deputandam, id sine dubio tenentem quod ecclesiæ ab apostolis, apostoli a Christo, Christus a Deo accepit; reliquam vero omnem doctrinam de mendacio præjudicandam.—*Ibid.*]

Irenæus, from whom Stapleton quotes some words, which, it must be allowed, have very little force in them. For we confess with Irenæus, that the authority of the church is a firm and compendious demonstration of the canonical doctrine *a posteriori*, but not *a priori*: but we deny that this is the sole, or the greatest, or the strongest argument. This Stapleton could not prove from Irenæus. Besides, when Stapleton concedes out of Irenæus, that heretics who denied some scriptures were refuted by the scriptures which they received, does he not affirm, exactly as we would have it, that scripture may be proved by scripture, and that scripture may be otherwise recognised and proved than by the testimony of the church?

His fourth testimony is taken from the first council of Toledo, the twenty-first canon of which is to this effect: " If any shall say or believe that any other scriptures are to be received, save those which the church hath received, let him be anathema[1]." I answer: I do not see why I and all good Christians may not be permitted to say Amen to these words. For we think no otherwise than we are directed in this canon, and receive or reject no book without the testimony and example of the catholic church. Wherefore this denunciation of an anathema touches us in no way. But I wonder that Stapleton should be so stupid as not to understand or remark how weak is this argument of his: No scriptures should be received, which have not been received and approved by the church: therefore, scriptures are only to be received on account of the church's testimony. No scriptures should be rejected, but those which the church hath rejected: therefore the apocryphal writings are to be rejected solely on that account, because the church hath rejected them.

And of this testimony enough hath been said. Now follows the fifth and last, which is that of a certain Serapion, bishop of Antioch, of whom Eusebius speaks H. E. Lib. VI. c. 11, taken from an epistle of his: " We," says Serapion, "refuse certain books falsely inscribed with the names of the apostles, knowing that we have never received such[2]." Now he speaks of the gospel of

---

[1 Si quis dixerit aut crediderit alias scripturas recipiendas esse præter illas quas ecclesia recepit, anathema sit.—Anathem. XII. col. 328. Collect. Cann. Eccles. Hispan. Matriti. 1808.]

[2 'Ημεῖς γάρ, ἀδελφοὶ, καὶ Πέτρον καὶ τοὺς ἄλλους ἀποστόλους ἀποδεχόμεθα ὡς Χριστόν· τὰ δὲ ὀνόματι αὐτῶν ψευδεπίγραφα ὡς ἔμπειροι παραιτούμεθα, γινώσκοντες ὅτι τὰ τοιαῦτα οὐ παρελάβομεν.—H. E. Lib. VI. c. 12. pp. 177—8. T. II. ed. Heinich.]

Peter, which used to be read in some churches. I answer: That book was rejected by Serapion on account of the many falsehoods which were found in it, as is plain from the words which follow: therefore it was not rejected merely on account of the authority of the church. In this place Stapleton hath, as he often does, made use of a notable artifice. We, says Serapion, have not received the book, ὡς ἔμπειροι, as being *skilful* and *expert*; γινώσκοντες ὅτι τὰ τοιαῦτα οὐ παρελάβομεν. And Eusebius says that he refuted τὰ ψευδῶς ἐν αὐτῷ εἰρημένα, "the falsehoods contained in it." The book, therefore, was interspersed with some falsehoods and impostures. Besides, Stapleton omits some words which have great force in them, as will manifestly appear to any one who will look at the passage. For Serapion says[3], at the end of that chapter, that he had found very many things ὀρθοῦ λόγου, *sound*, in that book, but some also προσδιεσταλμένα, foreign from and at variance with the orthodox faith, and therefore had rejected it. He therefore did not reject it merely on account of the church's judgment, of which no mention is here made, but on account of the doctrine delivered in the book itself. This seventh argument, and the sixth also, which immediately preceded it, were merely human; and how weak such arguments are in causes of faith, every one must understand.

CHAPTER X.

OF THE TWO REMAINING ARGUMENTS OF OUR ADVERSARIES.

I COME now to the eighth and last argument, which Stapleton considers the weightiest and most important of all. It is stated in the eleventh chapter of his ninth book, and is drawn from the rule of faith, thus: The rule of faith which is lodged with the church, and delivered by the church, is the means by which the masters and pastors of the churches distinguished true scriptures from false. Therefore the church only should determine of the canonical books of scripture. I answer: if by the rule of faith we understand the articles of faith, then this reason of our adversary is not sufficient for the confirmation of his cause, nor is there any consequence in

[3 καὶ εὑρεῖν τὰ μὲν πλείονα τοῦ ὀρθοῦ λόγου τοῦ Σωτῆρος, τινὰ δὲ προδιεσταλμένα.—*Ibid.* p. 179.]

his argument. For this is no reason : Such a book teaches things in harmony with the articles of the faith; therefore it is canonical. For many books expound that sound doctrine which is in perfect harmony with the articles of the faith, and nevertheless should not be received into the canon. The reason is indeed good negatively the other way : such a book delivers something repugnant to the articles of the faith; therefore it is not canonical. But affirmatively, it does not hold. But what is that rule of faith? Undoubtedly the rule of faith is the scripture itself: if therefore, the canon of scripture be consigned by the rule of faith, then the scripture is confirmed by the scripture, which is the very thing we maintain. But he means far otherwise. The rule of faith, says he, is not the scripture, but a certain previous, presupposed, and pre-existing faith, which, being prior to the scripture, is neither included in, nor convertible with, the scripture. This is certainly an impious and blasphemous fiction of Stapleton's. For it is to be held undoubtingly, as we shall hereafter prove most largely, that the revealed and written word of God is the sole rule of faith, which is a thing prior to the faith of the church. For all " faith is by hearing, and hearing by the word of God," Rom. x. 17 : that is, our hearing hath regard to the word of God, as its object, and objects are prior to the senses perceiving them ; therefore the word is prior to faith. If he feign another rule of faith besides the written word of God, we reject, repudiate, and refuse to acknowledge any such, and reduce the whole rule of the catholic faith to the scripture alone.

But I ask whether it is by this rule, or without this rule, that the church distinguishes true scriptures from false? Stapleton answers thus, at the close of the chapter: "The rule of faith," says he, " delivered and accepted by the church, is the sole and most certain mean, whereby the pastors and governors of the church distinguish the true scriptures from the false: therefore, without this rule the genuine scriptures cannot be distinguished from the spurious." I derive then from this statement four observations.

Firstly, if true scriptures are discerned from false by the rule of faith, then it no less appertains to the whole body of the church to consign the canon of scripture, than to the pastors and governors of the church themselves. For all the faithful have this rule, not alone the pastors, governors and prelates ; because the faith is common to both laymen and ministers. Now this makes against Stapleton, who does not attribute this power to the whole body of the church, but only to the prelates and pastors.

Secondly, if it be not by its own authority, but by the rule of faith, that the church distinguishes the true scriptures from the false, then all Stapleton's former arguments, drawn from the authority of the church, are of no avail; because the church does not rest simply on its own authority, but on some certain rule of faith in adjudicating and discriminating scripture. Thus the previous arguments, which are founded on the bare authority of the church, are altogether avoided, and the whole judgment of the church is tied to the rule of faith.

Thirdly, how can these things agree, or in any wise stand together? He says that the pastors and masters of the church do, by means of the rule of faith delivered and received by the church, distinguish the true scriptures from the false; and under this name of the church he understands the pastors only, and prelates, and masters (as he calls them) of the churches. Therefore, he says nothing else but this, that the pastors do, by means of the rule of faith delivered and received by the pastors, discriminate the scriptures. But, in the first place, the pastors do not always think alike concerning the canonical scriptures, (if by the pastors he understand the bishops and doctors,) as may be proved from antiquity. If therefore this rule be delivered by the pastors, it will be changeable and uncertain. Yea, even the pastors of the present day do not think alike of the canonical books. It is necessary, therefore, that at length they should betake themselves to the pope alone, as to (in their own phrase) the chief pastor, make him the church, and make all depend upon his caprice. Again, how absurd is it, that pastors should receive from pastors, that is, from themselves, the most certain mean of discerning the scriptures! These things are of such a nature, that certainly they can in no way be reconciled.

Fourthly, I ask what this rule is? and where we may find it containing a certain and definite enumeration of books? is it written or unwritten? If he say, written; I demand where it is written. If it be not written, we may easily despise it, as a thing of no credit or importance: for we make no account of their pretended unwritten traditions. But he says that it is written in the hearts of the faithful, and to this purpose he adduces the testimonies of Isaiah, Jeremiah, and others, where the Lord says that he will write his laws in the hearts of the faithful. We for our parts approve all this. But, in the meanwhile, he does not perceive that he is overturning all that he had previously

established. For he said above, that the testimony of the Holy
Spirit is therefore to be rejected because not an external, but an
internal, evidence. But if this rule of faith be written in the
hearts of the faithful, how, I beseech you, will it be more certain
than the testimony of the Spirit? And wherein does it differ
from the testimony of the Spirit? since faith is the work and
effect of the Holy Ghost in the hearts of the faithful, received from
the word of God, whereby all saving truth is proved and confirmed
to us. Therefore, Stapleton hath at length of his own accord
passed over entirely to our opinion.

Stapleton next handles two subjects at the end of this book.
The first is, that not only the ancient apostolical church, but this
present church also, may consign and constitute the canon of
scripture. Wherein he hath for opponents Durandus and Driedo,
two very learned papists, who contend that this power related
only to the apostolical church ; and that the office of the present
church was only to receive the canon consigned by that other more
ancient church. With these he enters upon a very severe encounter and contention, of which I shall not be a sharer, but a
spectator only.

The second is, that this present church also might even now add
other books to the canon, as the book of the *Shepherd*, and the
Apostolical Constitutions written by Clement, and other books also,
which were formerly doubtful, but never condemned : which indeed,
it is manifest, is said and maintained absurdly. But, it seems, they
have gone to such a length of impudence, that nothing is so revolt-
ing to be said, as to make them ashamed of affirming it. Certainly
the book of the *Shepherd* is altogether unworthy of such great
authority ; and the Apostolical Constitutions of Clement have not
even a grain of the apostolic spirit. The church, therefore,
neither can, nor should, receive these books into the canon. Stapleton, while he asserts the competency of the church to do this,
is at variance both with very many papists (Thomas à Walden[1],
for example, and others), and even with himself; since he had
already alleged a testimony from Augustine, whence it appeared
that the canon of scripture was consigned by the apostles, who
excluded this book from the canon. But I would fain have him
answer, whether the canon of scripture was settled heretofore, or
not ? He cannot deny that it was : for he has already confessed
it out of Augustine ; and there are some councils too, which the

[1 Doctrin. Fidei, T. i. L. 2. Art. 2. c. 23. N. 9.]

papists object to us, in which they say that the canon of scripture
was consigned. If, therefore, the canon of scripture was consigned
formerly, certainly a canon settled by so great authority cannot
be changed, or this or that book introduced into it. For how
grossly absurd would it be, either that a book intrinsically canonical should be for so many ages not received into the canon; or
that it should now, so late, in the very last age of the world, be so
received! As to the Constitutions of Clement, they were even condemned by the judgment of some councils, as is shewn above.
They were deemed, therefore, wholly unworthy of having rank or
place in the canonical scriptures : yea, they certainly can never be
received into the canon by the church. For the church cannot
make non-canonical books canonical, but only cause those books to
be received as canonical, which are really such in themselves.
Augustine, at least, was so far from thinking that this most venerable canon could be changed, or increased by any new accession
of books, that in his 129th sermon upon the Times [2] he does not
hesitate to denounce an anathema upon all who believe that any
scriptures should be held in authority, or reverence any but those
which the church *had received*. Therefore, if the church were to
receive any new books into the canon, it would act against the
faith itself, and deserve the severest censure, nay, execration.
Now that it hath this power is boldly maintained by Stapleton :
whence it is plain enough how great an injustice he does the
church. But we have answered Stapleton's arguments already at
sufficient length.

There remains now one other argument, which Stapleton indeed hath not made use of : but I perceive that some other papists
are exceedingly delighted with it. It is to this effect : The church
is more ancient than the scripture ; therefore it ought to have more
authority in respect of us than the scripture. So Eckius, in his Enchiridion : so Hosius, Lib. iii. *de Auctoritate Scripturæ :* so Lindanus, in his Panoply, in many places : so Andradius in the third
book of his Defence of the Council of Trent : so Schröck the Jesuit,
in his 13th Thesis ; and some others beside. I answer : In the first
place, I confess that there was a time when the word of God was not
written, and that the church existed then : but it does not, therefore, follow that the church was more ancient than the word. For
the doctrine was the same when not written, as it is now when it
is written ; and that was more ancient than all churches. For the

[2 Col. 876. Opp. T. x. Basil. 1569.]

word of God is the seed of the church. Now the seed is always
more ancient than that progeny of which it is the seed. When I
speak of the word of God, I mean no other than that which is now
written : for the unwritten word was the same with that which is
now written. Secondly, Neither is that assertion true, that all
things that are junior are of less authority. For Christ was later
in time than John. Shall then the authority of John be greater
in respect of us than that of Christ? No one in his senses will
affirm that. This argument therefore is but slight, and of no importance whatsoever, although it be handled very shewily by some
authors. Some of the papists have laboured, as if they were on a
question of chronology, to shew that the word was unwritten for
more than two thousand years, and that the gospel was preached
about thirty years before it was written. But there is no reason
why we should give this argument a larger answer in this place.

CHAPTER XI.

OUR ARGUMENTS, WHEREBY WE PROVE THAT THE AUTHORITY OF
THE SCRIPTURE, IN RESPECT OF US DOES NOT DEPEND UPON
THE JUDGMENT AND AUTHORITY OF THE CHURCH.

HITHERTO we have spoken of the arguments of the papists,
and have given such answers as are sufficient to satisfy all impartial persons. Now follow the arguments of our defence.

Our first argument is to this effect : If the scripture had divine
authority before any public judgment of the church, then it hath
of itself in respect of us canonical authority, and its authority
does not depend upon the church. But the former is true ; therefore also the second. The major proposition is manifest. The
minor is confirmed by four reasons. The first : The papists themselves confess that the church does not make the scripture authentic, but only declares it. But if the scripture be first authentic
of itself, then certainly it necessarily follows that it must be authentic also to us ; for nothing can be called authentic, which
seems authentic to no one. That is called authentic, which is
sufficient to itself, which commends, sustains, proves itself, and hath
credit and authority from itself; the contrary of which is ἀδέσ-

πότον and ἄκυρον, that, namely, which is uncertain and hath no authority of itself. Therefore, if the scriptures were authentic before the church declared them to be authentic, they were authentic also to us; otherwise they were absolutely incapable of being declared authentic.

The second. The judgment of fathers, councils, and the church, is but recent, if we respect the antiquity of scripture. If therefore the authority of scripture depend upon the public judgment of the church, then doubtless for many centuries there was no certain canon of scripture. Fathers, indeed, and councils enunciate the canonical books; but those books both were, and were esteemed, previously authentic, and canonical, and sacred, as is plain from those fathers and councils themselves. Let them produce any public judgment of the church, and it will readily appear that the scriptures were deemed canonical before that judgment.

The third. I demand what this judgment of the church was, or where it can be found? If they answer, In the books of the fathers, and the decrees of the councils: I desire to know, how we are more sure of the authority of the fathers and councils than of that of scripture? For example, whence are we more certainly assured that these are the books of Augustine, those of Jerome, than we are that this is the Gospel of Matthew, and that of Mark? If they urge, that the living voice of the church is necessary, then they must needs abandon the support which they are wont to build upon in the authority of the ancient church. If they say, that this is certain from the voice of the present church; I ask again, whence it appears that this is the voice of the true church? They must prove this from the scriptures; for the true church can no otherwise be proved but from the authority of scripture. Now from thence it will follow that the authority of scripture is more certain than that of the church.

The fourth. If the church be gathered together to consign the canon of scripture, it must needs be so by some authority. I demand, therefore, by what authority it is so collected? If they answer, by some internal impulse or revelation of the Spirit, we entirely reject such revelations which are besides the word, as fanatical and anabaptistical and utterly heretical. If they say that it is collected by the authority of scripture, then they concede that which we demand: for it will thence follow, that the scripture had a canonical authority before it was confirmed by the judgment of the church. If they allow only this part of scripture which

gives such an authority to the church to have been previously
canonical, but deny the rest to have been so, they do this without
any certain reason. Suffice it to say so much of our first argument.

Our second argument is to this purpose. *That* is the true
and proper cause of that authentic authority which the scripture
holds with us, which produces this effect perpetually and necessarily ; that is, which always causes the scripture to have an
authentic authority with us. But the necessary and perpetual
cause of this is only the testimony of the Holy Spirit, not the
public judgment of the church. Therefore, the testimony of the
Holy Spirit, and not the public judgment of the church, is the true
and proper cause of that authentic authority which the scripture
hath with us. Concerning the major there can be no doubt ; and
the minor is easily established. For if the judgment of the church
always rendered the authority of scripture canonical in respect of
us ; then all who heard this from the church would presently believe
it, and immediately all, to whom this judgment of the church came,
would receive that canon which the church had established. But
the church hath long since consigned the canon of scripture, and
nevertheless the Jews, Turks, Saracens, and even many Christians
do not heartily assent to it : it is, therefore, evident that the
judgment of the church is not the certain, necessary, solid and
perpetual argument of that authority which the scripture obtains.
But the Holy Spirit always produces this effect : his testimony,
therefore, is the true and proper cause of the authority of scripture
in respect of us.

Our third argument stands thus : If the authority of the church
in respect of us depend upon the authority of scripture, then the
authority of scripture in respect of us does not, on the contrary,
depend upon the authority of the church. But the first is true,
and therefore also the second. The consequence of the major is
sufficiently strong of itself; and the assumption may be easily
established. For I demand, whence it is that we learn that the
church cannot err in consigning the canon of scripture? They
answer, that it is governed by the Holy Spirit (for so the council
of Trent assumes of itself), and therefore cannot err in its judgments
and decrees. I confess indeed that, if it be always governed by
the Holy Spirit so as that, in every question, the Spirit affords it
the light of truth, it cannot err. But whence do we know that it
is always so governed? They answer that Christ hath promised
this. Be it so. But where, I pray, hath he promised it? Readily,

and without delay, they produce many sentences of scripture which they are always wont to have in their mouths, such as these : " I will be with you always, even to the end of the world." Matth. xxviii. 20. " Where two or three are gathered together in my name, there I will be in the midst of you." Matth. xviii. 20. " I will send to you the Comforter from the Father." John xv. 26. "Who, when he is come, will lead you into all truth." John xvi. 13. I recognise here the most lucid and certain testimonies of scripture. But now from hence it follows not that the authority of scripture depends upon the church; but, contrariwise, that the authority of the church depends on scripture. Surely it is a notable circle in which this argument revolves ! They say that they give authority to the scripture and canonical books in respect of us ; and yet they confess that all their authority is derived from scripture. For if they rely upon the testimonies and sentences of these books, when they require us to believe in them ; then it is plain that these books, which lend them credit, had greater authority in themselves, and were of themselves authentic.

Our fourth argument stands thus : If the scripture have so great force and virtue in itself, as to draw up our souls to itself, to infuse into us an intimate persuasion of its truth, and of itself to commend itself to our belief; then it is certain that it is to us of itself αὐτόπιστον, canonical and authentic. Now the first is true ; therefore also the second. There is no controversy about the major. The minor may be confirmed by testimonies of scripture. In Luke viii. 11 the word of God is compared to seed, and 1 Pet. i. 13 is called " immortal seed." Now then as seed displays itself, and issues forth, and bears fruit in its season, so the word of God resembles the nature of seed ; it springs up, and breaks forth, and manifests its energy. Besides, 1 Cor. ii. 4, Paul says : " My speech and my preaching was not in persuasive words of man's wisdom, but in demonstration of the Spirit and in power," ἀλλ᾽ ἐν ἀποδείξει Πνεύματος καὶ δυνάμεως. In Luke xxiv. 32, those two disciples, to whom Christ appeared on their way to Emmaus, conversed thus with one another, after Christ had vanished from their sight : " Did not our heart burn within us, καιομένη ἦν ἐν ἡμῖν, whilst he spake unto us by the way, and whilst he opened unto us the scriptures ?" Heb. iv. 12, " The word of God," says the apostle, " is quick and powerful, ζῶν καὶ ἐνεργὴς, and quicker than any two-edged sword, and pierceth even to the dividing asunder of the soul and spirit, and of the joints and marrow, and is a

discerner of the thoughts and intents of the heart." 1 Cor. xiv.
24, 25, " If all prophesy," says Paul, " and there come in one that
believeth not, or one unlearned, he is convinced of all, he is judged
of all ; and *so are the secrets of his heart made manifest*, and so,
falling down on his face, he will worship God, and report that God
is in you of a truth." From all these places we understand, that
there is a certain divine force, virtue, and efficacy in scripture, which
reaches not the ears only, but even the soul itself, and penetrates
to the inmost recesses of the heart, and proves the most certain
divinity of scripture. The scripture, therefore, which hath such
a force in itself, and which so openly shews, proves, establishes
itself, and persuades us of its own truth, is by all means of itself
canonical and authentic.

Our fifth argument is taken from the words of Christ, John v.
34, where Christ says : " I receive not witness of men," ἐγὼ οὐ
παρὰ ἀνθρώπου μαρτυρίαν λαμβάνω. Hence we draw an argument
to this effect : Christ is known of himself; he depends not on the
testimony or authority of any man. Therefore, neither does the
scripture. For the authority of scripture is not less than that of
Christ, whose word it is. But here they will object thus : Did not
Christ use the honourable testimony of John ? Why then may not
also the scripture be commended by the testimony of the church ?
I answer, that John did indeed give testimony to Christ, but not
any authority, not even in respect of us. The same may be said
of the church ; that is, that it gives testimony to the scriptures;
that it commends and declares them authentic, and yet imparts to
them no authority, not even in respect of us. Christ's saying, " I
receive not witness of man," is the same thing as if he had said : I
need not that any should give me authority by his testimony ; I
am sufficiently fortified on all sides by mine own authority ; I will
abundantly gain authority for myself by mine own testimony. As,
therefore, Christ could of himself demonstrate that he was the
Messiah, so the word of Christ can of itself produce the belief that
it is the word of God. Its being commended by the church is not
for the purpose of receiving greater authority, but in order that its
authority may be the more recognised by men. Canus, Lib. II.
cap. 8, seeks to break the force of this testimony, thus : The sense
is, says he, I do not receive witness of man; that is, I do not need
the witness of any man, but I allege the witness of John for your
sakes. Be it so. Then also it will follow, that neither does
scripture need the witness of the church.

Our sixth argument is taken from the same chapter, verse 38, where Christ says : " I have greater testimony than that of John ;" —ἔχω μαρτυρίαν μείζω 'Ιωάννου : and then he recites three such testimonies, namely, his works, the testimony of his Father, and the scriptures. Hence I conclude thus : If the testimony of scripture concerning Christ be more certain than the judgment and witness of John, then is it also much more certain and valid than the judgment and witness of the church. For the papists dare not say, that the judgment of the church concerning scripture is more certain than was that testimony of John concerning Christ. But the former is true, and therefore also the latter. Nay, the written word of God is even more certain and firm than a divine revelation and a celestial voice : for so we read, 2 Pet. i. 19. Does the church dare to attribute more to her judgment than to a divine voice and heavenly revelation ? Peter was with Christ upon the mount, and there heard the voice of God the Father ; and yet he says, " We have a more sure word of prophecy," βεβαιότερον τὸν προφητικὸν λόγον. If then the scripture be more certain than divine revelations from heaven, much more must it needs be more certain than the judgment and testimony of the church. Whence it is plain that no authority can be conceived greater or more certain than that of scripture. Beza indeed hath translated βε-βαιότερον most firm ; but it comes to the same thing : for if the word of prophecy be most firm, then certainly it is more firm than any revelation, and contains the highest degree of strength in itself.

Our seventh argument is taken from 1 Thess. ii. 13, where Paul addresses the Thessalonians thus : " We give thanks to God always, because that, when ye received the word of God which ye heard of us, ye received it not as the word of men, but (as it is in truth), the word of God, ἐδέξασθε οὐ λόγον ἀνθρώπων, ἀλλὰ λόγον Θεοῦ, which also worketh effectually in you that believe." From this place I argue thus : If the Thessalonians, when they only heard Paul, received the doctrine of scripture as divine, and so embraced it, then, without the judgment of the church, the scripture ought to have a divine authority with us. But the former is true ; for the Thessalonians had then heard of no pro-phecy or testimony of any church, but had only received the word from the lips of Paul : therefore also the latter. Ambrose writes thus upon that place : " They received the word with such devotion as to prove that they understood it to be the word of

22

God[1]." But whence could they understand it to be such? Certainly
from the doctrine itself, and the testimony of the Holy Spirit; not
from the authority of any church, or of the apostle himself. For
what church could persuade the Thessalonians by the weight of
its testimony to receive Paul, or assent to his discourses as divine?
The apostle himself was unknown to them, and had nowhere any
authority but on account of that doctrine, the minister and herald of
which he was. Therefore, the doctrine itself gained for him all his
authority and credit. We read in like manner, Gal. iv. 14, " Ye
received me," says Paul, "as an angel of God, yea, as Christ
Jesus." Whose commendation was it, I beseech you, which procured for Paul this authority and dignity with the Galatians? No
man's. Therefore that doctrine which the apostle brought with
him excited in the strongest manner the minds of the Galatians to
welcome and respect Paul, and sufficiently of itself commended itself
and its minister. So Acts xvii. 11, the Berœans, when they heard
Paul, examined his teaching not by the judgment of any church, but
by the standard of the scripture itself. It appears, therefore, that
scripture of itself, without the testimony and authority of the
church, hath a divine, canonical and authentic authority even in
respect of us.

Our eighth argument stands thus: The authority of the unwritten word did not depend upon the authority of the church.
Therefore neither does the authority of the written word now
depend upon the church. The argument is conclusive, because
the reason is the same in both cases. The major is proved because, when as yet the word was not published in the scriptures
or written documents, God used to speak immediately to the patriarchs, and this word was not commended or received by any
authority of the church, but by that of God alone: therefore also
the written word of God should be received in like manner: unless it be said that it is of less authority since it hath been consigned to books than it was before; which is the height of absurdity.
Paul, Rom. ii. 15, affirms of the law, that it is *written* in our
hearts. I believe the law, therefore, not on account of the testimony or judgment of the church, but because we retain the light
of the law impressed and inscribed upon our hearts. Now then,
if the law, which is one portion of the word of God, be acknowledged of itself and by its own light, which is impressed upon our

[1 Tanta devotione receperunt verbum, ut probarent se intellexisse esse
Dei verbum.—Opp. T. ii. App. p. 279. Paris. 1670.]

souls, and easily proves itself to all, and shews that this is the will of God; much more is the gospel sealed in our hearts by the Holy Spirit, and received on account of the Holy Spirit's authority. For, if we understand that the law is the will of. God, not persuaded by the authority of the church, but by the internal light of the law; how much more need is there that we be illuminated by the light of the Holy Spirit, before we believe the gospel; since the law is natural, but the gospel transcends all nature, and therefore needs some greater kind of confirmation!

Our ninth argument is taken from 1 John v. 6, where these words are found: τὸ πνεῦμά ἐστι τὸ μαρτυροῦν, ὅτι πνεῦμά ἐστιν ἡ ἀλήθεια. "It is the Spirit that beareth witness that the Spirit is truth;" that is, by a metonymy, that the doctrine delivered by the Spirit is true. The old translator somewhat otherwise: *Spiritus est qui testatur, quoniam Christus est veritas.* But it comes to precisely the same thing. For the sense is plain, that it is the Spirit which testifies of the Spirit, that is, of the heavenly doctrine whereof he is the master, and of Christ: where the testimony of the Spirit in confirming doctrine is established.

Our tenth argument is taken from the same chapter, verse 9, where these words are contained: " If we receive the witness of men, the witness of God is greater;" ἡ μαρτυρία τοῦ Θεοῦ μείζων: whence we understand that no testimony can be either greater or more certain than the divine. But the testimony of the church is human : for if they would have the testimony of the church to be divine, they must mean thereby the testimony of the Spirit, and so they will assert the same thing as we. Thomas Aquinas by "the testimony of men " in this place understands the testimony of the prophets; but the testimony of the church cannot be more certain than the testimony of the prophets. If, therefore, there be, as Thomas implies, something greater than the testimony of the prophets, then it will follow that the testimony of the church is not the greatest whereby we are convinced of the truth of faith and doctrine.

Our eleventh argument is taken from the last words of the fifth chapter of the gospel according to St John, which are these : " If ye believe not Moses' writings, how shall ye believe my words ?" εἰ τοῖς ἐκείνου γράμμασι μὴ πιστεύετε, πῶς τοῖς ἐμοῖς ῥήμασι πιστεύσετε ; They are Christ's words to the Jews : whence I conclude thus : They who do not believe the scriptures themselves, will not even believe the testimony of Christ; much less will be capable of being induced to repose faith in the voice and

words of the church. Jansenius, himself a papist, observes that
it is an argument *a fortiori*, because " as that is firmer which
is consigned to writing, so it is more censurable and a greater
fault, not to believe writings than not to believe words[1]." And
Theophylact interprets this place in the following manner : " If
ye believe not words written, how shall ye believe my words that
are not written ?" Οὐ πιστεύετε τοῖς γράμμασι, καὶ πῶς πιστεύσετε τοῖς ἐμοῖς ἀγράφοις ῥήμασιν; It is evident, therefore,
that those who are not moved by the authority of the scriptures
themselves, to embrace them with a pure faith, can be moved
or induced by no other argument or authority to believe.

Stapleton does not touch upon the foregoing arguments, whereby it is plain that our cause is abundantly demonstrated : but now
follow some which he endeavours to obviate. For, Lib. IX. c. 2,
he proposes six arguments of the Protestants, as he calls them,
which he answers severally, c. 3. The first four arguments are
taken from Calvin, *Instit.* Lib. I. c. 7,[2] the remaining two from
others, which we shall join to the foregoing along with the defence of them.

Calvin's first argument, therefore, shall be our twelfth, which
is this : If the canon of scripture depend upon the determination
of the church, then the authority, verity, and credibility of all
the promises of salvation and eternal life contained in scripture
depend upon a human judgment; because we believe those promises on account of the canonical authority of the scriptures in
which they are contained. But it is absurd, that the promises
of God should depend upon men, that the eternal truth of God
should rest upon the will of man, because then our consciences
can have no confidence, no security. Therefore the canon of scripture does not depend upon the determination of the church.

Stapleton answers, that the judgment of the church in this matter
is not merely human, but divine and infallible, so as that the faithful
soul may most safely acquiesce in it, and therefore that Calvin's
argument is inconsequential. But what is the meaning of this assertion, that the church's judgment is not merely human ? Be it
so. But is it merely divine ? For surely it is requisite that the
truth of the promises of eternal life should be propped and supported by a testimony purely divine. This Stapleton does not
openly affirm, but afterwards seems to wish it to be understood,

[1 Comment. in Concord. Evang. p. 241. Lugd. 1606.]
[2 Tom. I. pp. 57—62. ed. Tholuck. Berol. 1834.]

when he says that it is divine and infallible, and that faithful souls may safely acquiesce in it. But here he does not answer candidly ; for the question is, whether those things which are promised in the scriptures are believed by us to be true solely on account of the church's authority, or on account of some more certain judgment? Stapleton says that the judgment of the church is divine, because God speaks through the church, and that so we may acquiesce in the voice and sentence of the church. Be it so ; let the judgment of the church be divine. Well, is not the judgment of scripture divine also in Stapleton's opinion? Why then may we not acquiesce in the judgment of scripture as well as in that of the church? But indeed, when he answers thus, he accomplishes nothing. For the question is not, whether the judgment of the church be divine in itself, but whence it is that we are assured of its being so ;—unless perhaps he has forgotten his own Thesis. This latter question he gives us no information upon. He says only, that God speaks through the church, which we, for our parts, confess ; but we ask further, whether those things which God speaks and teaches through the church are believed by us to be true solely on account of the church's authority, and whether it be not proved in some other way than by the church's own testimony that God speaks through the church? By not telling us this, nor shewing how we know the church's judgment to be divine, he is guilty of manifest tergiversation, and fails to prove that which was the real question. For there is a wide difference between these two propositions ; God speaks through the church, and, We cannot be otherwise certain of the scriptures and doctrine of God, but because the church attests them.

Cochlæus indeed, of whom we have heard before, asserts that we cannot be certainly persuaded of the doctrine of scripture otherwise than by the testimony of the church. For that dishonest writer enumerates many strange and incredible things in scripture, which he falsely pretends to be believed solely on account of the church's authority. Stapleton thinks in the same way, and speaks in the same way in this chapter : for he says, that the church does not make the contents of scripture true, yet does cause them to be believed by us as true. From which statement it is apparent that Calvin's objection is just, that in this way our whole faith depends upon the authority and human judgment of the church. But the scripture teaches us far otherwise and better. For thus we read, 1 John, v. 10, "He who believeth not God, makes him a liar."

He therefore who no otherwise believes God promising, but on account of the authority of some one else, certainly believes that other person more than God, and so makes God a liar. Besides, in this way, the church would be mistress of our faith, which is repugnant to that saying of Paul, 2 Cor. i. 24, "We have not dominion over," οὐ κυριεύομεν, "your faith;" τῇ πίστει ἑστήκατε, "by faith ye stand." We stand, indeed, by faith, and that is the gift of the Holy Ghost, not of the church. We see, therefore, that it is not on the church's, but on the Holy Spirit's authority, that we persevere stable and constant in the faith, and fall not from divine grace. Besides, by this way of reasoning, it would follow that the ultimate issue and resolution (as they call it) of our faith would be into the voice and judgment of the church. This indeed some of the schoolmen, and those of great name too, have long since not been ashamed to affirm in express words; but the later papists deny it, and Stapleton himself elsewhere disputes against it. But how can it be denied, if, as Stapleton will have it, we believe whatever we believe on the church's authority? For if the judgment of the church causes the books of scripture to be canonical to us, then it certainly is the cause why those things which are contained in scripture are judged and believed true by us. And if this be so, is not our faith ultimately resolved into the voice of the church? On account of the church we believe the scriptures and every thing contained in scripture; for this is the meaning of Stapleton's assertion that the church causes those things which are found in scripture to be believed and held for true. Thus he does not perceive that he overturns his own opinion. Besides, he says that the judgment of the church is *divine* and *infallible*, and that the minds of the faithful may safely acquiesce in it. Why, therefore, should he not also concede, that the ultimate resolution of faith is placed in the judgment of the church?

From what hath been said it appears that all the promises of scripture are, in Stapleton's opinion, confirmed by no other authority than that of the church; whence what Calvin says follows, that our consciences are despoiled of all security, and that nothing certain is left to us in religion. But why, asks Stapleton, when the testimony of the church is divine? I answer: We confess, indeed, that the testimony of the church is divine in a certain sense; not absolutely, but in some respects, that is, so far as it agrees with scripture, with the Holy Spirit, with the will of God. But then we say that that judgment is not to be received on account of the church, but on account of the will and authority of God with which it agrees. Alphonsus de Castro, Lib. i. c. 8[1], answers this argument of Calvin's in another way; namely, that we owe it to the church indeed that we know what is divine scripture, but that afterwards, when we have been assured that scripture is divine, then we have from itself the obligation to believe it thoroughly in all respects. He thought that which Stapleton hath ventured to defend grossly absurd. But there is this also in de Castro's answer, that, if the church make scripture authentic to us, then it also makes authentic to us, and true, all the things which are written and taught in scripture. Whereupon Stapleton did not choose to make use of this answer; and preferred openly enunciating its consequence, that all things are believed by us on account of the church. What Stapleton subjoins out of Ephes. iv. 11, that Christ left to his church apostles, prophets, evangelists, pastors, doctors, that the people might be kept in the faith, and not carried about with every wind of doctrine, is of absolutely no weight. For although the people be retained by pastors and doctors in faith and obedience, it does not therefore follow that it is solely by their authority that the permanence of the people in their duty is effected. For the christian people acknowledges and reverences a greater authority than that of the pastors, namely, that of God himself; which unless it were of more avail than that of the pastors, the people could never be so retained. So, in precisely the same way, the people are kept in peace by the magistrates and ministers of the king; but yet there is a greater authority than that of these magistrates, on account of which they are kept in peace,—namely, that of the prince himself, whose authority and dominion extends far and wide through all the parts of his realm.

Our thirteenth argument, which was Calvin's second, is this: In this way the truth of divine scripture would be exposed to the mockeries of impious men, and would in great measure be brought into even general suspicion, as if it had no other authority than such as depended precariously upon the good will of men, if it be said to be received only on account of the judgment of the church. Therefore, &c. And this is most true; for who fails to perceive that, in this way, scripture is exposed to infinite reproaches and calumnies from men? Here Stapleton, overcome by the force of truth, is compelled even against his will to speak the truth. He says that it is not by the good will of men, but the testimony of

[1] [Opp. Paris. 1571. p. 46.]

God speaking through men, that both the scriptures and all the
rest of our faith have their authority. This we willingly embrace.
For we confess that the scripture hath its authority from the testimony of God; and we confess also what he adds, that God speaks
through men: for God uses no other ministry than that of men,
when he now addresses us in this world. But of what sort is this
testimony of God speaking through men? Let them tell us, and
they will find that the testimony of God speaking through the
church is one thing, and the church itself another. And if they
shall say that we believe the church on account of the testimony of
God, what else do they say but what we say also? But nevertheless we say further, that we ought to believe those things which
God speaks through the church, on account of the authority of
God himself who speaks, not on account of the authority of the
church through which he speaks. Stapleton, under the pressure of
this argument, betakes himself for refuge to his old distinction.
The scripture, says he, does not receive from the church any precarious authority, since it depends not upon the church in itself, but
only in respect of us; when yet he had said only a little before,
that we believe on the testimony of God speaking through the church.
Doubtless that authority cannot be called precarious, which rests
upon divine testimony. The man absolutely knows not whither to
turn himself, and yet he calls Calvin a caviller. Then he tells us
how scripture hath authority with us by means of the church;
because God speaking through the church commends it to us, and
makes it conspicuous. If he distinguishes God speaking through
the church from the church itself, we concede all this, and then
conclude that scripture rests upon the authority of God. If he do
not distinguish, then he makes God speaking through the church,
and the church through which he speaks, the same thing; that is, he
confounds the principal efficient cause with the instrument. I demand of him, therefore, whether he distinguishes that testimony of
God speaking through the church from the actual judgment and
testimony of the church, and makes the former something different
from the latter; or confounds the one with the other, and determines them to be absolutely the same? If he distinguish, then he
concedes what we wish, namely, that the authority of scripture in
respect of us rests upon the testimony of God. But if he confound
them, then he absurdly commingles things which ought to be kept
separate. For he who speaks is one, and that through whom he
speaks is another. If therefore God speaks through the church,

this is not properly the witness of the church, but rather of God. Now if it be the testimony of God himself, it follows that God, not the church, gives authority to the scripture even in respect of us. And now we have said enough upon this argument.

Our fourteenth argument, which is Calvin's third, runs thus: The testimony of the Holy Spirit is more excellent than all authority: therefore the same Spirit can best persuade us that it is God who spoke in the scriptures. We say that the scriptures are proved to us by the witness of the Holy Spirit: therefore, we apply the most certain testimony, even in the judgment of our adversaries themselves, who dare not deny this. For God is alone a fit witness of himself. Stapleton concedes that the testimony of the Holy Spirit is the best and most certain; but he concedes this only in words, and in reality breaks down the whole force of this testimony. For he subjoins that this testimony of the Spirit should be public and manifest, not private and secret, lest seducing spirits should introduce themselves under the title of the Spirit of God; and this public testimony of the Spirit he would have to be the judgment of the church. Here meanwhile he is compelled to confess, that there is need of the witness of the Spirit, and that this witness of the Holy Spirit is the most certain testimony. Thus then he affirms a testimony of the Spirit, but of such a kind as does not really exist, namely, a public and manifest one; so as that the external judgment of the church shall be holden to be the public judgment of the Spirit, and whatever the church determines and deems, this shall be believed to proceed from the testimony of the Spirit. Christ instituted no such tribunal, as will be shewn hereafter in its place. For I ask, whether it be public and manifest to all, or only to a few? Certainly, it is not manifest to all publicly; for then all would acknowledge and submit to it. If they say, it is public to a few, I would fain know of them how it can be called public and manifest at all? But I demand besides, who these few are to whom it is public? They will say, to the pastors, or, under the pressure of argument, to the pope alone. But we seek for such a public judgment as is open to all the faithful; and Stapleton should either shew us such, or confess that he is playing with us in a serious matter. For our dispute is not about the question how the pope or the pastors only, but how all the faithful universally, may understand the scriptures to have divine authority. Wherefore they are at length reduced to confess that they rest upon a different testimony from that of the church, and that a private one,

since it lies hidden in a single person. But it is absurd to dream of
any public tribunal of the Holy Spirit; yea, the scriptures themselves plainly teach the contrary, that the testimony of the Holy
Spirit is only private, internal, and secret. In 2 Cor. i. 21, Paul
says that God hath sealed us, and given to us the earnest of the
Spirit: but where? *in our hearts.* In Rom. viii. 16, the Spirit of
God is said to testify not openly, not externally, but internally,
that is, *in our spirit,* that we are the sons of God. In 1 John v.
10, he who believes upon the Son of God is said to have the testimony, not in any external tribunal, but ἐν ἑαυτῷ, *in himself.* In
Matth. xvi. 17, Christ says to Peter, "Flesh and blood have not
revealed this unto thee, but my Father which is in heaven." In
which words he unquestionably implies that the persuasion was
wrought, and the revelation made inwardly to Peter, by the Holy
Spirit, which he had just before confessed concerning Christ. In
1 John ii. 20, John addresses all the faithful in this manner : "Ye
have an unction from the Holy One, and ye know all things."
ὑμεῖς χρίσμα ἔχετε, καὶ οἴδατε πάντα. And at verse twenty-seven
of the same chapter, "The anointing which ye have received remaineth in you," ἐν ὑμῖν μένει. He does not mean any external
and manifest unction, but an internal one, entering in our minds
and establishing all truth to us internally. So Isaiah lix. 21 :
"My Spirit, which is within you," &c. And it is certainly repugnant to the nature of the Spirit, that this testimony should be
external and public. For such as the Spirit is himself, such should
also be his testimony. But the Spirit himself is hidden and secret,
and blows where he listeth, as Christ taught Nicodemus, John iii.
8 : therefore his testimony also is occult; yet occult in such a sense
as to admit of its being clear and certain to those persons themselves who are anointed with this unction. Indeed this is so manifest that the very papists themselves are compelled to acknowledge
it. For so Hosius in his *Confessio Petrocoviensis,* cap. 16 : "Now
we willingly concede that the gospels are to be received as the
word of God, who teaches and reveals truth to us internally, and
that they are not to be believed but on account of the voice of God
speaking to us within[1]." But certainly the testimony of the church
cannot be called the testimony of the Spirit in a strict sense, but
only by way of similitude, or in so far as it agrees and harmonises

[1] Nos vero libenter concedimus, accipienda esse evangelia ut verbum
Dei intus docentis et revelantis, neque credendum illis esse nisi propter Dei
vocem intus loquentis.—p. 21. Opp. Lugd. 1564.]

with the testimony of the Spirit. For we do not deny that the public judgment of the church may agree with the secret testimony of the Holy Spirit; but we say that then it is received for the sake of the testimony of the Spirit, not for the sake of the church.

But as to what Stapleton subjoins, that the public judgment is necessary on account of false and *seductive* spirits; we answer, that this man would fain seem wiser than Christ. For Christ, when he had a full prospect and foresight of this evil, nevertheless left no remedy against these deceiving spirits except the scripture, in whose judgment whosoever refuses to acquiesce will certainly contemn equally the authority of the church. He slanderously pretends also that we make the judgment of the church merely human; which is not true. For although we say that the church is composed of men, yet when its testimony agrees with the judgment and testimony of the Holy Spirit, and is in harmony with the word of God, we then confess that it is divine. Nevertheless we do indeed in the meanwhile say, that it is then believed not on account of the church itself and its authority, but on account of that truth which it follows and pronounces, and on account of the authority of God, whom, in that judgment, the church merely serves as a ministering agent. But all are not churches of God, which assume and arrogate to themselves this privilege, but those only which determine what Christ determined, and teach the same as he taught. But our dispute here is not concerning the true church, what and of what sort it is: this is the sole question before us,—whence we are assured that the judgment of the church is true and divine? This is the very point at issue. Let them then produce some argument whereby this may be cleared up for us; otherwise they do nothing. But assuredly they can produce none; nor hath Stapleton himself produced any, but only taken things for granted. He only says that we are impudent, if we do not believe, and unworthy of being disputed with; or else proves the conclusion by itself after this fashion: It is true that the judgment of the church is divine, because the church itself says so; it is governed by the Holy Ghost, because it says that it is so governed. We may, however, much more justly reply, that they are impudent if they do not believe the scripture, and that the scripture is divine because it affirms itself to be so. Nor is there any reason why we should say more upon this argument.

Now follows our fifteenth argument, the fourth of Calvin, which is this: The church is said (Ephes. ii. 20) to be built upon the

foundation of the prophets and apostles, that is, upon the prophetic
and apostolic doctrine : therefore the prophetic and apostolic doctrine, that is, the whole scripture, and the approbation of the same,
preceded the church, without which the church could never have
existed.   Stapleton answers, that Calvin misleads his reader by a
double equivocation concealed in these two words, *foundation* and
church.   For he says, in the first place, that the *foundation* in
this place does not signify the doctrine written by the prophets and
apostles, but their preaching : next, he says, that by the *church* in
this place are not understood the masters, prelates, and superiors, but
the faithful themselves as they constitute the body of the church.

As to the first equivocation, I return a fourfold answer. *First*,
what if we concede, that in this place the foundation of the prophets
and apostles is meant of the apostolic and prophetic preaching? This
will avail nothing against us : for the preaching of the prophets and
apostles was precisely the same as the scripture itself. This is manifest from Acts xxvi. 22, where Paul speaks thus : " Having obtained
help from God, I continue unto this day, witnessing these things to
both small and great, saying none other things than those which
the prophets and Moses did say should come ;" οὐδὲν ἐκτὸς λέγων.
Whatever, therefore, the apostles taught, they derived from the
prophets and Moses, and beyond them they taught nothing.   The
same may also be confirmed from Acts xvii. 11, where the Berœans
are said to have examined the preaching of the apostles by the
scripture ; which they certainly could not have done if they had
preached anything beside or without the scripture. *Secondly*, I
say that the foundation of the prophets and apostles in this place
actually does denote the scripture : which I prove from the circumstance that Paul here joins the prophets with the apostles.
Now the prophets were not then preaching, but only their writings
were extant.   Stapleton foresaw this, and therefore determines
that, in this place, it is not the prophets of the old Testament that
are meant and designed, but those of the new, who lived and
taught along with the apostles, such as those who are mentioned,
Ephes. iv. 11, and 1 Cor. xii. 28.   But under the name of prophetic doctrine always in the scriptures the whole doctrine of the
old Testament is wont to be understood. So 2 Pet. i. 16, where the
apostle says : "We have a more sure word of prophecy ;" ἔχομεν
βεβαιότερον τὸν προφητικὸν λόγον. So Heb. i. 1, where the
apostle says that God had spoken formerly in divers ways to the
fathers by the prophets.   So Rom. i. 2, where Paul says, that

God had before promised the Gospel διὰ τῶν προφητῶν αὐτοῦ ἐν γραφαῖς ἁγίαις. So Luke i. 70, where Zacharias, the father of John the Baptist, says that God had "raised up a horn of salvation for us in the house of his servant David, as he had spoken διὰ στόματος τῶν ἁγίων τῶν ἀπ᾽ αἰῶνος προφητῶν αὐτοῦ." Therefore in this place also, under the name of prophets are understood the old, and not the new prophets. For if Paul had understood those prophets of the new Testament, why not equally mention the evangelists, pastors and doctors, who were also preaching the word, and united their labours with the apostles and prophets in this work? Chrysostom opposes Stapleton, and teaches us that none other are here understood but the ancient prophets: for he says that the apostles were posterior in time to those prophets whom Paul names here, and yet are set in the first place: Πρῶτον τίθησι τοὺς ἀποστόλους ἐσχάτους ὄντας τοῖς χρόνοις[1]. Thirdly, I say, that the preaching of the apostles and prophets, as it was their action, continued only a short time. But the apostle speaks of a perpetual foundation which should consist and endure to the end of the world, and upon which the church of all times should always rest. This is the doctrine which the apostles first delivered by word of mouth, and afterwards in books that were to remain for ever. How then can the church be now founded upon that preaching, which hath ceased and come to an end many ages ago? Fourthly, Ambrose says that by the foundation in this place is understood the old and new Testaments, and that other prophets are here designated than those of whom we read Ephes. iv. 11, and 1 Cor. xii. 28. The same is the opinion of Thomas Aquinas; the same of Dionysius the Carthusian, and of some other papists: so that we may perceive that Stapleton is here at variance with his own men. We have discussed the first ambiguity; it remains that we come now to the second.

The second equivocation which Stapleton remarks in Calvin's argument is in the word Church. Stapleton wishes to understand in this place by the church, not the pastors, but the people. But it is plain that the apostle is here laying the foundation of the whole church, and therefore of the pastors also; unless perhaps they are no members of the church. Indeed it would be absurd that he should except the masters and prelates of the church more than the rest of the faithful, as if they had another foundation to rest upon besides the prophetic and apostolic doctrine; whereas absolutely all the

[1 In Ephes. Hom. vi. T. II. p. 39. B.]

faithful are settled upon this foundation, of which Christ is the corner-stone. Since this is so, it is idle in Stapleton to say, that the church, as it denotes the body of the faithful, is founded upon the doctrine of the apostles and prophets, but not as it denotes the prelates and governors. Hence it is manifest that Calvin's reasoning stands firm ;—namely, scripture is the foundation of the church; therefore, scripture and its approbation is prior to the church.

But Stapleton still defends himself with that worn-out distinction. He says that the scripture is posterior to the church in regard of its acceptation in respect of us : as if approbation and acceptation were not the same thing, or scripture were not then accepted when it was approved. The adversary, therefore, cannot elude Calvin's argument by this distinction. What he subjoins, namely, that the pastors are known before the scriptures, is utterly false, and a barefaced begging of the question. For we ought first to know how good pastors should feed their flocks, (a point of knowledge only attainable from scripture, which most clearly describes the pastoral office), before we can recognise the actual good pastors. So we know a governor, a general, a professor of any art, from the matters themselves which they handle, and which are the subject of their art, and in no other way : unless, indeed, he understand merely a confused sort of knowledge, such as that of which Aristotle speaks, Physic. I. cap. 1. But that is rather a sort of mere uncertain conjecture or guess, than any clear and certain knowledge. As to his remark that the church itself also, in the sense of the pastors and rulers, is sometimes compared to a foundation and a gate, as by Augustine in his exposition of Ps. lxxxviii. we allow it and concede it readily : but the reason is because that by their constancy the weaker are sustained and strengthened ; by their preaching the gates of heaven are, in a manner, opened, so as that, without the ministry of the word, no access to salvation could lie open to any one. In the meanwhile, however, what we have before laid down is true, that the pastors are founded upon the word, and it cannot be determined otherwise than out of the word itself, who are true, good, and faithful. Therefore it must ever be held as most true, that the approbation of scripture precedes this discrimination of the pastors. For if we approve them for pastors, then before that, and much rather, must we approve the scriptures, which have made them pastors, and taught us not only what their office is, but also our own; and without which neither would they know how to feed the flock, nor could we esteem them as our pastors. In like manner, since the church depends upon the scriptures, the knowledge of the scriptures must needs precede the knowledge of the church.

Our sixteenth argument is this: Scripture in the doctrine of religion hath the rank and place of a principle; all its declarations are, as it were, axioms and most certain principles, which neither can, nor ought to be proved by other things, but all other things to be proved and confirmed by them. If this hold in human sciences, whereof men are the authors, much more does it hold in scripture, whose author is the Holy Ghost, the Spirit of truth. Whoever is the author of this argument, it is most true. It seems to be Musculus's. Stapleton answers by a distinction (for he is very copious in distinctions, which he generally abuses greatly,) in this manner: The principles of sciences, says he, are in themselves indemonstrable with respect to the nature of things; but in respect of us they may be demonstrated, on account of our great dulness, by a demonstration shewing simply that they exist. Such is the case of scripture. I answer: We confess that the scriptures may be demonstrated by an argument *a posteriori*; and that this argument is especially useful to us on account of the slenderness of our intellect; and so that we are much aided in this matter by the voice and testimony of the church. But nevertheless we deny that the scripture needs this testimony of the church, or that it is on no other grounds authentic to us. We receive indeed the axioms of the sciences, when they are first delivered, and believe them to be true, induced by the words and authority of the professors of those sciences: but when we understand the reason of them, then we believe rather on account of the plain and necessary truth of the axioms themselves, which we perceive; for they have an infallible reason in themselves which commends them to our belief. The existence of the principles of the sciences may be explained to us; but are they understood to be true no otherwise than because the professors have so delivered them? Yea, the axioms themselves mutually demonstrate each other. In like manner, the scriptures may be illustrated and commended by the voice of the church, although they are in themselves most firm and certain principles, which are both proved by the authority of God himself, and fortify each other by their mutual testimony. Stapleton subjoins that the scripture is in such a sense a principle in religion as yet to allow that the church's voice is prior to it. Which is utterly false, since all the voice of the church arises from the scripture. Besides, that which is taught is always prior to that which teaches. Now the

scripture is taught, and the church teaches : therefore the scripture
is prior to the church.

But Stapleton proceeds, and proves that the church is prior
to the scripture, and even of greater authority; because the scripture (says he) is one of those things which are believed; but
the church is the rule of all those things which are believed.
Where we may observe a two-fold self-contradiction. The *first*
is, that whereas, in the chapter immediately preceding, he had
denied that the scripture was believed, and said that though we
professed in the Creed a belief in the church, we did not in the scripture ; now, on the contrary, he says that the scripture is one of
the things believed, and so appertains to the Creed. Thus does he
contradict himself, nor attend at all to what he says. The *second*
is, that he says that the scripture is one of the things to be believed,
and, therefore, cannot be the rule of those things which are believed; while yet he determines the church to be that rule, although
it be itself one of the things which are believed. For do we not
plainly in the Creed profess that we believe in the catholic church?
If, therefore, scripture be not the rule of faith, because it is an
article of faith, why does not the same argument hold also against
the church ? But is the voice of the church indeed the rule of
faith ? Yea, rather, on the contrary, scripture is the rule of the
church. Does scripture follow the voice of the church, or the contrary ? These men themselves say that the scripture is not squared
to the voice of the church, but the testimony of the church to
scripture ; so as that, since it is canonical scripture, therefore the
church can do no otherwise than declare it to be scripture. Thus
the church is not the rule, but a thing directed by the rule. The
scripture itself is the rule of faith, as we shall hereafter shew
more clearly : for the voice of the church ought to be governed by
scripture, and the church is the effect of faith, and therefore cannot
be the rule of faith. For the church is the multitude of the faithful ; and therefore ought to be governed by faith, to follow faith,
to depend upon the rule of faith, and adjust all things by it. But
the voice of the church is an act of the church, and posterior to the
church. The voice of the church is the voice of men : but the rule
of faith is the voice of God. Thus are they not ashamed of any
absurdity or blasphemy : to such a pitch of desperation are they
come. But we have spent words enough upon this argument.

Now follows our seventeenth argument, which stands thus : The
church is subject to the scripture ; therefore it ought not to judge

of scripture. The argument is perfectly conclusive, if we understand an authoritative judgment, as the lawyers express it, which is
what the papists would have. The antecedent is proved by a twofold testimony of Augustine. The first is contained in his treatise
against Faustus the Manichee, Lib. xi. c. 5, where Augustine says
that "the scripture is settled upon a certain lofty throne to command the service of every faithful and pious understanding[1]." The
second is in his book *de Vera Religione*, c. 31, where the same
Augustine says that "it is lawful for pure minds to know the eternal
law of God, but not lawful to judge it." Here also Stapleton seeks
to escape under the screen of one of his customary distinctions.
He says that the church, as it denotes the body of the faithful, is
subject to the scriptures; but, as it denotes the pastors, governors,
and prelates, is not subject, because they rather judge of the scripture not yet accepted, in order to its acceptation : and thus he
seeks to elude both passages from Augustine. But Augustine undoubtedly speaks of the whole body of the church, when he says
that every faithful understanding should serve the scriptures; in
which words he embraces the bishops and prelates. And certainly
in that chapter he speaks especially of those whose office it is to
expound the scriptures, that is, of the pastors themselves. Are not
these also obliged to be subject to the scriptures, and to submit
their understandings to them? See what things these popish prelates arrogate to themselves! Augustine therefore would not have
even these exercise what is called an *authoritative* judgment upon
scripture, but rather do it service. Next, as to his assertion that
it is the privilege of the pastors to judge of scripture not yet
accepted; I demand whether scripture be yet accepted or no?
They cannot deny that scripture hath been long ago accepted. It
follows, therefore, that this judgment of the church is at an end.

Nor is the sense of Augustine different in the second passage, as
may easily be perceived from observing his own words. He says
that the church does not judge the scripture (which he calls the
law, rule, and truth), but only according to the scripture. For he
uses there a similitude taken from the civil laws, which agrees excellently well with our defence. "Just as it happens in the case of
temporal laws (says Augustine), although men judge of them when
they institute them, yet when they are instituted and confirmed, it
will not be lawful even for the judge to judge concerning them,

[1 *Excellentia canonicæ auctoritatis veteris et novi Testamenti . . . tanquam in sede quadam sublimiter constituta est, cui serviat omnis fidelis et
pius intellectus.*—Cont. Faust. Manich. xi. c. 5. T. x. p. 267.]

but according to them[1];" the same is the case of the divine law. For such is the gist of his comparison. But who hath authority to establish divine laws? Not men, but God alone. If therefore God hath made and promulgated these laws, then they are laws without the judgment and acceptation of the church. Forasmuch then as the scriptures are made and promulgated by God, they ought not to be subjected to human judgment, nor can any one lawfully sit in judgment upon them. God hath established these laws. It is our part to receive, acknowledge, venerate, obey, submit ourselves to them, and judge of every thing according to them, not to exercise judgment upon them. And this all men without exception are bound to do; yea, the prelates themselves, and those who hold the highest authority in the church.

But here he declares that he will immediately close the mouths of us heretics. Let us attend and see how he performs his promise. Calvin, Instit. Lib. I. c. 9, disputes against those who introduce enthusiasm, and shews that their enthusiastical spirits, of which they boast, are to be judged of by the scriptures. They say, that it is unjust to subject the Holy Spirit to scripture. Calvin answers, that no injury is done to the Holy Spirit, when he is examined by scripture, because in that way he is tried by no foreign rule, but only compared with himself. Now he is always equal to, and like himself; he is in every respect at perfect harmony and agreement with himself, and nowhere at variance with himself: this, therefore, is not injurious to him. These things are most truly spoken by Calvin. Hence Stapleton gathers this argument: As, says he, it is no insult to the Holy Spirit to be examined by the scriptures, so it is not an insult to the scripture to be examined by the voice and testimony of the church. But this reasoning of Stapleton will then only be conclusive, when he shall have shewn and proved, that the analogy and proportion of the church to the scripture is similar to that of the scripture to the Holy Spirit; which is what he will never be able to prove. For the whole scripture is divinely inspired, and ever in harmony with the Spirit. Therefore every spirit which agrees not with scripture is to be rejected: but all churches do not agree with scripture. Here then halts this so boasted argument of Stapleton's, wherewith he hoped to be able to close our mouths.

[1 Sicut in istis temporalibus legibus, quanquam de his homines judicent cum eas instituunt, tamen cum fuerint institutæ atque firmatæ, non licebit judici de ipsis judicare, sed secundum ipsas . . . . . Æternam igitur legem mundis animis fas est cognoscere; judicare non fas est.—August. De Ver. Relig. cap. xxxi. T. I. p. 977.]

And thus far Stapleton, who is bold in words, but in argument loose and weak, as we have seen. Let us now dismiss him.

Now follows our eighteenth argument, which is this: The papists say that we believe the scripture upon the word and authority of the church. I ask, therefore, what sort of faith is this,—whether acquired or infused? They call that acquired which is gained by our own exertions, and human topics of persuasion; that infused, which the Holy Spirit hath disseminated and inspired into our hearts. If they say that it is acquired (as they must needs say, because the authority of the church is in the place of an external means of persuasion), I say, that is not sufficient of itself to produce in us a certain conviction; but in order that we should believe any thing firmly, there is need of the internal infusion of the Spirit. This appears readily from the following passages. Deut. xxix. 4: "Ye have seen all these miracles," says Moses to the Israelites; "but God hath not given you a mind to understand, eyes to see, and ears to hear, unto this day." Whence we perceive that we believe nothing as we ought without infused faith, not even things the most manifest, such as were the miracles which Moses mentions. Matth. xvi. 17: "Blessed art thou, Simon Bar-jona, because flesh and blood hath not revealed these things unto thee, but my Father which is in heaven," saith Christ to Peter. Peter, indeed, had heard John the Baptist; he had heard Christ himself, and had seen many of his miracles: yet Peter nevertheless could not believe before a divine revelation was added to all this; and therefore Christ attributes the whole of Peter's faith to revelation. To the same effect is what we read of Lydia, Acts xvi. 14, whose heart God is said to have opened. 1 Cor. xii. 3: "No one," says Paul, "can call Jesus Lord, but by the Holy Ghost." And, verse 9 of the same chapter, faith is reckoned amongst the gifts ($\chi\alpha\rho\acute{\iota}\sigma\mu\alpha\tau\alpha$) of the Holy Spirit; and he speaks there of justifying faith, not of the faith of miracles. From these premises it is manifest that the faith upon which we rest is infused, and not acquired. But if they say that we believe the scriptures by an infused faith, they say precisely the same as we. For what else is that infused faith but the testimony of the Holy Spirit, on account of which we believe even the scriptures and the doctrine of scripture, and which seals the whole saving truth of scripture in our hearts?

Our nineteenth argument is taken from the authority of the fathers, who testify that the scripture and its truth are no otherwise ascertained for us, and can no otherwise be confirmed in our souls, but by the witness of the Holy Spirit. There is a notable

passage of Augustine's, Confession. Lib. XI. c. 3 : "I would hear
and understand," says he, addressing God, "how thou madest
heaven and earth. Moses wrote this : he wrote, and departed : he
passed from hence to thee ; nor is he now before me. For, if he
were, I would hold him, and ask him, and beseech him for thy
sake, to unfold these things to me, and I would lend the ears of
my body to the sounds which should issue from his lips. But if he
were to speak in the Hebrew tongue, it would strike my senses in
vain ; nor would any of his discourse reach my understanding : but if
he spoke in Latin, I should know what he said. But how should I
know whether he spoke the truth ? And even if I knew this, should
I know it from him ? Surely within, inwardly in the home of my
thoughts, truth, which is neither Hebrew, nor Greek, nor Latin,
nor barbarian, without the organs of mouth or tongue, without the
sound of syllables, would say, He speaks the truth; and I, rendered certain immediately, should say confidently to that man of
thine, Thou speakest truth. Since then I cannot interrogate him,
thee I entreat, O Truth, filled with whom he uttered words of
truth ; thee, O my God, I entreat, have mercy on my sins, and do
thou, who didst grant to him thy servant to speak these things,
grant to me also to understand them[1]." Thus Augustine. In which
place he teaches us, that that public and external judgment of
the church, which the papists have so often in their mouths, hath
not strength sufficient to engender faith. For they will not, I
suppose, attribute more to the church than to Moses and the prophets. If therefore, although Moses and the prophets too were to
rise from the dead and declare that what they wrote was true, yet
their testimony would not suffice us for faith, but we should require
in addition the internal testimony of the Holy Spirit, and a divine

[1 Audiam et intelligam quomodo fecisti cœlum et terram. Scripsit hoc
Moses, scripsit et abiit; transivit hinc ad te. Neque etiam nunc ante me
est : nam si esset, tenerem eum, et rogarem eum, et per te obsecrarem, ut
mihi ista panderet, et præberem aures corporis mei sonis erumpentibus ex
ore ejus. At si Hebræa voce loqueretur, frustra pulsaret sensum meum, nec
inde mentem meam quicquam tangeret. Si autem Latine, scirem quid
diceret: sed unde scirem an vera diceret? Quod si et hoc scirem, num
ab illo scirem? Intus utique mihi, intus in domicilio cogitationis, nec
Hebræa nec Græca nec Latina nec barbara veritas sine oris et linguæ organis,
sine strepitu syllabarum diceret, Verum dicit; et ego statim certus confidenter
illi homini tuo dicerem, Verum dicis. Cum ergo illum interrogare non possum,
te, quo plenus vera dixit, Veritas, rogo ; te, Deus meus, rogo, parce peccatis
meis, et qui illi servo tuo dedisti hæc dicere, da et mihi hæc intelligere.—Aug.
Confess. XI. iii. T. I. p. 232.]

persuasion of the truth itself; then certainly neither shall we believe
the church's testimony, unless the same testimony of the Holy
Spirit be, in the same manner, added.

The same Augustine says also, in his book *Contra Epist. Fund.*
c. 14, that, " in order that we may obtain an understanding of what
we believe, it is requisite that our minds should be inwardly confirmed
and illuminated by the Deity himself[2]." And in his book *De Vera
Religione*, c. 31, he writes thus, as we have just heard : " It is lawful for pure minds to understand the eternal law [of God], but to
judge it is unlawful[3]." Where then are those who arrogate to themselves this judicial power, which they would exercise upon the scriptures, whose authority is supreme ? Basil, upon Ps. 115, writes of
faith thus beautifully and truly : " Faith," says he, " is that which
draws the soul to assent by a force transcending the methods of
logic : faith is that produced, not by the necessary demonstrations
of geometry, but by the energy of the Holy Spirit[4]." Thus we
believe not till the Holy Ghost—not the church—hath inspired us
with faith.   Hereto appertains also what Ambrose says, *De Fide
ad Gratian.* Lib. I. c. 5 : " Do not," says he, " O Arian, estimate
divine things by our (sayings, or writings, or authorities, or
words); but believe them divine, when you find that they are
not human[5]."   Divine things, therefore, are proved by themselves, are believed on their own account.   Salvian, the bishop,
De Providentia, Lib. III., writes thus : " All human sayings need
arguments and witnesses, but the word of God is its own witness ;
because it must needs be, that whatever incorruptible truth speaks,
should be the incorruptible testimony of truth[6]."

We have besides the testimonies of papists themselves. For the
chief popish writers may be cited in this cause. Gabriel Biel, *in
Sentent.* Lib. III. Dist. 25, in Dub. 3, speaks thus : " Catholic verities, without any approbation of the church, are by their own nature immutable, and immutably true, and so are to be considered

[2 Ut . . . quod credimus intelligere mereamur, non jam hominibus, sed ipso
Deo intrinsecus mentem nostram firmante atque illuminante. T. x. p. 192.]

[3 Vide supra, p. 354.]

[4 ἡ ὑπὲρ τὰς λογικὰς μεθόδους τὴν ψυχὴν εἰς συγκατάθεσιν ἕλκουσα, κ.τ.λ.—
T. I. p. 313, B.   Whitaker, in making this citation, writes incorrectly συγ-
κατάβασιν for συγκατάθεσιν.]

[5 Noli, Arriane, ex nostris æstimare divina, sed divina crede ubi humana non invenis.—Opp. T. IV. p. 122. Par. 1603.]

[6 Humana omnia dicta argumentis et testibus egent, Dei autem sermo
ipse sibi testis est : quia necesse est quicquid incorrupta veritas loquitur, in-
corruptum sit testimonium veritatis.—Salv. Opp. Par. 1684, p. 43.]

immutably catholic[1]." But this is a catholic verity about which we
inquire : it is, therefore, immutable in its nature, and immutably to be
considered catholic, and that, without the approbation of the church.
Hosius in his *Confessio Petrocoviensis,* cap. 16, says that we believe
the gospel on no other score, but on account of the voice of God
speaking within and teaching us[2]. This he affirms more than once
in that book, although afterwards he tries in some degree to
correct and excuse himself. Melchior Canus, *Loc. Commun.* Lib.
II. c. 8, disputes upon this question at great length, and, though
differing from us in words, agrees with us in substance. For he
says, that, without infused faith we can believe nothing necessarily,
nor be persuaded of any thing certainly. But that faith which
springs from the church's judgment is acquired; whereas infused
faith proceeds from the Holy Spirit. Therefore, even by the confession of the papists themselves, the scripture is to us what it is,
that is, the scripture, on account of the authority of God; and in
order that we should certainly believe what we receive in scripture,
we have need of the internal testimony of the Holy Spirit. Canisius, in his Catechism, in the chapter upon the precepts of the
church, sect. 16, says that we "believe, adhere, and attribute the
greatest authority to scripture on account of the testimony of the
divine Spirit which speaks in it[3]." Hence two things are collected :
first, that the Holy Spirit speaks in scripture; secondly, that the
Holy Spirit, speaking in scripture, persuades us to believe scripture
and assign to it the greatest authority. So Stapleton in the last
chapter of his first book: "It is not derogatory to the sacred scripture that it receives witness from the church, although it have greater
testimony from the Spirit of God, who is its author." If this be
true, why hath Stapleton afterwards disputed so keenly against this
testimony of the Spirit, which he had himself confessed to be greater
than the testimony of the church? And Bellarmine himself, in his
MS. lectures upon Thomas' *Secunda Secundæ,* Quæst. 1, Art. 1, Dub. 1,
teaches that we believe, not on account of the church, but on account of the revelation of God; and refutes the contrary opinions
of certain others. Thus we conclude that our opinion is true not only
in itself, but even in the judgment of our adversaries themselves.

And so much upon the third question.

[1 Sicut veritates catholicæ absque omni approbatione ecclesiæ ex natura
rei sunt immutabiles, et immutabiliter veræ, ita sunt immutabiliter catholicæ
reputandæ.—p. 253. Brixiæ, 1574.]

[2 .. propter Dei vocem intus loquentis.—p. 21. Opp. Lugd. 1564.]

[3 Scripturæ propter testimonium divini Spiritus in illa loquentis credimus, &c.—Opus Catech. p. 157. Colon. 1577.]

THE FIRST CONTROVERSY.

QUESTION IV.

CONCERNING THE PERSPICUITY OF SCRIPTURE.

CHAPTER I.

OF THE STATE OF THE QUESTION.

In commencing to speak of this question, we must return to that foundation which was laid at the beginning. In John v. 39, Christ says, " Search the scriptures," ἐρευνᾶτε τὰς γραφάς. The precept of Christ, therefore, is plain, declaring that the scriptures should be searched : whence the question arises, whether those sacred scriptures, which we are commanded to search, are so full of obscurity and difficulty as to be unintelligible to us ; or whether there be not rather a light and clearness and perspicuity in scripture, so as to make it no useless task for the people to be engaged and occupied in their perusal. Here, therefore, we have to dispute concerning the nature of scripture. But, before coming to the argument, we must see what is the opinion of our adversaries upon this matter, and what is our own. As to our own opinion, the papists certainly either do not understand it; or, if they do, treat us unfairly and slander us in an impudent manner. For we never said that every thing in scripture is easy, perspicuous, and plain ; that there is nothing obscure, nothing difficult to be understood ; but we confess openly that there are many obscure and difficult passages of scripture : and yet these men object to us this, and affirm that we maintain the scriptures to be perfectly easy.

The council of Trent hath defined or expressly determined nothing upon this matter. We must, therefore, investigate the opinion of our adversaries by the help of other writings of papists, so as to be enabled to discover the true state of the controversy. Eckius, the most insolent of popish writers, in his Enchiridion, Loc. IV., writing of the scripture, objects to us this opinion,—that the scripture is so easy, that even the ignorant people may and ought to read it.

His words are these: "The Lutherans contend that the sacred' scriptures are clear ; and accordingly laymen and doting old women treat of them in a style of authority [1]." Whence we understand that their mind and opinion is, that the people are to be kept from reading the scriptures, because they are so obscure as that they cannot be understood by laics, women, and the vulgar. We hold the contrary, that the scriptures are not so difficult but that they may be read with advantage, and ought to be read, by the people. Hosius also, in his third book of the authority of the church against Brentius, is copious in proving and establishing the exceeding great obscurity of the sacred writings. So the Censors of Cologne, against Monhemius, write to precisely the same effect : for they say in their preface, that the difficulty of scripture "may be argument enough that all are not to be indiscriminately admitted to the reading of it." Hence they conclude that the unlearned are to be prohibited reading scripture, even the history of Christ's passion ; in which they say that there are so many doubtful points, that even the learned can hardly reconcile them. Thus they permit no part of scripture to the people, not even that most sweet and easy narrative, altogether worthy of our perusal and meditation, which contains the history of the death of Christ. Andradius, *Orthodox.* *Explic.* Lib. ii., disputes largely upon the obscurity of scripture. Lindanus, in his Panoplia, Lib. iii. c. 6, affirms of all scripture that which Peter said only of certain subjects handled in Paul's Epistles : for he says that there are, throughout the whole body of scripture, many things "hard to be understood," and that such is the unanimous opinion of divines. Stapleton, Lib. x. c. 2, says that the church ought to interpret scripture on account of the difficulties which present themselves generally and in most places. The Rhemists, in their annotations upon 2 Pet. iii. 16, say that the whole scripture is difficult, but especially the Epistles of Paul ; whereas Peter, as shall appear hereafter, affirms neither : all that Peter observes is, that there are some things in Paul's Epistles "hard to be understood, which the unlearned wrest, as they do the other scriptures, to their own destruction." What they subjoin out of Augustine, that of all things which Paul taught, nothing is more difficult than what he writes concerning the righteousness of faith, can by no means be conceded. For if Paul ever said any thing plainly, he hath declared his mind upon this subject in a perspi-

[[1] Lutherani contendunt scripturas sacras esse claras ; ideo laici et deliræ anus eas tractant imperiose.]

cuous discourse. The same Rhemists, in their marginal annotation upon Luke vi. 1, attribute to us this opinion, "that all things are very easy." The Jesuit Bellarmine affirms that there are many obscurities in scripture; which we also concede: but when he determines the state of the question to be this, whether scripture be so plain of itself, as to suffice without any interpretation for deciding and putting an end to all controversies of faith of its own self, he fights without an adversary: at least he hath no adversaries in us upon this point. Prateolus, in his *Elenchus Hæreticorum*, Lib. XVII. c. 20, says that it is the common article of all sectaries to affirm that the scriptures are clear of themselves, and need no interpretation. Sixtus Senensis, in his Bibliotheca, Lib. VI. Annot. 151, objects to us this error,—that we say that the whole scriptures are so clear and perspicuous of their own nature as to be capable of being understood by any one, however illiterate, unless some external obstacle be interposed. Costerus the Jesuit, in his Enchiridion of Controversies lately published, confesses that many things in scripture are plain; but adds that many things are not of such a nature as to be intelligible to every body without any trouble.

But they do us injustice, and openly preach falsehood concerning us, when they affirm us to say that all things in scripture are so plain that they may be understood by any unlearned person, and need no exposition or interpretation. Hence we see, both what they think, namely, that the scriptures are so obscure that they ought not to be read by the unlearned; and what they say, but falsely say, that we think, that all things are plain in the scriptures, and that they suffice without any interpretation to determine all controversies. Let us now see what our opinion really is.

Luther, in his assertion of the articles condemned by Leo X., in the preface, says that the scripture is its own most plain, easy, and certain interpreter, proving, judging, and illustrating all things. This is said by him most truly, if it be candidly understood. The same author, in his book of the Slavery of the Will against the Diatribe of Erasmus, writes almost in the beginning, that in the scriptures there is nothing abstruse, nothing obscure, but that all things are plain. And because this may seem a paradox, he afterwards explains himself thus: he confesses that many places of scripture are obscure, that there are many words and sentences shrouded in difficulty, but he affirms nevertheless that no dogma is obscure; as, for instance, that God is one and three, that Christ hath suffered, and will reign for ever, and so forth. All

which is perfectly true : for although there is much obscurity in
many words and passages, yet all the articles of faith are plain.
Stapleton, Lib. x. cap. 3, interprets these words of Luther, as if he
said, that all the difficulty of scripture arose from ignorance of
grammar and figures ; and he objects to us Origen and Jerome,
who certainly were exquisitely skilled in grammar and rhetoric,
and yet confess themselves that they were ignorant of many things,
and may have erred in many places.   We answer, that what he
blames in Luther is most true, if it be rightly understood : for
he who can always arrive at the grammatical sense of scripture,
will, beyond all doubt, best explain and interpret the scriptures.
But hitherto no one hath been able to do this every where and in
all places.   Certainly the grammatical meaning of scripture, as it
is ever the best and truest, so is it sometimes the hardest to be
found ; so that it is no wonder that Origen and Jerome himself,
although both of them most skilful grammarians, may have erred
in the interpretation of scripture.   Luther adds besides, that the
things themselves are manifest in scripture ; and that therefore we
need not be put to much trouble, if the words be sometimes in
many places less manifest.   His words are these : " The things
themselves are in light ; we need not care, therefore, though some
signs of the things be in darkness[1]."   But some persons complain
greatly of the obscurity of the things also, so that this distinction
of Luther's between the things and the signs of the things may
seem to be idle.   Luther answers that this occurs, not from the
obscurity and difficulty of the things themselves, but from our
blindness and ignorance.   And this he very properly confirms by
the testimony of Paul, 2 Cor. iii. 14, 15, 16, where Paul says that
" the vail is placed upon the hearts of the Jews until this very day,
which vail is done away in Christ ;" and from 2 Cor. iv. 3, where
the same apostle says, " If our gospel be hid, it is hid to them
which are lost :" and he illustrates the same thing by the similitude of the sun and the day, both of which, although very clear in
themselves, are invisible to the blind.   " There is nothing," says he,
" brighter than the sun and the day : but the blind man cannot
even see the sun, and there are some also who flee the light[2]."
Stapleton endeavours to take this answer from him.   He says that

[1 Nihil refert, si res sit in luce, an aliquod ejus signum sit in tenebris.—
Opp. Witeberg. T. II. p. 459. 2.]

[2 Eadem temeritate solem obscurumque diem culparet, qui ipse sibi
oculos velaret.—Ibid. p. 460.]

Luther, in this way, condemns all the fathers, and so all antiquity, of error and blindness. But I answer, that Luther is speaking of things, that is of the nature of the doctrine and of the articles of the christian religion : the truth of which (though not of all, yet of those which are necessary to salvation), it is manifest from their writings, was thoroughly seen by the fathers. He is not speaking of the several words and passages wherein they might sometimes easily err, without, nevertheless, in the least incurring the blame of blindness on that account.

But Erasmus, in his Diatribe, contends that even some dogmas are obscure, as the doctrine of the Trinity, of the distinction of Persons, of sin against the Holy Ghost, and such like ; and to this sense he tortures that passage which is contained in Rom. xi. 33, where Paul says that the "judgments of God are unsearchable, and his ways past finding out." Luther answers, that these doctrines are indeed obscure in themselves ; but that they are plain so far forth as they are proposed in scripture, if we will be content with that knowledge which God hath propounded and conceded to his church in the scripture, and not search into every thing more curiously than becomes us. But as to the passage from Paul, he answers, that indeed the things of God are obscure, but that the things of scripture are clear ; that the judgments of God concerning the number of the elect, the day and hour of the judgment, and such-like, are unknown and inscrutable ; but that those things which God hath revealed in his word are by no means inscrutable to us ; and that Paul in that place spoke of the things of God, not of the things of scripture. Furthermore he says, that the reason why so many dispute about the things of scripture is to be found in the perversity and depraved desires of men, especially the sophists and schoolmen, who, not content with the simplicity of scripture, have rendered every thing obscure and intricate by their traps and devices ; but that the scripture must not be falsely blamed on account of men's abuse of it. Luther uses another distinction also in that place. He says that the perspicuity or obscurity of scripture is either internal or external ; the internal is that of the heart itself, the external is in the words. If we speak of the internal obscurity or perspicuity of scripture, he says that not even one jot is in this way clear in the scripture without the internal light of the Holy Spirit ; for that all things in this view and respect are obscure to the fleshly understanding of men, according to that which is said in Ps. xiv. : " The fool hath said in his heart, that there is no God." But if we understand the exter-

nal clearness or obscurity of scripture, he says that all doctrines
are in this way clear, and brought to light in the ministry of the
word. And this distinction is very necessary : for although, in
the external way, we perfectly hold all the doctrines of religion,
we yet understand nothing internally to salvation, nor have learned
any dogma aright, without the teaching of the Holy Spirit.

Assuredly, this is the difference between theology and philosophy : since it is only the external light of nature that is required
to learn thoroughly the arts of philosophy; but to understand theology aright, there is need of the internal light of the Holy Spirit,
because the things of faith are not subject to the teaching of mere
human reason. We may, in a certain manner, be acquainted with
the doctrines of scripture, and obtain an historical faith by the
ministry of the word, so as to know all the articles of faith, and
deem them to be true, and all without the inward light of the
Spirit, as many impious men and devils do ; but we cannot have
the πληροφορία, that is, a certain, solid, and saving knowledge,
without the Holy Spirit internally illuminating our minds. And
this internal clearness it is, which wholly flows from the Holy
Ghost. Other arts serve our purpose when only externally understood; but this is of no avail unless understood internally. Meanwhile Luther was far from such madness as to say, that there was
nothing difficult in scripture, or that it did not need an interpretation. Yea, on the contrary, in the preface to his Commentary
upon the Psalms, he acknowledges that there are many obscurities and difficulties in the scripture, which God hath left us,
as if on purpose to keep us constantly scholars in the school of
the Holy Spirit. And in the same place he affirms, that a
man must be impudent who would say that he understood even
any one book thoroughly : and the same hath ever been the
opinion of us all.

The state of the question, therefore, is not really such as the
papists would have it appear ; but our fundamental principles are
these : First, that the scriptures are sufficiently clear to admit of
their being read by the people and the unlearned with some fruit
and utility. Secondly, that all things necessary to salvation are
propounded in plain words in the scriptures. Meanwhile, we concede that there are many obscure places, and that the scriptures
need explication; and that, on this account, God's ministers are to
be listened to when they expound the word of God, and the men
best skilled in scripture are to be consulted. So far concerning
the state of the question.

CHAPTER II.

WHY GOD WOULD HAVE MANY OBSCURITIES IN THE SCRIPTURES.

We should carefully bear in memory the preceding distinctions drawn by Luther; for they are sufficient to obviate almost all the arguments of the papists in this question. But before proceeding to their arguments, I have thought it proper to set forth the reasons on account of which God was willing that there should be so many things of considerable obscurity and difficulty in the scriptures. This contributes much to the better understanding of the matter upon which we treat. The fathers write excellently well upon this subject, as Clemens Alexandrinus, Stromat. Lib. vi.[1], Augustine, *de Doct. Christ.* Lib. ii.[2], Gregory, Homil. vi. in Ezechiel[3], and others.

Now the causes are such as follow: *First*, God would have us to be constant in prayer, and hath scattered many obscurities up and down through the scriptures, in order that we should seek his help in interpreting them and discovering their true meaning. *Secondly*, he wished thereby to excite our diligence in reading, meditating upon, searching and comparing the scriptures; for, if every thing had been plain, we should have been entirely slothful and negligent. *Thirdly*, he designed to prevent our losing interest in them; for we are ready to grow weary of easy things: God, therefore, would have our interest kept up by difficulties. *Fourthly*, God willed to have that truth, so sublime, so heavenly, sought and found with so much labour, the more esteemed by us on that account. For we generally despise and contemn whatever is easily acquired, near at hand, and costs small or no labour, according to the Greek proverb, ἐπὶ θύρας τὴν ὑδρίαν. But those things which we find with great toil and much exertion, those, when once we have found them out, we esteem highly and consider their value proportionally greater. *Fifthly*, God wished by this means to subdue our pride and arrogance, and to expose to us our ignorance. We are apt to think too honourably of ourselves, and to rate our genius and acuteness more highly than is fitting, and to promise ourselves too much from our science and knowledge. *Sixthly*, God willed that the sacred mysteries of his word should be opened freely to pure and holy minds, not exposed to dogs and swine. Hence those things which

[1 P. 677, et seqq. ed. Morell. Paris. 1629.]
[2 cap. 6, pp. 35, 36. ed. Bruder. Lips. 1838.]
[3 Opp. p. 1261, A. Paris. 1705.]

are easy to holy persons, appear so many parables to the profane.
For the mysteries of scripture are like gems, which only he that
knows them values; while the rest, like the cock in Æsop, despise
them, and prefer the most worthless objects to what is most beautiful and excellent. *Seventhly,* God designed to call off our minds
from the pursuit of external things and our daily occupations, and
transfer them to the study of the scriptures. Hence it is now
necessary to give some time to their perusal and study; which
we certainly should not bestow upon them, if we found every thing
plain and open. *Eighthly,* God desired thus to accustom us to a
certain internal purity and sanctity of thought and feeling. For
they who bring with them profane minds to the reading of scripture, lose their trouble and oil: those only read with advantage,
who bring with them pure and holy minds. *Ninthly,* God willed
that in his church some should be teachers, and some disciples;
some more learned, to give instruction; others less skilful, to receive
it; so as that the honour of the sacred scriptures and the divinely
instituted ministry might, in this manner, be maintained.

Such was the wisdom of the Holy Spirit, wherewith, as Augustine expresses it, *De Doctrina Christ.* Lib. II. c. 6, he hath
modified the scriptures so as to maintain their honour and consult
our good. Other causes more besides these might be adduced;
but it is not necessary to enumerate more.

CHAPTER III.

WHEREIN THE ARGUMENTS OF THE PAPISTS ARE OBVIATED.

LET us come now to the arguments of our adversaries; which
indeed might be omitted, as neither injuring, nor even touching our
cause, nor having any force against us whatsoever: for all that they
prove is, that there are some difficult passages in scripture, which
we concede. Costerus, a papist, in his Enchiridion, cap. 1, mentions and sets forth some places full of obscurity and difficulties, as
1 Pet. iii. 19, where Christ is said to have "preached to the spirits
in prison, which were sometime disobedient in the days of Noah,"
&c.; and 1 Cor. xv. 29, "What shall they do who are baptized
for the dead, if the dead rise not at all?" 1 Cor. iii. 15, "If any
man's work be burned, he shall suffer loss; yet he himself shall be

saved, yet so as by fire." He might verily have produced a thousand such passages; but, in order to dispute pertinently against Luther and us, he ought to have shewn some doctrines or articles of faith not openly and plainly set forth in scripture. Bellarmine alleges five arguments in order to prove the scriptures to be obscure, which we acknowledge in some places to be true. But let us see of what sort these arguments are.

His FIRST argument is taken from the authority of scripture, from which he cites some passages. In the first place he reasons thus: David was ignorant of many things, therefore much more we; consequently, the scriptures are obscure. Now that David was ignorant of many things, he proves from Psalm cxix., where it is said, "Give me understanding, and I will search thy law;" where also the psalmist entreats God "to teach him" his law, to "illuminate his eyes;" and in many places of that same Psalm he ingenuously confesses his ignorance of many things. To the same purpose he alleges what Jerome writes of David, to Paulinus, Ep. 13, *de Institit. Monachi:* "If so great a prophet confesses the darkness of ignorance, with what night of ignorance do you suppose that we, mere babes and hardly more than sucklings, are surrounded[1]?" From all which he concludes that the scriptures are obscure. I answer, in the *first* place, these things do not touch the question. There is no one amongst us who does not confess with David, that God is to be constantly besought to teach us his law, to illuminate our hearts, &c. Therefore the example of David is objected to us in vain. Who would believe that these men know what they are saying? Do we indeed affirm that the scripture is so plain, that God needs not to be prayed to to teach us his law, his will, and his word? No one was ever so impious and so mad. Therefore we ought continually to pray with David, that God would give us understanding, that he would open our eyes, illuminate our minds, and teach us himself: otherwise we shall never understand any thing aright. For it is not enough to know the words, the letter or the history, but a full persuasion is required. This it was that David sought, that he might more and more make progress in true understanding and faith. *Secondly,* David speaks there not principally of the external understanding (for doubtless he knew the letter, and the grammatical and historical sense of most passages), but of that internal full assurance whereof we read Luke i. 1, in

[1 Si tantus propheta tenebras ignorantiæ confitetur, qua nos putas parvulos et pene lactentes inscitiæ nocte circumdari?—Opp. T. I. p. 323. Veron. 1734.]

order to the obtaining of which we maintain that we must labour with continual prayers. Thus David was ignorant of some things, and did not perfectly penetrate the meaning of God and the mysteries of his word ; which is plain from Jerome himself in that same place quoted by Bellarmine. For thus he subjoins : " Unless the whole of what is written be opened by him who hath the key of David, who openeth and no man shutteth, and shutteth and no man openeth, they can be unfolded by no other hand[1]."

The second passage of scripture which he objects is Luke xxiv. 27, from which place he reasons thus : Christ interpreted the scriptures to his disciples : therefore the scriptures are not easy, but need an interpreter. I answer, in the *first* place, which of us ever took away the interpretation of scripture ? Certainly, none of us ; for we all readily confess that the scriptures need interpretation. *Secondly*, those disciples were crushed and stricken at that time with a sort of amazement, and slow and unapt to understand any thing ; so that it is no wonder that they could not understand the scriptures without an interpretation. Thirdly, those who understand the grammatical sense of scripture, ought nevertheless to hear the exposition of scripture, to help them to a better understanding. This we never denied.

In the third place, he objects to us the case of the eunuch, Acts viii., whom he states to have been a pious man and studious of the scripture; and to prove this he cites the superfluous testimony of Jerome, from his epistle to Paulinus concerning the study of the scriptures. He, being asked by Philip if he understood what he was reading, replied, " How can I understand, unless some man declare it unto me ? " Therefore, says Bellarmine, the scriptures need interpretation. I answer, in the *first* place, we concede that many things in scripture are obscure and need interpretation ; therefore this place concludes nothing against us. *Secondly*, although this eunuch was pious and very studious of scripture, he was yet unskilful and not much familiar with scripture, as is plain from his question ; for he asked Philip whether the prophet spoke of himself, or of some other person. Now, we do not say that every thing is immediately plain and easy in the scriptures, so as to be intelligible to every one ; but we say that those things which at first seem obscure and difficult, are afterwards rendered easy, if one be diligent in reading

[1 Nisi aperta fuerint universa quæ scripta sunt, ab eo qui habet clavem Davidis, qui aperit et nemo claudit, claudit et nemo aperit, nullo alio reserante pandentur.—Ibid. p. 324.]

them, and bring with him a pure and pious mind. *Thirdly*, as to Jerome, we say that he speaks of a certain higher understanding and illumination, as is manifest from his own words in that place. For thus he writes of that eunuch[2]: " While he held the book, and conceived in thought, uttered with his tongue and sounded with his lips, the words of the Lord, he knew not him whom in the book he ignorantly worshipped. Philip comes, shews him Jesus, who lay concealed in the letter. O wonderful power of a teacher ! In the same hour the eunuch believes, is baptized, and becomes faithful and holy, a master in place of a disciple."

In the fourth place, he objects to us the words of Peter which are contained in 2 Epistle iii. 16, where Peter says expressly that there are δυσνόητά τινα (some things hard to be understood) in Paul's epistles. And the Jesuit bids us observe, that Peter does not say that there are some things hard to be understood merely by the *unlearned and unstable*, but simply and absolutely δυσνόητα, difficulties ; whence he wishes to infer that they are difficult to all, though especially to the unlearned. And to this purpose he alleges the testimony of Augustine, *De fide et operibus*, c. 16, where he confesses that a certain place in Paul seems to him very difficult. I answer, *first*, We concede that some places are hard to be understood: therefore, this passage does not make against us. *Secondly*, Peter does not say that πάντα, all things, but only τινὰ, some things, are hard to be understood. And what if some things be obscure ? Yet it follows that the greatest part is plain and easy. *Thirdly*, Although Peter inveighs against the ἀμαθεῖς καὶ ἀστηρίκτους, " the unlearned and unstable," who στρεβλοῦσι " wrest" the scriptures, he nevertheless does not debar them altogether from the reading of the scriptures. *Fourthly*, Peter does not say that Paul's epistles are obscure, nay, not even that there are some obscurities in Paul's epistles, but only in those things concerning which he himself writes in his own. Now Peter speaks of the last judgment, and the destruction of the world, about which unlearned men had at that time many ridiculous fictions. That Peter is speaking of the subjects, not of the epistles of Paul, is manifest from the very words : for he does not say, ἐν αἷς, but ἐν οἷς, which plainly refers to the τού-

[2 Cum librum teneret et verba Domini cogitatione conciperet, lingua volveret, labiis personaret, ignorabat eum quem in libro nesciens venerabatur. Venit Philippus, ostendit ei Jesum, qui clausus latebat in litera. O mira doctoris virtus! Eadem hora credit Eunuchus, baptizatur, et fidelis ac sanctus factus est, ac magister de discipulo.—Ibid. p. 272. Ep. 53.]

24

[WHITAKER.]

των immediately preceding. In these matters and articles of our faith we confess that there are many difficulties, as also in other mysteries of our religion. The occasion of the mistake arose from the vulgate version, which renders *in quibus*, which is ambiguous. Beza much more properly, in order to remove the ambiguity, translates it, *inter quæ*. Peter, therefore, speaks not of the character of Paul's epistles. But the Rhemists endeavour to overturn this reply, in which attempt they shew how stupid they are, while they desire to exhibit their acuteness. They say there is absolutely no difference between these two assertions : This author is difficult and obscure, and, There are many things difficult and obscure in this author. I answer, first, Peter does not say, as they would have him, that *all*, or *many*, but only *some* things in Paul's epistles are obscure : he narrows his expression as much as possible. Secondly, these two assertions are not equivalent: for an author may speak perspicuously and plainly of things most obscure and difficult. What is harder to be understood than that God made the world out of nothing ? that God took flesh of a virgin ? that God and man were one person ? That this world shall be destroyed, and our bodies restored again to life after death, surpass our understanding ; and yet concerning these the scriptures speak with the utmost clearness and explicitness. So much for Bellarmine's first argument.

His SECOND argument is taken from the common consent of the ancient fathers, of whom he brings forward eight, Irenæus, Origen, Ruffinus, Chrysostom, Ambrose, Jerome, Augustine, Gregory; all of which very learned fathers may be passed over by us, since they say absolutely nothing that makes against us. For they either say that there are some obscurities in scripture, or that, without the internal light of the Spirit, the scriptures cannot be rightly understood by us as they ought : both of which propositions we concede. However, let us return some reply, as briefly as we can, to each of the testimonies of these fathers.—The first is Irenæus, who, in his second book against heresies, cap. 47, after shewing that there are many things, even in the creatures themselves, obscure and difficult, as the origin of the Nile, the vernal visits and autumnal departures of the birds, the ebb and flow of the sea, and other such like things, finally accommodates all these to scripture. "Likewise," says he, "in the scriptures we understand some things, and some things we commit to God[1]." I answer, that nothing could

[1] Si ergo et in rebus creaturæ quædam quidem eorum adjacent Deo, quædam autem et in nostram venerunt scientiam ; quid mali est, si et eorum

be said more truly; for never any man attained to all things that are delivered in scripture. But we speak of things necessary. This testimony of Irenæus avails against those, who, elate with pride and carried further than behoves them by curiosity, attribute to themselves a knowledge of all things, and especially of the scriptures: but it in no way touches us, who confess that there are many matters in scripture too abstruse to be perfectly understood by any man in this life.

The second testimony is that of Origen, who in his twelfth Homily on Exodus says, that in the case of the scriptures we should not only employ study, but pour forth prayers also day and night, that the Lamb of the tribe of Juda may come and open for us the sealed book[2]. So, in his seventh book against Celsus, he says that the scripture is in many places obscure[3]. I answer, We say also that study and diligence are required in reading the scriptures, and that assiduous prayers are also necessary. The papists, therefore, are impertinent, who say that we affirm that any one may treat the scriptures negligently and without prayer, and yet understand them correctly, or that the scripture is not in many places obscure.

The third father whom Bellarmine cites is Ruffinus. He, Lib. XI. c. 9, writes that Basil and Nazianzen were both bred at Athens, both colleagues for many years; and, setting aside the books of the philosophers, applied themselves with the utmost zeal to the scriptures, bestowing their whole attention upon them, and learned them from the writings and authority of the fathers, not from their own presumption. Hence the Jesuit concludes that the scriptures are obscure. I answer, that these distinguished men bestowed this so great labour and such extraordinary diligence in the study of scripture, not to obtain any moderate or vulgar knowledge, but that they might understand the scriptures accurately, and prove fit to instruct others. Similar study and diligence should be applied by all those who would discharge the office of pastors and teachers in the church, as was the case of Basil and Nazianzen; but so great labour is not necessarily required in the people. It is sufficient for them to understand and

quæ in scripturis requiruntur, universis scripturis spiritualibus existentibus, quædam quidem absolvamus secundum gratiam Dei, quædam autem commendemus Deo?—p. 203. B.]

[2 Opp. T. II. p. 174. Par. 1733.]

[3 pp. 338, 9. ed. Spencer. Cantab. 1658.]

hold aright the articles of faith, and the things which are necessary to salvation.

In the fourth place, Bellarmine objects to us Chrysostom. He
in his fortieth Homily on the fifth chapter of the gospel of St John,
upon these words,—ἐρευνᾶτε τὰς γραφὰς, "search the scriptures,"
—says that there is need of great labour and the utmost diligence in
the sacred scriptures, and that it behoves us to dig deep, to search
and investigate diligently to find those things which lie concealed
in their depths. For it is not (says he) what lies ready to hand
and at the surface that we dig for, but what is profoundly buried
like a treasure. I answer, these words do not prove that the scriptures are so obscure that the laity ought not to read them. We,
for our parts, confess that the scriptures ought not to be read carelessly, or without faith, as they were read by the Jews; but we
judge both diligence and faith to be required in the reading of
them. The Jews read the scriptures negligently and without faith:
we say that the scriptures are easy to the studious and faithful.
But Bellarmine produces another testimony also, from Chrysostom's
Opus Imperfectum upon Matthew, Hom. 44; where two reasons
are brought why God chose that the scriptures should be obscure.
The first is, that some might be teachers and others learners;
because if all knew all things equally well, a teacher would not
be necessary, and good order would not be maintained amongst
men. The second reason is, lest scripture should be not so much
useful as contemptible, if it were understood promiscuously by all.
I answer: This is precisely the same as we say ourselves, that God,
induced by the fittest reasons, chose that there should be many
obscurities in scripture. But what hath this to do with the cause
in hand?

In the fifth place, he objects Ambrose, Epist. 44 *ad Constan-
tium Episcopum*, where these words are found: "The holy scripture
is a sea, having in it deep meanings, and the profundity of prophetic
enigmas, into which sea have entered many streams[1]." I answer:
We readily confess with Ambrose, that there are many obscure
meanings in scripture, and that scripture is like a sea: but the
same Ambrose says also presently in the same place, that "there
are also in the scriptures rivers sweet and clear, and pure fountains
springing up unto eternal life." So he compares scripture to rivers

[1 Mare est scriptura divina, habens in se sensus profundos, et altitudi-
nem propheticorum ænigmatum; in quod mare plurima introierunt flumina.
—Class. 1. Ep. II. § 3. T. VIII. p. 181. Ambros. Opp. ed. Caillau. Paris. 1839.]

also.   There are, I confess, in the scripture, as in the ocean, many depths; but yet the same Ambrose himself says a little afterwards: "There are different streams of scripture. You have what you may drink first, what second, and what last[2]."

In the sixth place he objects Jerome, from whom he cites three testimonies.   The first is taken from the Epistle to Paulinus on the Study of the Scripture, where[3] he writes that we cannot possibly learn and understand the scriptures, without some one to go before and shew the way, that is, without a master and interpreter; and, running through all the books, he shews in each that there are many things mystical and obscure.   The second testimony of Jerome is contained in the preface to his commentaries upon the Epistle to the Ephesians, where he says that he had bestowed much labour upon the scriptures, always either reading himself or consulting others; upon which latter account, he had gone as far as to Alexandria, to consult there a certain learned man called Didymus.   The third testimony of Jerome, which Bellarmine cites is taken from his Epistle to Algasia, Quæst. 8, where Jerome writes, that the whole Epistle of Paul to the Romans is involved in exceeding great obscurity[4].   I answer: We willingly acknowledge and concede all these things; that is, firstly, that the scriptures cannot be perfectly understood without a master; next, that there are some obscure and difficult places in scripture, and that teachers and masters should be consulted upon them; lastly, that the Epistle to the Romans is obscure; and so that some books are more obscure than others.   Yet, meanwhile, it does not follow that all things in scripture are so obscure that laymen should not touch it, and the people should be wholly prevented and repelled from its perusal: for in this way it would not be lawful for any man whatsoever to read the scriptures.

In the seventh place, he objects Augustine, from whom he produces four testimonies.   The first is cited from his work *De Doctr. Christ.* Lib. II. cap. 6, where Augustine teaches that the obscurity of scripture is of use " to tame our pride and to rouse our understanding from listlessness, since things easily investigated are

[2 Sunt ergo et fluvii dulces atque perspicui, sunt et fontes nivei, qui saliant in vitam æternam . . . Diversa igitur scripturarum divinarum fluenta. Habes quod primum bibas, habes quod secundum, habes quod postremum.—Ibid.]

[3 Hæc a me perstricta sunt breviter . . . . ut intelligeres, te in scripturis sanctis, sine prævio et monstrante semitam, non posse ingredi.—Ut supra, p. 369.]

[4 T. I. pp. 864—70.]

generally held cheap[1]." I answer: Yet the same father says in
the same chapter, that the Holy Spirit provides for our hunger in
the plainer places, and that hardly any thing can be obtained from
those obscurer passages, which is not found said elsewhere with
the utmost plainness. The same father, in the ninth chapter of
the same book, says, that amongst those things which are *plainly*
set down in scripture, are to be found *all those things* which make
the sum of our faith and practice[2]. The second testimony of Augustine is taken from his Confessions, Lib. XII. cap. 14, where
he says, that "the depth of the divine words is wonderful[3]."
I answer: we confess this to be most true in many places. But
as there are some places such as that an elephant may swim in
them, so there are others so disembarrassed, plain, and utterly free
from prejudices or danger, that a lamb may, as it were, easily
wade over them. The third testimony cited from Augustine is
contained in his third Epistle to Volusianus, where he says that
"the depth of the christian scriptures is such, that one may every
day make new progress in them, although he should endeavour to
study them alone from his earliest childhood to decrepit age, in
the amplest leisure, with the closest study, and a genius of the
highest order." I answer: Here the Jesuit betrays his remarkable
unfairness, and really singular dishonesty: for there follow immediately these words which he hath omitted: "Not that one comes at
those things which are necessary to salvation with so much difficulty[4]." Besides, the same father says in the same epistle, that
"the scripture, like a familiar friend, speaks without disguise
to the heart, not of the learned only, but of the unlearned also;
nor elevates with proud diction what it conceals in its mysteries, so
as to make the duller and unlearned minds afraid to approach,
like the poor to the rich; but invites all by its humble style, whom
it feeds with its manifested truth, and exercises with that which is

[1 Quod totum provisum divinitus esse non dubito ad edomandam labore
superbiam et intellectum a fastidio revocandum, cui facile investigata plerumque vilescunt.—Opp. T. III. p. 27.]

[2 In eis enim quæ aperte in scripturis posita sunt, inveniuntur illa omnia
quæ continent fidem moresque vivendi.—Ibid. p. 31.]

[3 Mira profunditas eloquiorum tuorum, quorum ecce ante nos superficies
blanditur parvulis: sed mira profunditas, Deus meus, mira profunditas.—T.
I. p. 253.]

[4 Tanta est enim christianarum profunditas literarum, ut in eis continuo pro-
ficerem, si eas solas ab ineunte pueritia usque ad decrepitam senectutem, maximo
otio, summo studio, meliore ingenio addiscerem. Non quod ad ea quæ necessaria sunt saluti tanta in eis perveniatur difficultate.—Ep. 137. n. 3. T. II. p. 526.]

hidden." He says, moreover, that the scripture hath in its *ready* places whatever it hath in the *recondite* ones: " but that, lest men should grow weary of what is plain, the same things again when covered are desired, when desired are, as it were, renewed, and renewed are intimated with pleasure[5]." When the Jesuit passes all this over in silence, he displays his own extraordinary desire to deceive us. The fourth testimony of Augustine is found in *Epist.* cxix. c. 21: "In scripture," says Augustine, "there are many more things that I know not, than that I know[6]." I answer: This ought to be the true and ingenuous confession of all, to acknowledge that they are very far distant from the perfection of knowledge: yet Augustine both professes that he himself knew whatever was necessary, and concedes that it might be easily understood by others.

The eighth testimony cited by the Jesuit is that of Gregory the great, in his sixth Homily upon Ezekiel, where he writes thus: " The very obscurity of the words of God is of great use, because it exercises the perception so as to be enlarged by labour, and, through exercise, be enabled to catch that which a lazy reader cannot. It hath besides this still greater advantage, that the meaning of the sacred scripture would be lightly esteemed, if it were plain in all places. In some obscure places the sweetness with which it refresheth the mind, when found, is proportionate to the toil and labour which were expended upon the search[7]." I answer: Nothing could be said more truly. We confess with Gregory, that there are many obscurities in scripture, and that this hath happened through the divine wisdom, partly to exercise us in scripture, partly to prevent its being despised, partly that the

[5 . . . . . quasi amicus familiaris sine fuco ad cor loquitur indoctorum atque doctorum. Ea vero quæ in mysteriis occultat, nec ipso eloquio superbo erigit, quo non audeat accedere mens tardiuscula et inerudita, quasi pauper ad divitem; sed invitat omnes humili sermone, quos non solum manifesta pascat, sed etiam secreta exerceat veritate, hoc in promptis quod in reconditis habens: sed ne aperta fastidirentur, eadem rursus operta desiderantur, desiderata quodammodo renovantur, renovata suaviter intimantur. —Id. ibid. prop. fin.]

[6 Et miror quia hoc te latet, quod non solum in aliis innumerabilibus rebus multa me latent, sed etiam in ipsis sanctis scripturis multo nesciam plura quam sciam.—Ep. 55. c. 21. n. 38. p. 190.]

[7 Magnæ utilitatis est ipsa obscuritas eloquiorum Dei, quia exercet sensum, ut fatigatione dilatetur, et exercitatus capiat quod capere non potest otiosus. Habet quoque adhuc aliud majus, quia scripturæ sacræ intelligentia, si in cunctis esset aperta, vilesceret. In quibusdam locis obscurioribus tanto majore dulcedine inventa reficit, quanto majore labore fatigat animum quæsita.—Opp. T. I. p. 1213. Paris. 1705.]

truth when discovered might give us greater pleasure. But, in
the meanwhile, Gregory does not say, that every thing is obscure
in scripture: yea, he plainly reclaims against such an assertion;
for he says, " In some obscure places." Therefore it is not all, but
some places in scripture, that are obscure, if we believe Gregory.
But what man in his senses would reason thus: Some things in
scripture are obscure, so as not to be understood in a moment;
therefore either nothing can be understood, or the scriptures are
not to be read?   And so much for the Jesuit's second argument.

Bellarmine's THIRD argument is founded upon necessary reasoning.   In scripture, says he, we must consider two things, the
things spoken, and the way in which they are spoken.   Whichever
we regard, there is the greatest difficulty.   For, firstly, the things
are most difficult, namely, the divine mysteries which are delivered
in the scriptures of the Trinity, the incarnation of Christ, and
such like; and Bellarmine asks, why metaphysics are more obscure
and difficult than the other sciences, but because of their subject-
matter?—because, that is, they treat of more obscure and difficult
things? In the same way he concludes that the scriptures are hard
and dark, because hard and dark subjects are treated of therein.   I
answer, by observing that the subjects of scripture are indeed
obscure, hidden, abstruse, and mysterious, yet not in themselves
but to us.   When I say, in themselves—I do not mean to say it
of the nature of the things themselves, as if the things were not
all obscure (for I confess that they are obscure); but what I mean
is, that the subjects of scripture, as they are set forth and delivered
in scripture, are not obscure.   For example, that God is one in
substance and three in persons, that God was made man, and such
like, although they be in themselves, if we regard the nature of the
things themselves, so obscure that they can by no means be perceived by us; yet they are proposed plainly in scripture, if we will
be content with that knowledge of them which God hath chosen to
impart to us.   As to the fact, that many have written with great
acuteness and subtlety of these matters, I say that these subtleties
are of no concern to the people, who can be saved without a
knowledge of them.   Yea, I say besides, that some of them are
impious, and destructive to the very persons who invented them.
Scripture would have us be contented with this plain, perspicuous,
and simple doctrine, which it delivers.   All difficulty therefore, if
difficulty there be, in the things, is ours, and springs from ourselves.
And so much of the obscurity of the things themselves.

Now as to the manner of expression, he proves the scriptures

to be obscure by six reasons. The *first* reason is, because there
are many things in the scriptures which may seem at first sight
contradictory and plainly repugnant to each other ; such as these
two places, Exod. xx. 5, where God threatens that he " will
visit the sins of the fathers upon the children, unto the third and
fourth generation ;" and Ezekiel xviii. 20, where we read that the
very soul which sinneth shall die, and that " the son shall not bear
the iniquity of the father." I answer : Some things may seem
contradictory in scripture, to a man who does not consider
them with sufficient attention ; yet it is certain, nevertheless, that
scripture is in perfect harmony with itself. God willed that some
such shews of contradiction should occur in scripture, that we might
be so the more excited to diligence in reading, meditating upon,
and collating the passages together : wherein whosoever shall use
diligence, as Augustine formerly did in harmonizing the evangelists,
will easily reconcile all those places which seem repugnant to each
other. As to these passages, one readily perceives that they
agree. For it is certain that God punishes men for their own,
and not for other people's sins, as we are told, Ezek. xviii. 20.
Therefore, what is said of the punishment of parents being derived
upon their posterity, Exod. xx. 5, must needs be understood with
this condition, if their posterity continue in their wickedness : for
if they avoid their parents' sins they will not be subjected to their
punishments.—The *second* reason, to prove that the scriptures are
obscure in their manner of expression, is this : because many
words in scripture are ambiguous, and many whole discourses also,
as John viii. 25 : *Principium, qui et loquor vobis.* I answer :
This is, indeed, ambiguous, and false, and utterly ridiculous,—but
only in the Vulgate version : for it should be translated, *quod
loquor*, not *qui loquor*. But in the Greek text all is easy ; for
the words are τὴν ἀρχήν ὅ τι καὶ λαλῶ ὑμῖν, that is, κατὰ τὴν
ἀρχήν. Of which words this meaning is obvious enough : I am
no other than what I have said that I was from the beginning.—
The *third* reason is, because there are many imperfect speeches
and sentences in scripture, as in Rom. v. 12, ὥσπερ occurs without
any thing to correspond to it : where the Jesuit says that the
principal word is wanting. I answer, that I cannot discover what
word he means. I confess that there is a want of an apodosis ;
but the sentence is not so obscure as to be unintelligible, and the
apostle seems afterwards to have subjoined the other member
which corresponds to this.—The *fourth* reason is, because there
are in scripture many sentences put out of order ; as Gen. x. 31,

we find it written thus, " These are the children of Shem, according to their families and their tongues:" but in chap. xi., at the very commencement, the whole earth is said to have been at that time of one lip and one tongue. I answer, first, that in every discourse, and especially in histories, some inversion of the order of time (ὕστερον πρότερον) is common. The rule of Ticonius given long ago[1] was : That some things are related in scripture by way of anticipation, so as to be told briefly before they occurred, in order to prepare and make more intelligible a fuller exposition of each circumstance in its proper place. And Augustine hath admirably explained that place in the following manner, *De Civit. Dei*, Lib. XVI. c. 4 : " Although, therefore, these nations are said to have had their several languages, yet the historian returns back to that time, when they all had but one language ; and setting out from thence, he now explains what occurred to produce a diversity of languages[2]." Secondly, it should not be translated, " The people was of one speech," but, " had been of one speech :" and so indeed Tremellius most fittingly and correctly renders it, so as to remove all ambiguity ; to which version the Hebrew text is no way repugnant.—The *fifth* reason is, because there are in the scriptures some phrases proper and peculiar to the Hebrew tongue, which are to us very hard to be understood, as Ps. lxxxix. 29, " like the days of heaven ;" as if there were day and night in heaven, or as if heaven lived by day and night like men. So Ps. cxix. 108 : " My soul is alway in my hand[3]." I answer, that there are, indeed, in the Hebrew, as in other tongues, certain idioms and phrases proper and peculiar to that language ; yet such nevertheless as to be readily intelligible to those who are practised in the scriptures, and such as express the meaning with a singular sort of emphasis and grace. For who is so dull as not to understand what such modes of speech as these denote ? God spake by the hand of Jeremiah, or, The word of the Lord came by the hand of Zechariah, that is, by the ministry of that prophet. So,

[1 Sextam regulam Tichonius *recapitulationem* vocat . . . . Sic enim dicuntur quædam, quasi sequantur in ordine temporis, vel rerum continuatione narrentur, quum ad priora quæ prætermissa fuerant, latenter narratio revocetur.—Augustin. de Doctr. Christ. Lib. III. c. 36. T. III. p. 81.]

[2 Cum ergo in suis linguis istæ gentes fuisse referantur, redit tamen ad illud tempus narrator, quando una lingua omnium fuit; et inde jam exponit, quid acciderit, ut linguarum diversitas nasceretur.]

[3 This phrase, however, is not peculiar to the Hebrew. It occurs in a fragment of Xenarchus' Pentathlus, preserved by Athenæus, ἐν χειρὶ τὴν ψυχὴν ἔχοντα, δεδιότα.—Deipnos. Lib. XIII. § 24. p. 569. ed. Casaub.]

" His throne is like the days of heaven," that is, shall endure perpetually like heaven itself: and, "my soul is in my hand," that is, is exposed to every danger.—The *sixth* reason why the scriptures are obscure in their mode of expression is this, because there are many tropes, many figures and schemes of rhetoric in scripture, as metaphors, ironies, metonymies, inversions, and such like. I answer and say that scripture is not obscured, but illustrated, by these tropes and figures. For even the rhetoricians themselves teach, that tropes are to be employed for the purpose not of obscuring speech, but of lending to it ornament and light. Augustine, *de Doctr. Christ.* Lib. II. c. 6, writes thus upon this subject: " No one doubts that things are more pleasantly understood by similitudes[4]." Chrysostom, upon Isaiah viii. [v. 7], treating of these words, " Behold the Lord will bring upon them the waters of the river, strong and many, the king of the Assyrians," &c., writes thus : " He hath in a metaphorical way used terms to express both the manners of a native prince and the power of a barbarian. This he does in order (as I have all along told you) to make his discourse more plain[5]." And a little after : " Whenever scripture uses metaphors, it is wont to explain itself more clearly." In the same way Thomas Aquinas, in the first part of Summ. Quæst. I. Artic. 9, respons. ad Arg. 2 : " Whence those things that in one place are spoken under metaphors, are expressed more clearly elsewhere[6]." Therefore, although the scriptures are rendered more obscure in some places by metaphors, yet those metaphors are elsewhere explained so as to leave no obscurity in the discourse or sentence. So much for Bellarmine's third argument.

His FOURTH argument is taken from common experience, and stands thus : If the scriptures (says he) be not obscure, why have Luther himself and the Lutherans published so many commentaries upon the scriptures, and interpreted them so variously, that Osiander asserts that there are twenty most different opinions upon justification subsisting amongst the Confessionists or Lutherans alone? I answer, *first*, that the multitude of commentaries was perhaps not very necessary, because the scriptures might have been understood without so many of them : although those who

[4 Nemo ambigit per similitudines libentius quæque cognosci.—T. III. p. 28.]

[5 ποιεῖ δὲ αὐτὸ, ὅπερ ἔφην ἀεὶ, τὸν λόγον ἐμφαντικώτερον κατασκευάζων . . . πανταχοῦ ἐν ταῖς μεταφοραῖς ἑαυτὴν ἑρμηνεύειν εἴωθεν ἡ γραφή.—Opp. T. I. p. 1084. Eton. 1612.]

[6 Unde ea quæ in uno loco sub metaphoris dicuntur, in aliis locis expressius exponuntur.—Quæst. I. Art. ix. Resp. ad Arg. 2. p. 4. Par. 1639.]

write learned and elaborate commentaries upon scripture deserve
special gratitude from all students of scripture. *Secondly*, I say
that commentaries were published in order that the scriptures might
be better and more easily understood. *Thirdly*, I say that there
is the utmost unanimity amongst the Confessionists (as they call
them) in all things necessary, that is, in the articles of faith, and
especially concerning justification; although perhaps there may be
some dissension amongst them about smaller matters, as the explication of some rather obscure place; which proves not the
obscurity of scripture, but our slowness and inconstancy. *Fourthly*,
it is little matter what Osiander, a man of the utmost levity and
audacity, may have said; whose calumnious temper appears from
his saying, that two methods of justification are collected by the
confessionists from these words, "Abraham believed God, and it
was imputed unto him for righteousness;"—one, of faith; the other,
of imputation: as if, forsooth, being justified by faith and being
justified by imputation were not absolutely the same thing. Certainly there is no difference between these two. These, therefore,
are not two different methods of justification; and the objection of
variety of opinions in a matter of the utmost moment is not true.
This calumny is mentioned by Hosius, in his third book against
Brentius. So also Lindanus, in his *Dubitantius*, and *Prateolus*, in
his *Elenchus Hæreticorum*, Lib. IX. c. 35. And so much of Bellarmine's fourth argument.

   Now follows his FIFTH and last argument, which is taken from
the confession of protestants. Protestants themselves, says he,
confess this same thing, that there are many obscurities in scripture;
as Luther, Brentius, Chemnitz, and the centuriators. I answer : Now
then they absolve us, and openly shew that they themselves are false
and slanderous. What now hath the Jesuit gotten, when through this
whole disputation of his he hath sought to prove and persuade us
by many arguments of that which we concede of our own accord,
and hath bestowed so much trouble upon refuting that which we,
for our parts, never defended? When, therefore, they prove that
the difficulty of understanding scripture is great, they dispute not
against us, who confess that what they conclude from argument,
is affirmed and determined by us already. What our adversaries
ought to have proved was, either that all was obscure, or so few
things plain in the scriptures, that the people ought not to meddle
with them.

   Thus far then we have replied to the arguments of our adversaries.

CHAPTER IV.

THE ARGUMENTS OF OUR WRITERS ATTACKED BY BELLARMINE ARE DEFENDED.

Now follow the arguments upon our side. We shall use in this place those very arguments which Luther and Brentius formerly used against the papists, and to which our Jesuit endeavours to reply. They are nine in number, to which we will add three; and so this whole cause will be concluded in twelve arguments.

We have explained the state of the question above, and have shewn what the papists and we hold respectively. Our opinion is, that the scriptures are not so difficult, but that those who read them attentively may receive from thence advantage and the greatest edification, even laymen, plebeians and the common mass of mankind. This we establish by the following arguments, whereof the FIRST is taken from Deut. xxx. 11, where we read it thus written: " This commandment which I command thee this day is not hidden from thee, nor far from thee : It is not in heaven, that thou shouldest say, Who shall ascend for us into heaven, and take it for us, and tell it unto us that we may do it ? Neither is it beyond the sea, that thou shouldest say, Who shall pass over for us beyond the sea, and take it for us, and tell it unto us that we may do it ? But this word is very nigh thee, in thy mouth, and in thy heart, that thou mayest do it." From which words it is evident that the scriptures may be easily understood. The Jesuit alleges a two-fold answer.

First, he says that the ancients interpret this place, not of the facility of understanding the commandments of God, but of the facility of fulfilling them ; and he brings Tertullian, *contra Marcion*. Lib. iv. Origen, Ambrose, Chrysostom, *Comment.* in 10 Rom. as testimonies ; and he says that thus this place makes against the Lutherans, who deny that the law of God can be fulfilled. I answer, *first*, that it belongs to our purpose now to dispute of the meaning of this place, and inquire how it is used by the apostle in the 10th chapter of the Romans. We have only to see whether it can be concluded from this place that the scripture is easy : which indeed is plain from the words themselves ; first, because it says, that " the commandment is not hidden ;" next, because it says that there is no need that any one should "ascend into heaven and declare it unto us, or that we should *pass over the sea*" and seek it in foreign regions : whereby the sacred writer

takes away the excuses which men are wont to make ; and concludes
that this word is near, in the mouth and in the heart : therefore,
it was not unknown.   Thus the meaning is, that the will of God
was so opened to them in the scriptures, that they could not be
ignorant of it, or allege any excuse of ignorance.   *Secondly*, if that
be true which these fathers say, then that which we contend for
must so much the rather be conceded.   For if the commandments
of God can be easily obeyed, then certainly they can more easily
be understood.   For it is much more easy to understand God's
precepts than to fulfil them ; and one cannot possibly do that which
he does not understand.   But the true meaning of the place is, that
the will of God is plainly revealed to us in the scriptures.   *Thirdly*,
the Lutherans truly deny that the law of God can be fulfilled by
us : nor is it they only that deny this, but those very fathers also
whom Bellarmine alleges, as shall appear afterwards when we come
to that controversy.

The Jesuit's second answer (for he distrusts the former one)
is this, that those words are to be understood of the facility of
understanding the decalogue only, not the whole scripture : for
that the decalogue may be easily understood, since the precepts
of the decalogue are natural laws, and those Jews could easily
know them who had heard them explained by Moses.   I answer :
It is certain that Moses is there speaking of the whole will of
God, which is declared in the whole of the word and scriptures,
and so that this place relates to the entire scripture.   For he carefully exhorts the people to walk in all the ways of the Lord, and
keep all his precepts, ceremonies and judgments.   And, in order
that these might be the better understood, the monuments of scripture are delivered by Moses, as we find in chap. xxxi. 9.   But let
us take what he gives.   For, if he concede the Decalogue to be
plain and clear, it will follow that the historic and prophetic books
are still more easy; which are, for the most part, a sort of commentary upon the Decalogue, and contain in them a plainer and fuller
exposition of its meaning.   The Decalogue is everywhere repeated,
inculcated, explained in the other books of scripture.   Now no one
will say that the text is more easy than the commentary.   But that
Moses does not speak only of the Decalogue is clear from the preceding verse, and from Augustine, Quæst. 54 in Deut. and De Lyra
upon the place, and Hieronymus ab Oleastro, a papist himself, who
says, in his commentary on these words, that Moses speaks of "the
whole law," and then subjoins, "that we should be very grateful to
God for making those things which are necessary to salvation easy,

and reducing them to a small number :" and in what sense he calls them easy, he shews before, where he says, " that the commandments of God are not difficult and hidden, but easy to be understood, said, and done." There is no reason why I should make any larger defence or discourse upon our first argument.

Our SECOND argument is to this effect : In Ps. xix. 9, the word of God is called *clear ;* and Ps. cxix. 105, it is called a *lamp* to our feet, and a *light* to our paths ; and Proverbs vi. 22, Solomon says, " The commandment is a lamp, and the law is light." From these and similar places it is evident, that the word is not so obscure as to be unintelligible, but perspicuous and plain. The Jesuit's answer to this argument is twofold. *First*, he says that this is to be understood of the Lord's precepts, not of the whole scripture. I answer, this is manifestly false : for, in Ps. cxix, the prophet David praises the whole word of God at great length, and prays of God that he may understand it all, not merely some part of it ; and in Ps. xix, he speaks of those two things which manifest and declare God to us, and by which men attain to a knowledge of God, the creatures and the word of God, which latter is there described by him under many titles. For it is called the *Law* or *Doctrine of the Lord, the Testimony of the Lord, the Statutes of the Lord, the Precepts of the Lord, the Fear of the Lord*, by a metonymy, because it teaches the fear and reverence of the Lord ; and this doctrine he declares to be *sound* and *perfect*, and to *give wisdom to the simple.* He therefore did not mean any part, but the whole scripture, the teacher of true and perfect wisdom. Genebrard, upon Ps. xviii, testifies that some interpret the place of the whole scripture ; nor is he speaking of our writers, but either of his own or of ancient ones. Indeed, Jerome is plainly of that opinion, and Lyra and many others. Now the third place is likewise to be understood of the whole doctrine of scripture, which the wise prophet calls a *lamp* and a *light*. *Secondly*, the Jesuit says, that, if these places be understood of the whole scripture, then the scripture is called *clear* and a *lamp*, not because it is easy to be understood, but because it illuminates men when it is understood. I answer, and affirm, that it is therefore called a lamp, because it hath in itself a light and brightness wherewith it illuminates others, unless they be absolutely blind, or wilfully turn away their eyes from this light. A candle is not kindled that it should be set under a bushel, but that it should shine on all who are in the house. The same is the case of the word of God. Ambrose, in his fourteenth discourse

upon Ps. cxviii, writes thus upon this subject : " Our mouth is fed
by the word, when we speak the commandments of the word of
God : our inward eye also is fed by the light of the spiritual lamp,
which shines before us in the night of this world, lest, as walking in
darkness, we should stumble with uncertain steps, and be unable to
find the true way [1]." And Augustine, Concio 23 in Ps. cxviii. hath
these words : " The saying, ' Thy word is a lamp to my feet and
a light to my paths,' denotes the word which is contained in all the
holy scriptures [2]." This entirely overturns the Jesuit's first reply,
wherein he determines that this place and others like it are not to
be understood of the whole scripture, but only of the precepts of
the Lord; for Augustine expressly expounds it of the whole
scripture. The comparison, therefore, of scripture to a lamp is to
be understood to mean that we are thereby illuminated, who by
nature are plunged in utter darkness, and see and understand
nothing of what is pleasing to God. A lamp hath light in itself,
whether men look upon that light or not : so also the scripture is
clear and perspicuous, whether men be illuminated by it, or receive
from it no light whatever. As to what Bellarmine says,—that the
scripture gives light when understood,—it is most certain ; for it
can give no light otherwise. But we affirm that it may be understood by all who desire to know it, and bestow the pains they
ought ; even as a lamp may be seen by all who choose to open
their eyes. Then the scripture is called *lucid*, not only because it
hath light in itself, but because it illuminates us, dispels the
darkness of our minds, and brings us new light, which is what no
lamps can do. For a lamp is beheld by those who have eyes ; but
to those who are blind no lamp shews light. But the scripture is
so full of divine light as to dispel our blindness with its rays, and
make us who before saw nothing in this light to see light. Therefore, Ps. cxix. 130, it is said to illuminate, or bring light to babes.

Our THIRD argument is taken from Matthew v. 14, where Christ
thus addresses his apostles : "Ye are the light of the world."
Therefore, the apostolic doctrine, and consequently the scripture,

[1 Pascitur enim os nostrum verbo, cum loquimur mandata Dei verbi.
Pascitur et oculus noster interior lucernæ spiritalis lumine, quæ nobis in hac
mundi nocte prælucet: ne sicut in tenebris ambulantes, incertis titubemus
vestigiis, et viam veram invenire nequeamus.—§ 5. T. IV. p. 288, ed. Caillau.
Paris. 1836.]

[2 Quod ait, Lucerna, etc. . . . . verbum est quod scripturis sanctis omnibus continetur.—Opp. T. VI. p. 705.]

hath light in itself. So Brentius argues against Soto, and not ill.
The Jesuit answers *first*, that this is not spoken of the light of
doctrine or of the scriptures, but is to be understood of the light of
example and probity of life; and that therefore there is subjoined a
little after, " Let your light so shine before men that they may see
your good works," &c.   I answer, and confess that these words
may be understood of the light of conduct: but I say besides, that
they ought to be understood also of the light of doctrine. And this
is manifest from the circumstance that the apostles are, in the same
place, compared to salt, in respect of their doctrine and preaching.
As the doctrine of the apostles was the salt of the world, so was it
also the light of the world. And whereas the Jesuit objects the ensuing words, " Let your light so shine," &c., I say that those words
also ought principally to be understood of the light of doctrine,
inasmuch as doctrine is the principal work and fruit of an apostle.
And so indeed by the fruit of heretics or false apostles, Matth. vii.
20, their false doctrine and heretical preaching is signified. And in
this manner some of the fathers also expound this place.

Secondly, the Jesuit admits that these words may also be understood of the preaching and doctrine of the apostles, but that this
is there called light, as he before observed that the word was called
a lamp, not because it is easily understood, but because, when understood, it illuminates the mind and instructs us upon the sublimest
subjects. I answer, that nothing can be more futile than this reply.
As if forsooth the sun had no light in itself, unless blind men could
see it.   For scripture in this matter is like the sun, because it
illuminates with that light which it hath in itself all but those who
are either blind, or do not choose to turn their eyes towards it.
Hosius, however, gives another answer, in his 3rd book against the
Prolegomena of Brentius[3], namely, that the preaching of the
apostles was plain and luminous, but that the scripture is not
equally plain; that they preached plainly, but that their writings
are more obscure.   And he uses a comparison to illustrate this:
for the orations of Demosthenes now written are much more
difficult to be understood than when they were delivered, because
many things in them are not now apparent which were then
manifest; so as that it may be truly said that a great part of
Demosthenes is lacking in the orations of Demosthenes: and the
case is the same, he says, with the apostolic writings. Now, as to
the solution of this argument, I wish to know, in the first place,

[3 Opp. Lugd. 1563. p. 550.]

why the Jesuit, who doubtless had it before him, did not choose to
make use of it? It is probable that the cardinal's reply seemed
weak to that acute polemic, and that he therefore chose to go in
quest of another. However, I answer thus: although the living
voice of the apostles, when they preached, had more force in it to
move the passions of men; nevertheless, in regard of the sum of
evangelic doctrine, the same facility and perspicuity appears in
their writings. For if "the word of prophecy" be like a lamp,
that is, clear and plain, as Peter expressly affirms, 2 Pet. i. 19,
(where he understands the writings, not the preaching of the prophets, as we shall afterwards prove,) then certainly the apostolic
word must needs be still clearer and more illustrious. And hence
springs our next argument.

For thus we reason in the FOURTH place: It is written, 2 Pet.
i. 19, "We have a more sure word of prophecy, whereunto ye do well
that ye take heed, as to a lamp shining in a dark place, until the
day dawn and the day-spring arise in your hearts." The prophetic
scripture is like a lamp shining in a dark place; therefore, it is
illustrious and clear. The Jesuit applies precisely the same answer
which he used before, namely, that the words of the prophets are
compared to a lamp, not because they are clear and plain and easy
to be understood; but because then, when they are understood,
they give us light and shew us the way to Christ, who is the sun
of righteousness. I answer: it is nevertheless certain that scripture
is compared to a lamp, because it hath light and clearness in it,
which it also shews to men, unless they are either blind or turn
away their eyes from it, as was said before. For as the sun is
obscure to no one, nor a lamp when lit and set in the midst, save
to the blind and those who shut their eyes; so also is the scripture.
Here also the Jesuit hath departed from Hosius' answer, and made
use of another almost contrary to it, and far more futile. The
prophetic word illuminates us, and leads to Christ, the sun of righteousness, and is therefore called a lamp: as if one used to kindle
a lamp in order to look upon the sun. Hosius says that it is called
a lamp, because there are many things in it clear, and because
what were formerly shadows and enigmas are now declared by the
gospel. What else is this but what we maintain, that there are
many things in scripture so clear that any one may understand
them? Although, indeed, the apostle said that the scripture was
like a lamp, even then when those shadows were not entirely dispelled; for he mentions the prophetic word. The cunning Jesuit

saw that our cause was confirmed by this answer : and therefore he devised another, that it is called a lamp because it illuminates if it be understood ; although it be plain that it is called a lamp because it shines brightly and speaks perspicuously, so as to be capable of being easily seen and understood : as if he were to say, it is not a lamp, unless you see it shining ; whereas it is a lamp, and shines, whether you see it or will not see it. The apostle says that it shines in *a dark place :* therefore it dispels the shades. So the scripture dispels the darkness from our mind, by propounding a clear and luminous doctrine, which refutes our errors and shews to us the certain paths of truth.

Our FIFTH argument is taken from the words of the apostle, 2 Cor. iv. 3, which are these : " If our gospel be hid, it is hid to them that are lost." Therefore the gospel is plain and manifest, and, consequently, also the evangelic scripture, save only to those who, with a blind impulse, rush headlong upon their own destruction. The Jesuit answers, that Paul in that place speaks not of the knowledge and understanding of scripture, but of the knowledge of Christ ; and he says that this book was closed to the people of old, but is open to us. I answer, and say in the first place, that it is evident from the second verse of the same chapter, that Paul speaks of the knowledge of scripture, and therefore of the whole doctrine of the gospel. For he says that he delivered to the Corinthians the gospel most sincerely, without any deceit or false colouring, μὴ δολοῦντες τὸν λόγον τοῦ Θεοῦ, and then presently follow these words : " If our gospel be hid, it is hid to them that are lost ;" as if he had said, our doctrine and preaching was so full and clear that none can fail to understand it, but those who choose to perish and have minds averse to God. Besides, if he confess that the knowledge of Christ is manifest in the scriptures, we desire no more : for this is as much as we require or contend for, that all things necessary to salvation may be easily known from scripture. For if we openly and easily know Christ from the scriptures, we certainly understand from the scriptures all things necessary to salvation. These men concede that Christ is openly set forth in the scriptures : from which admission we shall easily prove that the scriptures should be diligently read to the people, that they may understand Christ from the scriptures ; since they who have obtained him, and learned him aright, want nothing for eternal salvation. The fathers also interpret this place of the perspicuity of the doctrine itself. Chrysostom, in his 8th Homily upon these words,

says, that the apostles had nothing *dark*, συνεσκιασμένον, either in
their life, or in their *doctrine and preaching*, ἐν τῷ κηρύγματι.
Ambrose also understands these words of the whole gospel delivered
by the apostles. So also Œcumenius; for he observes, that it is
as much as if the apostle had said : The fact that many believe not
comes not from our fault, or from the obscurity of the gospel, but
from this, that they are reprobate and unfaithful. Οὐχ ἡμῶν
ἔγκλημα ἢ ἀσαφείας τοῦ εὐαγγελίου, ἀλλὰ τῆς ἐκείνων ἀπωλείας
καὶ τυφλώσεως. Theophylact also says upon this place, that the
light and brilliancy of the gospel is such as to dazzle the eyes of
the impious[1]. Thomas Aquinas upon these words says, that the
cause why many understand it not is not in the gospel, but in the
malice and incredulity of men. Likewise also Cajetan and Catharinus and other papists. Thus the confession of our adversaries
confirms our cause, that the evangelic scripture and doctrine is
clear in itself, obscure or unknown to none but those who are not
of the number of the faithful. Therefore the whole cause of obscurity or ignorance is not the difficulty of the things, but the
blindness and incredulity of men.

Our SIXTH argument is as follows : The sum of the whole scripture, which consists in the precepts of the Decalogue, the Creed, the
Lord's prayer and the sacraments, hath clear testimonies in the
scriptures : therefore the scriptures are clear. The Jesuit puts in
this conclusion,—therefore the whole scripture is manifest ; and
denies the consequence. I reply, if by the whole scripture he understands every several passage of scripture, we frame no such
argument ; but if by the whole scripture he means the sum of
doctrine necessary for any man's salvation, then we acknowledge
the argument, and say that the whole is clear. As to what he subjoins,—that, if the articles of faith were clear in scripture, then there
would not be so many controversies about them, and hence collects
that there are not such luminous testimonies to them in scripture ;
I answer, that this is weak reasoning ; because on these grounds
the scriptures would have nothing whatever certain, plain, or
evident. For there is nothing in scripture so plain that some men
have not doubted it ; as, that God is Almighty, that he created
heaven and earth, that Christ was born of the Virgin Mary, conceived of the Holy Ghost, and so forth : these are indeed plainly
and openly set down in scripture, and yet there are controversies

[1 ὥσπερ εἴ τις ὀφθαλμιῶντά τινα ἀποκλείσειε τοῦ μὴ τὰς ἀκτῖνας τοῦ ἡλίου
ἰδεῖν, ἵνα μὴ καὶ προσβλαβείη.—p. 355. Lond. 1636.]

about them. Things therefore are not presently obscure, concerning which there are many controversies; because these so manifold disputes arise rather from the perversity and curiosity of the
human mind, than from any real obscurity. The apostle says that
the minds of infidels are blinded by the devil, lest they should see
that brilliant light and acquiesce in it : which is most true of our
adversaries.

Our SEVENTH argument stands thus : There is this difference
between the new and the old Testaments, that the old Testament
is like a book closed and sealed, as we find in Isaiah xxix. 11, but
the new Testament is like a book opened, as we read, Revel. v.
We do not use this argument to prove that the whole scripture
was obscure and unknown to the old Jewish people, but to shew that
the knowledge of Christians is now much clearer than was formerly
that of the Jews. The Jesuit answers by saying that this is true,
not of the whole scripture, but only of the mysteries of our redemption which is wrought by Christ. I answer, if he confess that
the scripture is like a book opened, so far as the mysteries of our
redemption are concerned, there is certainly no more that we
need to demand : for from this admission it will follow immediately
that all things necessary to salvation are plain in the scriptures;
which is the foundation of our defence. Surely he was overcome
and constrained by the force of truth to publish this open and ingenuous confession. But now, if the mysteries of our redemption
are clear in the scriptures, why should it not be lawful for the
people to read the scriptures and have them constantly in their
hands, so as to recognise the goodness of Christ, and understand
the plan of their redemption and salvation ? Jerome, in his Commentary upon Ezekiel xliv. writes thus upon this subject : " Before
the Saviour assumed a human body, and humbled himself to receive
the form of a servant, the law and the prophets and the whole
knowledge of scripture was closed up, Paradise was shut up. But
after that he hung upon the cross, and said to the thief, 'To-day
shalt thou be with me in Paradise,' immediately the vail of the
temple was rent, and all things were set open ; and, the covering
being removed, we can say, 'We all with open face beholding the
glory of the Lord are changed into the same image from glory to
glory'[2]." As to what the same Jerome writes elsewhere (namely,

[2 Priusquam Salvator humanum corpus assumeret, et humiliaret se for-
mam servi accipiens, clausa erat Lex et Prophetæ, et omnis scientia scripturarum, clausus erat Paradisus. Postquam autem ille pependit in cruce, et

in his Epist. 13, de Instit. Monach. to Paulinus), that a vail is placed
not upon the face of Moses only, but of the apostles and evangelists
also ; he speaks there of the difficulty of believing without the Holy
Spirit, but not of the difficulty of understanding, as is plain from
that same place. Let it suffice to have said so much upon our
seventh argument.

Our EIGHTH argument is to this effect : The fathers proved their
opinions out of the scriptures. Therefore the scriptures are clearer
than the writings and commentaries of the fathers : for no one proves
what is unknown by what is still more unknown. Luther hath this
argument in the Preface of his Articles condemned by Leo X. The
Jesuit answers, that the scriptures are indeed, in respect of their
truth, clearer and more open than the writings of the fathers, but
not in respect of the words. Which surely is a foolish answer : for
to say that the scriptures are clearer than the fathers in respect of
their truth, is nothing more than saying that they are truer. But
what sort of a distinction is this ? If the truth of scripture be
clearer, how can the words be more obscure ? For it is from the
words that the truth arises. If therefore he confess that the scriptures are plainer than the commentaries of the fathers, in respect
of their truth, then he concedes that the truth is plainer in the
scriptures than in the writings of any father ; which is sufficient.
And doubtless if we will compare the scripture with the writings of
the fathers, we shall generally find greater obscurity and difficulty
in the latter than in the former. There is no less perspicuity in
the Gospel of John or in the Epistles of Paul, than in Tertullian,
in Irenæus, in certain books of Origen and Jerome, and in some
other writings of the fathers. But in all the schoolmen there is such
obscurity as is nowhere found in scripture. " The words of scripture," says he, " are more obscure than the words of the fathers."
Even if there were some obscurity in the words of scripture greater
than in those of the fathers, it would not nevertheless be a just
consequence, that the scriptures were so obscure that they should
not be read by the people. This should rather rouse men to an
attentive reading than deter them from reading altogether. Besides,
the scriptures speak of necessary things no less plainly than any
fathers, or even much more plainly, because the Holy Spirit excels
in all powers of expression. Where has Augustine or Chrysostom,

locutus est ad latronem, Hodie mecum eris in Paradiso, statim velum templi
scissum est, et aperta sunt omnia, ablatoque velamine dicimus, Nos omnes
revelata facie gloriam Dei contemplantes in eandem imaginem transforma-
mur, a gloria in gloriam.—Opp. T. v. p. 536.]

or any father, written more plainly that Christ hath delivered men from their sins and from eternal punishment, than the evangelists, than Paul, than Peter, than the rest of those whose ministry the Holy Ghost hath used in writing the scriptures? Surely all necessary things are so plainly set forth in the scripture, that he who does not understand them in scripture will never be instructed by any commentaries of the fathers.

Now follows our NINTH argument, which is this: Formerly, in the earliest times of the church, there were no commentaries upon the scriptures extant, but the fathers read them without commentaries; and yet, even then, the scriptures were understood: therefore they are plain and easy in themselves. This is also an argument of Luther's. The Jesuit answers, that the first fathers consulted the apostles themselves, and learned from them the sense of scripture, and afterwards wrote commentaries. And he shews out of Jerome, that commentaries on the Apocalypse were published from the very first by Justin Martyr and Irenæus. I answer: It is certain that there was a time when the church both read and understood the scriptures without commentaries. For they can produce none before Origen, who published any commentaries upon the scriptures; and he lived two hundred years after Christ. Therefore the church was all that time without commentaries. As to his objection from Jerome's catalogue, article Jo-HANNES[1], that Justin and Irenæus wrote commentaries on the Apocalypse, the statement is untrue. For Jerome does not affirm this, but only says that they interpreted the Apocalypse. Perhaps, therefore, they expounded some obscure places in the Apocalypse; but how correctly, appears from the circumstance of their establishing the error of the Chiliasts by the authority of this book. But let us grant them to have written something upon this book: will it therefore follow that they published commentaries upon the whole scripture? By no means. Certainly the Apocalypse is a small book compared with the whole of scripture. Besides, the Jews before Christ had no commentaries on the prophets, and yet they understood them. The scriptures, therefore, are not so obscure as the papists wish them to appear. We confess, indeed, that we owe a deep debt of gratitude to those who have written learned commentaries, because by their means we understand scripture with increased facility; but yet that the scriptures may be understood without them, is clear from the fact that they were understood

[1] Scripsit Apocalypsim, quam interpretantur Justinus Martyr et Irenæus.]

before any commentaries were published : and if at the present day
no commentaries remained, the scriptures would nevertheless be
understood.

These are the arguments of Luther and Brentius. We will
now add three arguments of our own : whereof the first, which
shall count as the TENTH, is this : If the scriptures be so obscure
and difficult to be understood, that they cannot be read with advantage by the people, then this hath happened, either because the
Holy Spirit could not write more plainly, or because he would not.
No one will say that he could not : and that he would not, is
repugnant to the end of writing ; because God willed that they
should be written and committed to letters for the very end, that
we should learn what was written, and thence derive a knowledge
of his will; as is plain from Rom. xv. 4, "Whatsoever things were
written, were written for our learning :" where Paul speaks not
only of the learned, but of the whole multitude of the faithful.
The scriptures, therefore, are clear.   Besides, God does not mock
us when he bids us read the scriptures ; but he would have us read
the scriptures in order that we may know and understand them.
Again, the scripture is called a rule, a standard, a mark, laid open
to the eyes of all: it is, therefore, of necessity easy and clear. Thus
then we briefly conclude this argument.   The Holy Spirit willed
the scriptures to be consigned to writing in order that we might
understand them ; and that this was the end which he proposed
there are many things in the scriptures themselves that testify :
therefore, they are so written as to be intelligible by us, or else the
Holy Spirit hath not gained his end; which cannot be thought
without impiety.

Our ELEVENTH argument is on this wise. There are two classes
of men,—the faithful, and the infidels.   To infidels everything is
obscure; for they understand nothing aright, but are involved in the
thickest darkness.   But the faithful understand every thing, the
not understanding of which would involve the loss of true salvation :
they are ignorant of nothing necessary to salvation.   So Christ,
John x. 27, " My sheep hear my voice ;" that is, they understand
it.   So Jeremiah xxxi. 34, " All shall know the Lord, from the
least to the greatest."   So Christ says to his disciples, Luke viii.
10, " To you it is given to know the mysteries of the kingdom of
God," &c.   So Paul, 1 Cor. ii., last verse, "We have the mind of
Christ."   The faithful, therefore, understand, acknowledge, approve
the scriptures.   And the scriptures are such in themselves as by

IV.]QUESTION THE FOURTH.393

their own light to turn the eyes of all towards them, and cause themselves not only to be understood, but also to be received with faith. For they not only have light in themselves, but they illuminate others also with their light. So the Apostle, 2 Cor. iv. 6, attributes not only φῶς [light], but φωτισμὸς [illumination] also to the scripture. So great, then, is the brightness of scripture, that it opens even the eyes of us who are blind by nature, and restores clear sight to us.

There remains now our LAST argument, which is founded in human testimonies, that is, those of the fathers; which, although it have no great force in itself, must yet be of great avail against our adversaries, who studiously affect such arguments in every question. First, Augustine upon Psal. viii. says: "God hath made the scriptures stoop to the capacity of babes and sucklings[1]." And, *de Doctr. Christ.* Lib. II. c. 6, he writes thus: "The Holy Spirit hath so modified the scriptures, combining ornament with utility, as to provide for our hunger in the easier places, and prevent satiety by the more obscure. For scarce anything can be gotten out of those obscurities which may not be found spoken elsewhere with the utmost plainness[2]." The Jesuit says that it is not for nothing that Augustine added here the qualification *fere;* because, says he, there are many things obscurely propounded in scripture, which are nowhere explained in other places. I answer: Though I should concede this, yet are these things such as may be unknown without loss or danger of losing salvation. Meanwhile he gives no answer to Augustine, who says in express words, that the Holy Spirit hath provided for our hunger in the plainer places; that is, that we can draw and obtain from the open places of scripture what suffices to dispel our hunger. But that hunger is not removed before we thoroughly understand the things necessarily required for our salvation. The same Augustine also, in his discourse of Blasphemy against the Holy Spirit, says that "we are fed in the plain places of scripture, and exercised in the obscure ones." Precisely to the same effect, Tract. 44. in Johan.: "He feeds us with the clear, and exercises us with the hidden[3]." Therefore those things which can feed

[1 Inclinavit ergo scripturas Deus ad infantium et lactentium capacitatem.—T. v. p. 54.]

[2 Magnifice et salubriter Spiritus Sanctus ita scripturas modificavit, ut locis apertioribus fami occurreret, obscurioribus autem fastidia detergeret. Nihil enim fere de illis obscuritatibus eruitur, quod non planissime dictum alibi reperiatur.—T. III. p. 28.]

[3 Pascit manifestis, exercet occultis.]

us to life and salvation are set down plainly in the scriptures; and those which are not so plain are yet not such as to be unintelligible, but to require greater diligence and industry. And, *de Doctr. Christ.* Lib. II. c. 9, he writes thus: "Amongst those things which are clearly set down in scripture, are found all those which make the sum of faith and practice, that is to say, hope and charity[1]." Wherein we may observe four things. *First*, what things are necessary to salvation,—namely, a right faith and a pious life. *Secondly*, whence these may be learned,—namely, from the scriptures. *Thirdly*, If we ask whether all things requisite for these two may be learned from the scripture, or only some? Augustine answers, that all things necessary both for a right faith and pious life are delivered in scripture. *Fourthly*, If we ask, whether they are set down plainly or obscurely in scripture? Augustine answers, Plainly. What could possibly be more clearly expressed?

The same author, in his piece *de Peccat. meritis et remissione*, Lib. II. c. 36, discoursing of the generation of the soul and of other sublime and difficult matters, observes: "Although I could not tell concerning any of these how it could be demonstrated or explained, yet I believe that here also the authority of the divine oracles would be most clear, if a man could not be ignorant of them without the loss of promised salvation[2]." Where he declares that he does not doubt but that those points, which cannot be unknown without the loss of salvation, may be proved by the clearest authority of scripture. So constant is he to his principle, that all things necessary to salvation are plainly set down in scripture. So also in his Book *de Utilitate credendi*, c. 6, he writes thus of this matter: "Trust me, what is in those scriptures is lofty and divine. There is in them certainly truth, and instruction most suited to refresh and restore the soul, and so modified as that no one shall be unable to draw thence enough for himself, if he only approach to draw with piety and devotion, as true religion demands[3]." If there

[1 Vide supra.]

[2 Etsi enim quodlibet horum, quemadmodum demonstrari et explicari possit, ignorem, illud tamen credo, quod etiam hinc divinorum eloquiorum clarissima auctoritas esset, si homo illud sine dispendio promissæ salutis ignorare non posset.—Opp. T. XIII. p. 88.]

[3 Quidquid est (mihi crede) in scripturis istis, altum et divinum est. Inest omnino veritas, et reficiendis instaurandisque animis accommodatissima disciplina, et plane ita modificata, ut nemo inde haurire non possit quod sibi satis est, si modo ad hauriendum devote ac pie, ut vera religio poscit, accedat.—T. X. p. 63.]

be no one who cannot draw what is sufficient for him from the
scriptures, they are certainly impious who pluck and steal them
away from the people under the pretext of their being obscure and
difficult. Why do they not permit men to draw their salvation from
the scriptures, but because they are enemies to men's salvation?
And, in his fifth Book against Julian the Pelagian, c. 1, he blames
that heretic for exaggerating the difficulty of the scriptures, and
saying that they were only suitable for the learned[4]: which Thesis
when our adversaries maintain, they resemble the heretical more
than the catholic doctors. Let these testimonies suffice from
Augustine.

We bring forward Chrysostom in the second place, who hath
clear testimonies in our favour. He, in his third Homily upon
Lazarus, compares the apostles with the philosophers, and says
that the philosophers wrote obscurely, but the prophets and apostles
so plainly, that any one may learn and understand them by themselves. His words are these : " What then, they say, if we do not
understand what is contained in books? Yet by all means, although
thou understandest not what is hidden there, yet great sanctity is
gained by the very perusal of it. Although indeed it is impossible
that you should be equally ignorant of all. The grace of the
Spirit hath so disposed and arranged them, that publicans, fisher-
men, tent-makers, pastors and apostles, the ignorant and illiterate,
may be saved by these books, lest any of the uninstructed should
fly to this excuse of difficulty ; that the things spoken might be
easily discerned by all ; that the craftsman, and the servant, and
the widow, and the most unlearned of men, might gain some benefit
and advantage from hearing them read[5]."

Then he subjoins the comparison of the philosophers with the
prophets and apostles. " For not, like the Gentiles, for vain glory,
but for the salvation of their hearers, did they whom God from the
beginning deemed worthy of the grace of the Holy Spirit, compose all their works. The philosophers indeed, who are strangers
to God, the masters of speech, the orators and writers of books,
seeking not the common good, but aiming only at gaining admiration for themselves, even when they said something useful, yet
even this an obscurity which they ever affected involved as in a
certain cloud of wisdom. But the apostles and prophets took the

[4 Exaggeras quam sit difficilis paucisque conveniens eruditis sanctarum
cognitio literarum.—Opp. Anti-Pelag. T. II. p. 241. Lovan. 1648.]
[5. Tom. I. pp. 737. 740. Paris. 1718. 38.]

contrary way, and exposed to all the clear and open declarations which they made, as the common teachers of the world, so as that every one, by the mere perusal, might be enabled to understand what was said." Thus Chrysostom. The Jesuit endeavours to break the force of this testimony, and maintains that Chrysostom said this in order to rouse many from their lethargy, and excite them to read the scriptures, who could, if they chose, read them with benefit and advantage. Where he confesses that many can read the scriptures with advantage; which is sufficient: for these many are not only learned, but unlearned also; since it is plain enough that Chrysostom speaks not merely of the learned, but of the unlearned also: otherwise his comparison would be utterly inept and improper, because even the philosophers themselves were intelligible to the learned. Chrysostom says that the scriptures are plainer than the books of the philosophers; therefore, the scriptures may be read with benefit even by the unlearned. As to what Chrysostom advises in the same place,—that we should go frequently over the obscure passages, and, if we cannot even so understand what is said, then repair to some learned men and consult them,—this we also willingly concede, and earnestly approve, and consider ourselves very fortunate if by any means, after frequent reading and long meditation, we can obtain a knowledge of those matters. However, the same father elsewhere asserts that all things necessary to salvation are plain and manifest in the scriptures; for thus he writes in his 3rd Homily upon 2 Thessalonians: "All things are clear and plain in the divine scriptures[1]." And because this might seem a paradox, he afterwards explains himself by saying, πάντα τὰ ἀναγκαῖα, "all necessary things are clear and plain;" so that we have no need of homilies and sermons, except διὰ τὴν ῥαθυμίαν ἡμῶν, that is, on account of our own sloth and negligence. And he removes that objection which the people are wont to make: "But, you will say, I know not what is set down in the divine scriptures. But why? Are they in Hebrew, or Latin, or any foreign language? Are they not spoken in Greek? Yes, you say, but obscurely. Tell me, I beseech you, what is that obscurity?" The Jesuit answers, that he is speaking only of the historical books; which is false: for he says of *all things necessary to salvation*, πάντα δῆλα, σαφῆ, εὐθέα, "they are all manifest,

[1 Πάντα σαφῆ καὶ εὐθέα τὰ παρὰ ταῖς θείαις γραφαῖς· πάντα τὰ ἀναγκαῖα δῆλα.—T. XI. p. 528.]

clear, easy," which are contained not only in the historical, but also in the other books and parts of scriptures. The same father writes thus in the Prologue to the epistle to the Romans : " Wherefore, if ye also will resolve to bestow a studious and diligent perusal upon this piece, there will be nothing more required by you, οὐδενὸς ἑτέρου δεήσεσθε, for true is the word of Christ, who says, ' Seek and ye shall find ; knock and it shall be opened to you '."

And, whereas some suppose the reading of the scriptures to be pernicious to the people, Chrysostom in the same place removes this scruple also, and says that this knowledge is highly necessary for all, and removes infinite evils ; but that ignorance of the scriptures is the mother of all errors and heresies. For thus he writes : ἐντεῦθεν τὰ μυρία ἔφυ κακά, ἀπὸ τῶν γραφῶν ἀγνοίας. " Hence have sprung infinite evils, that is, from very ignorance of the sacred scriptures ; hence hath grown the prevailing pest of heresies ; hence in many the neglect of life, hence useless and unprofitable labours. For even as those who are deprived of the use of the light of this world can never go straight ; so they who do not turn their eyes to the rays of the scriptures of God, do of necessity run frequently into many errors, just as if they walked in darkness replete with perils." The same author, in his first Homily upon John, writes thus : " Therefore he (John) covered not his doctrine in mist and darkness, as they (the philosophers) shrouded their perverse opinions in obscurity as in a vail. But his doctrine is clearer and more lucid than the rays of the sun, and therefore propagated to all men." And, in his first Homily upon Matthew, he says, that " the scriptures are easily intelligible and plain even to the slave, the rustic, the widow, the child, and the man of weakest intellect." What class of men, therefore, is there to whom the scriptures are so difficult as our adversaries slanderously pretend. Slaves, rustics, women, boys, and people of the meanest understanding, may be engaged with advantage in the perusal of them. Therefore the scriptures have great perspicuity and facility, and should not be taken away from the people on the pretext of their obscurity.

Justin Martyr, in his Dialogue with Trypho the Jew, when employed in proving the Deity of Christ, thus addresses those with whom he held the conference : " Attend to those things which I shall quote from the sacred scriptures, and which are such as to need merely a hearing, and not any exposition[2]." Where he says that the scriptures are so easy that he who hears them merely, im-

[2 Pag. 274, E. Paris. 1636.]

mediately understands them.   For the Greek words shew that this
is affirmed of the scriptures themselves, not merely of those matters
which he mentioned out of the scriptures: προσέχετε οἷς μέλλω
ἀναμιμνήσκειν ἀπὸ τῶν ἁγίων γραφῶν, οὐδὲ ἐξηγηθῆναι δεομένων,
ἀλλὰ μόνον ἀκουσθῆναι.   Irenæus, Lib. III. 15, affirms the doctrine of the apostles to be "manifest and firm, keeping nothing
back[1]."   Thus it is both perspicuous and perfect.   Clemens Alexandrinus, in his προτρεπτικὸς λόγος, or exhortation to the Gentiles,
writes thus: "Hear ye that are far off, hear also ye that are nigh.
The word is concealed from none; the light is common, it beams
on all men; there is nothing Cimmerian in the word.   Let us haste
to salvation, to regeneration[2]."   Jerome, in his Commentary upon
Psalm lxxxvi., compares the apostles and prophets with the philosophers, as Chrysostom did above, and says that Plato wrote for few,
because scarcely three men understood him; but the apostles and
prophets, whom he there calls the princes of the church and the
princes of Christ, "wrote not for a few, but for the whole people,
that all might understand."   Ambrose, in his seventh epistle, at the
beginning, says that Paul so explains himself in most of his discourses, that he who treats of him finds nothing to add; "and, if he
would say something, must discharge the office of a grammarian
rather than of a reasoner[3]."

Basil, in his shorter definitions, Quæst. 45, where he handles
the question,—If a man, having heard the Lord (who had said,
"The servant that knew his Lord's will and did it not, neither prepared himself to do his will, shall be beaten with many stripes; but
he who knew not, and did things worthy of stripes, shall be beaten
with few stripes,") should on that account studiously neglect the
knowledge of the divine will, hath he any comfort?—declares it evident, that he who is such, falsely pretends ignorance, and inevitably
incurs judgment for his sin.   For, saith the Lord, "if I had not
come among them and spoken to them, they had not had sin; but
now they have no cloak for their sin."   Then he subjoins what makes

[1 Igitur testificatio ejus [Lucæ] vera, et doctrina Apostolorum manifesta
et firma, et nihil subtrahens.—Pag. 273, B. Paris. 1675.]

[2 Ἀκούσατε οὖν οἱ μακρὰν, ἀκούσατε οἱ ἐγγύς· οὐκ ἀπεκρύβη τινὰς ὁ λόγος·
φῶς ἐστι κοινὸν, ἐπιλάμπει πᾶσιν ἀνθρώποις· οὐδεὶς Κιμμέριος ἐν λόγῳ. σπεύ-
σωμεν εἰς σωτηρίαν, ἐπὶ τὴν παλιγγενεσίαν.—p. 56, D. Paris. 1629.]

[3 In plerisque ita se ipse suis exponit sermonibus, ut is qui tractat nihil
inveniat quod adjiciat suum; ac si velit aliquid dicere, grammatici magis quam
disputatoris fungatur munere.—Ep. 37. (class. 1.) T. VIII. p. 448. Paris. 1839.]

for us in this controversy : τῆς ἁγίας γραφῆς πανταχοῦ πᾶσι τὸ θέλημα τοῦ Θεοῦ διαγγελλούσης⁴. " The sacred scripture every where declares to us the will of God. Therefore he who is such will not be condemned with a lesser judgment along with those who are in ignorance, but with a severer, with those of whom it is written, 'They are like the deaf adder that stoppeth her ears, lest she should hear the voice of the charmers and the enchanter, while she is skilfully charmed by him'." The same author, in the beginning of his Commentary upon the Psalms, observes : " From scripture, as from a common repository of drugs to heal our souls, ἐν κοινῷ τῶν ψυχῶν ἰατρείῳ, every man may choose a remedy suited to his complaint, each may be his own physician." Epiphanius, Hæres. 69, says : " All things are clear and full of light in the divine scripture⁵," &c. And Hær. 76, " All things are clear in the divine scriptures to those who will approach with pious reasoning to the divine word :" πάντα σαφῆ ἐν τῇ θείᾳ γραφῇ τοῖς βουλομένοις εὐσεβεῖ λογισμῷ προσέρχεσθαι τῷ θείῳ λόγῳ⁶.

Cyril of Alexandria, in his seventh Book against Julian, answering an objection from the simplicity of the scriptures, says that they were so written purposely, in order that they might be known and understood by every one. His words are these : " But some one will say, that the divine scripture hath a style and diction common to all, vulgar and trite ; whereas the things of the Greeks are expressed elegantly, and abound in grace and eloquence. We say, therefore, that the prophetical and Mosaic books are expressed in the Hebrew language ; and, in order that they might be known to all, small and great, are usefully committed to a familiar diction, so as to transcend no man's capacity⁷." The same father also, in his ninth book against the same antagonist, says that nothing in the scriptures is difficult to those who use them as they ought ; but that every sentence in them is inaccessible to Julian and such as he.

[⁴ Basil. Opp. T. II. p. 542, A. B. 1618.]
[⁵ τῶν ῥητῶν πάντῃ ἐν Πνεύματι Ἁγίῳ κατηυγασμένων.—T. I. p. 763. ed. Petav.]
[⁶ Ibid. p. 920, A.]
[⁷ Sed dicet aliquis quod divina scriptura communem omnibus et vulgarem ac protritam habet dictionem, res autem Græcorum diserte dicuntur, et abundant gratia et eloquentia. Dicimus igitur, quod lingua quidem Hebræorum Prophetica dicta sunt et Mosaica: ut autem omnibus essent notæ parvis et magnis, utiliter familiari sermone commendatæ sunt, ita ut nullius captum transcendant.—col. 160. Basil. 1569.]

Fulgentius, in his discourse concerning the confessors, writes thus upon this subject: " In which commandments (that is, the divine), as in most rich viands, the spiritual abundance of heavenly dainties is so exuberant, that there is in the word of God plenty for the perfect to eat, and plenty also for the babe to suck. For there is both the milk of the suckling, whereby the tender infancy of the faithful may be nourished, and the solid food whereby the robust youth of the perfect may gain spiritual increase of holy vigour. There provision is made universally for the salvation of all whom the Lord designs to save. There is what suits every age ; there is what fits every profession. There we hear the precepts which we should perform : there we know the rewards we are to hope for. There is the command which teaches by the letter, and instructs us unto knowledge : there the promise which draws us by grace, and leads us to glory[1]." Gregory the great, in the epistle to Leander, which may be found at the end of the works of Gregory, compares the scripture to a river, in which " the elephant may swim, and yet the lamb may walk."

Bernard, in his discourse upon those words of Wisdom, " The Lord hath led the just by straight paths," writes in this manner : " The ways of the Lord are right ways, fair ways, full ways, plain ways : right, without error, because they lead to life ; fair, without soil, because they teach purity ; full in multitude, because the whole world is now within the net of Christ ; plain, without difficulty, because they freely bestow sweetness[2]."

The same may be proved even from the papists themselves. For Andradius, in his second book of orthodox explications, says that those things which are the chief heads of faith are to be held explicitly even by the ignorant people; and that there is no degree of rudeness so

[1 In quibus denuo mandatis, tanquam ditissimis ferculis, sic cœlestium deliciarum copia spiritalis exuberat, ut in verbo Dei abundet quod perfectus comedat; abundet etiam quod parvulus sugat. Ibi est enim simul et lacteus potus, quo tenera fidelium nutriatur infantia, et solidus cibus quo robusta perfectorum juventus spiritualia sanctæ virtutis accipiat incrementa. Ibi prorsus ad salutem consulitur universis quos Dominus salvare dignatur. Ibi est quod omni ætati congruat: ibi quod omni professioni conveniat, etc.— p. 649. Antwerp. 1574.]

[2 Viæ Domini viæ rectæ, viæ pulchræ, viæ plenæ, via planæ : rectæ sine errore, quia ducunt ad vitam; pulchræ sine sorde, quia docent munditiam; plenæ multitudine, quia totus jam mundus est intra Christi sagenam ; planæ sine difficultate, quia donant suavitatem.—Sermones de Divers. Serm. xx. 1. Bernard. Opp. T. iii. p. 41. Paris. 1835.]

great as to exempt an ignorance of these from crime, though it suffice
to hold the rest implicitly. Therefore the chief heads of faith,
even according to Andradius, are plainly proposed in scripture, and
none ought to be ignorant of them, however rude and unlearned.
Catharinus, in his commentary on 2 Tim. iii. says, that to him who
hath faith the scriptures " make themselves easy, as much as may
be, and familiar to be understood." Likewise Sixtus Senensis,
Biblioth. Lib. 6, Annotat. 151, distributes the scriptures into two
classes, one of which he allows to be " plain and clear, as containing the first and highest principles of what should be believed,
and the chief precepts of good morals, and easy examples; of which
kind are the moral sentences, and some of the sacred narratives,
useful for moulding our manners[3]." Thus our opponents confess
that those things are plain in scripture, which contain the chief
heads of faith, and precepts and examples of practice. We accept
this admission ; nor did we ever think or write that every thing
was plain in scripture. For it is sufficient for the people to learn
from the scriptures those chief principles of faith, which are necessary for every man's salvation, and imitate the precepts and examples of a life becoming Christians, which occur everywhere in the
sacred pages. For we do not say that the scriptures are simply or
universally plain, but in the chief and most necessary things, so as
to be capable of being read with benefit by the people. Our
adversaries allow that the scriptures are clear in those things
which are the chief and highest principles of faith or elements of virtue, and yet do not permit the people to read the
scriptures. What can be more iniquitous ? Indeed all the papists
in their books, when they seek to prove any thing, boast everywhere that they can bring arguments against us from the most
luminous, plain, clear and manifest testimonies of scripture : therefore, there are many very clear passages in scripture. For in
every dispute their common phrases are,—This is clear,—This is
plain,—This is manifest in the scriptures, and such like. Surely
when they speak thus, they ignorantly and unawares confess the
perspicuity of the scriptures even in the greatest questions and controversies. And so far of the fourth question.

[3 Utpote quæ prima summaque rerum credendarum principia, ac præci-
pua bene vivendi præcepta et exemplo cognitu facilia complectantur, ut sunt
morales sententiæ, et sacræ quædam historiæ formandis moribus utiles.]

[WHITAKER.]   26

THE FIRST CONTROVERSY.

QUESTION V.

CONCERNING THE INTERPRETATION OF SCRIPTURE.

CHAPTER I.

THE STATE OF THE QUESTION.

It is written, John v. 39, Ἐρευνᾶτε τὰς γραφὰς, " Search the scriptures." Christ our Saviour said this to excite the Jews, and all of us also, to investigate the true sense of scripture. For the scripture consists not in the bare words, but in the sense, interpretation, and meaning of the words. This is plain from Basil, in his second book against Eunomius, where he says, that " piety is not in the sound of the air, but in the force and meaning of the things denoted[1]." The same appears also from Jerome's commentary upon the first chapter of the Galatians, where he writes thus : " Let us not think that the Gospel is in the words of scripture, but in the sense ; not on the surface, but in the marrow ; not in the leaves of speech, but in the root of reason[2]." Since scripture therefore is concerned not merely with the words, but the true sense of the words, which we may rightly call the very life and soul of scripture ; it is plain that this precept of Christ, wherein he bids us " search the scriptures," is to be understood of the sense and meaning of the scriptures, and not of the bare words alone. Hence arises this question, concerning which we dispute with the papists, — Whence the true interpretation of scripture is to be sought? Here we must seek first the state of the question ; and then come to the arguments on both sides. The Tridentine fathers, in their fourth session, command that no one shall dare to interpret holy scripture contrary to that sense which holy

[1 I cannot find this in the place specified; and suppose there is a mistake in the reference.]

[2 Ne putemus in verbis scripturarum esse evangelium, sed in sensu; non in superficie, sed in medulla; non in sermonum foliis, sed in radice rationis. —T. VII. p. 386.]

mother church hath held, and holds, to whom (as they say) it belongs to judge of the true sense and interpretation of scripture; or contrary to the unanimous consent of the fathers. They seem, therefore, to determine that the interpretation of scripture is the privilege of the church, and that that is the true one which agrees with the fathers. But still the matter is left in doubt. For we inquire further, what is this church; and who are these fathers? We must, therefore, consult other papists in order to gain a full and perfect knowledge of the true state of the question. I mean to follow in this matter especially the Jesuit Bellarmine and Stapleton: and I will divide the whole course of this question into two parts, treating, first, of the authority and supreme tribunal for interpreting scripture, with whom it is lodged; next, of the means to be used in the interpretation of scripture. But first we must premise something in the way of prolegomena, which are of great importance to the understanding of the question.

CHAPTER II.

OF CERTAIN PRELIMINARIES, NECESSARY FOR UNDERSTANDING
THE STATE OF THE QUESTION.

OUR FIRST preliminary observation shall be upon the number of the senses of scripture, which the fathers determine to be various; that is, the historical, which they have styled also the grammatical or literal sense, the ætiological, the analogical, and the allegorical. Upon this fourfold interpretation of scripture consult Augustine, *de Utilitate Credendi*, c. 3 : where he says that it is the historic sense, when we are told what was done, and what not done ; that scripture is expounded ætiologically, when it is shewn why any thing was done or said; analogically, when the agreement of both Testaments is explained ; allegorically, when we are taught that some things which are written are not to be taken in the letter, but understood figuratively. Others, however, enumerate other kinds of mystical senses, as the tropological, the allegorical, and anagogic; of which we read a great deal in Origen and the rest. The Jesuit divides all these senses into two species; the historic or literal, and the mystic or spiritual. He defines the historic or literal, as that which the words present immediately ; and the mystic or spiritual, that which is referred to something besides what the words express ; and this he says is either tropological, or anagogic, or allegorical.

26—2

Thomas Aquinas, in the first part of his Sum. Quæst. I. Art. 10, says out of Gregory, Moral. Lib. xx. c. 1, that it is the peculiar property of scripture, and of no other authors, that not only the words, but the things also, have a signification; and this he says is denoted by that book mentioned Ezek. ii. 10, and Revel. v. 1, which was "written within and without." The words of Gregory cited by Thomas are these: "The sacred scripture transcends other sciences in the very manner of its expression, since in one and the same discourse it discloses a mystery while it narrates an event[1]." Nazianzen compares the literal sense to the body, the mystical and spiritual to the soul. The Jesuit uses a different simile: "As," says he, "the begotten Word of God hath two natures, the one human and visible, the other divine and invisible; so the written word of God hath a two-fold sense: the one outward, that is, historic or literal; the other, inward, that is, mystic or spiritual." Then he determines that this spiritual sense is three-fold, allegorical, anagogic, and tropological, as we have said before that others had determined also. These things we do not wholly reject: we concede such things as allegory, anagoge, and tropology in scripture; but meanwhile we deny that there are many and various senses. We affirm that there is but one true, proper and genuine sense of scripture, arising from the words rightly understood, which we call the literal: and we contend that allegories, tropologies, and anagoges are not various senses, but various collections from one sense, or various applications and accommodations of that one meaning.

Now the Jesuit's assertion, that the literal sense is that which the words immediately present, is not true. For then what, I beseech you, will be the literal sense of these words, Ps. xci. 13, "Thou shalt go upon the adder and the basilisk; the lion and the dragon shalt thou trample under foot?" For if that be the literal sense of these words, which the words immediately present, let them shew us the lion on which Christ trampled, the adder or basilisk on which he walked. Either, therefore, the literal sense is not that which the words immediately present, as the Jesuit maintains; or these words have no literal sense, which he dares not affirm. For they say that all the senses mentioned above are to be found in every passage of scripture. Besides, what will they

[1 Sacra scriptura reliquas scientias ipso locutionis suæ more transcendit, quia uno eodemque sermone, dum gestum narrat, prodit mysterium.—p. 4. Par. 1639.]

make the literal sense of Isaiah xi. 6, 7, 8, and lxv. last verse? where the prophet says that "the wolf shall dwell with the lamb, and the leopard lie down with the kid, the calf and the lion and the sheep shall dwell together, and the calf and the bear pasture together," &c. Certainly no one can shew where and when this prophecy was fulfilled according to the letter, if we determine the literal sense to be that which the words immediately suggest. Finally, if this Jesuitical definition of the literal sense be true, what literal sense, I pray you, will remain in those words of Christ, Matth. v. 29, 30, "If thy right eye offend thee, pluck it out; if thy right hand offend thee, cut it off?" Origen, indeed, though elsewhere too much given to allegories and mystical senses, interpreted these words according to the letter, but absurdly. The literal sense, then, is not that which the words immediately suggest, as the Jesuit defines it; but rather that which arises from the words themselves, whether they be taken strictly or figuratively. If the discourse be figurative, it is not to be explained according to that meaning which the sound of the words would at first and immediately suggest. This is what Alphonsus de Castro seems to affirm, *Contra Hæres.* Lib. I. c. 3, where he defines the literal sense better than the Jesuit, making it that which either the words, or the things expressed by the words, denote. For example, the literal sense of these words, "The seed of the woman shall crush the serpent's head," is this, that Christ shall beat down Satan, and break and crush all his force and power; although the devil neither is a serpent, nor hath a head.

As to those three spiritual senses, it is surely foolish to say that there are as many senses of scripture as the words themselves may be transferred and accommodated to bear. For although the words may be applied and accommodated tropologically, allegorically, anagogically, or any other way; yet there are not therefore various senses, various interpretations and explications of scripture, but there is but one sense, and that the literal, which may be variously accommodated, and from which various things may be collected. The apostle, indeed, Galat. iv. 24, interprets the history of Abraham's two wives allegorically, or rather typically, of the two Testaments; for he says in express words, ἅτινά ἐστιν ἀλλη-γορούμενα, &c. But there he does not make a two-fold sense of that history, but only says that it may be allegorically interpreted to his purpose, and the illustration of the subject which he hath in hand. Indeed, there is a certain catachresis in the word ἀλλη-γορούμενα, for that history is not accommodated by Paul in that place allegorically, but typically; and a type is a different thing from an allegory. The sense, therefore, of that scripture is one only, namely, the literal or grammatical. However, the whole entire sense is not in the words taken strictly, but part in the type, part in the transaction itself. In either of these considered separately and by itself part only of the meaning is contained; and by both taken together the full and perfect meaning is completed.

The same is to be thought of all those places in which scripture interprets any thing in an allegoric sense. Hence we perceive that there is but one true and genuine sense of scripture, namely, the literal or grammatical, whether it arise from the words taken strictly, or from the words figuratively understood, or from both together; and that allegorical expositions are not various meanings, but only various applications and accommodations of scripture. Such allegories, indeed, we may sometimes use with profit and advantage to give pleasure, not to coerce assent; especially when scripture explains a thing allegorically, for otherwise we should be frugal of inventing allegories. David fought with Goliah. David was a type of Christ, and Goliah of the devil. Therefore, this fight and victory of David may be typically accommodated to denote the combat of Christ with Satan, and his victory. One may also give an allegorical accommodation of the same narrative, thus: David overcame Goliah. So ought we to overcome our passions, which wage a kind of giant war within us against the Spirit of God. I confess that these are true and may be fitly said: but it would be absurd to say that either the one or the other was the sense of this history. So much upon allegories.

Tropology hath still less claims to be esteemed a new sense, because it flows plainly and necessarily from the very words, and is therefore collected from the text itself. It is nothing more than an ethical treatment of scripture, when we collect from the scriptures what is suitable to direct our lives and form our morals, and hath place in common life: as, Abraham overcame five kings with a small band; therefore we should neither trust too much to a great number, nor despair with a few. David, given up to inactivity, was entangled by love, and so fell into adultery: therefore we should shun idleness. Noah, when drunk, lay shamefully exposed, and so became the sport of his own son: therefore we should beware of drunkenness, lest we fall into disgrace and mischief. "Thou shalt not muzzle the ox that treadeth out the corn:" therefore ministers are to be supported and supplied with all things needful. This is what Paul collects from the words, 1 Cor, ix. 9, and 1 Tim. v. 18. Peter in the hall of the high priest denied Christ, but went out and repented : therefore the company of evil men is to be avoided. Christ also hath used this mode of interpretation, Matth. xii. 41, 42, where he accommodates to the case of the Jews then present the repentance of the Ninevites immediately upon hearing Jonah, and the long journey of the queen of Sheba to Solomon. In this treatment of texts, and such educings of various admonitions and exhortations, the greatest part of the minister's function lies. But all such things flow and are concluded from the very words themselves. This, therefore, is not a new or various meaning, foreign to the words themselves, but absolutely one and the same with the literal sense.

We should form a like judgment of the type or anagoge. In Psalm xcv. God says, " I sware in my wrath, that they should not enter into my rest." There the rest may be understood both of the land of Canaan, and typically also of the kingdom of hea-ven : for the realm of Canaan was a type of the kingdom of heaven. Yet this is not a twofold sense ; but, when the sign is re-ferred to the thing signified, that which was hidden in the sign is more openly expressed. When we proceed from the sign to the thing signified, we bring no new sense, but only bring out into light what was before concealed in the sign. When we speak of the sign by itself, we express only part of the meaning ; and so also when we mention only the thing signified : but when the mutual relation between the sign and the thing signified is brought out, then the whole complete sense, which is founded upon this simili-tude and agreement, is set forth. Paul says, 1 Cor. x. 11, " All these things happened to them for ensamples," or typically, τύποι συνέβαινον ἐκείνοις, &c. : the meaning of the place is, that we should accommodate the events of the ancient Jewish people to our instruction, so as that, admonished by their example, we may learn to please God, and avoid idolatry and other sins ; not that we are to collect from all these things I know not what new and spiritual mean-ing. For although this sense be spiritual, yet it is not a different one, but really literal ; since the letter itself affords it to us in the way of similitude or argument. The Jews were punished when they sin-ned : therefore, if we sin in like manner, we shall bear and pay to God similar penalties. He hath set before us the punishment of the Jews pourtrayed as it were in a picture, that we may constantly have it before our eyes. They had indeed many things of a typical nature, the cloud, the passage through the sea, the water from the rock, the manna; which all were symbols to the pious of heavenly things. As the water flowing from the rock refreshed the weary people, and the manna fed them, so Christ cheers and preserves us. As they were enveloped in the cloud, and set in the midst of the waves of the great deep, so all the godly are washed by the blood of Christ. These were all sacraments to them, and so the pious understood them. When, therefore, these are expounded literally of the things themselves, spiritually of celestial graces, we do not make two diverse senses; but, by expounding a similitude, we compare the sign with the thing signified, and so bring out the true and entire sense of the words. So in our sacraments there are not two senses, the literal and the mystical; but one only, founded in the comparison and conjunction of the signs and things. As our bodies are washed with water, so our souls are purified by the blood of Christ: as our bodies are strengthened with bread and wine, so are we wholly sustained by the flesh and blood of our Saviour. So from these types Paul argues : If the Jews perished for their crimes, we also shall perish, if we commit the same offences. Paul does not there deliver a twofold sense, but he draws and sets forth an example from those things which befel the Jewish people, by which he admonishes the Corinthians to take warning.

The sense of scripture, therefore, is but one,—the literal; for it is folly to feign many senses, merely because many things follow from the words of scripture rightly understood. Those things may, indeed, be called corollaries or consequences, flowing from the right understanding of the words, but new and different senses they are by no means. Thomas Aquinas himself appears to have seen this; for, in the 1st part of his Sum. Quæst. I. Art. 10, he writes thus : " Since the literal sense is that which the author intends, and the author of holy scripture is God, who comprehends all things together in his mind; there is nothing improper in saying that, even according to the literal sense, there are several meanings of scripture in one text[1]." Since then that is the sense of scripture, and the literal sense, which the Holy Spirit intends, however it may be gathered ; certainly, if the Holy Spirit intended the tropologic, anagogic, or allegoric sense of any

[1 Quia sensus literalis est quem auctor intendat, auctor autem sacræ scripturæ Deus est, qui omnia simul suo intellectu comprehendit; non est inconveniens, si etiam secundum literalem sensum in una litera scripturæ plures sint sensus.—p. 4. Par. 1639.]

place, these senses are not different from the literal, as Thomas hath
expressly taught us. So also Alphonsus de Castro, Lib. I. *contra
Hœres.* cap. 3. " He that shall choose to confine the sense of a
parable within the letter, will not do amiss[2]." So much for the
first preliminary.

We must note and observe in the SECOND place, that it is only
from the literal sense that strong, valid, and efficacious arguments
can be derived; which is the concession even of our adversaries
themselves. It follows, therefore, that this and no other is the
genuine sense of scripture. For a firm argument may always be
derived from the genuine and proper sense. Since, therefore,
firm inferences cannot be made from those other senses, it is evident that they are not true and genuine meanings. Therefore,
tropology, allegory, and anagoge, if they are real meanings, are
literal ones. Now the reason why sound arguments are always derived
from the literal sense is this, because it is certain that that which is
derived from the words themselves is ever the sense of the Holy
Spirit; but we are not so certain of any mystical sense, except when
the Holy Spirit himself so teaches us. For example, it is written,
Hosea xi. 1, " Out of Egypt have I called my son;" and Exod.
xii. 46, " Thou shalt not break a bone of him." It is sufficiently
plain that the former is to be understood of the people of Israel,
and the latter of the paschal lamb. Who, now, would dare to
transfer and accommodate these to Christ, if the Holy Spirit had
not done it first, and declared to us his mind and intention?—
namely, that the *Son* in the former passage denotes not only the
people of Israel, but Christ also; and the *bone*, in the latter, is to
be understood of Christ as well as of the paschal lamb. They who
interpret those places merely of the people of Israel or the paschal
lamb, bring only part of the meaning, not the whole: because the
entire sense is to be understood of the sign and the thing itself
taken together, and consists in the accommodation of the sign to the
thing signified. Hereupon emerge not different senses, but one entire sense. However, we must argue from the literal sense: and
hence comes that vulgar and trite proverb, that metaphorical and
symbolic theology is not argumentative; which Thomas, in the
place quoted above, proves out of Augustine, Epist. 48, *contra
Vincent. Donat.*, as also Jerome on the 13th of Matthew. Hence
also Dionysius the Areopagite says in a certain place, that " mystical

[2 Sensum parabolæ qui intra literalem circumsepire voluerit, non abs re
faciet.—De Sensu Parab. p. 5. Par. 1564.]

theology does not prove any thing." Alphonsus discourses copiously upon this subject, Lib. I. c. 3 ; and Andradius says, *Trident. Defens.* Lib. II., that " the literal sense alone supplies arguments to confirm the doctrines of religion[1]."

Our THIRD preliminary observation is, that we must not bring any private meanings, or private opinions, but only such as agree with the mind, intention, and dictate of the Holy Spirit. For, since he is the author of the scriptures, it is fit that we should follow him in interpreting scripture. This our adversaries concede : for both plain reason convinces them, and that passage in 2 Pet. i. 20, makes the matter sufficiently clear, where Peter says no scripture is ἰδίας ἐπιλύσεως. But what is the sense of the Holy Spirit ? what his mind and intention, wherewith all our interpretation should suit and agree ? In this the controversy consists. Now therefore we must proceed to the discussion.

CHAPTER III.

THE STATE OF THE FORMER PART OF THIS QUESTION TREATED
MORE AT LARGE.

WE have already made two divisions of this question ;—the former, concerning the authority of interpreting the scriptures, with whom it is vested ; the latter, concerning the means by which we may come to the true sense of scripture. We have now to treat of the former, in the first place, and afterwards we shall consider the latter also in its proper place.

As to the former part of this controversy, our adversaries, upon their side, attribute this authority of which we speak to the church, and pronounce it to be the church's privilege to interpret scripture. So the council of Trent, Sess. 4[2], whose judgment Stapleton affirms and explains, Lib. x. c. 11, with a copiousness excelled

[1 See also Thomas Aquinas, Summ. Theol. Pars. 1. q. 1. Art. 10. Sixtus Senensis. Bibl. S. Lib. III. p. 141. Vega, de Justificatione, Lib. IX. c. 44. Salmeron. Comment. in Heb. i. Disp. 7. § idem.]

[2 Nemo . . . . . contra eum sensum quem tenuit et tenet sancta mater ecclesia, cujus est judicare de vero sensu et interpretatione scripturarum sanctarum, ... ipsam scripturam sacram interpretari audeat.—Sess. iv. Decret. 11. p. 20, 21. Lips. 1837.]

by no other writer. However, here too a question arises. For we also say that the church is the interpreter of scripture, and that this gift of interpretation resides only in the church : but we deny that it pertains to particular persons, or is tied to any particular see or succession of men. We must see, therefore, what is the sense borne by that axiom or postulate of the papists, wherein they assert so confidently that the church hath the authority of interpreting the scriptures. The intent of this assertion, it seems, we may seek and find in Stapleton, who (as was said above) interprets the council of Trent in a large exposition. Now Stapleton says, that the sense of scripture is not that which is given by any bishop or catholic pastor, but teaches us that we must apply certain cautions, such as these.

The *first* caution is, that the enemies of the church are not to be listened to. This we also concede;—that when the sense of scripture is sought for, the enemies of the church are not to be consulted. But which is that church? He takes it for granted that their church is the true church ; which none of us will ever grant. The *second* caution is, that we are not bound to believe any catholic, however learned, if he be only a private person. He must, therefore, bear a public character, and be a magistrate, whom we are obliged to believe in this matter. The *third* caution is, that we should consider what the bishops and pastors of the church have thought, delivered, and determined, concerning the interpretation of this or that scripture. The *fourth* caution is, that what they have determined should be received and held without hesitation. But here he interposes two conditions : the first is, Provided they have remained in catholic unity,—that is, have quietly and contentedly subjected themselves to the authority of the pope, and not revolted from him : the second is, If they have agreed with all their colleagues in the episcopate. But, in this way, even the common expositions of the fathers are not to be received and held, because we do not know whether they agreed with their brother bishops. For there were many other bishops of those times, of whom no writings or monuments whatever remain. Whence can we know that Augustine, Ambrose, and others agreed with their colleagues in the episcopate, whose books are not now in our hands?

The *fifth* caution is: We ought to refer an opinion about which we entertain doubts to a council. But we cannot always and immediately, when we are in doubt of the meaning of a place, assemble a council; and councils may err, as we shall prove hereafter in its proper place. There follows, therefore, *another* caution, which is to this effect : Since it is very difficult to assemble councils, and they have not supreme authority, and sometimes even err, it behoves us to await the sentence of the supreme pastor, or (as he expresses it) the supreme head, upon understanding which all doubt will be put an end to. But where was the need of these long circuits ? Why are we not sent straight at once to the supreme pastor and pontiff, without minding fathers, bishops, and councils ? Why not repair to and consult him in the first place ? Why not, at the very outset, lay before him our questions and doubts, since everything must finally of necessity devolve on him ? Perhaps it would be too troublesome for the pope to have frequently to give answers upon the sense of scripture, especially since he is busily employed with other more weighty matters, in which he loves better to be occupied. But at present, I suppose, we must stop here. For, when we have come to the pope, what more can we desire ? Still not even yet have we done enough. Stapleton perceives that neither of fathers, nor councils, nor Roman pontiffs are all the expositions true ; and therefore there is still need of fresh cautions. Still many doubts occur concerning these cautions, and the affair is not yet brought to an end.

Accordingly he adds a *seventh* caution, which is this : that the sense of scripture is so to be embraced and held as the church would have it held, and in the same degree as the church : that is, what the church declares to be held as matter of faith, we also should hold as of faith ; what she hath willed and taught to be held as probable and useful, is to be held similarly by us. But how shall we know what the church holds as matter of faith, and what as only probable ? This he explains in the next caution. The *eighth* caution is : that the church holds that as of faith, and propounds also to us to be held as of faith, firstly, which she proposes under an anathema ; secondly, which she constantly maintains against heretics ; thirdly, which she delivers as the orthodox sense ; fourthly and lastly, which is elicited by the application of those means which Stapleton is afterwards to deliver.

The *ninth* caution is : that whatever bishops may have written or said, or howsoever they may have expounded scripture, their exposition is not necessarily to be received, if they have only written, spoken, or expounded by the way. But this involves us in still greater doubts. For how shall we certainly understand what things are written by the way, what seriously, carefully, and professedly, unless the men themselves who write shall tell us ?

Surely we must here stand in endless hesitation. But, in the meantime, what are we to think of the schoolmen? This he explains in the next caution. The *tenth* caution therefore is: that the schoolmen have no certain or infallible authority of expounding scripture. Thus the schoolmen are deprived of authority. You see what a matter it is amongst them to be a bishop. All the fathers, who were not bishops, have their authority lowered by Stapleton. Such are Origen, Tertullian, Jerome, Bernard, Lombard, all the monks, Aquinas, Bonaventura, Scotus, Stapleton himself, and all such writers who are not yet advanced and promoted to the episcopal function. Their interpretation, therefore, he says, is not to be followed under pain of infidelity, but only of gross contumaciousness. But what is to be thought of the bishops? He shews this in the next caution. The *eleventh* caution, therefore, is; that whatever even the bishops themselves may have said or written, if they did not teach it as bishops *ex cathedra*, hath no certain authority, and is not of necessity to be received by us. But we have not heard Augustine and the other fathers teaching from the chair, and therefore are ignorant what they taught from the chair, what not, or whether they taught from the chair at all. We have only their books. What are we then to determine concerning them? Forsooth, that those are to be received which the church hath received and approved; whereof a catalogue is set forth by Gelasius in Gratian, causa 15. Tit. *Ecclesia Romana*[1]. But are all these to be received? They will not themselves say this either: for they do not receive all. Yea, there are many things in all those books which the papists themselves are compelled to reject; and, therefore, he adds a *twelfth* caution, which is to this effect: that a certain argument cannot immediately be gathered from every interpretation of the fathers. Next follows the *thirteenth* caution, not much unlike the preceding; namely, that we must not bind ourselves absolutely to the opinions of any doctor, or schoolman, or churchman. What then,—where shall we stop at last? *Finally*, he adds, that we should make recourse to the church, follow her authority, and acquiesce in her judgment. This is taking a long circuit for nothing. Why did he not bring us straight at once to this point? He might at the beginning have sent us to the church, and dispatched this whole business in a few words.

[1 The reference should be, Gratian. Decret. *Distinct.* xv. c. 3. *Sancta Romana Ecclesia.* Whitaker has, by a mistake, quoted the second for the first part of the Decree.]

But what is this church, to which we are to repair in the last resort, and by whose interpretation we ought to abide? Forsooth, the Roman; for they mean no other whenever they speak of the church. The sense of scripture, therefore, must be referred to the Roman church. But what is this Roman church? Must all be consulted who belong to it? By no means; for no one could do this, though he spent his life in it. What then? perhaps we should only consult the bishops and pastors; for they always mean these by the Roman church. But even these we could never meet personally. Therefore, finally, the church is the supreme pontiff. To him we must repair, hang upon his lips, and seek from him the interpretation of scripture. But do the papists make a reasonable demand, when they would have us submit ourselves to his judgment, and depend upon his interpretation, whom we accuse as a false interpreter of scripture, yea, whom we affirm to be the very antichrist himself? Surely, they are very unjust, and plainly betray their own want of confidence, when they confess that they cannot prove their cause to us without appealing to him, and referring all to the judgment of him whom they know willing always to be on their side, and unwilling ever to pronounce anything against them and himself. Such then are Stapleton's cautions.

But the Jesuit comprises the matter in a smaller compass. *First*, he says that the sense of scripture is to be sought in the fathers when they agree. But they seldom agree. How, therefore, shall this agreement be made certainly evident to us? Besides, even when they agree, why should we rather believe them so agreeing than scripture agreeing with itself? *Secondly*, if we are still doubtful of the sense of scripture, he desires us to seek it from a council confirmed by the chief pastor. *Thirdly*, if even thus all doubt be not removed, we must seek it from the chief pastor himself with his council of pastors. Mark how cautiously and with what hesitation he speaks of his supreme pontiff! But hath not the pope of himself authority to interpret scripture? He dares not to affirm this; and yet doubtless this is what he means. He was ashamed, it seems, to ascribe such great authority to the pope alone. Yet neither did he dare to deny it altogether; and therefore timidly and confusedly he names the pope together with a council of pastors. It was once a great question, whether the authority of a council or of the pope was greater in interpreting scripture. Formerly they used to believe that the authority of a council was greater than that of the pope; but, since the councils of

Constance and Basle, a greater authority hath been attributed to the pope. Yet here, I know not how, the Jesuit joins a council of pastors to the pope. Alphonsus, *contra Hæres.* Lib. I. c. 4, seems to follow the old opinion : for he says that a council alone hath this supreme authority, because a council alone is *the church represent-ative.* And, chap. 8, he says that the apostolic see hath the next place after a general council in making definitions. Afterwards he explains what he meant by the apostolic see : " The apostolic see," says he, " comprehends not only the supreme pontiff, but also that council which the pontiff uses, and by which he is aided in making a definition." And this too is perhaps the council which the Jesuit means in this place, when he joins a council of pastors with the pope. But all the cardinals are not pastors ; for some are pres-byters, some only deacons ; and these men call none but bishops pastors. Besides, the cardinals attend the pope only in the way of ornament and pomp, and have no place in the settling of any definition. Yea, although all the cardinals were to say nay, yet the pope can define what he will. Therefore, although the Jesuit puts a council of pastors along with the pope, yet in reality this authority of interpretation is lodged with the pope alone ; because, however much the rest oppose, yet his opinion shall always stand and prevail. The question then is, whether the authority of inter-preting scripture be lodged with the church thus understood ? The papists hold the affirmative ; we the negative.

We have heard now their opinion. It remains to see what ours is. Now we determine that the supreme right, authority, and judgment of interpreting the scriptures, is lodged with the Holy Ghost and the scripture itself : for these two are not mutually repugnant. We say that the Holy Spirit is the supreme interpreter of scripture, because we must be illuminated by the Holy Spirit to be certainly persuaded of the true sense of scripture ; otherwise, although we use all means, we can never attain to that full assu-rance which resides in the minds of the faithful. But this is only· an internal persuasion, and concerns only ourselves. As to external persuasion, we say that scripture itself is its own interpreter ; and, therefore, that we should come to the external judgment of scrip-ture itself, in order to persuade others : in which proceeding we must also use means ; of which more hereafter. But that the interpretation of scripture is tied to any certain see, or succession of men, we absolutely deny. Here, therefore, we have specially to discuss and prove two points : first, that the pope cannot claim for himself this power of interpreting the scriptures : secondly, that scripture is to be interpreted by scripture.

Now, having proposed the state of the question, we must come to the contest and disputation.

CHAPTER IV.

THE ARGUMENTS OF OUR OPPONENTS TAKEN FROM THE OLD TESTAMENT ARE SET ASIDE.

STAPLETON hath treated this question at once loosely and confusedly. The Jesuit hath drawn his arguments into a conciser form. With him, therefore, our present contest shall principally be maintained. He adduces four arguments, whereof the first is from the authority of the old Testament, the second, from the authority of the new Testament ; the third, from the common practice of the church, and the testimonies of the fathers ; the fourth, from necessary reason. He cites seven testimonies from the old Testament, which we will examine in order.

The first place is, Exodus xviii. 13, 26, from which he argues thus : after the people of God were collected and reduced to the form of a church, Moses sat as supreme judge; and afterwards also, though other judges were established, yet he reserved the more difficult causes for his own decision. Therefore, now also there ought to be in the church one common tribunal, and some supreme judge and moderator of all controversies, from whom no appeal is to be permitted.

I answer, first; Moses was a prophet, endowed with singular wisdom, adorned with extraordinary gifts of God, commended also to the people by divine testimonies, and sent immediately by God himself. Now the pope hath no such qualifications. If he be such, let him shew us those extraordinary gifts wherewith he is endowed, and those testimonies by which he is by God commended to the church, and so enable us to believe him.

Secondly, I confess that in every republic there ought to be judges to determine and put an end to such disputes as arise amongst men, although not with so much authority as Moses : I confess also, that, in every particular church there should be ministers to interpret the scriptures to the people, and answer those who inquire concerning the will of God. But an argument from particular churches to the whole universal church does not hold: for then one might also conclude from this place, that there ought to be amongst Christians one supreme political judge (since Moses was such in the Israelitish republic), who should examine every thing that was brought into controversy. But even the papists themselves do not require this.

Thirdly, I affirm that this should be attributed to Aaron rather than to Moses, and that for two reasons : first, because Aaron was the ordinary priest and had successors ; not Moses, whose function was extraordinary : for Moses had no successors in his office. Now many of the priests, who in fixed succession after Aaron held the chief place in the church, were impious men and idolaters, as is clear from the sacred text. Secondly, because Moses was not a priest, after the law was published and Aaron consecrated and anointed, nor discharged any priestly function, but was merely a prophet: therefore we must not ascribe to him a judicial power, which, according to them, belongs only to a priest. As to our reading, Ps. xcix. 6, " Moses and Aaron amongst his priests :" I answer, either that the Hebrew word[1] denotes chief men of the people, as in 2 Sam. viii. 18, where David's sons are said to have been *Cohenim* ; and Samuel was not a priest, nor born in a priestly family, as we see in 1 Chron. vi. 27 : or that Moses is called a priest, because he had been a priest before the consecration of Aaron ; for afterwards he ceased to be a priest, and was only a prophet and magistrate. But the Jesuit says that Moses was an extraordinary priest, and greater than Aaron : and he illustrates this by a comparison to this effect,—namely, that in the new Testament Peter was an ordinary pastor, but the rest of the apostles extraordinary, because Peter had successors, but the rest none : so that Aaron was an ordinary priest, but Moses an extraordinary, because Aaron had successors, but Moses none. But this is a mere dull fiction. For who can say that Peter was an ordinary pastor, while the rest were extraordinary, when they all received the same vocation and the same charge from Christ, Matt. xxviii ? Besides, Jerome, Ep. 85, plainly refutes this ; for he says, that "all bishops are successors of the apostles[2]," not of Peter

---

[1 כֹהֵן Gesenius owns that "admodum vetus est sententia Hebræorum, כֹהֵן etiam *principem* notare," though he rejects it himself.]

[2 Apud nos Apostolorum locum episcopi tenent.—Ep. 41. T. I. p. 187. ed. Vallars.]

[WHITAKER.]

alone. So Cyprian, Ep. 69[1]: and the same author, in his book *de Simplicitate Prælatorum*, writes thus: "The other apostles were the same as Peter was, endowed with an equal share both of honour and of power[2]." Besides, if there be any force in the Jesuit's comparison, why, as Moses was superior to Aaron, because the latter was the ordinary priest, and Moses the extraordinary, were not also the other apostles superior to Peter; since he was the ordinary pastor, and they the extraordinary? Thus, either the other apostles were superior to Peter, or this comparison of the Jesuit's suits his purpose in no way.

Fourthly, if the authority of Moses was extraordinary, it cannot surely be dragged to establish any such ordinary authority as that which the papists maintain.

Fifthly, it may be that Moses in this respect represented Christ, and was a type of him who is the supreme Judge of all controversies. But now all types are taken away; and it is a trite saying, that we cannot argue from types.

Sixthly, if Moses were supreme judge, and a priest higher than Aaron, then there were two judges and two chief priests also in that people: yea, there was a priest higher than the chief priest; which is impossible.

The second place of the old Testament alleged by Bellarmine is contained in Deut. xvii. 8—13: "If there arise a matter too hard for thee in judgment between blood and blood," &c. "We see from this place," says the Jesuit, "that all who are in doubt on any matter, are sent to a living judge, not to their own private spirits." I answer: It is a malicious assertion of the Jesuit to say that we send men in doubt on any matter to their own private spirits: for we send no man to his own private spirit, but to scripture itself, and the Spirit of God speaking clearly in the scripture. But, to give a distinct answer, I say, first, that this precept was conditional, as appears from the very words themselves. For they who consulted that supreme judge were ordered to do according to "that *sentence of the law* which he should teach them." All, therefore, are commanded to obey the decree of the judge, but with this condition, provided that he judge according to the

[1 Potestas ergo peccatorum remittendorum Apostolis data est, et ecclesiis quas illi a Christo missi constituerunt, et episcopis qui eis ordinatione vicaria successerint.—Ep. 75. ed. Fell. p. 225.]

[2 Hoc erant utique et ceteri Apostoli quod fuit Petrus, pari consortio præditi et honoris et potestatis.—pp. 107, 108. This treatise is now more commonly (and more correctly) cited under the title, *De Unitate Ecclesiæ*.]

law of God, that is, shew from the law that it is the will of God. This we also willingly concede, that every priest and minister, and not the pope alone, is to be obeyed whenever he judges according to the law. Meanwhile this place does not establish any such supreme judge as may determine what he pleases at his own caprice, and by whose judgment, though destitute of all scripture authority, we are bound to stand : yea, rather, when it requires him to answer according to the law, it assigns the supreme judgment to the law and not to him. Here the Jesuit brings many things to elude and overturn this answer. For he says, *first*, that those words, " and shall teach thee according to the law," are not to be found anywhere but in the Vulgate edition. I answer, first, that this is enough, since they hold that edition for authentic. Secondly, this condition is plainly expressed in the Hebrew copies, v. 11, *al pi hathorah asher jorucha*[3] : in which words the priest is bound to the mouth, that is, the sentence and declaration of the law, so as to decree nothing but what the law itself dictates and declares. Thus the priest ought to be a second mouth to this divine mouth. *Secondly*, he says that this is not a condition, but an assertion or promise : for Moses did not mean to say, Abide by the judgment of the priest, if he teach thee according to the law ; for then men would have been reduced to greater doubts than before, and the priest would not be the judge, but they themselves, who would have to judge of the sentence of the priest. I answer, men are remitted to the priest only in ambiguous and doubtful causes, and then required to abide by his judgment. What? Simply by whatever judgment he may pass? God never gave so great a power to any man ; and the priest in this case he hath expressly tied to the law, to prevent his saying a word and making an answer beyond the law. Were men bound to abide by the judgment of the priest, even when he taught not according to the law ? Who would say so ? Therefore the condition is necessary : and yet men are not thereby involved in greater doubts or made judges themselves : for there was great judicial weight in the priest ; and whatever he had once determined was held for rule to all external intents and purposes, in order that so controversies and disputes might be removed. *Thirdly*, he concludes from the premises, that it is not a condition, but a promise : as if God had said, Do thou abide by the judge's sentence, and I promise that the judge shall

[3 עַל־פִּי הַתּוֹרָה אֲשֶׁר יוֹרוּךָ.]

always determine rightly. I answer, If such a promise be made
to the priest, then the same pertains also to the political judge,
because he is joined with the priest; and so the political judge also
will be infallible in civil matters: which (I suppose) the papists will
not allow. But he says that the judge here mentioned is ecclesiastical, and not civil: whereas the falsehood of this pretence is
plain from the context. Moses speaks there of controversies between
blood and blood, plea and plea, which are forensic and civil actions:
therefore he speaks of the civil judge. But, says he, if the civil
judge be there spoken of, then the definitive sentence is assigned to
the priest, but the *execution* to the judge: which is also manifestly
false. For, first, these words are there contained in the Vulgate,
Ex decreto judicis morietur. Therefore, the judge himself should
pass sentence and adjudge the accused to death; and consequently
the definitive sentence also is assigned to the judge. Again, there
is a fault in the Vulgate edition. For in v. 12, *ex* occurs for either *et*
or *aut*, as is clear from the Hebrew and Greek texts. In the Greek
there is ἤ, *or;* and the Hebrew word also denotes *or*, but never
from; so that the words should be read thus: " He who will not
obey the priest or judge shall die." And that a disjunctive particle
is required, is plain from v. 9: for they are ordered to come to
the priests and to the judge; so that he who should *presumptuously*
despise the priest or the judge should be put to death. Thus it is
not every dissent from the decision, however modest, and with
probable grounds, pious and reasonable; but such as was bold, presumptuous, headlong and frantic, that was punished capitally. The
words of the text stand thus in the Vulgate: v. 12, *Qui autem
superbierit, nolens obedire sacerdotis imperio, qui eo tempore
ministrat Domino Deo tuo, ex decreto judicis morietur.* Hence
the Jesuit gathers, that the definitive sentence belonged to the
priest, the execution to the magistrate. But the Hebrew verity
teaches us otherwise, which is to this effect: " And the man that
will do presumptuously so as to refuse to hearken to the priest who
stands to minister there before the Lord thy God, or to the judge,
that man shall die." This law gives as much definitive authority
to the judge as to the priest. The Hebrew has, *o el hashophet*[1].
Upon which place Cajetan writes thus: " The translator hath
made a change: for in the Hebrew it is, *or to the judge.* The
expression is disjunctive, ' in not obeying the priest or the judge.'

[1 אוֹ אֶל־הַשֹּׁפֵט.]

Where I would have the intelligent reader observe, that the decision of an ambiguous case is not described as being made by a single person, but by many priests and the judge. The ordering execution is ascribed to the pontiff or the judge. Like penalties are decreed against the opposer of the priest and the judge[2]." The Jesuit hath spoiled the cardinal's argument: for he says, first, that the particle is disjunctive; secondly, that the execution belonged to the pontiff or the judge; thirdly, that the same penalty was prescribed for him who resisted the judge as for him who resisted the priest; fourthly, that the definitive sentence was not of one priest, but of many, and of the judge. Jerome ab Oleastro, in his commentaries, gathers from this passage: "That it is not free to judges to judge as they will, but according to the laws; and that we are commanded to obey them when they judge according to the same[3]." But these men require obedience to whatever they prescribe, and will by no means suffer their decrees to be examined. Cyprian also, Ep. 69, cites this place thus: "It behoves us to hearken to the priest or the judge[4]." And so much for our first general reply to this testimony of the Jesuit's.

Secondly, I answer, that these words are not to be understood of a perpetual right of interpreting the scriptures, but only of an authority of determining difficult disputes and controversies; if ecclesiastical, by the minister; if political or civil, by the magistrate; so as that, in either case, there might be some one from whom there should be no appeal; for otherwise there would be no end of litigation. But now, there is no consequence in such an argument as this: disputes of murder, assault, blood, leprosy, and such like, are always to be determined by some judge, and there ought to be some certain tribunal for controversies at law: therefore, there ought to be some supreme judge with whom shall reside the power of interpreting scripture, and from whom no appeal shall be permitted. For no tribunal concerning religion

[2 Interpres mutavit: nam Hebraice habetur, *vel judici*. Disjunctive enim dicitur, non obediendo sacerdoti vel judici. Ubi, prudens lector, adverte, quod definitio ambiguæ causæ non ab uno sed a multis sacerdotibus et judice describitur. Præcipere executionem attribuitur pontifici vel judici. Par pœna decernitur opponentis se sacerdoti vel judici.]

[3 Non est judicibus liberum judicare ut volunt, sed juxta leges; et illis parendum præcipit, cum secundum eas judicaverint.—Comment. in Pentateuch. Lugdun. 1586.]

[4 Cum Dominus Deus in Deuteronomio dicat, Et homo . . . . ut non exaudiat sacerdotem aut judicem.—Ep. 66. p. 166. ed. Fell.]

hath been constituted by this law. God hath reserved this to himself, and hath allowed it to no man, knowing as he does how easily men corrupt religion with their perverse opinions. But this law is promulgated to establish external judgments of controversies at law, which either the magistrate or the priests are to judge. Now, no commonwealth can subsist, unless it have some supreme tribunal from which no appeal can be made; but still, in such cases, where it is consistent with religion, and not impious, to obey even an unjust sentence. But Bellarmine says that the law is general concerning all doubtful questions which arose out of the law; and that the occasion of the law was the case of those who served strange gods. I answer, first, there is no mention in the law of doubts arising out of the law; for in it none but external and forensic disputes are spoken of. Secondly, what he adds, of the occasion of the law, is false, and would be of no value if it were true.

The third place which the Jesuit cites is taken from Ecclesiastes xii. 11, where we read thus: "The words of the wise are as goads, and as nails driven deep, which by the counsel of the masters are given from one shepherd. Seek, my son, no more than these[1]." Solomon, says he, teaches us that we should thoroughly acquiesce when sentence is pronounced by the chief pastor, especially combined with the advice of sage councillors. And if these things are said of the priest of the old Testament, how much more may they be said of the priest of the new Testament, who hath received greater promises from God! I answer: The meaning is, that the doctrine and heavenly wisdom which the prophets delivered, and which the ministers of God teach and expound, is like to goads, because it strikes, excites, and urges us, and so rouses us from our sloth; and to nails, because it keeps us fixed and firm in piety; and that one shepherd, who is there mentioned, is neither the pope, nor the priest of the old Testament, but Christ himself. For so Salonius, an old father, writes upon this place: " Who are these wise men? who is this one pastor? The wise men are the prophets, the one pastor is God[2]." And Jerome says also

[1 Verba sapientium sicut stimuli, et quasi clavi in altum defixi, quæ per magistrorum consilium [aliter et rectius concilium] data sunt a pastore uno. His amplius, fili mi, ne requiras. Vulgate translation.]

[2 Qui isti sapientes sunt? Quis iste unus pastor? Sapientes sunt prophetæ, unus pastor Deus.—Bibliothec. Patrum. T. VIII. Salonius was son of Eucherius of Lyons, and flourished about A. D. 453.]

upon the same place : " Although several teach the word of God, yet there is but one author of that teaching, namely, God." Where he refutes the Manicheans, who made the author of the new Testament a different being from the author of the old. Others suppose this one pastor to be the Holy Spirit, as Vatablus; others, Christ, as Mercerus; none the pope, except senseless papists. The place, therefore, is not to be understood of the pope, as Bellarmine would have it, but of God. But the Jesuit foolishly subjoins, if this be understood of the priest of the old Testament, much more of the priest of the new Testament. I answer : I do not understand it of the priest of the old Testament. But as to the new, who, I beseech you, is the priest of the new Testament, but Christ alone? We at least recognise no other High Priest of the new Testament. What did ever God, or Christ, or any apostle promise to the pope? Let them produce the records, and shew us there, if they can, that any such promise was made.

The fourth place which the Jesuit alleges is taken from Haggai ii. 11. The words are these : " Thus saith the Lord of hosts, Ask the priests concerning the law." I answer : In the first place, we confess this, namely, that the ministers, bishops and doctors, should be inquired of concerning the law; and that, when inquiries are made, they should answer them; otherwise they would not do their duty. But does it thence follow that they have therefore the power of defining anything just as they choose? Far from it. Yea, it is incumbent upon them to answer according to the law. Whence it is manifest that authority is lodged with the law ; and that they have no authority, but only a ministry. Secondly, it will follow from this place, that there ought to be not one supreme judge of scripture, but many, because God says through the prophet in the plural number, "Inquire of the priests," not in the singular, " Inquire of the priest."

The fifth place cited by the Jesuit is contained in Malachi ii. 7, where are these words: " The priest's lips shall keep knowledge, and they shall require the law from his mouth." I answer : In these words is shewn, not what sort of persons the priests always *would be,* but what they always *ought to* be. Therefore this is a fallacy founded upon a figure of speech. There is a precept in these words (let the priests be always such), not a promise (they shall be always such); for it follows immediately : " But ye have wandered from the way and made many to stumble :" as much as to say, Ye should have been endowed with knowledge, and skilful in the law, so as to be able to teach others also; but ye are unlearned and ignorant of the law, and have caused many to sin and violate my laws. Now, if the prophet affirmed this truly of those priests of the old Testament, it may certainly be said with even more truth of the popish clergy. So Hosea iv. 6, God thus addresses such priests as were in that time : " Because thou hast spurned knowledge, I also will spurn thee from being a priest unto me :" and Hosea v. 1, God calls the priests of that time *snares*.

The sixth place which the Jesuit cites (though he hath omitted it in his published edition) is Ezek. xiii. 3, where the words are as follows : " Woe to the foolish prophets, that follow their own spirit." Hence we see, says the Jesuit, that private spirits are not to be followed in the interpretation of scripture. I answer : We also deny that each man is to follow his own private spirit. But to follow scripture itself, and the Spirit of God speaking publicly in the scriptures (which we exhort all men to do), is not to follow a private spirit.

The seventh and last place cited by the Jesuit is contained in 2 Chron. xix. 10, 11, where Jehoshaphat makes Zebadiah judge of civil suits or controversies, but Amariah, the pontiff and priest, of those matters which pertain to God ; and distinguishes the office of the pontiff from the office of the king, assigning to the pontiff alone the cognisance of the doubtful points about the law. I answer : We confess that the functions of king and priest are distinct, and that they should not be confounded together. Nor is there need of our here making any large reply, because the same answer which we made to his second passage will suffice also for this,—namely, that, indeed, there ought to be some judges, not of scripture, but of suits and controversies, as well ecclesiastical as civil. We say that ecclesiastical disputes should be determined by the minister out of the divine law, and political disputes by the civil judge out of the laws of the state. But meanwhile, to end or determine controversies is one thing, and to interpret scriptures a very different one. And so much in reply to the Jesuit's first argument.

CHAPTER V.

AN ANSWER IS GIVEN TO THE TESTIMONIES TAKEN FROM THE NEW TESTAMENT.

His second argument is taken from the authority of the new Testament. Now from this he alleges nine testimonies, which we must examine severally in their order.

The first testimony is contained in Matth. xvi. 19, where Christ says to Peter, "I will give unto thee the keys of the kingdom of heaven; and whatsoever thou shalt bind on earth shall be bound in heaven, and whatsoever thou shalt loose on earth shall be loosed in heaven." From these words the Jesuit infers that the authority of interpreting scripture is given to Peter and all his successors, and, as it were, the chief judgment of scripture. I answer: We shall have to speak elsewhere at large of the power of the keys; however, sufficiently for the purposes of the present place, we thus briefly reply. *First*, the keys do not here denote, as the Jesuit would have it, the authority of interpreting the scriptures and opening all those things which are obscure in scripture, but they denote the authority of preaching the gospel. For when the gospel is preached, the kingdom of heaven is opened to those who believe, but closed against those who will not believe. *Secondly*, That authority of the keys was not committed to Peter alone, but to the rest of the apostles also. For in this place he did not give the keys, but only promised that he would give them: but afterwards, when he actually gives them (Matth. xxviii. 18, 19; John xx. 21, 22, 23), he addresses all the apostles equally. Therefore, if the pope have the authority of interpreting the scriptures, because the keys were given to Peter, then also other bishops and ministers, who were successors of the rest of the apostles, received the same authority, because the keys were given to the rest of the apostles as well as to Peter. *Thirdly*, Augustine says in his 124th Tractate upon John, as in many other places, that "Peter signified the universal church[1]," when the keys were given to him: therefore this power of the keys was given not to the pope alone, but to the whole church. But of this place we shall speak elsewhere more copiously.

The second place which Bellarmine cites from the new Testa-

[1 Ecclesia quæ fundatur in Christo, claves ab eo regni cœlorum accepit, id est, potestatem ligandi solvendique peccata.—Cf. Augustin. de Baptism. III. 17. In Johan. Tract. 50. In Psal. cviii. c. 30.]

ment is contained in Matth. xviii. 17: "If he will not hear the
church, let him be unto thee as a heathen man and a publican."
The Lord, says he, speaks of private injuries; but much rather is he
to be understood of public injuries, such as heresy is: and by the
church he denotes not the whole body of the faithful, but only the
pastors and bishops.   I answer : Christ speaks there not of the interpretation of scripture, but of fraternal correction and admonition,
which those who despise and make light of, are to be brought before the church itself ; and if they will not hear even the church
and acquiesce in the church's admonitions, then they are to be excommunicated.   Secondly, I confess that the church is to be heard,
and always to be heard, but under two provisions.   *First*, it behoves us to be certain that the church which we hear is the true
church of Christ, and that from the scripture's testimony ; for this
cannot be proved by any other means, and otherwise it is not to
be listened to.   *Secondly*, The church is to be heard, not simply in
all its dogmas, declarations, decrees, sentences and injunctions, but
then, and then only, when it enjoins what Christ approves and
prescribes : for if it enjoin anything of its own, in that it is
not to be heard.   The church is to be credited only on account
of Christ and Christ's word : therefore, if it once diverge from
the mind of Christ, it is not to be heard ; yea, we must not believe even an angel from heaven, if he teach otherwise than the
scripture hath delivered, as Paul warns us, Gal. i. 8.

The third place of the new Testament cited by the Jesuit is
Matth. xxiii. 2.   The words are these : " The scribes and Pharisees sit in Moses' seat ; all, therefore, that they command you to
observe, that observe and do."   Therefore, says the Jesuit, if they
must be obeyed who sit in the chair of Moses, much more they
who sit in the chair of Peter.   I answer : To sit in Moses' seat is
to succeed Moses as teacher ; for by the seat of Moses is understood
the doctrine delivered by Moses and the function of teaching.   In
this chair of Moses the scribes and Pharisees sat, and taught some
things legitimately and correctly.   They were to be heard, therefore, yet not in all, but then only when they taught according to
the law, and when they followed Moses in their teaching, not in
whatsoever simply they commanded.   For then Christ would have
contradicted himself ; since, in the 6th and 7th chapters of Matthew,
he refutes their false interpretations, and wholly sets aside certain
dogmas introduced by them into the church contrary to the true
sense of the law.   Who, indeed, would say that those scribes and

Pharisees always in their teaching sat in Moses' seat, when Moses, Deut. xviii. 15, had foreshewn that a prophet like unto him was to be raised up by God, whom he warned them to hear; whereas the scribes and the Pharisees continually, with all their authority and the most pertinacious obstinacy, exclaimed that Christ was not to be listened to? Wherefore Christ desired his disciples to beware of the leaven of the Pharisees, Matth. xvi. 6. The sum is this: That teachers and pastors are always to be heard, when they prescribe what is right and true, although in the meanwhile they do not those things which they enjoin upon others, nor lead a life agreeable to their profession: which is of force against those who will not use the ministry of wicked pastors. This we readily concede, which the Jesuit desires to be observed.

Afterwards the Jesuit remarks out of Cyprian, Epist. Lib. iv. Ep. 9[1], that Christ never blamed the priests and pontiffs but under the name of scribes and Pharisees, lest he should seem to blame the chair and priesthood itself. I answer, *first*, that the right itself and function of teaching is in truth not to be blamed, but those who do not rightly discharge that function; not the chair, but those who abuse the chair. The interpretation of the law was divinely instituted. If true, therefore, it is not to be blamed: but if false, the perverse interpretation of the law ought to be censured. Christ does not blame the priests when they interpret the law correctly; but when they mingled false doctrines and corrupted the law by their decisions, he censures them freely and with severity. *Secondly*, I say that the Jesuit misrepresents Cyprian. For that father does not write to the effect which this man pretends, as may appear by the place itself, if any one choose to examine it. But, as to his accommodation of this *a fortiori* to the chair of Peter, in this fashion, If those were to be heard who sat in the chair of Moses, much more those who sit in the chair of Peter; I answer, That they are indeed to be heard, but with that previous condition before laid down concerning those who sat in the chair of Moses, —namely, provided that be true which they teach: otherwise they are not to be heard. However, he goes on to object Augustine, Epist. 165[2], where he says, that in the succession of the Roman church, from Peter to Anastasius, who was then bishop of Rome, there was no traditor, no Donatist. I answer: That testimony of Augustine is nothing to the purpose. For we confess that up to

[1 i. e. in Erasmus' edition. It is Ep. 66, in bishop Fell's, and the passage referred to will be found in p. 166.]

[2 i. e. in Erasmus' edition, Basil. 1596, T. ii. col. 751.]

that time the Roman bishops were devout and good men ; but we say that afterwards evil men succeeded them and crept into the church.   Augustine's meaning is, that the church or Christians are not contaminated, if perchance a bishop should have been a traditor, since the Lord says, that even bad men are to be heard, and we should do not what they do, but what they say.   He says therefore, firstly, that there was no traditor in that succession from Peter to Anastasius : secondly, that even had there been one, yet the church would not be injured, since the Lord had provided for his church, saying of wicked prelates, Do what they say ; do not what they do.   Augustine neither mentions the argument *a fortiori*, nor says that the successors of Peter cannot possibly misinterpret the law ; but only that, while they teach aright, the church is not defiled by their evil life.   And so much for the third passage.

The fourth place of the new Testament, which the Jesuit brings to confirm his opinion, is written in the last chapter of John, verse 16, where Christ thus addresses Peter : " Simon Peter, lovest thou me ? Feed my sheep."   From these words the Jesuit would have three observations drawn.   The first is, that what was said to Peter was said also to Peter's successors.   I answer, *firstly*, that these words belong properly to Peter alone.   For in these words, Peter is restored to his former dignity in the apostolic office, from which he had then fallen ; and so the fathers themselves have interpreted this place : for they say that Peter is therefore thrice commissioned to feed, because he had thrice denied Christ, that so his triple confession might answer his threefold denial.   *Secondly*, I allow that these words, in the way of accommodation or inference, may be applied also to the successors of Peter.   For if it behoved Peter to feed Christ's lambs and sheep, therefore also the successors of Peter should resemble Peter in this respect.   *Thirdly*, I say that this appertains as much to all bishops and ministers as to the pope of Rome himself ; because they all succeed Peter in this matter, that is, in the preaching of the word, and should imitate his diligence in feeding the sheep of Christ.

The second point which the Jesuit observes, and would have us to observe, in the above passage, is this ; that the action of feeding in this place principally denotes the office of teaching, because here it is only *rational sheep*, that is, men, that are fed by the spiritual pastor. I answer, that this is correctly enough remarked ; and therefore I say that these words appertain least of all to the Roman pontiff, because he is least of all engaged in teaching.

Thirdly, the Jesuit observes, that *sheep* in this place denotes all the faithful, and therefore all Christians. I answer : Christ does not say to Peter, Feed all my sheep ; for neither Peter nor any other apostle could do that ; but he speaks indefinitely, " Feed my sheep." Christ gives the same command to Peter concerning feeding his sheep, as he gave to the other apostles, that each, according to the portion assigned to him, should feed the flock of Christ. For since to feed is, as Bellarmine hath reminded us, to teach, Christ hath thus in the last chapter of Matthew, v. 19, equally granted to all his apostles the pastoral authority, saying to all indifferently, " Go, and teach all nations." Therefore, if feeding and teaching be the same, the same authority was granted also to the other apostles as to Peter ; and if sheep denote all Christians, the other apostles also were commanded to teach all Christians. But that injunction is to be understood of all the apostles together and conjointly ; not of the several apostles separately, because they could not each severally run through all nations, and teach all Christians. Hence the Jesuit concludes, that the Roman pontiff cannot teach all by preaching, which we for our part allow to be most true, (for neither the pope, nor any other sole individual can preach to all men ;) but he adds, yea, nor yet by writing commentaries ; because then (says he) we should have to blame many pious popes, who have bestowed no pains on this employment. But we will deliver him from this apprehension : we freely and of our own accord confess that Christ did not mean that method of feeding. Therefore he determines that some singular kind of teaching was in these words commended to Peter and his successors, namely, one which consisted in establishing and decreeing what each person ought to teach and believe. I answer : In this way they ascribe to their pope, not a prætorian, but absolutely a dictatorial power, such as God claims for Christ alone, when he says (Matt. xvii. 5), " Hear him :" from which words Cyprian, Epist. 63, concludes, " that Christ alone is to be heard, because of him alone God said, ' Hear him ;' and therefore that we need not be solicitous what others said before us, but what Christ said, who was before all[1]." Surely this is an admirable and truly singular function of teaching, not to preach, not to write commentaries, but determine and prescribe what others are to believe !

[1 Quare si solus Christus audiendus est, non debemus attendere quid alius ante nos faciendum putaverit, sed quid, qui ante omnes est, Christus prior fecerit.—p. 155. ed. Fell.]

A monstrous fiction! Who instituted this office, that there should be one man who should prescribe what all others should teach, and not teach himself? This office is recognised neither by scripture, nor the fathers, nor the church. Christ commended nothing to Peter alone; and committed to him no such popish species of pastorate. For Peter, in fact, both taught, as much as he could, by word of mouth, and wrote epistles: which would not have been necessary for him to do, if he had been only bound to determine and fix what others should teach.

The fifth place which the Jesuit cites from the new Testament is Luke xxii. 32, and contains the words of Christ to Peter a little before his death, which are these: " I have prayed for thee, Peter, that thy faith fail not." From these words, says the Jesuit, Bernard, Epist. 190[1], deduces that Peter teaching *ex cathedra*, and consequently also his successors, cannot err; with which Epistle the decretals also agree. I determine here nothing of the authority of Bernard and the decretal epistles; but as to the matter itself I briefly answer, and say, in the *first* place, that this, whatever it was, pertains to Peter alone, and not to his successors: for Christ says, " I have prayed for thee, Peter,"—not for thy successors. He prayed indeed, doubtless, for the other apostles also, but specially for Peter, because he was about to suffer the assault of a temptation more perilous than befel the rest, and therefore required to be assisted by some peculiar aid of prayer. *Secondly,* I affirm, that this faith, of which Christ here speaks, is true faith, whereby one perseveres firm and constant to the end; actually justifying faith; in a word, faith of the heart and not of the mouth, as the place itself shews, and the comments also of the fathers thereupon. But the papists do not mean this faith, but an historical faith, which merely holds the true sense of doctrine: for they confess that the pope may be an impious and wicked man; but hold nevertheless that he cannot err in the interpretation of scripture, whensoever he seats himself in the chair. *Thirdly,* if Christ asked this for all the Roman pontiffs, that they should be exempt from error, then he did not obtain what he asked. For it is certain that many Roman pontiffs have erred, even when teaching *ex cathedra*, that

[1 Dignum namque arbitror ibi potissimum resarciri damna fidei, ubi non possit fides sentire defectum. Hæc quippe hujus prærogativa sedis. Cui enim alteri aliquando dictum est, *Ego pro te rogavi, Petre, ut non deficiat fides tua?*—Bernard. Opp. De Erroribus Abælard. Præf. p. 52. T. ii. Paris. 1835.]

is, determining controversies ; as Alphonsus asserts, *Contra Hœres.*
Lib. i. c. 4[2], where he affirms that the pope not only may err, but
even be a heretic[3]. The same is written and held by other papists
also. Then who, I pray you, will be the supreme judge of the
church, when the supreme pontiff hath fallen into heresy ? Is he a
fit person to be the supreme judge in religion, and one in whose
judgment we should acquiese, who may be, and is a heretic, as the
very papists themselves confess ? Surely, never. The supreme
judge of all controversies must be such an one as can neither err
nor prove a heretic : and such is Christ himself, that true High
Priest, and the sacred scripture. But now, since the pope may err
and fall into heresy,—the possibility of which our adversaries concede,—what shall we pronounce concerning Christ's prayer ? He
prayed that Peter's faith might not fail, which these men will have
extend to Peter's successors also. But faith cannot consist with
heresy. Therefore Christ could not obtain what he sought, if their
interpretation be received.

The sixth place which the Jesuit objects out of the new Testament is contained in Acts xv. 5, 6, 7, 28 ; where, upon a question
arising about the law of Moses and circumcision, the Christians who
disputed amongst themselves, are not remitted (says the Jesuit) to
a private spirit, but to a christian council over which Peter presided, which came to this conclusion, ver. 28 : " It seemed good
to the Holy Ghost and to us," &c. Hence the Jesuit gathers, that
the Holy Spirit is always present in a council where Peter or
Peter's successors preside. I answer, *first,* that we do not send
any one who is in doubt on any matter to his private spirit, neglecting all means of finding truth, as the Jesuit falsely objects to
us ; but to scripture itself, and the Holy Spirit speaking publicly
in the scripture, who, we say, ought to be heard, and by whose
authority we maintain that all controversies should be decided :
which also was the very thing done in this council. Let the same
thing, if possible, be now done as was done here. Let the pastors
and bishops be gathered together to consider and define some
question not by their own judgment, but by the authority of the
Holy Spirit speaking in the scriptures. For thus they defined that
controversy out of the scriptures, that we might understand that the
supreme judgment is to be given to the scriptures. Nor was there

[2 Omnis homo errare potest in fide, etiamsi Papa sit. He gives as instances the cases of Liberius and Celestine.—Lugd. 1564.]
[3 See Delahogue, de Ecclesia, pp. 386, et seq. Dublin. 1815.]

anything there concluded but by the authority of scripture. *Secondly,* the Jesuit's assertion that Peter presided over this council is false. For James presided rather than Peter; for it was in the words proposed by the former that the decree was drawn up, as appears from verses 13 and 22, and there are no vestiges whatever of a precedence or presidential right being assigned to Peter in that assembly. As to his attempt to prove that Peter presided from the circumstance of his having spoken first, I answer, that although Peter's words are recited first by Luke, yet it is plain from verse 7, that many had spoken before Peter: for it is said there, that after long disputing upon both sides Peter rose up. Πολλῆς, says Luke, συζητήσεως γενομένης. *Thirdly,* I confess, that the Holy Ghost was present and presided in this council, and that this sentence was that of the Holy Ghost, since it is proved by the testimony of scripture. But what hath this to do with the popish councils over which Peter presides not, and in which the Holy Spirit hath no share?

The Jesuit's seventh place is written Gal. ii. 2, where Paul says that he, at Jerusalem, compared his gospel σὺν τοῖς δοκοῦσι, that is, with those who were in some estimation, or who were held of some value. From this place, says the Jesuit, the fathers conclude that the church would not have believed Paul's gospel, if it had not been confirmed by Peter: therefore, it was then the privilege of Peter, and is now that of Peter's successor, to judge of the doctrine of faith. I answer, *first :* Paul went to Jerusalem, not to meet Peter alone, and compare his gospel with him solely, or borrow from him authority, but to treat publicly with the whole church concerning that doctrine which he preached. For so, v. 2, Καὶ ἀνεθέμην αὐτοῖς τὸ εὐαγγέλιον, which the old translator renders, *Et contuli cum illis evangelium,* that is, " with the whole church ;" which also is plain from his subjoining, κατ' ἰδίαν δὲ τοῖς δοκοῦσι, " privately with those who were of reputation :" therefore what follows, μὴ εἰς κενὸν τρέχω ἢ ἔδραμον, " lest I should run, or had run in vain," pertains no more to Peter than to the whole church, or those principal apostles. *Secondly,* therefore, although we should not interpret the place of the whole church, yet we cannot interpret it of Peter alone. For Paul says expressly, that he compared his gospel not with Peter alone, but with several, namely, σὺν τοῖς δοκοῦσι, and he afterwards shews who these were, namely, James, Peter, and John. Therefore it is false that Paul's gospel was confirmed by Peter alone : it was the privilege of these others, as much as of Peter, to judge concerning doctrine. *Thirdly*, as to the Jesuit's assertion, that the church would not have believed Paul's gospel unless it had been confirmed by Peter, it may bear two senses. If he mean, that the church ought not to have believed it, unless Peter had approved it, it is false; for the church ought always to believe an apostle preaching the truth. But if he mean that it would not have believed so readily, I assent: for this was the reason why Paul wished to go to Jerusalem, and there explain his gospel to those who were there, because some supposed that he preached and taught otherwise than the rest of the apostles; which suspicion entertained by many he thus entirely removed.

The eighth place produced by the Jesuit is contained in 1 Cor. xii. 8, 9, &c., where Paul says that "to some is given by the Spirit the word of wisdom, to others the word of knowledge, to others faith, to others the interpretation of speeches." From this place he concludes, that the spirit of interpretation is not given to all, and therefore that all cannot interpret the scriptures. I answer, this we spontaneously concede. But the Jesuit deceives us by the ambiguity of a word. For there is both a public and a private interpretation. We confess that all have not the gift of publicly interpreting the scriptures; but in private all the faithful, taught by the Holy Ghost, can understand the scriptures and recognise the true sense of scripture.

The ninth and last place, which the Jesuit adduces from the new Testament, is contained in 1 John iv. 1, where we are admonished "not to believe every spirit, but to try the spirits whether they are of God:" therefore (says the Jesuit) a private spirit can not be the judge or interpreter of scripture, because it is to be judged itself. I answer : The Jesuit does not understand the state of the question. We do not say that each individual should acquiesce in that interpretation which his own private spirit frames and dictates to him ; for this would be to open a door to fanatical tempers and spirits : but we say that that Spirit should be the judge, who speaks openly and expressly in the scriptures, and whom all may hear ; by him we desire that all other spirits, that is, all doctrines, (for so the word is to be taken in this place,) should be examined. We recognise no public judge save scripture, and the Spirit teaching us in scripture : yet this man speaks as if we made the spirit within the judge of others ; which should never be done. For we are not so mad or foolish as to deal thus : You ought to acquiesce in this doctrine, because my spirit judges it to be true; but we say, You should receive this doctrine because the Holy Spirit in the scriptures hath taught us thus to think and to believe.

Let it suffice to have said thus much against the Jesuit's second argument, which is that drawn from the authority of the new Testament.

CHAPTER VI.

OF THE THIRD ARGUMENT OF OUR ADVERSARIES.

His third general argument is from the practice of the church in councils, and the testimonies of the fathers : and here he makes a large enumeration of councils by which controversies were decided. I answer, that I do not understand what concern all these have with the argument. For we allow that it is a highly convenient way of finding the true sense of scripture, for devout and learned men to assemble, examine the cause diligently, and investigate the truth; yet with this proviso, that they govern their decision wholly by the scriptures. Such a proceeding we, for our parts, have long wished for; for it is attended with a twofold advantage : first, that what is sought by many is found the more readily; second, that errors, and heretics the patrons of errors, are the more easily repressed, when they are condemned by the common consent and judgment of a great number. This course, however, is not open to us in all controversies and at all times : for one cannot always, when in doubt of the interpretation of a passage, immediately convoke a council. We shall have a second opportunity of speaking about these matters, and therefore I now answer all with this one word; that, indeed, the weightiest controversies have been determined and settled in councils, but not by the absolute authority of the council itself, but by the judgment and authority of scripture in the council. Pious bishops never assembled to define a point themselves by their own authority, but by that of scripture. Therefore all religious councils have ascribed the supreme decision to the scriptures. Such we see to have been the case in Acts xv.; for there the maintainers of circumcision were refuted out of the Law of Moses. So the Novatians were refuted by authority of scripture. So the Anabaptists, as is plain from Augustine. So finally the Arians, in the council of Nice, were refuted and condemned by the authority of scripture. For thus the emperor Constantine addresses the fathers assembled in that Synod : "There are the prophetic and apostolic books, which plainly teach us what should be believed. Laying aside, therefore, all hostile feelings of enmity, let us derive from the inspired scriptures, λύσιν, the solution or decision of those matters about which this controversy hath arisen[1]." This is the very thing which we demand. Since, then, councils, whenever they are good and pious, follow the scriptures, it is manifest that the supreme authority of judging belongs to the scriptures.

The Jesuit proceeds to cite the Roman pontiffs, and emperors and fathers in great number, concerning whom also we will briefly reply in order. The popes alleged are, Damasus, Epist. 3. ad Stephanum ; Innocent. I. in Epist. ad Concil. Carthag. et Milevit. apud August. 91 and 93[2] ; Leo I. Epist. 81 and 89 ; Gelasius, Epistol. ad Episcopos Dardaniæ ; Gregory, Lib. IV. Ep. 52. These instruct us that weighty causes, especially of faith, pertain to the cognisance of the apostolic see. I answer, *first*, that formerly weighty causes were referred to the Roman church by the agreement and arrangement of the bishops, for the better maintenance of the peace of the church, and the easier repression of heretics and schismatics ; as also because it seemed unjust to determine anything which concerned the public profession of the faith, without consulting the bishop of Rome, who occupied the principal see. Hence it came to pass that by degrees those prelates seized and arrogated to themselves still greater authority, and laid claim to a divine right, the catholics meanwhile raising no very strong reclamations, as supposing that they possessed in the Roman church a great protection against heretics. *Secondly,* that these decretal Epistles of the popes Damasus, Julius, and others, are merely supposititious, of no sense or genius, but wholly made up of ignorance, arrogance, and antichristianism. Erasmus deems the Epistles of Innocent unworthy of so great a prelate, and misses in them " style and genius and erudition[3]." Gelasius everywhere exaggerates the dignity and

[1 Vide supra.]

[2 Aug. Opp. T. II. p. 88. Paris. 1555. See Coke, Censura quorundam Scriptt. Vett. p. 219. (Helmstadt. 1683). Papebroch himself (Catalog. Roman. Pontific. p. 61. ap. Cave, Hist. Liter. Art. *Innocentius I.*) confesses that many of this pope's epistles may be proved spurious by chronology.]

[3 In hac epistola et dictionem et ingenium tali dignum Præsule desiderare cogimur.—Censura in Ep. xciii. inter Epp. Augustini ut supra, p. 86. 2.]

privileges of his see without any moderation. Leo and Gregory, indeed, write with considerably more modesty, and yet transgress far and widely the limits of christian humility. *Thirdly*, that these bishops are not to be heard in their own cause, who were manifestly too deeply interested on their own side, and too deeply prejudiced in their own favour, even to the manifest injury of other churches and bishops.

Let us come now to emperors, the first of whom is Constantine. He, says Bellarmine, would not sit down in the Nicene synod before the bishops had given him leave to be seated[1]. So Eusebius tells us in his life of Constantine, Lib. III. : which conduct shewed that he was not president of that council. In the Epistle also to all churches, given in that same place, he says : "Whatever is decreed in the holy assemblies of the bishops, should wholly be ascribed to the divine will[2]." Ambrose says of him, Ep. 32 : "Constantine left the judgment free to the bishops[3]." And Augustine, Epist. 162, writes that the Donatists were by him referred to their own proper judge, Melchiades bishop of Rome[4]. I answer, that these things are irrelevant to the matter in hand. We do not say that Constantine was president of the Nicene council, in which, perhaps, he was never present more than once. But what then? Neither was the Roman pontiff president, as we shall prove in its proper place. That he did not sit down until desired by the bishops, proved his singular urbanity and respect for Christ's bishops,— nothing else. As to his writing in his epistles to the churches, that what the holy assemblies of bishops determine should be ascribed to the divine will, we acknowledge it. For holy bishops determine nothing but what the words of sacred scripture sanction, which is the rule they follow in their decrees ; otherwise they are not holy. Neither are all the decrees of all councils to be esteemed divine, but those which are supported by the authority of scripture,

[1 οὐ πρότερον ἢ τοὺς ἐπισκόπους ἐπινεῦσαι ἐκάθιζε. Euseb. de Vita Constant. Lib. III. c. 10. p. 402. D. Ed. Vales. Paris. 1678.]

[2 πᾶν γὰρ εἴ τι δ᾽ ἂν ἐν τοῖς ἁγίοις τῶν ἐπισκόπων συνεδρίοις πράττεται, τοῦτο πρὸς τὴν θείαν βούλησιν ἔχει τὴν ἀναφοράν. Ibid. cap. 20. p. 407. c.]

[3 Sicut factum est sub Constantino augustæ memoriæ principe, qui nullas leges ante præmisit, sed liberum dedit judicium sacerdotibus.—Class. I. Ep. xxi. n. 15. p. 339. T. VIII. Paris. 1839.]

[4 Neque enim ausus est Christianus imperator tumultuosas et fallaces querelas suscipere, ut de judicio episcoporum qui Romæ sederant ipse judicaret : sed alios, ut dixi, episcopos dedit.—Al. Ep. xliii. cap. 7. T. II. p. 97.]

as we shall shew hereafter in its fitting place. What says Ambrose of Constantine ? What if Constantine left the judgment free to the bishops, and himself prescribed nothing to them : will it therefore follow that they should not judge according to the scriptures ? Furthermore, Augustine does not write that Constantine referred the Donatists to the bishop of Rome as their proper judge : for the bishop of Rome was not the proper judge of the Donatists ; and if he were, Constantine would have compelled them to acquiesce in his sentence : whereas afterwards he assigned other arbitrators, and finally took cognisance of the cause himself; which fact Bellarmine omitted, because plainly repugnant to the plea which he had undertaken to defend.

The second is Gratian, in his Epistle to the bishop of Aquileia, in which he allows " the cognisance of altercations" to the bishops[5]. I reply : Who denies that the bishops can judge of such causes ? or what hath this to do with a question about the interpretation of scripture ? The third is the younger Theodosius, in an Epistle to the council of Ephesus, wherein he says that those who are not of the episcopal order " should not intermeddle in ecclesiastical matters[6]." I answer : There will be another place for discussing the question, whether it be lawful for none but bishops to treat of ecclesiastical affairs : meanwhile, what does this contribute towards confirming the supreme authority of the Roman pontiff in the interpretation of the scriptures ? The fourth is Martian, who, *L. Nemo. C. de Summa Trinit.* declares that nothing " once adjudicated should be gone back upon or subjected to fresh disputation[7]." I answer, that whatever things have been once adjudicated in a synod according to the scriptures cannot be called a second time in question without injury to the synod. But must, therefore, whatever judgment the Roman pontiff hath passed prevail even against the plain evidence of scripture ? The fifth is Valentinian the elder, who permits bishops to assemble when they would, and denies that such

[5 Neque enim controversiæ dubiæ sententiæ rectius poterant expediri, quam si obortæ altercationis interpretes ipsos constituissemus antistites.— Rescript. Gratian. Imp. ad Conc. Aquileg. inter Opp. Ambrosii. T. VIII. p. 230. Paris. 1839.]

[6 ἀθέμιτον γὰρ τὸν μὴ τοῦ καταλόγου τῶν ἁγιωτάτων ἐπισκόπων τυγχάνοντα τοῖς ἐκκλησιαστικοῖς σκέμμασιν ἐπιμίγνυσθαι. Ap. Labb. et Cossart. Concill. T. III. coll. 442, 3.]

[7 Nam et injuriam facit judicis reverendissimæ synodi, si quis semel judicata ac recte disposita revolvere ac publice disputare contenderit.—Cod. Justinian. Lib. I. Tit. iv. l. 111. Lugd. 1585.]

matters appertain to him; as we see in Sozomen. Lib. vi. c. 7¹. I
answer : Valentinian denies that it was lawful for him μετὰ λαοῦ
τεταγμένῳ τοιαῦτα πολυπραγμονεῖν, " who was ranked amongst
the laity to busy himself with such matters :" what then? The
Roman bishop is the judge of all interpretations of scripture and all
controversies? Surely a beautiful conclusion! The sixth is the
emperor Basil², in the 8th synod, and the seventh, Theodoric, king
of the Goths, in the fourth Roman synod under Symmachus³; who
say nothing more than that laymen should not presume to decide
church-controversies, but should leave them to the bishops. Yet it
does not follow from this, either that the bishop of Rome is the
supreme interpreter of scripture, or that bishops can define controversies of faith and religion any otherwise than out of scripture.

Let us now see how the case stands with the fathers. In the
first place he objects to us Irenæus, contra Hær. Lib. iii. c. 2,
where, he says, that father lays it down that controversies cannot
be determined out of the scriptures alone, because they are variously
expounded by heretics ; and that therefore, in the next chapter, he
sends the heretics against whom he disputes to the Roman church,
and shews them that controversies are to be determined by the
doctrine of that church⁴. I answer : Whoever will look at the place
itself in Irenæus, will readily perceive the fraud and prevarication
of the Jesuit. For there Irenæus finds fault with those heretics
with whom he was engaged, on the very score of not receiving the
scriptures, but rather pressing and adhering to tradition. Now
their reason was, that scripture admits various senses and no fixed
interpretation. This the Jesuit ascribes to Irenæus, as if it were
his own opinion ; whereas Irenæus in that place is not speaking his

[¹ 'Εμοὶ μὲν, ἔφη, μετὰ λαοῦ τεταγμένῳ οὐ θέμις τοιαῦτα πολυπραγμονεῖν· οἱ
δὲ ἱερεῖς οἷς τούτου μέλει καθ᾽ ἑαυτοὺς ὅπη βούλονται συνίτωσαν.—p. 525. B.
Paris. 1686.]

[² Labb. et Cossart. Concill. T. viii. col. 1157.]

[³ Ib. T. iii. col. 1333.]

[⁴ Cum enim ex scripturis arguuntur, in accusationem convertuntur ipsarum scripturarum, quasi non recte habeant, neque sint ex auctoritate, et
quia varie sint dictæ, et quia non possit ex his inveniri veritas ab his qui
nesciant traditionem.—p. 230. Paris. 1675. In the next chapter, p. 232, we
find : Maximæ et antiquissimæ et omnibus cognitæ, a gloriosissimis duobus
apostolis Petro et Paulo Romæ fundatæ et constitutæ ecclesiæ, eam quam
habet ab apostolis traditionem et annunciatam hominibus fidem, per successiones episcoporum pervenientem usque ad nos, indicantes, confundimus
omnes eos, &c.]

own sentiments, but proposing the judgment and opinion of the heretics, and censuring it. And as to cap. 3 of the same book, Irenæus does, indeed, send those heretics to the Roman church, and with good reason; because that church was then the most illustrious and noble of all churches, and retained, at that time, the tradition of the apostles uncorrupted. But it hath now fallen, and become much changed from what it was in the early ages.

Next he objects Athanasius, in his Epistle to the Hermits, wherein, speaking of the Arian Constantius, he says : " When was it ever heard that the judgment of the church received its authority from the emperor⁵?" I answer : The legitimate judgments of the church upon matters which concern faith borrowed their force and authority from none but from God himself. Therefore, whoever assumes the right of determining concerning the faith as it may seem good to himself, as the impious Constantius did, he seizes upon divine authority, even though he were the Roman pontiff, or all pontiffs together ; since it is their duty not to pronounce according to their own pleasure, but to unfold what God hath determined, and that not otherwise but by the scriptures ; so as always to acknowledge that their opinion is to be squared by the rule of scripture, and approved as it accords with scripture.

In the third place, he objects Basil, Epist 52, to Athanasius, where he says that it seems to him advisable that the Roman bishop should be written to, that he might of his own authority send some persons into the East to dissolve the acts of the council of Rimini⁶. I answer : I confess, indeed, that Basil writes that he thought this advisable ; but what is that to the purpose ? Ought not catholic bishops to condemn heretical opinions, and provide for the peace and tranquillity of the church ? Basil requires that a message should be sent to the Roman bishop in order that, as it was difficult to send persons " by public decree and consent," ἀπὸ κοινοῦ καὶ συνοδικοῦ δόγματος, he might of himself choose and send certain men fit for the office, and who understood the whole transactions at Rimini in

[⁵ T. I. p. 371. Ed. Benedict.]

[⁶ Ἐφάνη δὲ ἡμῖν ἀκόλουθον ἐπιστεῖλαι τῷ ἐπισκόπῳ Ρώμης, ἐπισκέψασθαι τὰ ἐνταῦθα, καὶ δοῦναι γνώμην· ἵνα ἐπειδὰν ἀπὸ κοινοῦ καὶ συνοδικοῦ δόγματος ἀποσταλῆναί τινας δύσκολον τῶν ἐκεῖθεν, αὐτὸν αὐθεντῆσαι περὶ τὸ πρᾶγμα, ἐκλεξάμενον ἄνδρας ἱκανοὺς μὲν ὁδοιπορίας πόνους διενεγκεῖν, ἱκανοὺς δὲ πρᾳότητι καὶ ἀπονοίᾳ ἤθους τοὺς ἐνδιαστρόφους τῶν παρ' ἡμῖν νουθετῆσαι· ἐπιτηδείως δὲ καὶ οἰκονομικῶς κεχρημένους τῷ λόγῳ, καὶ πάντα ἔχοντας μεθ' ἑαυτῶν τὰ ἐν Ἀριμίνῳ πεπραγμένα, ἐπὶ λύσει τῶν κατὰ ἀνάγκην ἐκεῖ γενομένων. T. II. p. 825. B.]

Italy, ἐπὶ λύσει τῶν κατ᾽ ἀνάγκην ἐκεῖ γενομένων, "to dissolve what was there done by force;" that is, inform the people that it was not reason or scripture, but violence and fraud, that prevailed in that council, and so impair the authority of that council. What could any one collect from this to confer the supreme right and dictatorship in the interpretation of all parts of scripture upon the bishop of Rome?

The fourth father whom he objects to us is Nazianzen, in his oration upon his flight[1], and again in his oration to his panic-stricken fellow-citizens[2], where there is nothing whatever to favour the opinion of our adversaries. He bids them not " to feed the pastor, or judge the judge :" not as if the bishops were allowed to establish any thing just as they pleased, while the people were forbidden to contradict or examine it; but because rashness in judging is to be guarded against. For the people, if they desire not to be involved in error and perdition, are bound to judge heretical bishops who discharge the office of pastors and judges.

Chrysostom follows in the fifth place, who, in his last Homily upon St John, says that Peter was set as a master over the whole world by Christ[3]. I answer, but not as sole master. Neither does this avail any thing towards establishing the pope's authority. For Chrysostom does not say that the pope was set as a master over the world.

Cyril is the sixth, whom Thomas cites in his small treatise[4] on the errors of the Greeks. I answer, that testimony is not extant in Cyril's Thesaurus, which Thomas hath cited against the Greeks, so that it may justly be asked where Thomas found it. It is some apocryphal and supposititious testimony, such as the rest upon which the papal primacy is founded.

Bellarmine now proceeds to the Latin fathers, and, in the seventh place, he objects Tertullian in his book of Prescriptions against Heretics, where he teaches that we should not dispute

[1 Orat. I. T. i. p. 1.]
[2 Orat. XVII. T. i. p. 265.]
[3 Chrysostom there says of Peter, τὴν προστασίαν ἐνεπιστεύθη τῶν ἀδελ-φῶν, in v. 21. But he adds afterwards of him and the other apostles generally, ἐπειδὰν γὰρ ἔμελλον τῆς οἰκουμένης τὴν ἐπιτροπὴν ἀναδέξασθαι, οὐκ ἔδει συμπεπλέχθαι λοιπὸν ἀλλήλοις, in v. 23.]
[4 Dicit enim Cyrillus in libro Thesaurorum: Ut membra maneamus in capite nostro, apostolico throno Romanorum pontificum, a quo nostrum est quærere quid credere et quid tenere debemus.—Thomæ Aquinat. Opp. T. xvii. p. 9. Venet. 1593.]

against heretics out of scripture[5].   I answer : Tertullian says that
some heretics do not receive some parts of scripture ; that against
such we must not dispute out of the scriptures, but use other arguments.   This we also allow, conceding that with such men, who
deny and reject the scriptures, we must argue not from the scriptures but from the testimony of the church, or contend in some
other way.   For he who disputes only of scripture against those
who deny the scripture loses his pains ; and who denies that the
truth was specially to be sought for in the apostolic churches ?
Can it be proved from this that the Roman bishop is the supreme
judge of controversies and interpreting of scripture ?

To Tertullian succeeds Cyprian, Lib. I. Epist. 3, where he says
that " heresies and schisms arise from this, that God's priest is not
obeyed, and that one priest at a time in the church, and one judge at
a time, is not considered as representing Christ[6]."   I answer, that
this priest and judge is not the sole bishop of Rome, as Bellarmine
feigns, but each catholic bishop of the church : for Cyprian is now
speaking of himself, against whom the Novatians had created another
bishop, and introduced schism and heresy into that church.   So
Lib. IV. Epist. 10 : " Thence," says he, " schisms and heresies have
sprung and do spring, that the bishop, who is but one and presides
over the church, is despised by the arrogant presumption of certain
persons[7]." He speaks of the particular bishops of particular churches,
to whom even Bellarmine himself does not ascribe an absolute
power of interpreting scripture.   And even should we concede that
Cyprian speaks of Cornelius, what will follow but that he was the
sole priest of the Roman church, not of all churches ?   Ambrose,
indeed, Ep. 32, to Valentinian[8] the younger, blames him severely
and justly for wresting the cognisance of matters of faith from the
catholic bishops and assuming it himself.   For who can doubt that
it belongs to the bishops and pastors to judge of matters of faith ?

[5 Hunc igitur potissimum gradum obstruimus, non admittendos eos ad
illam de scripturis disputationem, si hæ sunt illæ vires illorum, uti ne eas
habere possint.   c. xv. p. 11.]

[6 Neque enim aliunde hæreses obortæ sunt aut mota sunt schismata,
quam inde quod sacerdoti Dei non obtemperatur, nec unus in ecclesia ad
tempus sacerdos et ad tempus judex vice Christi cogitatur.   Ep. lix. p. 129.
Ed. Fell.]

[7 Inde schismata et hæreses obortæ sunt, dum episcopus, qui unus est et
ecclesiæ præest, superba quorundam præsumptione contemnitur.]

[8 Quando audisti, clementissime imperator, in causa fidei laicos de
episcopo judicasse ?—Class. I. Ep. xxi. n. 4. p. 337. T. VIII. Paris. 1839.]

But will this make the bishop of Rome supreme judge, or permit bishops to judge as they please?

Augustine is next objected to us, who, in his first book against Cresconius the grammarian, cap. 33, says, " Let him who fears he may be deceived, consult the church[1]." I answer : This we allow, but under the condition which Augustine subjoins; namely, that that church is to be consulted "which the scripture points out." For otherwise than by the scriptures it cannot certainly be known which is the true church. We say that the church should be consulted in every cause which concerns faith, and that the church ought to consult the scriptures. And truly they are justly deceived who do not consult the church, and obey her pious counsels and admonitions. But, although pious doctors are to be sought for and inquired of, and all proud and perilous temptations to be avoided, as Augustine hath reminded us in the Prologue to his books of Christian Doctrine; yet we should consider both what they answer, and how truly, lest our faith should rest upon human teaching rather than upon divine testimony. That is not really faith, which is founded upon the authority of men ; and upon such authority is founded whatever depends not on the word and voice of God.

But Jerome, says Bellarmine, writes thus to Damasus : " I shall not be afraid to speak of *three hypostases*, if you desire me[2]." Therefore he entirely acquiesced in the authority of the Roman pontiff. I answer : Jerome was, indeed, in great doubt and anxiety, whether he ought to say with the Greek bishops that there were three hypostases. He recognised three persons : but this term ὑπόστασις he regarded with suspicion, supposing that perhaps some poison lay concealed in it; and when constantly in the writings of the Greeks meeting with the assertion that there are three hypostases, he feared that he might involve the doctrine of three Gods. Upon this subject he consulted the bishop of Rome, being himself in total seclusion, and having, in that place where he was, no learned man whose advice he could ask. He was the more inclined to consult him rather than any other person, because he was himself a presbyter of the Roman church, and Damasus, as bishop of that

[1 Ut quoniam sancta scriptura fallere non potest, quisquis falli metuit hujus obscuritate quæstionis, eandem ecclesiam de illa consulat, quam sine ulla ambiguitate sancta scriptura demonstrat.—T. VII. p. 168. Paris. 1637.]

[2 Discernite, si placet, obsecro : non timebo tres hypostases dicere, si jubetis.—Ep. lvi. Opp. T. II. p. 131. Basil. 1565.]

church, was in the best condition to know the sense of that church which Jerome would desire to follow. The controversy, therefore, was about words, not things: for Jerome was perfectly master of the thing meant, but wished to know what Damasus and the Roman church thought of the expression, because he was desirous of acquiescing in the consent and custom of that church.

In the next place, as to what Sulpitius Severus tells us, *Historiæ Sacr.* L. II., of Martin, how he told the emperor Maximus, " that it was impious for the temporal judge to take cognisance of an ecclesiastical cause[3];" I answer, that Martin did indeed assert the church's right to judge of doctrine, and allowed no such right to the emperor. And who denies that this judgment belongs to the bishops? But must therefore the Roman pontiff alone engage in such judgments, or be the supreme judge of the church and interpreter of scripture? Bellarmine should consider what enormous licence he allows himself in controversy. There is a wide gap between such premises and any conclusion suitable to the question proposed.

Furthermore, Prosper, who comes next, does not, as Bellarmine affirms, prove, in the end of his book against Cassian, that the Pelagians are heretics on no other score than because they had been condemned by the Roman bishops. For throughout the whole of the book he had been contending against the Pelagians with arguments for the most part taken from Augustine; and then in the end he mentions how the Pelagians had been condemned by Innocent, Zosimus, Boniface and Celestine. Is this nothing else but proving that the Pelagians were heretics upon no other account than because they had been condemned by the Roman bishops?

Afterwards the Jesuit alleges Vincentius Lirinensis, who, in his commentary, teaches us that besides the scriptures we should apply " the rule of catholic understanding[4]." I answer: that each man is not to be left to his own private opinions, but that the analogy of truth is to be retained, and " the line of prophetic and apostolical interpretation." What then is this? He shews, says Bellarmine, that it is the decrees of councils, the consent of the fathers, and

[3 Namque tum Martinus apud Treveros constitutus non desinebat increpare Ithacium, ut ab accusatione desisteret: Maximum orare, ut sanguine infelicium abstineret: satis superque sufficere ut episcopali sententia hæretici judicati ecclesiis pellerentur: novum esse et inauditum nefas, ut causam ecclesiæ judex seculi judicaret.—p. 161. Amstel. 1641.]

[4 Idcirco multum necesse est, propter tantos tam varii erroris anfractus, ut propheticæ et apostolicæ interpretationis linea secundum ecclesiastici et catholici sensus normam dirigatur.—Commonit. c. 2. p. 325. Paris. 1663.]

such like. We also value these things highly; yet not promiscuously, but with discrimination. For the decrees of councils are
not always perfectly entire, and the consent of the fathers can
never be proved. But wherefore did Vincentius say nothing of
the Roman pontiff, when he was disputing of the true interpretation of scripture? Who does not perceive that this glorious
interpreter of scripture was unknown to Vincentius?

Gregory follows, who, Lib. v. Epist. 25, says: "We know that
the most pious lords keep strict discipline, observe order, respect
the canon, and intermeddle not with the business of the priest[1]."
I answer: Pious princes use not to meddle with the affairs of the
priesthood, and this is said to be unlawful for them to do. But
what is this to the Jesuit's cause? Will it therefore follow, that
the supreme right of expounding scripture and the final judgment
of all controversies appertains to the bishop of Rome? These testimonies respect rather another question, whether a prince ought to
undertake the care of religion. But such is the acuteness of the
Jesuits, that they can prove anything by anything.

I pass over Anselm and Bernard, and excuse them, considering
the time they lived in, if perchance they ascribed some extravagant
prerogatives to the Roman pontiff. If he had produced even more
numerous and stringent arguments than these, yet, since they are
merely human, they could make no reason of demonstrative force.

And so much upon the Jesuit's third argument.

CHAPTER VII.

OF THE JESUIT'S FOURTH ARGUMENT.

His fourth and last argument is drawn from the reason of the
thing. God, says he, was not ignorant that there would be in his
church at all times many controversies and difficult questions concerning the faith. Therefore he would not have well provided in
things necessary for his church, if he had not established and left
to it some judge of those controversies. But God hath excellently
well provided for his church always, especially in respect of things
necessary. Therefore he hath left some judge. I answer: God

[1] Notum est piissimos dominos disciplinam dirigere, ordinem servare,
canones venerari, et se sacerdotalibus negotiis non miscere.—Opp. T. I. p.
838. Basil. 1564.]

hath, indeed, left his church a judge; but the question now is, who is that judge? upon which a controversy is raised between us and the papists. We say that the judge is the Holy Spirit speaking in the scriptures. But the Jesuit draws up three assertions upon this subject. First, he says that this judge is not some spirit of private revelation. I answer: We concede this. The authority of such a spirit is secret, hidden and private; but the judge sought should possess a public, open, and universally notorious authority. Secondly, the Jesuit affirms that this judge is no secular prince. I answer: We concede this also. For we ascribe the supreme decision solely to the scripture and the Holy Spirit; and yet the papists object to us that other sentiment and opinion, as if it were ours. Thirdly, the Jesuit concludes that the supreme judge must be an ecclesiastical prince, such as is the Roman pontiff. I answer: Whatever, then, the papists talk so vauntingly of fathers and of councils, yet it is to their ecclesiastical prince, that is to the pope, that all controversies are finally referred, and with that prince and supreme interpreter rests the whole meaning of scripture and the right of adjudicating upon it. But we do not acknowledge that prince, whom Christ never constituted; and we say that the scripture itself publicly set forth and propounded is its own interpreter.

It remains now that we see with what sort of reasons he endeavours to overturn this opinion of ours. Now the Jesuit proves that scripture cannot be its own interpreter, by three arguments. His first reason is, because scripture hath various meanings; and, therefore, since it cannot speak, it cannot inform us which of these is the true and genuine sense. I answer: Scripture, as we have already said, hath one simple meaning, which may be clearly gathered also from the scriptures themselves: and although the scripture hath not voice and speech like a man, yet does it speak plainly as a law; and God himself speaks in the scripture, and scripture is on that account styled the word of God. With no less certainty, therefore, may we elicit a true meaning from scripture, than if God himself were to address us with an audible voice. Do we then desire a better judge and interpreter than God himself? He who reads the letter of a friend, does he fail to understand his friend's meaning, because the letter itself does not speak, or because he does not actually hear his friend speaking to him? No man in his senses would say that. Since the scriptures, then, are as it were a letter sent to us from God, we can from them understand the will of God, although they do not speak to us. "The heavens" (says the prophet, Ps. xix.) " declare the glory of God;" and yet they speak not: the scriptures have a yet more glorious and distinct utterance. " In the beginning God created the heavens and the earth." What ? shall we not know the meaning of these words, unless we consult the pope ? And no less plain are all the chief articles of our religion.

The second argument wherewith the Jesuit proves that scripture cannot be its own judge and interpreter, is this : because in every well-constituted state there is careful distinction made between the law and the judge ; and therefore the scripture cannot be the judge, since it is the law. I answer: In no commonwealth should any judge be constituted, who might expound the law according to his own will and pleasure : for then what will be the use of laws ? On the contrary, the judge, in every state, is bound to expound the law by the law ; otherwise he will prove an unrighteous magistrate, if he follow his own mind and not the law. So in the church bishops and pastors ought to interpret scripture and expound the will of God, but yet by the law of God itself, that is, the scriptures : although, in truth, we allow to no man so much authority in respect of the scriptures as may be ascribed to the judge of civil matters in regard of the laws of men. Human laws may with much greater safety be entrusted to a single judge than the divine law. The divine law is both the judgment and the judge, the interpreter and the rule. For what rule shall that judge whom the papists feign propose to himself in the interpretation of scripture ? Hath he none ? That, I hope, they dare not affirm. Now if he follow any rule, it must needs be either a public or a private one. If he follow a private and hidden rule, it should not be received, because doubtful and uncertain, and no better than the private testimony of the Spirit; whereas every rule ought to be certain and known. But if it be a public rule which he follows, it must needs be scripture : for what other can it be ? Now he that follows scripture as his rule, and squares and conforms his interpretations to it, confesses that he hath no power to interpret the scriptures otherwise than as the rule of scripture itself prescribes. Thus he does not judge of the sense of scripture with an absolute authority, but submits his judgment to the scriptures.

The Jesuit's third reason upon this subject is to this effect: A judge ought to have a coactive authority ; otherwise his judgment will have no force, nor will any one acquiesce in his sentence. I answer : Scripture, indeed, hath no external power of compulsion, but only internally compels the mind to assent. But if there were any external judge of this sort, who could compel all persons, then there would be no controversies, which yet have always been and always will be, and now too are almost infinite. The Roman pontiff can indeed compel in one sense, that is, terrify, and restrain by fear, and punish with death; but he cannot compel us to believe that this is the will of God, and to receive the scripture as the voice of God. It is the Holy Spirit who persuades us to believe this, who leads our minds to form true opinions, and makes us hold them firm even to our last gasp. The pontiff, therefore, is not the judge, because he cannot compel us to believe. For that coaction of his, which he uses when he gags our mouths, and strangles our very throats, so as to prevent us even from muttering, is mere violence, and can avail nothing without the inward persuasion of the Holy Spirit. Yea, unless that inward persuasion of the Holy Spirit be superinduced, the mind can never securely and resolutely acquiesce in any interpretation.

So far then we have spoken of the arguments of the papists; which are, for the most part, irrelevant, being directed against the private spirit, which is not the judge whom we recognise.

CHAPTER VIII.

OUR ARGUMENTS WHEREBY WE PROVE THAT THE SUPREME DECISION IN INTERPRETING SCRIPTURE BELONGS NOT TO THE CHURCH, BUT TO THE SCRIPTURES THEMSELVES AND TO THE HOLY SPIRIT.

OUR opinion is, that the supreme decision and authority in the interpretation of scripture should not be ascribed to the church, but to the scripture itself, and to the Holy Spirit, as well speaking plainly in the scriptures as also secretly confirming the same in our hearts. This opinion of ours we now establish by some arguments.

Our first argument depends upon the conclusion of the third question. For if scripture cannot otherwise be known but by scripture and the Holy Spirit, which was the conclusion we have arrived at already, in the third question; then certainly neither should we seek the sense of scripture from any other source than from scripture and the Holy Spirit speaking in scripture. For the sense of scripture is the scripture itself. Hither, therefore, may be referred all those arguments which we used in the third question.

Our second argument is this : That which alone hath power to engender faith, hath alone the supreme authority of interpreting the scriptures, and defining and deciding all controversies. Now it is only the scripture and the Holy Spirit that have this power. Therefore this authority is to be ascribed only to them. The major is sufficiently plain. For faith (says Paul, Rom. x. 17) "cometh by hearing," that is, from the sense of scripture duly perceived. Now the sense of scripture is only to be sought from scripture itself and the Holy Spirit. The minor is also manifest : for it is only the Holy Ghost that can infuse into our hearts that saving faith which is therefore called by the schoolmen *Fides infusa.* The church cannot infuse this faith : for that faith which we obtain from the church is not called infused, but acquired, and the papists themselves allow that it is not sufficient to a full assurance or certain persuasion. The gospel is called "the power of God unto salvation," Rom. i. 16 ; and if this be true, then it is certainly sufficient to engender faith. And the apostle testifies that he preached the gospel without any ornaments of speech, in order that it might be evident that the people's faith was the mere result of the gospel itself. Faith, therefore, is not the gift of the church, except improperly and in a mere ministerial capacity ; but it is properly and necessarily the gift and effect of the Holy Spirit speaking through the scriptures. The sum of the matter is this : faith is produced by scripture alone ; therefore the true sense of scripture is to be discovered from the scripture itself alone.

Our third argument stands thus : The supreme judge of controversies and legitimate interpreter of scripture should have these three properties : the first is, that we should certainly know that the sentence which he delivers is true, and that we can acquiesce in it ; the second, that no appeal from that sentence shall be lawful ; the third, that he be influenced by no partiality. Now the church or the pope possess none of these ; whereas the scripture, and the Holy Spirit speaking in the scripture, have them all. Therefore the supreme decision is to be given to them, and not to the church or the pope. The major is self-evident. The minor, namely, that none of these properties exist in any visible church or in the pope, is clear also. For by the church the papists mean, first, the fathers and the unanimous sentences of the fathers ; since unless they agree, they do not assign to them such great authority. But how can we be certain whether all the fathers agreed amongst themselves or with their brother bishops ? In order to know this for certain we

should have to read all the fathers. Besides, there are no books
extant of many fathers, so as to leave us totally ignorant what their
opinion was. Secondly, by the church they mean councils. But
how shall we know certainly that councils were legitimately assembled? And without this we can have no certain persuasion of the
presence of the Holy Spirit. Besides, councils were not assembled
or held to define all controversies and interpret all obscure parts of
scriptures, but to condemn and refute two or three heretical doctrines. So in the council of Nice Arius was condemned, who denied
the divinity of the Son. In the council of Constantinople Macedonius
was condemned, who impugned the divinity of the Holy Spirit. So
in other councils other opinions of heretics were refuted out of the
scriptures. But how small a part is this of those things which
require a legitimate interpretation! In the third and last place,
therefore, by the church they mean the pope. But there are
grounds of hesitation also with respect to his sentence. For how
can we be certain that he does not himself err? How shall it be
made plain to us that he hath any such authority? They say, from
scripture. I ask, from what scripture? Forsooth from this: " I
have prayed for thee, Peter, that thy faith fail not." Luke xxii. 32.
Be it so. But who shall judge of the sense of this passage? How
shall I know that it is spoken of the pope? My ears tell me that it
is said of Peter; but of the pope I hear nothing. For Christ says,
" I have prayed for thee, Peter," not " I have prayed for thee,
pope." And Peter, indeed, did remain firm and constant in the
faith to the very end of his life; but many popes have not had the
like perseverance. How then shall I know that these words are
meant of the pope? Who shall be the judge of this controversy?
The pope, they tell us. But it is unjust that he who is the subject
of the controversy should be the judge of the controversy; and I
am in greater doubt of the pope's authority than of the sense
of this passage. There is need, therefore, of some other and more
impartial judge. For who could say this was a legitimate interpretation;—since the pope says that infallibility is promised to him in
this text, therefore he is infallible? Surely he needs some greater
authority and testimony than his own word to prove that such a
promise hath been made to him. Besides, the papists themselves
acknowledge, that the pope may not only err, but even be a heretic,
and so completely overturn this interpretation of the passage.

Finally, councils, fathers, popes, are men; and scripture testifies
that all men are deceitful. How then shall I acquiesce in their sen-

tence? How can my conscience certainly determine, so as to leave no room for my faith to waver, that whatever they may pronounce is true? This is surely to leave no difference between God and men. For I believe what God says to be true, because he says it, and seek no other reason; but when I hear scripture saying that "all men are liars," I dare not ascribe so much to man, lest I make him equal to God. If they say that it is true, not because they pronounce it, but because scripture says it, then they give the supreme authority to another, that is, to scripture. Thus, what we said was the first requisite in every judge, we have shewn impossible to be found in this judge whom our adversaries have set up.

But now, as to the second part: if we cannot certainly know that their judgment is true, and that we may acquiesce in it, much less can we be so certain of their sentence as to make it unlawful for us to appeal against it. They appeal from fathers to councils, from councils to the pope; why then should it not be lawful for us to appeal from the pope to God, that is, to the Holy Spirit speaking in the scriptures? But, says the papist, God does not speak; the Holy Spirit does not speak; it is foolish, therefore, to appeal to him. I answer, that such an assertion is false and impious. For God speaks with us in the scriptures as it were face to face, as much as he formerly spake out of the cloud, Matth. xvii. 5; nor would he speak otherwise than he hath spoken in the scriptures, if he were now to utter a voice from heaven. Consequently we are commanded, John v. 39, to "search the scriptures:" and Matth. xxii. 29, Christ thus addresses the Sadducees: "Ye do err, not knowing the scriptures." So that errors spring from ignorance of the scriptures. And, 2 Pet. i. 19, Peter praises those to whom he writes, saying: "Ye do well that ye take heed to the word, λόγῳ, of prophecy." And on this account pious pastors do not say, you must believe because we say it, but because God hath said it; and if we ask of them how this may be known, they tell us, from the scriptures,—from this or that place of scripture. The Levites are commanded, Deut. xvii. 11, to judge according to the law; and, Joshua i. 7, Joshua is ordered to decline from the law neither to the right hand nor to the left. He is therefore permitted to determine nothing of himself, but is bound most closely to the scripture as his rule. Also, that scripture is not dumb or mute, but utters a clear voice which, if we be not deaf, we may easily hear, is manifestly shewn by the following texts: Rom. iii. 19, Paul says, ὅσα ὁ νόμος λέγει τοῖς ἐν τῷ νόμῳ λαλεῖ, "Whatever the law saith, it speaketh to those who are under the law." So Moses ascribes to it a *mouth*, Deut. vii. 11, where Pagninus hath translated it, *ex ore legis*. Heb. xii. 5, " Ye have forgotten the exhortation which speaketh, διαλέγεται, unto you as unto children : My son, despise not thou the chastening of the Lord," &c. John vii. 42 : " Hath not the scripture said, εἶπεν; &c." And afterwards, verse 51, Nicodemus asks, Μὴ νόμος ἡμῶν κρίνει τὸν ἄνθρωπον; " Doth our law judge the man," &c. If the law condemn, it certainly speaks. John xix. 37, ἑτέρα γραφὴ λέγει, " another scripture saith." Paul asks, Rom. iv. 3, τί γὰρ ἡ γραφὴ λέγει; " What saith the scripture ?" And *discourse*, λόγος, is everywhere ascribed to scripture, so as plainly to convict those of folly and audacity who deny the power of speech to the scriptures. Since it is certain, therefore, that scripture speaks, what sort of voice shall we ascribe to it ? Is it such as none can understand without the pope's help as interpreter ?

Our fourth argument is to this effect : If the scriptures should be interpreted and understood by the same Spirit whereby they were written, then it is necessary for all who would interpret or understand them to consult the Holy Spirit. But the former is true, and therefore also the latter. There can be no doubt of the consequence in the major; and as to the minor, it is evident from 2 Tim. iii. 16, and 2 Pet. i. 21, that the Holy Spirit is the author of scripture. Now that the same Spirit is required for the understanding of scripture, the papists themselves acknowledge, as Stapleton, Andradius, and others, but in a somewhat different way from us. For they say that this Spirit, by whose teaching the scriptures are to be rightly understood and interpreted, resides only in the pope; whereas we say that he resides in every pious man who duly interprets scripture. This also Bernard asserts in his discourse to the fathers of the mountain, where these words occur : " You will never be able to enter into Paul's meaning, unless you imbibe Paul's spirit[1]." But, you will ask, how am I to imbibe this spirit ? Can this spirit be infused by the pope ? Bernard subjoins, that it is to be gotten " by the use of a devout intention in reading, and by meditation;" therefore from the scripture itself. He adds something of the same kind respecting David : " You can never understand David, until by actual experience you feel the

[1 Nunquam Pauli sensum ingredieris, donec usu bonæ intentionis in lectione ejus, et studio assiduæ meditationis, spiritum ejus imbiberis.—Opp. T. I. p. 1171. Basil. 1566.]

29—2

affections which the Psalms express¹." Each man therefore needs
the Holy Spirit for the scriptures. This is what Jerome affirms in
his commentary upon the first chapter of the Galatians : " He that
understands scripture otherwise than the sense of the Holy Spirit,
by whom it was written, demands, may be called a heretic²."
To this also relates that saying of Paul, 1 Cor. ii. 15, "He that is
spiritual judgeth all things," ἀνακρίνει πάντα. Who is this spiritual man? The Jesuit wishes it to be understood only of a few
perfect persons, who can even predict future events. But the falsity
of this appears from the very words themselves : for πνευματικὸς,
or *the spiritual man*, is there opposed to τῷ ψυχικῷ, or *the carnal
man*, and therefore denotes all the faithful who are regenerate and
have received the Holy Ghost ; as by *the carnal*, on the contrary,
all those are meant who have not yet obtained the spirit of regeneration.

So 1 John ii. 20, "Ye have an unction from the Holy One,"
that is, ye have the Holy Spirit. What follows? What is it
we have obtained by him? It follows, "and ye know all things,"
that is, all things necessary. Therefore he says, verse 27, "Ye
have no need that any one teach you." The Jesuit thus endeavours
to elude this passage. He interprets the clause, "that any man
teach you," as if now any one were to say, Ye who are catholics
have no need that any Calvinist should teach you. So he would
have John address the Christians of his time to this effect: ye who
are Christians have no need that any false prophet or false apostle
should teach you. But Augustine expounds this text very differently in his third Tractate upon the Epistle of John, where his
words are as follows: "'The anointing teacheth you all things.'
What then, brethren, are we about who teach you, if his anointing
teacheth you of all things? We seem to labour in vain. And why
do we spend our breath in this manner? Let us dismiss you to his
anointing, that his own anointing may teach you. But as I have
now proposed this question to myself, I propose it also to the
apostle. Let him vouchsafe to listen to one of his little children
asking him. I say to John himself, They to whom you spake had
the anointing. You said, His own anointing teacheth you : wherefore then did you compose this Epistle? Why teach, instruct, and

[¹ Nunquam Davidem intelliges, donec ipsa experientia Psalmorum affectus indueris. This piece, however, is not by Bernard.]

[² Qui scripturam aliter intelligit, quam sensus Spiritus Sancti efflagitat,
a quo scripta est, hæreticus appellari potest.]

edify them³?" Hitherto he hath proposed the doubt; now he subjoins the reply.   There follow therefore in Augustine these ensuing
words: "Now," says he, "behold, brethren, this great mystery.   The
sound of our words strikes the ear; the teacher is within.   Suppose not that any man learns of man.   We may admonish you by
the noise of our voice; but unless there be one within to teach you,
it is an empty noise.   Would ye, brethren, know it still further?
Have ye not all heard this discourse?   Yet how many will go
hence uninstructed!   As far as in me lies, I have spoken to all:
but they to whom that unction speaks not internally, they whom
the Holy Ghost does not teach internally, they go forth uninstructed.   External instructions are a sort of help and admonition:
but he who teaches hearts hath his chair in heaven⁴."   What is
this chair in heaven?   Wherefore, O most holy Augustine, dost
thou place this chair in heaven?   Knowest thou not that this chair
is found on earth?   Wert thou never at Rome, or sawest thou
never the chair of Peter, wherein whosoever sits can teach thee
all things?   Why not rather in the earth?   Doubtless Augustine
knew nothing of that chair.   But he goes on still farther, and refers
to the same purpose that saying of Christ, which is related Matth.
xxiii., " Call no man master on earth; for one is your master, even
Christ."   " He therefore," says Augustine, "speaks internally to
you, when no man is there.   For although one may be beside you,
yet is there no one in your heart.   But let it not be so that there
should be no one in your heart; let his own unction be in your
heart, lest your heart should be desert and thirsty and without

[³ Quid ergo nos facimus, fratres, qui docemus vos, si unctio ejus docet
vos de omnibus? Quasi nos sine causa laboramus. Et ut quid tantum clama-
mus? Dimittamus vos unctioni illius, ut doceat vos unctio ipsius. Sed modo
mihi facio quæstionem, et illi ipsi apostolo facio. Dignetur audire parvulum
quærentem a se: ipsi Joanni dico, Unctionem habebant quibus loquebaris? Tu
dixisti, quia unctio ipsius docet vos de omnibus: ut quid talem epistolam
fecisti? quid illos tu docebas? quid instruebas? quid ædificabas?—Opp.
T. IX. p. 129, 2. Paris. 1555.]

[⁴ Videte magnum sacramentum, fratres. Sonus verborum nostrorum
aures perculit: magister intus est. Nolite putare quemquam hominem
aliquid discere ab homine. Admonere possumus per strepitum vocis nostræ:
si non sit intus qui doceat, inanis fit strepitus noster. Adeo, fratres, vultis
nosse? Nunquid non sermonem istum omnes audistis? Quam multi hinc
indocti exituri sunt! Quantum ad me pertinet, omnibus locutus sum; sed
quibus unctio illa intus non loquitur, quos Spiritus Sanctus intus non doceat,
indocti redeunt. Magisteria forinsecus adjutoria quædam sunt et admoni-
tiones: cathedram in cœlo habet, qui corda docet.—Ibid.]

any springs to irrigate it. The inward master therefore teaches; Christ teaches, his inspiration teaches." Thus Augustine upon that place; whence it appears that he differs widely from the Jesuit.

To the same purpose also is that saying, Isaiah liv. 13, " They shall be all taught of God;" which passage is cited by Christ, John vi. 45 : where we must note, that Isaiah does not say, they shall be all God's disciples, but, they shall be all *taught of God*, Θεοδίδακτοι, or διδακτοὶ τοῦ Θεοῦ, which is something more. None, therefore, are truly taught but such as God teaches internally by his Holy Spirit. The Jesuit says, that we are therefore said to be taught of God, because Christ hath now taught us in his own person, and not through the prophets, as formerly : but absurdly. For it is manifest that the prophet speaks of all the faithful, and Christ also, John vi., applies it to all believers. But the faithful do not now hear Christ speaking in his proper person; are they, therefore, not Θεοδίδακτοι? Surely no discreet man will say so. However the Jesuit is obliged at length to confess that, *in a more subtle and close* (yea, rather in a correcter and truer) sense, it is meant of the Holy Spirit. Augustine, *de Grat. Christ.* cap. 12, 13, 14[1], compels him to make this admission. A somewhat similar passage occurs, Jeremiah xxxi. 33, 34, " I will put my law in their hearts, and they shall all know me from the least to the greatest." The Jesuit interprets that place to mean that all will believe in the unity of God, as now (says he) the Jews and Turks and all nations do. But this is mere playing with the subject : for the text means to refer to saving faith, as is manifest from the context; for there follows immediately : " They shall all know me from the least to the greatest, saith the Lord : for I will pardon their iniquity, and their sin I will remember no more." This is what he promises to inscribe upon their hearts. Is this to believe as the nations, Jews and Turks, believe? Who would say it? Again, Luke x. 21, 22, Christ gives thanks to the Father that he had " hid these things from the wise and prudent, and revealed them unto babes," &c. From which place it may be gathered, that faith is the work of God and of the Holy Spirit, not of any man; and that whoever really knows the religion of God, hath learned this knowledge from God. And let so much suffice for our fourth argument.

[1 Sic enim docet Deus eos qui secundum propositum vocati sunt, simul donans et quid agant scire, et quod sciunt agere . . . . . Isto modo sunt omnes secundum propositum vocati, sicut scriptum est in prophetis, *Docibiles Dei.*— De Gratia Christi. c. 13. Opp. T. vii. p. 166, 2.]

Our fifth argument stands thus : When we demand of our opponents how scripture ought to be interpreted, they always answer at first and say, by the unanimous expositions of the fathers. But we immediately again demand of them, when we are to know that the fathers agree ? For certainly in most places they are at variance; so that their authority will be but small. To make this better understood, I will propose one or two examples, from which the rest may be conjectured. Origen, Jerome, Athanasius, Ambrose, explain those words, Rom. vii., " I am carnal, sold under sin," in such a manner as to make Paul speak not of himself, but in the person of an unregenerate man. But Augustine against Julian the Pelagian, Lib. ii. c. 2[2], will have them to be understood of a regenerate man, and therefore of Paul himself. And in other places also he expounds that passage of the apostle in the same manner : which exposition Thomas confesses to be the preferable one. Let us consider another instance of the discrepancy of the fathers' interpretation of scripture. Paul says, 1 Tim. iii. 2, " that a bishop should be *the husband of one wife.*" Upon this place, as appears from Gratian, Dist. 26. C. *Unius* and C. *Acutius*[3], the opinions of Augustine and Jerome were contrary to each other. Let us add a third example. Chrysostom and Jerome excuse the dissimulation of Peter related by Paul, Gal. ii. ; on the other hand Augustine and Ambrose think it sinful. Add now a fourth : " We conclude," says Paul, (Rom. iii. 28,) " that a man is justified by faith ;" which place Ambrose expounds of the heathen only, Chrysostom most truly of all men universally, because he says, a man simply, τὸ κοινὸν τῆς φύσεως ὄνομα θείς. So, to prove the same thing by yet other examples, in the same place by " the works of the law" Jerome understands ceremonies, circumcision, the sabbath, and such like ; but Augustine and Ambrose the whole law, even the Decalogue. Hilary (Can. 30 in Matth.) thinks that Judas did not take the eucharist with the rest of the apostles, whom even some papists also follow : Augustine in many places, and almost all the other fathers, determine the contrary. Ambrose supposes that in Coloss. ii. 21, in those words, " taste not, handle not," we are warned to have no hope in worldly things ; but Augustine, Ep. 59, and Chry-

[2 It should be c. 3.]

[3 The opinion of Jerome, in Dist. 26, c. 1, is : Unius uxoris virum, id est, monogamum post baptismum. That of Augustine, ibid. c. 2, is, Acutius intelligunt qui nec eum, qui catechumenus vel paganus habuit alteram, ordinandum censuerunt.]

sostom, and Theophylact, teach us that rather they contain a censure of those who issued such prohibitions. Why should I enumerate more such expositions of fathers dissenting from each other, when they sometimes are at open variance with themselves? Erasmus, in his annotations on Luke xxii., upon these words, " But now he that hath a purse," &c. declares that Augustine is inconsistent with himself upon the question whether Christian men may engage in war[1].

Who then is so stupid or so void of common sense as that, when he sees the fathers agreeing neither with each other nor with themselves in the interpretation of scripture, he should nevertheless rest in their interpretations? But even though we were to concede to them that the fathers agree upon all points (which they however cannot prove), yet, even from this, the conclusion which they seek to draw will never follow; and this we prove by the following argument : Whatever is of such a nature that it could not have been always the rule of scriptural interpretation, and had not always a judicial authority, ought not now to have the force of a rule or judicial decision : for the rule ought to be always one and the same, certain, firm and perpetual. But the unanimous exposition of the fathers was not always the rule of interpreting scripture; and, therefore, neither is it the rule now. That it was not the rule always, appears readily ; since there was a time when none of the writings of the fathers were extant. Most of them wrote four hundred years after Christ, some five or six hundred years after Christ. Now what, I beseech you, was the rule of scriptural interpretation before that time? There certainly was some, and yet this was not then in existence.

Our sixth argument stands thus : Scripture hath greater authority in judging than the present church : therefore scripture ought to be the judge rather than the church ; for this judgment ought to go along with the greatest authority. Now that the church hath not as great authority as the scripture, is manifest from Gal. i. 8, where Paul says : " If we, or an angel from heaven, preach unto you any other gospel than that we have preached unto you, let him be accursed!" The papists (I suppose) will not ascribe more to the modern church than to that ancient one which flourished in the apostle's time. Now it had no such authority, and could no otherwise interpret scripture than according to scripture. There-

[1 Jam illud videndum, an de bello satis sibi constet Augustinus; qui cum tot locis Christiane bellum detestetur, nunc adversus Manichæos ac Donatistas belli patronus esse videatur.—p. 212. Basil. 1535.]

fore neither can any church do otherwise. Upon this passage we shall speak hereafter.

Our seventh argument is taken from Acts xvii. 11, where the Bereans are praised for searching the scriptures whether those things which Paul taught were so. From which place we argue thus : If the doctrine of the apostle was examined by scripture, then the doctrine of the church should also be examined by scripture. The antecedent is true ; therefore also the consequent. The Jesuit here hath but one reply. He says that the person of the apostle was not known to the Bereans, and that they did not understand whether Paul was an apostle or not ; and therefore that they did well in judging his doctrine by the scriptures : but we do know (says he) that the church cannot err, and therefore we ought not to examine its teaching. I answer : It makes little matter whether the Bereans knew Paul to be an apostle or not. The question is not about persons, but about the kind of teaching. The Bereans are praised for not rashly and hastily receiving whatever Paul taught them, but diligently examining his doctrine by scripture. Whence we draw two inferences : First, that all doctrine is to be judged by the scriptures. For, if the Bereans compared the preaching of an apostle with the rule of scripture, shall we embrace without any examination whatever the pope may please to maintain ? Secondly, That the apostles preached nothing which could not be established by the scriptures of the prophets, and did perfectly agree with them. But we (says he) know that the church cannot err. But we (say I) know that the pope errs shamefully, and they who think otherwise err also to the eternal ruin of their own souls. Whether the church may err or not, shall be treated of in its proper place. Verily, the church, that is, the pope, would be a kind of God if he could not err.

Our eighth argument is taken from 1 Thess. v. 21, where Paul says, " Prove all things," πάντα δοκιμάζετε : and from 1 John iv. 1, where John says, " Believe not every spirit, but try the spirits whether they be of God ;" δοκιμάζετε τὰ πνεύματα. Hence I conclude, that the teaching of the church should be examined. The Jesuit says that this precept does not refer to all, but only to the learned and well instructed ; which he illustrates by the following comparison. If a book, says he, were sent to an university to be examined, all the members of the university would not examine it, but only the doctors of some one faculty. I answer, that the book should be examined and perused by all who ought

458 THE FIRST CONTROVERSY. [CH.

to approve it. But as to the present subject, I allow that all
cannot try every doctrine; for the ungodly cannot do so. But all
pious and faithful men both ought and can discharge this duty, as
is plain from 1 Thess. v. For if all good Christians are commanded
" to pray always, to rejoice evermore, to give thanks, not to quench
the Spirit, to hold fast that which is good," which are the common
duties of piety; then also all good Christians ought to " try all
things." Now those former injunctions concern all the faithful.
Therefore also this latter. For John in that place addresses ἀγα-
πητούς and παιδία, his *beloved* and *little children*, that is, all
devout and faithful Christians. Therefore all pious people are commanded by the apostle to take heed to themselves, and diligently
to examine every doctrine, lest, peradventure, they receive false for
true. Secondly, Bellarmine says that it is only doubtful doctrine
that is here treated of. I reply, that we also mean no other.
For that which is either plainly false, or undoubtedly true, is not
commonly brought in question or examined by those who are
already taught what they ought to think. But how are we to
ascertain that any doctrine is not doubtful? Without examination
we can never be able to determine that any dogma is absolutely
certain and beyond all doubt. It is this trial (δοκιμασία) which
enables us to distinguish true doctrines from false, to hold fast the
true and to reject the false. Is any one so mad as to say that the
doctrines of Christianity are no otherwise certain and indubitably
true, than as the pope of Rome hath affirmed them in a response
from his chair? But first we must, at least, examine the privilege by
which he pretends that he is exempted from error in passing judgment. Will he remove this too from our cognisance? Surely, unless this be clear, we shall be always in uncertainty. What then?
Must he be interpreter of his own privilege also? The pope hath
the privilege of infallibility. Whence doth this appear? From
the opinion and exposition of the pope himself. Those who can
assent to so slight an inducement truly deserve never to think
correctly of anything. Besides, what else is this, but to ascribe our
faith, not to God, but to the pope? Similar to these passages is
that, Matth. vii. 15, where Christ orders all to beware of false
prophets. But how shall we know them? He tells us, " by their
fruits." But what are these fruits? Are they bad morals? By
no means; for many false prophets seem to live a life of greater
sanctity than some good or true teachers. They are to be known,
therefore, not merely by their morals, but still more by their false

interpretations and expositions. And so Vincentius Lirinensis, whom
the papists highly esteem, expounds this place, capp. 36 and 37.

Our ninth argument is this: If the fathers, the councils, and
the pope have the supreme authority of interpreting the scriptures,
then our faith is ultimately resolved into their judgment. But the
consequent is false, and therefore also the antecedent. The consequent in the major is manifest. For whatever hath the supreme
authority of assigning the sense of scripture, upon that our faith,
in the last resolution, must bottom itself and rest. For our faith re-
poses upon that which gives the most certain sense of scripture, and
judges of all doctrine. The papists themselves concede the minor:
for they deny, as was already remarked in the third question, that
our faith is ultimately resolved into the sentence of the church.

Our tenth argument stands thus: He who made the law alone
hath supreme authority to expound the law. But God alone made
the scriptures. Therefore God alone hath supreme authority to interpret the scriptures. The major is plain by the very light of
nature. The minor is also manifest. So the apostles confirmed all
their doctrine by the authority of the divine law, that is, by the old
Testament. So Nehemiah, as we read, Nehem. viii. 9, read the law
of God plainly to the people, and in expounding the sense "gave
the meaning by the scripture itself." So Tremellius translates that
passage, and correctly. The scripture itself, therefore, is its own
faithful and clear interpreter, and the Spirit of God in the scriptures illustrates and explains himself.

I form our eleventh argument thus: If the supreme judgment
of scripture belong to the church, then it will follow (though our
adversaries intimate that they do not like the consequence), that the
authority of the church is greater than that of scripture; which is
made plain by the following considerations. The sense of scripture
is the scripture itself. They, therefore, who embrace and retain
any sense for no other reason but because the church hath so determined and taught, and not on account of the prophetic or apostolic
scriptures, these not only ascribe a more august authority to the
church than to the scripture, but also rest their salvation upon the
voice and sentence of the church. For to faith are incident these
two things, *what* we believe, and *why*. The *what* contains all the
integral parts of the thing believed. Now what is the *why*? Is it
the authority of the pope or the church? Do we then upon no
other account believe that the world was made, that Adam sinned,
that the Redeemer Christ was promised, came into the world in

his proper time, undertook and accomplished the business of our salvation, and that he will return again at the end of the world, but because thus speaks the church, and thus the pope of Rome? O noble basis of the christian faith! O glorious faith of papists!

I propound our twelfth argument thus: If the pope be the supreme judge of controversies and interpreter of scripture, then every definition of the pope's is as authentic as the scripture. The force of the inference is manifest, but the consequent is plainly false. For then all the definitions of the popes would have equal authority with the scriptures, and should be ranked in the sacred canon of scripture, and should be searched with still greater diligence than the scriptures: all which conclusions are monstrously shocking and absurd.

Our thirteenth argument is to this effect: No man is a sufficient judge of controversies or interpreter of scripture: therefore, not the pope. For no man ought to decide controversies by his own authority, but by that of another, namely, of God and the scriptures. So formerly the Nicene fathers condemned Arius by divine testimonies; so the holy bishops condemned Macedonius, Nestorius, Eutyches, by the authority of scripture, and not by their own. Besides, if a man could define controversies by his own authority, he would have a sort of lordship over our souls and faith, which the apostle plainly denies, 2 Cor. i. 24. οὐ κυριεύομεν ὑμῶν τῆς πίστεως. Furthermore, if we were placed in the power of a man, to remove all controversies and determine what should be believed, then the sentence of a man would be the matter of our faith.

Our fourteenth argument is as follows: If the scriptures do not interpret themselves or judge controversies, this is because they are either obscure or imperfect. But neither impediment exists: for we have shewn before that they are plain in all necessary things; and that they are perfect in all respects, we shall demonstrate hereafter.

Our fifteenth argument is this: Every one ought to rest upon his own faith and his own judgment, and not depend upon another's will and pleasure. Therefore the Roman pontiff is not the sole judge of controversies in the church. For each individual should be his own judge, and stand by his own judgment, not indeed mere private judgment, but such as is inspired by God: and no one can bestow the Holy Spirit save God who infuses it in whom he will. Nor can any one man render another certain in matters of religion, with whatever authority he may be invested. Christ says, John vi. 44, 45, " No man can come unto me unless my Father draw him : wherefore whosoever hath heard and learned of the Father cometh unto me." John the Baptist says also, John iii. 33, " He that receiveth his testimony hath set to his seal that God is true." There is, therefore, need of Christ's testimony before we can truly and aright believe anything.

There remains now our last argument, which is drawn from human testimony, and the authority of the ancient fathers. Irenæus, in his 4th book against Heresies, cap. 63, says that " the legitimate and safe exposition of the scriptures is by the scriptures themselves[1]." Hilary, in his 1st book upon the Trinity, writes thus upon this subject : " The best reader is he who rather waits for the meaning from the words than imposes one, who takes instead of giving it, nor forces that to seem to be contained in the expression which, before reading it, he had presumed to be the sense. When, therefore, the discourse shall be of the things of God, let us allow to God the knowledge of himself, and wait upon his words with a pious veneration. He is a sufficient witness to himself, who is not known but by himself[2]." So Hilary.

Augustine hath many testimonies in our favour. In his book of Marriage and Concupiscence, Lib. II. cap. 33, he writes thus : " This controversy requires a judge." But who shall be the judge? He replies, " Let Christ be the judge." And a little after : " With him let the apostle judge also ; for Christ himself speaks in the apostle[3]." Why did he not say, Let the Roman pontiff, or, at least,

[1 Agnitio vera est apostolorum doctrina, et antiquus ecclesiæ status in universo mundo, et character corporis Christi, secundum successiones epis-coporum, quibus illi eam, quæ in unoquoque loco est, ecclesiam tradiderunt, quæ pervenit usque ad nos, custodita sine fictione scripturarum tractatione plenissima, neque additamentum neque ablationem recipiens, et lectio sine falsatione, et secundum scripturas expositio legitima et diligens, et sine periculo et sine blasphemia.—p. 400. A. ed. Fevard.]

[2 Optimus lector est, qui dictorum intelligentiam exspectet ex verbis potius quam imponat, et retulerit magis quam attulerit, neque cogat id videri dictis contineri, quod ante lectionem præsumpserit intelligendum. Cum itaque de rebus Dei erit sermo, concedamus cognitionem sui Deo, dictisque ejus pia veneratione famulemur. Idoneus enim sibi testis est, qui nisi per se cognitus non est.—pp. 776, 777. Opp. Paris. 1693.]

[3 Ista controversia judicem quærit. Judicet ergo Christus, et cui rei mors ejus profecerit, ipse dicat: hic est, inquit, sanguis meus, qui pro multis effundatur in remissionem peccatorum. Judicet cum illo et apostolus, quia et in apostolo ipse loquitur Christus.—Opp. T. VII. p. 185.]

Christ speaking in the Roman pontiff, be judge? Doubtless,
because he acknowledged no such judge. The same father, in his
book of Grace and Free-will, cap. 18, writes in almost the same
terms: " Let the apostle John sit as judge between us[1]." But
where? Surely nowhere else but in the scriptures : for he immediately produces a place from 1 John iv., " Beloved, let us love
one another." Also, in his books of Christian Doctrine, he writes
more than once, that scripture is to be expounded by scripture. In
the 11th book of his City of God, c. 33, there occurs the following
testimony. "We," says he, " have supposed that there are two societies of angels, different and opposed the one to the other,—the one
both by nature good and upright in will, the other though good by
nature, yet perverted in will—which are plainly spoken of in other
more clear testimonies of scripture, to be here, in this book, called
Genesis, designated by the words light and darkness, although
perhaps he who wrote it had another meaning in this passage. This
obscure passage hath not been considered without profit; for even
though we have failed to discover the meaning of the author of this
book, we have not swerved from the rule of faith, which is sufficiently
known to the faithful by means of other parts of sacred scripture
which have a like authority[2]." The same author also, in his book
de Genesi ad Literam, Lib. i. c. 21, tells us how the sense of scripture may best be found : " When we read the divine books, where
the number of true meanings which may be drawn from a few words,
and are fortified by the integrity of the catholic faith, is so great,
let us especially choose that which it shall appear certain that he
whom we read intended ; but if this be hidden from us, yet that
which the context does not forbid, and which is in harmony with a
sound faith : but if the context too cannot be considered and
sifted, at least only that which a sound faith prescribes. For it is
one thing not to distinguish what the writer principally intended,

[1 Sedeat ergo inter nos judex apostolus Joannes, et dicat nobis : Carissimi, diligamus invicem.—Opp. T. vii. p. 284. 2.]

[2 Nos has duas societates angelicas, inter se dispares atque contrarias,
unam et natura bonam et voluntate rectam, aliam vero natura bonam, sed
voluntate perversam, aliis manifestioribus divinarum scripturarum testimoniis declaratas, quod in hoc libro, cui nomen Genesis, lucis tenebrarumque
vocabulis significatas existimavimus, etiamsi aliud sensit hoc loco forte qui
scripsit. Non est inutiliter obscuritas hujus pertractata sententiæ, quia etsi
voluntatem auctoris libri hujus indagare nequivimus, a regula tamen fidei,
quæ per alias ejus auctoritatis sacras literas satis fidelibus nota est, non
aberravimus.]

and another to swerve from the rule of piety. If both faults be avoided, the fruit to the reader is perfect. But if both cannot be avoided, even though the intention of the writer be uncertain, yet it is not without use to have gained a meaning congruous with a sound belief[3]." The same father, Epistle 19, indicates plainly enough what we should determine of the expositions of the fathers, when he says: "Other authors, however excellent their sanctity and learning, I read so as not to credit their assertions merely because they thought thus; but because they have been able to persuade me that they were not repugnant to truth, either by means of the canonical writers or some probable process of reasoning[4]." In these words Augustine teaches us three things: First, that, in matters of faith, we ought to depend upon the authority and judgment of no men, however holy or learned, much less upon that of a single impure and illiterate pontiff. Secondly, that no human expositions are to be received but as they are confirmed either by the scriptures or by probable reasoning. Thirdly, that we require to have a full persuasion, such as cannot be thought to be in those who, knowing nothing accurately themselves, hang the whole of their faith and salvation on the opinions of other men.

Basil, Epist. 80[5], ascribes the authority of deciding and defining controversies, in these words: "We do *not* think it just that that custom of speaking, which hath obtained amongst them, should be esteemed the law and canon of correct doctrine. For if custom is sufficient to be the test of right doctrine, it is doubtless lawful also for us to imitate them herein. Let us stand therefore by the judgment of the scripture inspired by God; and let, by all means, truth

[3 Cum divinos libros legimus, in tanta multitudine verorum intellectuum qui de paucis verbis eruuntur, et sanitate catholicæ fidei muniuntur, id potissimum deligamus, quod certum apparuerit eum sensisse quem legimus: si autem hoc latet, id certe quod circumstantia scripturæ non impedit, et cum sana fide concordat: si autem et scripturæ circumstantia pertractari ac discuti non potest, saltem id solum quod fides sana præscribit. Aliud est enim, quid potissimum scriptor senserit non dignoscere, aliud autem a regula pietatis errare. Si utrumque vitetur, perfecte se habet fructus legentis. Si vero utrumque vitari non potest, etiamsi voluntas scriptoris incerta sit, sanæ fidei congruam non inutile est tenuisse sententiam.—Opp. T. III. p. 116, 2.]

[4 Alios autem ita lego, ut quantalibet sanctitate doctrinaque præpolleant, non ideo verum putem, quia ipsi ita senserunt; sed quia mihi vel per illos auctores canonicos, vel probabili ratione, quod a vero non abhorreat, persuadere potuerunt.—Id. Ad Hieronym. T. II. p. 15, 2.]

[5 Quæst. IV. c. 17.]

of opinion be ascribed to those with whom are found doctrines consonant with the divine oracles." It is admirably well expressed in
the Greek: ἡ θεόπνευστος ἡμῖν διαιτησάτω γραφή. Καὶ παρ᾽ οἷς
ἂν εὑρεθῇ τὰ δόγματα συνῳδὰ τοῖς θείοις λόγοις, ἐπὶ τούτοις
ἥξει τῆς ἀληθείας ἡ ψῆφος. From these words two things are
to be gathered : first, that in every question the judgment of the
scriptures is supreme ; secondly, that those are to be judged to
have the truth whose doctrines agree with the divine oracles.

Optatus Milevitanus, in his 5th book against Parmenianus, disputing upon this question, whether a baptized person might be
rebaptized, illustrates our cause admirably in these words : " Some
judges must be sought of this controversy. If Christians, they cannot be assigned by consent of both sides, because truth is obstructed
by party zeal. A judge must be sought without. If a pagan, he
cannot know the Christian mysteries. If a Jew, he is an enemy of
Christian baptism. Therefore no tribunal can be found on earth
to take cognisance of this matter. A judge must be sought from
heaven. But why do we knock at heaven's gates, when we have
his Testament here in the gospel ? The Testament, I say ; for in
this place earthly things may rightly be compared with heavenly[1]."
Thus Optatus ; from which passage we derive three observations :
first, that in every religious controversy some impartial and competent judge must be sought for, who is not engaged in the interest
of either party. At that time there was a dispute between the
catholics and Donatists. No Christian judge, says Optatus, could
be found competent to decide the controversy ; because all Christians
favour one side or the other, so as to approach the decision with
some degree of prejudice. Whence I draw this conclusion : if the
Roman pontiff was not then a competent judge of those controversies which then subsisted between the catholics and the Donatists, because he might seem attached to one side ; how much less
can the final decision be allowed him in these which are now
agitated, wherein he is under the influence of still stronger party
feeling, inasmuch as it is his own interest that lies at stake !

[1 Quærendi sunt aliqui hujus controversiæ judices : si Christiani, de
utraque parte dari non possunt, quia studiis veritas impeditur. Deforis
quærendus est judex. Si paganus, non potest nosse christiana secreta. Si
Judæus, inimicus est christiani baptismatis. Ergo in terris de hac re nullum
poterit reperiri judicium. De cœlo quærendus est judex. Sed ad quid pul-
samus ad cœlum, cum habemus hic in evangelio testamentum ?—Optat. c.
Parmen. Don. Lib. v. c. 3.]

Secondly, that no judge of religion is to be sought for, as the papists would have it, upon the earth, but from heaven. If Optatus had thought that any judge had been constituted on earth by Christ, he would surely never have said that a judge was to be sought in heaven, but would have appealed to this legitimate judge of the church. Thirdly, that it is not necessary to elicit any divine voice or response from heaven itself; but that the scriptures should be consulted, and a certain decision of the controversy sought in the gospel and derived from the gospel: for he says that we then have a celestial judge, when the scripture is the judge.

Ambrose, in the 5th book of his Epistles, in a certain oration against Auxentius the Arian, which is contained in the 32nd and 33rd Epistles[2], desires the people to be the judge of that dispute which he had with Auxentius, because he knew them to be skilled in the scripture. Auxentius was unwilling that the people should hear the dispute, and on that account Ambrose censures him. Theophylact says upon John x., "Since it is, when made intelligible and opened by the Holy Spirit, that the scriptures shew us Christ, probably the porter is the Holy Spirit:" where he sufficiently indicates, that the scriptures are only unfolded by the Holy Ghost, and that therefore the Holy Ghost is the porter of the scriptures. Therefore, those who are without this Spirit can never understand the scriptures.

Lyra, having raised the question whether the truth of faith can be sufficiently proved by the sacred scripture, answers thus, as we read in Pelbart's Golden Rosary, Tom. III. c. de Fide, Art. 9. "The efficacy of proof through scripture may be otherwise taken thus, that, although scripture may in some sense be otherwise explained so as at least to escape without a manifest contradiction, yet, speaking simply, it cannot so reasonably be explained in any other manner but that the exposition of the catholic faith shall always appear more reasonable[3]." So that, however heretics may turn and twist the scriptures, yet the scriptures shall assert of themselves their own truth from

[2 Hæc ego, fratres, coram ipso apud vos plenius disputarem: sed certus non ignaros vos esse fidei, vestrum refugit examen.—Sermo c. Auxent. n. 26. p. 353. T. VIII. Paris. 1839.]

[3 Alio modo potest accipi probationis efficacia per scripturam sic, quod licet scriptura possit aliter exponi aliquo modo, saltem ad evadendum absque contradictione manifesta, tamen simpliciter loquendo, non potest alio modo rationabiliter exponi, quin semper appareat expositio fidei catholica rationabilior.]

[WHITAKER.]   30

the false expositions of heretics in such a manner as to make the
catholic truth ever seem more probable to any man not wholly
estranged from it.   Cajetan, in the preface to his commentaries
upon the books of Moses, says, that the exposition of scripture is not
tied by God to the sense of the fathers ; and he therefore admonishes his readers not to take it ill, or blame him, if he sometimes
dissent from *the torrent of the fathers,* that is, from their unanimous
opinion.   Canus, in his Common places, Lib. VII. c. 3, censures the
cardinal severely , and charges him with arrogance ; but it is not
necessary that I should appear in his defence, whom Andradius
vindicates in the second book of his *Defensio Tridentina,* subjoining
also some reasons to shew that he could say truly what he actually
hath said.   For he alleges, firstly, that the fathers were too much
given to allegorical expositions ; and, consequently, that since the
sense of scripture is but one, Cajetan is not to be blamed for under-
valuing the allegories of the fathers.   Secondly, he says, that the
ancient fathers, however united in their sentiments upon the mysteries of religion, did yet assign different and dissimilar meanings
when they approached the interpretation of scripture.   Thirdly
and lastly, he affirms that the Holy Spirit is " the sole and faithful interpreter of scripture."

Let it suffice to have said thus much upon the former part of
this fifth question.   Now follows the second part.

CHAPTER IX.

THE STATE OF THE QUESTION, CONCERNING THE MEANS OF FINDING THE TRUE SENSE OF SCRIPTURE.

WE have spoken of the supreme authority for interpreting
scripture, which we have proved to belong to the Holy Spirit
speaking in the scriptures, not to fathers, or councils, or pope.   We
have now to treat concerning the means of finding the sense of scripture.   For since scripture hath no audible voice, we must use certain means to investigate what is the sense and what the mind of
the scriptures.   If Christ were now himself with us, if the apostles
and prophets were living amongst us, we might repair to them, and
entreat them to disclose to us the meaning of what they had written.
But since they have departed and left us only their books, we must

consider what means we should use to discover the true sense of scripture and the words of God. The church, indeed, hath always used some means in the interpretation of scripture. Here I will enumerate first those means which are proposed by our divines; which if we make a lawful and holy application of, we shall not miss of the true meaning, and which the church herself is bound to use, unless she prefer to go wrong in the interpretation of scripture.

In the first place, prayer is necessary for reading the scriptures so as to understand them; and on that account David so often begs of God to illuminate his mind and to open his eyes; and, in Matth. vii. Christ says, "Ask, and it shall be given you: seek, and ye shall find: knock, and it shall be opened unto you." And James, chap. i. v. 5, says: " If any of you lack wisdom, let him ask of God, who giveth to all men liberally, and upbraideth not, and it shall be given him." Whence a certain father said, that he profited more in the knowledge of scripture by prayer, than by reading and study. And Origen[1], in his 12th Homily on Exodus, says that we must not only apply study in order to learn the sacred word, but also supplicate God and entreat him night and day, that the Lamb of the tribe of Juda may come, and, taking himself the sealed book, vouchsafe to open it. Augustine too, in his book *De Scala Paradisi*, c. 2, writes thus admirably upon this subject : " Reading inquires, meditation finds, prayer asks, contemplation tastes : whence the Lord himself says, ' Seek, and ye shall find; knock, and it shall be opened unto you.' Seek by reading, and ye shall find in meditation : knock by prayer, and it shall be opened to you in contemplation. Reading does, as it were, set the solid food at the lips; meditation breaks and chews it; prayer gains a relish; and contemplation is the very sweetness itself which gives us pleasure and refreshment. Reading is in the rind, meditation in the marrow, prayer in the demand of desire, contemplation in the delight of the sweetness now acquired[2]." Thus far Augustine. And Jerome says

[1 Unde ostenditur non solum studium nobis adhibendum esse ad discendas literas sacras, verum et supplicandum Domino, et diebus ac noctibus obsecrandum ut veniat agnus de tribu Judæ et ipse accipiens librum signatum dignetur aperire. Origen. Opp, p. 61. Paris. 1604.]

[2 Lectio inquirit, meditatio invenit, oratio postulat, contemplatio degustat; unde ipse Dominus dicit: Quærite, et invenietis; pulsate, et aperietur vobis. Quærite legendo, et invenietis meditando : pulsate orando, et aperietur vobis contemplando. Lectio quasi solidum cibum ori apponit, meditatio masticat et frangit, oratio saporem acquirit, contemplatio est ipsa dulcedo

to Læta : " Let reading follow prayer, and prayer reading[1]." This
should be always the first means, and the foundation of the rest.

Secondly, we ought to understand the words which the Holy
Spirit hath used in the scriptures ; and therefore we ought to know
the original languages. We should consult the Hebrew text in the
old Testament, the Greek in the new : we should approach the
very fountain-heads of the scriptures, and not stay beside the
derived streams of versions. Indeed, the ignorance of these languages, the Hebrew and the Greek, hath been the source of many
errors ; at least, those who are not acquainted with them are destitute of the best helps and assistances, and are involved in frequent
and unavoidable mistakes. Augustine, in his books of Christian
Doctrine, exhorts all students of theology to the study of these
languages. And upon this account in the council of Vienna[2] (however otherwise superstitious, as held under pope Clement V.) a
decree was made that there should be professors of these tongues in
all universities. For, unless we understand the words, how shall we
find the sense ? And indeed many errors are refuted by the mere
understanding of the words themselves. Thus we often refute our
adversaries. For example, Luke ii. 14, the Rhemists make out
the freedom of the will from the Vulgate Latin version, which is
this : *Pax in terra hominibus bonæ voluntatis.* But they are
easily refuted by the original : for in the Greek it is $\epsilon \dot{\upsilon} \delta o \kappa \acute{\iota} a$,
which never denotes the free will of man, as the Rhemists absurdly
explain it, but the gratuitous goodness of God toward men : and this,
indeed, some of the papists themselves concede. Eph. ii. 10 is thus
read in the Vulgate Latin version : *Creati in Christo Jesu in operibus bonis ;* whence some papists gather, that we are justified by
good works. But they are easily refuted out of the original Greek ;
for $\dot{\epsilon} \pi \acute{\iota}$ there denotes *ad*, not *in*. In Coloss. iv. 16, there is mention made, in the old version, of a certain epistle of the Laodiceans ;
from which many have thought that there was some epistle of Paul

quæ jucundat et reficit. Lectio in cortice, meditatio in adipe, oratio in
desiderii postulatione, contemplatio in adeptæ dulcedinis delectatione. The
Benedictines ascribe this work to Guigo or Guido Carthusianus (flor. circ.
1120), and place it in the appendix to T. VI. of their edition of Augustine,
Par. 1679. It is often printed amongst the works of St Bernard.]

[1 Orationi lectio, lectioni succedat oratio.—Ad Læt. Ep. 57. (al. 7.) T. IV.
p. 596.]

[2 The council of Vienna, counted as the 15th general, was held in the
year 1311. See its decrees in Labbe's collection of the Councils, T. XI
part 11.]

written to the Laodiceans. But this mistake is corrected by the original : for in the Greek text it is read ἐκ Λαοδικείας. In 1 Cor. xiv. 16, the words stand thus in the old version: *Si benedixeris Spiritu, qui supplet locum idiotæ, quomodo dicet Amen?* Hence the papists gather that there ought to be some person to make responses to the priest in behalf of the whole congregation, such as those clerks, whom they hire for a groat to stand beside the priest at mass. But this admits an easy refutation from the Greek text : for ὁ ἀναπληρῶν τὸν τόπον τοῦ ἰδιώτου does not mean him who *supplies* the place of the unlearned (since the verb ἀναπληροῦν never occurs in that sense[3]), but rather one that fills the place of the unlearned, that is, one who sits amongst the unlearned, and is really unlearned and a layman. In 1 Sam. xxi. 13, it is said that David, in the house of Achish king of Gath, was mad, or played the madman in their hands, that is, pretended madness. The old translation hath, *collabebatur inter manus eorum.* Of these words Augustine, in his Commentary on Psalm lxxxiii.[4], produces a strange exposition suggested by the faulty translation of some obscure interpreter, who had rendered them thus : *ferebatur in manibus suis.* Hence Augustine refers these words to Christ, and says that they are true if accommodated to the holy supper, because Christ did, after a certain manner (*quodammodo*), carry himself in his own hands, when he said to his disciples, " This is my body." However, he puts in the word *quodammodo*, so that the papists should not suppose that he favoured their opinion. Now Augustine fell into this mistake from not understanding the Hebrew term. Bellarmine, *De Ecclesia*, Lib. iii. c. 12, proves the visibility of the church by the testimony of Psalm xix., *In sole posuit tabernaculum suum*, according to the version of the old translator, who hath followed the Septuagint. Yet Jerome, twelve hundred years ago, had rendered it from the Hebrew thus : *Soli posuit tabernaculum in eis* (the heavens); so as to shew that this text testifies not that the tabernacle of the church was pitched in the sun, but that of the sun in the heavens. Such faults and blemishes in versions the heretics, and above all the papists, abuse to the confirmation of their errors ; which, however, are most easily removed by an inspection

[3 But see Schwartz. Comment. Ling. Græc. p. 98.]
[4 Quomodo ferebatur in manibus suis ? Quia cum commendaret ipsum corpus suum et sanguinem suum, accepit in manus suas quod norunt fideles, et ipse se portabat quodammodo.—Augustin. Opp. T. viii. col. 234. Basil. 1569.]

of the originals and a knowledge of the languages. It is therefore principally necessary that, as Augustine somewhere says, we should have a just and correct knowledge of the signs of things, that is, of words.

Thirdly, in dealing with the words we should consider which are proper, and which figurative and modified. For, when words are taken figuratively, they should not be expounded strictly. "It is," says Augustine, in his books of Christian Doctrine, "a wretched bondage of the soul, when signs are taken for things[1];" that is, when what is spoken figuratively is expounded as if spoken strictly. Hence hath arisen that difficult and long-continued dispute between us and the papists about the words of consecration, which we would have understood figuratively, and they strictly. But how shall we know whether words be taken figuratively or strictly? This inquiry suggests the addition of a fourth mean.

Fourthly, therefore, we ought to consider the scope, end, matter, circumstances (that is, as Augustine says, the persons, place and time), the antecedents and consequents of each passage; and by this means it will be no hard matter both to refute many errors, and to arrive at a clear understanding of those things which seemed at first obscure. The Rhemists conclude from 1 Pet iv. 8, (where Peter writes, that charity covers the multitude of sins,) that charity hath the power of taking away and extinguishing sins, and thereby of justifying us before God; and therefore, that faith alone does not justify. Now, if we consider the occasion, scope, preceding and following context, and the other circumstances of this passage, we shall find that the apostle is not speaking of our charity as justifying us before God or procuring remission of our sins, but of that fraternal love which represses many occasions of offence, and so quenches feuds and enmities amongst brethren. But how shall we understand that this is the sense of the passage? Why, from the context itself. The apostle says, in the words immediately preceding, " having sincere love one towards another." He is speaking, consequently, of the love wherewith we should embrace and respect our brethren. And, if we compare this place with another, namely, with Prov. x. 12, whence Peter took these words, this will appear still more plainly. There we read thus : " Hatred stirreth up strifes and contentions, but love covereth the multitude of sins:" where, by reason of the antithesis between the

[1 Ea demum est miserabilis animæ servitus, signa pro rebus accipere. Lib. III. c. 5, ad fin.]

first and second clauses of the sentence, the meaning of the latter may easily be gathered from that of the former. Christ says, Matt. xix. 17 : " If thou wilt enter into life, keep the commandments." From this all the papists collect that we are justified by the merit of our works, but, in the meanwhile, they reflect not what sort of person it was to whom Christ said this; a person, namely, who had come to Christ resting upon the opinion of his own righteousness, and, elevated with pride, had asked, what he ought to do to obtain eternal life. Such persons, who trust in their own merits, are deservedly referred to the law ; that so they may come to understand how far they are from perfect righteousness. Indeed, the ancients frequently fell into mistakes from not attending to the series and connection of the text. In Job xxi. 13, we read, " They pass their days in wealth, and go down in a moment to the grave:" which words many have understood to mean that the holy author affirmed that the rich, after spending their whole life in luxury, were suddenly plunged into eternal punishment; whereas it readily appears from the words, that his meaning is very different, and almost the contrary of this. He means that those wicked rich men, the enemies of God and piety, are happy not only in life, but in death also; since after they have filled themselves with all kinds of pleasures, they die without any protracted pain, while others pine under lingering diseases, and are tortured with keen agonies in death. Hence then springs the fifth mean.

For, in the fifth place, one place must be compared and collated with another ; the obscurer places with the plainer or less obscure. For though in one place the words may be obscure, they will be plainer in another. For example, James, chap. 2, verse 21, affirms that Abraham was justified by works. The place is obscure, and seems to favour the papists. Whence, then, shall we know the true meaning of this passage ? Why, we must compare it with the second verse of the fourth chapter of the Epistle to the Romans, and so it will readily appear how this place is to be understood. For Paul, in Rom. iv. 2, expressly says, that Abraham was not justified by works, because then he would have whereof to glory : and it is sufficiently plain that the apostle Paul is speaking, in that place, of the works which followed the call of Abraham : first, because he says, " Abraham believed God, and it was counted unto him for righteousness;" which every body knows to have taken place after his call: secondly, because afterwards he proceeds to the example of David, whom all know to have been a holy man, regenerated by the Spirit of God, and called by God. We must needs therefore confess that the term 'justification' is taken in different senses, unless we choose to suppose that the apostles are at variance, and pronounce contradictory declarations. In James, therefore, *to be justified* means to be declared and shewn to be just, as Thomas Aquinas himself confesses upon that place; but, in Paul, *to be justified* denotes the same as to be absolved from all sins, and accounted righteous with God.

Sixthly, in the comparison of places, we must observe that not only similar passages are to be compared with similar, but dissimilar passages also are to be compared together. Like places are to be compared with like; as, for example, John vi. 53, " Unless ye eat the flesh of the Son of man, and drink his blood, ye have no life in you;" with John iv. 14, " Whosoever shall drink of that water that I will give him, shall never thirst; but the water that I will give him shall be in him a well of water springing up unto everlasting life." This water is spiritual, and the mode of drinking it is spiritual; and the same holds as to the eating of his flesh: for to eat and to drink are similar kinds of expression. Therefore as the water which causes that we never thirst is drunk in a spiritual manner; so the flesh of Christ must be eaten, and his blood drunk, only in a spiritual manner. Unlike places are to be compared together : for example, if that same passage, John vi. 53, be compared with the sixth precept in the Decalogue, "Thou shalt do no murder;" (for if it be a crime, yea, an enormity, to slay a man, it is certainly a far deeper crime to eat and devour a man;) hence Augustine concludes, *de Doct. Christ.* Lib. iii. c. 16, that these words must be understood and explained figuratively, because otherwise they would command a flagitious crime.

Seventhly, all our expositions should accord with the analogy of faith, which we read of, Rom. xii. 6. Now the analogy of faith is nothing else but the constant sense of the general tenour of scripture in those clear passages of scripture, where the meaning labours under no obscurity; such as the articles of faith in the Creed, and the contents of the Lord's Prayer, the Decalogue, and the whole Catechism : for every part of the Catechism may be confirmed by plain passages of scripture. Whatever exposition is repugnant to this analogy must be false. For example, the papists elicit transubstantiation from the words, " This is my body," making the meaning of them this, This bread is transformed into my body. The Lutherans adopt another interpretation, namely, The body of Christ is under this bread; and hence infer their doctrine of consubstantiation. Both expositions are at variance with the analogy of faith. For, first, the analogy of faith teaches that Christ hath a body like to ours : now such a body can neither lie hid under the accidents of bread, nor be along with the bread. Secondly, the analogy of faith teaches that Christ is in heaven ; therefore he is not in the bread or with the bread. Thirdly, the analogy of faith teaches that Christ will come to judgment from heaven, not from the pix. Similar is the case of the popish doctrine, that we are justified by works; which is likewise repugnant to the analogy of faith. For in the Lord's Prayer we ask for the remission of sins, and in the Creed we profess belief in the forgiveness of sins, and that, as long as we live ; nor merely of other people's sins, (for that is the faith of devils,) but also of our own. Therefore, we cannot believe that God will deem us just on account of our own works.

Eighthly, since the unlearned know not how to make a right use of these means, they ought to have recourse to other persons better skilled than themselves, to read the books of others, to consult the commentaries and expositions of learned interpreters, and to confer with others. Such was the practice of Jerome, of Augustine, and of other fathers. But, in the meanwhile, care must be taken that we do not ascribe too much to them, or suppose that their interpretations are to be received because they are theirs, but because they are supported by the authority of scripture or by reason, so as to allow them no weight in opposition to the scripture. We may use their labours, advice, prudence, and knowledge; but we should use them always cautiously, modestly, and discreetly, and so as still to retain our own liberty. He that shall be content to make such a use of these means, and will lay aside his prejudices and party zeal, which many bring with them to every question, will be enabled to gain an understanding of the scriptures, if not in all places, yet in most ; if not immediately, yet ultimately.

CHAPTER X.

THE GENERAL ARGUMENTS OF OUR OPPONENTS AGAINST THESE MEANS ARE OBVIATED.

WHAT? Do our opponents find fault with these means? Not altogether; but yet neither do they entirely receive them. Stapleton, Lib. II. c. 9, admits that they are highly conducive, but says that they are not firm, certain, or of uniform avail; and that those who seek to interpret scripture in this way are sometimes deceived: which points he endeavours to prove and demonstrate by many arguments adduced against these means of exposition. These we proceed now to obviate, briefly, and conformably to the plan of our discourse. In that chapter he tries to shake our means by three arguments.

The first is, that these means of ours are subordinate to the means which they maintain; which (as ye shall hear afterwards) are the rule of faith, the practice of the church, the unanimous opinion of the fathers, the definite interpretation of councils. For, unless they agree with the rule of faith and the other means settled by them, they are neither just nor salutary. I answer, firstly, by conceding that all our methods of exposition should be in harmony with the rule of faith, and that we must not depart a hair's breadth from that rule. But what is that rule? Upon that we shall speak hereafter. In the meanwhile we lay it down that the rule of faith is no other than the constant tenor of the sense of scripture, to which special regard must be had in every exposition of scripture. This mean we have ourselves laid down; and to this all the interpretations of all men should agree. Whatever is not combined with this rule must be rejected as illegitimate. But Stapleton will not allow that this rule is contained in the scriptures, as will appear afterwards, where also I shall give a larger reply to the objection. Secondly, I answer, that the practice of the church is uncertain, mutable, and often wrong; that an unanimous opinion of the fathers or a definite interpretation of councils is boasted of and pretended in words, but cannot be shewn in fact. The fathers do not all interpret scripture by the same rule, nor have councils defined all controversies; and the later fathers and newer councils differ widely from the more ancient. Thirdly, that the practice of the church, the opinions of the fathers, and the definitions of councils, should be examined by the standard of scripture, not the contrary. It is therefore a preposterous proceeding to interpret scripture by these things which are themselves to be judged of by scripture.

His second argument is, that these means of ours are common to all heretics and Jews and pagans, while his are peculiar to the catholics and orthodox. I answer: If the meaning be that all can use these means, I acknowledge the fact upon which this argument is founded; for the means of interpreting scripture should be such as are not peculiar to certain men, but plain and public. But if the meaning be, that heretics, making use of these means, can confirm their heresies out of scripture, the assertion is utterly false. And if this be not the meaning, Stapleton brings this allegation to no purpose. Now this is so far from being true, that heretics, if they would make a legitimate application of these means, would see that their heresies were condemned by the scriptures; and, in like manner, the Jews and pagans would understand that their impious and profane opinions were refuted by our scriptures. If Stapleton indeed thought, as he appears to have thought, that these means favour the heretics, or can give them any aid in maintaining their cause; he hath put a great and unworthy insult upon the scriptures, as if they could be, in any question, more favourable to heretics than to catholics. But the scriptures are the bulwarks and muniments of the catholics, the torment and destruction of heretics. Wherefore, heretics may indeed use these means: but, if they use them aright, they will no longer continue heretics as they were, or they will be absolutely self-condemned. Yea, if the heretics might lawfully interpret scripture otherwise than by scripture, they might defend their cause with much greater ease and probability than they have ever yet been able.

His third argument is, that our means are human, his divine; because the church cannot err damnably in its public faith or practice. I answer: If they are called human because they are used by men, I confess them to be in this sense human; and, in this sense, their own means also are no other than human. But if Stapleton calls them human under the notion that nothing but human industry is required in their application, he is grievously mistaken: for with these means must of necessity be combined the teaching of the Holy Spirit, without which we shall ever expend labour in vain upon the study of the scriptures. It was upon this account that we said, that we should before all things pray that we might, in searching the scripture, hold that way which was most direct, and that the Holy Ghost might always shew us

his illumination. For the practice of the church is the custom of
men ; the sense of the fathers is the opinion of men ; the definition
of a council is the judgment of men ; the decree of a pope is the
will of man, yea, of one single individual. But, say they, the
church never errs ; the pope never errs. We shall shew both
assertions to be false in the proper place. We say that scripture
never errs, and therefore judge that interpretation to be the
truest which agrees with scripture. What have we to do with
churches, or councils, or popes, unless they can shew that what
they define is in harmony with the scriptures? And what, at the
last, must we say that this church really is which they object to us?
Here certainly you will find nothing but what is human, and, consequently, uncertain and altogether unsafe.

CHAPTER XI.

THE PARTICULAR ARGUMENTS OF OUR ADVERSARIES ARE REFUTED.

LET us now reply severally to each of his special objections.
The means against which he disputes are principally four. First,
the consideration of what goes before and what follows : secondly,
the observation of the phrase and style : thirdly, the comparison,
of passages : fourthly, the inspection of the originals.

[I.] Against the first he objects, that such a consideration is uncertain, because the context of scripture is various and miscellaneous,
the order of discourse in the scriptures often interrupted ; that Paul
often imperceptibly, and without any notice, passes from one subject
to another ; that in the same sentences some things are said literally,
and some figuratively ; nay, that the same word is taken in different
senses in the same sentence. Therefore, this consideration is uncertain, and (to use his own words) " misleads the reader in many
ways, when taken separately." I reply, that Stapleton hath answered himself. For we do not say that each of these several
means, taken by itself and applied separately, is always sufficient for
discovering the true sense of scripture ; but that they, all taken
together, are sufficiently efficacious when properly handled. Indeed
we ought to think we have prospered well, if after the long and
diligent use of these means we at length attain to the true sense of
a difficult passage of scripture. When Stapleton, therefore, ad-

duces examples to shew that we cannot, by this consideration alone, find what we seek, he wastes his pains and only amuses his reader. But if he join the others with this, then he will easily perceive what great efficacy there is in these means for the opening out and illustration of the scripture. For example, Gen. iii., we read, that Adam and Eve "saw the fruit of the tree, that it was fair to the eye," &c., and yet that, immediately after eating it, "their eyes were opened." *Eyes* are here spoken of, first in a figurative, and then in a strict sense. Who does not know this, or what end was the exhibition of this instance designed to serve? Why, Stapleton gathers from this, that the consideration of the context, preceding and consequent, is no firm and *infallible* rule for understanding scripture. As if we said so, or depended upon this rule alone! For when we approach the interpretation of difficult scriptures, we do not separate and divorce these means from each other, as if each were sufficient separately and of itself for each passage: but we say that everywhere those means are to be applied which are fit and necessary; and that if one give us not adequate assistance, we should take in the rest also; as he who cannot open a door with one key, applies another, and tries many, nor stops trying until he hath found the true one. Even so, when considering the antecedents and consequents is insufficient, we must compare the passage before us with others, or sift the style and phraseology, or examine the original. But, to answer this particular instance of Stapleton's,—who does not see that the consideration of the context is here specially useful and efficacious in ascertaining the true meaning of the passage? For, if one were to argue that Adam or Eve were blind at first, because their eyes are said to have been opened after they had tasted of the fruit, he might be easily refuted from the words immediately preceding. For the woman saw the fruit, which was in appearance fair and delightful; and this must needs be so understood as to imply that Eve really had eyes and the power of vision, since she was so influenced by this sight as to be unable to restrain herself from immediately gratifying her desires: and consequently, what follows concerning the opening of their eyes can only be taken figuratively. Thus the place itself shews, that this second statement must be understood of some other kind of seeing. Stapleton brings another example from Ps. xxii: *Deus, Deus meus, respice in me; quare me derelinquisti? Longe a salute mea verba delictorum meorum.* These words, says he, are spoken in the person of his body and of

the whole church : upon which point we will plainly refute him by
the application of two of our means, the comparison of places, and
the examination of the originals. For, first, in Matth. xxvii. 46,
Christ himself, who is the head of the church, hath proved this to
be his own voice and complaint, by exclaiming as he hung upon
the cross, " My God, my God, why hast thou forsaken me ? " In
the next place, if we look into the original Hebrew verity, we shall
understand that the second member of this verse should be translated, "Thou art far from my help, from the words of my roaring."
However, our opponent's argument labours under the fallacy of
division and composition : These means do not suffice separately ;
and therefore not taken together.

[II.] His objections to the observation of the style and phraseology are of a similar character ; which, although he allows it to
be an excellent and very useful mean, and one which may not un-
frequently be applied with advantage, he nevertheless contends is
doubtful, ambiguous and deceitful, *if taken alone and by itself.*
We accept his praises of this mean, and are glad that we may use
it with Stapleton's good leave ; but, as to his affirming it not to
be sufficiently efficacious, taken by itself alone, for gaining the
authentic sense of scripture, this is precisely our own judgment. We
ascribe no such great force to these several means when applied
singly ; but think that each hath its weight, and contributes much
help, and that all taken together are sufficient. Stapleton, being
unable to break them down when united and joined together, does
his best to separate them, and attack them in detail ; which is a
plain proof of his distrusting his own cause : just as they who are
afraid of, and dare not stand before, united and collected forces,
yet venture to fall upon them when they are scattered. But let
us hear what sort of argument Stapleton broaches against this
method. First, the scripture hath not one, but many different
authors, who have each their own manner of expression. Isaiah's
style differs from that of Amos ; Peter and Paul do not write in
the same manner. I answer, that, indeed, the styles in scripture
are various, but that nevertheless that variety is not so great as
to baffle observation. Although Isaiah, who was educated in the
royal court, hath a much purer and more elegant diction than
Amos, who had lived amongst shepherds, yet this shepherd speaks
in such a manner as to be intelligible to all who can understand
anything : for he had learned to speak from the best master of
speech, even the Holy Spirit. So, although Paul, brought up by

Gamaliel, the most learned of the Pharisees, speaks otherwise than
Peter or James, who had passed almost all their lives in fishing;
yet the difference is not very great, since Peter and James did not
learn to speak Greek in their fishing occupations, but were taught
by the Holy Spirit, a much better and more eloquent instructor
than Gamaliel. But let us grant that the style of scripture is different in many books: yet how does this prevent either that such
differences should be marked, or that, when marked, they should
yield great help in the interpretation of scripture? Certainly the
fathers are much more unlike each other than the prophets or
apostles. Augustine is copious, Jerome succinct; Lactantius imi-
tates Cicero; Tertullian affects obscurity; Chrysostom is ornate
and clear; Nazianzen compressed and acute. In a word, they have
not all the same character, and yet all speak so as to be easily
intelligible when read with attention. Secondly, says Stapleton,
the variety of the interpreters and of the originals produces uncertainty. I answer: Translators, indeed, we often see go wrong;
on which account it is not always safe to acquiesce in them. But
there is no such variety in the originals as Stapleton pretends.
Thirdly, The rules which respect the phraseology of scripture are
not universal. I answer: Although they are not absolutely universal, yet are they such as may assist the students of scripture;
and, whatever they be, the scripture must not be accommodated to
them, but they to the scripture. Upon this point Stapleton hath
used no examples, and he produces no phrase that may not be
explained by the scriptures themselves. What? must we wait until
the pope tells us the force of Hebraisms, who, generally, knows
nothing of either Greek or Hebrew? A worthy judge of style
forsooth!

[III.] He disputes against the comparison of passages in c. 10.
We say that a diligent and judicious comparison of places is a good
means of interpretation; while he maintains that, *taken alone and
by itself*, it is not only fallacious but pernicious. What then? We
do not suppose that either this, or any mean whatever, should be
used and applied alone; and I wonder that he did not hence perceive the egregious sophistry of his proceeding. For, when our
assertion is, that all these means should be used, when necessary,
to unfold the involved meanings of scripture, and not that any one
should be trusted alone, this man comes and disputes against us as
if we determined that each several mean by itself was strong enough
and sufficient for all purposes. Furthermore, we require a fair,

judicious, and diligent comparison ; and, therefore, his long discourse of the wrong feelings under which many labour, of the ambiguity of words, and of the customs of heretics, is beside the question. Heretics, and those who are led by party-spirit, or their own feelings, search scripture either carelessly or perversely. However, let us briefly refute the reasons of our opponent from point to point.

First : In a comparison, private feeling and prejudice generally prevail. I answer : If there be any so perverse as to yield no assent to the scriptures when duly and accurately compared, such persons will respect no authority, unless influenced either by fear or shame, or in some hypocritical manner. Can he who is not moved by almost innumerable testimonies of scripture, appositely and judiciously collated, to believe the deity of Christ, can he be persuaded by the authority of the church or the opinion of the Roman pontiff? Assuredly, that man will never be a good catholic, whom well collated scriptures cannot bring to adopt a catholic opinion ; and such are the popish pseudo-catholics, who have derived their catholic errors not from the scriptures, but from the inventions of men.

Secondly : The same words and phrases have not always everywhere the same sense and signification. I answer : Although words and phrases may in one place have some ambiguity, on account of their being taken variously, yet the difficulty may be freed from embarrassment either by considering the things themselves, or by the comparison of other places, or by recurring to the analogy of faith. " The flesh " and "the world" are taken in various senses, and so are many other terms. Who denies it ? But whence hath the observation of this variety been derived ? Is it not from the scriptures themselves and the comparison of places ?

Thirdly : Some places occur but once in scripture. I answer : These are either plain or not necessary to salvation. For those common phrases of the apostles, " being buried with Christ ;" " being crucified with Christ ;" " living with him ;" " reigning with him ;" " being baptized into his death," and such like, are plain enough in themselves, and may also have light thrown upon them by the comparison of other sentences.

Fourthly : Because all heretics, by using great diligence in comparing scripture, have nevertheless erred most foully in the sense of scripture. I answer : They did not compare scripture with great diligence, but for the most part, slightly and carelessly. And his assertion, that " by a most diligent collation of scripture they fell into shameful errors," is an outrageous insult upon the scriptures. For even though it might be said that they fell into error while using the comparison of parallel passages, yet they did not err by means of that comparison; since, however those may go most shamefully wrong who collate scripture, yet a careful collation is never the cause of their mistakes. Stapleton proposes an example of such a comparison. The Arians compared that saying of Christ in John x., "I and my Father are one," with those other words of Christ in John xvii., "Father, I will that they all may be one, as thou, Father, art in me, and I in thee;" nevertheless, says he, that interpretation hath obtained, which is prescribed by the rule of faith. I answer by demanding, whence the church derived its proofs of this interpretation? Stapleton says, from the rule of faith. Well then, was it from the scripture? By no means, if we are to believe Stapleton; for it would then follow that the Arians were confuted by the comparison and testimony of the scriptures. Now it is certain that the Arians *were* refuted by the church and the holy fathers out of the scriptures, and specially by the collation of scripture, as is plain from Hilary de Trin. Lib. VIII. And if this very place, John x., be duly weighed, it will sufficiently establish the consubstantiality of Christ with the Father. For Christ promises that none shall snatch his sheep out of his hand, because none can snatch them out of his Father's hand. And, in order to give us an intimate persuasion of this truth, he subjoins, "I and my Father are one;" which must necessarily be understood of an unity of nature and of power. Also when Christ says that he will give his sheep eternal life, he gives no obscure evidence of his being God. Besides, as Chrysostom hath observed, the Jews immediately perceived that Christ had pronounced himself consubstantial with the Father; and on that account rushed upon Christ in a transport of frantic fury, and sought to stone him. So it presently follows in the evangelist: "They therefore took up stones to stone him." This also follows, which is still plainer. The Jews being asked by Christ wherefore they sought to stone him, replied, *for blasphemy*, and because he, being a man, *made himself God*. Upon which place Augustine, in his 48th Tractate upon John, discourses thus: "Thus far the Jews were able to bear him; but when they heard, 'I and my Father are one,' they could bear it no longer, and, hard as ever, rushed to take up stones[1]."

[1] Hucusque Judæi tolerare potuerunt: audierunt, Ego et Pater unum sumus, et non pertulerunt, et more suo duri, ad lapides cucurrerunt.—Opp. T. IV. p. 816.]

31

[WHITAKER.]

Then, a little lower down: "Lo, the Jews understood what the Arians understand not. For they were enraged upon that very account, because they perceived that the words, 'I and my Father are one,' supposed an equality of the Son with the Father[1]." Thus, from a comparison of places, and a consideration of the context, and strict inference, the fathers concluded that Christ here speaks of unity of nature, and so condemned the Arians by a most righteous sentence. Augustine teaches well, that both Arians and Sabellians are refuted by these words. Thus he speaks, as quoted in the Catena of Thomas Aquinas: "If you mark both terms, both the *one* and the *are*, you will escape both Scylla and Charybdis. His saying *one* saves you from Arius: his saying *are* saves you from Sabellius. If *one*, then not different: if *we are*, then Father and Son are distinct persons[2]." Thus always the catholic and pious fathers in every question and dispute refuted the heretics by the words and collation of the scriptures.

In the eleventh chapter Stapleton adduces one example to shew how pernicious the collation of scripture may be. Chemnitz, says he, relying upon such comparisons, perverts a notable passage of the apostle, where we are taught that a vow of celibacy should not be violated, 1 Tim. v. : "Having damnation because they have cast off their first faith." This *first faith*, says he, the church understands of a vow of celibacy and widowhood : whereupon he cites many fathers and councils. We shall elsewhere have to discuss this passage, when we shall shew that Chemnitz has advanced nothing inconsistent with the scriptures or piety. However, a prudent and fair comparison of a single passage of scripture hath more force in it than the bare opinions of many fathers. To understand by the "first faith" a vow of celibacy or widowhood is repugnant not only to the parallel passages, but even to the analogy of faith. Wherefore if all the fathers had said that such a vow is here sanctioned, they might better be excused than defended. But some of the fathers have passed a sounder judgment upon this passage, taking *the first faith* to mean, not any vow of abstaining from marriage, but sincere religion and piety. So Jerome, in the preface to his commen-

[1 Ecce Judæi intellexerunt, quod non intelligunt Ariani. Ideo enim irati sunt, quoniam senserunt non posse dici, Ego et Pater unum sumus, nisi ubi est æqualitas Patris et Filii.—T. IV. p. 817.]

[2 Utrumque audi, et *unum*, et *sumus;* et a Charybdi et a Scylla liberaberis. Quod dixit, unum, liberat te ab Ario : quod dixit, sumus, liberat te a Sabellio. Si unum, non ergo diversum; si sumus, ergo Pater et Filius.—Fol. 306, 2. Paris. 1537.]

tary upon Titus; Athanasius de Trin. Lib. vi.; Vincentius Lirinensis, Commonit. c. 12. For they say that heretics cast away their first faith, not when they contract marriage after a vow of celibacy, but when they fall away to infidelity or heresy after having made a profession of the true faith. No faith is prior to that faith in the Trinity which we profess in baptism. This first faith heretics violate and annul, when, forgetting their pure and sound profession, they take up false and impious notions in religion. And in this manner wanton widows cast away their first faith : for, after having devoted themselves to the service of the church, being entangled in the seductions of lust, they first abandon their ministry, which can only be discharged by chaste matrons ; and then, perceiving themselves to have lost their character amongst Christians by their unchastity, pass over to the enemies of the christian faith. So the apostle explains himself, verse 15, where, speaking of such widows, he says : " For some already ἐξετρά-πησαν ὀπίσω τοῦ Σατανᾶ³." The apostle therefore immediately tells us the meaning of the phrase πρώτην πίστιν ἀθετεῖν. It is nothing else but ἐκτραπῆναι ὀπίσω τοῦ Σατανᾶ, that is, to turn from the right way, and follow Satan as a guide ; which is what those do who persevere not in their faith pledged to God and in a holy profession. For to take faith for a vow is to assign it a sense unheard of in the scriptures. But we will speak at large of this passage in its proper place.

[IV.] In his last chapter he disputes against the inspection of the originals, concluding that it is not now as necessary as it was formerly, because there is now one certain and authentic version of both Testaments, expressly approved by the church in a general council. I answer, that the synagogue of antichrist in their pretended council of Trent did that which the true church of Christ never in any council dared to attempt or think of,—namely, made the originals of scripture in both Testaments unauthoritative and non-authentic, and pronounced the authenticity of the vulgate Latin version, than which nothing can possibly be more faulty and corrupt. However, we have largely treated this whole matter in the first part of the second question, where we have proved, not only by strict reasoning, but even by the confession of the papists themselves, that the Latin copies should be amended from the originals. There is no necessity for entering now into a fuller reply to this argument.

[³ Compare also v. 8 : τὴν πίστιν ἤρνηται, καὶ ἔστιν ἀπίστου χείρων, said of one who provides not for his own.]

CHAPTER XII.

THE ARGUMENTS BY WHICH OUR OPPONENT ENDEAVOURS TO ESTABLISH HIS OWN MEANS ARE EXAMINED.

HAVING heard what he hath alleged against the means which we employ, let us now see how he defends and confirms his own. Stapleton, then, Lib. II., proposes four means. The first is, the rule of faith, c. 1 and 3; the second, the practice of the church, c. 4; the third, the unanimous interpretation of the fathers, c. 5; the fourth, the interpretation prescribed and decreed by councils, c. 6. These he pronounces to be the only certain and authentic means. Here you perceive that there is no express mention of the pope, which I know not whether to ascribe to forgetfulness or to design. I suspect that either the reason is, that the pope is implied in all these means, (for the rule of faith is that which the pope approves; the practice of the church that which the pope observes; the exposition of the fathers that which the pope follows; the definition of councils that which the pope confirms;) or that these are mere means, while the pope is the judge who forms his judgment by them. Thus Stapleton seems here to overturn the position maintained by Bellarmine and Stapleton himself elsewhere, which attributes a judicial and definitive authority to the practice of the church. For if there are means of interpreting scripture, then the supreme judicial authority resides not in them, but in the scriptures; and if the pope himself be understood to be included in these means, then he disowns this authority as his, and gives it to the scriptures. We have already spoken of Stapleton's three latter means, and intend to speak again in the proper place. Let us now consider the rule of faith whereof he boasts.

What rule, then, does he mean? If the scripture, we gladly recognise it as the interpreter. And, assuredly, the rule of faith is either the scripture itself, or the sum and epitome and ascertained sense of scripture, not any thing beside or beyond the scripture; and so the fathers thought when they mentioned the rule of faith. Tertullian, in his book *de Virginibus Velandis*, thus explains that rule: "The rule of faith," says he, "is but one, immoveable and incapable of reformation, that is, the rule of believing in one God almighty, the Maker of the world, and in his Son Jesus Christ, who was born of the virgin Mary, crucified under Pontius Pilate, rose again from the dead on the third day, was taken up into heaven, and is now sitting at the right hand of the Father, and will come to judge the quick and the dead by means of the resurrection also of the flesh[1]." And this he calls also *the law of faith.* So Augustine, in his Enchiridion, c. 56 : " Unless the Holy Ghost were God, he would not be placed before the church in the rule of faith[2]." Gerson, upon Communion in both Kinds, understands the scripture by the rule of faith, when he says : " Holy scripture is the rule of faith, against which, when rightly understood, no human authority may be admitted[3]." We always appeal to this rule, and it is this which our adversaries fear and shun. Stapleton says, Lib. VII. c. 1, that the rule of faith is more extensive than the Creed, and denotes that doctrine which the apostles delivered to the churches, and which was publicly received by all, that is to say, all tradition written or unwritten. We, however, make no account of those pretended traditions, and demand a known, open, clear, certain, immutable rule. The unwritten rule is uncertain, and known only to a few ; whereupon we shall treat in the question next ensuing. In the meanwhile, it is either repugnant to the scriptures, or not. If it be repugnant, it is to be rejected without hesitation : if it agree, that must be perceived and judged of by the scriptures. Since, therefore, the scriptures are the line and measure for judging things unwritten, unwritten traditions cannot be the rule of interpreting scripture.

Stapleton, however, contends that his unwritten rule is that analogy of which the apostle speaks, Rom. xii.[4], the *measure of the rule* mentioned in 2 Cor. x.[5], and *the rule*, Galat. vi.[6], and Philipp.

[1 Regula quidam fidei una omnino est, sola immobilis et irreformabilis, credendi scilicet in unicum Deum omnipotentem, mundi Conditorem, et Filium ejus Jesum Christum, natum ex virgine Maria, crucifixum sub Pontio Pilato, tertia die resuscitatum a mortuis, receptum in cœlis, sedentem nunc ad dexteram Patris, venturum judicare vivos et mortuos per carnis etiam resurrectionem.—c. 1. p. 201.]

[2 Ne per hoc Spiritus Sanctus, si creatura, non creator esset, profecto creatura rationalis esset. Ipsa est enim summa creatura ; et ideo in regula fidei non poneretur ante ecclesiam, quia et ipse ad ecclesiam pertineret in illa ejus parte quæ in cœlis est.—p. 207. ed. Bruder. Lips. 1838.]

[3 Scriptura sacra est regula fidei, contra quam bene intellectam non est admittenda auctoritas.—Gerson. Opp. T. I. p. 521. Paris. 1606.]

[4 κατὰ τὴν ἀναλογίαν τῆς πίστεως.—Rom. xii. 6.]

[5 κατὰ τὸ μέτρον τοῦ κανόνος.—2 Cor. x. 13.]

[6 ὅσοι τῷ κανόνι τούτῳ στοιχήσουσιν.—Gal. vi. 17.]

iii.[1] But it is manifest, that it is not that popish rule of ecclesiastical
tradition that is meant by the apostle, but the sense and force of
the apostolic preaching, which they afterwards set forth plainly and
copiously in written documents, and handed down to the perpetual
memory of all generations. Stapleton, Lib. II. c. 3, enumerates
many testimonies from Augustine to commend his fictitious rule of
faith : but, if we sift them each thoroughly, it will be plain that
such a rule as they dream of never entered into the head of
Augustine. The rule of Augustine is no other than a profession
of religion, agreeing in all respects with the scriptures ; nor does
Augustine acknowledge any rule save that which the sound and
catholic doctrine of the scriptures embraces, and nowhere desiderates
these unwritten rules of the papists. So in his imperfect work upon
Genesis *ad literam*, c. 1, he expounds the catholic faith ; where
(says Stapleton) he comprises in the rule of the catholic faith not
only those things which are laid down in the Creed, but many
others which the church had recently defined against the Manicheans
and Pelagians. But Stapleton did not observe, that Augustine puts
nothing in the rule of faith which is not contained in the scriptures.
Whatever the church defined against the Manicheans or Pelagians,
it took from no other source than the canonical scriptures ; which
were called canonical upon that very account, because they contain
a certain necessary, perfect, and infallible rule of all faith and
religion. And although all things are not plainly and explicitly
laid down in the Creed, which are of avail to the refutation of those
heretics ; yet the principles of that faith are delivered in the Creed,
which is found more largely expounded in the scriptures. Indeed
the first article of the Creed sufficiently refutes the Manicheans :
for, if we believe in God, the Maker of heaven and earth and all
creatures, then there is but one God, the Creator of the world, and
not two gods, nor was the world made by an evil deity, as the
Manicheans blasphemously taught. The article which teaches that
Christ was conceived by the Holy Ghost of the virgin Mary condemns the Pelagians, who deny original sin : for if Christ were
thus conceived and born, to escape being tainted with any spot of
original sin, then it follows that the rest of mankind must be born
universally infected by that sin : and the Creed, as understood and
explained by the scriptures, refutes also the other Pelagian errors.

But what are those many points, not set down in the Creed,
which Augustine enumerates ? Forsooth, he introduces some things

[1 τῷ αὐτῷ στοιχεῖν κανόνι.—Philipp. iii. 16.]

concerning sin and the punishment of sin gainst the Pelagians, and concerning the creation of all things against the Manicheans. Now these may be learned even from the Creed, and are most plainly delivered in the scriptures. Let Stapleton, if he can, produce even a single passage from Augustine, wherein that holy father declares that the rule of faith contains any dogma which is not delivered in the scriptures. For these testimonies which he hath produced make mention of no rule not circumscribed by the boundaries of scripture. The most stringent of all is that which is objected to us from the third Book of Christian Doctrine, c. 2, where Augustine writes, that "the rule of faith is learned from the plainer parts of scripture and the authority of the church[2]:" where note (says Stapleton), that the rule of faith is to be derived not from the scriptures alone, but also from the authority of the church. But Augustine does not attribute to the church the authority of determining or defining any thing beyond the scriptures, nor does he say that the rule of faith is to be drawn from the scriptures and the authority of the church; but he reminds the student of theology, that whenever he lights upon a passage which admits of an ambiguous stopping, he should consult that rule of faith which he hath learned from the plainer parts of scripture and the authority, that is, the teaching, of the church. Not that we are to deem the church's authority absolute, but that the church leads us by her voice and guidance, and protects us by her authority from the craft of heretics. The church hath authority to interpret scripture; not, indeed, an uncontrolled and indefinite authority, but tied to certain bonds and conditions, so as to be obliged to interpret scripture not by her own caprice, but by the scriptures themselves : which legitimate and authentic expositions of the church must needs have very great weight with all the faithful, and especially with candidates for the ministry. It would be an heretical punctuation of the words to read thus, *In principio erat Verbum, et Verbum erat apud Deum, et Deus erat ;* so as to make the sense to be, The Word was in the beginning with God, but was not God. "Now this," says Augustine, "is to be refuted by the rule of faith, wherein faith in the coequality of the Persons of the Trinity is prescribed." Indeed, both the scripture and the church prescribe faith in the equality of the Trinity, but not with the same weight of authority. The church prescribes it, because it hath received it all from scripture : scripture prescribes as the

[2 Consulat regulam fidei quam de scripturarum planioribus locis et ecclesiæ auctoritate percepit.—p. 78.]

self-credible and supreme verity. Thus the church prescribes nothing beyond the scripture, and whatever authority the church hath to prescribe any thing is included within the boundaries of scripture; nor will Stapleton find in Augustine any other rule of faith than that which is derived from the catholic exposition of the scriptures themselves.

CHAPTER XIII.

THAT SCRIPTURE IS TO BE INTERPRETED BY SCRIPTURE.

It remains now in the last place for us to prove that these means are to be used; which is a corollary from the conclusion already demonstrated, that scripture is its own interpreter. For if scripture interpret itself, then we must apply these means to obtain the interpretation of scripture; since those who would use other means do not allow to scripture the power of expounding its own meaning. But scripture does indeed explain itself with the utmost plainness and perspicuity, if we will only attend to scripture thus explaining itself; and although it may not in all places leave absolutely no room for doubt, yet it does so in most, and the most necessary places, and in the principal articles of our faith.

We have examples of this sort of interpretation in the scriptures. For the scripture, where it speaks with some obscurity, explains its meaning sometimes immediately after in the very same place, sometimes accumulatively in several other places. This I will briefly illustrate by examples of both sorts of interpretation. In Isaiah li. 1, we have: "Look unto the rock whence ye were hewn, and to the hole of the pit whence ye were digged." The language is obscure and ambiguous; but the obscurity is wholly removed by the words which follow: "Consider Abraham your father, and Sarah who bore you." What better expositor do we require? Gen. xv. 2, Abraham says to the Lord: "What wilt thou give me, seeing I go childless, and the steward of my house is this Eleazar of Damascus?" These words are somewhat dark, but light is thrown upon them presently after: "Behold, thou hast given me no seed, and lo, my servant born in my house is my heir." What could possibly be spoken more plainly? Gen. xi. 1, the whole world is said to have been *of one lip;* and, to make this better understood, it is immediately subjoined, that their *speech was the same.* Exod. xx. 4, in the second precept of the decalogue, we are commanded to " make no graven image, nor likeness of any thing ;" and, to put us completely in possession of the drift of this law, a lucid exposition is added in the way of commentary. Deut. vii. 3, the Israelites are forbidden to unite themselves with the Canaanites by affinity. This might be plain enough by itself, but is rendered still more clear and definite by what follows in the same place, " Thou shalt not give thy daughter to the son of any of them, neither shalt thou take the son of any of them for thy daughter :" and the reason of the law, subjoined immediately in a large exposition, makes the meaning of the law still more evident. Isaiah i. 2, " I have brought up children, and they have rebelled against me," saith the Lord ; and then immediately shews that this declaration concerns the Israelites : " Israel doth not know, my people doth not consider." Isaiah liii. 1, " To whom is the arm of the Lord revealed ?"—the meaning of this is plain from the preceding clause, " Who hath believed our report ?"—so as to make it evident, that the gospel is denoted by the arm of the Lord. In the sixth of John Christ is described as having discoursed at large of eating his flesh and drinking his blood, and having given grievous offence by that discourse not only to the Capernaites, but also to his own disciples. Wherefore, to prevent that offence from sinking too deep or dwelling too long in pious minds, Christ himself at the last explains himself, saying, that the time should come when they should see the Son of man ascending up ; that it is the Spirit that quickens, while the flesh profits nothing ; and still more plainly, that those words which he had spoken *were Spirit and life.* So plainly, so carefully, so largely does Christ remove that stumbling-block from his discourse, and teach us that he spoke of a spiritual, not a carnal and bodily, sort of eating and drinking. Paul says, 1 Cor. v. 9, " I wrote unto you in an epistle not to keep company with fornicators :" but what sort of fornicators he meant, he presently indicates ; not those who were strangers to the christian name and profession, but those who, professing to be Christ's adherents, abstained not from fornication and such-like similar enormities ; with such he hath forbidden us to have any familiarity, and hath clearly explained his mind upon that subject. So, in the fifth chapter of the Epistle to the Ephesians, speaking of marriage, he drops these words, " This is a great mystery :" where, foreseeing that some would hence infer that marriage was a sacrament, he subjoined what absolutely removes the ground of such a surmise, "But I speak concerning Christ and the church;" in which words he protests that it is not matrimony, but the union of Christ and the church, that is styled by him a mystery. Such examples are innumerable, wherein it is apparent that the Holy Spirit hath been careful that what he might seem at first to have expressed with some obscurity, should afterwards be clearly explained, so as to free the reader from all difficulty.

Now if I were to attempt to prove by examples, how those things which are expressed with some obscurity in one place are explained with the utmost clearness in other parts of scripture, I should scarcely come to any end. For the usage of scripture is to send us, for the true meaning of one part of scripture, to another; so that, in this way, we do not rest or acquiesce in any single portion, but embrace the whole body of the sacred volumes in our reading and meditation. Passages must therefore be compared with one another, if we desire rightly to understand or gain a firm hold of scripture. The prophetic scriptures illustrate the books of Moses, and the whole old Testament is opened out in the new. In Exod. iii. we have the words, "I am that I am," and, "I am hath sent me to you." What is the meaning of these expressions? What else but this, that God is eternal and immortal, unlike the other deities of erroneous creeds? Now this is elsewhere expressed without any ambiguity of phrase. Isaiah xliii., "Before me there was no God formed, neither after me shall there be any;" and Isaiah xlviii., "I am the first, and I am the last:" and in infinite other passages of both Testaments the same truth is most manifestly established. When the devil abused the scriptures, Christ restrained him by the authority of the scriptures, Matt. iv.; thus instructing his church to refute those opponents who torture scripture into various senses by testimonies of scripture compared together, skilfully applied and correctly understood. Christ condemns and sets aside that licentious custom of divorce, which the Jews had taken up from a false exposition of the Mosaic law, no otherwise than by interpreting the law and explaining it by another passage of scripture, Matt. xix. Christ refutes and convinces by the testimony of scripture the Sadducees who denied the resurrection, and founded their denial upon a subtle piece of reasoning, Matt. xxii. The apostle in his epistles to the Romans, Corinthians, Galatians, Hebrews, and in almost all the rest, quotes frequently sentences from the old Testament, and explains them;

so as that if we were not (as he says of the Jews) "dull of hearing," and were earnestly desirous, without pride or prejudice, to
handle, peruse, revolve, search, examine the scriptures, to learn the
scriptures from the scriptures themselves, and to deem no expositor of the Holy Spirit better than the Holy Spirit himself, we
should assuredly be seldomer at a loss to understand the scriptures.
But, whereas we read or consider the scriptures with but slight
attention, and follow the changeful and manifold opinions and interpretations of men, we are distracted by doubtful and almost
infinite judgments, and imagine I know not what obscurities, and
become blind as the bats, seeking light in the very blaze of noon.

Let us next see briefly what the fathers determined respecting
these means of interpretation. Basil, in his treatise of the Holy
Spirit, c. 1, bids us "investigate the meaning concealed in every
word and syllable[1]." The expediency of doing this he proves
thus : The scope of scripture is, that we may be made like to
God ; such a likeness cannot have place without knowledge : now
" knowledge comes by instruction," and " of instruction the beginning is speech, the parts whereof are syllables and terms." The
same Basil, in his Ascet. Quæst. 267, hath these words : " Whatsoever seems to be spoken ambiguously or obscurely in some places
of holy scripture, is cleared up by what is plain and evident in
other places[2]." What is this, but the very thesis which we maintain ? So then, if we would understand the ambiguities and obscurities which meet us in every direction in the study of scripture,
we must consult other passages, and compare scripture with itself.
Irenæus, Lib. II. c. 47[3], says that all scripture is in harmony with
itself, and that the parables (that is, the more obscure sentences)
are in harmony with the places perspicuously expressed, *et quæ
manifesta sunt absolvent parabolas;* that is, that light is so re-

[1 Τὸ γὰρ μὴ παρέργως ἀκούειν τῶν θεολογικῶν φωνῶν, ἀλλὰ πειρᾶσθαι
τὸν ἐν ἑκάστῃ λέξει καὶ ἑκάστῃ συλλαβῇ κεκρυμμένον τὸν νοῦν ἐξιχνεύειν, οὐκ
ἀργῶν εἰς εὐσεβείαν, ἀλλὰ γνωριζόντων τὸν σκόπον τῆς κλήσεως ἡμῶν· ὅτι πρό-
κειται ἡμῖν ὁμοιωθῆναι Θεῷ κατὰ τὸ δυνατὸν ἀνθρώπου φύσει. ὁμοίωσις δὲ οὐκ ἄνευ
γνώσεως· ἡ δὲ γνῶσις ἐκ διδαγμῶν· λόγος δὲ διδασκαλίας ἀρχή· λόγου δὲ μέρη
συλλαβαὶ καὶ λέξεις.—T. II. p. 143. B.]

[2 τὰ ἀμφίβολα καὶ ἐπικεκαλυμμένως εἰρῆσθαι δοκοῦντα ἔν τισι τόποις τῆς
θεοπνεύστου γραφῆς ὑπὸ τῶν ἐν ἄλλοις τόποις ὁμολογουμένων σαφηνίζεται.
—T. II. p. 632. c.]

[3 Omnis scriptura a Deo nobis data consonans nobis invenietur, et
parabolæ his quæ manifeste dicta sunt consonabunt, et manifeste dicta
absolvent parabolas.—p. 203. c. ed. Fevard.]

flected upon the obscure places from the clear, that no one who does not choose it, can possibly err and be misled.

Origen, in his 24th Homily upon Numbers, tells us : " The discovery of what we seek in the scriptures is much facilitated by adducing from several places what is written upon the same subject[1]." Tertullian, in his book de Virginibus Velandis : " Arise, O truth, thyself expound thine own scriptures, which custom knows not; for had it known them, it would not have existed[2]." And in his book against Praxeas : " Scripture is in no such peril as to need help from thy reasoning, lest it should seem to contradict itself. It hath reason, both when it determines God to be but one, and when it shews the Father and the Son to be two, and is sufficient for itself[3]." Hilary, in his 9th book upon the Trinity : " Let the meaning of what is said be gathered either from the preceding, or from the following context[4]." Ambrose, Epist. 7, Lib. II.[5], says that Paul interprets himself in most passages ; and likewise Chrysostom, Hom. 9, upon 2 Cor. : " Every where, when he uses any obscure expression, he presently again explains himself[6]." Cyril, in his Thesaurus, Lib. VIII. c. 2, says that " we must observe the circumstances, time, subject, and person, in order that we may investigate the true meaning[7]."

But most clearly of all Augustine, in his four books of Christian Doctrine ; in three of which he treats of the method of finding out the true sense of scripture, and in the fourth, the mode of teaching

[1 Facilius in scripturis quod quæritur invenitur, si ex pluribus locis quæ de eadem re scripta sunt proferantur.]

[2 Exsurge igitur, veritas, et quasi de patientia erumpe : nullam volo consuetudinem defendas; nam jam et illa consuetudine, sub qua te fruebaris, expugnatur. Te esse demonstra quæ virgines tegis. Ipsa scripturas tuas interpretare, quas consuetudo non novit; si enim nosset, nunquam esset. —c. 3. p. 204. P. II.]

[3 Porro non periclitatur scriptura, ut illi de tua argumentativa succurras, ne sibi contraria videatur. Habet rationem, et cum unicum Deum statuit, et cum duos Patrem et Filium ostendit, et sufficit sibi.—c. 18. p. 270. P. IV.]

[4 Dictorum intelligentia aut ex præpositis aut ex consequentibus exspectetur.—Hilarii Opp. p. 116. Basil. 1570.]

[5 In plerisque ita se ipse suis exponit verbis, ut is qui tractat, grammatici magis quam disputatoris fungatur munere.—T. VIII. p. 448. Paris. 1839.]

[6 πανταχοῦ ὅταν τι ἀσαφὲς εἴπῃ, ἑαυτὸν ἑρμηνεύει πάλιν.]

[7 Ante omnia quando locum scripturæ aliquem recte intelligere volumus, tria diligenter consideranda sunt; tempus quando scriptum est quod dicitur ; persona quæ dicit, vel per quam, aut de qua dicitur.—Opp. T. II. col. 284. Paris. 1573.]

others what we now understand. And forasmuch as the end of all
scripture is, as Augustine observes, the love of God and of our
neighbour, he therefore treats of this in his first book, and determines that without any doubt that is no true interpretation
which does not serve to build up the edifice of this genuine charity.
Having handled this matter, he comes closer to his subject, and
pronounces the difficulty of understanding things to lie in the signs
wherewith the things are denoted. Such signs he distinguishes
into the unknown and the ambiguous.

He treats of the unknown in the second book, and of the ambiguous in the third. He first defines and divides a sign in several
chapters, teaching us that it is sometimes taken strictly and sometimes figuratively; whence he says that the obscurity of the scriptures is occasioned, of which obscurity he sets forth the various
uses. Then, c. 8, he enumerates the canonical books; because, as
he says, the first task is to know the books, to read them through,
and commit them to memory. Then he exhorts us to seek in
those passages which are clearly expressed the precepts of living
and the rules of faith; since all that make the complex of faith
and a good life may be found in what is so expressed. Having
mastered these, which are the plainer parts, he bids us proceed to
the more obscure; and in c. 10, he returns to signs, which he says
are unknown either in the words or in the sentence. Lest any
one, therefore, should err on account of his ignorance of the signs,
he delivers in cc. 11, 12, the general precepts for acquiring an
acquaintance with the art of grammar, which is a requisite condition
for learning the sense of scripture. He affirms skill in the three
languages to be greatly needed, and bears his testimony to the
great aid to be derived from a multitude of learned interpreters:
but if interpreters do not agree, he teaches us that recourse must
be had to the Hebrew and Greek originals. Afterwards he shews
that physics, and arithmetic, and music, and specially logic, upon
which he speaks largely, are useful to a divine for understanding
the scriptures; and, whilst he maintains that these philosophic arts
are of great advantage to the students of theology, he yet reminds
us that we do not addict ourselves to them immoderately; because
many, though not all, of the discourses of the philosophers are
superstitious, false, and impious. He directs the reader also to
study history, through ignorance of which many persons have
fallen into error, cc. 27, 28; and concludes that the philosophers
have many things agreeable to our religion.

In his third book he discusses the ambiguity of signs, which
happens in many ways: for sometimes they are taken strictly, sometimes metaphorically and figuratively ; sometimes it is doubtful how
the sentence should be stopped or pronounced ; upon which subject
he lays down this general rule, that we must never depart from the
rule of faith: furthermore, that we must take care not to understand
strictly what is spoken figuratively, c. 6 ; for it is a pitiable bondage
of the soul to take signs for things. Many chapters and many rules
are occupied with this subject. He subjoins another general rule,
that some precepts are proposed to all in common, some privately
to special persons ; and that these are to be diligently distinguished
the one from the other. Then he adds another, that we ought
not to imitate every thing that is related or even praised in the
scriptures ; and this other, that the clear places must be applied to
understand the obscure ; which point he frequently repeats. Then
follow the rules of Tychonius, seven in number, which may be
read in Augustine himself. These rules he calls the keys whereby
the mysteries of the holy scripture are unlocked. It is surprising that Augustine, when anxious to prescribe the best method of
understanding and expounding scripture, did not remind us that the
bishop of Rome was the sole certain interpreter of scripture.

The same Augustine, in his Book of 83 Questions, Qu. 69, says:
" The circumstances of scripture generally throw light upon the
meaning, when those things which lie round the scripture and
touch upon the present question are handled in a diligent discussion[1]." Jerome too, on Isaiah, c. 19 : " It is usual in scripture to
subjoin plain words to obscure ones, and to express in a clear form
what was first spoken enigmatically[2]." In his epistle to Pammachius, which is prefixed to his commentary upon Hosea, he says
that " the scriptures are the sealed book," which none could open,
or unlock its mysteries, but the Lion of the tribe of Judah. Jerome, therefore, does not recognise the pope as the public interpreter of scripture. But how then shall we understand the
scriptures ? He subjoins : " We must pray to the Lord, and say
with Peter, ' Declare unto us this parable '."

Why should I enumerate other authors, even papists ? Gerson,

[1 Solet circumstantia scripturæ illuminare sententiam, cum ea quæ
circa scripturam sunt, præsentem quæstionem contingentia, diligenti discus-
sione tractantur.]

[2 Moris est scripturarum obscuris manifesta subnectere, et quod prius sub
ænigmatibus dixerint, aperta voce proferre.—Opp. T. IV. p. 201. Veron. 1735.]

in his treatise *Quæ Veritates sunt Credendæ*, says, p. 1 : " The scripture expounds its own rules by themselves, according to the several passages of scripture[3]." And in his book of Communion in one Kind, he says that the scripture is " like one connected speech, whereof one part confirms, elucidates, and explains another[4] :" and hence he concludes with Augustine, that " one scripture should be compared with other passages of holy scripture." Again, upon Canticles, p. 3 : " One passage of scripture can lend an exposition to another[5]." Augustinus Steuchus, upon Genesis, c. 2, says : " God was not so unmerciful as to wish that men should be tortured throughout all generations by ignorance of this matter ; since he did not permit the existence of any one place in scripture which we cannot understand, if we will only weigh it carefully. For, as Theodoret says in this place, ' Holy scripture, when it designs to express any thing of importance, explains itself, and does not suffer the hearer to go wrong[6]'." Hieronymus ab Oleastro prescribes sixteen canons, in the beginning of his commentary upon the five books of Moses, highly useful for the reading and understanding of the scriptures; the drift of all which canons is to enable us to interpret scripture by scripture, not to direct us to have recourse to external means whenever we would expound a difficult place in scripture.

Thus then we close this question.

[3 Whitaker was deceived by the running title in Gerson (Opp. T. i. Basil. 1488); for the citation is really from the tract, *Casus contra Propositiones Magistri Johannis Parvi*: Unde propositiones universales de sacra pagina possunt et debent aliter exponi quam oppositiones Magistri Johannis Parvi, primo quia scriptura exponit regulas suas per semet ipsas secundum diversos passus scripturæ, *et juxta sacros doctores*.]

[4 Quarum una pars confirmat, elucidat, exponit alteram.]

[5 Unus potest passus in scripturis mutuo ceteros exponere.]

[6 Non adeo inhumanus fuit Deus, ut voluerit hujus rei ignoratione per omnes ætates homines torqueri; cum neque ullum in sacris scripturis esse passus sit locum, quem si accurate pensitemus, intepretari non possimus. Ut enim hoc loco ait Theodoritus, ἡ ἁγία γραφὴ ἐπειδὰν βούληταί τι τοιοῦτον ἡμᾶς διδάσκειν, ἑαυτὴν ἑρμηνεύει, καὶ οὐκ ἀφίησι πλανᾶσθαι τὸν ἀκροατήν· id est, sacra scriptura cum explicare aliquid grande vult, se ipsa declarat, neque patitur errare auditorem.—Opp. T. i. p. 106, 2. 1578. The citation should have been from Chrysostom. The passage occurs, Hom. xiii. in Gen. ii. T. iv. p. 103. Paris. 1718-38.]

THE FIRST CONTROVERSY.

QUESTION VI.

CONCERNING THE PERFECTION OF SCRIPTURE, AGAINST HUMAN TRADITIONS.

CHAPTER I.

THE QUESTION IS PROPOSED.

OUR Saviour Christ says, John v. 39, ἐρευνᾶτε τὰς γραφὰς, " Search the scriptures." From these words certain questions concerning the scriptures were taken at the commencement of our inquiries, which embrace the whole controversy about scripture debated between us and our opponents. Of these questions, five have already been handled; the sixth still remains, upon which we are now about to enter. Here we have to inquire, whether the scripture contained in the books of the old and new Testaments comprehend a full and perfect body of teaching, or whether unwritten traditions are requisite to complete this necessary doctrine. In this place, therefore, we have to dispute against the popish traditions, about which they are no less anxious than about the scriptures themselves, which they defend with the most eager vehemence, and in which they repose much greater confidence than in the scriptures. Lindanus, in his Panoplia, Lib. II. c. 5, says that tradition is that Homeric Μῶλυ, which preserves the christian faith against the spells of heretics; intimating thereby that the papists would be presently slain by our spells, that is, the scriptures, if they did not apply this *Moly* as an amulet. And, Lib. I. c. 9, he calls it the *Lydian stone*, that is, the test of true and false doctrine; and, Lib. II. c. 9, he says that it is *the shield of Ajax*, which should be presented against all heretics; and, Lib. v. c. 2, he styles it *the foundation of the faith :* which opinion of Peter Soto he praises and defends. Canus, in his Common Places, Lib. III. c. 3, says that traditions are of greater efficacy than scripture for the refutation of heretics. Whence we understand in what account and value the papists hold traditions. Assuredly they do find more support in them than in the scriptures. These traditions they call divine, sacred, holy, apostolic, and ecclesiastical; but we style them human, secret, obscure, silent, unwritten. Now in the handling of the present question we mean to observe the following order: First, we will explain what they denote by the term tradition: secondly, how they classify their traditions: thirdly, what rules they propose for distinguishing true traditions from the false and spurious: fourthly, what are the dogmas which are founded upon the authority of tradition: fifthly, we will state the question: sixthly, we will obviate the arguments of our adversaries: seventhly, we will set forth our own arguments which we use in this question against the papists. We shall treat severally of these in the order wherein we have proposed them.

CHAPTER II.

WHAT THE PAPISTS DENOTE BY THE TERM TRADITION.

TRADITION is a general term, and denotes a doctrine handed down in any manner, whether in words by the mouth, or in written documents. In Acts vi. 14, the Vulgate version hath *traditiones*, but the Greek text τὰ ἔθη. By that term are understood the legal ceremonies, all of which Moses hath comprised in his books: for there follows immediately ἃ παρέδωκεν ἡμῖν Μωυσῆς, that is, which he consigned to writing. The fathers too sometimes understand written teaching by this term. So Cyprian, Epist. 74, ad Pompeium, in these words: "If it be enjoined in the Gospel or in the Epistles or Acts of the Apostles, that those who come from any heresy should not be baptized, but only have hands laid upon them, in token of their repentance, let this also be observed as a holy tradition[1]." Hence we may observe the ignorance of Lindanus, who, in his Panoplia, Lib. II. c. 5, would have unwritten tradition to be denoted and highly praised by Cyprian in this same epistle and place; whereas Cyprian is speaking of the apostolic and evangelical scriptures. So

[1 Si ergo aut in evangelio præcipitur, aut in apostolorum epistolis aut actibus continetur, ut a quacunque hæresi venientes non baptizentur, sed tantum manus illis imponatur in pœnitentiam; observetur divina hæc et sancta traditio.—p. 211. ed. Fell.]

[WHITAKER.]

32

again : "Whence is that tradition ? Does it descend from the
authority of the Lord by the gospels, or comes it from the commandments and epistles of the apostles ? For God is witness that
those things should be done which are written[1]." But there is no
need for dwelling longer upon this matter, since the papists themselves concede that this term is sometimes so used. Basil, in his
third book against Eunomius, speaking of baptism, writes thus :
"This is plainly repugnant to the tradition of holy baptism[2] :"
τοῦτο σαφῶς μάχεται τῇ παραδόσει τοῦ σωτηρίου βαπτίσμα-
τος : which is meant to apply to the scripture itself, as is plain
from what follows afterwards in that same place. For he adds, that
infants should be baptized *in the name of the Father, and of the
Son, and of the Holy Ghost*, κατὰ τὴν τοῦ Κυρίου παράδοσιν,
"according to the tradition of the Lord." Now Christ and the
apostles left this doctrine consigned to writing. We must carefully
bear this in memory ; for the papists sometimes object to us the
name of tradition as signifying unwritten teaching, when in point of
fact it denotes written teaching.

Nevertheless, tradition is frequently taken also in scripture
and in the fathers for unwritten teaching, as in Matt. xv. 2, "Why
do they transgress the tradition of the elders ?" For that *tradition
of the elders* here mentioned never occurs in scripture. So also
this term is taken in the third and sixth verses of the same
chapter ; for there Christ opposes "the commandment" to the
"tradition." So 1 Cor. xi. 23, ὃ καὶ παρέδωκα ὑμῖν : he had
delivered it to them, but had not yet written it. However, these
things are now all committed to writing. The fathers frequently
thus use this term. Bellarmine brings an example from Cyprian,
Epist. 63, *contra Aquarios*, where these words are found : "I
would have you know that we have been admonished to preserve
the tradition of the Lord in offering the cup[3]." Chemnitz, however,

[1 Unde est ista traditio? utrumne de dominica et evangelica auctoritate
descendens, an de apostolorum mandatis atque epistolis veniens? Ea enim
facienda esse quæ scripta sunt, Deus testatur.—Ibid. paulo ante.]

[2 Τοῦτο δὲ σαφῶς μάχεται τῇ παραδόσει τοῦ σωτηρίου βαπτίσματος· πορευθέντες,
φησὶ, βαπτίζετε εἰς τὸ ὄνομα τοῦ πατρὸς καὶ τοῦ υἱοῦ καὶ τοῦ ἁγίου πνεύματος.....
τὸ δὲ βάπτισμα ἡμῶν ἐστι κατὰ τὴν τοῦ Κυρίου παράδοσιν, εἰς ὄνομα πατρὸς καὶ
υἱοῦ καὶ ἁγίου πνεύματος.—T. II. p. 84. A. B.]

[3 Admonitos autem nos scias, ut in calice offerendo Dominica traditio
servetur.—p. 148. The point which Cyprian is there pressing is not the use
of water, but the absolute necessity of mixing it with *wine*. The "Dominica
traditio" is referred to for establishing this latter, as appears manifestly from

proves from that same epistle, that tradition is sometimes taken for teaching delivered in writing, not by word of mouth. For he contends, that Cyprian in those same words affirms that it is delivered in scripture, that water should be mingled with the wine. Bellarmine says that he was deceived : but he is much more deceived, as is plain from the passage itself. For although the mixture of water with the wine in the holy supper be approved by Cyprian and the other fathers ; yet it is not confirmed by unwritten tradition, but by the scriptures themselves, and reason. To this they referred the circumstance that Christ's side, when it was transpierced as he hung upon the cross, poured forth blood and water ; and they rested also upon the fact that it was the custom of men in those warm countries to drink always their wine temperately diluted with a little water. However, we allow that the term is sometimes so taken by the fathers as to signify unwritten teaching. So Tertullian, in his book *de Corona Militis :* "You will find no scripture : tradition is alleged as authority[4]." So also Basil, upon the Holy Spirit, c. 27[5]. In this sense it is that the papists take this word in this controversy ; for they divide the word of God into the written and unwritten word : which distinction, indeed, Dionysius the Areopagite hath made use of. In the former class they rank the scripture ; in the latter, traditions. They call, therefore, those dogmas and points of doctrine which are nowhere found in scripture, *traditions.* But they style them *unwritten,* not because they are absolutely so, but because they were not written in the sacred books by the original authors. Thus Bellarmine determines, who proposes the baptism of infants as an example. But we shall shew in its proper place, that this tradition is delivered in the sacred writings. This then is the open and ingenuous confession of the papists, that they cannot find their traditions in the scriptures, or prove them by the scriptures.

what follows: neque aliud fiat a nobis, quam quod pro nobis Dominus prior fecerit; ut calix, qui in commemoratione ejus offertur, mixtus vino offeratur. Nam cum dicat Christus, Ego sum vitis vera; sanguis Christi, non aqua est utique, sed vinum.]

[4 Harum et aliarum ejusmodi si legum expostules scripturam, nullam invenies : traditio tibi prætendetur auctrix, consuetudo confirmatrix, et fides observatrix.—c. 4.]

[5 Τῶν ἐν τῇ ἐκκλησίᾳ πεφυλαγμένων δογμάτων καὶ κηρυγμάτων τὰ μὲν ἐκ τῆς ἐγγράφου διδασκαλίας ἔχομεν, τὰ δὲ ἐκ τῆς τῶν ἀποστόλων παραδόσεως διαδοθέντα ἡμῖν ἐν μυστηρίῳ παρεδεξάμεθα.—Τ. II. p. 210. c.]

32—2

We have explained then what the papists understand by the
term tradition. It follows now that we should mention their classification of traditions.

CHAPTER III.

HOW THE PAPISTS CLASSIFY THEIR TRADITIONS.

ALL the traditions of the papists are not of the same kind,
order, or authority, but admit various and manifold distinctions.
Lindanus, in the fourth book of his Panoplia, c. 100, is large in
discussing this question : but he treats everything in a coarse
method. Bellarmine proposes a twofold classification of traditions,
one derived from the authors, the other from the matter. Ranging
them according to the authors, he says that they are either
divine, apostolic, or ecclesiastical : wherein he follows Peiresius, who
gives precisely the same division of traditions in the second part
of his sixth assertion, where he says that there are three originals
of sacred traditions : first, divine authority ; second, apostolic teaching ; third, The power of bishops, and especially the Roman
bishops. He calls those divine which Christ himself instituted, and
which nevertheless are not found in the sacred writings ; of which
kind he says are all those things which appertain to the matter
and form of the sacraments : these things, says he, Christ did
undoubtedly institute, but yet did not leave consigned in writing.
Now we must believe that Christ instituted these things, because it
is certain that he did so. Hereupon I desire to know, whence
we can possibly know this for certain. No one indeed doubts that
Christ was the author of the sacraments : but we say that their
matter and form is found in the holy scriptures. Now Bellarmine and
the papists concede, that what they believe concerning the matter
and form of the sacraments can be found no where in the Bible ;
as, for instance, what they believe of the matter and form of confirmation, penance, matrimony, &c. But we affirm the whole
essence of the sacraments to be delivered in the sacred writings.
However, the argument by which he proves that all the things
which they use in baptism, confirmation, penance, matrimony, and
the rest of their sacraments, were instituted by Christ, is worth
observing. It is to this effect : Paul says, 1 Cor xi. 13 : " I

received of the Lord what I also delivered unto you:" therefore, we must believe that all these things were prescribed by the Lord. But how does this consequence follow? Paul received of the Lord those things which he delivered to the Corinthians to be observed by them: therefore every thing also which these men deliver, they have received from the Lord. Now, those things which the apostle delivered he left in his writings, and mentions in this very place. This they cannot shew of their traditions.

He calls those apostolical traditions, which the apostles prescribed not without the authority of the Holy Ghost, although they did not leave any mention of them in their epistles. Of this kind, he says, are the fast of Lent, the Ember days, and many other things of the same kind. Yet afterwards he forgets himself, and confesses that the fourth time of fasting was instituted by Calixtus. Here, however, we must note that Bellarmine concedes that Lent was not instituted by Christ, but by the apostles: whereas other papists usually defend Lent by the example and authority of Christ; contending that, as he fasted forty days, so we should also fast for the same period; and so making this tradition of Lent not apostolical, but divine. The Rhemists, upon Matt. iv., bring a passage from Jerome, to shew that Christ fasted forty days in order that by his example he might leave to us certain solemn days of fasting. Alphonsus de Castro, *contra Hæreses*, Lib. viii., says, that many grave divines affirm that Lent was instituted by Christ; and names one Maximus, who says that he has proved this number of forty to be sanctioned by examples in the scripture. But if that were true, this would no longer be a tradition, since it is written. Hosius, however, in his *Confessio Petrocoviensis*, c. 4, affirms this to be an ecclesiastical tradition, in these words: "Mother church hath instituted the fast of forty days[1]." Thus they are uncertain what to determine concerning this tradition.

He calls those ecclesiastical traditions, which by degrees, and by the consent of nations, obtained the force of laws. Of these he gives no example.

He proceeds to add, that divine unwritten scriptures have an authority equal to that of the scriptures; and, in like manner, that apostolical traditions rank along with the writings of the apostles. His reason is, because the authority of the word of God does not depend upon its being written, but upon its having proceeded from

[1 Mater ecclesia . . . quadraginta dierum jejunium instituit.—Opp. p. 4. Lugd. 1564.]

God. We allow that this is a good reason, provided he can prove
that these traditions were instituted by Christ or the apostles. But
now what is the authority of ecclesiastical traditions? He says that
they are of the same authority as the written constitutions and
written decrees of the church. But how great is that force? They
will not, I suppose, put the ecclesiastical traditions upon a par with
the divine. Yet the Tridentine fathers, in their fourth session,
command us to receive and reverence the unwritten traditions with
the same pious affections as the very books of holy scripture. We
should ask those fathers, what traditions it is they mean? They
make no distinction, they use general expressions. Perhaps, therefore, they desire that even the ecclesiastical traditions should have
equal authority with the scriptures of God. Those fathers do not
obviate this doubt. Yet surely they ought to have explained the
distinctions and degrees which were to be applied to traditions of
such a multifarious nature.

Bellarmine next proceeds to his second classification, founded
upon the matter of the traditions: and here he enumerates many
species. He says that some belong to faith, some to morals;
some are perpetual, others temporary; some universal, others particular; some necessary, others free. Some are matters of *faith*,
as that the blessed Mary was always a virgin, that there are only
four gospels and no more. As to the former tradition, Jerome,
Ambrose, and Epiphanius, who wrote against Helvidius upon this
subject, bring testimonies from scripture to prove the perpetual
virginity of Mary. Basil, however, in his homily upon the nativity of the Lord, affirms this dogma to be ἀπολυπραγμόνητον
τῷ τοῦ μυστηρίου λόγῳ[1], which is the same as saying that it
is no article of faith. The latter tradition (that there are four
gospels and no more) does not rest merely upon unwritten teaching: for the books themselves indicate that they were written by
divine inspiration; and if these men seek to obtrude upon us
more gospels, such gospels we can refute out of the scriptures.
Moral traditions are such as the sign of the cross, the celebration of festival days, and so forth. He makes those *perpetual*
traditions, which are never to have an end; of which nature
are those which he hath mentioned: and those *temporary*, which
belonged to those legal ceremonies which the Christians observed
for a while to enable the church, composed of Jews and Gentiles,

---

[1 Μηδὲν τῷ τῆς εὐσεβείας παραλυμαίνεται λόγῳ· μέχρι γὰρ τῆς κατὰ τὴν
οἰκονομίαν ὑπηρεσίας ἀναγκαία ἡ παρθενία, τὸ δὲ ἐφεξῆς ἀπολυπραγμόνητον τῷ
λόγῳ τοῦ μυστηρίου καταλείψωμεν.—T. I. p. 590. B.]

to unite into one body. But these are not unwritten : for we read of Timothy being circumcised, and of the injunction laid upon the Gentiles by the apostles to abstain from things strangled and from blood. But Bellarmine will say that they are written to us, not to them. Yea, they were written even to them : for that law which demands of us a mutual charity requires this too, that in matters indifferent we should help and consider the weakness of our brethren, and abstain from those things whereby they are offended. Therefore all these things depend not solely upon unwritten teaching. He calls those *universal*, which the whole church everywhere observes, such as the celebration of Easter and Whitsuntide : those *particular*, which only certain churches observe, as fasting upon Saturday was formerly peculiar to the Roman church. He styles those *necessary*, which are delivered in the form of a precept ; as that Easter is to be kept upon a Sunday : those *free*, which are delivered in the form of a counsel, not of a precept ; such as the sprinkling of holy water.

We have now explained what our opponents mean by the term tradition, and how many kinds of tradition they make : it remains, in the next place, that we inquire into the rules by which they tell us that true traditions are to be distinguished from spurious.

CHAPTER IV.

THE RULES WHEREBY THE PAPISTS DISTINGUISH GENUINE FROM SPURIOUS TRADITIONS.

BELLARMINE, Lib. IV. c. 9, proposes five rules whereby true and genuine traditions of the apostles may be distinguished.

The *first rule* is this : Whatsoever the universal church holds as an article of faith, and which is not found in the Bible, is without any doubt apostolical. The reason of this rule is, because the church cannot err. That the church cannot err, he proves by a twofold argument : first, because it is *the ground of truth ;* secondly, because, as Christ says, the gates of hell shall not prevail against that rock upon which the church is built. I reply : The present occasion does not permit me to handle the question, whether or not the church may err : there will be another fitting place for discussing that subject. Meanwhile, I return two answers.

First, I demand what they mean by the universal church ? For although a very great number of men everywhere throughout the churches may have embraced some practice or opinion, it does not therefore follow that it should be ascribed to the whole church; because there may be many who condemn it, and amongst these the church may subsist. So when Christ was upon earth, there were many traditions of the Pharisees which had become prescriptive, such as are mentioned Matt. xv. and Mark vii.; some of which related to faith, and some to practice. These were universal (if those are to be styled universal which are observed by the great majority), and had prevailed in the church through a long course of years and ages ; for they are called the traditions " of the elders." Does it therefore follow, either that these were divine, or that all men who belonged to the church held them, especially when it is certain that some of them were plainly impious ? Superstitious rites, then, and perverse opinions, and traditions repugnant to piety, may prevail amongst men professing God's holy religion. For the church does not always consist of the greatest or the most numerous, but sometimes of the fewest and the meanest.

Secondly, Bellarmine cannot prove that any popish tradition was observed in all churches. For, to take his own example, many churches have entertained doubts concerning the number of the canonical books, as we have shewn in the first controversy. It follows, therefore, that it was no apostolical tradition, because it was not received by the universal church, according to this rule of Bellarmine's. However, what he writes in this place, and hath taken from Canus, Lib. III. c. 4, must in nowise be passed over. He says that all points which the church holds as articles of faith were delivered by the apostles or prophets, in writing or by word of mouth, and that the church is not now governed by new revelations, but remains content with that which it received from the apostles. If this be true, then the church cannot now deliver any thing as an article of faith which was not heretofore, from the very times of the apostles, received and preserved as an article of faith. But the papists affirm that the church can now prescribe some new article of faith, which had not been esteemed in former ages as a necessary dogma. That the virgin Mary was conceived without original sin, was formerly thought a free opinion, not a necessary part of faith : upon which subject Canus hath copiously discoursed, Lib. VI. c. 1. But, at present, it is not permitted amongst papists to retain the ancient liberty of opinion upon this subject ; and he is hardly deemed a catholic, who ascribes any even the slightest taint of sin to Mary. The university of Paris admits no one to any of the higher degrees in divinity, who does not solemnly swear both that he believes that Mary was conceived in immaculate purity, and that he will constantly persevere in the assertion of the spotless conception of the virgin. So Canus informs us, Lib. I. c. 7, (*de Maria Deipara Virgine*); which custom he says is also received and tenaciously adhered to in Spain and in other popish universities. This then is at the present day one great article of the popish faith; and it is a new article, because no such formerly was publicly received. How then hath it constantly subsisted? Or how can Stapleton escape the charge of absurdity, who in the last three chapters of his ninth book endeavours to prove that the present church can add a book to the canon of scripture? The canon is an article of faith; for Bellarmine hath given it as an example of his rule. Stapleton adds: "If the Holy Spirit should so suggest." Now this is the very thing to which Bellarmine alludes, when he says that the church is not now governed by new revelations, but remains content with those things which they who were the ministers of the word handed down. So beautifully do they agree among themselves. Some say that a new dogma, which never was such before, may be prescribed by the church; others, that the church is not governed by new revelations, but remains content with those things which were delivered from the beginning. So that either Bellarmine's rule is false, or these articles of faith cannot and ought not to be considered necessary. But I demand of Bellarmine, whether it was delivered down by the apostles, that the epistle to the Hebrews was written by Paul. All the papists allow it. Lindanus, *Panopl.* Lib. IV. c. 100, affirms that it is no less necessary to believe it Paul's, than to believe its canonicity. If that be true, then this is an apostolical tradition: if it be apostolical, then it was always received by the universal church. But it may be easily shewn that many churches thought otherwise; yea, that the Roman church itself was once in the contrary opinion, as appears from Jerome's catalogue of illustrious men, under the title Caius. Either therefore the Roman church erred in the one tradition or in the other; or else at least this first rule of Bellarmine's is not true, certain, and perpetual.

Bellarmine's *second rule* is like the first, and runs thus: When the universal church observes any thing which is of such a nature as that it could not be instituted by any one but God, and yet is nowhere found mentioned in scripture, we must needs believe it to have been instituted by Christ himself, and delivered down by his apostles.   The reason is, because the church can no more err in act than in belief.   He produces Augustine as either the witness or the author of this rule; who, in his Epist. 118, declares that it is "a piece of the most insolent frenzy to dispute the propriety of doing that which the whole church throughout all the world is constantly doing every day[1]."

I answer : Our cause can receive no damage from this opinion of Augustine.   For he speaks of such traditions as were received and practised by the whole church.   His words are : "That which the whole church observes," it is a piece of the most insolent frenzy to question the propriety of doing.   But the papists have no such unwritten tradition which can be certainly shewn to have been always observed by the universal church; and those traditions which are here maintained by Bellarmine are of a different kind altogether.   The first is, the baptizing of infants : the second, the not re-baptizing those who were baptized by heretics.   These traditions, though not in so many words, may yet be found in scripture, and confirmed by the certain and express authority of scripture.   Therefore they should be styled written, and not unwritten traditions, inasmuch as they are gathered out of the scriptures.   As to the former, Augustine indeed, *de Genesi ad lit.* Lib. 10, c. 23, calls the baptism of infants an apostolical custom and tradition ; but he means a written tradition : for that such was Augustine's mind is evident from his fourth book against the Donatists, on Baptism, c. 24, where from the circumcision of God's former people he proves the baptism of infants.   Besides, the same thing may be established from that testimony of scripture, " I will be a God to thee and to thy seed," that is, to thy children.   This covenant is consigned in the holy scriptures, Gen. xvii.   The baptism of children, therefore, rests upon the written authority of the word of God.   Assuredly, if in this matter we had no other than the authority of unwritten tradition, we should be reduced to sad extremities in maintaining the dispute with the Anabaptists ; for they care nothing for unwritten traditions.   Yet these heretics our churches have refuted and condemned by the testimony of scripture, while the papists in the interim either keep a treacherous silence, or impiously, as well as falsely, pretend that they can be refuted no otherwise than by tradition.   As to Bellarmine's second instance, of not re-baptizing those who had been baptized by heretics ; although Cyprian contended that baptism administered by a heretic was null and void, (for that question was debated, with

[1 In the new editions, Ep. 54. Opp. T. II. p. 164. Bassan. 1797.]

great heat on Cyprian's part, between him and other bishops;) yet Augustine proved that Cyprian was in error by the authority, not so much of tradition as of scripture. For thus he writes, in his first book of Baptism against the Donatists, c. 7 : " Lest I should seem to prove my point" (he is speaking of this very thing) " by mere human arguments, I produce certain evidence from the Gospel[2]." In the second book of the same work, c. 3, he says that he did not doubt but that Cyprian would have corrected his opinion, if any one had shewn him that baptism is not lost by the heretics when they go out, and therefore can be given by them whilst they are without. But the plainest passage of all is in Lib. v. c. 26. Cyprian had said that we should appeal in this question to the fountain of apostolic tradition, that is, the scripture. This saying Augustine praises and highly approves in that chapter, and then produces from Eph. iv. the proposition, that there is *one baptism*, which consequently cannot be repeated. These two examples, therefore, are foreign from Bellarmine's subject, being written traditions; whereas he is delivering the rules of the unwritten.

Bellarmine's *third rule* is not very unlike the two former : Whatever the universal church hath observed through all former times and ages, is apostolic, although it be of such a nature as that it might have been instituted by the church. This rule, also, he confirms from Augustine, *contra Donat.* Lib. iv. c. 22, where he writes to the following effect: " That which the universal church holds, which, though never instituted by any council, was always retained, is with the utmost justice believed to be delivered by no less than apostolical authority[3]." I answer: We can only admit this sentence and rule of Augustine's with a twofold proviso : First, provided the thing in question were so retained as to make the manner of the observance always the same, that is, if it were always observed alike; secondly, if it were observed as necessary, not as free and indifferent. If there were a various practice and diversified custom of observing it, then it was not apostolical. If it were observed as a thing indifferent, we are ready to allow that the church hath authority to constitute and appoint such indifferent ceremonies. But I affirm that no popish tradition can be produced, which was observed uniformly, and as necessary at all times. Bel-

[2 Ne videar humanis argumentis id agere . . ., ex Evangelio profero certa documenta.—Opp. T. xii. p. 110.]

[3 Quod universa tenet ecclesia, nec conciliis institutum sed semper retentum est, non nisi auctoritate apostolica traditum rectissime creditur.—Opp. T. xii.]

larmine assigns Lent as an instance. But the manner of observing
Lent was formerly most various and uncertain. Bellarmine, how-
ever, proves it to be an apostolical tradition, because those who
trace it back, and seek the origin of the institution, can find it
no where but in the apostolic times. For, commencing with
Bernard, he ascends from him to Gregory, from Gregory to
Augustine, from Augustine to Jerome, from Jerome to Chrysostom,
from Chrysostom to Ambrose, from Ambrose to Epiphanius, Basil,
Nazianzen, Cyril, Origen, Irenæus, Telesphorus, Ignatius, Clement.
This seems indeed a striking enumeration : but I have two answers
to make. *First*, I desire to know what Lent he means? That
which the Roman church now observes, or another? He must
needs mean the former ; for otherwise he disputes absurdly. But
now it may be proved by those same testimonies which he hath
himself made use of, that Lent was formerly observed much otherwise than it is now observed, in respect of the number of the days,
the mode of fasting, and the kinds of food : this may be proved, I
say, if not from Bernard and Gregory, yet from Augustine, Jerome,
and the rest of the more ancient fathers. *Secondly*, I affirm that
an author may be found for the observance of Lent later than the
apostles' times. For Platina, in the life of that pope[1], writes, that
Lent was instituted by Telesphorus, who lived a hundred years
after Christ. They will find no more ancient author; yet the
papists make him to have been not the author, but the restorer
and asserter, of this fast instituted by the apostles. However, if
Christ and the apostles had instituted Lent, it would not, in those
early and pure times, have so quickly ceased to be observed as to
require to be restored by Telesphorus. The epistle of Ignatius to
the Philippians, wherein he mentions Lent[2], is spurious. The
book of Clement referred to is spurious also, and was condemned
in the sixth general council at Constantinople. The canons which
go under the name of the apostles are also supposititious, as we
have proved before. Bellarmine gives, as another instance, Ecclesiastical orders, which he will have to be likewise an apostolical
tradition, proving it by tracing them back to the apostles' times, as
in the former example. But here his own rule fails him ; for the
apostolic canons, to which he ascribes so much, name only five

[1 Telesphorus autem, quem diximus Xysto successisse, constituit ut sep-
tem hebdomadibus ante Pascha jejunium observaretur.—Platina Vitt. Pontiff. p. 28. Col. Ub. 1600.]

[2 τὴν τεσσαρακοστὴν μὴ ἐξουθενεῖτε· μίμησιν γὰρ περιέχει τῆς τοῦ Κυρίου
πολιτείας.—Ignat. ad Philipp. p. 111. ed. Voss. Lond. 1680.]

orders,—the bishop, priest, deacon, reader, and chanter, omitting the
exorcist, porter, and acolyth. So Ambrose, in his Commentary on
Ephes. iv., enumerates only five, and omits acolyths and porters
altogether. This instance, therefore, does not suit very well with
Bellarmine's rule.

The *fourth rule* is not more certain than the rest, and is to
this effect: When the doctors of the church, whether assembled
in council, or writing it in their books, affirm something to have
descended from apostolical authority, it is to be held apostolical.
He gives, as an example of the former sort, that the fathers
assembled in the second council of Nice taught the worship of
images to be an apostolical tradition. I answer: That the decree
of that council was against scripture, against other councils (as,
for instance, against the fourth Constantinopolitan synod, which was
more ancient than the Nicene, as being the seventh general council),
and finally, against other doctors and fathers of the church. For
Gregory the great, in the ninth Epistle of his seventh book of
Epistles[3], says that, although images should not be broken, yet
the people should be carefully taught and admonished not to
worship them; as, indeed, many churches to this day retain
images, but worship them not. However, it is much more prudent
and safe to remove them altogether. Thus the worship of images
is not an apostolic, but an antichristian tradition, if we believe
pope Gregory the first. He adduces no example of the second
sort; for he says that scarce anything of that kind can be found
expressly in the fathers, wherein they all agree. He therefore
delivers the following rule to meet that case: That which any
one father of great character writes is to be embraced as apostolical, if the others do not dissent. Surely an egregious rule!
But how shall we know that the others do not dissent? for
many books of the fathers are lost, and many fathers wrote none:
it may be that these dissented. Besides, many things are delivered
down even by some of the fathers, which by the confession of the
papists themselves are not apostolical, wherein nevertheless they
cannot shew that the rest dissented. But whom shall we call a
father of great character? Doubtless they will hold any one for
great who favours themselves, as Dionysius the Areopagite, than
whom no authority can be less respectable. So these men hold
the Decretal Epistles of the Roman pontiffs in great account and

[3 Tua ergo fraternitas et illas servare, et ab earum adoratu populum
prohibere debuit.—p. 1370.]

value, though nothing can be more futile and absurd than they
are.

Bellarmine's *fifth rule* is to this effect : That is to be held and
deemed undoubtedly apostolical, which is esteemed as such in those
churches wherein there is an unbroken succession of bishops from
the apostles. I answer : Where then was the need of all his previous windings ? At bottom he would have those only to be
apostolical traditions, which the church of Rome affirms to be
such. This was what he meant to say ; but lest we should not
bear it in this form, he set it forth in other words. However,
that such was his meaning appears most evidently from what
follows : for he subjoins that, although there were formerly in other
churches also unbroken successions of bishops from the apostles,
yet now this succession remains safe and entire only in the church
of Rome. But Lindanus, Lib. v. c. 7, says plainly (and indeed he is plain spoken upon all occasions), that he cannot see
any more certain rule than the judgment of the church ; he
means the church of Rome. However, I answer, in the *first* place,
that the succession even of that church is not entire and uninterrupted, as is plain from Platina and others. For Platina and
other historians testify that that see hath been vacant ten, yea,
twenty times over, not merely for a day, or a week, or a month,
but for one, two, or three years ; furthermore, that there were
frequent schisms, and sometimes two or three popes in existence
together. Nay, in one council[1] three popes were deposed, and
a fourth new one elected : upon which matters we shall have to
speak elsewhere. *Secondly,* though we should concede the succession of that church to have been unbroken and entire, yet that
succession would be a matter of no weight ; because we regard not
the external succession of places or persons, but the internal one
of faith and doctrine. *Thirdly,* an unbroken succession may be
found in other churches also. Our adversary will require to know
in what ? In the Greek churches. If he demand a particular
example, I instance in the most noble of them all, that of Constantinople, which was formerly called New Rome, and always
stood upon a par with Rome in dignity. Nicephorus, in his
History, Lib. viii. c. 6, describes the series of the Constantinopolitan
bishops from Andrew the apostle down to his own time. This also

[1 viz. That of Constance, which assembled in 1414. The popes deposed
were, John XXIII., Gregory XII., and Benedict XIII. The pope elected
was Otto de Colonna, who took the name of Martin V.]

was less interrupted than the Roman succession : for there were smaller intervals and less schisms in this church than in the church of Rome. But, because they can produce no traditions which suit exactly the preceding rules, they add this fifth one, in which they repose much more confidence than in the rest. How greatly they are deceived in this, appears from what we have said, and said but briefly, since these matters will demand a longer and more accurate discussion in their proper place.

So much then upon the rules which Bellarmine hath prescribed for distinguishing true from false traditions.

CHAPTER V.

WHAT DOGMAS ARE DEFENDED BY THE PAPISTS BY THE AUTHORITY OF TRADITIONS.

IT now remains that we inquire, what are those dogmas and institutions which the papists affirm are to be defended by the authority, not of scripture, but of unwritten traditions. It is but fit that we should have this matter perfectly cleared up. No one, however, as far as I know, hath drawn up a catalogue of them ; but they only affirm in general, that whatever they teach or do which is not found in scripture, is to be placed in the rank of traditions. The Tridentine fathers, Sess. 4, content themselves with ordering traditions to be received with the same pious affections as the holy scriptures.

In the meanwhile they explain not what these traditions are ; which explanation ought certainly to have been made. If there were extant a definite enumeration and list of these traditions, one would readily perceive that all the peculiar doctrines and practices of the papists, or at least most of them, are derived from some other source besides the scriptures. Now why are these monuments, so sacred and so necessary, not published ? Peter Soto, a popish author of great name, in his book against Brentius, says, that all those observances, the beginning, author, and origin of which cannot be found in scripture, are apostolical traditions. Of this kind, says he, are the oblation of the sacrifice of the altar, the unction of chrism, invocation of saints, prayers for the dead, the primacy of the Roman bishops, the consecration of water in baptism, the whole

sacrament of confirmation, orders, matrimony, penance and extreme
unction, the merit of works, the necessity of satisfaction, the necessity of enumerating one's sins to the priest. Thus he. But perhaps
other papists will not make equally large concessions. Nay, I may
say that all will, with the sole exception of the point of the merit of
works. We accept this confession, and congratulate ourselves upon
having to deal with adversaries who openly confess that none of
these things rest upon any certain authority of scripture. Hence
it is evident that, if not all, yet the most important dogmas of the
papists depend upon tradition, although, for the sake of appearance,
they generally cite scripture in defence of them; but if they reposed any real confidence in the scriptural proofs, they would not
press the slight and nerveless authority of tradition.

Canisius, in his Catechism, c. 5, (*de Præcept. Eccles.*) says that
the worship of images, stated fasts, Lent, all the rites in the office
of the mass, prayers and offerings for the dead, are traditions; inasmuch as these, and some others, are incapable of being defended upon
the foot of scripture alone : but he does not tell us what those others
are. But the author who has spoken most clearly and copiously upon
this subject is Lindanus, in his *Panoplia*, Lib. iv. c. 100, wherein he
comprises a farrago of traditions, upon which I beseech you to cast
your eyes. Meanwhile I remark, that he enumerates amongst traditions the fact of Peter's having been at Rome. Thus we derive
from tradition both points, Peter's having been at Rome as well as
his primacy. However, he enumerates his traditions with still
greater accuracy and distinctness at the end of that book, table C;
although there he hath omitted some, and set down some, as traditions, which are found in scripture, as the baptism of infants and
original sin. He counts also amongst traditions the seven sacraments.
This tradition rests upon the authority of the council of Florence,
held about a century ago. Verily, an ancient authority this for
a tradition! He enumerates besides, the consecration of water and
oil in baptism, the real presence, communion in one kind, the eucharist being a sacrifice, its reservation and adoration, private masses,
confession of sins, satisfaction, and indulgences. There is scarcely
any thing omitted, which is controverted between them and us.
Over and above these traditions, Peresius adds, part 3, the celibacy
of priests. But the papists are too shrewd to venture upon fixing
any certain list and catalogue of these traditions, but leave free to
themselves the power of having recourse to tradition in every question. When therefore they allege scripture in proof of these things,

they do violence to their own consciences; inasmuch as they know well, and even confess plainly, that these things are such as must be proved by a silent tradition, and not by the testimony of scripture. Our assertion, therefore, that these things cannot be established by scripture, is allowed by our adversaries themselves. I come now to the state of the question.

CHAPTER VI.

THE STATE OF THE QUESTION IS LAID DOWN.

WE say, in the first place, that every thing which the apostles either taught or did is not contained in the books of the old and new Testaments. We allow besides, that Christ said and did many things which are not written. Out of twelve apostles seven wrote nothing, who yet orally taught, and did many things in many places; for they were commanded to go into all the world, and preach the gospel to all nations : which command they sedulously performed. Indeed, it is plain from the last chapter of John, that all the things which Christ did are not committed to writing. Furthermore, we confess that the apostles established in the several churches some rites and customs, for the sake of order and decency, which they did not consign in their writings, because those rites were not to be perpetual, but free, and such as might be changed as convenience and the times required. Now that some such rites, suited to the seemly polity of the church, were prescribed by them, is manifest from 1 Cor. xi. and xiv. We have, however, in scripture only this general rule, that all those rites should be directed to the end of securing edification and decency, but the particular rites themselves are not set forth. But we say that all things that are necessary, whether they regard either faith or practice, are plainly and abundantly explained in the scriptures. Hence we say that the sum of our religion is written, being precisely the same as the teaching of those apostles who wrote nothing. For those who wrote not taught absolutely the same gospel as those who wrote : all preached the same Christ, and the same gospel, and the same way of salvation. Although indeed the precise words which they spoke are not extant, yet, as far as the thing itself and subject-matter is

[WHITAKER.]   33

concerned, that same unwritten preaching of the apostles is found in
scripture : all the words, indeed, of Peter, John and the rest, are
not written down, yet the substance of that teaching which those
apostles delivered is found in the scriptures.   Thus, although Christ
said and did many things which are not written, yet the sum of
all Christ's words and works is consigned in the monuments of
scripture.   It is without reason, therefore, that Bellarmine accuses
Brentius and Chemnitz of inconsistency, when they call it a piece of
signal impudence to compare unwritten traditions with written, or
affirm both to have the like authority; and yet confess at the same
time, that Christ and his apostles taught many things which are not
written.   This is a mere cavil : for although every single thing they
said and did be not written (for which no books would have been
sufficient), yet nothing necessary hath been omitted ; and, when the
chief heads and doctrines are written so clearly, it might be said
with perfect truth that all is written.   He who compares these unwritten things with the written, does only in other words praise
the written teaching.   But Brentius and Chemnitz affirm him to be
at once rash and impious, who would venture to set any unwritten
doctrine upon a par in point of authority with the scriptures :
wherein they say nothing that is not perfectly consistent with itself
and with right reason.   Bellarmine proceeds to censure some *lies*
(as he calls them) of Chemnitz and Calvin, which I will not examine in this place : most of them will recur again and be handled
in their proper places.

　　Bellarmine states the question thus : We, says he, assert that
the whole necessary doctrine, whether regarding faith or practice,
is not expressly contained in scripture ; and consequently that,
besides the written word of God, we require also the unwritten
word of God, that is, divine and apostolical traditions.   They, that
is, the heretics (meaning us), assert that all things which pertain
to faith and morals are contained in the written word, and that
there is no need of traditions.   I answer : The word *expressly* is
ambiguous.   If he mean that we affirm all things to be contained
directly and in so many words in scripture, he states the question
wrongly.   But if he mean under the term *expressly* to include what
is inferred and deduced by necessary argument from the scriptures,
we accept his statement.   For if that which is directly laid down
in scripture be true, then that also which is deduced from it by
necessary consequence must needs be true also.   So Nazianzen
rules, in his fifth book of theology, where he writes concerning

the Holy Spirit: "Inferences from scripture stand on the same footing with the actual words of scripture[1]." Some things are not, and yet are said in scripture to be; as that God sits, that he hath ears and eyes. Some are, and yet are not said, that is, expressly and in so many words; as that the Holy Ghost is God; while nevertheless something is said from which they may be certainly collected or inferred, even as he who says twice five says ten, and he who says twice two says four, though not in so many words. Some neither are nor are said. Lastly, some both are and are said. This division is Nazianzen's own: τὰ μὲν οὐκ ἐστί, λέγεται δέ· τὰ δ᾽ ὄντα οὐ λέγεται· τὰ δὲ οὔτε ἔστιν, οὔτε λέγεται· τὰ δὲ ἄμφω καὶ ἔστι καὶ λέγεται. So we say that all necessary things are contained in scripture, though not always in express terms. For example, infant baptism and original sin are not propounded directly and in set terms in the Bible, and yet they may be inferred from it by the strictest reasoning. Thus, to comprise the whole matter in a few words, we say that all things appertaining to faith and morals may be learned and derived from scripture, so as that traditions are in no way requisite. They, on the contrary, say that all things necessary to faith and manners are not contained in the written word of God, and that therefore traditions are necessarily required. There is no need of saying more upon the state of the question. It follows now that we set forth and weigh the arguments upon both sides.

CHAPTER VII.

THE ARGUMENTS OF OUR ADVERSARIES, WHEREBY THEY PROVE THAT THE SCRIPTURES WITHOUT TRADITION ARE NEITHER NECESSARY NOR SUFFICIENT.

At length our Jesuit opponent approaches the question itself, taking upon himself to make good two positions: First, that the scriptures are not necessary nor sufficient without traditions. Secondly, that there are many apostolical traditions respecting both faith and practice. He proceeds to prove them both in regular order. The first is manifestly twofold; first, that scripture is not necessary; and secondly, that it is not sufficient without tradition.

[1 Opp. T. i. p. 605. c.]

In the FIRST place, he proves that scripture is not *necessary ;* wherein you see to what a pass the thing is brought. For he makes tradition in such a sense necessary as to make scripture unnecessary, thus preferring tradition to scripture as a necessary thing to an unnecessary one. O Jesuit, what art thou doing, or what thing is this that thou attemptest ? Thou deniest the scriptures to be necessary, and, not satisfied with a mere denial, thou seekest even to prove and to establish the charge. How couldest thou wish thus to commence this dispute with blasphemy ? Here we understand what noble and honourable thoughts our adversaries entertain of the scriptures, when they say that they may be done without, that they may be set aside, that they are not necessary. Here he makes use of but one argument, but drawn from various times in the church's history.

In the first place he says, that there was no scripture from Adam to Moses, and yet, that there was then the word of God and pure religion ; and that therefore the scriptures are not absolutely necessary. He proves the antecedent from there being no mention of scripture in the book of Genesis ; while in Gen. xviii. God says, " I know that Abraham will teach his children." Thus, says he, religion was preserved pure for two thousand years before Christ without scriptures : why then might it not have been preserved also for fifteen hundred years after Christ ? I answer : I will not contest the truth of his assertion that there was no scripture before Moses, as I perceive that the same thing is said by Chrysostom in his 1st homily upon Matthew, and also by Theophylact. Augustine, however, in the 15th book of his City of God, c. 23, affirms that something was written by Enoch[1]. And Josephus, Antiquit. Lib. I. c. 3, tells us that the posterity of Adam before the flood erected two columns, one of stone, and the other of brick, and engraved certain inscriptions on them[2]. Pliny indeed affirms the use of written characters to have subsisted always, Lib. VII. c. 56[3]. And Sixtus Senensis, Biblioth. Lib. II., thinks that "the book of the wars of the Lord" was more ancient than the books of Moses. However, I concede that there was no scripture more ancient than

---

[1] Scripsisse quidem nonnulla divina Enoch illum septimum ab Adam negare non possumus.]

[2] στήλας δύο ποιησάμενοι, τὴν μὲν ἐκ πλίνθου, τὴν δ' ἑτέραν ἐκ λίθων, ἀμφοτέραις ἐνέγραψαν τὰ εὑρημένα.—Lib. I. c. 2. § 3.]

[3] Literas semper arbitror Assyrias fuisse. Where Perionius and some others read, *Assyriis.*]

the books of Moses, and that religion remained pure for so many years without scripture. What follows from that? Are the scriptures, therefore, unnecessary? By no means. For I perceive a twofold fallacy in this argument. The *first* lies in the consequent. Our opponent disputes thus : Scripture is not absolutely necessary; therefore it is not necessary at all. But here lies the Jesuit's error : for it is not every necessity that is absolute ; some is only hypothetical. God could teach us without the holy scriptures, and lead us to eternal life ; but he chose to propound his teaching to us in the scriptures. This, therefore, being supposed, it is necessary that we learn and derive the will and doctrine of God from the scriptures. Thus, not even food is simply necessary, because God could easily nourish us without food ; but only hypothetically. God indeed formerly shewed himself familiarly to our fathers, and, in a manner, conversed constantly with some distinguished men, to whom he immediately disclosed his will ; and then I confess that the scriptures were not necessary : but afterwards he changed this method of teaching his church, and chose that his will should be committed to writing ; and then scripture began to be necessary. The *second* fallacy is mistaking the question : for the time is changed, when he argues thus : Scripture was once not necessary ; therefore it is also unnecessary now. This reasoning is inconsequential. For though God once taught his church by oral instruction, yet now he hath pleased to choose another mode of teaching his people. These times, therefore, and those bear very different relations to the matter in hand. God hath now seen fit that all that teaching which he delivered of old orally to the fathers should be committed to books and writing. And the reason of the change was to provide more completely for the pure and uncorrupted preservation of his teaching. For doctrine delivered only orally without writing could not be so easily saved from corruptions ; and in fact it was soon depraved, and God's religion remained in its integrity with very few, so as that God was compelled frequently to repeat and renew it over and over again. The scriptures, therefore, are necessary to us, because God foresaw that we should need, for preserving the integrity of true religion, to have the scriptures in our hands ; so that to think otherwise is to accuse God of thoughtlessness or error.

The Jesuit next proceeds to the second age of the church, which intervened between Moses and Christ; wherein he cannot deny that scriptures were published by the holy prophets, which he nevertheless maintains to have been unnecessary. For he says in the *first* place, that at that time the scriptures belonged exclusively to the Jews, while yet there were, even amongst the Gentiles, religious persons who had not the scriptures in their hands, as is plain from the case of Job and his friends. To this purpose he alleges Augustine on Original Sin, Lib. II. c. 24 ; and in the City of God, Lib. XVIII. c. 47. I answer : We confess that there were amongst the Gentiles some pious persons really zealous for true religion : but that the scriptures were read by such persons, is also clear from the story of the eunuch in Acts viii. Besides, the number of such persons as the Jesuit mentions was very small. And, however the case be, those who appertained to the church were not ignorant of the scriptures. In the *second* place, he says that, although the Jews used to read the scriptures, yet they used tradition more than scripture : as appears from Ps. xliv. 1, 2, and lxxviii. 3, 4, where we read that fathers related the works of God to their children ; and from Deut. vi. 20, where the fathers are commanded to tell their children, when their children should ask them, what great things God had done in their behalf. I reply, that no conclusion can be drawn from such testimonies as these. For what if parents were commanded to tell God's works to their children, and children to ask them of their parents? Those things which the parents related were also set forth in scripture. In Ps. xliv. the prophet shews what it was they had heard from their fathers ; for it follows that God had cast forth the nations before them, and planted them in. Now, this is all written : every thing recited in Ps. lxxviii. is also written ; as the deliverance of the people from Egypt, &c. In the sixth chapter of Deuteronomy the people are commanded to converse about the scriptures, and to instruct their children in them. Thus it was from the scriptures that the fathers told these things to the children, and out of the scriptures that the children asked these questions of their fathers. *Thirdly*, this sagacious man assigns the reasons why the ancient Jews made greater use of tradition than of scripture. The first reason is, because at that time the scriptures were not yet reduced into the form of books, but were scattered about in loose papers. The second is, because the priests and Levites were neglectful of their duty to such a degree, as that sometimes the whole scripture disappeared, as is plain from 2 Kings xxii., where we read of the volume of the law being found. But after the captivity (says he) Ezra reduced the scriptures into the form of books, and added

many things, as the piece about the death of Moses at the end of
Deuteronomy. I answer: Although we were to concede the negligence of the priests and Levites, does it therefore follow either
that the whole scripture perished, or that it was unnecessary?
The negligence of the priests and Levites does not prove the
scriptures unnecessary, but themselves guilty of horrible sacrilege.
Thus, even now the papists pluck away the scriptures from the
people; but are they, for that reason, not necessary? A man
should be a fool to say so. The scriptures, however, were not altogether lost, nor does the finding of the book of the law prove that
they were. The book that was found in the temple, during its
purification, was the very autograph of Moses, or only the book of
Deuteronomy. As to his assertion, that the scriptures were so
scattered in loose pieces at that time that they could not be read,
it is a mere fiction, and made without any reasonable ground. For
although Ezra reduced the Psalms and other books to order, it
does not follow from that that the scriptures were before in such
confusion that they could not be read. As to the piece at the end
of Deuteronomy, some say that it was added by Joshua, as Sixtus
Senensis, Lib. I.; others by Moses before his death, so as to seem
rather to have been translated than to have died[1].

Bellarmine passes on to the third age of the church, which
takes its origin from the coming of Christ; and says, that the
church was without scriptures even for many years after Christ:
which assertion of his, however, every body perceives to be
utterly false. For the faithful had during all that time all the
books of the old Testament; and immediately after Christ the
scripture of the new Testament began to be published, and the
church always had the full teaching necessary to salvation in
written documents. Now, as far as the sum and substance of
teaching is concerned, there is no difference between the old Testament and the new. The promises are written in the old
Testament, and the fulfilment of them in the new. Nor was it
very many years after Christ that the church lacked the scriptures
of the new Testament. For Matthew wrote his gospel eight years
after Christ's ascension, if that be true which Theophylact tells us,
upon the 1st of Matthew: μετὰ ὀκτὼ ἔτη τῆς τοῦ Χριστοῦ
ἀναλήψεως. Nicephorus[2], however, says that it was in the fifteenth

[1 Ut raptus, non mortuus fuisse videatur.]
[2 Hist. Eccles. Lib. IV. c. 14.]

year; but Eusebius, Lib. v. c. 8[1], out of Irenæus, dates it after
the twentieth, when Peter and Paul had already come to Rome.
But the Jesuit proves his assertion from Irenæus, Lib. III. c. 4,
where that father writes, that in his time some barbarous nations
lived admirably without the scriptures, by the sole help of tradition.
I answer: I confess that Irenæus in that place does say, that some
nations, assenting to those traditions which the apostles delivered
to those to whom they committed the churches, had salvation
written in their hearts without ink or characters, by the power of
the Holy Ghost. But lest you should think that these were
the popish traditions, he subjoins a recital of the Articles of the
Faith, in one God, the Creator of heaven and earth, in Christ the
Son of God, his passion, resurrection, ascension, &c. Then he
adds: "Those who have believed this faith are indeed, in respect
of our language, barbarians; but as to their opinions, and customs,
and conversation, they are, on account of their faith, excellently
wise and well-pleasing to God, by reason of the righteousness
and chastity and wisdom of their whole behaviour[2]." But although
some barbarous people were for a time without the scriptures, it
does not therefore follow that the scriptures are absolutely unnecessary. Many persons know not how to read, and nevertheless
hold a sound faith from the preaching of pastors and teachers:
are the scriptures therefore not necessary? Whence then did
those very pastors and teachers derive that knowledge of religion
which they possess? Doubtless from the scriptures. The scriptures, therefore, are highly necessary. And although for a time
doctrine might be preserved intact without written monuments, it
is not safe to keep it so long, nor possible to keep it so always.
Besides, in a short time after the scriptures were translated into
those barbarous tongues, in order that, by the reading and expounding of them, they might the better preserve the teaching
which they had received. The conclusion he draws is, that the

[1 Ματθαῖος .... γραφὴν ἐξήνεγκεν εὐαγγελίου, τοῦ Πέτρου καὶ τοῦ Παύλου
ἐν 'Ρώμῃ εὐαγγελιζομένων.—T. II. p. 53. ed. Heinich.]

[2 Cui ordinationi assentiunt multæ gentes barbarorum, quorum qui in
Christum credunt, sine charta et atramento scriptam habentes per Spiritum
in cordibus suis salutem, et veterem traditionem diligenter custodientes, &c.
. . . Hanc fidem qui sine literis crediderunt, quantum ad sermonem nostrum
barbari sunt; quantum autem ad sententiam, et consuetudinem, et conversa-
tionem, propter fidem, perquam sapientissimi sunt, et placent Deo, conver-
santes in omni justitia et castitate et sapientia.—p. 242. B. D. ed. Fevard.]

scriptures are not simply necessary; and so far not amiss. But are they therefore not necessary at all? This is plainly what he means, but he dares not to speak out; since presently afterwards, replying to a citation from Chrysostom, who writes that the scriptures are necessary to us, though not to the patriarchs, he observes that this necessity must be understood to refer "to our well-being, that is to mean that they are useful." So that, according to him, the scriptures are merely useful, and contribute to our well-being, but are not necessary. From the whole reasoning of our opponent, therefore, we see the truth of what we read in this same author Irenæus, Lib. III. c. 2, that the heretics, when they are refuted out of the scriptures, turn round and accuse even the scriptures themselves.

CHAPTER VIII.

THAT THE SCRIPTURES ARE NECESSARY.

HERE I will briefly demonstrate the necessity of the scriptures, although we shall afterwards have to treat that question more at large.

In the first place, the scriptures contain that necessary doctrine without which we cannot be saved, that is to say, the teaching of the law and the gospel: therefore they are necessary. As to the law, the apostle tells us, Rom. vii.: "I had not known lust, except the law had said, Thou shalt not covet." Therefore, the doctrine of the law is learned from the scriptures, and indeed only from the scriptures, when rightly and solidly understood. Still less can we understand the doctrine of the gospel without the scriptures, because it is still more foreign and remote from our minds than the doctrine of the law, and our nature recoils from it still more than from the law. Besides, God does not teach us now by visions, dreams, revelations, oracles, as of old, but by the scriptures alone; and therefore, if we will be saved, we must of necessity know the scriptures.

Secondly, the scriptures preserve the doctrine and religion of God from being corrupted, or destroyed, or forgotten: therefore they are necessary. The antecedent is manifest. For God willed

that his word should be written by Moses, the prophets and the
apostles, for this very reason, that there was a certain risk that
the true teaching would be corrupted, or destroyed, or consigned
to oblivion, if it were not written and published in books.   In
Hosea viii. 12, God says, "I have written to them the great
things of my law ; but they were counted as a strange thing."
Luke says, chap. i. verse 3, "It seemed good to me to write
unto thee in order, most excellent Theophilus,"—for what purpose ?   The reason is subjoined : ἵνα ἐπιγνῷς περὶ ὧν κατηχήθης
λόγων τὴν ἀσφάλειαν.   Theophilus had before that been instructed in the true doctrine (as is plain from the words περὶ
ὧν κατηχήθης) ; but Luke chose to write for him the whole of
that doctrine in order, that he might know it better and more
certainly, and retain it when known more firmly.   The scripture
therefore is necessary *for certainty* : for those things which are
taught orally have not the same firmness and certainty as those
which are written and consigned in books.

Thirdly, in Matth. xxii. 29, Christ says to the Sadducees, "Ye
do err, not knowing the scriptures :" πλανᾶσθε, μὴ εἰδότες τὰς
γραφάς.   From which words we gather that the scriptures are necessary to us, lest we should fall into error.   In another evangelist
the words stand thus : "Ye therefore err, because ye know not the
scriptures :" οὐ διὰ τοῦτο πλανᾶσθε, μὴ εἰδότες τὰς γραφάς ; and
so the place makes still more clearly for our side.   The same is
the purport also of the passage in 2 Pet. i. 19, "We have also a
more sure (and firm) word of prophecy, whereunto ye do well that
ye take heed :" where Peter teaches us that nothing is surer than
the scriptures.   To them, therefore, as the solid, firm and perpetual monuments of the faith, it behoves us to cleave constantly.
In Luke xvi., when the rich reveller begs that somebody may be
sent to his brethren, Abraham replies : "They have Moses and the
prophets ; let them hear them."   From which words it is clear that
all things necessary are to be derived from Moses and the prophets,
that is, from the scriptures, and that there can be no more certain
or clearer method of learning than from the scriptures.   In John
xx. 31, we read thus : "They were written, that ye might believe
that Jesus is the Christ the Son of God ; and that believing ye
might have life by his name."   Whence it may be inferred that
the scriptures are necessary to us for the obtaining of faith and
eternal life ; since it was for that purpose they were written.   In
John v. 39, Christ says to the Jews, "Search the scriptures ;"—

wherefore? "Because in them ye think ye have eternal life." And indeed they were right in so thinking, and Christ approves their opinion. In Psalms xix. and cxix. the prophet David passes high encomiums upon the scriptures; from which praises and eulogies men's necessity may be gathered. He calls them *the law;* and what more necessary than law? Now, if the law be necessary in a state, then much rather in the church. For if in civil affairs men cannot be left to themselves, but must be governed and retained in their duty by certain laws; much less should we be independent in divine things, and not rather bound by the closest ties to a prescribed and certain rule, lest we fall into a will-worship hateful to God.

Fourthly, we can by no means do without the scriptures: therefore they are necessary. The Jesuit will deny the antecedent. But if we can do without the scriptures, why hath God delivered them to us? Thus the wisdom and counsel of God refute the foolish fictions of the papists.

Fifthly, ministers are commanded to read the scriptures, and to be assiduous and diligent in the study of them: therefore the scriptures are necessary. For if any persons could be free or discharged from the duty of reading the scriptures, who could be rather than the clergy? forasmuch as none are better acquainted with tradition than they are. In 1 Tim. iv. 13, Paul admonishes Timothy to be attentive to reading, πρόσεχε τῇ ἀναγνώσει· and in 2 Tim. iii. 14, 15, he shews what it was that he was to read so attentively, namely, the holy scriptures; for thus he writes: "But thou abide in those things which thou hast learned, and hast been entrusted with, knowing from whom thou hast learned them, and that from a child thou hast known the holy scriptures, which are able to make thee wise unto salvation through faith which is in Christ Jesus." Upon which place Chrysostom comments thus: "While the apostle speaks this to Timothy, he gives at the same time a wholesome admonition to all. And if he uttered such admonitions to one who could raise the dead, what are we now to say, who fall so miserably short of his excellence?" Thus Chrysostom. If, then, the scriptures are commended to Timothy, how much more to us? To the same purpose is the passage in Rom. xv. 4: "Whatsoever things were written of old time, were written for our learning, that we through patience and comfort of the scripture might have hope." It was, therefore, for our service that God provided in delivering his doctrine in a written form;—I had

almost said for his own too, since before that he had been compelled to repeat the same lessons frequently. So Thomas Aquinas
writes upon that passage: "There was," says he, "no necessity
for writing these things, but only on our account."

Sixthly, Chrysostom, in his 1st Homily upon Matthew[1],
expressly writes that the scriptures are necessary; and removes the
Jesuit's objection, that because scripture was not necessary in the
time of the patriarchs, neither is it so now. He says that the
patriarchs and apostles were exceedingly pure in soul, and that
God therefore addressed them immediately, and taught without the
medium of written documents; whereas, since we are rude and dull,
God hath chosen to instruct us by the scriptures. Bellarmine saw
this place, and endeavours to break the force of the argument.
He says that the scriptures are called necessary, because they are
useful. Excellent! But, then, they are so useful as to be necessary. Nothing, indeed, is more useful than what is necessary.

You have heard how admirably the Jesuit hath acquitted
himself of his first undertaking. I do not choose at present to pro-
secute the question more at large, or to illustrate it with testimonies
of the fathers, which shall be produced in their proper place.

CHAPTER IX.

THE ARGUMENTS OF OUR OPPONENTS, WHEREBY THEY PROVE THAT
THE SCRIPTURES ARE NOT SUFFICIENT WITHOUT TRADITION.

Now, then, in the SECOND place he proves that the scriptures are not *sufficient* without tradition, and do not contain all
things appertaining to faith and practice. This he does by
three arguments.

The first is to this effect: If the scripture be sufficient, then
it is either the whole canon which is sufficient, or the several
books contained in that canon: but neither is the case; and therefore the scripture is not sufficient. I answer: I confess that we
do not speak of each several book when we say that the scriptures
contain sufficient instruction, but mean the whole canon, whence we

[1 Tom. VII. p. 1. et seqq.]

affirm that all things necessary may be drawn. Nor is this to be understood, however, merely of the canon, which is now richer and more copious than it was formerly (for at one time the canon was by no means so large and full, since the Jews, who were without the new Testament, had not so many books as we have); but we say that the canon extant in the time of the Jews was then, and that the canon extant in our time is now, sufficient without tradition. When there were only the five books of Moses, they were sufficient. When they were increased by the accession of other books (those of the prophets namely), these were sufficient, but more abundantly sufficient. In each age and generation, according to the circumstances of the church, the books which were extant were sufficient. But the Jesuit endeavours to weaken the force of this, and proves that even the whole canon is insufficient, because many books which were really sacred and canonical have perished. This he proves from Chrysostom's 9th Homily upon Matthew, on these words : " He shall be called a Nazarene." I answer, *firstly,* Chrysostom thought that this sentence could no where be found in those books of the old Testament which are still preserved. There is another similar sentence of which he entertained the same opinion : " Out of Egypt have I called my Son." Indeed, the seventy translators whom he followed exhibit neither passage : but the Hebrew text does; with which he was not conversant, being ignorant of the Hebrew language. Jerome, in his work *de Optimo Genere Interpretandi,* says that both sentences are found in the Hebrew copies, the former in Isaiah xi. 1, the latter in Hosea xi. 1. *Secondly,* we concede that some pieces are now wanting which formerly stood in the canon of scripture ; while nevertheless we affirm that the canon which now remains is sufficient, and contains all things necessary. Some books of Solomon's have been lost, but without any injury to faith or risk of our salvation ; as that which he wrote concerning plants, springing herbs, and worms, and also many proverbs. For God knew that these things would not be necessary to us for salvation. *Thirdly,* we deny that so many pieces have been lost as the papists and the Jesuit suspect. For, as to the books of Samuel, Gad, Nathan and Ahijah, I reply, that they are not lost, but are the same as those books which we now have, namely, the books of Samuel, Kings, and Chronicles, which were written by those prophets. Bellarmine goes on to say, that it is certain from the new Testament that the epistle of Paul to the Laodiceans hath been lost, which piece he himself mentions in the last chapter to the Colossians. But nothing can be more uncertain than this. For we have before established, both by the words themselves and the testimonies of authors, that this was no epistle of Paul to the Laodiceans, but of the Laodiceans to Paul; unless indeed we translate ἐκ Λαοδικείας, " to the Laodiceans." For other people wrote letters to Paul, as is plain from 1 Cor. vii. 1 : " Now concerning those things whereof ye wrote unto me." The opinion arose from the ambiguous version *Laodicensium,* which they give a passive sense to : wherein I am surprised that a man so polished and learned in Greek literature as Bellarmine should not have perceived the shameful error into which many had fallen, and should have chosen rather to incur the blame of negligence than to omit a very foolish argument.

The Jesuit's second argument is as follows : If Christ or his apostles had intended to restrain the word of God to the compendious form of scripture, then Christ would have commanded the evangelists and apostles to write, and they would somewhere have indicated that they wrote in pursuance of the Lord's injunction. But we nowhere read of this : therefore they never designed to do this. I answer by pronouncing the assumption to be untrue. Can we suppose that the apostles and evangelists attempted to write without a command or authority? Was it under the impulse of some slight occasional motive that they wrote so many works ; or did they not rather follow therein the authority of the Holy Spirit? Surely we cannot entertain the former thought without impiety. We believe that they were induced and moved to write by the special authority of Christ and the Holy Spirit : for the scripture is called θεόπνευστος, that is, delivered by the impulse and suggestion of the Holy Ghost. And 2 Pet. i. 21, Peter testifies that holy men of God spake " as they were moved by the Holy Ghost." Which makes it plain that they followed the impulse and authority of the Holy Spirit, not their own will and choice. The men were merely the instruments ; it was the Holy Ghost who dictated to them.

Our opponents, however, will have it that they wrote of themselves, without any express command. In Exod. xxiv. 4, we read that Moses wrote all the words of God : and Canus expressly acknowledges that he wrote this pursuant to the command of God. In Hosea viii. 12, God says : " I wrote unto them the great things (as some translate it, but as others, the authentic things) of my law." God therefore says, that he wrote those things which Moses wrote. But had the apostles any express command ? Undoubtedly they had. For, in Matt xxviii. 19, we read that the last words of Christ to his apostles were these : " Go, teach all nations." Now the term μαθητεύειν, which is used in that place, denotes teaching both orally and by writing, as should seem best to the Holy Spirit. For the Holy Spirit governed their minds in the discharge of this office, and impelled them to writing as a thing most specially needful. For they were required not merely to give temporary instructions ; but it was a part of their office to leave a written teaching, which should suffice for all ages, and remain even unto the end of the world. In Rev. i. 11, it is expressly written, " Those things which thou hast seen, write in a book," γράψον εἰς βιβλίον. This is an express command. If this injunction was given to him, we cannot doubt but that the same injunction was in the same way given to the rest also. Again, in Rev. xiv. 13, John says : " I heard a voice saying, Write." These things sufficiently prove that the apostles and evangelists followed the divine authority, and were not moved to writing by certain exceeding slight and fortuitous circumstances, as the papists impiously pretend, especially Lindanus, who thinks that he can make this good in the case of every one of the books. The fathers were very far indeed from this notion of the papists. For Augustine, in the last chapter of his first book upon the Consent of the Evangelists, says expressly that Christ wrote all those things which the apostles and evangelists wrote ; because the apostles were only the hands, but Christ the head. Now the hands write nothing but as the head thinks and dictates. Therefore, says he, we should receive their books with the same reverence as if Christ had written them with his own hand, and we had seen him writing them. His words are as follow : " Through that human nature which he assumed, he is the head of all his disciples, as members of his body. When, therefore, they wrote what he shewed and spoke to them, we must by no means say that he himself did not write, since his members did that which they knew by the influence of their head. For whatever he willed that we should read concerning his deeds or words, he commanded them as his hands to write. He that understands this harmonious unity, this ministry of the members in divers offices, but agreeing under one head together, will receive what he reads in the gospel narratives of Christ's disciples no otherwise than as if he saw the very hand of the Lord, which was a part of his proper natural body, engaged

in writing it[1]." Thus Augustine. Irenæus also, Lib. iii. c. 1, says
that the gospel is delivered in the scriptures "by the will of God."
And Athanasius, in his epistle to Liberius, speaking of Christ, says:
" He composed both the old Testament and the new[2]." Finally,
Gregory, in his 4th book of Epistles, Epist. 84, says, that
the scripture is the epistle of God the Creator to his creature[3];
which assertion is also, in some places, made by Augustine and
Chrysostom. Now then, who dares to forge letters in a prince's
name? Much less would the apostles or prophets have dared to do
so in the name of God.

From these considerations, it is manifest, that all the books
of the old and new Testaments were written not merely by the
will and command, but under the very dictation of Christ; nor
yet merely occasionally, or under the suggestion of some slight
circumstance, but with the deliberate purpose of serving the church
in all ages : whence plainly appears the falsehood of Lindanus'
pretence. But, if this were so (he urges), they would have
written a catechism, or composed some document in common, or
else each severally would have published in writing the whole
evangelic doctrine. I answer : None of these is necessary. For
they knew well that God would so direct their wills and hands,
that those should write whom it behoved to write, and write just
so much as was sufficient, and do all things in the proper time.
And if that is true which is handed down, they published the
Creed before they separated to go into their several provinces,
which is indeed an epitome of the scriptures. But this (says he)
they delivered orally, and did not commit to writing : upon which

[1 Omnibus discipulis suis, per hominem quem assumpsit, tanquam mem-
bris sui corporis, caput est. Itaque cum illi scripserunt, quæ ille ostendit et
dixit, nequaquam dicendum est, quod ipse non scripserit, quandoquidem membra ejus id operata sunt, quod dictante capite cognoverunt. Quidquid enim
ille de suis factis et dictis nos legere voluit, hoc scribendum illis, tanquam suis
manibus, imperavit. Hoc unitatis consortium, et in diversis officiis concor-
dium membrorum sub uno capite ministerium quisquis intellexerit, non aliter
accipiet quod narrantibus discipulis Christi in evangelio legerit, quam si ipsam
manum Domini, quam in proprio corpore gestabat, scribentem conspexerit.—
Opp. T. iv. p. 33.]

[2 ὁ διαθέμενος τὴν παλαιὰν καὶ τὴν καινὴν διαθήκην. Whitaker translates
" composuit," which he perhaps meant to be taken in the sense of arrange:
but his argument seems to require what is given above. The passage may
be found in Athanas. Opp. T. iii. p. 669. Paris. 1698.]

[3 Imperator cœli, Dominus hominum et angelorum, pro vita tua tibi suas
epistolas transmisit.—Gregor. Opp. T. ii. col. 808. Basil. 1564. It is Lib. iv.
Ep. 31. ed. Benedict. Paris. 1705.]

point as I feel no solicitude, I will spend no arguments. Indeed, it is nothing to the purpose; and the whole creed is contained in the scriptures, as Augustine tells us, *ad Catechumen.* Lib. 1. *de Symbolo :* " These words (meaning the Creed) which you have heard, are scattered through the scriptures. Thence they have been gathered and reduced into a system, to help the memory of the weak[4]." But of the Creed hereafter.

The Jesuit's third argument, whereby he proves that the scriptures are not sufficient without tradition, is to this effect : There are many things which we cannot be ignorant of, that are nowhere found in the scriptures; therefore all things necessary are not contained in the scriptures. The Jesuit sets forth and discusses many examples, which we must sift and examine severally. *First,* he says, that there is no doubt but that women, under the old Testament, had some remedy against original sin as well as men, which supplied the place of circumcision : but there is nothing about it found in the scriptures. I answer, that circumcision regarded not only men, but women also in a certain sense. For although they were not circumcised in the flesh, nevertheless the efficacy of circumcision reached to them, and in the circumcision of the men they were consecrated to God : for woman was considered a part of man, and a partner and sharer in all his goods. Unmarried women appertained to their parents, married women to their husbands : of a surety they had no peculiar sacrament. Lombard, Lib. IV., distinct. 1, letter G, says, that faith and good works had the same efficacy in the case of women as circumcision in that of men, and so were justified although they had no sacrament. But others say (as appears from the same author, Lombard), that they were sanctified and justified by sacrifices and oblations. Bellarmine might therefore have learned from his own master, how frivolous was this pretence. Besides, he ought to have considered that circumcision was not merely a remedy against original sin, but also a sign of the derivation of sin. Now it is by men rather than by women that sin is propagated ; and therefore this mark was the rather imprinted upon them.

The Jesuit subjoins, there is no doubt but that infants dying before the eighth day had some remedy against original sin ; but this is nowhere found in scripture. I answer : This is futile,

[4 Illa verba quæ audistis per divinas scripturas sparsa sunt, inde collecta et ad unum reducta, ne tardorum hominum memoria labaret.—Augustin. Opp. T. VI. col. 399. Antwerp. 1701.]

34

and, like the former objection, unworthy of a reply.   For the salvation of infants depends not upon the sacraments.   Others, however, answer that they might be circumcised before the eighth day, if they were in any danger of losing their lives : how truly, I inquire not.   But as it was not all who were partakers of the sacraments that were saved ; so neither were all damned who had them not.   If God had determined that all who died before circumcision should be damned, he would not assuredly have deferred that rite until the eighth day.   The Jesuit's *third* example is no more suited to the purpose than the previous ones.   In the time of the old Testament, says he, many Gentiles were saved ; and yet we read nothing in the scriptures of their justification from original and other sins.   I answer, that we do so read : for they were justified by faith in the Mediator without the sacraments.   But, if he speak of external means, there is a law to be found in the books of Moses for incorporating proselytes into the Jewish state.   These three arguments are derived from that foul spring of error, the popish tenet of salvation being inclosed in the sacraments ; whence they conclude that there was need of external means and remedies. These men know nothing of the power of faith.   The Jesuit's *fourth* example is of this sort : We must believe the canonicity of the books in the old and new Testaments, which yet cannot be discovered from the books themselves.   I answer, that this may be known sufficiently from the scriptures themselves.   For the doctrine itself confirms itself, and bears most certain testimony to itself.   Do we not read that the whole scripture is given by inspiration of God ? But, says the Jesuit, how shall I know that this is scripture which affirms this ?   And here he brings in a comparison.   It is written, says he, in the Alcoran, that that book was sent down from heaven ; and yet we are by no means therefore to believe that it really did come from heaven.   In like manner, says he, I must be assured of the authority of this book from some other source.   I answer : Seest thou not, O Jesuit, that the books of scripture are impiously and absurdly compared by thee to the Alcoran ?   The Alcoran is replete with absurdities and manifest falsehoods : whereas every thing in scripture bears the stamp of divinity, and the whole scripture plainly shews itself to be given by inspiration of God, as we have proved in the third question ; so as that those who are endued with the Spirit of God cannot fail to recognise God speaking in the scriptures.   Thus the conclusion of the Jesuit is false.   For if that be the true faith which is delivered in the creed, then our faith rests upon the scriptures, and upon them alone, since all the articles of faith are contained in the scriptures. And this faith is sufficient for salvation, because this faith lays hold upon Christ, in whom are all the promises of eternal life. But these men argue as if the principle of faith were laid in tradition; and if this be true, then faith depends entirely upon tradition. In Luke xxiv. 45, we read that Christ opened the minds of the apostles that they might understand the scriptures. Whence we perceive that faith springs from a right understanding of the scriptures.

Fifthly, The Jesuit says that it is not only necessary to believe the existence of a canon of sacred books in the old and new Testaments, but also to know which those books are. For example, we ought to know that the gospel of Mark is genuine and true, and so also that of Luke, and so on through all the other books of either Testament. But how are we to be assured of this? The evidence certainly cannot be derived from scripture; as in the case of believing that the gospels of Bartholomew or Thomas are not genuine, whereas reason teaches that we should rather believe a book bearing the title of an apostle, than one which bore the title of one who was not an apostle. Besides, how (he asks) shall we know that the epistle to the Romans is Paul's, and that to the Laodiceans not his, when the latter is mentioned in the epistle to the Colossians and the former nowhere? I answer : This is a fine piece of theological reasoning ; as if it were not evident from the very inscription of the epistle to the Romans, that it was written by Paul ! His assertion that it is certain that Paul wrote an epistle to the Laodiceans hath been sufficiently answered by us already. The epistle to the Colossians mentions no epistle written by Paul to the Laodiceans, but rather hints (as we have shewn above from certain of the fathers) that some epistle had been written by the Laodiceans to him. This error was occasioned by an erroneous version and still more erroneous interpretation of it. Jerome, in his Catalogue, testifies indeed to the existence in former times of such an epistle, but testifies also that it was universally exploded. There is still extant a little epistle pretending to be that of Paul to the Laodiceans, but utterly unworthy of the apostle's name. However, the Jesuit says that we should not only know that there are canonical books, but also which they be. I answer : This is indeed necessary, but not simply and alike to all : which even the papists themselves may be compelled to own. For formerly many persons to whom they dare not deny the possibility of salvation, entertained doubts concerning

some of the canonical books.   This was therefore not necessary to
them.   Indeed, there is no consequence in this argument, The
Holy Spirit recognises all the canonical books ; therefore all who
have the Holy Spirit recognise them.   For the Holy Spirit does
not produce the same effect in all persons, nor have all the same
measure of the Spirit.   Thus all who have the Holy Spirit do not
determine exactly alike concerning all the parts of religion.   Some
know Christ more perfectly, and some less ; and this also is to be
ascribed to the Holy Spirit, for " no one can say that Jesus is the
Lord but by the Holy Ghost," and even many papists have removed
the apocryphal books from the canon of scripture.   Secondly, I answer, that this very thing may be learned from the scriptures, namely
from the very books themselves, as that the gospel of Mark is true,
and so also that of Luke, and so the epistle of Paul to the Romans.
For the books themselves prove themselves by their own testimony.
The purity, the truth, the wonderful character impressed upon these
writings, prove, at least to all those that have the Holy Spirit, that
they emanated from God and his holy inspiration.   For it is only
they who have received the Holy Spirit that can hear, recognise,
and understand his voice.   Then, secondarily, these books are confirmed by the authority of the church which hath received these
books, but constantly rejected those others, such as the gospels of
Bartholomew and Thomas.   This, however, is only a secondary evidence.   Augustine, *de Consent. Evangelist.* Lib. I. c. 1, replies to
a similar objection, namely, why the same faith is not reposed in the
other authors who wrote accounts of Christ and the apostles ? and
alleges two reasons why their books were rejected, lest any should
suppose that the church had rejected them merely on its own authority.   The first reason is, because they were not such as the church
in those times believed or approved : where he speaks of the church
of those times.   The second is, because the authors of those books
did not write with the requisite fidelity, but fallaciously introduced
into their writings matters which the rule of apostolic faith and
sound doctrine condemns.   But whence could this appear but from
the books themselves ?   Bellarmine pretends that there is no difference between those gospels and ours, between the epistle to the
Romans and that to the Laodiceans, save only this, that the church
hath received one set of gospels and rejected the other ; hath
admitted the epistle to the Romans into the canon, and exploded
that to the Laodiceans : which is plainly at once impious and absurd
in the highest degree.

The Jesuit's *sixth* example is this: We must not only know what books form the canon in both Testaments, we must also know in particular that these are the very same books; not only that the gospel of Mark is true, but that this which we now have is the gospel of Mark: now this cannot be proved from the scriptures. I answer: It is not simply necessary to salvation that we should believe that this book which is inscribed with the name of Mark was actually written by him. I say not this rashly, but with reason and judgment. It is indeed necessary for me to believe it to be true and divine; but every one who doubts whether it were written by Mark does not immediately fall from salvation, or deserve to be esteemed a heretic. We do indeed think that he would deserve blame who should entertain such doubts, because there is no reason for them: but nevertheless we do not on that account exclude him from life and salvation. The scripture receives not authority from men, but from the Holy Ghost: nor is it more necessary to believe that this is the gospel of Mark, than to believe that the epistle to the Hebrews was written by Paul, or the Apocalypse by John. The authors of many books are unknown, as of Joshua, Ruth, Chronicles, Esther, &c. But other books assert their own authors, as the Pentateuch, which no one doubts to have been written by Moses, because it bears his name, so that sometimes the whole Pentateuch is called by the name of Moses. So the gospel and epistles of John, of Paul, and of Peter: and yet the evidence with respect to all these is not precisely the same. The papists urge the same objection with respect to the Creed, as if it were necessary we should believe that the Creed was written by the apostles themselves. For so Lindanus argues, *Panopl.* Lib. III. c. 8. But if I doubt whether the Creed were written by the apostles, am I therefore a heretic? Surely not, if I hold and receive the doctrine delivered in the Creed. Augustine, *de Symbolo*, Lib. I. c. 1, says, that the contents of the Creed are scattered through the scriptures, and that the Creed was collected out of the scriptures. If this be true, it was not written by all the apostles; for James died before any, and many of the apostles before all the books of the new Testament were published. Bellarmine then subjoins some remarks which we have answered in the third question.

In the *seventh* place, the Jesuit says, that it is necessary that we should not only read, but understand the scriptures. Now, he says, there are many ambiguities in the scriptures which cannot be

understood until they are explained by an infallible guide. For
he says there are two things to be considered in the scriptures, the
words and the sense, the words being like a sheath, while the
sense is the sword of the Spirit; and, though the words may be
understood by every one, yet it is not so with the sense. To this
purpose he thinks is the saying of Basil, *de Spirit. S.* c. 27, that
the gospel "without an interpretation is a mere name[1]." He
enumerates many things of this kind, which are obscurely laid
down in scripture, as the equality of the persons of the Godhead,
the procession of the Holy Spirit, original sin, Christ's descent
into hell. These, he says, cannot be deduced from scripture without great difficulty. I answer: When our adversary confesses
that, with whatever difficulty, these things may be deduced from
scripture, he concedes that they are not unwritten verities, or such
as are to be counted amongst traditions. For the ancient fathers
teach most truly, that whatever is deduced from scripture, whatever
difficulty may attend the deduction, is all written. Secondly, I
say, that the Jesuit differs from other papists in this point. For
others write in a very different style about these matters, and rank
them in the number of unwritten traditions. Stapleton, Lib. XII. c.
5, says that the *Homoüsion* cannot be proved from scripture, nor
yet the Deity of the Holy Spirit. Nazianzen, *de Theolog.* Lib. V.
mentions certain heretics who maintained that the Holy Ghost was
ξένος καὶ ἄγραφος θεός, "a strange God unknown to scripture[2]."
They compare us to these heretics, because we receive nothing but
what is found in scripture; whereas they themselves much more
resemble those heretics, denying these things to be written which
indeed are so, because gathered by necessary inference from the
scriptures rightly expounded and understood. Cochlæus against
Bullinger affirms the Homoüsion to be a tradition, and declares
that he would find it easier to prove the sacrifice of the mass out
of the scriptures, than the Homoüsion or the Trinity. Yet the
fathers formerly proved it by the express testimony of scripture:
for although they could not produce the very terms from scripture,
yet they found the sense and meaning of the words in scripture.
Tertullian, in his book against Praxeas, proves by many testimonies

[1] εἰ γὰρ ἐπιχειρήσαιμεν τὰ ἄγραφα τῶν ἐθῶν ὡς μὴ μεγάλην ἔχοντα τὴν
δύναμιν παραιτεῖσθαι, λάθοιμεν ἂν εἰς αὐτὰ τὰ καίρια ζημιοῦντες τὸ εὐαγγέλιον,
μᾶλλον δὲ εἰς ὄνομα ψιλὸν περιϊστῶντες τὸ κήρυγμα.—T. II. p. 210. G.]

[2] πόθεν ἡμῖν ἐπεισάγεις ξένον θεὸν καὶ ἄγραφον; Orat. xxxvii.—T. I.
p. 593. B.]

of scripture, that God is one in substance and three in persons. So Epiphanius, in *Hæres*. 60,³ proves that the Homoüsion is in scripture, as to the sense, though not as to the term: ἔστι δὲ καὶ σαφῶς ἔγκειται ἐν νόμῳ καὶ παρὰ ἀποστόλοις καὶ τοῖς προφήταις. So also against the Sabellians. So in the Anchoratus we find that the Arians blamed that term because it was not found in scripture. But Ambrose, *de Fide, c. Arian.* c. 4 and 5, proves it by many testimonies of scripture ; and begins his fifth chapter with these words : " Knowing, therefore, this unity of substance in the Father and in the Son, on the authority, not only of the prophets, but also of the gospels, how canst thou say that the Homousion is not found in scripture⁴ ?" Then he adds more to the testimonies which he had used in the preceding chapter. Augustine, *c. Maximin. Arian. Lib.* III. c. 14, wishes the dispute concerning this doctrine to be managed, not by the testimonies of the fathers, or by councils, but by scripture itself. The catholics urged the council of Nice, wherein that term was approved and sanctioned : the Arians that of Rimini, consisting of twice as many bishops, who unanimously rejected that term. But Augustine, in the place referred to, writes thus : " Neither should I allege the council of Nice, nor you that of Rimini, prejudging, as it were, the question. I am not bound by the authority of the one, nor you by that of the other. By the authority of scripture, a witness not peculiar to either of us but common to both, let allegation be compared with allegation, cause with cause, reason with reason⁵." In this passage Augustine desires that this article may not be debated and defined by the testimonies of the fathers, but of scripture ; and therefore he appeals from councils to the bible. So in his dispute with Paxentius, he says, that although this term be not found in scripture, yet it is sanctioned by John and Paul : which is the plainest possible refutation of the papists, who pretend that the Arians were convicted by tradition rather than by the scriptures. For Augustine openly and confidently appeals to the scriptures, and all the fathers use arguments from the scriptures.

[³ He means Hæres. 69. §. 70. p. 796. B. T. 1. ed. Petro.]

[⁴ Cum ergo hanc unitatem substantiæ in Patre et Filio non solum prophetica sed et evangelica auctoritate cognoscas, quomodo dicis in scripturis divinis Ὁμοούσιον non inveniri?—Opp. T. IV. p. 280. Paris. 1603.]

[⁵ Sed nunc nec ego Nicænum, nec tu debes Arimense, tanquam præjudicaturus proferre concilium. Nec ego hujus auctoritate, nec tu illius detineris : scripturarum auctoritatibus, non quorumque propriis, sed utrisque communibus testibus, res cum re, causa cum causa, ratio cum ratione concertet.—T. VI. p. 306.]

The procession of the Holy Spirit from the Father and the Son the church hath always most truly held against the later Greeks, who affirmed that the Spirit proceeds from the Father only. That error was condemned in the council of Lyons, in the time of Innocent the Fourth. Thomas Aquinas was summoned to that council, but he died on the way; and his place was supplied by Bonaventure, who proved most learnedly from scripture that the Spirit proceeds from the Son as well as from the Father. Thomas Aquinas also proves this in many places, as in his *Quæstiones Disput.* Quæst. 10, and in *prima Secundæ*, Quæst. 36, Art. 2. And before Thomas Augustine, in his 99th Tractate upon John, affirms the Spirit to proceed from the Son, and proves it out of scripture.

As to the third example, of original sin, it can be proved expressly enough from scripture, although indeed the term never does occur therein: as, from Rom. v. 12, "As by one man sin entered into the world, and death by sin, &c.;" and Psalm li. 7, "I was shapen in iniquity, and in sin did my mother conceive me." Here Bellarmine favours the Pelagians, asserting that it is hard to prove original sin from scripture; whereas Augustine, in his books against the Pelagians, establishes the point abundantly from scriptural evidence.

As to the fourth example, Christ's descent into hell, I certainly do confess that he that shall seek to establish this article, as the papists hold it, by scripture, undertakes a difficult task. Andradius, *Defens. Trident. Concil.* Lib. II., says that it cannot be gathered at all from scripture. Bellarmine says that it may, but with difficulty. But if it can, with whatever difficulty, be deduced from the scriptures alone, then the evangelists and apostles must have written something about it. Andradius, however, honestly confesses that this point cannot be proved by any place in scripture; and thence he proves that something is necessary which is not delivered in the scriptures. Certain it is, however, that some of the papists abuse some passages of scripture in behalf of this doctrine, as Psalm xvi. 10, and Acts ii., in which chapter Peter recites some words out of that Psalm, and 1 Pet iii. 19, "By which also he went and preached to the spirits in prison, &c." Yet Andradius plainly denies that it can be inferred from scripture, and gives a far different interpretation to the place in Peter. However, says Andradius, this point is laid down most plainly in the Creed. I answer: Ruffinus, however, affirms that it was not laid down in the Roman creeds in his time, yea, that it was then wanting even in the creeds of the orientals[1]; adding, that nothing more is delivered in these words than is implied by the clauses immediately preceding, wherein we profess our belief that Christ was buried, making the meaning of both articles precisely the same. This is at least not unreasonable; which I say, without intending to determine any thing for certain upon the subject. The Nicene Creed does not exhibit this article. The Athanasian does: but this makes rather for us than against us; for Athanasius mentions the descent into hell, but not the burial. In the Nicene Creed, on the contrary, the burial is mentioned, but not the descent into hell: which seems to indicate the sameness of the articles.

Besides, there are almost infinite reasons assigned for this descent. The Roman catechism delivers two: the first reason is, in order that Christ might deliver the fathers; the second, that he might display his power and sway over the lower regions. Clemens Alexandrinus, *Stromat.* 6[2], maintains, that Christ and the apostles descended in order to preach the Gospel to the condemned souls, and bring the hope of salvation to the philosophers and others who might believe. Aquinas, in his Sum, part III. q. 52, art. 1, enumerates three reasons why Christ descended into hell. The first is, " Because, as it was suitable that he should die that he might deliver us from death, so it was suitable that he should descend into hell to deliver us from going down into hell:—" as if, forsooth, he who delivered us from eternal death did not so perfectly finish his work as to leave us in no danger of such a descent. " Secondly, because it was suitable that, when the devil had been vanquished, he should rescue his captives who were imprisoned in the pit. Thirdly, in order that, as he had shewn his power on earth by living and dying, so he might also shew his power in hell by visiting and illuminating it." In the exposition of the creed he adds a fourth reason: " That he might perfectly triumph over the devil." Augustine knew nothing of these fine reasons, since, Ep. 99, he writes that he had not yet discovered what advantage Christ's descent into hell conferred upon the just men of old time. These are his words: " I have not yet discovered what benefit Christ conferred upon the righteous who were in the

[1 Sciendum sane est, quod in ecclesiæ Romanæ symbolo non habetur additum, *descendit ad inferna;* sed neque in orientis ecclesiis habetur hic sermo.—Expos. Symb. §. 20.]

[2 Δέδεικται δὲ κἂν τῷ δευτέρῳ Στρωματεῖ, τοὺς ἀποστόλους ἀκολούθως τῷ Κυρίῳ καὶ τοὺς ἐν ᾅδου εὐηγγελισμένους.—p. 637. D. Paris. 1629.]

bosom of Abraham, when he descended into hell, since I do not
see that, as to the beatific presence of his divinity, he ever withdrew from them[1]." Besides, nothing is certainly defined as to the
period during which Christ remained in hell. The Roman catechism affirms that he remained in hell as long as his body lay in
the sepulchre. So Thomas, in his Sum, part 3, q. 52, Art. 4 : "At
the same time his soul was brought out of hell, and his body from
the tomb[2]." If this be true, how did he perform his promise to the
thief, "To day shalt thou be with me in paradise?" Unless,
indeed, they make a paradise in hell. The papists indeed place
paradise upon earth : but it is plain from 2 Cor. xii. 2, 3, 4, that
that paradise which we deem to be the seat of the happy souls, is
neither in hell, nor on earth, but in the highest heavens. Besides,
when the thief besought Christ to remember him when he was in
his kingdom, he surely never thought of this infernal kingdom. It
is not, therefore, necessary that we should believe that Christ
descended in this way into hell; nor can Christ's descent into hell
in this sense be proved either with ease or with difficulty from
scripture.

In the *eighth* place, the Jesuit objects thus : We must believe
that the essential parts of all the sacraments were instituted by
Christ : but no such thing is found in scripture, except with
respect to two, or three at the most. In the Sartorian edition this
argument is omitted. I answer : We recognise only two sacraments, which we maintain to have been instituted by Christ in
regard of both matter and form : for the whole entire essence of
these is set forth in the scriptures. As to the other popish sacraments, it is no wonder that their essence is not explained in
scripture, because some of them have no matter, some no form, and
some neither form nor matter.

In the *ninth* place, he frames this objection : It is necessary to
believe that Mary continued a virgin always. But this is not
certain from the scriptures : therefore, some necessary things are
known from some other source besides the scripture. Cochlæus adds
further, that the title of θεοτόκος or *Deipara* is not grounded
upon the scriptures : which is a notable calumny ; for the fathers
proved the virgin to be θεοτόκος from the scriptures, against

[1] Unde illis justis qui in sinu Abrahæ erant, cum ille in inferna descen-
deret, nondum quid contulisset inveni, a quibus eum secundum beatificam
præsentiam suæ divinitatis nunquam video recessisse.—Ep. 99. al. 164. §. 8.]
[2] Simul anima ejus educta est de inferno, et corpus de sepulchro.]

the Nestorians, namely, from Matt. i. 23, and Luke i. 35, and many other places. I answer: As to the perpetual virginity of Mary, it is no business of mine to meddle with that dispute. I content myself with saying, that the fathers, who managed the controversy with Helvidius, adduced not only some obscure traditions, which no one would rank very high, but made use also of testimonies from scripture. So Proclus Cyzicenus alleges a passage from Ezekiel about the gate which should be closed [3]. So Ambrose, Sermon 4 and 5. So also Ambrose, Epist. 31 and 79, proves the same from John, where Christ commends his mother to John's care; which he would not have done, if she had a family of chil-·dren. Epiphanius prosecutes this argument still more copiously against the Antidico-Marianites. Jerome contends against Helvidius with many passages of scripture; and in like manner other fathers. Therefore, if these fathers determined aright, this opinion is not absolutely without scriptural authority. Now, as to the Jesuit's assertion, that it is an article of faith to believe the perpetual virginity of the blessed Mary, I say that Basil thought otherwise: for, in his Homily on Christ's nativity, he says that we should not curiously dispute upon this subject, but that it is enough to know that she had no children before Christ.

In the *tenth* place, Bellarmine uses the following objection: We must believe under the new Testament that Easter is to be celebrated on the Lord's day, because the Quartadecimans were esteemed heretics by the ancient church. But this is by no means evident from scripture. I answer, that there was indeed a great contention formerly about this matter, but without reason; so that it is a wonder how there could have been such great and fierce dissension about a thing so slight and of hardly any importance. Pope Victor threatened to excommunicate all the eastern churches for keeping Easter upon another day than Sunday; but Irenæus and many other very holy bishops blamed Victor on that account, as appears from Eusebius, Lib. v. c. 25. The eastern churches said that they followed John and Philip; the western, Paul and Peter. Sozomen, Lib. vii. c. 19, says, that the controversy was settled by Polycarp and Victor upon the agreement that each should follow his own custom and judgment; deeming it " a piece of folly to be divided on account of customs," εὔηθες ἐθῶν ἕνεκεν ἀλλήλων χωρί-ζεσθαι. From whose words we perceive that the observance was free, and not necessary as Bellarmine says. Perhaps those apostles

[3 Ezek. xliv. 2.]

in the beginning, in compliance with men's weakness, observed
certain days, which afterwards through human error passed into a
law. If John kept the passover with the Jews, as Paul sometimes observed circumcision, does it thence follow either that the
passover is to be celebrated with the Jews, or that any celebration
of the passover is of perpetual obligation? I answer, therefore, in
the first place: That there was no reason why such learned fathers
should have contended so earnestly, or disputed so keenly upon this
subject. It is no point of necessity to celebrate it upon the Lord's
day, or some other day, or upon any day at all. For so Socrates,
Lib. v. c. 22, says, that the apostles determined nothing about
festivals: Σκοπὸς μὲν οὖν γέγονε τοῖς ἀποστόλοις οὐ περὶ ἡμερῶν ἑορταστικῶν νομοθετεῖν: on which point he discourses at
large, and says, that those fathers contended about this matter to
no purpose; since the passover was a type and ceremony, and all
types have now vanished. Secondly, I affirm, that this was indeed a very ancient custom, but still free: for such were the
terms of the agreement between Victor and the oriental bishops.
Thirdly, I say, that the Quartadecimans, that is, those who, in
imitation of the Jews, used to celebrate Easter upon the fourteenth
day of the first month, were opposed by scriptural arguments;
because Christ rose upon Sunday, and there ought to be a difference
between the Easter of the Jews, and that of the Christians.

In the *eleventh* place, Bellarmine objects that the baptism of
infants cannot be proved from scripture by the Lutherans and
Calvinists, though it can by the catholics. But why not by the
Lutherans and Calvinists? Because the Lutherans say that there
is need of faith, and that baptism is of no avail without actual
faith in the individual, with which the scriptures do not teach us
that children are endowed. I answer, first: That in asserting
that catholics can prove the baptism of infants from scripture, he
contradicts himself; for he had said before, that the baptism of
infants was an unwritten tradition. Bellarmine in his published
edition uses different language from that of his manuscript Lectures. For in the book printed at the Sartorian press his words
are these: " Now this the catholics do not, and the Lutherans cannot, prove out of the scriptures alone." But in the MS. copy thus:
" This though the catholics can prove out of scripture, yet the
Lutherans cannot." Thus he concedes that infant baptism may be
proved from scripture, although not from it alone. Secondly, the
Lutherans alone are concerned with the question about the faith of

infants. However, I do not think that they say that baptism is of
no avail if infants have not actual faith; but that it is possible
that infants may have faith, although it be not apparent to us.
But let the Lutherans answer for themselves upon this point. It
is enough for us that Bellarmine himself concedes the possibility
of proving infant baptism from scripture.

In the *twelfth* place, Bellarmine objects something about purgatory. Luther, says he, believed in the existence of purgatory,
as is manifest from his assertions, Art. 17. But he himself affirms
that it cannot be proved from scripture : therefore we should hold
something which is not contained in scripture. I answer : I confess
that Luther used such expressions, and professed belief in purgatory. But what sort of belief? I believe it, says he, not as
certain, but as probable. Besides, he says in the same place, that
he believes the existence of purgatory in the same way as he believes Thomas Aquinas to be a saint : which I do not think that
he believed very earnestly. Furthermore, he wrote that book at
an early period, when he first began to take pen in hand against
the papists ; afterwards he changed his opinion, and determined
otherwise about purgatory.

Bellarmine thinks himself very acute in his *thirteenth* objection,
supposing that he hath caught us in our own toils. It is this : We
say that nothing is necessary to be believed which is not contained
in scripture. He retorts this upon us, and asks us where we find
this written. I answer, in the first place : We do not say that
there is no unwritten word of God, but acknowledge that Christ
and his apostles said many things which are not contained in scripture. Our opinion is this ; that not every particular of all kinds,
but that all the general kinds of particulars, that is to say, all the
principal heads of doctrine, are in scripture. We say, that whatever cannot be unknown without making shipwreck of faith and
salvation, is fully found and explained in the scriptures. Secondly,
this word also is written, that all necessary dogmas may be drawn
from scripture ; as we shall prove hereafter. Thirdly, as to his
assertion, that the *word* mentioned by Moses, Deut. iv. 2, (where
he says, " Ye shall not add to this *word* which I speak unto you,
neither shall ye diminish from it,") is not written, it may be plainly
refuted from verses 8 and 9, where Moses says this word is the
whole law, and commands parents to teach it to their children.
Now all parents could not know the unwritten law, which we suppose to have been of a mysterious character, and concealed from the

people.   Besides, he divides this law into the ceremonial, judicial,
and moral : therefore he speaks of the written law, as we will shew
more clearly hereafter.

CHAPTER X.

THE ARGUMENTS TAKEN FROM SCRIPTURE, WHEREBY BELLARMINE PROVES THE EXISTENCE OF SOME TRUE TRADITIONS, ARE ANSWERED.

IT follows now that (to use his own language) he should prove
de facto the existence of some true traditions.   His FIRST argument
is taken from what hath been already said and argued.   If scripture
do not contain all necessary things, then there is some unwritten
word : otherwise God would not have well provided for his church,
if anything necessary were wanting.   I answer : That God hath
excellently well and wisely provided for his church by delivering to
it the scriptures, which contain in themselves a full and perfect body
of doctrine sufficient for every man's salvation.   For the things
alleged are either contained in scripture, or are not necessary.

The SECOND argument is taken from the authority of scripture,
out of which he quotes many testimonies.   The *first* place is John
xvi. 12, where Christ says to his disciples : " I have yet many
things to say unto you, but ye cannot bear them now."   From which
place the Jesuit concludes that there are many unwritten traditions,
because the Lord said many things which are not written.

I have four replies to this.   Firstly, these many things of which
Christ here speaks were no other than what he had previously
taught his apostles, and which required to be repeated and explained,
because the apostles then in consequence of the dulness of their
minds found some difficulty in understanding them.   On that account Christ (John xiv. 26) had promised to them the Holy Spirit,
who should bring all things to their remembrance : now what were
these " all things ?"   Were they anything more than he had previously taught them ?   By no means ; but precisely the same as
he had before said to them.   The Spirit was to enable them to
recollect what they had heard, to suggest to them, and to recall to
memory what they had forgotten, to explain to them what they had
not understood : διδάξει πάντα καὶ ὑπομνήσει ὑμᾶς πάντα ἃ εἶπον
ὑμῖν.   Therefore the Holy Spirit suggested nothing more than Christ

had spoken. We have a clear example of this in John ii. 22. Christ had said that he could in three days restore and rebuild the temple, if it were destroyed. The disciples did not understand these words at the time when they were spoken; but after his resurrection the evangelist says that they understood that he spake not of the temple reared by human hands, but of his own body. Jansenius, a popish author, commenting upon these words, "I have yet many things to say unto you," John xvi. 12, affirms that these "many things" are not "different from what he had previously taught them," but only a clearer "explication" of them; and to this he appositely applies 1 Cor. iii. 1, "I could not speak unto you as unto spiritual, but as unto carnal, even as unto babes in Christ." Indeed Christ in that discourse, which is contained in John xv., testifies that he had delivered all things to his disciples, when he says: "All things, which I have heard of my Father, I have made known unto you." Christ had declared all things: he had, therefore, reserved nothing, nor had the Holy Spirit any more or any different instructions to give the disciples than those truths which Christ had heard from his Father and had announced to them: but these things required to be repeated again and again, on account of the ignorance and slowness and sorrow wherewith their minds were at that time oppressed and encumbered.

Secondly, they cannot deny that the Holy Spirit taught the apostles these many things, and indeed all things, and that they delivered them to the churches, committing them, besides, to books and written documents, lest they should be consigned to oblivion; upon which topic we shall speak more at large hereafter. But what sort of an argument is this which the papists construct in this fashion,—I have many things to say unto you which I will not say, because ye are not capable of understanding them; therefore, all things are not written? Who does not perceive that there is absolutely no conclusiveness in this reasoning? Where is the middle term? What the tie by which these two things are bound together into coherence? Surely it is a palpable instance of the fallacy *ignoratio elenchi*. For Christ does not say, Ye shall not write all, or, ye shall not know all; but, I will not now say what I have to say, because you cannot now bear so many things. Does it therefore follow, that they afterwards did not know or did not write them all? By no means.

Thirdly, How do the papists infer that these things which Christ reserved are their traditions? Christ reserved many things; therefore he reserved what they hold. It is a mere fallacy of the

consequent. But in order to see that these were not the popish
traditions, let us consider the nature of these latter. Are they so
abstruse or so sublime, so difficult or so important, so arduous or
so divine,—are they pregnant with such deep and recondite meaning, as to meet the conditions of the context? Nay, they are so
easy, so almost futile and childish, as not only to be level to the
capacity of the apostles when still imperfectly instructed, but such
as almost any one may understand without an effort. Doubtless,
therefore, Christ was not thinking of them in this place. They are
all mere trifles, such as any the most dull and stupid is capable of
mastering. The most mysterious parts of the popish traditions are
those which pertain to the sacraments, the sacrifice of the mass, its
rites, ceremonies, gesticulations, and so forth. Yet these are of such
a nature that they may be easily learned and understood by any
ignorant priest, yea, by a boy. Are these the things which ex-
ceeded the reach and perception of the apostles? or were they
traditions about fasting, or about Lent, or feasts, or prayers? All
these are of such a character as to be intelligible to even the most
stupid of mankind. Therefore these are not the "many things"
which Christ reserved, but some greater things than these, which,
although they had often heard them, and although they were extant
in the scriptures, could not be understood without the assistance of
the Holy Spirit.

Fourthly, the papists, when they draw such an argument from
this place, plainly imitate the ancient heretics. So Augustine tells
us, *Tractat.* 97, *in Joan.*, that all the heretics abused these words
of Christ to persuade the people that their figments were those
things which Christ reserved. " All the most foolish heretics,
who would have themselves called Christians, endeavour to colour
their daring figments by the occasion of this passage in the gospel, where the Lord says, ' I have yet many things to say unto
you.'[1]" This is no slight blow the learned father deals to the
papists of our time ; whom, in *Tractat.* 96, he answers thus :
" Since Christ was silent, who of us will say they were these
or those things ? or, if he venture to say it, how can he prove it ?"
Then he subjoins : " Who is there so vain or rash, as that even
when he hath said what is true, what he pleases, and to whom he
pleases, without any divine testimony, will affirm that these are

[1 Omnes autem insipientissimi hæretici, qui se Christianos vocari volunt,
audacias figmentorum suorum . . . hac occasione evangelicæ sententiæ colorare
conantur, ubi Dominus ait, Adhuc multa habeo vobis dicere.—T. IV. p. 975.
Bassan. 1797.]

the things which the Lord was unwilling to say? Who of us can
do this, destitute of the extraordinary authority of a prophet or an
apostle, without incurring the severest blame for his temerity²?"
Where Augustine plainly condemns the papists as guilty of heretical
rashness and audacity. Then he says, a little after, "But what
those things were which he himself did not tell, it is rash to wish
presumptuously to say." And again, almost at the commencement : " Who of us would now venture to say that he was now able
to tell what they then were not able to bear? On this account
you must not expect that I should tell them to you." Augustine
affirms himself to be utterly ignorant what things these were; but
the papists of our time boast that they know all these things, and
are quite well able to understand them. Augustine bestows three
entire discourses upon these words, wherein he teaches us these
three points : First, that all the heretics were wont to abuse these
words to the support of their figments; secondly, that we should
not curiously inquire what those things were which Christ did not
tell ; thirdly, he thinks them greater and more mysterious than
the human mind, even when illuminated by the Holy Spirit, can
comprehend or understand, such as secrets of predestination, the
number of the elect, the joys of the kingdom of heaven ; in which
third point he was in error. However, the papists must make
good two things in order to prove that this place lends them any
help : first, that those things which Christ then reserved are
now also still unwritten ; the other, that they are the same they
boast of, and place amongst their traditions. But these things
they will never be able to prove.

The *second* place of scripture cited by the Jesuit is contained in
the last chapter of John, in the closing words, where the evangelist
writes thus : " There are also many other things which Jesus did,
the which if they should be written one by one, I suppose that even
the world itself could not contain the books that should be written."
Therefore, says Bellarmine, there are many things unwritten, since
even a single hand can contain all the books that have been written.
I answer, that there are many errors in this argument. Firstly,
John does not there speak of Christ's doctrine, but of his acts, that

[² Quis est tam vanus aut temerarius, qui cum dixerit etiam vera, quibus
voluerit, quæ voluerit, sine ullo testimonio divino, affirmet ea esse quæ tum
Dominus dicere noluit? Quis hoc nostrum faciet, et non maximam culpam
temeritatis incurrat, in quo nec prophetica nec apostolica excellit auctoritas?
—Opp. T. IV. p. 970.]

35

[WHITAKER.]

is, of his signs and miracles.   For he says, "which Jesus did,"
ὅσα ἐποίησεν, not, "which he said." This place is therefore irrelevant
to the question before us.   For we do not say that all the miracles
of Christ were committed to writing, since they were too many and
great to be contained in any books : but we affirm that the whole
doctrine of Christ, so far as it is necessary to our salvation, is
written in these books.   To this effect is what we read in John xx.
30, where the evangelist writes thus : " And many other signs did
Jesus in the presence of his disciples, which are not written in this
book."   Thus it is manifest, that the evangelist speaks of his signs
and miracles, not of his doctrine.   Is, then, anything wanting,
because his miracles are not all written?   By no means : for all
Christ's miracles had this scope, to prove the divinity of the Son,
to seal his doctrine, and finally, to shed a lustre round his person.
Now this " those miracles" which are related in scripture do most
evidently ; nor could these things be more firmly established, even
if all Christ's miracles were described in writing.   The learned,
however, recognise a certain familiar hyperbole in these words of
John, such as frequently occurs in scripture ; as when we read that
gold and silver were as plentiful as stones and earth, that the walls
of a city reached as high as heaven, that the Israelites were like
grasshoppers in the sight of the Canaanites.   John here obviates
a scruple which some, who prosecuted their inquiries with a greater
desire to gratify their curiosity than any prudent care for edification, might raise : did Christ live so long, and yet do nothing more
than these things which are related by the evangelists?   John
answers, that he did many other things, which are not written.
Yea, even all the words of Christ are not related one by one severally, but only in general.   The second error is no less glaring.
All things are not written : therefore, all necessary things are not
written.   The argument is inconsequential.   We confess that all
things are not written, but yet contend that all necessary things
are written.   In John xx. 30, 31, " Many other signs," says the
evangelist, " did Jesus in the presence of his disciples, which are
not written in this book ; but these things are written that ye
might believe that Jesus is the Christ, the Son of God, and that
believing ye might have life through his name."   John therefore
confesses that many other miracles were exhibited by Christ, and
that they are not written; and yet says, that these things which are
written are sufficient for faith and salvation ; for that all who believe these will obtain eternal salvation.   The fathers understood

these words to mean thus, that all necessary things may be derived from the scriptures. Augustine, *Tract.* 49 *in Joann.*, writes thus upon this subject: "Though the Lord Jesus did many things, yet all are not written (as this same holy evangelist testifies, that the Lord Jesus said and did many things which are not written); but those things were chosen to be committed to writing, which seemed sufficient for the salvation of believers[1]." Therefore, those things which are written suffice for the salvation of believers. Cyril, Lib. XII. in Joan. cap. ult., writes thus: "All those things which the Lord did are not written, but so much as the writers thought sufficient both for faith and manners; that, clothed with the glory of an orthodox faith and a virtuous life, we might reach the kingdom of heaven[2]." Nothing could be written more plainly. Many things were omitted, but nothing that was necessary. Therefore the evangelists and apostles wrote all those things which they thought sufficient either for manners or for doctrine. The third error in this reasoning is the most absurd. The evangelist says that the things unwritten are innumerable; therefore, if he mean the traditions of the papists, they must be infinite, so as that not even the whole world could contain them. They must, therefore, either confess their traditions to be infinite, and incapable of being enumerated by themselves, or else concede that this place does not refer to them.

The *third* passage of scripture cited by the Jesuit is from the beginning of Acts i., where Luke writes that Christ conversed with his disciples during forty days after his resurrection, and said many things to them, and taught them many things concerning the kingdom of heaven. Then, doubtless, says Bellarmine, Christ told his disciples what he would not tell them before; as, for instance, concerning the sacrifice of the mass, the institution of the sacraments, the ordination of ministers, &c. &c., which they delivered to the church. I answer: I readily confess that the apostles did deliver, with the utmost fidelity, to the church what they had received from Christ. But I can perceive no consequen-

[1 Cum multa fecisset Dominus Jesus, non omnia scripta sunt, (sicut idem ipse sanctus evangelista testatur, multa Dominum Christum et dixisse et fecisse quæ scripta non sunt;) electa sunt autem quæ scriberentur, quæ saluti credentium sufficere videbantur.—T. IV. p. 819.]

[2 Non igitur omnia quæ Dominus fecit conscripta sunt, sed quæ scribentes tam ad mores quam ad dogmata putarunt sufficere; ut recta fide et operibus ac virtute rutilantes ad regnum cœlorum perveniamus.—Cyril. Opp. col. 220. Paris. 1508.]

tial force in this argument. For how will he prove the very
thing which he makes the basis of his reasoning,—that it was his
traditions which Christ taught at that time? He says that this is
undoubtedly true. But we cannot take his assertion for an argument : we want reasons, not asseverations. Now where is the
consequence in this reasoning? Christ, after his resurrection, often
conversed with his disciples, (not indeed conversing with them constantly, but at intervals; for so Œcumenius; he had not, says
that author, συνεχῆ διατριβὴν with them, but διεσταλμένως; and
it is plain from John xx. 26, that he was for eight days together
absent from the disciples,) and spake unto them many things
concerning the kingdom of God : therefore, he delivered to them
those things which are not written. I confess that Christ said many
things about the kingdom, but of the popish traditions not a word.
We shall much better understand what it was he said, by consulting the scriptures, so that we have no ground for inventing any
unwritten verities. From Matt. xxviii., Mark xvi., John xx. and
xxi., Luke xxiv., and Acts i., we may gather the nature of his
discourses. He expounded to them the scriptures; he gave them
authority to cast out devils, to retain and remit sins; he attested
his resurrection to them; he bade them preach the gospel to all
nations, and said other things of the same kind, which we can
read in scripture, so that we have no need of such conjectures as
the papists rely upon in this question.

The *second* testimony of scripture cited by the Jesuit is taken
from certain words of the apostle, in 1 Cor. xi., where Paul handles
two questions,—one concerning the manner of prayer, the other
concerning the mode of receiving the eucharist. He commences
(says Bellarmine) both from tradition. The first thus : " I praise
you, brethren, that ye remember all my instructions." Now these,
says he, are not written; and to prove it he alleges Chrysostom, Theophylact, Epiphanius, and says that other fathers also
might be alleged. Therefore, there actually are some unwritten
traditions. I answer : It may be conceded that these things are
nowhere written in scripture; and yet nothing can be gathered
thence to the prejudice of the defence of our cause. For if the
apostle speak of free institutions and indifferent ceremonies, which
belong not to the class of necessary things, he touches not upon
our subject, nor censures the position which we maintain. For we
do not say that all indifferent ceremonies are expressly delivered
in scripture (as how men ought to deport themselves in the congre-

gation, and the like), which, we are well assured are various and mutable, according to the change of times and persons. We contend not, I say, about indifferent ceremonies, which appertain merely to external polity and order, but about necessary doctrine. This is perpetual; those are not perpetual, but suited to the times. But let us grant that necessary doctrine is here denoted by the term 'tradition;' and indeed, for my own part, I think that the whole teaching delivered by the apostle is meant, because he says, ὅτι πάντα μου μέμνησθε, and afterwards embraces the eucharist under the term 'tradition :' thus he speaks of the whole sum of his teaching, wherein some things were necessary and perpetual, some things left free, which (specifically, though not generally) might be altered and changed. For, in general, all things must always be referred to the ends of decency and edification. What then follows from all this? We confess that the whole doctrine of the apostle was not then written, when that epistle to the Corinthians was written: does it follow from this that it is not even now written? Surely, by no force of this place or argument. We allow, indeed, that all things were not written immediately; but we say that afterwards, when all the sacred books were published, all things were abundantly contained in them. If, then, this place be understood of doctrine, we say that it is now fully written, although it was not so then; if of indifferent ceremonies, it is still farther from touching us. For these may be changed, provided only the reason and end be preserved; nor are they necessary, as is plain from the place before us. For the apostle speaks of that modesty which women ought to observe in the congregation, and of that decency also which is required in men when they frequent religious meetings and assemblies. He desires men to pray with uncovered, women with covered heads : which injunctions are not of a perpetual obligation; for they are not now observed even by the papists themselves; so as to make it plain that all churches are not bound to the same ceremonies.

But, says Bellarmine, the apostle commences the second question also, which concerns the manner of receiving the eucharist, from the topic of tradition, thus: "I delivered unto you that which I also received of the Lord." So that in these words he praises them for holding tradition. I answer : Does it, therefore, follow that something unwritten is necessary? By no means. For immediately after the apostle tells us what that was which he had received of the Lord, and had delivered to the Corinthians, "that

the Lord Jesus Christ in the same night," &c., which not only he
writes in this place, but three evangelists, Matthew, Mark, and
Luke, have also written.   This, therefore, which Paul delivered is
assuredly not unwritten.   But there is another place in that
chapter, which the Jesuit presses very earnestly : " The rest will I
set in order when I come."   ' What it was he settled, says he, is
nowhere found written.   Catholics justly think, that he not only
settled rites and ceremonies, but also delivered matters of greater
importance, such as concerning the ordination of the clergy, the
sacrifice of the altar, the matter and form of the other sacraments ;
nor can the heretics shew the contrary.'   I answer, in the *first*
place, that the apostle speaks of comparatively slight matters,
namely, of some outward rites and ceremonies appertaining to
order and decency, as is indicated by the word $\delta\iota\alpha\tau\acute{\alpha}\xi\omega\mu\alpha\iota$.
Chrysostom seems to give no bad explanation of these words : he
supposes, that by this term either some clearer explanation of what
was written is denoted, or some matters of slight moment and
importance which did not require to be pressed.   Thus Chrysostom
understands $\tau\acute{\alpha}$ $\lambda o\iota\pi\acute{\alpha}$, " the rest," to mean either the clearer
elucidation of these same things, or else some other matters, which
were of no necessity and no great weight.   But the papists think
their greatest articles, the sacrifice of the altar, the form and
matter of many sacraments, and other very important things of the
same kind, are here denoted.   But *secondly*, let us grant that they
were necessary things which the apostle promises that he would
set in order when he came.   Are they nowhere written ?   And
if they be not written in this epistle, are they therefore
nowhere to be found in other passages of scripture ?   *Thirdly*, if
they be written neither here nor elsewhere, does it follow that
they were those things which they count amongst their traditions ?
Our adversaries (says Bellarmine) cannot in any way shew the
contrary : but it would have been more reasonable if he had shewn
what he maintains.   And yet I think it quite possible to shew
what he thinks impossible to be shewn.   I profess myself able to
shew it, not by uncertain suspicions, but by the clear testimony of
scripture.   For if those things be here understood which the
papists rate so high,—the sacrifice of the altar, the ordination of the
clergy, institution, and such like, then some necessary things were
not delivered to the Corinthians when this epistle was written.
For the papists say that these articles of theirs are necessary in
the highest degree.   Now all necessary things had been abundantly

delivered by the apostle to the Corinthians, before he sent this
epistle to them, as is plain from 1 Cor. i. 5, where he says that
they were enriched "in everything," ἐν παντὶ λόγῳ καὶ πάσῃ
γνώσει : and from chap. xv. 1, 2, where he writes, "I declare
unto you, brethren, the gospel which I preached unto you, which
also ye received, and wherein ye stand, by which also ye are
saved if ye continue therein, &c." Whence it is plain that the
apostle had before this delivered to them the whole complete body
of christian doctrine. The papists must, therefore, either deny
that their traditions are necessary ; or must say, in spite of Paul's
most express assertion, that all necessary things were not delivered
to the Corinthians. Although therefore it is preposterous and
unjust in Bellarmine to require us to prove any thing here, when
he himself cannot do it, and though it is a violation of the laws of
disputation; yet we have complied with his wishes, and have plainly
proved the contrary. Thus we see the papists have no grounds
for "justly thinking" that it is their traditions which the apostle
here tacitly implies. But mark, upon what a noble foundation
rest the popish dogmas, and those not the slighter ones, but the
most weighty of all, the sacrifice of the altar, the form and matter
of the sacraments ;—forsooth upon that here touched by Bellarmine in the words, "The Catholics justly think." This is to
suspect, to guess, to wish ; not to believe, to prove, to argue.
Teach, shew, demonstrate to me, that these things were instituted
by Paul.—You cannot do it, and you own you cannot do it.

    The Jesuit's *third* testimony is taken from 2 Thess. ii. 15,
where the apostle says, ἄρα οὖν, ἀδελφοί, στήκετε : "Therefore,
brethren, stand fast," hold firm, keep your ground, καὶ κρατεῖτε
τὰς παραδόσεις, "and hold the traditions which ye have been
taught, whether by our word or epistle." From these words, say
our adversaries, it is plain that all things are not written : and
indeed the papists find no more plausible passage than this in
scripture. I reply : Various answers are given to this testimony.
Some suppose that Paul speaks only of certain external rites and
ceremonies of no great moment : but the scope of the epistle and
the context refutes that opinion. For Paul, having mentioned the
horrible devastation which was to be occasioned by the coming of
antichrist, immediately subjoins, "Stand fast, and hold the traditions, &c." Therefore his doctrine is rather to be understood as
designated by the term 'traditions.' The apostle Paul had founded
the church of the Thessalonians, and had both taught them orally,

and written an epistle to them. Now, therefore, he exhorts them
to hold fast his whole teaching, as well what he had when present
delivered by word of mouth, as what he had committed to writing.
So that some things were delivered in discourse orally, and others
written in an epistle. Does not then this place establish traditions? Nay, our writers have returned a twofold answer to this
testimony. First, that the things which Paul delivered orally
were not different from, but absolutely the same with, those which
were written. Those who adopt this answer explain the passage
thus: Hold the traditions which ye have been taught, both orally
and by our epistle. But the Jesuit opposes two arguments to
this answer. First, he says that the apostle uses a disjunctive
particle, εἴτε, thereby indicating that the things which he had delivered, and those which he had written, were not the same, but
different. I answer, that the particle εἴτε hath not always a disjunctive, but sometimes a conjunctive force, as 1 Cor. xiii. 8: εἴτε
δὲ προφητεῖαι καταργηθήσονται εἴτε γλῶσσαι, παύσονται εἴτε
γνῶσις, καταργηθήσεται, which words are to be thus rendered:
" Both prophecies shall fail, and tongues shall cease, and knowledge
shall fail:" and of a similar kind are other instances in scripture;
so that nothing can be necessarily gathered from the force of the
particle. But the Jesuit brings forward another objection, namely,
that then the former epistle must needs contain all necessary doctrine, which, says he, it does not, nay, not the hundredth part of
necessary doctrine, as is manifest. I answer: I acknowledge the
justice of this reasoning. I confess both that the former epistle
does not contain the whole doctrine of the gospel and all things
necessary to salvation, and that many other things beside are requisite; as also that the matters delivered orally were different
from those which Paul wrote. This answer, therefore, on our
side, is invalid, and not sufficiently clear, although many learned
men of our party acquiesce in it. We must, consequently, seek
another reply. I answer, then : That the canon of the new Testament was not yet published and settled, when Paul wrote this
epistle to the Thessalonians; yea, I maintain, that no books of the
new Testament were then written, excepting only the gospel of
Matthew ; and, if we believe Irenæus[1], these two epistles to the
Thessalonians were more ancient even than the gospel of Matthew:

[1 Ὁ μὲν δὴ Ματθαῖος .... γραφὴν ἐξήνεγκεν εὐαγγελίου, τοῦ Πέτρου καὶ τοῦ
Παύλου ἐν Ῥώμῃ εὐαγγελιζομένων καὶ θεμελιούντων τὴν ἐκκλησίαν.—Lib. III.
c. 1.]

for he says that Matthew wrote his gospel whilst Paul and Peter were preaching the gospel and founding the church at Rome, which was more than twenty years after Christ's ascension. Now this epistle was written seventeen or eighteen years after Christ's ascension, whilst Paul was teaching at Athens. It is therefore inconsequential reasoning to say: When Paul wrote to the Thessalonians, all necessary things were not written; therefore not afterwards: or, The Thessalonians had not then received the doctrine complete, as being without the other books of the scriptures of the new Testament; therefore we, who have all the books, have not the doctrine entire: or, Paul did not write all necessary things in this epistle; therefore neither did all the others. Paul in this place mentions both traditive and written teaching, and that justly considering the time: but we have now more books than those Thessalonians had; and therefore it does not follow that all necessary things are not found in the canon as now published. The Jesuit makes two assaults upon this most reasonable reply of ours.

First, he says that something was proposed by Paul to the Thessalonians, as namely, the time of antichrist's coming, which is not contained in the rest of scripture. He proves this from 2 Thess. ii. 5; and he confirms it out of Augustine, *de Civit. Dei*, Lib. xx. c. 19,[2] where he endeavours to make that father say that, although the Thessalonians knew this, yet we do not, as having never heard the apostle. I answer: That he abuses the words both of scripture, and of Augustine. For, if the apostle had taught the Thessalonians what day or what year antichrist would come, which is what he maintains, they would not have expected Christ's second advent to judgment to take place suddenly and soon, as it is apparent from this second chapter that they did. And although Paul may have said something to them about the coming of antichrist, yet it does not follow that he had described or predicted any thing of the particular time when he was to come. So that those words, in the fifth verse, " Remember ye not that when I was with you I told you these things?"—must be understood of the whole preceding series and chain of subjects (namely, that antichrist should be revealed, that he should sit in the temple of God,

[2 Et nunc quid detineat scitis, id est, quid sit in mora, quæ causa sit dilationis ejus, ut reveletur in suo tempore, scitis: quoniam scire illos dixit, aperte hoc dicere noluit. Et ideo nos, qui nescimus quod illi sciebant, pervenire cum labore ad id quod sensit apostolus cupimus, nec valemus.— p. 689. Basil. 1511.]

that he should exalt himself above all that is called God, &c.), not of any certain or precise date of his coming, which the apostle had never assigned. But be it so, let it be true, that Paul delivered to the Thessalonians some certain day, month or year, when the coming of antichrist was to take place: it will then follow that this is a tradition. Now if it be a tradition, then the papists are able to shew the time when antichrist shall come, since they say that they possess all the apostolical traditions. But this they cannot do: yea, they deny that any one can do it. As to Augustine, Bellarmine abuses his words also most disgracefully. For Augustine does not say that the Thessalonians knew the time when antichrist was to come; but he says that they knew what it was that delayed his coming, which we are ignorant of: upon which point we raise no question. For whether the impediment delaying the coming of antichrist at that time were the circumstance of the Roman empire being still safe and entire, or the gospel being not yet preached in the whole world, we may be entirely ignorant of it without injury to our faith. Augustine therefore says nothing against our defence.

The Jesuit answers, in the second place, that, even though it were conceded that all is written in other books, yet this would be no objection to believing in traditions also. For (says he) the apostle does not say, I promise that I or the other apostles will commit all the rest to writing, but, "hold the traditions." I answer: Although Paul had never written or made such a promise, does it follow that all the rest were not written by other apostles? By no means. For they wrote according as they were commanded by the Holy Ghost. We confess that many things are found in other scriptures, which were not then committed to writing, concerning the birth, death, resurrection, future advent of Christ, and the whole mystery of our redemption by him accomplished. These things the apostle enjoins to be held no less than any of those which he had himself written, because no less necessary in themselves. How does he prove to us that, if these had been then fully, yea, abundantly set forth in writing, the apostle would have made any mention of traditions? But it was because he knew that these things had not yet been written, that he admonished the Thessalonians to hold fast the traditions. However, since he cannot prove what he desires from scripture, he brings in the fathers, Basil, Chrysostom, Theophylact, and others, to whose testimony we will give a satisfactory answer by and by. Meanwhile to these fathers we oppose Ambrose's commentary upon these words, who says, that by tradition in this place is meant the evangelical doctrine or tradition of the gospel[1], which is abundantly explained in the scriptures.

Although what we have already said is sufficient to explain this passage, yet, in order to make our reply firmer and fuller, we will subjoin three observations. First, we bid them prove the force of this argument: "Some things are not written: therefore these are the very points which they boast of and obtrude upon us." This they can never prove; and yet they must demonstrate this before they can establish their position. Secondly, if from this mode of speaking ("Hold fast the traditions which ye have been taught, whether by our word or epistle") it follows that some necessary things are not written, then from the same form of speech it will also follow that some necessary things were not orally delivered: whereas they will have it that all necessary truths are contained in tradition. Now let them choose which they please. Thirdly, I inquire to whom the apostle delivered those things which they maintain not to have been written? Certainly, if they wish to be consistent with themselves, they must needs reply that they were not delivered to all, but only to certain persons; namely, to the wise and perfect. For so Canus, Lib. III. c. 3, Fundament. 4, proves from Hilary and Origen, that Moses did not write the more secret exposition of his law, but delivered it orally to his servant Joshua: and thence he infers that the apostles also acted in the same way, and committed their more secret doctrines only to a few wise persons. But it is manifest that those things which the apostle here mentions were delivered to all the Thessalonians: for the apostle addresses them all, when he says, "Keep the traditions;" so as to make it impossible for us to understand in this place certain secret traditions delivered only to a few persons. From this it is plain that this place does not, as Bellarmine affirms, remain in its strength. We have already examined three testimonies of scripture which the Jesuit considers the strongholds of his cause. Now follows the fourth.

The Jesuit's *fourth* testimony is derived from certain injunctions given by Paul to his disciple Timothy. He proposes three injunctions; the first of which is contained in 1 Tim. vi. 20, "Keep that which is committed unto thee," or *the deposit*. Under the name *deposit* (says Bellarmine) is denoted not the scripture,

[1 In traditione evangelii standum . . . monet.—Opp. T. III. p. 567. Paris. 1603.]

but a treasury of unwritten doctrine, as some of the fathers have explained it: therefore, there are some unwritten traditions. I answer: If I chose to go through all the various interpretations of this place, I might easily stop the adversary's mouth. Cardinal Cajetan, a man of undoubted learning, would have us understand by this "deposit" *the flock* committed to Timothy, which Paul commands him to keep diligently. Which exposition overturns the Jesuit's argument. But I do not think that that interpretation suits the passage, and therefore will not use it. Let it be, then, that it denotes, as he desires, a treasure of sound and catholic doctrine: what will follow from that? Does it follow that all necessary doctrine is not written? How can Bellarmine join together things so distant as such a conclusion and such premises? I, for my part, do not think that the scripture is meant by the term "deposit," nor does any of our divines so explain the passage; but we understand by "the deposit" the sound and catholic doctrine itself. Now, then, such an argument as the following is inconsequential: Paul exhorts Timothy to preserve sound doctrine; therefore, it cannot be wholly derived from the scriptures. If I were to advise a person to keep fast the catholic faith, and beware of popish errors, would he immediately suppose that that faith could not be derived from scripture? Nothing less. But, says Bellarmine, if scripture be meant by "the deposit" (which none of our divines assert), it is much better kept in libraries and papers. From which answer we may see the profane temper of the Jesuit. Is scripture then indeed better kept in libraries than in the hearts of men? It is thus, forsooth, that they are wont to keep the scriptures, not in their minds, but in their chests. Paul, however, is not speaking of the external custody of books, but of that internal keeping, when the scripture is laid up in the hearts of the faithful. Here he cites certain fathers, to whom I will only oppose Tertullian[1]. He, in his Prescriptions against heretics, desires us to understand by the term "deposit," in this place, no remote or secret doctrine, but that which was written "above and below" by the apostle: so that, if we believe Tertullian, no other doctrine is here meant but that which is delivered by

---

[1 Quod hoc depositum est?....an illius denuntiationis, de quo ait, Hanc denuntiationem commendo apud te, filiole Timothee; item illius præcepti, de quo ait, Denuntio tibi ante Deum, &c..... Quod autem præceptum, et quæ denuntiatio? Ex supra et infra scriptis intelligere erat, non nescio quid sub-ostendi hoc dicto de remotiore doctrina, sed potius inculcari de non admittenda alia præter eam quam audierat ab ipso, et puto, coram multis, inquit, testibus.—c. 25.]

the apostle in this same letter.   However, I think myself, that not
only is sound doctrine here meant and denoted by the term "deposit," but also the office committed to Timothy, and all the gifts
of the Spirit bestowed upon him and necessary to the due discharge
of that office.

The second place cited by the Jesuit in this fourth testimony
is 2 Tim. i. 13, where Paul thus addresses Timothy : ὑποτύπωσιν
ἔχε ὑγιαινόντων λόγων, ὧν παρ' ἐμοῦ ἤκουσας, ἐν πίστει καὶ
ἀγάπῃ τῇ ἐν Χριστῷ Ἰησοῦ : that is, " Have a form or model
of sound words which thou hast heard of me, with faith and love,
which is in Christ Jesus." I answer, that ὑποτύπωσις here denotes
an express image shining forth either in the matter or the form.
The apostle, therefore, means that Timothy should make no change
in the matter, or even in the form, of the apostolic doctrine.   But
can any thing in favour of tradition be gathered from this place ?
Absolutely nothing.   For the principal heads of those same words
are proposed by Paul in that same place, and are the two things
πίστις and ἀγάπη, "faith and love."   Both of these may be
drawn from scripture.   For, firstly, the whole of love depends
upon those two precepts, " Thou shalt love the Lord thy God with
all thy heart," &c., and " thy neighbour as thyself;" upon which
subject Christ discourses, Matth. xxii. 37, and in verse 40 says, that
" upon these two commandments hang all the law and the prophets."
From the law and the prophets, therefore, all things may be
derived which concern love.   The same is also to be determined
concerning faith, since it hath no larger extension than charity.

The third place cited by the Jesuit in this fourth testimony is
contained in 2 Tim. ii. 2, where Paul thus addresses Timothy :
" Those things which thou hast heard of me before many witnesses,
the same commit thou to faithful men, who shall be able to instruct
others also."   These (says Bellarmine) must needs be understood
of traditions ; for if the apostle had meant the scripture, he
would not have said, " what thou hast heard of me before many witnesses," but, what I have written.   I answer : Bravely reasoned !
The apostle in these words commends sound doctrine to Timothy,
and that no other than what is contained in the scriptures.   But,
in the meanwhile, let Bellarmine shew the consequence of his argument : " What thou hast heard of me commit to faithful men :
therefore these things can nowhere be found in scripture."   The
apostle would not have that sound doctrine deposited, and in a
manner buried in books, but set forth before all men; so as that not

only should Timothy hold it himself, but commend and communicate it to others who might be the masters of many more. So also, in the present day, there are learned divines who can teach other men; but does it, therefore, follow that they do not derive their lessons from the scriptures? Nothing, therefore, can be weaker than this argument.

The Jesuit's *fifth* testimony is taken from 2 John, verse 12, where John writes thus: "Having many things to write unto you, I would not write with paper and ink; but I trust shortly to see you, and to speak with you face to face, that our joy may be full:" and from 3 John, verses 13 and 14, where he writes in almost the same words: "I have many things to write, but will not write unto you with ink and pen; but I hope to see you shortly, and to speak with you face to face." Therefore, says Bellarmine, John said many things to the disciples which are nowhere found in the scriptures. I answer: I confess that all things are not found in those very brief epistles of John; but are all necessary things therefore not found in the rest of the books of scripture, numerous and large as they are? Who can be so mad as to argue from so small a part of scripture to the whole? Surely this is just as if one were to say, that because a finger is not the whole body, therefore the nature of the whole body does not consist in all its parts. John says that he chose to put off many things till his arrival. What were these? Doubtless, no other than those which are most plainly proposed in the scriptures, as namely, concerning the nature and benefits of Christ, the mysteries of our religion, the way to life and salvation, or other things of the same kind.

These are all the testimonies of scripture cited by the Jesuit, which he hath borrowed from Canus in the end of the third chapter of his third book.

But the same Canus, in the sixth chapter of the third book, hath other testimonies, to which also we will reply in order. He snatches up one from 1 Cor. xi. 16, where Paul uses these words: "If any man seem to be contentious, we have no such custom, neither the churches of God." So great, says Canus, is the force of ecclesiastical tradition, that he refutes by custom and the tradition of the church those whom neither scripture nor natural reason could refute. Whence he concludes that tradition is far more prevailing than either scripture or natural reason. For the apostle had before proved that women should pray with covered heads by the voice both of scripture and of nature: then follow these words, as if he had said, If these things cannot prevail with you, if ye are not moved by these, yet the institution and practice of the church and tradition ought to have great weight with you.   I answer: Such talk befits a declaimer better than a divine.   It is surely strange that so great a man should fall into so egregious an hallucination. The apostle does not say, If ye despise scripture and nature, I present you with the custom of the church; but he says, that the church hath no such custom as that any man should be contentious, but rather that all should preserve the common peace.   But if any one be contentious, he is a stranger to the church of God.   The apostle does not argue as this man pretends, I will refute him who contends against scripture and nature, that women should pray with heads uncovered, by the practice of the church; but he says, that the churches of God have no custom of allowing any man to be contentious.   Thus he represses contentious spirits by the authority of the church, and does not confirm the dogma by mere custom.   Now that custom of avoiding contention in the church is abundantly sanctioned by testimonies of scripture.

The second passage of scripture cited by Canus is contained in 1 Tim. vi. 3, where Paul writes thus: "If any man teach any other doctrine, and consent not to the wholesome words of our Lord Jesus Christ, and the doctrine which is according unto godliness, he is proud," &c.   Paul, says Canus, speaks of oral discourses, not of the scriptures.   I answer: If Canus desires to prove that the scriptures are here excluded, because Paul mentions words only and not writings, then by the same reason traditions also are excluded, because they too are written somewhere.   But by words Paul means sound doctrine; not because it is not written, but because it ought not to be hidden and buried in books, but brought forth and set in the light, and held in the mind, the tongue and the lips, and communicated and published to others.

The third passage of scripture cited by Canus is found in Galat. i. 9, where Paul writes thus: "If any one preach unto you any other gospel than that ye have received, let him be Anathema." Paul says (remarks Canus) "that ye have *received*," not, "that I have written."   Upon this place we will speak hereafter; meanwhile I answer: Where is the consequence in such an argument as this, They received; therefore they did not receive it in a written form?   Or again, Since they received many things orally, therefore we also now hold many things on no other security than tradition?

Our Rhemists, in order to shew their great skill in scripture, propose some new testimonies. First, they allege 2 Tim. iii. 8, upon which place they write, that Paul received the names of the two magicians there mentioned from tradition : and they say that there are similar traditions of the names of the three kings who came out of the East to adore Christ, and who are elsewhere called by them Melchior, Gaspar, and Balthazar[1]; a similar tradition of the name of the penitent thief, whom they call Ismas[2]; and of the name of the soldier who pierced Christ's side, whom they pretend to have been called Longinus[3]. This name was doubtless given him ἀπὸ τῆς λόγχης, that is, from the lance by which Christ was transpierced. They pretend that he afterwards died a martyr : and many traditions of the same stamp have been invented in later generations. I answer : Though we should grant that the apostle knew the names of the magicians by tradition, yet the knowledge of these was not necessary to salvation, any more than it is necessary to our salvation to know the names of those three kings : for if this had been necessary, the evangelists would not have been silent upon that subject. Let the Rhemists bring us, if they can, any necessary dogma of the church, which stood upon the foot of mere tradition. It is not to be doubted but that some things were received by tradition. From this source was derived a great portion of the genealogy which Matthew and Luke give in their account of the birth of Christ ; which indeed ought to be thought much more necessary than any knowledge of the names of kings or wizards. Yet who will refuse to confess that the faith might be safe without it, provided only we assent to the scriptures which establish that Christ was descended by a regular succession from Abraham and David ? Though, indeed, that very accurate genealogy drawn out by the evangelists contributes much to the stability of this faith. And whatever necessity is in the thing itself, it may now be learned from the scriptures. For the names of Christ's ancestors are now published, and Paul hath indicated who those distinguished magicians were, who so boldly resisted Moses.

They allege also Acts xx. 35. There (they say) a saying of Christ

[1 Legends assign various names : Apellius, Amerus, and Damascus ; Magalath, Galgalath, and Saracin ; Ator, Sator, and Paratoras. See Casaubon. c. Baron. Exerc. xi. 10 : who observes in a MS. note of the copy before alluded to, that the most correct order and orthography is, Baltasar, Melchior, Jaspar.]

[2 In the gospel of Nicodemus (c. x. ap. Fabric. cod. Apocr. T. i. p. 260) the penitent thief is called Dimas, and the other Gestas. Gerard Vossius writes Gismas and Dismas. Whitaker, I suppose, meant to write *Dismas*.]

[3 Ibid. p. 259 ; where see Fabricius' note, as also T. ii. p. 472.]

is recited by Paul, which is nowhere found in the gospels : " It is more blessed to give than to receive." I answer : I confess that this is nowhere expressly and in so many words written in the gospels ; but yet something is found in the gospels which comes to the same thing. For the precept in Luke xvi. 9, to " make to ourselves friends of the mammon of unrighteousness, that they may receive us into everlasting habitations," is to the same effect as this sentence. So also, Luke vi. 38, " Give, and it shall be given unto you :" and in the same verse, " Lend, hoping for nothing again." There are scattered throughout scripture many similar expressions, so as to leave no necessity for going in quest of unwritten traditions. Besides, I say, that though all Christ's sayings are not written, yet all that were necessary are ; so that no injury hence accrues to our faith.

They allege, besides, 1 Cor. xv. 3, where Paul says to the Corinthians, " I delivered unto you that which I also received ;" and they will have it that their traditions are established by this expression. I answer : But they ought to have subjoined the sequel, namely, " That Christ died for our sins, according to the scriptures, and that he was buried, and rose again the third day, according to the scriptures." Let them deliver likewise doctrines according to the scriptures, and we will receive their traditions. Now when Paul so frequently repeats in this place, *according to the scriptures*, he means it to be understood that he had drawn from the scriptures whatever he had delivered to the Corinthians.

Fourthly, they allege something from the epistle of Jude, ver. 9, in favour of traditions, where Jude proves that we must not speak evil of magistrates by the example of Michael, of which he could know nothing but by tradition. I answer : I confess this to be most true : but yet we learn from other places of scripture also, that it is an impious thing to speak ill, yea, or even to think ill of the magistrate.

Finally, wherever the term παράδοσις occurs, the Rhemists seize upon it as an argument for tradition. But it will not be necessary to pursue their other testimonies in detail.

Other papists have still fresh testimonies. Lindanus seeks to establish the authority of unwritten traditions from Jeremiah xxxi. 32, 33 ; where the prophet speaks of that new covenant which God would make with his people, which he predicts should not be the same as the old covenant which he made with the Jews, because that was written upon tables of stone ; whereas the new covenant should be written upon men's hearts : therefore, says he,

36

[WHITAKER.]

the evangelical doctrine is written not in books, but on the heart. I answer : It is not conclusive to say, I will write upon the heart, therefore, not upon tables : for it is written both upon tables and in the heart. But the difference between the old and the new covenant is founded upon this, that most of the ancients had scarce any thing but the material tables, and had not the force of the covenant inscribed upon their hearts ; whereas he predicts that in the new Testament there will be far ampler gifts of the Holy Spirit, and many more who shall have the covenant of God impressed upon their hearts. The place must be understood as speaking comparatively, not absolutely or simply.

So far, then, concerning the second argument of our opponents, which is founded upon the authority of scripture.

CHAPTER XI.
BELLARMINE'S THIRD ARGUMENT IS OBVIATED.

Now follows Bellarmine's third argument, which depends entirely upon the testimony and authority of general councils : for we make no account of the decretal epistles of certain popes. He proposes three councils : the first Nicene, the second Nicene, and that of Constantinople, which was the eighth general.

As to the first council of Nice, he says that Theodoret, Lib. I. c. 8, writes plainly, that Arius was condemned in that council by unwritten tradition : for, says he, even the Arians themselves alleged some things from scripture ; therefore, they were condemned not by scripture, but by traditive doctrine. I answer, in the *first* place : What sort of an argument is this ? The Arians alleged many things from scripture ; therefore they could not be refuted out of scripture. If this be a firm inference, then certainly no heretics can be refuted out of scripture, since all heretics allege scripture. But the Arians wickedly wrested the scriptures into an improper sense ; whose impious expositions the fathers assembled in that council refuted out of the scriptures ; as is plain from Socrates, Sozomen, and Athanasius, who was himself present in the Nicene council, and disputed largely against Arius out of scripture. But perhaps the Jesuit argues upon the supposition that the Arians could allege more passages in their favour from the scripture, than the catholic fathers could bring against them, and that therefore the catholics could not safely trust the scriptures. But they could

not produce more passages. Nor yet is it always he who can heap
together most sentences of scripture, that maintains the justest
cause: for he who brings one sentence of scripture rightly understood, hath a better cause than he who abuses a great number
of scripture passages. Athanasius, for his part, refutes the Arians
out of scripture, and the other fathers trusted more to scripture
than to tradition. Otherwise Augustine, *c. Maximin. Arian. Lib.*
III. c. 14, would never have recalled him from councils to the
scriptures. In that passage is the celebrated saying: "Neither
should I allege the council of Nice to you, nor you that of Rimini
to me, as if we could prejudge the question. I am not bound by
the authority of the latter, nor you by that of the former. Let
the contest be matter with matter, cause with cause, reason with
reason, on the foot of scriptural authorities, which are witnesses
not peculiar to either side, but common to us both[1]." Augustine
therefore trusted most to the scriptures in this question. Besides,
Constantine (as Theodoret relates, Lib. I. c. 7) plainly says that
the doctrine of the Holy Ghost is *written*, ἀνάγραπτον. These
are his words: "The books of the evangelists and apostles, as
also the oracles of the old prophets, plainly teach us, what we
should think of divine subjects. Laying aside, then, all factious
contention, let us resolve the points of inquiry by the testimony of
the inspired words: ἐκ τῶν θεοπνεύστων λόγων λάβωμεν τῶν
ζητουμένων τὴν λύσιν[2]." So that Constantine exhorts the fathers
of that council to determine this whole controversy out of the
books of the prophets and apostles. *Secondly,* I reply, that his
assertion that Theodoret expressly writes that the Arians were
condemned by unwritten tradition, is untrue. For Theodoret writes
that a writing of Eusebius of Nicomedia was convicted of open blasphemy by the scriptures. His words are these: συνήγαγον ἐκ τῶν
γραφῶν, *they collected out of the scriptures* testimonies against
Eusebius and the other Arians[3]. I confess, indeed, that the term
ὁμοούσιος was proved orthodox out of antiquity, as having been
used 130 years before by bishops who then flourished in the church,

[1 Lib. II. c. xiv. §. 3. p. 848. Opp. T. x. Bassan. 1797.]

[2 ... τοῦ παναγίου πνεύματος τὴν διδασκαλίαν ἀνάγραπτον ἔχοντας. εὐαγγελικαὶ γάρ, φησι, βίβλοι καὶ ἀποστολικαὶ καὶ τῶν παλαιῶν προφητῶν τὰ θεσπίσματα σαφῶς ἡμᾶς ἃ χρὴ περὶ τοῦ θείου φρονεῖν ἐκπαιδεύουσι. τὴν πολεμοποιὸν
οὖν ἀπελάσαντες ἔριν, ἐκ τῶν θεοπνεύστων, κ. τ. ἑ.   Lib. I. 7.]

[3 αὕτη τῶν Ἀρειανῶν ἡ διεφθαρμένη διάνοια. ἀλλὰ καὶ ἐνταῦθα οἱ ἐπίσκοποι,
θεωρήσαντες ἐκείνων τὸ δόλιον, συνήγαγον ἐκ τῶν γραφῶν τὸ ἀπαύγασμα, τήν τε
πηγήν, κ. τ. ἑ.   Ibid. c. 8.]

since the Arians slanderously asserted it to be a new word. The
term, we confess, is not found in scripture; yet the meaning of the
term is found there. "The Arians," says Theodoret, in that same
place, "were condemned by the words of scripture rightly understood," ἐξ ἐγγράφων μετ᾿ εὐσεβείας ἐννοουμένων λέξεων κατεκρίθησαν. What could be written more expressly? He adds too
that the words of scripture alleged against the Arians had the same
force and meaning as the Homoüsios,—ταύτην ἔχει τὴν σημασίαν.

I come now to the second council of Nice, in the sixth session,
whereof these words occur: "Many things are observed by us
without the authority of scripture, as for example, the worship of
images[1]." I answer: We make no account of that council, and do
not acknowledge its authority; yea, we say that it was an impious
and wicked conventicle, wherein many things were concluded most
plainly against scripture. As the first council of Nice was truly
catholic, so this second council of Nice was absolutely heretical:
whereof we mean to speak in its proper place. If the papists had
any shame, they would themselves be ashamed of this council.
However, we take what he grants us, that these fathers have said
that the worship of images cannot be proved from scripture. Why
then is he not ashamed to abuse so foully so many places of
scripture for the support of this practice?

Thirdly, Bellarmine objects the eighth general council, in its
sixth action, where the fathers of that council say that they hold
the apostolic and ecclesiastical traditions. I answer in precisely
the same way as in the former case. We entertain no reverence
for the authority of this council, which was like the preceding, and
established a profane idolatry. It was held 900 years after
Christ. These were Bellarmine's councils. Hath he not given us
a beautiful demonstration of his thesis?

CHAPTER XII.

THE FOURTH ARGUMENT, FOUNDED UPON THE TESTIMONIES OF THE
FATHERS, IS ANSWERED.

In the fourth place, our opponent collects the testimonies of the
fathers; in the management of which argument he is large and

[1 καὶ ἐγγράφως καὶ ἀγράφως ἐκ τῶν ἀρχῆθεν χρόνων αὐτὰς.... ἐστήριξαν,
μεθ᾿ ὧν καὶ τὴν τῶν σεπτῶν εἰκόνων ἀνάδειξιν. Concill. Labbe et Cossart. T.
VII. p. 406. Paris. 1671.]

copious, yet so as to combine at the same time judgment and
selection. These we must needs answer, as well because our
adversaries repose on these their special confidence, as because it is
fit that all who are desirous of becoming learned divines should
be thoroughly acquainted with all these matters. Neither in this,
nor in any other controversy, can they possibly prevail against us
by the scriptures; and therefore they press us as closely as they
can with the authority of the fathers. Indeed, even though the
fathers were opposed to us, and we could give no answer to the
arguments drawn from them, this could inflict no real damage
upon our cause, since our faith does not depend upon the fathers,
but upon the scriptures. Nevertheless, I am far from approving
the opinion of those who think that the testimonies of the fathers
should be rejected or despised. Whether we regard then the
weakness of our brethren, or the confidence of our adversaries, we
should answer these testimonies also, nor deem our pains ill
expended upon such a task. However, we must take heed that we
do not, with the papists, ascribe too much to the fathers, but use
our rights and liberty when we read them; examining all their
sayings by the rule of scripture, receiving them when they agree
with it, but freely and with their good leave rejecting them whenever they exhibit marks of discrepancy.

He brings first into the field CLEMENS ROMANUS, a great man
undoubtedly, whom he sets upon a par with the apostles themselves.
What he hath written, says the Jesuit, in his book of the apostolic
canons, and his eight books of apostolical constitutions, he undoubtedly received from the apostles. I answer: Bellarmine's *undoubtedly*
is no sort of argument. We do not acknowledge this Clement, nor
make any account of the praises which Turrian[2] bestows upon him.
He praises and defends also the Decretal epistles, than which it is
quite certain that nothing is less deserving of praise. Eusebius,
H. E. Lib. III. c. 38, testifies that formerly many forged and adulterated pieces were published under the name of Clemens[3]. The
same historian affirms in the same chapter, that there is but one

---

[2 Pro Canon. Apostol. Florent. 1572.]

[3 ἰστέον δὲ ὡς καὶ δευτέρα τὶς εἶναι λέγεται τοῦ Κλήμεντος ἐπιστολή. Οὐ
μὴν ἔθ᾽ ὁμοίως τῇ προτέρᾳ καὶ ταύτην γνώριμον ἐπιστάμεθα, ὅτι μηδὲ καὶ τοὺς
ἀρχαίους αὐτῇ κεχρημένους ἴσμεν. Ἤδη δὲ καὶ ἕτερα πολυεπῆ καὶ μακρὰ συγ-
γράμματα ὡς τοῦ αὐτοῦ ἐχθὲς καὶ πρώην τινὲς προήγαγον ..... ὧν οὐδ᾽ ὅλως
μνήμη τις παρὰ τοῖς παλαιοῖς φέρεται· οὐδὲ γὰρ καθαρὸν τῆς ἀποστολικῆς ὀρθοδοξίας ἀποσώζει τὸν χαρακτῆρα.—Ed. Heinich. T. I. pp. 280—2.]

genuine epistle of this author, namely, that written to the Corinthians. Jerome testifies to the same point in his catalogue, under
the head of CLEMENS. Nicephorus also, Lib. III. c. 18, and
Epiphanius, *Hæres*. 30,[1] bear witness that the heretics formerly
took many things from the books of Clemens, but especially from
the book of the apostolical canons, which, together with the eight
books of Constitutions, was certainly condemned by the sixth
general council at Constantinople, Can. 2.[2] But when Bellarmine
affirms Clemens to have been the author of the apostolical canons,
he is at variance with the other papists, who say that these canons
were written by the apostles themselves, assembled at Antioch.
So Peresius[3], in the third part of his traditions, brings in Anacletus,
saying, that the apostles met at Antioch, and wrote these canons
there. But it easily appears that this is impossible : for in the
last canon is given an enumeration of the canonical books, many of
which were written after the death of some of the apostles : indeed,
James, the son of Zebedee, was slain by Herod Antipas, before any
book was written. These canons, therefore, were not written by all
the apostles. Besides, for what purpose should the apostles have
assembled ? Are we to say that it was to write their traditions,
when the papists maintain that the apostles judged that tradition
should be promulgated orally, and not by writing ? But if they
deemed it fit that traditions should be written, why did they not
write them in the books of scripture ? Farther, if these canons were
written by the apostles, they would have equal authority with the
canonical books, which even the papists themselves do not venture
to affirm. Again, there are some things in these canons which
even the papists do not approve ; as for example, in the fifth canon
these words occur : " If either a bishop or a priest dismiss his wife
under the pretext of religion, let him be excommunicated[4]." And,
in canon 8, we read thus : " If any priest, deacon, or bishop, doth
not join with him who communicates, let him be deposed from his

[1 c. 15, p. 139. ed. Petav. where, however, Epiphanius is not speaking of
these canons, but of the Recognitions of Clement.]

[2 He means the Quini-sext council *in Trullo* (Ann. 692). But there the
Canons are not condemned, but confirmed.—Bevereg. Pandectt. T. I. p. 158.]

[3 Peiresius Aiala, De Divin. Apost. atque Eccles. Traditionibus. Paris.
1550.]

[4 ἐπίσκοπος ἢ πρεσβύτερος ἢ διάκονος τὴν ἑαυτοῦ γυναῖκα μὴ ἐκβαλλέτω
προφάσει εὐλαβείας· ἐὰν δὲ ἐκβάλῃ, ἀφοριζέσθω.—It is can. VI. in Whiston's
Primit. Christ. Vol. II.]

office⁵." And in canon 9⁶ it is enjoined, that "the whole people should communicate with the minister who celebrates the eucharist; and if any do otherwise, let him be excommunicated." The papists do not observe these laws. Again, in canon 37, it is required that "councils should be held twice a-year⁷," which they themselves do not comply with. There is a matter in canon 46⁸ which they do not admit, as may readily be perceived from inspecting the canon itself. Finally, this book appears to be a farrago and patch-work, made up out of the acts of other councils, especially that of Antioch; for many similar things occur in the councils of Antioch. Now it is not probable that the Antiochene fathers took anything from these canons: for, if they had, they would not have concealed it, but rather have told it distinctly, in order to gain thereby the greater credit for their sanctions and decrees. They make, however, no mention of this book; a plain proof that it was then either not published or not allowed any apostolical authority.

I come now to the other book of Clemens, the Apostolical Constitutions; which also, if they really emanated from the apostles, would have equal authority with the canonical books. And indeed, in the last canon, these constitutions are ranked among the canonical books. The papists, however, do not yet venture to pass such a judgment upon this piece; which conduct cannot escape the charge of impiety, if the book is Clement's, and contains the constitutions of the apostles. It is a most weighty objection against the authority of this book also, that we read in the last canon, that this book should not be made public on account "of the mysteries which it contains," διὰ τὰ ἐν αὐτῷ μυστικά. This agrees better with the rites of Eleusis than with the christian religion. The apostles were sent to preach openly the message they had received from Christ, and to publish it to all, because necessary for all. "Those things which ye have heard in the ear, preach ye upon the housetops," says Christ to his apostles. And Paul says, 1 Cor. ii. 23: "I delivered unto you," that is, to you all, "that which I received of the Lord." Besides, even the papists themselves do

[⁵ εἴ τις ἐπίσκοπος ἢ πρεσβύτερος ἢ διάκονος..... προσφορᾶς γενομένης μὴ μεταλάβοι..... ἀφοριζέσθω.—can. ix.]
[⁶ can. x.]
[⁷ Δεύτερον τοῦ ἔτους σύνοδος γινέσθω τῶν ἐπισκόπων.—can. xxxviii.]
[⁸ ἐπίσκοπος ἢ πρεσβύτερος τὸν κατὰ ἀλήθειαν ἔχοντα βάπτισμα ἐὰν ἄνωθεν βαπτίσῃ, ἢ τὸν μεμολυσμένον παρὰ τῶν ἀσεβῶν ἐὰν μὴ βαπτίσῃ, καθαιρείσθω.—can. xlvii.]

not receive all the contents of this book, and many of them are manifestly false. In Lib. II. c. 59, Clemens, mentioning James the Lord's brother, excludes him from the number of the apostles[1]; whereas Paul, Galat. ii. 9, reckons him amongst even the leading apostles : yea, this author himself, Lib. vI. c. 14[2], as if he had forgotten himself, speaks of him as one of the apostles.   In Lib. II. c. 32, he mentions the Agapæ, and explains the manner of conducting them ; while Paul condemns them, 1 Cor. ii. 21 ; and it is certain that they were abolished long before.   In Lib. II. c. 63, he says that the people ought to assemble in the congregation twice a day, morning and evening[3]; which practice is not now observed even by the papists.   In Lib. v. c. 15, he says that those words which Christ spoke of Judas (" He that dippeth with me in the dish, the same is he that shall betray me") were uttered by Christ five days before the passover[4] : whereas it is evident from scripture, Matth. xxvi. 31, that Christ was betrayed that same night.   In the same book, c. 16, he affirms that Judas was absent when Christ celebrated the supper[5]; which contradicts not only scripture, but the fathers themselves.   Its repugnance to scripture is plain from a comparison of the three verses, 13, 14, and 15, of Luke xxii.   Nor is it less certain that it is opposed to the judgment of the fathers : for Dionysius, *Eccles. Hierarch.* c. 3, affirms him to have been present.   So Cyprian, in his discourse *de Ablutione Pedum.*   So Augustine, Epist. 163, and *Comment.* in Ps. 3, and in Ps. 10, and Tract. 63 in Joann.   So Chrysostom, in his Homily upon the thief.   So finally, Aquinas, in the third part of his *Sum.* Quæst. 81, art 2.   Pachymeres, indeed, upon Dionysius the Areopagite, *Eccles. Hierarch.* cap. 3, supposes Judas to have been absent; for thus he writes : " He delivered the mysteries to the disciples alone, after Judas had gone forth from supper, he being unworthy of them[6] :" but when he wrote this,

[1 Ἡμεῖς οὖν οἱ καταξιωθέντες εἶναι μάρτυρες τῆς παρουσίας αὐτοῦ, σὺν Ἰακώβῳ τῷ τοῦ Κυρίου ἀδελφῷ.—p. 259. c. 55.]

[2 p. 343; but that passage down to τὸ σκεῦος τῆς ἐκλογῆς is commonly thought an interpolation.]

[3 παραίνει τῷ λαῷ εἰς τὴν ἐκκλησίαν ἐνδελεχίζειν ὄρθρου καὶ ἑσπέρας ἑκάστης ἡμέρας.—c. 59, p. 267.]

[4 The constitutions speak only of its occurring, τῇ πέμπτῃ, i. e. the fifth day of the week.—p. 317.]

[5 Ἰούδα μὴ συμπαρόντος.—Ibid. See Jeremy Taylor's Life of Christ, Part 3. Sect. xv. §. 13, and the authors there cited.]

[6 τὰ μυστήρια μόνοις τοῖς μαθηταῖς μετὰ τὸ ἐξελθεῖν ἐκεῖνον ἐκ τοῦ δείπνου παρέδωκεν, ὡς ἀναξίου τούτων ὄντος Ἰούδα.]

he followed his own conjectures and opinion, not scripture. This same Clemens, Lib. v. c. 18,[7] enjoins observances of Easter which Epiphanius, writing against the Audians, blames as heretical, *Hæres.* 50 ; and, indeed, Epiphanius there tells us that the Audians defended their opinion by the authority of an apostolical constitution. Carolus Bovius writes thus upon that passage : " Wherefore it is so far from being true that the apostles established what we read in this chapter, that even the direct contrary seems to have been enjoined by them[8]." This is a fine author of apostolical traditions. Besides, in Lib. vi. c. 14,[9] he mentions an epistle which he states to have been written by all the apostles along with Paul; whereas James, the son of Zebedee, was dead before Paul came into the apostolic college. This, therefore, is demonstrably false. Finally, in Lib. vii. c. 24,[10] he brings forward several regulations void of all authority about fasting upon the fourth and sixth days of the week, and the observance of the sabbath (Saturday) and the Lord's day ; and he says that we should not fast upon any Saturday save that one whereon the Lord lay in the sepulchre : all which are now exploded by the papists. It is therefore manifest that this book is not genuine, but supposititious, and composed by some pretended Clemens. This is so clear, that Bellarmine himself hath thought fit to omit this author in his published edition, and brand him with this mark of insult.

In the second place he objects IGNATIUS, who, as Eusebius testifies, Lib. iii. c. 35,[11] exhorted all the churches to adhere to the apostolic traditions, which traditions he asserts that he had "also

[7 The constitutions there direct that Easter should *not* be kept with the Jews, which is directly opposed to the apostolical rule as given by Epiphanius, Hæres. lxx. §. 10 : ὁρίζουσι γὰρ ἐν τῇ διατάξει οἱ ἀπόστολοι, ὅτι ὑμεῖς μὴ ψηφίζητε, ἀλλὰ ποιῆτε, ὅταν οἱ ἀδελφοὶ ὑμῶν οἱ ἐκ περιτομῆς· μετ' αὐτῶν ἅμα ποιεῖτε.... κἄν τε πλανηθῶσι, μηδὲ ὑμῖν μελέτω.—Grabe, Spicil. i. 46. It is observable that Epiphanius does not venture directly to impugn this rule, though he is obliged to recur to a monstrous device to evade its natural meaning.]

[8 Quare tantum abest, ut ea quæ in hac capite legimus apostoli statuerint, ut etiam contraria horum ab ipsis præcepta videantur.]

[9 The names 'Ιάκωβος καὶ 'Ιωάννης, υἱοὶ Ζεβεδαίου, occur there in the enumeration of the apostles then assembled. But the passage is probably an interpolation.]

[10 ὑμεῖς δὲ ἢ τὰς πέντε νηστεύσατε ἡμέρας, ἢ τετράδα καὶ παρασκευήν.... τὸ σάββατον μέντοι καὶ τὴν κυριακὴν ἑορτάζετε.... ἐν δὲ μόνον σάββατον.... ὅπερ νηστεύειν προσῆκεν.—p. 369.]

[11 The Greek is given in the text, *infra.*]

left in writing by way of precaution, and lest posterity should be reduced to any doubt concerning them." I answer : First, the passage of Eusebius is either originally obscure or now corrupted, as is plain from an inspection of the Greek text. By the tradition thus mentioned, Eusebius means the sincere doctrine of the apostolic preaching, as is manifest from the place itself. His words are, ἀπρὶξ ἔχεσθαι τῶν ἀποστόλων παραδόσεως. If he had meant such numerous traditions as the papists dream of, he would not have said παραδόσεως, but παραδόσεων. Ignatius, perceiving that many heretics had at that time begun to corrupt the apostolic doctrine, declared that it seemed necessary to him that it should be committed to writing, " for the sake of security," ὑπὲρ ἀσφαλείας διατυποῦσθαι, and as a provision for posterity. Therefore, when he was at Smyrna, he wrote letters to various churches, wherein he comprised those traditions to which Eusebius here refers ; and that these were no popish traditions may be understood from the circumstance, that in these epistles Ignatius disputes against Simon, Cerinthus, Menander, and other heretics, who entertained impious sentiments concerning the person of Christ. Now against the heresies of such there is no need of unwritten traditions, inasmuch as they are plainly condemned in the scriptures. Bellarmine hath not followed Eusebius himself, but the faulty version of Ruffinus, where " traditions " are spoken of in the plural, whereas the Greek has "tradition" in the singular ; and certain words not found in the Greek are subjoined, to the effect that Ignatius "left these traditions in writing." Besides, Ruffinus says that the apostolic tradition required to be written for the benefit of posterity, that no doubt might remain with succeeding generations : but the traditions of the papists are, in the first place, most uncertain, so as that the interests of posterity seem not sufficiently therein consulted ; secondly, the papists cannot find all their traditions in these epistles of Ignatius ; nay, not the thousandth part of them. Bellarmine produces only three traditions out of Ignatius, namely, Lent, minor orders, and the Lord's day. As to Lent, I confess that it is mentioned in the epistle to the Philippians : but of that elsewhere. As to orders, he does indeed reckon a few of them, but not as sacraments ; nor does he enumerate them in the same manner as the papists do, since he mentions singers, whom they do not make even a minor order. However, the third tradition, of the Lord's day, is no unwritten verity, for it is contained in the scriptures ; as namely, Rev. i. 10. ἐν τῇ κυριακῇ ἡμέρᾳ. 1 Cor. xvi. 1 ; Acts xx. 7, μιᾷ σαββάτων. The words

of Eusebius, where he speaks of Ignatius, are these : προύτρεπέ τ᾽
ἀπρὶξ ἔχεσθαι τῆς τῶν ἀποστόλων παραδόσεως, ἣν ὑπὲρ ἀσφαλείας
καὶ ἐγγράφως ἤδη μαρτυρόμενος διατυπουσθαι ἀναγκαῖον ἡγεῖτο.
Which passage our countryman, Christopherson, hath thus translated:
" Then he exhorted them to adhere closely to the apostolic tradition;
to which having borne stedfast witness, he judged that, for its safer
preservation to succeeding time, it should be committed to writing[1]." The sense of which words is that, when Ignatius had borne
witness to and professed the apostolic faith by word of mouth,
he deemed it necessary to commit the same to writing also, in order
to check the heretics more effectually, and provide for the service of
the churches hereafter. Upon which account, as it follows immediately in that same place, he wrote various epistles. Hence we
gather against the papists, that Ignatius deemed it no way safe that
any doctrine should be left in an unwritten state. Yet these men
pretend that the apostles delivered down many things in an unwritten form, as if they could not have foreseen the necessity of
that which Ignatius, a very short time after the apostles, perceived
to be necessary in the highest degree.

Secondly, I say, that it may be doubted whether these epistles,
which are said to be Ignatius', are his or not. For Theodoret,
in his third Dialogue against the heretics, cites certain words
from the epistle to the Smyrnæans, which are not found in that
epistle as now extant. The words as they stand in Theodoret
are these : " They receive not eucharists and oblations, because
they do not confess that the eucharist is the flesh of our Saviour
Jesus Christ, which suffered for our sins, and which the Father
raised again in his mercy[2]." Theodoret cites this sentence from

[1 Deinde hortatus est, ut apostolorum traditioni mordicus adhærescerent:
quam quidem asseveranter testificatus, quo tutius posteritati reservaretur,
necessario scriptis mandandam existimavit. Valesius translates it thus:
Hortatusque est ut apostolorum traditionibus tenaciter inhærerent: quas
quidem ad certiorem posteritatis notitiam testimonio suo confirmatas, scriptis
mandare necessarium duxit. But may not ἤδη μαρτυρόμενος mean, " being now
upon the point of martyrdom?"—though I confess the active μαρτυρέω is the
regular form in such cases.]

[2 εὐχαριστίας καὶ προσφορὰς οὐκ ἀποδέχονται, διὰ τὸ μὴ ὁμολογεῖν τὴν
εὐχαριστίαν σάρκα εἶναι τοῦ Σωτῆρος ἡμῶν Ἰησοῦ Χριστοῦ, τὴν ὑπὲρ τῶν ἁμαρτιῶν
ἡμῶν παθοῦσαν, ἣν χρηστότητι ὁ πατὴρ ἤγειρεν.—c. 19. p. 106. Tigur. 1593.
These words are to be found in the shorter epistles, ad Smyrnæos. c. 6.
p. 412. ed. Jacobs: but it is to be remembered that the Florentine text was
first published by Is. Vossius, Amstel. 1646. The publication of the still

Ignatius' epistle to the Smyrnæans, which is nowhere to be discovered in the present epistle to the Smyrnæans.   Jerome also,
in his third Dialogue against the Pelagians, hath produced a testimony from the epistles of Ignatius which is not at present to be
found in them.   "Ignatius," says he, "an apostolic man and a
martyr, writes boldly, ' The Lord chose for his apostles those who
were sinners above all men'[1]."   Now in these epistles Ignatius hath
written nothing of the kind ; and if he ever wrote it, he did so with
more boldness than truth : for who would venture to say that the
apostles were the greatest sinners among all mankind ?   Eusebius,
Lib. III. cap. 36, testifies that Ignatius wrote seven epistles to certain churches : but there are now extant twelve.   Jerome too, in
his Catalogue under the title IGNATIUS, enumerates only seven[2] :
whence it is plain that the other five are undoubtedly spurious.
These are, the epistle to Mary, to the Tarsensians, to Hero, to the
Antiochenes, to the Philippians, from which last are derived almost
all the passages which our adversaries seize upon in Ignatius for
the defence of traditions.   Neither Eusebius nor Jerome makes any
mention of these epistles : therefore it is certain that they are
supposititious.   What we should determine about the rest, whether
they are Ignatius' or some other writer's, is far from clear ; since
some passages are cited by ancient authors from the epistles of
Ignatius, which are wanting in these pieces.   Eusebius, Lib. III. c.
36, testifies[3] that Polycarp, in his epistle to the Philippians, writes
that he had been requested by Ignatius to convey their epistle into
Syria.   This is not to be found in the epistle of Ignatius to Polycarp
which we now have.   Many proofs might be brought forward from
the epistle to the Philippians, which epistle the Papists principally
object to us, demonstrating it not to be the work of Ignatius, a man

shorter Syriac text by Cureton, Lond. 1845, has confirmed the suspicions
which most unprejudiced critics entertained of the integrity of even the
Florentine text.]

[1 Ignatius, vir apostolicus et martyr, scribit audacter, Elegit Dominus
apostolos qui super omnes homines peccatores erant.   But there can be
little doubt that Jerome here by mistake wrote Ignatius for Barnabas.—See
Barnab. Ep. c. 5, p. 131. Monach. 1844 : τοὺς ἰδίους ἀποστόλους . . . . ἐξελέξατο,
ὄντας ὑπὲρ πᾶσαν ἁμαρτίαν ἀνομωτέρους.]

[2 Scripsit unam epistolam ad Ephesios, alteram ad Magnesianos, tertiam
ad Trullenses, quartam ad Romanos.   Et inde egrediens scripsit ad Philadel-
pheos, et ad Smyrnæos, et proprie ad Polycarpum.]

[3 ἐγράψατέ μοι καὶ ὑμεῖς καὶ Ἰγνάτιος, ἵνα ἐάν τις ἀπέρχηται εἰς Συρίαν, καὶ
τὰ παρ' ὑμῶν ἀποκομίσῃ γράμματα.—T. I. p. 277.]

of the next age to the apostles. In it he writes: "If any one fast upon the Lord's day, or any sabbath but that only whereon the Lord lay in the grave, he is a murderer of Christ[4]." Now Augustine in his last epistle to Jerome affirms, that it was customary at Rome to fast on Saturday. And, in Epist. 86, he says that it is lawful also to fast upon the Lord's day. Again, Ignatius says in that same epistle[5], that if any one keep the passover with the Jews, he is partner and in communion with those who murdered Christ, κοινωνός ἐστι τῶν ἀποκτεινάντων τὸν Κύριον. Now it is certain that Polycarp kept Easter with the Jews, and (if we believe others) that John and Philip did so too. In his epistle to Mary he says that Clemens succeeded Anacletus[6]: but the papists make him to have succeeded Peter; and Peter in his own lifetime calls him bishop and citizen of Rome, Constit. Apost. Lib. VI. c. 8.[7] In the epistles to the Philadelphians and Antiochenes he assumes not to himself any apostolical authority; which he ought to have done, if he were prescribing apostolic traditions to the churches: for apostolical dogmas should be received as of equal authority with apostolical writings. In like manner Jerome, in his third Dialogue against the Pelagians, attributes to him no such great authority. But if Ignatius had published apostolic traditions, he should have claimed for himself the highest authority. Besides, although the papists sometimes object these epistles to us, and seem to set a high value upon them, they cannot deny that many things are found in them which they themselves do not approve. In the epistle to the Philadelphians, he says that a bishop ought to be chosen by the church itself. Then, in the same epistle, he maintains that a bishop is subject to no one, nor bound to render an account to any one but Christ himself. This, I am very sure, the papists will not bear, who would make all bishops responsible to the Roman pontiffs. In the epistle to the Trallians he writes, that there is no " elect

[4 εἴ τις κυριακὴν ἢ σάββατον νηστεύει, πλὴν ἑνὸς σαββάτου τοῦ πάσχα, οὗτος χριστοκτόνος ἐστίν.—p. 112. Ed. Voss. Lond. 1680.]

[5 εἴ τις μετὰ Ἰουδαίων ἐπιτελεῖ τὸ πάσχα, ἢ τὰ σύμβολα τῆς ἑορῆς αὐτῶν δέχεται, κοινωνός ἐστι τῶν ἀποκτεινάντων τὸν Κύριον καὶ τοὺς ἀποστόλους αὐτοῦ. —Ibid.]

[6 So in the Latin: adhuc existente te in Roma, apud beatum papam Cletum; cui successit ad præsens digne beatus.—Clemens. p. 72. But Vossius' Greek Text reads πάπᾳ Λίνῳ.]

[7 συμπαρόντων μοι (Petrus loquitur).... ἀδελφῶν Κλήμεντος τοῦ Ρωμαίων ἐπισκόπου τε καὶ πολίτου.—p. 387.]

church¹," ἐκκλησίαν ἐκλεκτήν, without a bishop, deacons, and presbyters : and in the same epistle he professes himself able to understand "heavenly things," τὰ ἐπουράνια, the whole celestial state,
and all the ranks of angels; and yet declares himself inferior to
Peter and Paul², who yet neither of them had much skill in such
matters.   In the epistle to the Magnesians he expresses an opinion
that greatly needs confirmation, that no presbyter, deacon, or
lay-man, should do anything without the bishop, even as Christ
does nothing without the Father³; and then he cites the passage,
"I can of mine own self do nothing." But we have said enough of
these epistles ; and it may be gathered sufficiently from the previous
remarks, what judgment should be formed of this Ignatius.   The
papists do not venture to defend these things : yet they ought to
defend Ignatius in everything, if there be any truth in their
assertion, that he committed the apostolical traditions to writing.

   In the third place follows HEGESIPPUS, a man undoubtedly of
great name and authority.   Eusebius, Lib. IV. c. 8, writes concerning
him, that he comprised apostolical traditions in five books⁴ ; and
although (says Bellarmine) those books are not now extant, yet we
may thence infer that the apostles did not themselves write everything that they taught.   I answer : I acknowledge that the testimony of Eusebius is clear ; but I reply, that under the term tradition
the doctrine of the apostles, and not unwritten traditions, is denoted.
For so Eusebius states that he comprised in those books the sincere
and undissembled exposition of the apostolic preaching, τὴν ἀπλανῆ
παράδοσιν τοῦ ἀποστολικοῦ κηρύγματος : whence it is plain that
he wrote no other things than those which are delivered in scripture.   Jerome, in his catalogue, under the head HEGESIPPUS⁵,
affirms that these books contain the history of what was done by
Christ, the apostles, and succeeding bishops, down to Hegesippus'
own time.   However, we should bear in mind Bellarmine's ad-

[¹ χωρὶς τούτων ἐκκλησία ἐκλεκτὴ οὐκ ἔστιν.—p. 157.]
   [² καὶ δύναμαι νοεῖν τὰ ἐπουράνια, καὶ τὰς ἀγγελικὰς τάξεις... ταῦτα γινώσκων ἐγώ,
οὐ πάντως ἤδη τετελείωμαι, ἢ μαθητής εἰμι οἷος Παῦλος καὶ Πέτρος.—pp. 158, 159.]
   [³ ὥσπερ οὖν ὁ Κύριος ἄνευ τοῦ Πατρὸς οὐδὲν ποιεῖ, οὐ δύναμαι γὰρ, φησὶ,
ποιεῖν ἀπ᾽ ἐμαυτοῦ οὐδὲν, οὕτω καὶ ὑμεῖς ἄνευ τοῦ ἐπισκόπου, μηδὲ πρεσβύτερος,
μηδὲ διάκονος, μηδὲ λαϊκός.—p. 146.]
      [⁴ ἐν πέντε δὴ οὖν συγγράμμασιν οὗτος τὴν ἀπλανῆ παράδοσιν τοῦ ἀποστολικοῦ
κηρύγματος ἀπλουστάτῃ συντάξει γραφῆς ὑπομνηματισάμενος.—T. I. p. 309. Ed.
Hein.]
      [⁵ Omnes a passione Domini usque ad suam ætatem ecclesiasticorum
actuum tenens historias.—c. 22.]

mission, that these books are not now extant. For there are now extant five books under the name of Hegesippus[6], which he does not venture to defend, because they contain a history, not from Christ to his own times, but from the Maccabees to the destruction of Jerusalem. Besides, the Hegesippus now extant informs us that many more books than five were written by him, while Jerome and Eusebius mention five only. Lastly, this Hegesippus, Lib. III. c. 5, makes mention of the city and church of Constantinople, and says that new Rome, that is Constantinople, was made equal to the old. Now this did not take place before the times of Constantine, by whom that name was given to the city : whereas the old Hegesippus lived long before Constantine's times. Hence it sufficiently appears that books do not always belong to the authors whose names they bear : for who would not suppose these books of Hegesippus to be genuine, if it were not manifest from their own contents that they are supposititious ? Let us come now to the remaining fathers.

I come therefore to DIONYSIUS the Areopagite[7], whom our opponent specially objects to us, as an author of undoubted excellence. From him he produces a clear testimony, taken from his book of the Ecclesiastical Hierarchy, c. 1, where Dionysius says, that " the chiefs of the sacerdotal function (that is the apostles) delivered these sublime and supersubstantial (ὑπερούσια) matters, partly in writing, and partly without writing[8]," ἐγγράφοις καὶ ἀγράφοις μνήσεσι. I answer, confessing that Dionysius is in some places a great patron of traditions. However, even if he were the true, and not a supposititious, false and pretended Dionysius, they would be able to allege but few things from him in defence of their traditions. Yet, since he undertook to write upon the Ecclesiastical Hierarchy, he would have been bound to develope accurately all the apostolical traditions, if any such there were, and if he were indeed the true Areopagite, the disciple of Paul, which for my part I am far from thinking; although I perceive that his defence hath been engaged in very zealously by some great men, and especially by Ambrosius

[6 Paris. 1511.]

[7 See Daillè De Scriptis quæ sub Dionysii Areopag. et Ignatii hominibus circumferuntur.—Genev. 1666. and compare Pearson, Vindic. Ignat. Part. 1. cap. 10. pp. 136—148. Cantab. 1672.]

[8 Σεπτότατα δὲ λόγια ταῦτά φαμεν, ὅσα πρὸς τῶν ἐνθέων ἡμῶν ἱεροτελεστῶν ἐν ἁγιογράφοις ἡμῖν καὶ θεολογικοῖς δεδώρηται δέλτοις, καὶ μὴν ὅσα πρὸς τῶν αὐτῶν ἱερῶν ἀνδρῶν ἀϋλωτέρᾳ μυήσει καὶ γείτονί πως ἤδη τῆς οὐρανίας ἱεραρχίας ἐκ νοὸς εἰς νοῦν, διὰ μέσου λόγου .... γραφῆς ἐκτός, οἱ καθηγεμόνες ἡμῶν ἐμυή-θησαν.—Dionys. Areop. Opp. T. I. p. 201. Paris. 1644.]

Conraldulensis. Bellarmine too waxes wroth with Luther and Calvin for denying these books to be the production of Dionysius the Areopagite. It is necessary therefore to say something upon the authority of these books: and I will bring forward, not conjectures or suspicions, but most certain demonstrations to shew that this is not the true Dionysius. *First,* Eusebius and Jerome make no mention of these books; which ought to be a very weighty proof that they were not composed by Dionysius. They used the utmost diligence in collecting and searching for the books of the ancients, so as that, if even a single epistle were written by any distinguished man, they took care not to omit mentioning it: and can we believe it possible that they either did not see such books as these, written upon such great and distinguished subjects, or judged them not worthy of being noticed? *Secondly,* no author of any considerable antiquity mentions these books: which proves sufficiently that they cannot belong to the same remote age as Dionysius the Areopagite. For many things therein occur which make against the ancient heretics, especially the Arians, and which certainly the Nicene fathers would not have failed to urge, if such books were then extant, or the author of them had been held in any estimation. *Thirdly,* the style of these books is not plain and simple, but too subtle, inflated and full of affectation, very unlike the apostolic. *Fourthly,* Erasmus, upon Acts xvii, is large in proving that this is not the true Dionysius. And before him Valla, upon the same place thinks that a heretic by name Apollinaris was the writer of these books which pass under the name of Dionysius. Theodore Gaza, too, in his Preface to the Problems of Alexander Aphrodisius, addressed to Nicholas V. denies that this is the true and ancient Dionysius. Likewise Cajetan, in his commentary upon Acts xvii, says, that "these books were not written by the apostolic Dionysius[1]." There were many Dionysiuses formerly in the church: perhaps these books were written by some of them, and afterwards, under a false impression, attributed to Dionysius the Areopagite, who was the most famous of that name. *Fifthly,* it appears most clearly from the books themselves, what opinion we should form of this sort of writers. In the books of the Celestial Hierarchy he treats a subject surely divine, the very order of the heavenly commonwealth; an argument full of difficulty and audacity. The apostle Paul, 2 Cor. xii. 14, says, that "these and

[1 An autem istemet sit ille Dionysius.... *certum non est.*—p. 495. 2. Paris. 1571.]

other such subjects are ineffable :" he adds besides, " that it is not lawful for a man to utter them." How then could Dionysius dare to utter these things, even if he knew them ? Or from what source could he possibly come to know them ? Whence, I beseech you, did he derive this wondrous knowledge ? From revelation ? How is this proved ? Why were they not rather revealed to the apostles, if it concerned us to know such things ? If we have no concern in them, then why hath Dionysius published these mysteries ? Irenæus, Lib. II. c. 55, expresses a noble sentiment condemnatory of these writers of hierarchies : " There is nothing sound in what they say : they are mad ; nor should we abandon Moses and the prophets to believe in them. Let them tell us the nature of things invisible ; let them tell the number of the angels, and the ranks of the archangels ; let them shew the mystery of the thrones, and explain the differences of dominations, princedoms, powers and virtues : but this they cannot tell us[2]." Whence it manifestly appears that such a subject was secret, unknown, unheard of, and as yet handled by no writer. Yet all these things are explained in the books of this Dionysius. Augustine, in his Enchiridion (*ad Laurent.*) c. 58, declares himself ignorant of the ranks of angels and their differences, what are thrones, what dominations, what principalities, what powers. " Let those," says he, " tell who can, provided they can prove what they say[3]." We return the same answer to the papists. Dionysius, indeed, tells all these things, but gives no proofs. Besides, Gregory the Great gives a different description of the ranks of angels from this Dionysius; and so Bernard also (as Eckius confesses) *Hom.* 4. *de Festo Michaelis.* Now if this Dionysius had obtained such high credit, or his books held such great authority, these writers would never have ventured to differ from him. So far concerning the Celestial Hierarchy.

Sixthly, in his book of the Ecclesiastical Hierarchy he writes largely of temples, altars, holy places, the choir, and the placing of catechumens without the portals of the temple. Now there was

[2 Non enim sunt magis idonei hi quam scripturæ, nec relinquentes nos eloquia Domini, et Moysem, et reliquos prophetas qui veritatem præconiaverint, his credere oportet, sanum quidem nihil dicentibus, instabilia autem delirantibus .... Dicant nobis quæ sit invisibilium natura, enarrent numerum angelorum et ordinem archangelorum, demonstrent thronorum sacramenta, et doceant diversitates dominationum, principatuum, potestatum atque virtutum. Sed hoc non habent dicere.—c. 54, pp. 212, 213, ed. Fevard.]

[3 Dicant qui possunt, si tamen possunt probare quod dicunt : ego me ista ignorare confiteor.—p. 209. Lips. 1838.]

[WHITAKER.]

37

nothing of the kind in existence in those times when Dionysius
lived.   In that age, by reason of their tyrannous oppressors, the
Christians were compelled to meet in hidden and concealed places,
and there to hold their prayers and sermons.   Besides, he mentions monks, *Hierarch. Ecclesiast.* c. 8.[1]   Now the papists grant
that Paul and Antony were the parents of the monks; and they
flourished some ages after Dionysius the Areopagite.   Certainly
there were no monks in the times of the apostles.   In his book of
the Divine Names, c. 4[2], he cites from Ignatius' epistle to the
Romans this very brief but very sweet sentence, ὁ ἐμὸς ἔρως
ἐσταύρωται, "my love is crucified."   Now Ignatius sent this
epistle to the Romans when he was on his journey to Rome with
the prospect of certain death, in the reign of Trajan, as we are
informed by Eusebius in his Chronicon, and in his Ecclesiastical
History, Lib. III. c. 36, and by Jerome in his Catalogue.   But
Methodius, in the Martyrdom of Dionysius, and Simeon Metaphrastes, in his Life, write that Dionysius the Areopagite was slain
in the reign of Domitian.   In the end of his book of the Ecclesiastical Hierarchy he calls Timothy his son, who nevertheless was his
equal in authority, weight, learning, and every kind of dignity.
In his seventh epistle, that to Polycarp[3], he writes that he was in
Egypt when that celebrated eclipse of the sun over the whole
world took place, at the time that our Lord Jesus Christ suffered
death upon the cross.   Yet Origen, *Tractat.* 35[4] *in Matth.* denies that this was an eclipse of the sun, because it was then full
moon, and an eclipse of the sun takes place only at the new moon.
He says besides, that the darkness spoken of by Matthew, xxvii. 45,
was not universal (for then some history would have mentioned it),
but local and confined to the land of Judæa.   Jerome[5], in his com-

[1] ἡ δὲ τελουμένων ἁπασῶν ὑψηλοτέρα τάξις, ἡ τῶν μοναχῶν ἐστιν ἱερὰ
διακόσμησις.—ut supra, p. 330.]

[2] γράφει δὲ καὶ ὁ θεῖος Ἰγνάτιος, ὁ ἐμὸς ἔρως ἐσταύρωται.—ibid. pp. 467,
477.]

[3] ἀμφοτέρω γὰρ τότε κατὰ Ἡλιούπολιν ἅμα παρόντε τε καὶ συνεστῶτε,
παραδόξως τῷ Ἡλίῳ τὴν Σελήνην ἐμπιπτοῦσαν ἑωρῶμεν, οὐ γὰρ ἦν συνόδου καιρός.
p. 775.]

[4] Quomodo ergo poterat fieri defectio solis, cum luna esset plena, et
plenitudinem solis haberet?.... Arbitror ergo, sicut cetera signa quæ facta
sunt in passione ipsius, in Hierusalem tantummodo facta sunt, sic et tenebræ
tantummodo super omnem terram Judæam sunt factæ usque ad horam nonam.
—Origen. Opp. part. II. p. 128.   Paris 1619.]

[5] Videturque mihi clarissimum lumen mundi, hoc est luminare majus,

mentary on Matthew, says that this was no eclipse, but that the sun wrapped in darkness withdrew his beams, and would not look upon so horrible a crime. If there had been such an eclipse, profane authors would certainly have mentioned it. But the probability is that, as Origen says, this darkness pervaded Judæa only, as formerly Egypt. Erasmus[6] is of the same opinion. I am not solicitous about the point; but hence I draw an inference, that these fathers had either not seen these books, or did not ascribe so much to them as the papists claim in their behalf.

Our countrymen, the Rhemists, in their annotations upon Acts i. cite a certain epistle of Dionysius to Timothy which is not to be found amongst those at present extant in Greek; for there are no more than ten epistles in the Greek copies: perhaps they would have this to be the eleventh. They say that a narrative is given in this epistle of the translation and assumption of the body of the blessed Virgin Mary : for Dionysius, as they affirm, writes that he and the twelve apostles were present at Mary's death. Now how was this possible, when they had before this parted company and gone into different parts and climes of the world? He says that they all assembled by a miracle, except Thomas, who did not arrive till three days after the Virgin's death. But these things can by no means be made to hang together. For the papists, as we read in the New Sacerdotale, part. i. p. 156, maintain that Mary conceived in the 14th year of her age, bore her son in the 15th, and it is certain that she lived thirty-three years with Christ. She was, consequently, 47 years of age when Christ died and ascended. Now they say that she died 16 years after Christ's ascension, in the 63rd year of her age. She lived therefore 15, or at most 16 years after Christ's ascension. But James, the brother of John, was put to death the third, or as some say the tenth year after Christ's ascension, in the reign of Claudius; and so say Genebrard in his Chronology, and Eusebius in his Chronicon. He died therefore six years at least before the death of Mary, and could not be present at her departure, unless indeed he dropped from heaven specially to attend her funeral. Besides, Dionysius' pretence that

retraxisse radios suos, ne aut pendentem videret Dominum, aut impii blasphemantes sua luce fruerentur.—Hieronym. Opp. T. IV. col. 139. Paris. 1706.]

[6 Indicat Origenes in nonnullis codicibus adjectum fuisse, tenebræ factæ sunt super totam terram deficiente sole, quasi solis deliquium eas induxerit. Atque ita certe tradit epistola quæ nomine Dionysii circumfertur, mihi ψευδεπίγραφος videtur.—p. 110. Basil. 1535.]

he was himself present is also false : for Dionysius was a senator
of Athens in the 17th year after Christ's ascension, which was certainly the year when Paul came to Athens. Mary therefore had
died before Dionysius was converted by Paul to the christian faith.
But this Dionysius, who is said to have been present at the death
of Mary along with the apostles, seems to have been a most zealous
adherent of the christian faith, and on familiar terms with the
apostles.

Lastly, even the papists themselves do not approve or receive
all the traditions of Dionysius. For, in the first place, he testifies
that Christians used in those times to receive the eucharist every
day. Besides, he describes a public not a private, a whole and
not a half-communion, *Hierarch. Eccles.* c. 3 ; and records in the
same place the reading of scripture and the public prayers to have
been made in the vulgar tongue. These points make against the
papists. In the seventh chapter of his Ecclesiastical Hierarchy
he relates a strange custom of the ancient church at funerals. He
says they used to salute the corpse, and then pour oil upon it ;
which customs are not practised by the papists now. They do
indeed diligently anoint the living, but bestow neither oil nor
salutations upon the dead. Bellarmine says that, although Luther
and Calvin reject these books, yet the circumstance of their being
quoted by Gregory the great in his Homily upon the hundred
sheep, and by others, proves that they are neither modern nor
despicable. I answer : I confess that they are not modern nor
despicable ; but the question is, whether they are the work of
Dionysius the disciple of Paul. Gregory the great, although he
mentions them, yet does not follow them in all things. Besides,
Athanasius, Jerome, Chrysostom, Augustine, and other fathers
older than Gregory, make no mention of these books. There is
no reason why we should not suppose that these books were published before Gregory, who gained the place and reputation of a
great doctor of the church after six hundred years had elapsed
from the time of Christ. But Bellarmine could produce or name
no author near the apostolic age, who hath mentioned these books ;
a sufficient evidence that they were unheard of in the more ancient
times, and are no genuine production of the Areopagite[1].

In the fifth place, he produces POLYCARP, a distinguished and

[1 See a curious discussion of the authenticity of these books in Hakewill's
Apologie (Lond. 1635.) Lib. v. pp. 208—226, between Hakewill and Good-
man, bishop of Gloucester.]

constant Christian, adorned with the illustrious crown of martyrdom. Eusebius, Lib. v. c. 20, relates of him out of Irenæus, that he was wont to repeat by heart many things which he had heard from the apostles concerning our Lord, and which he had written not on paper, but in his heart. I answer, in the first place: The passage in Eusebius should be referred to. Irenæus is writing against a certain heretic Florinus, who maintained that evil beings were created such by God. Then he desires him to remember Polycarp, the outlines and substance of whose teaching he recalls to his mind. For Florinus had been with Polycarp, and Irenæus also, in his youth, had heard Polycarp discoursing concerning the faith; and he goes on to speak of the place where Polycarp used to relate to the people many things about Christ, his miracles and his doctrine, which he had heard from those who had seen Christ, and which he had traced not on paper but on his heart[2]. Now why is all this alleged? Does it follow that because Polycarp said many things which he had heard from eye-witnesses, and because Irenæus engraved them upon his heart, therefore these things are not written, or unwritten traditions are necessary to salvation? His mention of eye-witnesses does not prove that the same things as he related were not written, but only that he wished to win the greater credit for what he said by this circumstance. Nor does the fact of Irenæus having inscribed these lessons upon his heart[3], prove that they could not have been written in books; but only that he, though a boy, had engraved the words of Polycarp so deeply upon his mind, that the memory of them remained perpetually fixed therein. Ought not all sound doctrine to be imprinted upon our minds, even though the sacred books deliver it also?

Secondly, Irenæus in that same place testifies that all the things which Polycarp used to relate from memory concerning Christ were "accordant with the scriptures," σύμφωνα ταῖς γραφαῖς. Let the papists introduce such traditions, and no others, and we will receive them willingly. But Bellarmine, in order to gain

[2 ὥστε με δύνασθαι εἰπεῖν καὶ τὸν τόπον ἐν ᾧ καθεζόμενος διελέγετο .... καὶ τὰς διαλέξεις ἃς ἐποιεῖτο πρὸς τὸ πλῆθος, καὶ τὴν κατὰ Ἰωάννου συναναστροφὴν ὡς ἀπήγγελλε, καὶ τὴν μετὰ τῶν λοιπῶν τῶν ἑωρακότων τὸν Κύριον· καὶ ὡς ἀπεμνημόνευε τοὺς λόγους αὐτῶν, καὶ περὶ τοῦ Κυρίου τίνα ἦν ἃ παρ' ἐκείνων ἀκηκόει, καὶ περὶ τῶν δυνάμεων αὐτοῦ, καὶ περὶ τῆς διδασκαλίας, ὡς παρὰ αὐτοπτῶν τῆς ζωῆς τοῦ λόγου παρειληφὼς ὁ Πολύκαρπος ἀπήγγελλε πάντα σύμφωνα ταῖς γραφαῖς.— T. II. p. 100.]

[3 ταῦτα .... ἤκουον, ὑπομνηματιζόμενος αὐτὰ οὐκ ἐν χάρτῃ, ἀλλ' ἐν τῇ ἐμῇ καρδίᾳ.—ibid.]

something from this passage, insists that Irenæus' saying that these things were consonant to scripture, is not inconsistent with their not being written. For it is not, says he, everything that is consonant to scripture, that can immediately be proved by scripture; for all truth is consonant to scripture, but all truth is not contained in scripture, nor can be proved by it. This he wishes to be taken as an answer to Chemnitzius. I answer : Firstly, that Irenæus in this place indicates plainly enough what he means by styling these things *consonant* to scripture. He had to deal with the heretic Florinus, who, as we have already said, asserted that evil things were created by God. This was the heresy he wished to refute : now this may be most plainly refuted by scripture. Secondly, whatever is consonant with scripture, may be proved by scripture : but there are many things not dissonant from scripture which cannot be proved by it. It is one thing to be consonant with scripture, and another to be not dissonant from it. That there is gold in the New Indies is not consonant with scripture, and yet is not dissonant from it. All truth that is consonant with scripture may be deduced from, and proved by scripture, because in accordance with scripture. So Irenæus, Lib. II. c. 47, says that " the parables are consonant with the plain expression." Thirdly, I affirm that some popish traditions are not only not consonant with scripture, but even altgether foreign from scripture ; such as the traditions of purgatory, indulgences, the mass, sacrifice for the dead, worship of images, and the merit of good works.

I come now to JUSTIN MARTYR, whom Bellarmine next objects to us. He brings against us many passages from his second apology : in the first place, that the Christians used then to meet upon the Lord's day[1] ; next, that they mixed water with the wine in the eucharist[2]. I answer : As to the former tradition, I say that it may be proved by scripture, and therefore is no unwritten tradition. As to the second, I confess that there was formerly such a custom, but maintain that it was a matter of no importance. It is no great matter if water be mixed with strong wine, such as the wine of those countries was, provided the substance of wine be not destroyed. Bellarmine then sets forth another tradition out of Justin ; that the eucharist is to be given to none but baptized per-

[1 τὴν δὲ τοῦ ἡλίου ἡμέραν κοινῇ πάντες τὴν συνέλευσιν ποιούμεθα.—p. 99. Paris. 1636.]

[2 προσφέρεται τῷ προεστῶτι τῶν ἀδελφῶν ἄρτος καὶ ποτήριον ὕδατος καὶ κράματος.—p. 97. ibid.]

sons. But I affirm that this may be gathered from scripture. However, he presses still more the following words of Justin : " The day after Saturday, which is Sunday, he appeared to his apostles and disciples, and delivered to them these things which we submit also to your consideration[3]," &c. I answer : In the first place, these words are of no service to the popish traditions. For Justin only says, that Christ rose on Sunday, which the scriptures tell us also ; and that he taught his apostles those things which Justin wrote in this book, and submitted to the consideration of Cæsar Antoninus. Now these are no other than we read delivered in the scriptures. For in this Apology Justin gives the emperor an account of the christian religion, wherein the papists have not been able to find any of their traditions. Secondly, I would not have them trust too much to Justin's traditions. For, in his Dialogue with Trypho, he keenly defends the error of the Chiliasts on the plea of apostolical tradition, and he hath some similar traditions which the papists at the present day do not own. There is, besides, a small book in Greek, bearing Justin's name, with the title Ζητήματα 'Αναγκαῖα, wherein he recites several traditions ; but it is no genuine piece of Justin's[4]. For in *Quæst.* 115, it mentions Irenæus, and in *Quæst.* 82, Origen, neither of whom could possibly have been known to him. Besides, it speaks also of the Manicheans, who arose some centuries after Justin. Finally, it is a very strong objection against the authority of this book, that it is not noticed by either Jerome or Eusebius.

IRENÆUS comes next to Justin. Bellarmine says that many noble testimonies might be cited from him, namely, from Lib. III. c. 2, 3, 4, where Irenæus writes that there is no more convenient way of arriving at the truth than by consulting those churches wherein there is a succession of bishops from the apostles. I answer : I confess that Irenæus appeals from the scriptures to the churches and apostolical traditions. Moreover, he writes that heretics are to be refuted not by scripture, but by tradition. Nevertheless our defence is no way prejudiced by Irenæus. We must see what the reason was, on account of which Irenæus spoke thus ; and when we have got a clear view of this, we shall readily understand that these statements yield little or no assistance to the

[3 καὶ τῇ μετὰ τὴν Κρονικὴν, ἥτις ἐστὶν ἡλίου ἡμέρα, φανεὶς τοῖς ἀποστόλοις αὐτοῦ καὶ μαθηταῖς ἐδίδαξε ταῦτα, ἅπερ εἰς ἐπίσκεψιν καὶ ὑμῖν ἀνεδώκαμεν. p. 99.]

[4 La Croze ascribes this piece to Diodorus Tarsensis. Thesaur. Epist. III. p. 280.]

papists. The reason why he appealed from scripture to apostolical traditions, and said that heretics were not to be refuted by scripture, was, because he disputed against heretics who slanderously contended that the scriptures were not perfect; yea, who lacerated, despised, corrupted, and denied them; who would not allow themselves to be pressed by their authority, but clave to their traditions, as the papists do now[1]. He rightly determines that it is not possible to dispute against such persons out of scripture. Read the second chapter of the third book. From that chapter it is apparent that those heretics were precisely similar to our papists : for they rejected the scriptures, firstly, because they were obscure; secondly, because they had various meanings and might be diversely understood; thirdly, because tradition was prior to scripture; fourthly, because the scriptures cannot be understood without traditions. For all these reasons they said that we should dispute rather out of tradition than out of scripture; in all which points the papists at the present day hold the same as they did : on which account, Irenæus appeals to the apostolical churches, and explains in c. 3, the grounds of this proceeding; namely, because, if the apostles had delivered any such traditions as the heretics pretended, they would doubtless have delivered them to those churches wherein they themselves had taught[2]. And accordingly he says, c. 3: "When we bring forward our succession, we confound the heretics[3]." He brings forward in that place the succession of the Roman church, because it was the most famous at that time.

But Bellarmine alleges some words from c. 4, to the effect that the apostles had laid up in the church, " as in a rich repository, in full abundance, all things which appertain to the truth, that every one that chose might thence derive the water of life[4]." I answer :

[1 Cum enim ex scripturis arguuntur, in accusationem convertuntur ipsarum scripturarum, quasi non recte habeant, neque sint ex auctoritate, et quia varie sint dictæ, et quia non possit ex his inveniri veritas ab his qui nesciant traditionem : non enim per literas traditam illam, sed per vivam vocem.—p. 230. ed. Fevard.]

[2 Etenim si recondita mysteria scissent apostoli, quæ seorsim et latenter ab reliquis perfectos docebant, his vel maxime traderent ea quibus etiam ipsas ecclesias committebant.—p. 232.]

[3 Fidem, per successiones episcoporum pervenientem usque ad nos, indicantes, confundimus omnes eos qui . . . . præterquam oportet colligunt.— ibid. B.]

[4 Non oportet adhuc quærere apud alios veritatem quam facile est ab ecclesia sumere, cum apostoli, quasi in depositorium dives, plenissime in eam

We also concede this.   But it is inconclusive arguing to say, They
bestowed all upon the church; therefore they did not write all.
Next he objects these words out of the same chapter: " If the
apostles had not left us the scriptures, ought we not to follow that
order of tradition which they delivered to those to whom they
committed the churches[5]?"   I answer : Surely we ought.   But
where is the force of this argument?   Though the apostles had
written nothing, we ought to follow the order of tradition; therefore the apostles have not written all that is sufficient for faith and
salvation!   In that chapter also Irenæus mentions certain barbarous
nations which served God and cultivated religion without the
scripture.   Had then no churches scriptures, or do the scriptures
not contain the entire doctrine of Christianity?   This conclusion
does not follow.   Bellarmine next alleges what Irenæus says,
Lib. IV. c. 45,[6] that the gift of truth was delivered to the churches
along with the succession of bishops from the apostles.   I answer :
Can it be probably concluded from this, that all necessary things
are not written?   By no means.   With the scriptures the apostles
delivered the truth to the churches ; and those apostles who wrote
nothing, delivered to the churches no other truth than that which
is contained in the scriptures.   Yet hence the papists may understand that succession is of no importance without " the gift of
truth."   Furthermore, our opponents should not lay too much
stress upon Irenæus, who was certainly deceived in the matter of
tradition.   For Eusebius, Lib. III. c. 39, says that he was a
Chiliast.   This may be proved from Lib. v. c. 23.   And Lib. II.
c. 39, Irenæus writes that Christ lived forty years; which he
affirms that he received by tradition not only from John, but from
the other apostles also.   Now this may be refuted by scripture ;
and, in fact, Epiphanius, *Hær.* 78, confutes this opinion.   And
Lib. II. c. 47,[7] Irenæus writes, that faith and hope remain in the
life to come, which the scriptures expressly deny.

contulerint omnia quæ sint veritatis; uti omnis quicunque velit, sumat ex ea
potum vitæ.—p. 242.]

[5 Quid autem? si neque apostoli quidem scripturas reliquissent nobis,
nonne oportebat ordinem sequi traditionis, quam tradiderunt iis quibus committebant ecclesias?—ibid.]

[6 Quapropter eis qui in ecclesia sint presbyteris obaudire oportet, his
qui successionem habent ab apostolis, sicut ostendimus, qui cum episcopatus
successione charisma veritatis certum secundum placitum Patris acceperunt.
—c. 43, pp. 381, 382.]

[7 Sicut et apostolus dixit, reliquis partibus destructis, hæc tunc perseve-

It follows that we go through the remaining supporters and
patrons of traditions ; the next of whom is CLEMENS ALEXANDRINUS.
He, as quoted by Eusebius, Lib. VI. c. 11, says[1] that he was obliged
to write a book concerning Easter, and to mention therein the traditions which he received from the presbyters, the successors of the
apostles.   I answer, that that book is not now extant, and consequently, that it is uncertain what traditions he therein related.
Secondly, it may well be supposed that it was traditions about
Easter, or some similar to these, that were treated of in that book,
traditions of no great importance, and no way necessary to salvation.
Thirdly, I affirm that this Clemens was not entirely orthodox,
having, as Eusebius testifies, shewn too great a disposition to make
use of apocryphal pieces.   In the first book of his Stromata he
says that the labourer, who is sent into the Lord's harvest, hath a
double husbandry, "written and unwritten," (ἔγγραφον and
ἄγραφον).   In the same book he says that Christ taught only
during one year, although it be manifest from the gospels that his
teaching lasted three years and upwards.   In the same book he
writes also that the Gentiles were saved by their philosophy.   In
the second book of the Stromata he hath laid the foundations of the
Nestorian heresy, as his translator Hervetus hath noted in the margin.   And in the same book he says that no one was saved before
Christ.   In his third book he says that Christ did not truly hunger
or truly thirst, but only seemed to be subject to hunger and thirst.
In the sixth book he says that Christ and the apostles converted
many to the faith in Hades by preaching to them.   And in his
Protreptical Discourse he makes "Eve" denote allegorically pleasure, and thus taught his disciple Origen to interpret scripture
allegorically; from which source almost all the heresies, ancient
and modern, have taken their rise.   He wrote also, and taught
that Christ is a creature, as Ruffinus tells us in the Apology for
Origen.

Next follows ORIGEN, the auditor of Clemens.   He tells us, in his
Commentary upon the Romans, c. 6, that the baptism of infants is a

rare, quæ sunt fides, spes, et caritas.   Semper enim fides, quæ est ad magis-
trum nostrum, permanet.—p. 203. c.   The schoolmen solve the difficulty by
determining that faith remains, *quoad habitum*, though not *quoad exercitium*.
They have other expedients indeed, but this seems the most plausible.]

[1 Καὶ ἐν τῷ λόγῳ δὲ αὐτοῦ τῷ περὶ τοῦ πάσχα ἐκβιασθῆναι ὁμολογεῖ πρὸς
τῶν ἑταίρων, ἃς ἔτυχε παρὰ τῶν ἀρχαίων πρεσβυτέρων ἀκηκοὼς παραδόσεις γραφῇ
τοῖς μετὰ ταῦτα παραδοῦναι.—c. 13. T. II. p. 182. ed. Heinich.]

tradition[2]. I answer : That it is indeed a tradition, but a written tradition, and capable of easy proof from scripture. Bellarmine next gathers another testimony from the same father's fifth Homily upon Numbers, where Origen says that many things are observed, the reason of which is not plain to all, as kneeling in prayer[3]. I answer : This is indeed a laudable tradition, but yet not a necessary one; for we read that some holy men have prayed standing. And Basil, *de Spirit. S.* c. 27, affirms that Christians used to pray erect, and not upon their knees, on Sundays, and from Easter to Whitsuntide. However, we need not defer much to Origen's authority, who is a writer full of blemishes and errors. Many of the ancient fathers wrote against him, as Epiphanius, Theophilus of Alexandria, and Jerome, who calls his writings " poisoned." Indeed, it is evident that there are many errors in his books. In his 35th Tractate upon Matthew, he writes that he learned from tradition that Christ's countenance assumed diverse appearances according to the worthiness of the beholders[4]; and says that it was upon this account that Judas gave a sign to the Jews, Matth. xxvi. For what need, says he, of a sign, when the Jews saw Jesus' face every day, if he had not a countenance that continually changed ? Now this is a ridiculous tradition.

Bellarmine next produces EUSEBIUS of Cæsarea. He, in his *Demonstratio Evangelica,* Lib. I. c. 8, confirms unwritten traditions : for he says that the apostles delivered down some observances in writing, and some orally[5]. I answer : That this testimony is clear enough, but unworthy of reception, because repugnant to

[2 Pro hoc et ecclesia ab apostolis traditionem suscepit, etiam parvulis baptismum dare.—Origen. Opp. T. IV. p. 565. Paris. 1733.]

[3 Sed et in ecclesiasticis observationibus sunt nonnulla hujusmodi, quæ omnibus quidem facere necesse est, nec tamen eorum ratio omnibus patet. Nam quod, verbi gratia, genua flectimus orantes . . . . non facile cuiquam puto ratione compertum.—T. II. p. 284.]

[4 Venit ergo talis traditio ad nos de eo, quoniam non solum duæ formæ in eo fuerunt, una quidem secundum quam omnes eum videbant, altera autem secundum quam transfiguratus est coram discipulis in monte. . . . Sed etiam unicuique apparebat secundum quod dignus fuerat.—T. III. p. 906.]

[5 οἱ δέ γε αὐτοῦ μαθηταὶ, τῷ τοῦ διδασκάλου νεύματι, κατάλληλον ταῖς τῶν πολλῶν ἀκοαῖς ποιούμενοι τὴν διδασκαλίαν, ὅσα μὲν ἅτε τὴν ἕξιν διαβεβηκόσι πρὸς τοῦ τελείου διδασκάλου παρήγγελτο, ταῦτα τοῖς οἵοις τε χωρεῖν παρεδίδου· ὅσα δὲ τοῖς ἔτι τὰς ψυχὰς ἐμπαθέσι καὶ θεραπείας δεομένοις ἐφαρμόζειν ὑπελάμβανον, ταῦτα συγκατιόντες τῇ τῶν πλειόνων ἀσθενείᾳ, τὰ μὲν διὰ γραμμάτων, τὰ δὲ δι' ἀγράφων θεσμῶν φυλάττειν παρεδίδοσαν.—p. 29. Paris. 1628.]

scripture. The same author says in the same place, that Christ did
not deliver all things to all persons, but reserved some points of
greater excellence for the perfect, and that the apostles also proceeded in the same manner. Irenæus gives a far different and
sounder determination, Lib. III. c. 15. And we read that the apostles made known the whole counsel of God to all the churches, and
concealed nothing that was necessary from any one. Besides, it is
absurd to suppose that the traditions pretended by the papists are
so excellent and sublime as not to be communicated to everybody.
For if we would judge aright, we must needs confess that much more
perfect and excellent matters may be found in scripture. Besides,
what that same author writes in the same place, of two ways of living amongst christian men, is a mere fiction.

In the next place follows ATHANASIUS. In the treatise which he
wrote in defence of the decrees of the Nicene Council against
Eusebius of Nicomedia, he says, that " that doctrine was delivered
down from hand to hand from fathers to fathers[1]." I answer : That
Athanasius speaks of the Homoüsion, which he proves to be no new
term, or then first invented by the Nicene fathers, but acknowledged
and used by the more ancient fathers also. But does it hence follow that the same term may not be justified out of the scriptures
too ? By no means. For it was in the scriptures that these fathers
learned to use it. We dispute not about words, but the sense of
words, the dogma, the doctrine which they convey. We reject not
certain words which are nowhere found in scripture, provided they
bear no meaning foreign from scripture. Such are the terms,
" Trinity," " person," " hypostasis," " consubstantial," and others
of that sort. But new dogmas, whereof the scriptures say nothing,
we do reject, and maintain that no article of faith is necessary which
is not delivered in the scriptures.

Bellarmine proceeds, and objects to us BASIL in the next place.
He writes thus, De Spirit. S. c. 27 : " Those things which we
observe and teach we have received partly from the written teaching, and partly delivered to us in a mystery from the tradition of
the apostles[2]." He remarks in the same place, that " both these

[1 ἰδοὺ ἡμεῖς μὲν ἐκ πατέρων εἰς πατέρας διαβεβηκέναι τὴν τοιαύτην διάνοιαν
ἀποδεικνύομεν.—Athan. Opp. T. I. p. 233. Paris. 1698.]

[2 τῶν ἐν τῇ ἐκκλησίᾳ πεφυλαγμένων δογμάτων καὶ κηρυγμάτων τὰ μὲν ἐκ τῆς
ἐγγράφου διδασκαλίας ἔχομεν, τὰ δὲ ἐκ τῆς τῶν ἀποστόλων παραδόσεως διαδοθέντα
ἡμῖν ἐν μυστηρίῳ παρεδεξάμεθα· ἅπερ ἀμφότερα τὴν αὐτὴν ἰσχὺν ἔχει πρὸς τὴν
εὐσέβειαν.—Basil. Opp. T. II. 210. Paris. 1618.]

have equal force to piety." He hath similar sentiments in c. 29.[3] The papists press with extraordinary earnestness these words and the passage adduced; and indeed they do seem to establish and sanction the decree of the council of Trent, wherein traditions are made equal to scripture. But I answer: Firstly, that it may be doubted whether these are the true and genuine words of Basil. Nor are we the first that have called this matter in question; since Erasmus, an acute judge of ancient writings, hath passed the same judgment in the preface[4] to his version of Basil, observing that he perceived a change of style from the middle of the book and onward. Damascene, indeed, in his first oration upon the Worship of Images, recites these words as Basil's: but we do not account his opinion of much consequence, since he came too late in point of time, and was excessively given to traditions; and this book of his is of no sort of authority. Secondly, if these be genuine words of Basil, then he is at variance with himself. For he elsewhere teaches that all things necessary to salvation may be found in scripture, and that the scriptures contain a full and perfect body of teaching; as will hereafter appear manifestly, when we come to propose the arguments upon our side. Thirdly, it is certain that Basil was sometimes too much addicted to traditions, and hence sometimes fell into mistakes. This may be plainly perceived from his Homily upon Christ's Nativity[5], where he writes, that the Zacharias mentioned in Matth. xxiii. 35, was the father of John the Baptist, and was slain by the Jews for having placed Mary the mother of Christ amongst the virgins after she had borne a son,

[3 ἀποστολικὸν δὲ οἶμαι καὶ τὸ ταῖς ἀγράφοις παραδόσεσι παραμένειν.— ibid. p. 217.]

[4 Rather, in his Dedicatory Epistle. His words are: Postquam dimidium operis absolveram citra tædium, visa est mihi phrasis alium referre parentem, aliumque spirare genium: interdum ad tragicum cothurnum intumescebat oratio, rursus ad vulgarem sermonem subsidebat, interdum subinane quiddam habere videbatur.... adhuc subinde digrediebatur ab instituto, nec satis concinne redibat a digressione. Postremo multa videbantur admisceri, quæ non admodum facerent ad id quod agitur; quædam etiam repetuntur oblivione verius quam judicio. Quum Basilius ubique sit sanus, simplex, et candidus, sibi constans, atque etiam instans, nunquam ab eo quod agitur excurrens temere, nunquam divinis mysteriis admiscens philosophiam mundanam, nisi per adversarios coactus, idque contemptim.—Cf. Stillingfleet. Ration. Account. P. I. c. 8. Works, Vol. IV. p. 235. Lond. 1709.]

[5 δηλοῖ δὲ καὶ ἡ κατὰ τὸν Ζαχαρίαν ἱστορία, ὅτι μέχρι πάντος παρθένος ἡ Μαρία· λόγος γάρ τίς εστι καὶ οὗτος ἐκ παραδόσεως εἰς ἡμᾶς ἀφιγμένος. κ. τ. λ.— Τ. I. p. 590.]

which the Jews could by no means tolerate. On this account he says that the Jews rushed upon him and slew him between the temple and the altar. This he calls an old tradition, λόγον ἐκ παραδόσεως ἀφιγμένον. I suppose he took it from Origen upon Matth. xxiii,[1] and Origen from I know not whom. However, we may see from Chrysostom and Jerome, what opinion we should form of this tradition. Chrysostom affirms that the person here meant was the son of Jehoiada, of whom we read, 2 Chron. xxiv. 20, 21. And Jerome says, that what we are told about the father of John Baptist is merely apocryphal, and rejected as easily as it is asserted, along with all the other things which rest upon no scriptural foundation. From which words it appears plainly what value is to be assigned to Basil's traditions, which are both condemned by ancient fathers and easily refuted by reason. Fourthly, I come to Basil's actual words : he says, that the gospel without unwritten tradition hath no force, but is a mere name, ψιλὸν ὄνομα. If he meant that it is of no avail without preaching and interpretation, he would have said something ; but he is speaking of certain rites and ceremonies not contained in scripture, which he there enumerates, and without which he pronounces the gospel to be of no avail. If Basil were now to rise from the dead, he would doubtless refuse to acknowledge such a sentiment, which deservedly merits to be exploded and condemned by all good Christians. However, let us see what sort of things are these traditions, so excellent, so necessary, so divine, and without which the gospel would lose all its efficacy : let us judge whether they possess indeed so much value and importance.

The first tradition which he proposes is *the sign of the cross :* for he says that those who have believed in Christ should be signed with the symbol of the cross, τῷ τύπῳ τοῦ σταυροῦ τοὺς ἠλπι-κότας κατασημαίνεσθαι. I acknowledge this to be an ancient ceremony, used from almost the earliest times of the christian church and religion, and used for this reason ; that Christians, who then lived in the midst of pagans and men most hostile to the faith of Christ, might by every means declare and publicly testify that they were Christians ; of doing which they supposed that there was no more convenient means than signing themselves with this outward symbol of the cross. Afterwards this sign was applied to other purposes, wherein there was more of superstition than of

[1 Tract. xxvi. cf. Huet, Origeniana. Lib. II. Q. iv. p. 66.]

religion.   For what? are we to think that piety and religion consist in outward things? Surely not.   " But the flesh is signed that
the soul may be protected," says Tertullian.   On the contrary, it
is by faith, not by the cross, that the soul should be protected.
The ancients, indeed, thought they were protected by this sign
against evil demons; but this had its origin in the Montanistic
heresy.   We read, however, in history, that many demons were
put to flight by this sign, as is narrated in the case of Julian the
apostate.   While he was celebrating some horrible rites, and a crowd
of demons had collected in the place where those impious ceremonies
were being performed, Julian, forgetting himself in his fright,
signed himself with the cross, as he used to do when he was a
Christian; whereupon forthwith all the devils betake themselves
to flight.   I am aware that these and similar accounts are delivered
down to us in history.   Meanwhile this should be deeply imprinted
upon the minds of us all, that the devil is a cunning, crafty, versa-
tile, deceitful and lying impostor.   He pretends therefore to fear
the sign of the cross, in order to lead us to place more confidence in
that outward sign than in Christ crucified himself.   But we shall
have to speak elsewhere of the sign of the cross.

Another of Basil's traditions is, that we should turn to the east
when we pray; πρὸς ἀνατολὰς τετράφθαι κατὰ τὴν προσευχήν.
I answer : This ceremony is of no importance whatsoever.   Can we
think that the apostles were anxious about such a matter as what
point of the compass men should turn towards in their prayers?
Does not God hear those who turn towards the south or west?   This
is surely more suited to Jews than Christians.   Eucherius, an
ancient father, in his Commentary upon the books of Kings, Lib. II.
c. 58, writes piously, that no precept directs us how to place our
body in prayer, "provided only the mind be present with God,"
and waiting upon him.   Socrates, Lib. v. c. 22, writes that the Antiochenes used to turn towards the west in their prayers, adopting a
custom directly opposite to what Basil tells us was commanded by
the apostles.   Must the gospel be ruined, if this glorious tradition
be taken away?   But let us consider the reasons of this tradition
broached by Basil.   " When we pray," says he, " we look towards the east; but few of us know the reason why we do so.
Now the reason is, because we seek our ancient country Paradise, which God is said to have placed, in the garden of Eden,
towards the sun's rising."   I answer : Is it then that earthly paradise in which Adam was placed, that we seek for?   Nay, we
seek another country, in the heavens, where there is neither east

nor west. This, therefore, was a reason absolutely ridiculous and unworthy of Basil.

Basil's third tradition relates to the words of invocation, when the bread and wine are exhibited in the eucharist. I answer : The papists themselves do not retain this form of invocation, nor understand any thing of its nature.

Fourthly, Basil says : " We bless the water of baptism." I answer : What does this mean ? Did not Christ by his authority and commandment, and by his word, sanctify all water for baptism? Is not all pure elementary water sufficient for baptism even without this benediction ? Is not baptism valid performed in any water ? We read in Acts viii. of the baptism of the eunuch : but neither there nor elsewhere in the sacred scriptures could we ever find a word of this sanctification of the water. Justin Martyr, in his second Apology, where he shews the manner and describes the form of baptism amongst the ancient Christians, makes no mention of blessing the water. We read in Eusebius, that Constantine always desired to be baptized in Jordan : but, I suppose, a whole river of running water could not be sanctified in this way. Chrysostom, (Hom. 25, in Joann.)[1] writes excellently well, that Christ by his baptism sanctified all waters : but these men are wont to apply exorcisms to water, salt, bells, as if all the creatures were full of devils. Yet, although they require exorcisms, they dare not deny that it is a legitimate, entire, and true baptism, which is performed even in not sanctified water.

Basil's fifth tradition is like the preceding, namely, that the persons to be baptized should be dipped thrice, τρὶς βαπτίζεσθαι, concerning which tradition we read also in the 50th canon of the apostles. I answer : Would the power of the gospel be impaired by the loss of this tradition ? Who would say so ? It is at least manifest that this tradition is neither apostolical nor necessary. For, in Acts ii., we read that three thousand men were baptized upon the day of Pentecost. So many persons could not be baptized on one day, if each were dipped three times. In the ancient and primitive church baptism was wont to be celebrated but twice in the year, at Easter and Pentecost, and then a vast multitude of persons was baptized on one day. How great a labour would this have been, if they had used the trine immersion with each ! Others, however, rather approve aspersion than immersion, as Cyprian, Epist. Lib. IV. Ep. 7. And Gregory, Epist. Lib. I. Ep. 4, says that it makes no matter whether we use the trine or simple immersion.

[1 Opp. T. IV. 654. Eton. 1612.]

Gratian, Dist. 4, *de Consecr. C. de Trina,* lays down the same
thing. But the fourth council of Toledo, can. 5, prohibits that trine
immersion : and, indeed, every one sees that even a single dip is
attended with danger to a tender infant. The papists themselves do
not now use a trine immersion, but a trine sprinkling, wherewith
they maintain that baptism is completely performed. Now if it be
an apostolic tradition that those who are baptized should be dipped
thrice, they ought not to have made any change.

Basil's sixth tradition is that those who are baptized should
ἀποτάσσεσθαι τῷ Σατανᾷ, renounce Satan. I reply, that this is
perfectly true. But do we not "renounce" Satan, when we profess
to believe in the Father, Son, and Holy Ghost?

From these instances we may judge of the rest. What? Are
these the things without which the gospel will lose all its efficacy?
Nay, the papists themselves retain not all these traditions of Basil's.
They do not dip, but sprinkle : they do not pray standing upon the
Lord's day, as Basil here determines that we ought ; for if we follow Basil, we ought to pray standing on all Sundays from Easter to
Pentecost. This the papists do not observe, shewing therein that
Basil is not to be listened to upon that matter. For Basil contends
most earnestly for this tradition, and adduces three reasons in support of the practice : 1. because Christ arose upon the Lord's
day : 2. because we seek the things that are above, τὰ ἄνω
ζητοῦμεν. But we should do this always; and according to this
reason, we should always pray standing : 3. because the eighth
day is a symbol of the world to come; and therefore, says he, the
church hath taught its nurslings to make their prayers in an erect
posture, and that upon a necessary obligation. A similar decree
was made in the first council of Nice, can. 20.[2] But a different
custom hath now for a long time prevailed. The papists themselves
have taught us by their own example to reject such traditions. For
these traditions of Basil's are either necessary, or they are not. If
they be necessary, why do they not themselves observe them all?
If they be not necessary, why do they press us with the authority
of Basil? For either we should not be attacked, if they be unnecessary ; or they sin in not observing them, if they be necessary.
Let them choose which they will.

The same Basil, however, in his Epitomized Definitions writes
much better upon the subject of traditions. He says that there
are some things enjoined in the scriptures, and some passed over

[2 Labb. et Cossart. T. II. col. 37.]

in silence : wherein though he may seem to favour the papists, he yet lends them no sort of countenance. For he afterwards teaches us what sort of things are those which are not mentioned in them, namely, things left free, of a middle and indifferent nature. Of all these he says that this is the rule, this the canon ; "all things are lawful for me, but all things are not expedient[1]." Now this rule must be understood of things indifferent. Whatever therefore is not set down in scripture must be looked upon as left free. This is our own opinion, that it is only things necessary, and not things indifferent, that are delivered in the scriptures. Since then we are disputing about things necessary, why do they press upon us Basil's traditions, which, being unwritten, are, in his own judgment, indifferent and not necessary ? Thus we see what opinion we should form of this place, than which the papists have none more urgent in favour of tradition. However, the Tridentine fathers would fain find sanction in this place for their decree, that traditions are to be received and reverenced with the same feelings of pious respect as the sacred books of the old and new Testaments themselves. But I answer, that no one is so foolish as to believe that these traditions of Basil's, just now set forth, have the same force and authority as holy scripture. Yet Bellarmine says, that they are of equal obligation, not indeed as to observance, but as to faith. So (he adds) some precepts of the Lord are greater than others, as, "Thou shalt love the Lord thy God with all thy heart," &c. ; and others of less importance, as that of avoiding idle words, Matth. xii. 36. These (says he) oblige us equally in respect of faith, though not equally in respect of observance. I answer : In the first place, the papists themselves have proved by their own example, that these traditions of Basil's are in no way to be treated as equal to scripture; for they have abrogated some of them both in respect of faith and of observance. Now not the smallest precept delivered in scripture can be abrogated, not even that concerning idle words. Secondly, if they could with so much clearness and authority prove their traditions to be as true as the precepts of scripture, we would willingly receive them as on the same footing with scripture : but, as we have already made appear, even they themselves do not certainly know their own traditions.

Hitherto we have been engaged in answering objections from

[1 τὰ μέν ἐστιν ὑπὸ τῆς ἐντολῆς τοῦ Θεοῦ ἐν τῇ ἁγίᾳ γραφῇ διεσταλμένα, τὰ δὲ σεσιωπημένα....περὶ δὲ τῶν σεσιωπημένων κανόνα ἡμῖν ἐξέθετο ὁ ἀπόστολος Παῦλος εἰπών· πάντα μοι ἔξεστιν, ἀλλ' οὐ πάντα συμφέρει.—T. II. p. 524.]

the fathers, and these matters have delayed me, though in haste to come to the arguments on our side. Yet there are still some testimonies remaining, which can by no means be passed over.

In the next place, Bellarmine brings NAZIANZENE into the field against us ; who, in his first Invective against Julian, declares that he admired the doctrine of the church, but especially the forms which the church had received by tradition and preserved[2]. I answer : Nazianzene by the word τύπους in that place means either the sacraments, which were indeed administered with the utmost sanctity and reverence, or some other rites and ceremonies which christian men used in the administration of the sacraments. But the other ceremonies which he mentions were free, not necessary, as the manner of singing, imposing penance, and such like. These were useful, and not to be blamed, but yet not absolutely necessary. They are consequently irrelevant to the present question, because our dispute is only about things necessary. Besides, even those ceremonies have certain rules in scripture, to which they must be squared and made conformable.

Next follows CHRYSOSTOM, who, upon 2 Thess. ii. 15, commenting upon the words, " hold the traditions," drops some expressions favourable to tradition. " Hence," says he, " it is plain that the apostles did not deliver everything in epistles, but many things also without writing[3]." I answer : Unless those many things of which Chrysostom speaks be founded upon the authority of scripture, he contradicts himself, as shall afterwards be made clear in the defence of our side. But Chrysostom says that both these classes are equally deserving of credit, ὁμοίως ἀξιόπιστα. And afterwards he says, " It is a tradition ; let that suffice." I answer : It was an inconsiderate word, and unworthy of so great a father. Must whatever is obtruded on us under the name of a tradition be immediately received ? Nay, the apostle tells us to " try the spirits," and to " prove all things." Theophylact and Œcumenius agree with him; but it is not necessary to answer them. The same Chrysostom also in his third Homily upon the Philip-

[2 ὁρῶν γὰρ τὸν ἡμέτερον λόγον μέγαν μὲν ὄντα τοῖς δόγμασιν . . . . ἔτι δὲ μείζω καὶ γνωριμώτερον τοῖς παραδεδομένοις καὶ εἰς τόδε τετηρημένοις τύποις τῆς ἐκκλησίας, ἵνα μηδὲ τοῦτο ἀκακούργητον μένῃ, τί μηχανᾶται.—Greg. Naz. Opp. T. I. p. 101. Colon. 1690.]

[3 ἐντεῦθεν δῆλον ὅτι οὐ πάντα δι᾽ ἐπιστολῆς παρεδίδοσαν, ἀλλὰ πολλὰ καὶ ἀγράφως· ὁμοίως κἀκεῖνα καὶ ταῦτά ἐστιν ἀξιόπιστα, ὥστε καὶ τὴν παράδοσιν τῆς ἐκκλησίας ἀξιόπιστον ἡγώμεθα. παράδοσίς ἐστι, μηδὲν πλέον ζήτει.—Chrysost. Comm. T. VI. p. 386. Paris. 1633.]

pians[1], and in his sixty-ninth Homily to the people of Antioch, declares that the apostles sanctioned the mentioning of the dead in the celebration of the holy mysteries ; which he also affirms to be salutary to the departed. I answer : I do not acknowledge that tradition, and have no doubt that, if the prayers of the living were so useful and salutary for the dead, scripture would have mentioned and even enjoined them. However, Chrysostom is scarce consistent with himself in this place. He says in a previous passage, that those who die in their sins are not to be helped by prayers, but perpetually mourned over. Afterwards, nevertheless, he pronounces that prayers are of great avail to these persons ; adding, however, that he speaks only of such as die in the faith, περὶ τῶν ἐν πίστει παρελθόντων. But how is it possible that one should die in faith, and yet die in sins ? For all their sins are remitted to those who die in faith.

In the next place Bellarmine objects THEOPHILUS of Alexandria. He in his first and third *Lib. Paschal.* says that the laws of fasting are apostolic. I answer : This was indeed an excellently learned writer, who refuted the Anthropomorphites; and yet he was a bitter enemy of Chrysostom, a person of the utmost sanctity and integrity, whom he ceased not from persecuting until he had glutted his hatred, and driven that most worthy prelate into exile. But to come to the question : I answer, in the first place, that those laws of fasting were not imposed by the apostles, but by the heretic Montanus. So Eusebius testifies, Lib. v. c. 18. " This," says he, (meaning Montanus), "is the person who prescribed laws for fasting," ὁ νηστείας νομοθετήσας. These laws, therefore, are heretical, not apostolical, being instituted by Montanus, and not derived from the apostles. Secondly, I say, that the rule of fasting prescribed by this Theophilus is such as the papists themselves do not observe. He would have us, when we fast, abstain not only from flesh, but from wine [2] : the papists abstain from flesh indeed, but in the meanwhile allow other dainties, and as large a quantity of wine as you please to fast on.

Next follows CYRIL of Jerusalem, whom Bellarmine declares to handle nothing else in his Catechetics but unwritten rites in the celebration of the sacraments. I answer : He produces however no traditions from this author, nor can he produce many. There are

[1 Ibid. p. 33.]
[2 Qui autem legum præcepta custodiunt, ignorant vinum in jejuniis.— Ap. Bibl. PP. T. v. p. 855. Lugdun. 1677.]

indeed a few, but those of no great importance. The book itself appeared in Greek only a few years ago, but seems quite worthy of Cyril: it is marked by singular knowledge, and piety and prudence. Let them, if they can, produce from him any traditions opposed to us. How far he is from approving unwritten traditions, he shews plainly in the fourth Catechesis, where he writes expressly, that in things appertaining to faith and religion nothing, however small, is to be established without the authority of scripture. His words are, δεῖ περὶ τῶν θείων καὶ ἀγίων τῆς πίστεως μυστηρίων μηδὲ τὸ τυχὸν ἄνευ τῶν θείων παραδίδοσθαι γράφων. The cause, then, of the popish traditions, which rest upon no testimonies of scripture, is lost. But Cyril adds further, that our faith must be proved by scripture, and from no other source: ἡ σωτηρία τῆς πίστεως ἡμῶν οὐκ ἐξ εὑρεσιλογίας, ἀλλ᾽ ἐξ ἀποδείξεως τῶν θείων ἐστὶ γραφῶν.

Next follows another CYRIL, namely of Alexandria, who in his sixth book against Julian the Apostate relates many things concerning the use of the image of the cross. I answer: We have already spoken of this tradition. It is not surprising that he should speak copiously upon this subject against Julian the Apostate; since the Christians of those times were wont to use this sign amongst the heathen as the banner of their profession. Meanwhile he defends the perfection of the scriptures, as shall be proved hereafter.—But Bellarmine hath omitted the testimony of this Cyril in his printed edition.

Next comes EPIPHANIUS, whom they make a great patron of traditions. He tells us, in *Hæres.* 75,[3] and 61 and 63, speaking against the Apostolici, that "we cannot take everything from the scriptures." And Bellarmine observes that the heretics (meaning us) have no answer to this but blasphemy. I answer: What blasphemy is it to say that Epiphanius delighted more in traditions than he ought, yea, even in those genealogies which the apostle condemns? Surely he that says this does no injury to Epiphanius: for the truth of this may be proved by such an instance as occurs in *Hæres.* 55, where he affirms that he knew by tradition who was the father of Daniel, and who of Elijah the prophet[4], and how old Lazarus was when Christ raised him from the dead[5].

[3 Hæres. lxxv. §. 6. p. 910. lxi. 6. p. 511. T. I. ed. Petav. The latter is the most important: οὐ γὰρ πάντα ἀπὸ τῆς θείας γραφῆς δύναται λαμβάνεσθαι. διὸ τὰ μὲν ἐν γραφαῖς, τὰ δὲ ἐν παραδόσει παρέδωκαν οἱ ἅγιοι ἀπόστολοι.]

[4 Hær. lv. §. 3. p. 470.]

[5 Hæres. lxvi. §. 34. p. 652: ἀλλὰ καὶ ἐν παραδόσεσιν εὕρομεν, ὅτι τριάκοντα ἐτῶν ἦν τότε ὁ Λάζαρος, ὅτε ἐγήγερται.]

However, my first reply is, that those things which Epiphanius
says cannot be derived from scripture, are either indifferent and
not necessary, as pertaining only to the external polity of the
church, or else Epiphanius is inconsistent with himself; for he says
elsewhere, that all things necessary are delivered in the scriptures.
Secondly, I say that those traditions which he styles apostolic have
been long since abrogated and disused by the papists. Why then
do they press us so urgently with the authority of this father,
when they themselves have long ago exploded his traditions? For
in *Hæres.* 51, he says that the wise men spoken of in Matth. ii.,
came two years after the birth of Christ. Now the fathers have
refuted this opinion, nor do the papists maintain it. The same
author tells us, *Hæres.* 80, that it is a tradition that men should
nourish beards[1]. Doubtless a noble one! Yet the papists neglect
this tradition, their clergy being all shaven and beardless. Thirdly,
as to the passage which Bellarmine adduces from *Hæres.* 61, it
may indeed be perceived from it that Epiphanius approved of some
traditions as apostolical, but yet not that he was so pertinacious
a maintainer of them as the papists are. For he says that it is
an apostolical tradition, " that no one should contract marriage
after a vow of celibacy[2]," and that to do otherwise is impious. So
far he and the papists agree. But in that same place Epiphanius affirms that it is better, if one fall in his course, that he should
take a wife, even after such a vow, and come at length, even
though halt, into the church, than suffer the daily wounds of secret
arrows. The papists merely provide that no man shall contract
marriage after a vow, but in the meanwhile escape not from those
" secret arrows." Epiphanius asserts that it is safer and better to
desist from the race begun, and contract marriage, than to go on
to destruction pierced by those deadly shafts of lust. Do they
approve of him here? Can they tolerate this opinion of his?
Far from it: they pronounce it an impious and sacrilegious crime
once to entertain a thought of marriage after such a vow, and they
annul such marriages though made and celebrated. However, he
hath one opinion sadly unauthorised: for he thinks this very act
of contracting marriage after a vow to be a sin; and nevertheless
he says that it is better to have one sin than many, κρεῖττον ἔχειν

[1 §. 7. p. 1073: ἐν τοῖς διατάξεσι τῶν ἀποστόλων φάσκει ὁ θεῖος λόγος καὶ
ἡ διδασκαλία, μὴ φθείρειν, τουτέστι μὴ τέμνειν τρίχας γενείου.]

[2 παρέδωκαν τοίνυν οἱ ἅγιοι Θεοῦ ἀπόστολοι τῇ ἁγίᾳ Θεοῦ ἐκκλησίᾳ, ἐφάμαρτον
εἶναι τὸ μετὰ τὸ ὁρίσαι παρθενίαν εἰς γάμον τρέπεσθαι.—ut supra, p. 511.]

ἁμαρτίαν μίαν καὶ μὴ περισσοτέρας. Who sees not how repugnant this is to sound divinity? For nothing wrong is on any account to be done.

The last of the Greek fathers cited by Bellarmine is DAMASCENE. In his book *de Fide Orthodox*. Lib. IV. c. 17, he says that the apostles delivered many unwritten traditions[3]. I answer : We make no account in this question of Damascene, a late author, superstitious, and devoted to the worship of images; so that it is no wonder that he should afford some patronage to tradition. He wrote indeed many things excellently well against the ancient heretics. Yet even the papists cannot venture to defend him upon every point : for in c. 18 of that same book he enumerates the Clementine Canons of the apostles along with the other canonical books of holy scripture; which the papists have not yet ventured on.

Thus far of the Greek fathers. Now follow the Latin; of whom our opponent produces first TERTULLIAN, citing his book *de Corona Militis*, wherein Tertullian contends vehemently for traditions : " Of these," he says, " and similar observances, tradition is the author, custom the confirmer[4]," &c. I answer in the first place, that Tertullian was a Montanist when he wrote that book; for he mentions the new prophecies, of which Montanus was undoubtedly the inventor. Now Montanus was the introducer of many traditions which could not afterwards be extirpated. He said that he had that Paraclete whom Christ promised; and relying upon the authority of this Paraclete, he introduced many things into the church without the authority of scripture. This wicked Montanus deluded Tertullian himself, whose loss and fall we may well lament : for at that time there was none more learned, none more holy, none more earnest in the defence of the christian faith, than Tertullian; yet this heresy of Montanism hath stripped this father of all his credit. So Hilary speaks, in his commentary on Matthew, canon 5 : " Although Tertullian hath written very suitable discourses upon this subject, yet the error which afterwards attached to him hath deprived even his commendable writings of all authority[5]." Jerome in his book against

[3 ὅτι δὲ καὶ πλεῖστα οἱ ἀπόστολοι ἀγράφως παραδεδώκασι γράφει Παῦλος. κ. τ. λ.—c. 16. T. I. p. 282. ed. Lequien. Paris. 1712.]

[4 Harum et aliarum ejusmodi disciplinarum si legem expostules scripturarum, nullam invenies; traditio tibi prætendetur auctrix, consuetudo confirmatrix, et fides observatrix.—c. 4.]

[5 Quanquam et Tertullianus hac de re aptissima volumina scripserit, sed consequens error hominis detraxit scriptis probabilibus auctoritatem.]

Helvidius denies him to have been " a man of the church ;" and in his Catalogue he says of Tertullian, that "he wrote many things against the church;" as indeed he did. This being so, how absurd it is to obtrude these Montanistic traditions upon Tertullian's authority! Vincentius Lirinensis, *Commonit.* c. 24, writes excellently of Tertullian, whom he compares to Origen : "What," says he, " could be more learned than this man ? Where could we find greater skill in all things human and divine ? &c. And yet, after all this, even he, this very Tertullian, losing his hold of catholic doctrine, and far more eloquent than fortunate, changed his opinion afterwards," &c.[1] Who would not fear in his own case when so great a man fell into heresy ?

Secondly, I reply that all those traditions which Tertullian here praises, with the single exception of the sign of the cross, are now abrogated by the papists themselves; and consequently, that their conduct is at once impious and impudent, when they object to us traditions which they themselves neither retain nor judge worthy of observance. Tertullian's traditions are such as these ; dipping thrice in baptism, presenting milk and honey to be tasted immediately after baptism, abstaining from the bath for a week after baptism, taking the Eucharist at meal-times, annual oblations to be made by every one in honour of the martyr's anniversaries, considering it a crime to worship kneeling on the Lord's day, or from Easter to Pentecost. These are the traditions which Tertullian mentions and praises so highly in this place, and not one of which is observed by the papists. Nay, he seems to have written this book expressly against the catholics. The very argument of the book seems to prove this, which is as follows : ' The soldiers were to receive a crown of laurel : one of them refused to wear that crown upon his head, because he was a Christian, and told the tribune of it ; whence ensued a great slaughter of the Christians. The catholics said that this was an ill-timed profession of Christianity. Tertullian defended it, and praises the soldier.' Besides, in that same book he speaks thus of the catholics : " I know them well, lions in peace, but harts in war[2]."

The other place cited by Bellarmine from this same Tertullian is

[1 Quid hoc viro doctius? quid in divinis atque humanis rebus exercitatius? .... Et tamen hic quoque post hæc omnia, hic inquam Tertullianus, catholici dogmatis parum tenax, ac disertior multo quam felicior, mutata deinceps sententia, &c.—Commonit. c. 24.]

[2 Novi et pastores eorum in pace leones, in prœlio cervos.—De Coron. Mil. c. I. p. 203. Col. Agripp. 1607.]

found in his book of Prescriptions against heresies, which he wrote before he fell into the Montanistic heresy. In that book he says that we should dispute against the heretics out of tradition, and not out of scripture. I answer : This seems, at first sight, to favour our opponents, and yet it inflicts a severe blow upon their cause. Tertullian had to deal with those same adversaries, as we have said before, that Irenæus also was engaged with. They denied the perfection of the scriptures ; and so do the papists. They said also that the apostles did not deliver everything to all, but some things only to the perfect : so do the papists at the present day. Besides, when Tertullian and Irenæus produced the scriptures, these men despised them. Furthermore, they mutilated and corrupted the scriptures, and denied some of the prophets, evangelists, and apostles. Hence Tertullian (as Irenæus did before him) appeals from the scriptures to the church and its discipline ; not to any unwritten doctrine, but to the defence, propagation, and promulgation of that doctrine which the apostles left delivered down orally in the churches founded by them. For, says he, the teaching which was first was true ; that which was later, false ; or, as he expresses it against Praxeas, " That was true which was first, that spurious which came later[3]." And he refutes those who said that the apostles had delivered certain secret doctrines to the perfect, by shewing that if there had been any doctrines of that sort, the churches founded by the apostles would have had and retained them.

CYPRIAN of Carthage, whom Bellarmine next objects to us, lived a century and more after Tertullian. In his epistles, Lib. I. Ep. 12, he declares it necessary that baptized persons should be anointed, and pronounces this to be a tradition. And Lib. II. Ep. 3, disputing concerning the mixture of water with the wine in the Eucharist, he says that " the tradition of the Lord should be observed." I answer, in the first place, that Cyprian was no apostle, and therefore his words should be examined, and not all received at once. So Augustine determines, contra Crescon. Lib. II. c. 32 ; where, speaking of an epistle of Cyprian's, he uses these expressions : " I am not bound by the authority of this epistle, because I do not hold the epistles of Cyprian for canonical scriptures; but I judge of them by the canonical books, and receive with approbation what in them agrees with the authority of the scriptures of God, but reject, without meaning him any disrespect, whatever does not agree[4]."

[3 Id esse verum quodcunque primum ; id esse adulterum quodcunque posterius.—c. ii. p. 606.]

[4 Ego hujus epistolæ auctoritate non teneor, quia literas Cypriani non

Secondly, I reply that Cyprian himself advises us to reject all customs which cannot plead for themselves the authority of scripture. Indeed, in that very same epistle he says that we ought to do as Christ did, and enjoined us to do, not minding what any one before us supposed ought to be done, but only what Christ, who is before all, first did. Let us, therefore, not mind what he himself said, but examine him by this very law laid down by himself.

First, then, let us see what he says of unction, Lib. I. Ep. 12 : "Those who are baptized must needs be anointed[1]." Whence, I beseech you, springs this necessity? Forsooth, that we may begin to be the anointed of God. Who sees not what a cold conceit is here? Can we not be the anointed of the Lord without this oil? If not, why did Christ give no precept to anoint when he commanded to baptize? and when we read in the Acts that so many were baptized, why do we not read that they were anointed also? If without this external oil we are not the anointed of the Lord, then Christ is not the Lord's anointed, since we nowhere read that he had this external unction : yet the Psalmist says that he was "anointed with the oil of gladness above his fellows." Perhaps Cyprian took this unction from Tertullian, from whom he derived much, and Tertullian from Montanus. Erasmus, in his book upon the purity of the tabernacle, says that formerly baptism was celebrated with water alone, but that afterwards the fathers added chrism. He says *the fathers*, not Christ or the apostles.

Next, as to the mixing of water with the wine in the Eucharist (which tradition Cyprian mentions, Lib. II. Epist. 3)[2], I reply, that Cyprian in that epistle is not so much solicitous about mixing water with the wine, as earnest to oppose the *Aquarii*, who rejected wine, and used nothing but water in the Eucharist : against these he says, " Let the tradition of the Lord be observed." However, I do not deny that the fathers used formerly to mix water with the wine. That is evident as well from Cyprian as from Justin's second Apology, besides the Pædagogus of Clemens Alexandrinus, Lib. II.

ut canonicas habeo, sed eas ex canonicis considero, et quod in eis divinarum scripturarum auctoritati congruit, cum laude ejus accipio; quod autem non congruit, cum pace ejus respuo.—T. VII. p. 177.]

[1 Ungi quoque necesse est eum qui baptizatus sit, ut accepto chrismate, id est, unctione, esset unctus Dei, et habere in se gratiam Christi posset.—Ep. 70. p. 190. ed. Fell. Amstol. 1691.]

[2 Admonitos autem nos scias, ut in calice offerendo Dominica traditio servetur, neque aliud fiat a nobis, quam quod pro nobis Dominus prior fecerit. Ut calix, qui in commemoratione ejus offertur, mixtus vino offeratur.—Ep. 63. p. 148.]

c. 2.   The reason was, because in those places the wine was so
strong that it could not be drunk conveniently unless tempered with
water : they therefore diluted their wine with water, because it
required such a mixture.   This is plain from the last chapter of
2 Maccabees, at the close : " Wine is not pleasing by itself, nor
water by itself; but wine mixed with water produceth a pleasant and delectable taste."   If wines were now so strong with us
as not to be fit to drink without water, it would be lawful even
in the Eucharist to use water with the wine, as a thing in itself
indifferent, provided only that the water destroyed not the nature
of the wine, but only tempered and diluted it.   Cyprian, however,
appears to value this custom too highly : for he says, If the wine
be without the water, then Christ is without the people ; if the
water be without the wine, then the people is without Christ.   But
Christ cannot be so easily severed from his church ; for the tie by
which Christ is united to the church is far too strong and binding
to be so readily broken asunder.   These therefore are mere figments.

Our opponent goes through the rest of his patristic testimonies,
and cites some from Hilary, Ambrose and Jerome, which might be
altogether omitted as impertinent to the present occasion.   For
HILARY[3], in that passage which Bellarmine urges, does not affirm
that any dogma not contained in scripture should be received; but
only that a term may be used, although it do not occur in scripture.
In that book he replies to Constantine, who was an Arian, and rejected the term *Homoüsion*, because it could not be found in scripture.
But this is of no force against us : for we readily receive even new
terms, provided they are such as expound the genuine sense of
scripture.   Such are *consubstantial, Trinity, person, supposition,
unbegotten,* θεοτόκος, and the like, which are convenient exponents
of the meaning of scripture.   But we should cautiously avoid those
terms which are foreign from the scriptures, such as *transubstantiation, consubstantiation, concomitance, ubiquity,* and the like.

AMBROSE is cited, in his book concerning the Initiate, c. 2 and
6,[4] where he explains the rites observed in baptism, which are
nowhere found written in the sacred pages.   The same author,

[3 Nolo, inquit, verba quæ non scripta sunt dici . . . Dic prius si recte
dici putas ; nolo adversum nova venena novas medicamentorum compara-
tiones . . . novitates vocum, sed profanas, devitare jubet apostolus.—Hilar.
c. Const. Imper. §. 16. coll. 1250, 1251. Paris, 1693.]

[4 Ambrosii Opp. T. VII. p. 4—14. Paris. 1839.]

Serm. 25, 34, and 36,[1] teaches us that Lent was instituted by Christ; and Ep. 81, and Serm. 38, he says that the Apostles' Creed is an unwritten tradition of the apostles. I answer, in the first place, that all Ambrose's statements are not to be received; for many both of the ancients and the moderns have justly censured him. Secondly, Ambrose recognises the perfection of the scriptures in all things necessary, as I shall hereafter make manifest. Thirdly, with respect to those traditions, I confess that the particular rites which the church of old used in the administration of the sacraments are not expressly prescribed in scripture. That Lent was prescribed by Christ, Ambrose does not teach, but only guess and conjecture: and if Christ enjoined Lent at all, it was by his example; which indeed is what Ambrose meant. For so he says, Serm. 34: "Thou subvertest the law, if thou keep not the example set by the Lord's fasting[2]." Ambrose supposed that the Lenten fast was enjoined by the example of Christ in the way of precept. He defends Lent, therefore, not by the authority of tradition, but of the scriptures; and accommodates to the same purpose other scriptures, wrested very unskilfully from their true drifts; as, for example, the account of the floods of rain-water which fell in the times of Noah, when the windows of heaven were opened forty days, and of Moses feeding the people of Israel forty years with manna from heaven in the wilderness. He heaps together other passages of scripture also with no greater wisdom. When he had these places of scripture to rely upon, might he not justly accuse of "contumacy and prevarication" all those who "subvert this law" of the Lenten fast, "given for our salvation, by eating dinners therein?" What? Do the papists eat never a dinner from one end of Lent to the other? Yea, verily, and every day. They are not then good Christians, if we believe Ambrose. For so says Ambrose: "What sort of Christian art thou, that dinest when thy Lord is fasting[3]?" But I forget that this is not dinner, but supper, even though they eat the meal at noon: for so they choose by a beautiful distinction to prove themselves good catholics, and turn dinner into supper, that is, noon into night. Behold the noble mirror of popish piety and conscientiousness! Could Ambrose recognise these men as catholics or Christians without abandoning his law? Now as to the Creed: I acknowledge it to be an apos-

[1 T. II. p. 291; I. 443; VI. 448; V. 126.]
[2 Rescindis legem, qui exemplum jejunii Dominici non custodis.]
[3 Qualis Christianus es, cum Domino jejunante tu prandes?]

tolical, but yet a written tradition; for there is not a word of the
Creed that is not found in the scriptures. Ambrose, not improperly,
calls the Creed the key of Peter, Serm. 38.

JEROME, in his epistle to Marcella, says that Lent is an apostolical tradition[4], and in his Dialogue against the Luciferians recognises the custom of the church[5]. To this I answer: With respect to
Lent, the objection hath been already satisfied; and as to the pious
customs of the church, who ever blamed, or did not rather highly
esteem them? But these customs are free, and by no means in the
class of necessary things: for Jerome taught that all necessary things
may be found in scripture, as we shall shew in its proper place.

I come now to AUGUSTINE, from whom our opponent adduces
various testimonies. *First* he cites the epistle to Januarius, Ep. 118,
where Augustine writes thus: "Now those which we observe,
handed down though not written, and which are indeed observed
by the whole world, may be understood to have been commended
and enjoined to be kept either by the apostles themselves, or by
general councils (whose authority is most salutary in the church);
as the anniversary solemnities in which we commemorate the passion
and resurrection of the Lord, and his ascension into heaven, and
the coming of the Holy Ghost, and anything else of the like
nature, which is observed by the whole church wheresoever diffused
throughout the world[6]." I answer, that Augustine's name stands
high in the church, and deservedly: yet we must remember that
he was a man, and therefore might err. And although he seems
in this place to favour traditions, yet in others he defends the
perfection of scripture with the utmost earnestness, as shall afterwards be more conveniently shewn. He was most clearly of

[4 Nos unam quadragesimam secundum traditionem apostolorum toto
nobis orbe congruo jejunamus.—Opp. T. IV. part. 2. coll. 64, 65. Paris, 1706.]

[5 Etiam si scripturæ auctoritas non subesset, totius orbis in hanc partem
consensus instar præcepti obtineret. Nam et multa alia, quæ per traditionem
in ecclesiis observantur, auctoritatem sibi scriptæ legis usurpaverunt.—Ibid.
col. 294. These words are put into the mouth of the Luciferian: but the
general principle is not disowned by the orthodox Dialogist.]

[6 Illa autem, quæ non scripta sed tradita custodimus, quæ quidem toto
terrarum orbe observantur, dantur intelligi vel ab ipsis apostolis vel plena-
riis conciliis (quorum est in ecclesia saluberrima auctoritas) commendata
atque statuta retineri; sicuti quod Domini passio et resurrectio et ascensio in
cœlum et adventus de cœlo Spiritus Sancti anniversaria solemnitate cele-
brantur, et si quid aliud occurrerit, quod servatur ab universa, quacunque se
diffundit ecclesia.]

opinion, that no dogma ought to be received which does not rest upon scripture. Either, therefore, he here speaks of traditions which are not necessary, or he is at variance with himself. But I come to the passage itself. Augustine speaks of traditions observed throughout the whole world. Now what are these? The solemn annual celebration of the passion, resurrection, ascension of the Lord, and the descent of the Holy Spirit from heaven. I answer, in the first place, that these traditions are of no great moment: for without these traditions our whole religion may be safe and sound; consequently these traditions are not necessary. We may confess and bear in mind all that relates to the death, resurrection, and ascension of Christ, without any solemnity of fixed and stated days. However, I do not condemn the practice of the ancient church, which, by a free custom, observed these days as festivals. I reply, secondly, that Augustine is ignorant and uncertain whether the observance of these days was instituted by the apostles or by general councils; which is a sufficient proof that the origin of this tradition was unknown. Yet the papists say that they are certain of its apostolical institution. Thus they know more about the matter than Augustine did. Thirdly, I reply, that Augustine does not prove these traditions to have been observed by all churches. He says so indeed, but he does not prove it, nor could he have proved it; for he did not know what was wont to be done by other churches. Perhaps the neighbouring churches observed this custom, and it is past doubt that the people of Hippo and the whole African church observed it : but he could not have been equally certain of all other churches.

However, the Jesuit endeavours to remove these answers of ours : and, firstly, argues that these customs were not free, because Augustine subjoins that those things which vary with places are free; but that those which are observed through all the world are necessary. I answer : Augustine calls those changeful customs free, and those which are fixed, necessary; but how necessary? To salvation? By no means; but because it was necessary for every one, wherever he went, to observe them, for the sake of avoiding disorder and shunning scandal. This we confess : but we say that such customs are always to be observed with a free conscience. Then, as to our assertion that the apostles did not institute these festival days, he endeavours to overthrow this also. Brentius proves from the fourth chapter of the Galatians, that the apostles did not institute them, because Paul in that chapter reproves the

Galatians for making a difference between days. Bellarmine answers out of Augustine's 119th Epist. *ad Januarium*, that the apostle speaks of those who observe times according to the rules of the astrologers. I reply, that the Galatians were more inclined to Judaize than to observe astrological rules. Therefore he brings another answer from Jerome, Chrysostom, and Augustine, upon the place. Those fathers say, that in this passage the festivals of the Jews, and not those of the Christians, are condemned. I answer: Yet even so the scope of the apostle is no less opposed to the papists. Paul disputes against those who suppose that any external ceremony is necessary to salvation, or to be conjoined with faith. If the papists hold this, he disputes against them: if they hold it not, then they confess what we desire, that these traditions are free, and not necessary. In that same epistle Augustine complains greatly of the multitude of ceremonies in the church. He says that the number of ceremonies had so increased in his time, as to make our state seem worse than that of the Jews had been. If he were now alive, and could see the state of the church, and the additional growth of ceremonies, he would say so still more. Socrates, Lib. v. c. 22, and Sozomen, Lib. vii. c. 19, and Augustine, Ep. 86, are clearly on our side in this matter: for they write that neither Christ nor his apostles prescribed any thing concerning festival days.

The *second* testimony cited by Bellarmine against us from Augustine, is from *de Baptism. c. Donat.* Lib. ii. c. 7, Lib. iv. c. 6, Lib. iv. c. 24, and Lib. v. c. 23. I answer: Chemnitz gives a correct and apposite reply (which I adopt), that Augustine in those passages is speaking of persons baptized by heretics, whose baptism he affirms ought not to be repeated. And although Augustine says that this is a tradition, yet he does not say that it is not in scripture; yea, he proves the same from scripture by many testimonies. Bellarmine spends many words to no purpose upon this point, and says that no sufficient proof can be brought from scripture; and that therefore Augustine, although he alleged reasons and scripture as much as he could find, yet placed his great foundation in tradition. I answer: Nevertheless, Lib. v. c. 4, he uses these expressions, "Supported by so many and such important testimonies of scripture," &c.—and subjoins, "the reasons of truth being so clear," &c. And Lib. v. c. 26, he says that what Cyprian advises, namely, "to recur to the fountain-head of scripture," is the best course, and what should be adopted without hesitation.

Here we must remark the impudence of Bellarmine. He says that Augustine does not prove his point from scripture, but only related by what scripture his opponents endeavoured to prove theirs; the falsehood of which is manifest. We read indeed, Lib. II. c. 8, that Cyprian was pressed with the authority of custom by the Roman bishop Stephen, and yet did not yield to it. Now if the authority of custom were as great as the papists wish to make it, he should have yielded. Andradius, however, *Defens. Con. Trid.* Lib. II. expressly says that Augustine pleaded many testimonies of scripture against the Donatists; whence I argue thus: Those testimonies which Augustine used were either apposite, or they were not: if they were, then he refuted the Donatists by scripture, which Bellarmine denies; if they were not, then he abused and played upon those passages, which would be a hard thing to say of so great a father.

But Bellarmine hath still another answer;—that Augustine brings conjectures out of scripture, which have indeed some efficacy towards establishing the truth after it hath been defined by a council, but are not sufficient of themselves. Nothing can be conceived more unworthy than this reply. For, first, conjectures drawn from scripture are so far from being sufficient to refute heretics, that they have absolutely no weight at all. Augustine would have done more harm than service to his cause, if he had brought nothing but conjectures. And, on the contrary, Lib. v. c. 47, he himself plainly declares, that he rests upon " most weighty testimonies of scripture" and " plain reasons of truth." Lib. v. c. 23, he writes that it is contrary to the commandment of God to baptize those who come from the heretics, if they have already received baptism amongst them, " because it is not only shewn, but clearly shewn by the testimony of scripture," &c. Bellarmine says that Chemnitz hath been dishonest in his citation of this passage. Why? Because those words " it is plainly shewn by the testimony of scripture" are not referred to the preceding but to the following point, namely, that many Christians baptized in the church lose charity, and yet do not lose their baptism. But here he is himself most outrageously dishonest. For Augustine is proving it repugnant to the commandment of God to rebaptize those who were baptized by the heretics, and afterwards come into the catholic church, " because it is not only shewn, but clearly shewn, by the testimony of scripture, that many false Christians, although they have not the same charity with the saints, have yet one common baptism with the saints[1]." Who sees not that Augustine applied these many and plain testimonies of scripture, whereby it is shewn that baptism remains entire without charity, to the confirmation of the cause which he defended against the Donatists, namely, that those who come from the heretics are not to be rebaptized, because the heretics may retain baptism, although they have made shipwreck of charity? Besides, if Augustine had adduced nothing but conjectures out of scripture, could he have used such words as these, " We may perceive by so many and great testimonies of scripture, and clear reasons of truth, that Christ's baptism cannot be destroyed by the perversity of any man[2]?" And elsewhere, " Because it is not only shewn, but manifestly shewn, by the testimony of the holy scriptures," &c. And elsewhere, where he praises the opinion of Cyprian, that we should recur to the fountain-head, that is, the scripture, he adduces that testimony, " one God, one baptism," and then goes on to mention other scriptures. Finally, if these conjectures are of no force until after the definition of a council, they were of no force then when Augustine disputed with them against the Donatists; for up to that time nothing had been defined in a council against the Donatists.

Afterwards Bellarmine adduces a testimony from Innocent's first epistle to Decentius[3]. However he hath omitted this testimony from Innocent, and the next from Leo, in his printed edition, although they appear in his MS. lectures. I answer briefly : Firstly, those decretal epistles are of no weight, no credit, no authority. Secondly, I say, that Innocent was wrong in his traditions, as is plain from Augustine, c. Julian. Lib. II. c. 2, and elsewhere. Thirdly, I affirm that the traditions recited in that epistle are frivolous and empty trifles ; such as that the kiss of peace is not to be given before the mysteries are completed, that confirmation is to be celebrated by the bishop, remarking that he dares not utter the words of confirmation, lest he should seem to betray the mysteries[4]. Now what, I pray

[1 Quia scripturarum sanctarum testimoniis non solum ostenditur, sed plane ostenditur, multos pseudo-christianos, quanquam non habeant eandem caritatem cum sanctis, baptismum tamen communem habere cum sanctis.]

[2 Tot tantisque scripturarum testimoniis et perspicuis rationibus veritatis intelligitur Christi baptismum non fieri cujuslibet hominis perversitate perversum.]

[3 Innocentii ad Decentium Ep. vi. inter Epp. Decret. ac Rescriptt. Rom. Pontiff. Matriti. 1821. p. 10.]

[4 Verba vero dicere non possum, ne magis prodere videar, quam ad consultationem respondere.—Ib. p. 11.]

[WHITAKER.]

39

you, are these so mystic words? *Confirmo te signo crucis, et ungo te chrismate salutis, in nomine Patris, et Filii, et Spiritus Sancti.* These words he dared not utter. Wherefore? He then adduces a testimony from Leo, Serm. 6. de Quadrag.[1] and elsewhere. I answer, in the first place, that Leo was wrong in saying that the apostles instituted fasts, which they never instituted. Secondly, I say that those fasts which Leo delivered are not now observed by the papists. For he speaks of fasts upon the fourth and sixth days of the week: but the papists do not fast upon the fourth day,

And let so much suffice for an answer to the testimonies of the fathers.

CHAPTER XIII.

BELLARMINE'S REMAINING ARGUMENTS ARE CONFUTED.

BEFORE coming to our own arguments, I must reply to the remainder of Bellarmine's. His fifth argument is taken from the testimony of heretics, which must needs be a strong one. The heretics, says he, of all times have rejected traditions; therefore those who despise traditions are heretics. That that was the case with Valentinus and Marcion, he proves out of Irenæus, Lib. III. c. 2, and Tertullian's Prescriptions. I answer: In the *first* place, it does not prove that the heretics of all times rejected traditions, that these men whom he names rejected them: yea, those very same heretics embraced traditions, as is abundantly evident from these same authors Irenæus and Tertullian. In the mean time, there is no consequence in such reasoning as this: All heretics rejected tradition; therefore all who reject tradition are heretics. *Secondly*, it is no way surprising that Valentinus and Marcion should have rejected such traditions as Irenæus means, and by which they clearly saw that they were refuted; for Irenæus produced the tradition of the apostolic churches. Now this tradition was no other than the conservation and propagation of the apostolic doctrine by the public ministry of the church. Nor is it wonderful that those men should have despised

[1 Quod ergo, dilectissimi, in omni tempore unumquemque convenit facere Christianum, id nunc solicitus est et devotius exsequendum, ut apostolica institutio quadraginta dierum jejuniis impleatur.—Leon. Opp. p. 40. Lugd. 1633.]

traditions, who made no account of scripture, and thought themselves wiser than the apostles. As to Cyprian, his error did not lie in rejecting custom and appealing to scripture, (for he is praised by Augustine for doing so,) but in thinking that his opinion could be established by scripture, whereas scripture is subversive of it. Even Gratian, Dist. 8 and 9, approves of Cyprian for refusing to yield to mere custom[2]. Bellarmine subjoins that the Arians (to mention no more) appealed to the scripture alone. I answer : The Arians clung to the bare words of scripture : we do not imitate them in that. We do not reject terms which never occur in scripture, provided the sense and force of those terms be contained in scripture, as we have frequently replied already : on which account we condemn the Arians for rejecting the *Homoüsion*. However, religion and piety do not consist in words ; and Luther said truly, that he should not be a heretic if he rejected the term *Homoüsion*, and yet so thought of the Son of God as the scriptures have delivered.

Bellarmine's sixth argument is taken from the custom of all nations, and specially of the Jews. Origen, Hom. v. in *Numeros*, Hilary, *in Ps. ii.*, and Anatolius, *ap. Euseb.* Lib. vii. c. 28, testify that the Jews had unwritten traditions. I answer : In the *first* place, it is a mere talmudical and cabbalistic fancy to suppose, that though the law was delivered in writing by Moses, the mysteries of the law were concealed by him, and entrusted only orally to persons wiser than the rest. Hence have arisen their exceeding foolish traditions of the Mishnah (δευτερώσεις), which Jerome and the other fathers so frequently deride. I reply, *secondly*, that the Jesuit himself confesses that some catholics have been in a different opinion, and that the Jews had no such traditions ; although he does not assent to their view. However, the reasons on which he grounds his dissent are very slight. The first reason is, because (says he) we have already shewn that all things are not contained in the law. I answer : But we have shewn before that you have shewn no such thing. What (I beseech you) were the points which you determined not to be contained in the law ? Expiation of original sin in the case of women, or of males dying before the eighth day. So Stapleton also, Lib. xii. c. 5, with whom Bellarmine agrees, as you have already heard. But we have sufficiently replied to these conjectures. Stapleton however adds, that " nei-

[2 Et certe, ut beati Cypriani utamur sententia, quælibet consuetudo . . . . veritati est postponenda.—Decret. Pars i. Dist. 8. c. 5.   Corp. Jur. Canon. Lugd. 1591.]

ther is faith in Christ as mediator ever written of in the whole old
Testament." Who can tolerate such an assertion as this, that the
faith of Christ in nowhere found in the whole old Testament? Why
then does Christ affirm that the scriptures testify of him? Or why
did the apostles establish the Christian faith by the old Testament,
and the fathers say that the new Testament was hidden in the old?
Bellarmine, I suppose, was ashamed of this notion of Stapleton's : and
indeed it is full of error and Jewish blasphemy. However, Bellarmine hath another argument against the opposite opinion. The
Jews, says he, must have had tradition, because, for a long time
after the birth of Moses the people lived without a written law.
I answer : It is true indeed that everything was not written immediately after Moses' birth ; but let him prove, if he can, that all
was not written when Moses had written the law. In Exodus xxiv.
3, we read that "Moses recited to the people all the words of
the Lord." Therefore he did not conceal those mysteries from
them. Christ also and the apostles always appeal to the scriptures,
urge the scriptures, expound the scriptures, and never make any
mention of these hidden mysteries. Besides, if there were such
hidden mysteries, then the better part of the divine law would have
been unwritten ; which is by no means to be thought.

But Bellarmine goes on to prove from Thucydides, Aristotle,
Lycurgus, Cicero, and Cæsar, that profane nations also were in
great measure governed by unwritten laws, and had their unwritten
customs. He adds proofs, besides, from the canon and civil law.
He produces all these testimonies to shew that the force of customs
and written laws is equal. I answer : In the *first* place, the church
is not governed in the same way as profane republics. Political
laws cannot provide for every individual case, or embrace all particulars; and therefore customs, having the force of laws, are necessarily required. But it was an easy thing for God to deliver all
things necessary for salvation in the scriptures. Yet even in the
state custom does not always prevail. Cicero says in his book *de
Claris Oratoribus*, "We must not use that most corrupt rule of
custom." Demosthenes too writes somewhere, that we must not do
as is often wont to be done, but as it is fitting should be done, οὐχ
ὡς γέγονε πολλάκις, ἀλλ᾽ ὡς προσήκει γίγνεσθαι. Tertullian in
his tract, *de Velandis Virginibus*, says most correctly : "Whatever
savours of opposition to truth is a heresy, although it be an old
custom." Old custom, therefore, is of no avail in religion, although
it have great weight in the commonwealth. He adds in the same

gospel of Christ, and Christ himself, was a scandal and stumbling-block to the Jews, and foolishness to the Greeks; but to the elect of both Jews and Greeks (for such are the perfect and the wise) it was "the power of God unto salvation." *Fourthly*, Bellarmine says, that almost all the fathers, when they speak of the eucharist and other sacraments, use such expressions as, "The faithful understand this ; the initiated know what is said[1]." I answer : I confess, indeed, that these words frequently occur in the fathers, and I know well that the fathers were very careful and anxious to afford no occasion to the Gentiles and profane of ridiculing those holy mysteries. They did not choose, therefore, to speak of them before all. But it does not therefore follow that the institution of the sacraments cannot be found in the bible.

These are all Bellarmine's arguments : let us now come to our own.

CHAPTER XIV.

SUCH OF OUR ARGUMENTS AGAINST UNWRITTEN TRADITIONS AS BELLARMINE HATH ANSWERED.

HITHERTO we have stood upon the defensive against our adversaries, and sustained their attack in such a manner as that none of their weapons have done any execution upon us. We will now begin to assail them in our turn. First, we will produce our arguments from scripture, as being far the strongest of all ; and of these scriptural arguments, we will place foremost those which Bellarmine hath attempted to answer.

The first passage of scripture is contained in Deut. iv. 2, " Thou shalt not add unto this word which I speak unto you, neither shalt thou diminish from it." Also in Deut. xii. in the last verse, similar expressions occur : "Do only this which I command you ; thou shalt not add thereto, nor diminish aught from it." From these passages we gather the following argument : If the Jews were not permitted to add anything to the books of Moses, then still less is it lawful for us to add anything to the canon of scripture, now increased by so many books since. But the former was not permitted : therefore still less is it now permitted to us. The consequence in the major is necessary ; for, if the five books of Moses

[1 ἴσασιν οἱ μεμνημένοι. This phrase, as observed by Casaubon, occurs at least fifty times in the writings of Chrysostom alone.]

contain a full and perfect body of doctrine, as they certainly do, and Moses therefore forbids any addition to be made, then surely a most abundantly perfect body of doctrine must needs be found in the whole circle of the books of the old and new Testaments. The minor rests upon the express words of scripture, "Thou shalt not add to this word, neither shalt thou diminish from it."

Our opponents have devised various replies, but Bellarmine shall stand in the place of all. He hath a twofold answer. In the *first* place, he says, that these words are not to be understood of the written word of God, but of the word orally delivered. This he proves by two reasons : first, because the scriptures were not then extant ; secondly, because Moses says "Which I command you," not, which I write. I reply to the first, that his assertion that the scriptures were not then published is manifestly shewn to be false by the scriptures themselves. But even if they had not been then written, yet Moses intended to write them. However, as I said, the scripture shews Bellarmine's assertion to be false ; for in Exod. xxiv. 4, we read, "Moses wrote all the words of the Lord." This was in the first or second year after the departure from Egypt. Now he delivered this discourse in Deuteronomy in the fortieth year after the Exodus, in the eleventh month, as appears from Deut. i. 3, a few days before his death ; for he died in the twelfth month of that same year. All therefore did not remain to be written at that time, since so short an interval as passed between this harangue and the death of Moses was not sufficient for committing all to writing. That the book of Deuteronomy was then written, appears from the book itself ; since we often read in it, "the words which are written in this book." This probably Bellarmine perceived on second thoughts ; for he hath omitted this reason in his late publication, although he presses it in the MS. He found out therefore afterwards, that it was no reason at all. Secondly, as to his observation that Moses says, "I command," not, "I write," it does not follow from this that the passage is not meant to refer to the written law. In Joshua i. 7, Joshua is commanded to do what the Lord had *commanded* him. What? Were these commandments therefore not written? On the contrary, it is plain from what follows that they were written : "This book of the law shall not depart out of thy mouth, but thou shalt meditate in it day and night." In the commencement of Deut. xxviii., it is thus written, "If thou wilt keep the things which I command thee this day," &c. And from verse 58 of the same chapter it appears that these were written ; for the same

Moses says to the same people, "If thou keep not all the things which are written in this book," &c. At the end of Deut. xxvii. we read thus : "Cursed be he who continueth not in all the words of this law ;" and Paul, Galat. iii. 10, interprets this to mean written words : "In all things which are written in the book of this law." Thus he implies that the whole law was written. There is no consequential force then in the argument, that because he says "which I command," not, "which I have written," therefore this word was not committed to writing, but delivered by oral tradition. Besides, if Moses had entrusted some things orally to certain persons, which he considered unfit to be written; to whom could he have committed them rather than to Joshua, to whom he imparted all his counsels, and who was his successor in office ? Yet Joshua himself is referred, and, as it were, tied to the book, Josh. i.: "This book shall not depart from thee, but thou shalt meditate therein day and night." In which words Joshua's meditation is referred to the book of the sacred scriptures which Moses himself had published, and not directed to those unwritten precepts. However, Bellarmine dismisses this reply of his as not sufficiently strong or safe, and betakes himself to another, which he says is the true one.

Secondly, then, he answers, that the Lord willed in these words, that his commandments should not be corrupted, but kept entire, as he enjoined them. In these things which I command you, you shall make no change, either by addition or diminution : but he does not say, you shall observe nothing else but what I now command you. I answer : I confess, indeed, that false interpretations of scripture are condemned in these words; but this is not the whole of what is here prohibited. For when God forbids them to add, he signifies that this body of doctrine was so perfect as that nothing could or should be added to it ; and that, therefore, we should acquiesce in it, be satisfied with it, and cleave to it alone. They *add*, therefore, who determine that this teaching is not complete and full. And when we shew that this word is written, we shew that the written word contains a full and perfect body of doctrine, to which nothing should be added. The ancient Jews understood and explained these words to mean that nothing should be added to the written word. So Josephus, quoted by Eusebius, Lib. iii. c. 8, testifies that the authority of their sacred books was so great, that nothing was added to, or taken from them, for so many ages. So the fathers also interpret these words. I will content myself with alleging Chrysostom, who, in his 52nd Homily

upon Matthew, says that the priests added many things to the
law, although Moses had enjoined them, with threats, not to do so.
Nor let any one suppose that Chrysostom speaks there of things
contrary to scripture; for he refers to those rites of frequent
washings used by the Jews. Those washings were not simply
contrary to scripture, but only because the Pharisees made holiness
consist in them; and yet Chrysostom confesses that, in this way,
an addition was made to the law, contrary to the command of God.
Hence it appears that this passage in Deuteronomy should be understood of the written word; since Chrysostom says that the Jews
made additions, because they used rites which were nowhere
written, although not absolutely contrary to scripture. Nay,
Thomas Aquinas himself explains this passage thus, " that nothing
should be added to the words of holy scripture, or diminished from
them [1];" and Cajetan, upon the place, says, " It may be gathered
from this that the law of God is perfect."

But let us see how Bellarmine establishes his interpretation.
Because otherwise, says he, the prophets and apostles would have
sinned, who afterwards added so much, if these words be understood to forbid any addition; therefore they ought to be understood not of not adding to, but of not corrupting what was written.
I answer, in the first place, that the prophets and apostles were
not to be ranked with other men, but had as much authority as
Moses himself, and therefore deserved as much credit as he. The
papists cannot establish their traditions by the same authority.
Secondly, that the prophets and apostles, when they wrote new
books, added nothing to the written word of God. For we must
distinguish two things in the word of God;—the sum of the
doctrine itself, and its principal heads,—and the explication of
these heads. As to the sum of doctrine, nothing was added by
the prophets and apostles; which may thus be easily proved. The
whole scripture is composed of two parts, the law and the gospel.
No one denies that the whole law of Moses, moral, judicial, and
ceremonial, is written. But perhaps doubts may be entertained
respecting the gospel. Nay, the whole of the gospel itself may
be found in the books of Moses. There is no article of the Creed
itself, for which there is not some illustrious proof extant in
Moses. Therefore, the whole doctrine of it, meaning the sum
of its teaching, is contained in the books of Moses. But as to
the clearer exposition and explication of this teaching, many ad-

[1 Sacra enim scriptura est regula fidei, cui nec addere nec subtrahere
licet.—Secunda secundæ, Quæst. I. Art. IX. Tom. II. p. 5, Antwerp. 1627.]

ditions were made by the prophets and apostles. The prophets illustrated Moses, the apostles the prophets : but neither the one nor the other added any dogma which is not found in the books of Moses; just as he who explains a law adds nothing to the law. On this account the apostles prove their gospel by the books of the old Testament; and Christ says, John v., "Search the scriptures ... for they testify of me."

But Bellarmine persists, and turns upon Chemnitz, Brentius, and Calvin, who had used this answer, thus: In the same way, says he, traditions are not additions to, but explications of, scripture: for traditions too are found in scripture, not in the particular indeed, but in the universal; and the new Testament is no otherwise found in the old. He uses a comparison to illustrate this answer of his : as the tree is in the seed virtually, so the new Testament is in the old, implicitly and potentially, in the universal, but not in the particular. And in the same way tradition is in scripture: for as Moses says generally, "A prophet shall the Lord your God raise up unto you like unto me; him shall ye hear;" so we are in the general commanded by the apostle to "keep the traditions." Thus he replies to Chemnitz, Brentius, and Calvin. But I undertake to obviate this reply. In the first place, I maintain that most of the popish traditions can by no means be expositions of scripture, because they most openly contradict and oppose scripture. Such are their worship of images, and sacrifice of the altar; as shall hereafter, if God permit, be made clear, when we come to those controversies. Concerning these and such-like expositions of scripture we may truly say : Woe to the gloss which corrupts the text! Secondly, I say that the Jesuit's pretence, that the new Testament is contained in the old, not in the particular, but only generally, is untrue. The comparison which he uses is impious and blasphemous, that the new Testament is no otherwise contained in the old, than as a tree in the seed, that is, only virtually and potentially : for all the dogmas and heads of the gospel are found in the old Testament, not in the universal merely, but also in the particular ; not only implicitly but explicitly, although indeed not so plainly and perspicuously. If we run through all the articles of our faith, we shall find them all, even in the particular, in the old Testament,— as that God is the Creator of heaven and earth, that Christ is the Son of a virgin, and so forth. All these are predicted in the old Testament, and the accomplishment related in the new. But they will say, perhaps, that the sacraments of the new Testament cannot be found in the old ; for this occurs to me as I ponder the subject.

Yet they can. For the sea and the rock prefigured baptism, and
manna the Eucharist, as the apostle testifies, 1 Cor. x. Otherwise
the apostles could not have proved all the dogmas which they
propounded out of the old Testament. Now it is certain that the
apostles confirmed all they said by its authority. Consequently,
the Bereans searched the scriptures (Acts xvii.) to see whether
those things which Paul preached were so. But if (as the Jesuit
says) the whole new Testament were comprehended in this sentence
only ("The Lord your God will raise up unto you a prophet like
unto me; him shall ye hear,") as the tree is in the seed, the
apostles could certainly never have persuaded the Jews that this
Jesus was the Messiah. But they used many other testimonies of
scripture. Paul says, Acts xxvi. 22, that he said "nothing but what
Moses and the prophets did say." So Christ, Luke xxiv. 27, "beginning at Moses and all the prophets, expounded in all the scriptures the things concerning himself." There were, therefore, other
testimonies, sufficiently clear, besides that single one which Bellarmine cites. And Rom. i. 2, Paul says, that the gospel was promised in the prophets. It is false then that the new Testament
is only potentially in the old. For the whole gospel is no less
perfectly in the old than in the new Testament, although not so
perspicuously. The tree is as much in the old Testament, as in
the new, though it spreads not its branches so diffusely.

Irenæus, Lib. iv. c. 66, after having shewn at large that Christ
accomplished all that the prophets had predicted, subjoins at length
at the close of that chapter: "Read more diligently the gospel given
us by the apostles, and read more diligently the prophets, and ye will
find that all that the Lord did and suffered and taught is preached
in them[1]." This passage subverts Bellarmine's reply. Augustine,
upon Psalm cv., says, that "the old Testament is unveiled in the
new, and the new veiled in the old." And, c. Faust. Manich.
Lib. xvii. c. 6, he writes thus: "Christ came not to add what was
wanting, but to do and accomplish what was written[2]." And he
says that Christ himself indicates this in his own words, when he
says, "One jot or one tittle shall not pass from the law" (not,
until what is wanting be added, but) "until all things which are

[1 Legite diligentius id quod ab apostolis est evangelium nobis datum, et
legite diligentius prophetas, et invenietis universam actionem, et omnem doctrinam, et omnem passionem Domini nostri prædicatam in ipsis.—p. 404.
Paris. 1675.]

[2 Venit Christus non ut adderentur quæ deerant, sed ut fierent et
implerentur quæ scripta sunt.]

written shall be accomplished." So that even Christ himself added
nothing, but all he taught, did, and suffered, was contained in the
old Testament. Jerome says in his Epistle to Damasus : " Whatever we read in the old Testament, we find also in the gospel ; and
whatever is read in the gospel, is deduced from the authority of
the old Testament[3]." Therefore whatever is found in the new
Testament may be confirmed, not only in respect of the universal
but of the particular also, by the authority of the old Testament.
We will support this answer of ours by only one testimony more.
Basil the Great, in his *Ascetics*, writes thus : " What is the property
of a believer ? To assent with the fullest persuasion to the word
of God, to reject nothing, and to superadd nothing." For this is
the very thing which the Lord forbids, Deut. iv. Then Basil
subjoins : " For if whatsoever is not of faith is sin, and faith be
by hearing, and hearing by the word of God, then whatsoever is
not derived from the scriptures is sin." Basil's own words are as
follow : Τί ἴδιον πιστοῦ ; τὸ ἐν τοιαύτῃ πληροφορίᾳ συνδιατί-
θεσθαι τῇ δυνάμει τῶν εἰρημένων, καὶ μηδὲν τολμᾶν ἀθετεῖν ἢ
ἐπιδιατάττεσθαι· εἰ γὰρ πᾶν ὃ οὐκ ἐκ πίστεως ἁμαρτία ἐστιν,
ὥς φησιν ὁ ἀπόστολος, ἡ δὲ πίστις ἐξ ἀκοῆς, ἡ δὲ ἀκοὴ διὰ
ῥήματος Θεοῦ, πᾶν τὸ ἐκτὸς τῆς θεοπνεύστου γραφῆς, οὐκ ἐκ
πίστεως ὄν, ἁμαρτία ἐστιν[4]. From which words I draw these
three inferences : First, that those words of Moses contained in
Deut. iv. and xii. should be understood of the written word of God ;
for it is to those words that Basil here alludes : secondly, that
the word on which faith is grounded is written : thirdly, that all
beside the scriptures, ἐκτὸς τῆς θεοπνεύστου γραφῆς, is sin because it is not of faith, and should be rejected. Let it suffice to
have spoken thus much upon the first place from scripture.

Our second passage of scripture is taken from Rev. xx. 18, and
is like the former. The words are these : " I testify to every man
that heareth the words of the prophecy of this book, If any man
shall add unto these things, God shall add unto him the plagues
that are written in this book : and if any man shall take away
from the words of the book of this prophecy, God shall take away
his part out of the book of life, and out of the holy city, and from
the things which are written in this book." Bellarmine replies,
that these words prohibit the corruption of this book, but not the

[3 Quidquid in vetere Testamento legimus, hoc idem in evangelio
reperimus; et quod in evangelio fuerit lectitatum, hoc ex veteris Testamenti
auctoritate deducitur.]

[4 Moralia, Reg. 80, T. II. p. 386, Paris. 1618.]

writing of new books, or the delivery of new doctrines. "For," says he, "John himself wrote his gospel after this." I answer: In the *first* place, every addition of books, provided they be prophetic or apostolic, is not indeed prohibited in these words: the prophets or the apostles might add other books. Yet the consequence will not hold, that the addition of the popish traditions is not forbidden here, unless they can prove that their traditions rest upon apostolical authority. *Secondly,* I confess that these words properly pertain to the confirmation of the authority of this particular piece of prophetic scripture, but they may also avail to the confirmation of the completeness of the whole canon. For we may, by parity of reason, argue thus: The authority and analogy of the other books is the same: if, therefore, it be not lawful to add to this book, then, by parity of reason, it will be unlawful to add to any other book, or detract from it. Hence it will follow that these books contain in them a full and perfect body of teaching, and that no dogma should be sought outside them. Now those who suppose that there is any other necessary article, add to these books. Solomon, Proverbs xxx. 6, writes thus: "Add thou not unto his words, lest he reprove thee, and thou be found a liar." So Ambrose gathers from this passage, *de Paradiso,* c. 12, that nothing should be taken away from the divine commands[1]. The same author, in his exposition of the Apocalypse, (if that piece be Ambrose's, which some doubt,) accommodates the words now before us to the other scriptures also; and our countrymen of Rheims allege his testimony in their annotations. Now in that exposition Ambrose affirms two things: First, that he who expounds the scriptures adds nothing; where he tacitly implies that whoever does more than expound the scriptures, makes an addition to them. In the next place, he says that those heretics are accursed, who added any thing to the scriptures, or diminished aught from them, for the confirmation of their heresies. Those, therefore, who add any thing to the scripture itself, or take any thing from it, are obnoxious to this denunciation. Augustine, likewise, in his exposition of this place, says that all *falsifiers* of scripture are condemned in these words. Thomas Aquinas in his commentary upon 1 Tim. vi., Lect. 1, says that the canonical scripture is the rule of our understandings; in confirmation of which he subjoins the two places of scripture which we have been handling, as well that from Deuteronomy, as this from the

[1] Si quid enim vel addas vel detrahas, prævaricatio quædam videtur esse mandati.—T. I. p. 62. Col. Agripp. 1616.]

Apocalypse. Therefore he understood these words to refer not merely to this book, but to the canon of the whole scripture.

We have now discussed two passages of scripture, wherein additions to, or diminutions from, scripture are forbidden; here follows a third, which is contained in Gal. i. 8, in the following words : " Though we, or an angel from heaven, preach any other gospel unto you than that which we have preached unto you, let him be accursed;" and afterwards, v. 9, " If any one preach any other gospel unto you than that ye have received, let him be accursed." It is a remarkable passage, and used by all our divines who write against the popish traditions. All those are obnoxious to this anathema, who preach any other gospel but that which is written. Now the popish traditions (even granting them to be not contrary to the scriptures) are yet wholly beside the scriptures : those therefore who defend them, lie under the weight of this anathema. Whoever preach any thing as gospel besides Paul's gospel, are pronounced accursed. The patrons of unwritten traditions preach as gospel something beside, yea, con- trary to Paul's gospel, since the whole of that is contained in the scriptures : therefore the patrons of popish traditions are declared accursed. Our argument from these words is confirmed also by the judgment of Augustine, c. *Liter. Petilian.* Lib. iii. c. 6 ; and of Basil, *in Summa,* Moral. 72, c. 1. Bellarmine returns two answers. *First,* that these words are not to be understood merely of the written word, but of the whole word of God, whether written or unwritten, and only orally delivered ; and he denies that the fathers are opposed to this exposition. I answer : I confess that the apostle denounces an anathema against those who add any thing to that word of God which he preached ; but I maintain that the whole of that word is contained in the scriptures. For from what source did the apostle confirm his gospel ? Assuredly, from the scriptures of the old Testament. How does this appear ? From Acts xvii. 10, where we read that the Bereans examined the gospel and doctrine of Paul by the scriptures ; which they would not have done, if all that Paul had delivered were not contained in the scriptures. In Acts xxvi. 22, 23, a still plainer testimony occurs : in that place the apostle declares to Festus, that he, having received help of God, had continued up to that day, testifying to all, but saying *nothing else* than what Moses and the prophets had said ; and then he enumerates certain heads of his teaching, Christ's death, resurrection, &c. It is manifest, therefore, that the apostle never spoke a word, or taught a single point, which might not be proved by the evidence of Moses and the prophets. The whole of Paul's Gospel can therefore be proved by the certain and clear authority of the old Testament.

Now as to Bellarmine's pretence, that Augustine and Basil offer no obstacle to our understanding this place as he would have it understood, let us see what is in it. Those fathers, says he, do not infer from this passage that nothing is to be delivered beside the scriptures, but only nothing contrary to them. Now these are the words of Augustine in the place cited above: " Whether the subject be Christ, or his church, or anything else appertaining to our faith and life; if (I do not say we, who are no wise comparable to him who said, 'though we,' but even what he there immediately subjoins, if) an angel from heaven preach to you anything besides what you have received in the scriptures of the law and of the gospel, let him be accursed!" In these words we should observe and consider the following points : First, that all that Paul taught may be found in the scriptures. This Augustine expressly affirms, dividing the scriptures into the law and the gospel. Secondly, that all things necessary may be found in these legal and evangelical scriptures. For, says Augustine, " Whether the subject be Christ, or his church, or anything else appertaining to our faith and life." Thirdly, that whatever is preached or announced besides what is contained in these scriptures, is to be wholly rejected. His words are, " besides what is written:" therefore not only that which is contrary to, but that also which is beside the scriptures, should be refused. Fourthly, it is worthy of observation that Augustine joins Paul in anathematizing the patrons and preachers of unwritten traditions. Now Basil's words, *Moral.* 72, are to this effect : " It behoves those hearers who are skilled in scripture, to examine what is delivered by their teachers, and to receive whatever is consonant to scripture, but reject whatever is alien from it[1]." And in confirmation of this he cites, amongst others, this testimony of Paul to the Galatians. Whence it manifestly appears, that Paul is here speaking of the scriptures, and condemning every doctrine not therein delivered : otherwise, if a teacher might allege other things beside the scriptures, Basil would have cited this passage to no purpose. In that case, he should

[1] δεῖ τῶν ἀκροατῶν τοὺς πεπαιδευμένους τὰς γραφὰς δοκιμάζειν τὰ παρὰ τῶν διδασκάλων λεγόμενα· καὶ τὰ μὲν σύμφωνα ταῖς γραφαῖς δέχεσθαι, τὰ δὲ ἀλλότρια ἀποβάλλειν.—Opp. T. ii. p. 372.]

have proposed some other test besides the scriptures, by which those skilled in scripture should examine the sayings and teachings of their instructors. For how can those who are only skilled in the scriptures examine those things which their masters deliver beside the scriptures? It appears therefore hence, that whatever is beside the scriptures, is alien from them, and therefore should be rejected. Thus those fathers say precisely what we say, and maintain the same tenets as we maintain.

But, says Bellarmine, the fathers have used this passage to confirm tradition, as Athanasius in his book of the Incarnation of the Word, and Cyril in his book upon the Orthodox Faith. I answer: Traditions are either consonant to scripture, and then they should be received, and those who do not receive them are condemned in these words; or they are, as Basil expresses it, alien from scripture, and then they should be rejected. These fathers speak of those traditions which are consonant to scripture, not of such as are alien from it. So much for Bellarmine's first reply to the passage alleged from Gal. i. 8. I come now to his second reply.

He says, in the *second* place, that the word "beside" in this place is equivalent to "against:" so as that Paul here anathematizes those who deliver anything *against*, not *beside*, the scriptures; consequently, that new doctrines are not here prohibited, provided they do not contradict the scriptures. The Rhemists explain the passage in a similar way; and so does Stapleton, Lib. XII. c. 10. We, however, take the word "beside" in its strict sense, so as to bring under this denunciation whatever is delivered *beside* that gospel delivered by the apostle. But let us see the reasons by which Bellarmine seems to confirm this reply of his. He hath four of them. The *first* is, because Paul himself taught and wrote many things beside; and after this Epistle, John wrote his Apocalypse and his Gospel. I answer: I maintain that Paul did not afterwards teach other, that is, new and different doctrines (as Bellarmine wishes to be supposed), but taught the same things to other persons; for, since he went afterwards into other regions he was obliged to repeat the same things frequently. Thus he taught other persons, but not other things. Now that he neither ought to have taught, nor actually did teach, anything different, but always one and the same thing, is evident from this, that the gospel of Christ is one, and that he always taught the gospel of Christ. Bellarmine's *second* reason is drawn from the drift and design of the apostle, because, says he, the apostle there disputes

[WHITAKER.]

40

against those who maintained the obligation of the law : now to maintain this was against, and not merely beside, the gospel preached by Paul.   I answer : But Paul not only proves that the rites of the law should not be observed, nor is this his whole design ; but affirms also, that he had delivered to the Galatians the gospel in its whole, perfect integrity, so as that whatever was thereto added, was false and impious.   For the apostle says that the false apostles had transferred the Galatians to " another gospel, which," says he in that same chapter, " is not another ; but there are some that trouble you, and would pervert the gospel of Christ."   It was not, therefore, another gospel which these false apostles preached, but only a corruption and depravation of that gospel which Paul preached ; and, whereas the apostle had delivered to the Galatians that gospel of Christ, wherein our salvation is fully and perfectly set forth, these false apostles endeavoured to introduce their legal observances, which was a thing both *beside* and *against* Paul's gospel.   But the apostle does not use the term *against*, because the false apostles would have denied that it was against that gospel which Paul himself had delivered.   In order, therefore, to obviate this false pretence, the apostle says, " beside what I preached unto you, and ye received :" as if he had said, I taught you nothing of the kind ; therefore those who introduce such things are to be avoided, and by no means to be listened to.   Thus it is certain that *beside* suits the apostle's design much better than *against*. Bellarmine's *third* reason is taken from Rom. xvi. 17, where the apostle writes thus : " I beseech you, brethren, mark those who cause divisions and offences, *beside* the doctrine which ye have learned ;" where, says he, Erasmus translates it, *against*.   I answer : I confess it, and so does Beza : for whatever is against scripture is also beside it ; and, conversely also, whatever in our holy religion is taught beside the scriptures, is against the scriptures too, if it carry with it any notion of necessity, that is, if it be proposed as a necessary doctrine.   Since the apostles delivered abundantly all necessary things in the scriptures, whatever is urged as necessary beside the scriptures is justly deemed contrary to them.   I confess that παρά may sometimes be conveniently translated *against*, but not in this place.   Bellarmine's *fourth* reason is taken from the authority of the fathers.   Of these he brings forward Ambrose, Jerome, Chrysostom, Theophylact, Œcumenius, and Augustine.   These all, says he, explain "beside" by "against." I answer, that in religious matters *beside* is equivalent to *against* the scriptures: but we have already shewn the reason why the apostle uses the term *beside* rather than *against*, because it suited his purpose better. There is no necessity for answering his patristic authorities. However, Chrysostom is most plainly for us, and against our opponent: for thus he writes upon the present passage: "The apostle said not, if they tell you all the contrary, or subvert the whole gospel, but even if they preach you any (that is, even a slight and minute, even the smallest) thing beside that gospel which ye have received, if they shake any portion of it, let them be accursed." And, to make it still more clear that he is upon our side, he subjoins: "Abraham, when he was asked to send Lazarus, answered, They have Moses and the prophets; if they believe not them, neither will they be persuaded though one rose from the dead. Now Christ introduces Abraham speaking thus in the parable, to shew that he would rather that more faith should be reposed in the scriptures than in even men raised from the dead: νεκρῶν ἐγειρομένων ἀξιοπιστοτέρας βούλεται εἶναι τὰς γραφάς. And Paul (and when I say Paul, I say Christ, since it is he who directed the mind of Paul) prefers the scriptures even to angels descending out of heaven, καὶ ἀγγέλων ἐξ οὐρανοῦ καταβαινόντων αὐτὰς προτίθησι, and that very properly; since angels, however great, are but servants and ministers; whereas the whole scripture hath come to us not from servants, but from God the Lord of all." Thus it is certain that Chrysostom maintains the perfection of scripture, and is on our side against the papists: for in these words he subverts both the Jesuit's answers, since he determines that the apostle both speaks of the written word of God, and condemns whatever is preached not only against, but beside the scriptures. So Œcumenius upon this place, τὸ παρ' ὃ δηλοῖ τὸ ὅσον δήποτε μικρὸν τοῦ κηρύγματος· "How small soever it be, let him be accursed." So Theophylact remarks that the apostle does not say "contrary to," but "beside."

I come now to Augustine, some of whose words Bellarmine cites from his ninety-eighth Tractate upon the gospel of John; and the same words are cited also by the Rhemists in their note upon this place to the Galatians. There Augustine writes, that the apostle said not, "Above what ye have received, but beside what ye have received[1]. For had he said the former, he would have

[1 Nam si illud diceret, sibi ipsi præjudicaret, qui cupiebat venire ad Thessalonicences, ut suppleret quæ illorum fidei defuerunt. Sed qui supplet, quod minus erat addit, non quod inerat tollit.]

answered himself by anticipation, who desired to come to the Thessalonians that he might supply what was lacking in their faith." I answer : This testimony is of no weight against us and our exposition, because although Paul meant to go to the Thessalonians to give them more instruction, yet it was in the same, and not in different points. As to the apostle's saying that something was still lacking to their faith, I use a distinction. There was something lacking to their faith subjectively, not objectively. The apostle had delivered to them the whole doctrine, but they had not received it all ; consequently he desired to come to them again, that they might more fully receive the doctrine delivered, and that their faith might be rendered more stable. In like manner we also need daily fresh instruction, that we may make every day new advances in the faith, since our faith is not perfect in this life. Meanwhile Augustine does not say that it is only contrary doctrines that are condemned by the apostle ; for the additional teaching of which he speaks may be such as is not beside, but contained in the scriptures. So much for our third testimony from scripture. Next follows the fourth.

Now the fourth passage of scripture which we cite against traditions is contained in the last verse of the twentieth chapter of John, and runs thus : " These are written that ye might believe that Jesus is the Christ the Son of God, and that believing ye might have life through his name." It is manifest from these words, that all necessary things may be found in those which are written, because by these a full and perfect faith may be produced, inasmuch as such a faith is capable of procuring eternal life. This interpretation of ours is supported by the authority of Augustine, *Tractat. 49 in Joan.* and *de Consensu Evangel.* Lib. I. c. 35, and of Cyril upon John, Lib. XII. c. ult. Bellarmine is here upon the rack, and turns himself on all sides to evade the difficulty. At last he gives five answers, which we will examine in order.

First, he says that John speaks of Christ's miracles, and asserts that miracles numerous enough to prove and persuade us that Christ was the Messiah are committed to writing. I answer: Although the evangelist does mention miracles in the preceding verse, yet the word ταῦτα, which he subjoins in this, is to be understood of doctrine rather than of miracles. For miracles do not properly produce faith in us, but rather confirm and support it when it hath been produced, and miracles minister to and win credence for the doctrine. Here, therefore, the end of the whole gospel is indicated : for the scope of the gospel is that we should believe, and so have life eternal. So Augustine upon this place, Tractat. 122 ; so de Lyra; so cardinal Hugo ; so Jansenius. Augustine says that the end of the book is indicated in these words. De Lyra says that in these words the utility of this doctrine is pointed out. Cardinal Hugo writes thus : " In these words is declared the end of scripture in general, and of this book in particular." Jansenius in like manner says the end and drift of this book are designed in these words.

Secondly, Bellarmine answers that John speaks only of the things written by himself; and that therefore if these are sufficient, the other scriptures will be superfluous. I answer: If the things written by John are such as that we may by them reach faith and salvation, then much more may we reach faith and salvation by all the books and the whole canon of the scriptures. Besides, we may give a far correcter explanation of this passage, if we say that John speaks here not only of his own book, but of all the books of the new Testament : for he had seen them all, and this gospel was written last ; and even though perhaps some of the books were published after it, yet it does not thence follow that all necessary things were not then written. But when he says, " These are written that ye might believe that Jesus is the Christ the Son of God," he is not to be understood to assert that faith or salvation could in no way be received without these scriptures. For faith and life may be obtained from the old Testament ; and those who had only the old Testament were believers and in a state of salvation : but by this present way we reach faith and salvation with greater clearness and plainness, in a better and surer method. These writings of John are therefore necessary, like the other books of the new Testament, only upon the preliminary supposition that God chose to teach us now under the gospel in a clearer way, and afford us most manifest evidence of the redemption which hath been wrought.

Thirdly, Bellarmine pretends that John does not affirm that these by themselves are sufficient to salvation, but that these and other things which have been written are referred and subordinated to the end of producing faith, and so putting us in possession of life. I answer : Scripture is not only one of those means which relate to salvation, but the entire and sole medium, the perfect and complete medium, because it produces a perfect faith. For that faith which brings salvation is perfect ; and consequently the medium whereby that faith is produced is also perfect. An argument may be framed thus : All things necessary to salvation are contained in believing that Jesus is the Christ, the Son of God. Now all things requisite

for our believing that Jesus is the Christ are written : therefore all
things necessary to salvation are contained in the scriptures.

Fourthly, Bellarmine endeavours to evade the testimonies of
Augustine and Cyril. He says, in the first place, that those fathers
speak only of the miracles of Christ, or, at most, of his words and
actions. I answer : This is enough. For if John hath sufficiently
written all Christ's sayings, then he hath sufficiently for our purposes committed his whole doctrine to writing. He says, in the
second place, that they do not affirm, upon the evidence of this
passage, that all things are sufficiently written which are absolutely
necessary to salvation ; but that all things which the evangelist
deemed fit to be written are written sufficiently. I answer : This
is surely a ridiculous fiction, which he hath learned from Canus,
Lib. III. c. ult. However, if we consult Augustine and Cyril, we
shall easily perceive the falsehood of this interpretation. Augustine says (*Tract. 49. in Joan.*) that "those things which seemed
sufficient for the salvation of believers were chosen to be committed
to writing[1];" and does not say that what was written was sufficiently written. Therefore all things are sufficiently written, which
are sufficient for our salvation and necessary to it. The same
father (*de Consensu Evangel.* Lib. I. c. ult.) writes thus : " Whatsoever he (i. e. Christ) wished that we should read concerning his
words or works, he enjoined the task of committing to writing upon
the apostles, as if they were his hands." Perhaps they will seize
upon the expression, " What he wished that we should *read.*"
But this makes signally against themselves. For their traditions
are written somewhere, although they are called unwritten. Now
Augustine says Christ committed to his apostles the writing of all
those things which he wished us to read. Therefore he gave no
commandment either to write or read more traditions. For if he
had wished them to be either written or read, who should have
written them rather than the apostles who wrote the rest ? or
where should they have been read rather than in the canonical
books and writings ? Cyril upon John, Lib. XII. c. ult., says that
those things are written " which the writers deemed sufficient both
for morals and for doctrine." Two things offer themselves for
consideration in this testimony : first, that these words should be
understood not of the books of John only, but of the rest also ;
therefore he says, " which the *writers,*" that is the apostles,

[1 Electa sunt . . . quæ scriberentur, quæ saluti credentium sufficere cre-
debantur.—Opp. T. III. col. 2163. Paris. 1837.—The other references are
cited more largely below, chap. 17.]

deemed sufficient : secondly, that the things which are written are sufficient both for morals and doctrine.

Fifthly, Bellarmine answers, that all things are sufficiently written in the general, but not in the particular; because we are commanded in the scriptures to hold traditions : where we have a recurrence of the same subterfuge as he had previously used. I answer : If all things are thus only written in the general, why, I beseech you, was so much written ? A few things would have been sufficient, from which the rest might have been taken. Yea, this one single sentence might have been enough, " Believe what the church teaches :" just as he had before said, that his traditions were, in the gèneral, enjoined by Paul in those words, " Hold the traditions," so as to leave nothing more to be desired. Augustine however, as ye have heard but now, determines far otherwise : " Whether the subject be Christ, or his church, or any other matter appertaining to our faith or life, I say not, Though we, who are in no wise comparable to him who said, Though we; but assuredly I do say what he added in that place, Though an angel from heaven preach any thing beside what ye have received in the scriptures of the law and the gospel, let him be accursed." Therefore all things are particularly, and that too with the fullest sufficiency, consigned to writing. Andradius in his Orthodox Explications, Lib. II. gives a different answer, but one so ridiculous and foolish that Bellarmine did not choose to make use of it. He says that Augustine and Cyril write, that those things which are written are sufficient, not because the evangelists have comprised all the mysteries of our faith in this small volume, but because those most holy persons had committed to writing " what might be sufficient to establish the credit of all the other things which were not contained in written documents." Thus, if we believe Andradius, these fathers meant that the evangelists wrote, not what was sufficient for our faith (which however Augustine expressly affirms), but what was sufficient to settle the credit of traditions;— an assertion destitute of all reasonable support ! For how can these things which are committed to writing establish the credit of those which are nowhere written ? Augustine says besides, that the apostles wrote by divine authority whatever Christ " wished us to read concerning either his words or works." Andradius is moreover at variance with himself; since, after having first said that "most holy persons" had written what sufficed to establish the credit of other things, he so far forgets himself afterwards as to maintain that Cyril spoke here " of the gospel of John only." We have said enough upon this testimony.

I come now to the celebrated passage of the apostle which is contained in 2 Tim. iii. 16, 17 : " All scripture is given by inspiration
of God, and is profitable for doctrine, for reproof, for correction, and
for instruction in righteousness ; that the man of God may be perfect,
throughly furnished for every good work." I will not here dispute
whether the apostle speaks here only of the books of the old, or of
the books of both Testaments. My opinion is that these words
refer to the new Testament also : for although the books of the new
Testament had not yet been published when Timothy was a child,
yet some of them had already seen the light when the apostle wrote
these words. However, if he spake only of the books of the old
Testament, then our argument may be pressed still more closely.
For if the books of the old Testament are of themselves sufficient
for all the ends here enumerated, then much rather do the scriptures of the old and new Testaments together contain a full body
of doctrine. But I do not choose to moot this question ; though I
think that this is a general sentence referring to the whole scripture.
From this passage we draw the following conclusion: The whole scripture is useful for the end of rendering the man of God perfect for
every good work : therefore, the scriptures are sufficient for all things
necessary for us. Our opponent hath a twofold reply : first, by conceding a certain sort of sufficiency ; secondly, by denying that sufficiency which we maintain. Let us examine these replies.

First, he says, it may be replied that the scriptures do, in
a certain sense, sufficiently instruct and perfect a man of God,
forasmuch as many things are " expressly " contained in scripture, and the same scripture teaches us also whence the " rest
may be derived." We have already answered this reply, by shewing that the scripture cannot be called sufficient only because it
sufficiently delivers some necessary things in the general, and indicates the source whence the rest may be derived ; because then
there would have been no need that the Holy Spirit should have
published so many books of scripture. The Decalogue, the Creed,
and the Lord's Prayer would have been enough, and there would
have been no necessity for so many pieces. But the Holy Spirit
willed that we should be most fully instructed, and therefore caused
so many books to be published, and referred us to the scriptures
wherein a clearly sufficient explication of all parts of our faith is to
be found. This reply therefore was an absurd one, Yet this is
the only one which Canus had to give, Lib. iii. c. ult. Bellarmine,
however, was not satisfied with it. Indeed, the second epistle to the
Thessalonians contains some things expressly, and refers us to the

source whence the rest may be derived, as the papists themselves
confess, when it says, " Hold the traditions." Therefore, if this
reply were sound, that epistle would have been sufficient. The
same might be said of the book of Ruth, Joshua, and others. Bellarmine, therefore, was obliged to seek another reply.

Secondly, then, Bellarmine denies that sufficiency which we
maintain, and that for three reasons. *First*, he remarks that the
apostle does not say " the whole," but " all " scripture. Therefore
the apostle ascribes his commendation not only to the whole scripture, but to all, that is, to each several book. Every part of scripture, then, and each several book, must be perfect, if he speak of
such a perfection of scripture. So Stapleton, Lib. XII. c. 8, expounds this place not of the " whole," but of " every " scripture.
I answer : " All " in this place is equivalent to " the whole," and
is frequently so used ; as, " all " life is full of wretchedness, that
is, " the whole " of life. So Coloss. ii. 9, " In him dwelleth πᾶν
τὸ πλήρωμα[1], 'all the fulness' of the Godhead ;" that is, " the
whole." So 2 Thessalon. i. 11, " To fulfil πᾶσαν εὐδοκίαν," that
is, " the whole." And frequently in scripture we read " all Israel,"
meaning the whole house of Israel. So Luke xxi. 31, πᾶς ὁ λαός,
" the whole people :" and Ephes. iv. 16, πᾶν τὸ σῶμα, " the whole
body :" and Matth. iii. 5, πᾶσα ἡ Ἰουδαία καὶ πᾶσα ἡ περίχωρος
τοῦ Ἰορδάνου, " the whole of Judæa and the whole region," &c.
Acts xx. 27, Paul says that he had declared πᾶσαν τὴν βουλὴν
τοῦ Θεοῦ, " the whole counsel of God." Rom. iv. 16, παντὶ τῷ
σπέρματι, " to the whole seed." And that this place must needs
be so understood, is manifest ; for otherwise each several Psalm,
yea, every chapter, every verse, every word, would be useful for
all these purposes : for these are all parts of scripture, all γραφαὶ
θεόπνευστοι. But this the papists do not concede. Our interpretation may also be confirmed from the preceding context ; where
the apostle shews that he is speaking of the whole body of scripture.
For Paul says above, that Timothy was skilled in the scriptures
from a boy. Now it was not in only some one part of scripture, or in
some single book that he was conversant, but in the whole scripture.
The same may be gathered also from what follows : for Paul says
that " Scripture is useful for doctrine, for reproof, for correction,
for instruction in righteousness :" now this great ability of scripture must be gained from the whole of it, not from any one book or

[1 The reader, however, needs hardly to be reminded that πᾶς with the
article is a very different thing from πᾶς without the article. There could be
no doubt of the meaning of πᾶσα ἡ γραφή.]

part of a book. So Dionysius Carthusianus, no bad expositor :
" All, that is, the whole canonical scripture." Bellarmine's pretence,
that all these uses may be found in each several book, is absurd.
He proves, in the case of the second epistle of John, which is the
shortest, that all these things may be found there, because we read
there that " Christ is the Son of God," which appertains to doctrine ;
that " antichrists are in the world," which appertains to reproof:
In the same epistle also the apostle enjoins us " to love one another,"
which appertains to instruction ; and says also, " Take heed unto
yourselves that we lose not what we have wrought," which appertains to correction. Now he ought to have shewn that all these
things were contained in each particle and member of the books, if
he meant to defend his interpretation. Besides, although some
things which serve all these purposes may be found in each of the
books of holy scripture, yet not so as to " perfect " ($\dot{\epsilon}\xi\alpha\rho\tau\iota\sigma\eta$) the
man of God. *Secondly*, Bellarmine disputes thus : When Paul wrote
these words, the gospel of John, the Apocalypse, and other books
also, were not written : therefore, he cannot be understood to speak
of the whole canon of scripture. I answer : The apostle speaks
of the canon which was then extant, and contained a full and
perfect body of doctrine. For the books written afterwards do
not prove that that body was not perfect, but only that what we
now have is more perfect. For the additional books do not add
any thing to the doctrine of scripture, but only to the explication
of the doctrine previously delivered. And the apostle speaks
not only of those books, but in general of the whole scripture.
Since, therefore, these books have been added to the body of scripture, this judgment appertains by a parity of reason to them also.
Finally, Bellarmine collects what he desires from the reasoning
of the apostle. The apostle, says he, argues from the universal
to the particular. All scripture is useful : therefore the old Testament is useful. I answer : The apostle does not argue from the
universal to the particular, but from the efficient and the final
cause. From the efficient thus : All scripture is divinely inspired;
therefore do thou read the scriptures from which thou mayst learn
divine wisdom. From the end, thus : Scripture is profitable for
many purposes; therefore do thou read the scriptures, that thou
mayst derive these many and great advantages from the study
of them. The old version (which however Bellarmine follows)
requires emendation : *Omnis scriptura divinitus inspirata utilis
est;* whereas it is in the Greek, $\pi\hat{\alpha}\sigma\alpha$ $\gamma\rho\alpha\phi\dot{\eta}$ $\theta\epsilon\acute{o}\pi\nu\epsilon\nu\sigma\tau\sigma\varsigma$, $\kappa\alpha\grave{\iota}$
$\dot{\omega}\phi\acute{\epsilon}\lambda\iota\mu\sigma\varsigma$. And although we must allow that when Timothy was

a child, some books of the new Testament were not extant, yet
when this epistle was written, and Timothy now grown up, many
were extant and in the hands of pious persons, as namely, the
gospels of Matthew, Mark, Luke, and all the epistles of Paul; for
this was the last epistle which Paul wrote a short time before he
departed out of this life. What! did not this apostle commend
these scriptures also to Timothy? Undoubtedly he did.

Now, after obviating the sophistry of Bellarmine, let us proceed
to confirm our own argument, which we state thus: The whole
scripture is useful for all these purposes: therefore it is perfect and
sufficient, and contains all necessary things. Bellarmine, however,
laughs at reasoning which concludes *sufficiency* from *utility*. So
the Rhemists upon this place, and the defender of the censure
against William Chark[1]. With this reply they seem to stop our
mouths; yet is it a mere subterfuge. For we do not argue that
scripture is sufficient because it is useful; but we prove its perfection and sufficiency from the magnitude of that utility which
may be obtained from scripture. For although everything that is
useful is not sufficient, yet if all sufficient things are useful, then,
conversely, some useful things are sufficient, and some kind of
usefulness is sufficient and complete. Now, such is the usefulness
mentioned in this place: and that it is such, is clear from the
words and the design of the apostle; since he speaks of such an
usefulness of scripture as proves the scriptures to be sufficient also.
For so, in the words immediately preceding, the apostle testifies of
the scriptures that they are able σοφίσαι, that is, ' to make a man
wise' unto salvation. Therefore they are sufficient. For wisdom
contains the perfection of knowledge. Now, from the scriptures
everything may be derived which can render men wise: therefore
all things requisite to perfect knowledge are contained in the scriptures. Neither Bellarmine, nor the Rhemists, nor the censor and
defender of the censure above cited, nor (as far as I am aware)
any papist, hath touched this argument: The scriptures teach perfect
wisdom: therefore the scriptures are sufficient for our salvation.

Besides, the apostle illustrates this utility by saying that the
scriptures are useful for all purposes; which is assuredly a sufficient
utility. But how is this proved, that the scriptures are useful for
all purposes? By this, that in the four heads here enumerated
are contained and included all things requisite to our salvation.

[1 W. Chark was one of the disputants against Campian in the conference
held in the Tower, Sept. 27, 1580.—Strype, Ann. Vol. II. Book ii. c. 22. p.
646. Life of Parker, App. 74.]

What we are obliged to do is, either to teach truth, or to refute errors, or to direct life aright, or to reprove vice. The papists themselves concede that all things are comprised in these four points, since the pastors of the church are engaged in nothing else besides these. Διδασκαλία denotes sound doctrine; ἔλεγχος, the refutation of false opinions; παιδεία, the godly direction of life; ἐπανόρθωσις, the correction of manners. Scripture is profitable for all these purposes. Yes, you may say,—but not sufficient. Yea, I affirm, profitable and sufficiently profitable; which is even still more evident from what follows. For he subjoins, " that the man of God may be perfect (ἄρτιος ᾖ), thoroughly furnished (ἐξηρ-τισμένος) unto every good work." The phrase, "man of God," is taken here in the same sense as in 1 Tim. vi. 11. It denotes a minister or pastor, as Melchior Canus confesses, Lib. III. c. ult. Hence, therefore, we may reason thus : The scriptures render a minister thoroughly furnished unto every good work : therefore they are sufficient. For if a minister can derive from the scriptures all things which are necessary for his function, then the people also may find in the scriptures all things necessary for salvation: for nothing is necessary to be believed by the people, which it is not necessary for the minister to teach and deliver. The measure of doctrine in the minister and of faith in the people is one and the same : so much as the pastor ought to teach, just so much, and no more, the people ought to know and believe. Now, he is called ἄρτιος, or perfect, who lacks nothing. The scriptures make a pastor perfect. Therefore they place him in a condition in which he is in need of nothing more. But, if there be no deficiency in the pastor, then there can be no deficiency in the scriptures, which have rendered him thus complete. And although the old translator hath rendered ἐξηρτισμένον by instructum, yet he undoubtedly means perfectly furnished. So in Matth. xxi. 16, where Christ cites a passage from the eighth Psalm, ἐκ στόματος νηπίων καὶ θηλαζόντων κατηρτίσω αἶνον, the old interpreter translates it, Ex ore infantium et lactentium perfecisti laudem. So in Luke vi. 40, where the disciple who shall be as his Lord is called ἐξηρ-τισμένος, the old interpreter renders it by perfectus. The meaning of the term is precisely the same in the present passage. Since then the scripture is needful for these four purposes, since it renders the man of God perfect, since it teaches a wisdom perfect to the end of salvation, it must needs itself be perfect and sufficient. No papist ever hath or will frame a full and pertinent answer to this argument. Chrysostom sheds some light upon this reasoning of ours in his commentary upon this place, Homil. 9. He says that Paul commended the scriptures to Timothy, because he knew that he himself must shortly die, and that this would plunge Timothy in the deepest affliction. He therefore comforts him in these words, commending to him the scriptures as capable of standing in the place of all other masters. So solicitous was Paul to remove this anxiety from Timothy's mind. Chrysostom subjoins that it is as if Paul had said : " Thou hast scripture for a master instead of me ; thence thou canst learn whatever thou wouldest know :" ἀπ' ἐμοῦ (φησὶ) τὰς γραφὰς ἔχεις· εἴ τι βούλει μαθεῖν, ἐκεῖθεν δυνήσῃ. Whence it may be inferred, that all things can be learned from the scriptures which could have been learned from the apostles if they had still lived. Jerome, explaining those words, " which are able to make thee wise," &c., says that the scriptures are not sufficient without faith. I grant it ; but in saying this he shews that they are sufficient if one believes them. Even papists themselves do not blame this interpretation. One Augustinus Villavicentius[1], who wrote four books upon the method of studying theology, which are really deserving of being perused by all students of theology, hath, Lib. I. c. 3, these words: " The scriptures can even by themselves instruct us to salvation." However, those books were really written by Hyperius, and Villavicentius says in the title of the work, that they were so corrected by him as to allow of their being read by catholics without danger ; yet he made no change in these words, although they make most decisively against the papists.

I come now to another argument, the last of those touched upon by Bellarmine, and derived from various passages of scripture wherein traditions are condemned: as, Matth. xv. 6, " Ye have made the commandment of God of none effect by your traditions ;" and the words of Isaiah, c. 29, alleged by Christ in that same chapter, " In vain do they worship me, teaching for doctrines the commandments of men :" and Galat. i. 14,[2] where Paul says that, before his conversion, he was " zealous for the traditions of his

[1 Whitaker has mistaken the name of this author, as appears from Placcius (De Scriptor. Pseudon. p. 609); which reference I owe to the kindness of my friend Mr Gibbings. The title of the work referred to is— De recte formando studio theologico libri quatuor ; ac de formandis sacris concionibus libri tres : omnes collecti et restituti per fratrem Laur. a Villa-vincentio, Xerezamum, Doctorem Theologum, Augustinianum, Eremitani, nunc denuo diligentissime correcti et emendati.—Colon. 1575. See the Literary History of the Book in Bayle, Art. HYPERIUS.]
[2 In the text the reference is by a mistake to verse 20.]

elders." From these and the like places, we reason thus : Christ
and the apostles condemn traditions : therefore, they are not to
be received ; and consequently scripture is sufficient. Bellarmine
hath but one reply, namely, that Christ and the apostles did not
condemn those traditions which the Jews had received from Moses
and the prophets, but those which they had received from certain
later persons, whereof some were idle, and some impious. This he
confirms by the authority of Epiphanius, Irenæus, and Jerome.

I answer: Firstly, it is false that the Jews received any traditions
from Moses and the prophets. He himself does not prove they did,
and even some papists (as he owns) determine the contrary way.
Finally, it is evident from the scriptures : for Christ says, " Search
the scriptures," not tradition ; and Abraham says, " They have
Moses and the prophets, let them hear them." Now by Moses and
the prophets the scriptures are meant, as in Luke xxiv. 27. There
is no mention in scripture of these traditions : the scriptures say
not a single word about them : there were, therefore, none. Besides, who were the guardians of these traditions ? They must needs
say, the priests. But they had corrupted even the scripture itself :
much more then tradition. Besides, to what part of the law did
they relate ? for to some part of it they must have had reference.
Not to the moral ; for that was perfectly delivered in the decalogue,
and expounded in the other books : nor to the ceremonial ; for
the ceremonial law is also perfectly delivered in the books of Moses,
wherein not even the minutest ceremony is omitted. Now although
the explication of these ceremonies is nowhere contained in the
scriptures, yet that is nothing to the purpose : for it is manifest
from the scriptures that the death of the Messiah, and the other
benefits which are derived from him to us, were signified and
declared by these rites. The judicial law is not concerned in the
present question, regarding, as it did, the mere external polity, and
not faith and religion, which form the subject of this dispute. This
therefore is irrelevant to the question before us. Further, let them
now produce, if they can, any of these traditions. They cannot.
Therefore they have all perished, while the scriptures meanwhile
have been preserved entire.

Secondly, when he says that Christ condemns vain and impious
traditions, I allow the truth of that assertion : but it does not thence
follow that he does not condemn the popish traditions ; since (as shall
appear hereafter) some of them are idle, and some pernicious.

Thirdly, I say that not only are impious traditions condemned by Christ, but all which do not rest upon the authority of scripture. For those frequent washings of the Pharisees, mentioned in (Matth. xv. and Mark vii.) who used to wash themselves, their vessels, and their couches so diligently, were not openly impious or pernicious, if they had not drawn after them an impiety of another kind: yea, they seem to carry a sort of piety upon the face of them; for the reason of this custom was their fear of having met with an unclean person, and so contracted some impurity. Surely this tradition hath a more specious reason, and borders more nearly upon piety, than most of the popish traditions.

Fourthly, when Christ objects the commandment of God, and opposes the scriptures to tradition, it is plain that he condemns all unwritten traditions.

Fifthly, if the authors of these traditions had lived only a short time before Christ, he would not have called them the traditions of *the elders*, τῶν πρεσβυτέρων. This shews plainly that these traditions were not very recent, but sufficiently ancient in their date. And Christ by citing Isaiah indicates that he is not speaking of a certain sort of modern traditions, but of all unwritten traditions in general. Undoubtedly therefore Christ condemns all doctrines which are the decrees of men, such as the papists have introduced in great numbers into the church,—the distinction of days, places, persons, meats, and such like; all which we pronounce pernicious, on account of these three evils following: first, because they draw and lead us away from the scriptures, as if they were insufficient, and contained not all necessary things; whereas Christ and the apostles always remand us to the scriptures; secondly, because those who are devoted to them place some of their hope of salvation in them, which must needs be displeasing to God; and thirdly, because those who are occupied in keeping such things, omit, neglect and despise the study of true godliness, and apply themselves wholly to some external rites and exercises devised and invented by themselves. The truth of this is witnessed by experience in the case both of the Jews and papists. For in the papacy the splendour of those works which human rashness and superstition have invented hath eclipsed those works of charity which are truly pleasing to the Deity.

Sixthly, as to the fathers here cited by Bellarmine, there is no necessity for making any reply to them, since we have shewn above that all unwritten traditions are condemned by Christ. I too can bring forward fathers. See Cyprian, Ep. 63 and 74, where this testimony of Isaiah is plainly used to prove that nothing should be received that is not based upon the authority of scripture. Elsewhere also he uses these testimonies for the same purpose. So Chrysostom, Hom. 52 in Matth., lays down the following points: first, that the priest and ordinary pastors made many innovations; therefore those who hold the office and succession of priests are not always faithful: secondly, that in doing so they transgressed the precept, Deut. iv., to make no additions to, or diminution from, the word of God; therefore those who make any change or innovation other than the Lord hath appointed in the scriptures, add to, or detract from, the word of God: thirdly, that this is done not only by those who introduce things contrary to the scriptures, but also by those who enjoin things not contrary to them; for he says, "that tradition was not contrary to the law," that is, openly and in every respect, but only consequentially. Those who will not eat without washing their hands first, do nothing simply contrary to any divine precept; but to make any part of godliness consist in this rite, or to be more solicitous about this precept than about God's commandments, this is to make the law of God of none effect, and to incur his severe displeasure. Now the papists have run into still more intolerable errors in this matter than the Jews of old, since their religion is wholly occupied in observing and performing not those things which Christ sanctioned and enjoined, but those which man's boldness and curiosity have devised. For example, those who are esteemed *religious* amongst the papists observe the rules of their founders far more punctiliously than the commands of God: the truth of which remark hath been now for a long time no secret to all the world.

Thus far we have defended those testimonies of scripture which Bellarmine endeavours, but ineffectually, to wrest from our hands.

CHAPTER XV.

WHEREIN OTHER TESTIMONIES OF SCRIPTURE AGAINST TRADITIONS, NOT NOTICED BY BELLARMINE, ARE EXPLAINED.

I WILL now add others which he hath not touched. Did Bellarmine suppose that we had no more testimonies of scripture? I will now then set forth those which he hath omitted, and draw arguments from the several passages.

The first is taken from Ps. xix. 8, where these words are read: "The law of the Lord is entire, and giveth wisdom to babes." By

the law the prophet means the old Testament, or the doctrine delivered in the old Testament. This the Rabbins themselves perceived, as is plain from the commentary of David Kimchi upon Ps. cxix.
The term, the Law, is used thus also in scripture itself, as in Rom.
iii. 19, John xv. 25 ; and the usage is so established, that the name
of the law is given even to the gospel, Rom. iii. 27. In this place
two attributes of the law are explained, which shew it to be perfect : in the first place, it is called *entire ;* in the second, it is said
to give wisdom to babes. *Temimah*[1] is by Tremellius, Bucer, and
Vatablus rendered *integra;* by Pagninus, Arias Montanus, and Calvin,
perfecta. The term denotes that nothing is lacking in the old
Testament, but that in it is contained a full, perfect, and absolute
body of doctrine ; for the books which were published afterwards
added no new dogma. The old translator renders it *immaculata,*
incorrectly. Yet the censor before alluded to abuses this translation to his own purpose : he concedes that the law of God is un-
defiled, but denies that it is perfect. However, that it is perfect
appears plainly from the other attribute, in that it is said to give
wisdom to babes or infants,—that is, to bestow divine knowledge
and wisdom upon those who had no understanding previously.
Now wisdom contains the height and perfection of knowledge.
From this place I argue thus : If the doctrine of the old Testament
was thus *perfect* and complete, so as fully to furnish the students
of it with all the parts of true wisdom, then much more is the
doctrine of both Testaments perfect. The antecedent is true, and
therefore also the consequent.

The second place is taken from Luke i. 3, 4, where Luke in
his preface writes thus : " It seemed good to me also, having had
perfect understanding of all things from the very first, to write unto
thee in order, most excellent Theophilus, that thou mightest know
the certainty, τὴν ἀσφαλείαν, of those things wherein thou hast been
orally instructed." Theophilus had been previously instructed in
the christian religion, and taught concerning Christ, (as appears
from the words, περὶ ὧν κατηχήθης ;) yet Luke thought himself
obliged to write to him the same things as he had learned : and
why ? that he might perceive τὴν ἀσφαλείαν, the sure and ascertained certainty of those things. Out of scripture therefore there
is no, or no great, " certainty." From these words the following

[1 תְּמִימָה the feminine of תָּמִים which Gesenius translates in this
place, *perfectus, absolutus.*]

argument may be drawn : If it was needful to Theophilus, to give
him adequate certainty, that those things which he had before
heard and learned should be reduced to writing; then all things universally which the apostles taught are written.   For we are bound
to have a certain knowledge of all things necessary.   Now that
was necessary to Theophilus.   Therefore all necessary points are in
writing.   And if it was necessary to Theophilus, who had heard the
apostles themselves, to have what he had learned from them reduced to writing, in order that he might know the full truth and
certainty of their teaching ; then this must be deemed still more
necessary for us, and the churches of subsequent time.   The former
is true : therefore also the latter.

The third place is taken from Luke xvi. 29, where Abraham
says to the glutton, " They have Moses and the prophets; let them
hear them."   It is plain enough that all the scriptures of the old
Testament are meant by Moses and the prophets.   And when he
says that these should be listened to, he indicates that a perfect
body of teaching may be found in them.   This, says Stapleton, Lib.
XII. c. 8, does not follow : for it is one thing, says he, to hear
Moses and the prophets, and quite another to hear nothing else.
By the latter the new Testament would be excluded as superfluous.
I answer : In the *first* place, the command to hear them denotes
that they only should be listened to ; because this teaching obtained
from Moses and the prophets is opposed to all other revelations and
visions.   The glutton desired that his brethren should be so admonished and instructed as to be enabled to obtain eternal life, and
escape those punishments wherewith he was then tormented.   Abraham rejoins, " They have Moses and the prophets ; let them hear
them:" as if he had said, If they hear them, they can from them learn
and know all those things by which they may shun this death and these
torments.   It is as much as to say, The teaching of those books which
Moses and the prophets have written is perfect ; there is no need
of seeking other masters or monitors.   Otherwise Abraham would
not have answered pertinently to the glutton's sense and meaning.
Secondly, because when the glutton still pressed his petition and
said, " Nay, father Abraham, but if one went unto them from the
dead, they will repent ;" Abraham replies, " If they hear not
Moses and the prophets, neither will they be persuaded though one
rose from the dead."   In which words he implies that those who
will not be satisfied with the teaching of scripture, can be persuaded
by no teaching at all.   *Thirdly*, when Abraham says, ἀκουσάτωσαν,

"let them hear them," he means them "alone;" just as when God
from heaven orders us to hear his Son Christ, Matth. xvii. 5,
"Hear him," he means that Christ should be heard alone. So
Cyprian, Ep. 63, expressly infers from that place in Matthew, that
Christ only should be listened to[1]. In Deut. x. 20, we are commanded to worship God, and serve him: Christ, explaining that
place, Matth. iv. 10, properly added the word "only." So in this
passage, "let them hear them," means, let them hear them "only."
As to his objection, that this would make the new Testament superfluous, I answer, firstly, that the new Testament was not then published; secondly, that these scriptures and traditions do not stand
upon the same grounds; thirdly, the gospel only explains Moses and
the prophets: but this exposition is not like a mere commentary,
being inspired and credible upon its own authority. De Lyra gives no
bad explanation of this passage in the following words: "They have
Moses, who taught moral and practical things: they have the prophets, who taught mysteries and points of faith; and these are sufficient
for salvation. Therefore he subjoins, 'Let them hear them.'[2]" No
words can be plainer. Jansenius, in his Commentary on the Evangelists[3], c. 97, says that all which we are required to know concerning
a future life may be learned from the scriptures. This is enough;
though it is not this alone which is sufficiently taught in scripture:
for the glutton did not merely desire that his brethren should
know this, but also the means of escaping those penalties. However, upon this admission, it is at least not necessary to believe
either purgatory, or *Limbus Patrum*, or *Limbus puerorum*: for
these they determine to be traditions. Now Jansenius says that
we may learn from the scriptures all that we need to know concerning the condition of the future life. From this place, I draw
the following syllogism: If those who wish to know any thing
necessary to salvation are referred to the scriptures, then the scriptures contain the whole of saving doctrine. The antecedent is true,
and therefore the consequent.

The fourth place is taken from Luke xxiv. 25 and 27. Christ,
in verse 25, blames the disciples for being slow "to believe all that

[1] Et quod Christus debeat solus audiri, Pater etiam de cœlo contestatur,
dicens .... Ipsum audite.—p. 155, ed. Fell. Amstel. 1691.

[2] Habent Mosen, qui docuit moralia et agenda: habent prophetas, qui
docuerunt mystica et credenda; et ista sufficiunt ad salutem: ideo sequitur,
Audiant illos.]

[3] Louvain, 1571; together with his Harmony.]

41—2

the prophets have spoken." But where can those things be found? This appears from verse 27. There it follows : " Beginning at Moses and all the prophets, he expounded to them in all the scriptures the things concerning himself." Hence we frame the following argument : If all the things that the prophets spoke may be found in the scriptures, then may those also which the apostles spoke be found in the scriptures also. The first is true : therefore also the second. The force of the consequence is manifest. For the same reason which impelled the prophets to commit all they said to writing, led the apostles also to take a similar course. For if the prophets wrote all that they spoke, why should we not suppose that the apostles and evangelists, proceeding with the same prudence, governed by the same Spirit, and having the same end in view, committed likewise to writing the sum of that doctrine which they delivered to the churches ? The same judgment should be passed where the cases are the same. And hence those are refuted, who dream of the existence of some unwritten prophetic traditions. For Luke makes all that the prophets spake to be comprised in the scriptures. Therefore, there were no unwritten traditions of the prophets. Therefore, there were no unwritten traditions of the apostles. The reason is precisely the same. If the ancient church had every thing in scripture, the christian church likewise hath every thing in scripture. The antecedent is plain ; therefore also the consequent. Otherwise God provided better for the Jews than for us.

The fifth place is taken from John v. 39, where Christ says, " Search the scriptures." The Jews read the scriptures, but did not understand them aright. Christ therefore exhorts them to give more diligent attention to the search. He adds as a reason, " For in them ye think that ye have eternal life." And they thought so truly, nor does Christ blame that opinion, So Psalm cxix. 2, " Blessed are they who ' search ' his testimonies[1]." If felicity and salvation may be derived from the scriptures, then every thing is contained in the scriptures. So Psalm i., " Blessed is the man who meditates in the law of the Lord day and night." If the Jews could have made a right use of the scriptures, they would

[1 The quotation is from the Vulgate, "Beati qui *scrutantur* testimonia ejus ;" which, as usual, follows the LXX. who have, οἱ ἐξερευνῶντες. But the Hebrew word is נֹצְרֵי, rightly translated in the English version, "who keep." However, the radical idea is to watch or look at narrowly ; which might yield the thought of *searching*, if there were evidence of such an usage.]

have found life in them.   And on this account Christ exhorts
them to *search* the scriptures.   From this place I reason thus :
If by searching the scriptures we can find all things requisite to
salvation and eternal life, then all things necessary are written.   Besides, if this benefit could have been obtained from the scriptures
of the old Testament, then much more certainly may the same
benefits be now obtained, after the addition of the scriptures of the
new Testament.

The sixth place is taken from Acts i. 1, where Luke writes
thus : " The former treatise have I made, O Theophilus, of all
that Jesus began both to do and to teach," &c.   Now whatsoever
things concerning Christ are necessary to be known, are contained
under these two heads, namely, the sayings and the acts of Christ ;
on which account Luke says in the beginning of his gospel, that he
had made himself perfect master of them all, and committed them
to writing.   From this passage we argue thus : If all things that
Jesus said and did are written, then all things which necessity
requires us to know concerning Christ are written.   Now the first
is true; therefore also the second.   Here perhaps some one may
object, Did he really write *all ?*   Nay, he hath omitted many
things written by Matthew and the rest, as the story of the Magi,
the cruelty of Herod, &c.   Besides, John says that if *all things
were* written, the whole world could not contain so many books.
What then ?   Are those things superfluous, which are written by
the other evangelists ?   I answer : Nothing less.   But if we had
only the gospel of Luke or of Matthew, we should be content with
it, and that one would be sufficient.   Nevertheless, the rest are not
therefore superfluous : first, because God willed that these things
should not be written by only a single author, in order that our
faith should stand upon the firmer evidence ; secondly, because he
willed that those things which are written by one with some
obscurity, should be more clearly treated by another, so that we
might thus have not only sufficient, but most abundant instruction.
Luke did not write all things absolutely that Jesus said and did,
but the chief and most necessary things (as even the Rhemists
themselves explain the words), and what might be sufficient.   And
so our argument will be perfectly conclusive, as follows : If all the
chief and necessary things are found either in one, or more of the
evangelists, then, much rather, in the whole scripture.   Now the
first is true, and therefore the second.

The seventh place is taken from Acts xvii. 2, 3, where Luke

writes that Paul reasoned for three sabbath-days *out of the scrip-tures*, ἀπὸ τῶν γραφῶν, that Christ had suffered; so that this was the Christ whom he preached unto them. Paul then discoursed from the scriptures, and confirmed his whole doctrine by the scrip-tures. Hence we gather the following argument: If Paul used no other evidence than that of scripture in teaching and delivering the gospel, and refuting the Jews; then all testimonies which are re-quisite either to confirm the true doctrine of the gospel or to refute heresies may be taken out of scripture. The former is true, and therefore the latter. The consequence is manifest. For if any other testimony had been necessary, the apostle would have used it. But he confirmed his doctrine only by the scriptures; and therefore, in verse 11, the Bereans are praised for having searched the scrip-tures, and examined Paul's teaching by them. Therefore we ought to do likewise. Now no heretics are more keen disputers, or more difficult to be refuted, than the Jews.

The eighth place is taken from Acts xviii. 24 and 28. Apollos was mighty in the scriptures, and refuted the Jews forcibly, εὐτό-νως, out of the scriptures. We may argue here as in the former case: If Apollos made use only of the scriptures in refuting the Jews and confirming the doctrine of the gospel, then the gospel may be confirmed and heresies refuted by the scriptures alone. The former is true, and consequently the latter also.

The ninth place is taken from Acts xxiv. 14, where Paul testifies before the governor, that he believed all things which are written in the law and the prophets: in which words Paul designed to give evidence of his faith, religion and piety. For the reason why he said this was to persuade the Jews that he was a believer and a Christian. It follows from this, that all articles of faith are contained in the books of Moses and the prophets. Thus, then, we argue: If all things that should be believed by a faithful and godly man are delivered in the books of Moses and the prophets, then all necessary things are found in the scriptures. Now the former is true, and therefore also the latter. The consequence holds; be-cause the whole worship of God consists in believing those things which are delivered by Moses and the prophets, and faith embraces these alone. So Paul says: " So worship I the God of my fathers, believing all things which are written in the law and in the prophets." He indicates that the true worship of God consists in believing what Moses and the prophets taught. If any other things were necessary, then he would not have used a pertinent argument to prove his piety. But hence it is plain that God willed nothing but the faithful reception of whatever is delivered in the scriptures, and that he is truly and perfectly a believer, who believes all things contained in the scriptures.

The tenth place is taken from Acts xxvi. 22, where Paul says, that through the divine assistance he continued up to that very day, witnessing both to small and great, saying nothing beside, οὐδὲν ἐκτὸς, " those things which Moses and the prophets did say should come." Therefore Paul in preaching the gospel uttered not a word extraneous to the scriptures of the law and the prophets. From this passage we reason thus : If Paul, when he preached the gospel, uttered not a word *beside* the Mosaic and prophetical scriptures, then all things necessary to the preaching of the gospel are contained in the scriptures. Now the former is true, and therefore also the second. The consequence holds : for Paul preached the whole gospel, being designed for this special purpose by God, and in the whole explication of it spoke nothing beside the scriptures. In Acts xx. 27, he says that he declared to the Ephesians " the whole counsel of God." Therefore the whole counsel of God in announcing the gospel may be learned from the scriptures. Hence another syllogism follows : If Paul taught nothing beside the scriptures, then neither is it now lawful for any one to deliver anything beside the scripture. But the former is true, and therefore the second. For who will dare to assume to himself what Paul could not or ought not to do ?

The eleventh place is taken from Rom. i. 2, where Paul says that the gospel which he preached was before promised in the prophets. But perhaps it may be said that these prophets did not write ; for the papists are continually falling into this delusion. Now, to prevent the suspicion that the prophets made this promise only orally, and did not commit it to writing, it follows, that the gospel was promised by the prophets ἐν γραφαῖς ἁγίαις, " in the holy scriptures." Hence we argue thus : If that gospel which Paul preached was promised in the scriptures, and Paul preached the whole gospel ; then the whole gospel was promised in the scriptures, and may be found in them. The former is true, and consequently the latter also. What will they deny here ? Did he preach the whole gospel, or only a part of it ? Did he not preach the whole ? Nay, he was specially appointed to the office of preaching, not a part of the gospel, but the whole. If they say that only part of the gospel was preached by Paul, let them specify how large a part that was. But they cannot. Chrysostom writes admirably upon this place : " The prophets did not merely speak, but committed what they spoke to writing; nor did they merely write, but pre-figured future events also in real types. Such was Abraham's leading his son Isaac to sacrifice; Moses' lifting up the brasen serpent, and stretching forth his hands over Amalek, and slaying the Paschal lamb." So Chysostom, and so, chap. xvi. 26, we read that this gospel was declared διὰ γραφῶν προφητικῶν.

The twelfth place is taken from Rom. x. 17 : " Faith cometh by hearing, and hearing by the word of God." Whence it appears that faith is conceived by hearing. But many things are heard : which, then, are those the hearing whereof begets faith ? The word of God, ῥῆμα τοῦ Θεοῦ, says Paul. From which words we argue thus : If faith is conceived by hearing the word of God, then all things which are necessary to faith are contained in the word of God. The former is true, and therefore the latter. But they will say that the whole word of God is not written. Now, I under-take to prove that the word of God in this place denotes the scrip-ture. It is written in 1 Peter i. last verse, " The word of the Lord abideth for ever ; and this is the word which by the gospel is preached unto you." In Matth. v. 18, Christ says : " Until heaven and earth shall pass away, one jot or one tittle shall by no means pass from the law till all things be fulfilled." This is the very same as Peter says : for the law in this place denotes the written teach-ing. So Matth. xxiv. 35, Christ says, " Heaven and earth shall pass away, but my words shall not pass away." Now we have be-fore shewn and proved that all Christ's words, or at least all that were necessary, are written. Peter himself makes this clear when he says, " This is the word which by the gospel is preached unto you." So Paul, Rom. x. 8, " That is, the word of faith which we preach." For the whole gospel is promised, as we learnt above, in the prophetic scriptures, and declared in the apostolic. Basil in his *Ascetics* excellently well confirms our interpretation; for he says, " Whatsoever is beside the divinely inspired scriptures is sin, because it is not of faith ; and faith is by hearing, and hearing by the word of God." Where he determines that that word whereby faith is begotten is by no means to be sought without the divinely inspired scriptures.

The thirteenth place is taken from Rom. xv. 4 : " Whatsoever things were written of old time were written for our learning, that we through patience and comfort of the scripture might have hope." In which words the apostle shews, by using the term προεγράφη, that he is explaining the utility of the old Testament.

Now, what was this utility? Our instruction; for he says, εἰς ἡμετέραν διδασκαλίαν. Whence it appears that there is no part of the old Testament idle or unfruitful. From this place we argue thus: If the Lord willed that so many things should be written for our instruction, that we might so be the better advanced in learning, then he willed that all necessary things should be written. The first is true; therefore also the latter. The force of the inference is manifest: for if he willed that not merely one or two, but so many books should be written, it follows necessarily that all necessary things are written in them; for we cannot suppose him to have chosen to repeat the same things so often, and yet omit what was necessary. This is confirmed by the consideration that God hath added the new to the books of the old Testament, so as to put us in possession of a most lucid body of teaching. This is afterwards made still clearer; for Paul subjoins, " that we through patience and comfort of the scriptures might have hope." If hope springs from the scriptures, then faith; for hope is supported by faith. Therefore all things necessary may be derived from the scriptures.

The fourteenth place is taken from Eph. ii. 19, 20: " Ye are no longer strangers and foreigners, but fellow-citizens of the saints, and of the household of God; and are built, ἐποικοδομηθέντες, upon the foundation of the apostles and prophets, Jesus Christ himself being the chief corner-stone." By the foundation of the apostles and prophets he means the prophetic and apostolic doctrine; as not only our divines, but Aquinas also, and Cajetan, and all the papists, confess. It will not be necessary, therefore, to stand upon the proof of this. Cajetan says that we are built upon Christ by means of the doctrine of the prophets and apostles. But why hath Paul coupled the prophets with the apostles? The reason of this may be learned from Thomas, who says that Paul names both, because the doctrine of both is necessary to salvation, and to shew the harmony between them. " For," says he, " the apostles preached that those things had been done which the prophets predicted should occur[1]." Hence then I draw the following inference: The prophets foretold all things necessary to salvation; therefore the apostles preached all things necessary. But the papists confess this of the apostles' preaching, and so I seem to prove nothing against them. Well, upon this I frame another argument, to this effect: Whatever the prophets preached they also wrote. So says Chrysostom, ἅπερ

[1 Nam quæ prophetæ futura prædixerunt, ea apostoli facta prædicarunt.—In Ephes. ii. 20. Comm. Lect. vi. Expos. in Pauli Epp. Basil. 1475.]

ἔλεγον καὶ ἔγραφον. They wrote therefore all necessary things. Now whatever the prophets foretold and wrote, the apostles preached and wrote to have been fulfilled. Therefore all necessary things are contained in the prophetic and apostolic scriptures; in the former as future, in the latter as done; in the former predicted, fulfilled in the latter. And it is sufficient for our purpose, if it be allowed that the prophets wrote all; since it is most certain that nothing is predicted in the prophetic books, the fulfilment of which may not be read in the apostolic. Hence, therefore, I gather a fresh argument : If the church rest only upon the written teaching of the prophets, then it rests also wholly upon the written teaching of the apostles. Now the former is true; for they can produce no unwritten teaching of the prophets : therefore also the latter.

The fifteenth place is taken from 2 Pet i. 19 : " We have also a more sure word, λόγον, of prophecy; whereunto ye do well that ye·take heed, as to a light shining in a dark place, until the day dawn, and the day-spring arise in your hearts." In which words the state of this life is compared to a dark place, which needs the light of a candle; but the state of the life to come, to the clear day, when Christ our day-spring shall arise and shed his divine light upon our minds. Peter then exhorts us, whilst we sojourn in this life, to turn our eyes continually towards this lamp of the prophetic word. Hence I argue thus : If in this dark life no other light is proposed or shewn to us but that of the scriptures, then we should be engaged with the scriptures alone, acquiesce in them, and betake ourselves wholly to them alone. Now the antecedent is true; therefore also the consequent. The minor is proved by observing that the apostle assigns as our lamp the prophetic word, λόγον προφητικὸν, or the holy scripture, as Cajetan interprets it, and all concede. For that λόγος is frequently used for scripture, is evident from many passages. Acts i. 1, τὸν μὲν πρῶτον λόγον ἐποιησάμην : where λόγος means the book. Luke iii. 4, ὡς γέγραπται ἐν βίβλῳ λόγων Ἡσαΐου. And Acts xiii. 27, φωναὶ τῶν προφητῶν, the *voices* of the prophets are said to be read.

The sixteenth place is taken from 1 John i. 4, " And these things we write unto you, that your joy may be full." In the first verse he mentions the word of life, and says, " That which we have seen and heard declare we unto you." But do we only declare it? Yea also, γράφομεν, we write it; for he speaks not merely of himself, but of the other writers too. Whatsoever things, then, the apostles heard and saw, they announced; and whatever they announced, they wrote. Now, as the papists confess, they announced all necessary things; therefore they wrote all necessary things. This is still more clearly shewn by the end proposed, "that your joy may be full." Thus then I reason: Full joy is procured by the scriptures: therefore scripture is perfect.

The last testimony is taken from the title of the scriptures, which are called the old and new Testaments. The prophetic books form the old Testament, the evangelical books the new. This is plain from 2 Cor. iii. 14 : "In the *reading of the old Testament*, even unto this day remaineth that same veil untaken away ; which veil is done away in Christ." Paul speaks of the prophetic books. Therefore the prophetic books bear the title of the old Testament. Hence I draw the following conclusion : If the books of holy scripture are rightly called the old and new Testaments, then they contain the full and perfect will of God and Christ. For it is the very notion of a testament to declare the perfect will of the testator, that is, of the Maker of the Testament. For even in the case of man's testament, no man disannulleth or addeth thereto, as Paul observes, Gal. iii. 15. If then this be really God's Testament, then it contains the full will of God ; and consequently none should add to or diminish from it, or seek the will of God elsewhere. Now it is the Testament of God; for no one hath hitherto blamed that title : therefore it contains the entire will of God. And, indeed, the covenant unfolded in these books Christ hath confirmed and established in his own blood.

CHAPTER XVI.

UNWRITTEN TRADITIONS ARE OPPOSED BY REASONS.

HITHERTO we have defended our opinion of the perfection of scripture by many testimonies from scripture. It follows now that we allege some REASONS suited to our purpose. We might produce many such, but will content ourselves with a few, namely, those which Bellarmine endeavours to answer, Lib. IV. c. 12. They are four in number.

The FIRST is this. Unwritten traditions cannot belong preserved : for such is the perversity, negligence, and ignorance of

men, as readily to subvert the best established things. Matters
entrusted to men's memories are easily consigned to oblivion.
These are notorious truths. Let us see how our opponent meets
this argument. He answers very confidently, that it is impossible
that these traditions should not be preserved, because the care
of them rests not on men, but on God. Here he notices God's
care in preserving his church; how God preserved traditions in-
violate from Adam to the time of Moses, and the scriptures from
Moses down to our times. Therefore, says he, God can now also
preserve unwritten traditions. I answer: In the *first* place, I
confess that the divine Providence can preserve from destruction
whatever it chooses; for God can do whatever he wills. But
if we choose thus to abuse the divine Providence, we may, in
the same manner, infer that there is no need of the scriptures,
that every thing should be trusted to the Divine Providence, and
nothing committed to writing, because God can preserve religion safe without the scriptures. As to what he says about the
church, I confess indeed that it can never perish; because God
hath promised that he will always preserve and defend his church
against all the attempts of those who seek to crush and destroy
it. But God hath nowhere promised that he will save and protect
unwritten traditions from being lost: consequently, the church
and tradition are not parallel cases. I can produce innumerable
testimonies and promises wherewith God hath bound himself to the
church to preserve it : let them produce any such promises of God
respecting the preservation of traditions. Now this they cannot
do. *Secondly*, I confess that God preserved his doctrine from
Adam to Moses orally transmitted, that is, in the form of unwritten
tradition. It cannot be denied. But then it was amongst exceeding few persons: for the great majority had corrupted this doctrine.
Besides, God frequently and familiarly shewed himself to the holy
fathers who then lived ; conversed with them, and often renewed
and restored the doctrine orally delivered, and brought it back to
its integrity and purity, when not preserved from all corruption
even by those godly men themselves. Thus God conversed familiarly with those ancient patriarchs : and if the reasoning of our
opponent were of any weight now, God would still treat us in the
same manner. But there is the greatest difference between those
things and ours ; and consequently his reasoning hath no weight.
Thirdly, the fact of Moses having written his heavenly doctrine is
a point of great importance against tradition, and strongly confirm-

atory of our opinion. For if God had seen that religion could
have been preserved entire and uncorrupted without the scriptures,
he would not have enjoined Moses to consign it in the lasting
monuments of written records: but perceiving that religion was
more and more corrupted every day, and that he was obliged to
repeat the same revelations very often, he devised a remedy in the
shape of writing. Although, therefore, formerly, when the body
of the church was scattered, and the worshippers of God but few,
there was no scripture; yet afterwards, when the body of the
church was collected, God willed that his doctrine should be written.
Fourthly, when he says that God preserved the scriptures from
Moses to our time, and therefore can now preserve unwritten traditions, his argument will be allowed to be of force when he can
shew that God feels the same solicitude for unwritten as for written
doctrine, and embraces both with the same care. But God hath no
such design. God protects the scriptures against Satan, as being
their constant enemy. Satan hath frequently endeavoured to destroy the scriptures, knowing that they stand in his way: but he
hath never spent any trouble or thought upon these unwritten
traditions; for he supposed that his whole object would be gained
if he could destroy the scriptures. In pursuance of this plan he
hath raised up such impious tyrants as Antiochus, Maximin, Diocletian, and others, who have endeavoured utterly to quench the light
of scripture. Now, if religion could remain entire even when these
books were lost, it would be in vain for Satan to labour with such
furious efforts to remove these books.

As to his assertion that it is impossible that traditions should
perish, I press him in turn with the inquiry, who was the guardian
of these traditions? If they are preserved, they must be preserved by somebody. Had they then but one guardian, or several?
If many, who were they? Perhaps he will say, the fathers. But
the fathers are at variance amongst themselves, and do not determine unanimously upon tradition. One affirms this to be an apostolical tradition; another denies it: now, if they were the guardians, they would agree. There must then be but one guardian;
who is he? The pope forsooth. But how hath he kept them,—
in a book, or in his mind? Not in a book; for no pope ever had
such a book, and no one pretends such a thing: nor yet in his
mind; for then, when the pope died, traditions would perish with
him, and the church lose a great part of necessary doctrine. Besides, when a person is chosen pope, he brings no other mind with

him to the papacy than he had formerly when he was a cardinal
or a monk; whereas this hypothesis would require that his mind
should be immediately illuminated with the ideas of these traditions. Since, then, we can find no competent guardians of these
traditions, it is plain that they must have long since perished, or
been very negligently kept. Our reasoning, therefore, is certain
and perfectly clear. Whatever is not committed to writing easily
perishes. Where now are the laws of Lycurgus? They have
perished. Where the unwritten dogmas and secret institutions of
Pythagoras? They are nowhere to be found. Where the discipline
of the Druids? It lies utterly extinguished; nor does a single vestige of it remain, save, perchance, some slight traces which we owe
to writing and to books. Yea, where are those traditions of the
Jews which Bellarmine tells us they received from Moses and the
prophets? Assuredly they are either kept in writing in the books
of the old and new Testaments, or else they have perished utterly
because not committed to books: for Bellarmine, I suppose, will
not venture to say that the church is the guardian of these traditions. If the trite proverb,

Vox audita perit, litera scripta manet,

be true in any case, its truth is most strikingly illustrated in the
present; and that the more, in proportion as our minds are usually
most prone to forget those things which are most excellent and
relate to God. All things which are not written are on the brink
of death and oblivion. In Isaiah xxx. 8, God says: " Go write
it in a table, and note it in a book, that it may be for the time to
come, for ever and ever." Thus he intimates that things which
are to last for a constancy must be committed to writing. And it
is plain that the Lord is speaking of his word; for he says in the
next verse, that " this is a rebellious people, lying children, children
that will not hear the law of the Lord." Job, that pious and holy
man, says in his book, xix. 23, 24: " Oh that my words were now
written! Oh that they were printed in a book! that they were
graven with an iron pen and lead in the rock for ever!" Where
is shewn the great efficacy of scripture, and how those things require to be written, which we wish to be kept safe throughout all
ages. In Psalm cii. 19, the prophet says: " Let this be written
for a memorial to those that come after." If we wish, then, that
anything should go down to posterity, it must be committed to
writing. We may adduce with the same view the passage, Luke i.
1, 2, where Luke says that it behoved him to write these things, in

order that Theophilus might be put in possession of the certainty of that doctrine which he had received. And the cause impelling Luke to this course confirms this: "Forasmuch," says he, "as many have taken in hand" to write, that is to corrupt the gospel, such as Ebion, Cerinthus, Apelles and the rest. It is on this account, Luke says, that it became needful for him to write. Consequently it is necessary that the gospel should be written; since otherwise it could not be preserved entire. Theophylact explains these words intelligently and perspicuously in his commentary upon this place: "Now, in delivering to you the gospel in a written form, confirm and assure your reason, lest you should forget what was orally imparted to you[1]." Writing, then, is in the nature of a muniment to keep safe the memory of things. So the apostle, Philipp. iii. 1 : "To write the same things unto you, to me is not grievous, and for you it is safe." Therefore it is safe for us that teaching should be written, and that often. The old interpreter hath translated it, *mihi necessarium est:* where Thomas Aquinas remarks, "Words pass easily away, but those things which are written remain[2]." In Exod. xvii. 14, the Lord says, "Write this for a memorial in a book." Upon which place Cajetan observes thus: "He orders the achievement to be written for a continual record of it[3]." Thus it plainly appears that our reasoning is founded upon the clearest lessons of common experience. For when memory fails, then those things which are committed to memory fail also. Hence conditions of peace, treaties, covenants, and whatever we wish to be safe and lasting, we commit to writing lest they should be lost, distrusting our memories. Now if our memory is so frail in outward things, then much more have we need of all helps and remedies for the support of our memories in the case of heavenly things. Thomas, in the proem to his *Catena Aurea* upon the gospel of Matthew, relates, out of Jerome, two reasons why Matthew wrote his gospel: the first was, that he might leave his gospel in men's memories; the second, that he might guard against the heretics. On both accounts it is plain that the scriptures are necessary for us in every part of religion.

But in addition to the reason drawn from a consideration of the divine Providence (which he thinks the most important, and to

[1] Νῦν ἐγγράφως σοι παραδιδοὺς τὸ εὐαγγέλιον, ἀσφαλίζομαι τὸν σὸν λογισμόν, ἵνα μὴ ἐπιλάθηται τῶν ἀγράφως παραδεδομένων.]

[2] Verba de facili transeunt: ea vero quæ scripta sunt permanent.]

[3] Rem gestam scribi jubet, ad perpetuam rei memoriam.]

which he trusts principally), Bellarmine adduces four others, to prove that traditions cannot perish. These we will briefly review. The first is *scripture* itself. But hereby he does not mean the holy scriptures : for although, says he, traditions are not found in the sacred books, yet they may be found in the monuments of the ancients and the ecclesiastical writings. I answer : In the *first* place, if God willed traditions to be written by any men, he doubtless willed that it should be by the apostles and evangelists, who were the fittest of all men to execute that work. Let them specify some cause, or allege some reason, why he should not rather have chosen that they should be written by Matthew, Mark, Luke, and the other apostles, than by Dionysius the Areopagite, Clemens Romanus, Irenæus, Augustine, and the like. *Secondly*, this answer puts those ecclesiastical writers whom they style *classics*, upon a par with the divine writers, the prophets, evangelists and apostles. For when they wish to prove any tradition, what reason, what authority, what demonstration do they allege ? They bring forward Dionysius, Irenæus, Cyprian, Tertullian, Clemens, and other such fathers of the church ; and by their authority they seek to persuade us, that these traditions are as certainly apostolic as if the apostles themselves had affirmed it. Consequently they give them no less credit, and demand for them no less than for Paul, Peter, and the other apostles. *Thirdly*, these monuments of the fathers differ about traditions, and make us still more uncertain. For when some affirm a thing to be an apostolical tradition, while others deny it, who sees not that the whole subject may be reasonably called in question ?

The second cause, whereby he proves the possibility of preserving traditions, is *continual usage*. In this way, says he, the vulgar languages are preserved, although there are no grammars of them. I answer : Nothing surely can be more futile than this reply. For, *first*, some traditions are secret, and in no way resting upon common usage, but far removed from daily practice, being used only at certain times, and not by many but a few. *Secondly*, these vulgar languages are changed almost every age, even those which are in daily and most frequent use. So the English and the Italians and other people have several times changed their languages. Consequently, if those things which are in the greatest use of a whole people, undergo such manifold changes and variations, how much more is it credible that those which are remote from popular use, and belong to the abstruser parts of scientific theology, are liable to be easily altered, unless defined by the certain rules and laws of scripture! If languages, which all men use, cannot be protected from alteration, how much less traditions which but few understand!

The third cause why traditions may be preserved is founded in certain *ancient monuments*. Here he relates a story about an altar in Flanders, which the heretics (he tells us) ordered to be overturned, saying, that altars were a modern invention: but whilst they were at work, they found some ancient characters graven upon the altars, from which they perceived that it was an ancient monument. I answer : This is a very foolish reason. For, firstly, this cannot be affirmed of all traditions, since it is not possible that there should be external monuments of them all; secondly, if traditions are preserved in dumb monuments, why are they not rather inscribed in the scriptures?

The fourth cause which enables traditions to be preserved is *heresy*. Heretics, says he, have aroused the church to seek into and preserve all traditions. For, he adds, those who live in peace are apt to neglect the instruments which confirm the possession of their goods ; but they who are engaged in perpetual contention and strife keep them diligently. I answer : Firstly, if this be a true reply, then nothing needed to have been written, because heretics are always in the church, and always engaged in strife. Secondly, if the fathers said truly, that the gospel was on that very account committed to writing because the heretics would constantly oppose it, then those traditions also should have been written, because (as he tells us) the heretics endeavour likewise to corrupt traditions. Luke speaks in a very different tone at the beginning of his first chapter. " Forasmuch," says he, " as heretics have attempted to corrupt the sacred history, I have therefore determined to put it in writing." So Jerome and others[1] interpret this passage in Luke. These reasons of Bellarmine's therefore are obviously weak.

Our SECOND REASON is this : The scriptures were delivered to us that we might possess a rule of faith. Consequently, the scripture is sufficient, and therefore there is no need of unwritten traditions. See Augustine, *contra Faust. Manich.* Lib. XI. c. 5, and *de Civit. Dei*, Lib. XIX. c. 18. Now, a rule of faith must be adequate, for otherwise it will be no rule at all. Bellarmine makes two replies, and assuredly with equal impudence and hardihood. *First* he says, that the proper end of scripture is not to be a rule

---

[1] [Hieron. Praef. in Matth. Origen. Hom. in Luc. i. 1. Theoph. in Luc. i. 1.]

of faith, but a kind of commonitory to help us to retain and cherish the doctrine orally delivered. I answer : In the *first* place, this reply is confuted by the very common title of scripture : it is called canonical, because it contains the canon, that is, the rule of faith and life. No one ever found fault with that inscription. The fathers always call it the canonical scripture. If it be a rule, then it is either no rule of our faith, or a perfect and adequate one. Thus Bellarmine removes that common title, confirmed by universal approbation ; since according to him we should call the scripture *commonitory*, and not *canonical*. *Secondly*, if the scripture were published not to serve as a rule of faith, but as a sort of commonitory, then there would have been no necessity for writing so many books ; for a few books would have sufficed for such a purpose. *Thirdly*, we have already proved by many arguments and testimonies that the scriptures are perfect, as from Deut. iv. and Psalm xix. and other passages : therefore they do not merely remind, but perfectly instruct and teach us. In Psalm cxix. 132, the prophet says : " Direct my feet in thy word :" therefore the scripture is a rule by which we may direct the whole course of our faith and life. In Matth. xxii. 29, Christ says to the Sadducees, " Ye do err, not knowing the scriptures ;" and in Luke xvi. 29, Abraham says to the glutton, " They have Moses and the prophets :" therefore the canonical books of scripture are not only our monitors, but our masters also. Besides, they are " written for our learning ;" and therefore not only for our admonition, as appears from Rom. xv. 4. And in 2 Tim. iii. 16, 17, the apostle says that the scripture is useful not for commonition only, but " for doctrine, for reproof, for correction, and for instruction," that is, for all the functions of the ministry : for he subjoins, " that the man of God may be *perfect, throughly furnished* unto every good work." Is this nothing more than a commonitory ? The scripture is also called the Testament. Therefore this assertion of our adversary's, that the scripture is not a *rule*, but only a sort of *commonitory*, is absurd in the highest degree, and not far removed from blasphemy.

Fourthly, the fathers themselves also teach most plainly, why the scripture is called canonical. Cyprian, in his discourse on the baptism of Christ, says that " all the rules of doctrine have emanated from scripture[1]." Basil, *contra Eunom.* Lib. i., calls scripture " the

[1] Inveniet ex hac scriptura omnium doctrinarum regulas emanasse ; et hinc nasci, et huc reverti, quidquid ecclesiastica continet disciplina.—In Fell's Cyprian, App. p. 33. inter Opp. Arnoldi Abb. Bonæ-Vallis. V. sup. p. 28.]

canon of right and the standard of truth². " Chrysostom, *Hom.*
13, *in Genes.* says : " The scripture, when it would teach us any
thing of this kind, explains itself, and suffers not the hearer to fall
into error.   I pray, therefore, and beseech you that, closing your
ears to all these, you would follow exactly the rule of holy scrip-
ture³." Augustine, *De baptismo, c. Donat.* Lib. II. says that the
scriptures are " the balance of God.   Let us not," he proceeds,
" bring deceitful balances, where we may weigh what we choose
and as we choose, saying at our own pleasure, this is heavy, and
this is light : but let us bring the divine balance from the holy
scriptures, as from the treasury of the Lord, and therein weigh
which is weightiest ;—or rather, not weigh it ourselves, but mark
how it is weighed by the Lord⁴." As, therefore, when we would
discover the weight of any thing, we apply a balance ; so, if we
know not whether this or that doctrine be true, we should try it
by the balance of the scripture.   Augustine elsewhere (*De perfect.
Viduit.* cap. I.) writes thus upon this subject : " The holy scripture
hath fixed the rule of our doctrine, that we may not seem to be
wiser than we ought, but be wise, as the apostle says, soberly,
according as God hath given to every man the measure of faith.
Let me not then think, that in teaching you I am doing any
thing more than expounding to you the words of the great
Teacher, and discoursing of that which the Lord hath given⁵."
The same author, *contra Crescon. Grammat.* Lib. II. c. 31, writes
thus concerning the same subject : " It was not without cause that
the ecclesiastical canon was with such wholesome vigilance established, to which certain books of the prophets and apostles appertain ; which books we must by no means dare to judge of, and

[² The reference is, I suppose, to T. II. p. 8. c.   But Basil is there
speaking of the Creed, not of the scripture.]

[³ τῆς ἁγίας γραφῆς, ἐπειδὰν βούληταί τι τοιοῦτον ἡμᾶς διδάσκειν, ἑαυτὴν
ἑρμηνευούσης, καὶ οὐκ ἀφιείσης πλανᾶσθαι τὸν ἀκροατήν.—T. IV. p. 103.]

[⁴ Non afferamus stateras dolosas, ubi appendamus quod volumus, et
quomodo volumus, pro arbitrio nostro dicentes, hoc grave, hoc leve est : sed
afferamus divinam stateram de scripturis sanctis tanquam de thesauris Dominicis, et in illa quid sit gravius appendamus ; imo non appendamus, sed a
Domino appensa recognoscamus.—T. VII. p. 43. Paris. 1635.]

[⁵ Sancta scriptura doctrinæ nostræ regulam figit, ne audeamus sapere
plus quam oportet sapere, sed sapiamus, ut ipse ait, ad temperantiam, sicut
unicuique Deus partitus est mensuram fidei.   Non sit ergo mihi aliud te
docere, nisi verba tibi Doctoris exponere, et de iis quod Dominus dederit
disputare.—De Bono Viduit. c. 1.]

according to which we may freely judge of all other writings of believers or unbelievers[1]." Therefore scripture is the rule by which we must try all things. Thus, whatever disagrees with scripture should be rejected; whatever agrees with it, received. Nay, Thomas himself, in his Comment. on 1 Tim. c. vi., Lect. 1, says that "scripture is as it were the rule of our faith[2]." He does not say "as it were," to diminish the dignity of scripture, but to shew that he is drawing a comparison. *Quasi* is here a mark not of diminution, but of comparison. And that he means that scripture is a perfect rule, is evident from his subjoining that nothing should be added to or diminished from it : to which purpose he alleges Deut. iv. 2, and Rev. xxii. 18, 19.

Let us now look at the causes and reasons which induce Bellarmine to style scripture a commonitory, rather than a rule. The *first reason* is, because in the latter case only necessary things should have been written : but now, says he, many things not necessary have been written ; as all the histories of the old Testament, many of the new, some of the Acts of the Apostles, and all the salutations in the apostolic epistles. But every rule comprises only things necessary. I answer : In the first place, no one can fail to observe how impious and profane is his assertion, that none of the histories of the old Testament are necessary. Is it not necessary for us to know the commencement of the church, its propagation, and continual conservation and government, and the promises made to the patriarchs concerning the Messiah ? Surely he blasphemes who denies this. Secondly, although it may be conceded that all the histories are not equally useful and necessary, because many may be saved without the knowledge of many histories ; yet in reality they are all not only useful, but necessary also. For although they are not all requisite to the being of faith, yet they contribute greatly to its better being. Thirdly, although perhaps more things than can be styled simply necessary are delivered in scripture, yet it does not therefore follow that the scripture is not a rule. For although the scripture contains some things which are not simply and absolutely necessary ; nevertheless, it is a rule to which all doctrine ought to be conformed. We say

[1 Neque enim sine causa tam salubri vigilantia Canon ecclesiasticus constitutus est, ad quem certi prophetarum et apostolorum libri pertineant; quos omnes judicare non audeamus, et secundum quos de ceteris literis vel fidelium vel infidelium libere judicemus.—T. VII. p. 177.]

[2 Scriptura est quasi regula fidei nostræ. Vide supra, p. 28.]

that the scriptures are a rule, because they contain all things necessary to faith and salvation, and more things may be found in them than absolute necessity requires. We do not attach so strict and precise a notion to the term 'rule,' as to make it contain nothing but what is necessary : and as to many things being frequently repeated, this makes it still more a rule ; since that repetition is profitable to our better and surer understanding of what is said.

Our adversary's *second reason* is, because the scripture does not contain all necessary things, as, says he, we have already proved : for there are many necessary things which are not in scripture. I answer : And we have already sufficiently replied, that the things which he deems necessary are useless and ridiculous : such are the remedy whereby women were cleansed from original sin under the old Testament, and others of the like sort, upon which we have spoken before. Bellarmine's *third reason* is, because scripture is not one continuous body, as it ought to be, if it were the rule of faith, but several. I answer : Although scripture contains many bodies, yet all these make up one continuous and entire body. The men indeed were various, whose service the Holy Spirit used in writing these pieces, and the hands which wrote them were many : but it was one Spirit which governed their hands and tongues. We should not regard the various men who wrote, but the one Spirit under whose direction and dictation they wrote. Thus there is one continuous body of doctrine in these books, various as they are. *Finally*, Bellarmine produces certain passages from scripture to prove that scripture is a commonitory, and not a rule ; as Rom. xv. 4, where the apostle says that all things which were written were written for our learning ; and 2 Pet. i. 12, and iii. 1, where Peter says that it was needful for him to *remind* and *stir up* those to whom he wrote. Therefore, (says he) it is commonitory, and not a rule. I answer to the first place, that the apostle says that all things which were written of old time were written for our *learning*. Now to be written for our *learning* is something more than *commonition*. We are commonished or reminded of things which we knew before ; but we learn things of which we were previously ignorant. As to the place of Peter, I allow that the scripture is profitable for monition ; but I say that this is not the only use it serves. For although Peter says that it was needful for him to remind those to whom he wrote, yet he does not merely do this, but teaches them also what it behoves them to know : and thus the scripture, when teaching us what we ought to know, exhorts us also to stand fast in this doctrine. *Secondly*, Bellarmine replies that scripture is a rule indeed, but *partial*, not *complete;* and that the whole and entire rule is the word of God, which is divided into the written and the unwritten word ; and that Augustine must be understood in this sense. I answer : It is unwillingly that he concedes to us that scripture is a rule ; and therefore he afterwards denies it again, by saying that it is only a *partial* one, thus taking away what he had previously given. For unless scripture be a whole and perfect rule, it cannot be a rule at all ; because there ought to be the exactest agreement between the rule and the thing to which it is applied. If, therefore, our faith be longer or broader than the scripture, then the scripture is not its rule ; because a rule should be adequate to the thing measured by it. A rule is thus defined by Varinus : "A rule is an infallible measure, admitting no addition or diminution[1]." So Theophylact, upon Phil. iii. : " A rule or standard admits neither addition nor abstraction[2]." And Basil, *Adv. Eunom.* Lib. I. blames Eunomius severely and justly for saying that the faith of the fathers is a rule or standard, and yet maintaining that something should be added to it : τὴν αὐτὴν καὶ κανόνα λέγει, καὶ προσθήκης φησὶν ἀκριβεστέρας δεῖσθαι[3]. In the same way Bellarmine says that scripture is a rule, and yet needs some addition and emendation. Consequently, he denies it to be a rule at all. Chrysostom, *Hom.* 13 *in* 2 *Cor.* says that "the sentence of the divine words" is " the exact balance and standard, and rule of all things." And, to let us know that he is speaking of the scriptures, he subjoins : " Inquire concerning all these things of the holy scriptures." So Photius, cited by Œcumenius upon Phil. iii. : " Faith is like a rule : for, like as if you take any thing from a rule, or add any thing to it, you entirely spoil the rule ; so it is with faith[4]." Thus it is manifest that the scriptures are either a perfect rule, or no rule at all. See also upon this subject Vincentius Lirinensis, c. 41. Why need I add, that Andradius himself testifies that

[1 Κανών ἐστι μέτρον ἀδιάψευστον, πᾶσαν πρόσθεσιν καὶ ἀφαίρεσιν μηδαμῶς ἐπιδεχόμενον.]

[2 ὁ κανὼν γὰρ οὔτε πρόσθεσιν ἔχει οὔτε ἀφαίρεσιν.—Theophyl. In Philipp. iii. 16, p. 611. Lond. 1636.]

[3 Basil. Opp. T. II. p. 9. A.]

[4 ὥσπερ γὰρ ἐπὶ τοῦ κανόνος κἂν ἀφέλῃς, κἂν προσθῇς, ἐλυμήνω τὸ πᾶν, οὕτω καὶ ἐπὶ τῆς πίστεως.]

scripture is a rule sufficiently perfect? For thus he writes, in the beginning of the third book of his *Defensio Tridentina :* "I am far from disliking the opinion of those who say that the scriptures are called canonical, because they contain the canon, that is, the amplest rule and standard of faith, piety, and religion, brought down to us from heaven by the exceeding goodness of God[5]." Thus he confesses that the scriptures are not only a rule, but a very ample rule of faith, piety, and religion.

Secondly, I demand why he affirms the scriptures to be a partial rule, or a rule only in part, and not throughout and altogether? If, because they contain only some necessary things, he is utterly mistaken in the matter of fact. For if God willed to give us a rule in the scriptures, he certainly willed to give us a perfect one. This may be gathered from the ends to serve which, and the causes on account of which, the scriptures were published. For why was this teaching committed to writing? First, that it might remain more fixedly in our memories. Now this reason teaches us that all necessary things ought to have been written; because all necessary things should be retained as firmly as may be in memory. Secondly, lest the doctrine should be corrupted. But nothing necessary ought to be corrupted. Thirdly, that we might the better and more surely know the sacred and heavenly doctrine. But all necessary things we ought to know rightly and surely. Wherefore all the reasons for publishing the scriptures will establish, that all necessary things are delivered in them, and that scripture is a perfect rule : for whatever reason there was for delivering a rule, held also for making that rule complete.

Thirdly, I answer, with respect to Augustine. Our adversary pretends that, though Augustine calls scripture a rule, he does not mean that it is the sole or perfect rule. Thus then speaks Augustine, *Contra Faust. Manich.* Lib. II. c. 5 : "The canonical scripture is placed upon an elevated throne, demanding the obedience of every faithful and pious understanding[6]." If this be true, then is it certain that scripture is as it were the queen and mistress which ought to rule and govern human in-

[5 Minime illorum mihi displicet sententia, qui canonicas ideo appellari dicunt, quia pietatis, fidei et religionis canonem, hoc est, regulam atque normam, e cœlis summo Dei beneficio ad nos delatam, continent amplissimam.—Andradii, Defens. Trid. Lib. III. prope init.]

[6 ... in sede quadam sublimiter constituta est, cui serviat omnis fidelis et pius intellectus.—Vide supra, p. 353.]

firmity, and to which our whole intellect, all teaching, every
thought and opinion, should be conformed in dutiful submission.
In the other place, which is taken from his *City of God,* Lib. XIX.
c. 18, he says that that faith " by which the just lives, and by
which we walk without doubting so long as we sojourn absent
from the Lord[1]," is engendered by the holy scriptures.   Whence
it follows, that scripture is a perfect rule both of faith and life.

Fourthly, it may be answered, that Bellarmine contradicts
himself.   He said before that scripture could not be a rule, because it is not one continuous body.   But the written and unwritten word are still less a continuous body ; and yet he makes
them both together form a rule.

Our THIRD REASON is drawn from the inconveniences which
traditions bring with them.   For if we allow so much to unwritten
traditions, we shall often err, and be always in uncertainty ; because
traditions are various and uncertain.   This is manifest from the
books of the fathers, as we have before shewn.   The fathers are
witnesses of the variety and uncertainty of traditions.   Now in the
doctrine of faith we ought to be certain and constant : therefore
we ought not to depend upon unwritten traditions.   The extreme
variety of traditions might be illustrated by many testimonies, and
in many words ; but I will touch it only briefly.   Papias was the
father and master of tradition.   Eusebius, Eccl. Hist. Lib. III. c. 39,[2]
writes copiously concerning him.   He says that he wrote many
things derived from unwritten tradition, ἐκ παραδόσεως ἀγράφου,
but that they were full of commentitious fables.   He wrote, as
Eusebius tells us, five books concerning the Lord's discourses :
but these, through the goodness of God, are now lost.   What
sort of pieces they were, appears from Eusebius, who says that
they were full of fables.   He first invented the heresy of the
Chiliasts, and that doubtless much more from unwritten tradition
than scripture, although perhaps he seized upon some occasional
support of that error from the scriptures.   Œcumenius[3] brings
forward another tradition from this Papias concerning Judas, —
namely, that he was not strangled, but, the rope breaking, lived in
a most wretched condition for some time after, and at length

[1 Credit etiam scripturis sanctis, et veteribus et novis, quas canonicas
appellamus ; unde fides ipsa concepta est, ex qua justus vivit ; per quam
sine dubitatione ambulamus, quamdiu peregrinamur a Domino.]

[2 T. I. p. 281, ed. Heinichen.]

[3 Apud Grabe, Spicil. II. p. 34.]

expired upon the road, crushed to death by a chariot which happened to pass by : which is also alluded to by Theophylact upon Matt. xxvii. But scripture opposes this, and the fathers form a different judgment. This Papias was the first who taught that Peter was at Rome, taught, lived, and died there[4] : for no author more ancient than he can be named for that tradition. To him the papists stand indebted for the primacy of their pontiff. Tertullian, c. Judæos, c. 5, says that Christ died in the thirtieth year of his age[5]; and Clemens Alexandrinus, Strom. 1,[6] says the same. But Irenæus, Lib. xi. c. 4, says that he lived to be fifty years old[7]. Both assertions are false; and yet both are supported by tradition.

There was formerly a great dispute about the time of celebrating Easter. The Western churches said that they followed Paul and Peter, keeping Easter upon the Sunday after the fourteenth day of the third month, to avoid any conformity with the Jews. The Orientals and Asiatics, however, alleged John, as ample and sufficient authority as could be desired, and Philip, in defence of their practice of observing it after the Jewish manner, upon the actual fourteenth day of the third month. There were also, as will hereafter appear, many disputes and differences in former times concerning Lent. The papists, and even some of the fathers, say that stated fasts were instituted by the apostles. But Augustine, Ep. 68, ad Casulan. denies that the apostles determined any thing about fasting. So Socrates, Lib. v. c. 22.[8] Indeed, it is certain that it was Montanus who instituted them, as we learn from the testimony of Apollonius, cited by Eusebius, Lib. v. c. 18. There, speaking of Montanus, he adds: " This is he who introduced fasts[9]." This may be perceived also from Tertullian, who in his book de Jejunio, which he wrote when a Montanist

[4 I can nowhere find that Papias said a word of Peter's having been at Rome, and cannot guess the grounds of this strong assertion.]

[5 Hujus [Tiberii] quinto decimo anno imperii passus est Christus, annos habens quasi xxx, cum pateretur.—c. 8, p. 234. ed. Seml. Lips. 1828.]

[6 Page 340. A.]

[7 The reference should be. xi. 39. Quia autem triginta annorum ætas primæ indolis est juvenis, et extenditur usque ad quadragesimum annum, omnis quilibet confitebitur a quadragesimo aut quinquagesimo anno declinat jam in ætatem seniorem, quam habens Dominus noster docebat, &c.—p. 192. A. ed. Fevard.]

[8 Δῆλον ὡς τῇ ἑκάστου γνώμῃ καὶ προαιρέσει ἐπέτρεψαν οἱ ἀπόστολοι.—p. 235. ed. Vales. Paris. 1686.]

[9 οὗτός ἐστιν ... ὁ νηστείας νομοθετήσας.—T. II. p. 85.]

against the catholics, blames the catholics for saying that men should " fast, each of his own free choice, as in a matter indifferent[1]," and that we should not be obliged to fast " at stated times according to the institution of the new discipline." This Tertullian objected to the catholics; and this is the very thing which we affirm and maintain against the papists, that each man should fast as time and occasion shall require, not at fixed seasons. Thus it was that the catholics then fasted; but afterwards, when the heresy of Montanus had secretly diffused itself more extensively, fasts began to be observed according to the institution of the new discipline. In the same book, Tertullian[2] praises the practice of mortification by hard fare (ξηροφαγίαν), in conformity with which Epiphanius, *in Epilog.*[3], makes it an apostolical institution.

Tertullian, in his book *de Corona*[4], and Basil, in his treatise of the Holy Spirit, c. 27,[5] enumerate various traditions, which they would have to be apostolical, but which are, nevertheless, not at all observed by papists at the present day: for example, that we should stand at prayer on Sundays, and from Easter to Pentecost. Basil adduces some reasons in confirmation of this, upon which we have spoken above. Tertullian pronounces it a piece of impiety to do otherwise. So even the first council of Nice, Canon 20, says that we ought to pray standing at that season[6]. But the present practice is different, even amongst the papists; who upon Sundays, and from Easter to Pentecost, do not pray in an erect posture, but kneeling, as at other times and seasons of the year. Of old they used to give the Eucharist to infants, as is manifest from Cyprian, *De lapsis*[7], and Augustine, in many passages. But this practice is now abolished. Epiphanius, against Aërius, writes that Christians in his time, upon the authority of apostolic tradition, used to eat nothing but bread and salt for some days before Easter[8]. Do the papists do so now? Jerome,

[1] Itaque de cetero (i. e. exceptis diebus in quibus sponsus ablatus) indifferenter jejunandum, ex arbitrio, non ex imperio.—c. 2, p. 181.]

[2] Ibid. c. 9.]

[3] Exposit. Fidei Catholicæ, c. xxii. p. 1105. T. I. ed. Petav.]

[4] c. 3. But Tertullian does *not* there pretend these traditions to be apostolical: he defends them on the plea of custom.]

[5] Basil. Opp. T. II. pp. 110, 111.]

[6] Apud Labb. et Cossart. T. II. col. 37.]

[7] p. 132, ed. Fell.—The passage referred to is the story of an infant which, after having eaten something offered to an idol, refused the eucharistic cup, and turned sick when forced to drink of it.]

[8] καὶ περὶ τῶν ἐξ ἡμερῶν τοῦ Πάσχα πῶς παραγγέλλουσι (apostoli scil.)

in his discourse on the nativity of Christ (though Erasmus writes that that piece is attributed by some to Leo, and by others to Maximus), says : " There is a difference of opinion in the world amongst men, whether this be the day whereon Christ was born, or whereon he was baptized[9]." So that he was ignorant whether Christ was born or baptized on that day, and whether they ought on that day to celebrate the memory of his nativity or of his baptism. So admirably did they preserve and understand their traditions. The papists celebrate the feast of the assumption of the blessed virgin Mary with the utmost honour, and the Rhemists in their notes on Acts i. praise this custom exceedingly: yet Jerome, in his book to Paula and Eustochium, concerning the assumption of the blessed virgin, says that " what is told about the translation of her body is apocryphal." Erasmus, indeed, writes that that book is not by Jerome, but by Sophronius, who, however, was contemporary with Jerome.

Such are the popish traditions which they maintain to be necessary, and deserving to be put on an equal footing with the scriptures. To all these things Bellarmine makes no other reply than that the church can discern true traditions from false. I answer, that this is the very point in debate ;—whether that church, to which they ascribe this power of judgment, be the true church, and not another, which hath now of a long time put off false, lying, and heretical traditions upon us for apostolical. Assuredly, since she is the very party accused, she can be no fit person to discharge the function of a judge.

I come now to our FOURTH REASON, which is derived from the custom and practice of heretics. It is the wont of heretics to affirm that Christ and the apostles delivered some things to all, and some secretly to certain persons only. This Irenæus tells us, Lib. I. c. 23, of the Basilidians, and Lib. I. c. 24, of the Carpocratians. In like manner speaks Tertullian, in his Prescriptions against Heretics. Bellarmine replies, out of Cyprian, that heretics are the apes of catholics[10]. However, says he, there is this difference, that the heretics conceal their traditions and mysteries on account of their

μηδὲν ὅλως λαμβάνειν, ἢ ἄρτου καὶ ἁλὸς καὶ ὕδατος;—Hær. LXXV. c. 6. p. 910, B.]

[9 Sive hodie natus Christus sive baptizatus, diversa fertur hominum opinio in mundo.]

[10 Novatianus, simiarum more, quæ cum homines non sint, homines tamen imitantur, vult ecclesiæ catholicæ auctoritatem sibi et veritatem vindicare. Ep. 73, p. 198.]

shamefulness and obscenity, whereas the catholics hide theirs, either because it is not necessary to disclose them, or because all are not capable of receiving them.   I answer: I confess, indeed, that heretics desire to seem like catholics, but they do not imitate them in this particular point.   For it is no practice of catholics, that is, of those who profess sound, solid, and pure doctrine, to hide and conceal the mysteries of Christ: yea, they keep back no part of sound doctrine, but propose the whole to all.   Irenæus tells us that Carpocrates maintained that Christ delivered some things to his disciples apart secretly.   But Irenæus himself, Lib. III. c. 15, writes very differently, denying that Christ and his apostles delivered one set of things openly, and another secretly[1].   Tertullian, in his Prescriptions, pronounces it an heretical proposition to say either that " the apostles did not know every thing, or did not deliver every thing to all[2]."   Yet so say the papists now: for although they concede that the apostles knew all, yet they do not concede that they delivered and promulgated all to all.   Doubtless Irenæus and Tertullian would never have blamed the heretics for concealing their traditions, if the catholics for any reason concealed theirs.   Therefore, whatever be the reason of concealing traditions, the very concealment itself is heretical.   Christ says, Matt. x. 27: " What I say unto you in darkness, that speak ye in the light; and what ye hear in the ear, that preach ye upon the house-tops." Therefore we ought not to hide or conceal any thing: for things which should be spoken on the house-tops should be delivered and divulged to all; not so as that this man and the other, but so as that *all* may hear them.

But here let us mark Bellarmine's exposition, and observe how neat an interpreter he is of scripture: " Preach ye upon the house-tops; that is," says he, " *if need so require;*"—so as to save his former reply, that the catholics conceal some traditions because there is no necessity for disclosing them.   I answer: What sort of an exposition is this?   As if it might be doubted whether there were any necessity for performing the command!   Yea, it is necessary because Christ hath enjoined it.   If they were allowed to interpret scripture thus, they might

[1 Igitur testificatio ejus vera, et doctrina apostolorum manifesta et firma, et nihil substrahens, neque alia quidem in abscondito, alia vero in manifesto docentium.—p. 273, B. ed. Fevard.]

[2 Sed eadem dementia, cum confitentur quidem nihil apostolos ignorasse, ... sed non omnia volunt illos omnibus revelasse, quædam palam et universis, quædam secreto et paucis demandasse.—c. 25, T. III. p. 17.]

easily corrupt any passage. " Preach upon the house-tops"—
that is, says Bellarmine, if there be any need! We may then put
a similar meaning upon the words, " Feed my sheep,"—that is, if
there be any need: and, " Teach all nations,"—that is, if there be
any need! From this it appears how absolutely, without any conscience, the papists are accustomed to deal with scripture. But
Theophylact gives a better explanation of this place: " What ye
have heard from me, teach with the utmost freedom and clearness
of speech, so as that all may hear[3] :" and he observes, that because
dangers attend upon this free speaking, therefore the Lord subjoins, " Fear not those who kill the body." The words are plain.
To the like effect Christ speaks of himself, John xviii. 20 : " I
spake openly to the world : I taught ever in the synagogue and in
the temple, whither the Jews always resort, and in secret have I
said nothing." Bellarmine explains it thus ;—that is, I said
nothing in secret which might not be said everywhere, as far as the
truth and purity of my sayings were concerned. But it does not
therefore follow, says he, that Christ taught his disciples nothing
apart. I answer : This is not what Christ says; but he affirms
that he spoke every thing openly in the midst of the synagogue,
and surrounded by the Jews. They could testify to his teaching;
and therefore he desires that they might be asked what they had
heard. From these premises I conclude that the whole teaching of
Christ was public and common to all, and that Christ taught
nothing to his disciples privately, which was not to be published to
all Christians.

CHAPTER XVII.

TESTIMONIES OF THE FATHERS.

I COME now to our LAST ARGUMENT which is founded upon the
testimony of the fathers. The fathers most clearly favour our
opinion. However, I bring them forward not to confirm a thing
in itself dubious and uncertain, but to shed light upon a truth
already ascertained, and to shut the mouths of our adversaries, who
loudly, in every question, claim the fathers as their own. I should

[3] Ἅπερ μόνοις ὑμῖν εἶπον, μετὰ παρρησίας διδάξατε καὶ μεγαλοφώνως, ὥστε
πάντας ἀκούειν ὑμῶν.—Theophyl. in Matt x. 27.]

never make an end, were I to seek to enumerate all who stand on
our side in this matter. There is almost not one single father,
hardly any author of any kind, who does not support our opinion
in this controversy. Here I might distribute my testimonies into
classes, since some tend to prove the perfection of scripture ; some
that all faith and religion should be based on scripture ; some that
the fathers are at variance about traditions : but I choose rather
to handle those cited by Bellarmine, Lib. IV. c. 11, and which he
endeavours to wrest out of our hands. I will prove that those
testimonies, the force of which he hath undertaken to obviate, are
fit and sufficient for the confirmation of our opinion.

The first testimony is that of IRENÆUS. He writes thus, Lib. III.
c. 1 : "It is by no other that we have gained the knowledge
of the economy of our salvation than by those by whom the
gospel reached us ; which gospel they then preached, and afterwards by the will of God delivered to us in the scriptures, to be
the bases and pillar of our faith[1]." We must remark three things
in these words : first, that the apostles and evangelists of Christ
preached and published the gospel orally as Christ had commanded
them ; and that this was the entire gospel : secondly, that these
same persons afterwards wrote it, and delivered it to us in the
scriptures ; and that by the divine will and authority : thirdly, that
the gospel by them committed to writing is the basis and column
of our faith. What does Bellarmine say in reply to these things?
Forsooth he tells us, that all things are written which the apostles
preached commonly and openly to all, but not all other things. So
that Irenæus says, not that the apostles wrote all, but all that they
preached to the people ; for they did not preach all to the people !
He lays down, then, two propositions : one, that all things are not necessary to all; the other, that the apostles preached to all, and left also
in the scriptures, all those things which were necessary for all persons.

First, he says that some things are simply necessary to
all ;—such as the Articles of the Creed, the ten Commandments,
and some of the sacraments, (but what sacraments, he does not
tell us ;) while the rest may remain unknown without any damage
to salvation. I answer : This distinction rests upon no authority
or foundation of scripture, but rather plainly contradicts and

[1 Non enim per alios dispositionem salutis nostræ cognoscimus, quam
per eos per quos evangelium pervenit ad nos ; quod quidem tunc præconia-
verunt, postea vero per Dei voluntatem in scripturis nobis tradiderunt, fir-
mamentum et columnam fidei nostræ futurum.—p. 229, A.]

opposes it, even in the highest degree. For the scripture testifies that the same things are necessary for all. There is not one faith of a prelate or bishop, and another of a private man or laic, but the same of both. The Apostles' Creed, and the other orthodox creeds, pertain not more to the people than to the prelates and masters of the church, and were published chiefly for their benefit. That the faith of all is one and the same, the apostle testifies, Ephes. iv. 5: " One Lord, one faith, one baptism, one God and Father of all, &c." As there is, therefore, not one baptism for a bishop, and another for a layman, but the same for both; nor one God of a layman, another of a bishop, but the same of both; so there is not one faith of a bishop, and another of a layman, but the same of both. Here the apostle affirms the faith of all Christians to be one and the same. But, lest the papists should suppose that I abuse this passage of scripture, I will bring forward expositors whom they dare not reject. Thomas Aquinas writes thus upon this place: " There is one faith, because one and the same thing is believed by all the faithful, whence it is called the catholic faith[2]." So Cajetan: " One faith, because we all believe one and the same thing[3]." Catharinus, too, hath almost the very same words upon this passage. Thus these men acknowledge that the faith of all is one and the same. Therefore, all things are equally necessary for all.

Secondly, he concedes that a knowledge of the articles of the creed, and of the decalogue, and of some sacraments, is necessary. I ask what sort of knowledge he means? Assuredly he must mean an explicit knowledge; for he says that an *explicit* knowledge of the rest is not necessary. Now, what knowledge should be called explicit? Is it the mere power of repeating these words? By no means, for any one could most easily do that; but there is required besides understanding and assent. Now I ask, is it possible, that he who rightly understands the articles of the creed, that is, who understands the sense of all those articles, and perfectly assents to their truth, and understands in like manner the ten commandments, can perish, whether he be bishop or layman? Surely not; since he embraces with his understanding and faith all things which pertain to salvation. Thus this first reply of Bellarmine's hath no strength in it. But how

[2 Una fides, quia unum et idem creditur a cunctis fidelibus, unde catholica dicitur.—Comment. in Eph. iv. 5. Basil. 1475.]

[3 Una fides, quia unum et idem omnes credimus.—Comment. ibid.]

does Bellarmine prove his distinction? From Acts ii. 41, where
Luke tells us three thousand men were baptized in one day, and
added to the church. These (says he) without doubt understood
not all, but only those necessary things; wherefore they are said,
after baptism, to have persevered in the doctrine of the apostles,
that is, to have learned the rest which they had not yet heard. I
answer, firstly: This is indeed to handle scripture like a Jesuit!
He writes to prove that all things are not simply necessary to all;
and for this purpose he brings forward Acts ii. 41. But nothing
of the kind can be inferred from this place: for does it follow that
these men knew what was necessary for them, therefore not what
was necessary for all? I see, however, what he means; that they
could not learn from one discourse all things necessary, and therefore, that they learned only what were necessary for themselves.
But he might have understood from the very words of the text, that
this was an extraordinary case; for under ordinary circumstances
they could not have learned so speedily even those necessary things.
And this is plain from verse 38, where Peter said: "Ye shall receive the gift of the Holy Ghost." Secondly, his expounding "they
continued," to mean, they learned what they previously were ignorant
of, is ridiculous. To continue is to abide and persevere in known
doctrine, not to learn new matters which we had not yet heard.

What then, somebody will ask, is not a different sort of knowledge required in a bishop from what is demanded in a laic? I
answer: One knowledge is not necessary to salvation in a bishop,
and another in a layman, but the same. If it were another, then
it would differ in kind; but there is no difference of kind in this
knowledge, but only of greater and less. And here we must note a
self-contradiction in the Jesuit. First he concedes that these persons
knew all things necessary before they were baptized: then he says
that afterwards they continued, that is, learned the mysteries of the
christian religion. But these are necessary things. Now why should
men, especially laymen, learn some necessary things afterwards, if
they had before learned all that was needful for them?

Bellarmine proceeds to prove the same point from 1 Thes-
sal. iii. 10, where Paul wishes to come to them, that he might
supply what was lacking to their faith. I answer: We have
already replied to this passage. However, I ask whether these
things which Paul wished to teach them were necessary or not?
If necessary, then they ought not to have been baptized before
they had learned them: Bellarmine himself confesses that adult

persons should not be baptized without an explicit knowledge and belief of what is necessary. But if they were not necessary, the apostle would not have been so eager to come to them. In neither way can this reply, or rather tergiversation, of our adversary stand consistently. The apostle, therefore, wished to come in order to teach them more certainly what they had previously learned, to confirm the faith which they had received, and not to deliver a new one.

Bellarmine replies in the second place, that the apostles preached to all the things which are simply necessary, but some things only to the prelates, bishops and presbyters. I answer: This is absolutely false and heretical. For Tertullian, in his Prescriptions, declares it to be the opinion of the heretics, "that the apostles either did not know all, or did not deliver all to all." And Paul, Gal. i. 8, 9, denounces an anathema against all those, even though they were angels, who should preach anything beside what he had preached and they had received; implying that he had preached nothing but what they had received. Now they were the people: the people therefore received that gospel which Paul preached, and received it entire. Here we must notice a remarkable contradiction in our opponents. They say that all things are not delivered to the people, because all things are not necessary for them: and yet they produce, in proof of their traditions, such scriptures as 1 Cor. xi. 2, "I praise you that ye remember me in all things, and keep the traditions even as I delivered them unto you." But these words are addressed to the people, as is plain from the first chapter. They produce also 2 Thess. ii. 15, "Hold the traditions." Now the apostle speaks these words to the laity and the people, as is clear from the first verse of the first chapter. Since, therefore, these traditions were preached to the people, they cannot confirm their traditions by the testimony of these places. Now that the apostle preached these to the people, is manifest from the consideration that otherwise he would not have praised the people for holding them. But if they were preached, then they were written too, according to the evidence of Irenæus and the consent of Bellarmine. Besides, we should carefully remark and remember that Bellarmine, coerced by inevitable force of reason, confesses that all those things which are simply necessary, and for all, are written: whence it follows that no traditions are necessary either simply or for all.

But let us look at the reasons by which he seeks to prove that

43

[WHITAKER.]

the same things are not necessary for all persons. The *first* is, because what are taught in the schools, and what are preached in sermons to the people, are not the same things : therefore the same things are not necessary for all.   I answer : The mode of treating them is different, but the things handled are the same.   The same things are taught in the schools and in the churches, but in a different manner ; popularly in the churches, accurately and precisely in the schools.   The *second reason* is taken from Acts xx. 17, 18, where Paul taught the elders of the church of Ephesus apart from the people.   I answer : He did indeed teach them apart, but nothing else than what he had taught all : for being unable to address the whole church, he sent for the elders.   Now that he taught them nothing else is clear from Luke, who hath set forth the sum of that discourse.   The *third reason* is taken from 1 Cor. ii. 6, " We speak wisdom amongst them that are perfect."   I answer : Irenæus, Lib. iii. c. 2,[1] bears witness that the heretics formerly abused this passage to support the same opinion (or rather madness) as the papists of the present time, as we have before observed.   The *fourth reason* is taken from 2 Tim. ii. 2, " Those things which thou hast heard of me before many witnesses, the same commit thou to faithful men, who shall be able to teach others also."   I answer : I have already given a sufficiently large reply to this place.   The *fifth reason* is taken from Irenæus, Lib. iv. c. 43[2], where Irenæus says that the apostles delivered to their successors along with the episcopate a certain gift of truth, according to the good pleasure of the Father. I answer, that the apostles delivered to their successors the gift of knowledge not only orally, but by writing also : for he says, Lib. iii, c. 1, that they not only preached, but delivered it also in the scriptures.

These pretences then being refuted, the testimony of Irenæus stands unimpeached.   The apostles preached and wrote the gospel ; they preached it all ; they wrote it all : and therefore he sub-joins, that it is the basis and pillar of our faith.   And to make

[1 Cum enim ex scripturis arguuntur, in accusationem convertuntur ipsa-rum scripturarum, ... quia non possit ex his inveniri veritas ab his qui nesciant traditionem : non enim per literas traditam illam, sed per vivam vocem ; ob quam causam et Paulum dixisse, Sapientiam autem loquimur inter perfectos.—p. 230. B.]

[2 Quapropter eis qui in ecclesia sint presbyteris obaudire oportet, his qui successionem habent ab apostolis, sicut ostendimus, qui cum episcopatus successione charisma veritatis certum, secundum placitum Patris, acceperunt. —pp. 381—2.]

it evident that Irenæus in this place speaks of no mere popular gospel, that is, of something suited merely to the people, he says, "*we* know the economy of our salvation," and "it hath reached *us*." Now he was a bishop; therefore he speaks of that gospel which contained all that was necessary, even for bishops. Besides, Irenæus writes in other places also against traditions. In Lib. II. c. 47, he says that "the scriptures are perfect, being spoken by the Word of God and his Spirit³." And, Lib. III. c. 2, he refutes the assertion of the heretics, that the apostles delivered some things secretly and apart; which subject he pursues at greater length in the third chapter of that same book. And, Lib. IV. c. 26, he says that "the precepts of a perfect life are the same in both Testaments⁴." Therefore all things which pertain to doctrine or morals are contained in the scriptures, and not merely some of them: for he says " of a perfect life," which is the thing denied by the papists. And, Lib. V. c. 17, he says that we should " betake ourselves to the church, be reared in its bosom, and nourished by the scriptures of the Lord." Then he subjoins: " For the paradise of the church is planted in this world. Therefore, says the Spirit of God, 'of every tree of the garden thou mayest freely eat;' that is, eat of every scripture of the Lord: but eat not of the transcendental sense, nor touch any heretical heterodoxy⁵." Therefore, as there was no other food whereof Adam could eat in paradise but the fruit of the trees, so he that is placed in the garden of the church should desire no other food for his soul beside the scriptures. Thus it is clear that Irenæus is opposed to unwritten traditions; and his custom was to use no other arms against the heretics save those of scripture; as Erasmus hath truly remarked in his preface to Irenæus: " He fights with no other defence than scripture against a host of heretics."

Our second witness against traditions is ORIGEN, who opposes them in many places: for example, in his Commentary on Rom. iii., Hom. 25 in Matth., Hom. 3 in Genes., Hom. 31 in Gen., Hom. 7

[³ Scripturæ quidem perfectæ, quippe a Verbo Dei et Spiritu ejus dictæ. —p. 203. A.]

[⁴ Consummatæ enim vitæ præcepta in utroque testamento cum sint eadem, &c.—p. 344. A.]

[⁵ Fugere igitur oportet sententias ipsorum .... confugere autem ad ecclesiam, et in ejus sinu educari, et Dominicis scripturis enutriri. Plantata est enim ecclesiæ paradisus in hoc mundo : ab omni ergo ligno paradisi escas manducabis, ait Spiritus Dei, id est, ab omni scriptura Dominica manducate : superelato autem sensu ne manducaveritis, neque tetigeritis universam hæreticam dissensionem.—c. 20, p. 466. B.]

43—2

in Ezech., Hom. 1 in Jerem. In the last-mentioned place he
writes as follows: " It is necessary for us to cite the testimony
of the holy scriptures. For our opinions and discourses have no
credit, unless confirmed by their witness. And that saying, ' By the
mouth of two or three witnesses shall every word be confirmed,'
agrees rather to the proof of an interpreter than to any number
of mere human testimonies; and means, that I should establish the
word of my understanding by taking two witnesses from the old
and new Testaments; or taking three, from the Gospel, from the
prophets, and from the apostles. For so shall every word be
established[1]." In these words Origen testifies that our judgments,
discourses, and opinions have no credit without scripture. Bellarmine
replies, that he speaks of certain very abstruse questions, of which
nature those generally are not which rest upon the testimony of
tradition. I answer : In the first place, it is absurd that those
things which rest on tradition should be not as abtruse and obscure
as those which were delivered in the scriptures. For what ? Are
those things which pertain solely to prelates and bishops easier
than those which are openly propounded to the people ? Who can
fail to perceive that Bellarmine here talks contradictions ? Secondly,
Origen speaks generally of all questions, whether clear or obscure.
And the same thing appears also from his Commentary upon
Rom. iii., where he has an admirable remark ; saying that Paul
" sets an example to the teachers of the church to bring forward
what they say to the people" (not meaning therefore obscure
questions), " not as presumed by their own reasonings, but fortified
by divine testimony." Besides, he subjoins : " If even the apostle
himself, such and so great as he was, thinks that the authority of
his words is not sufficient without shewing that what he says is
written in the law and the prophets ; how much rather should we,
who are the least, observe, when we teach, not to bring forward
our own judgments, but those of the Holy Spirit[2]!"

---

[1] Μάρτυρας δεῖ λαβεῖν τὰς γραφάς· ἀμάρτυροι γὰρ αἱ ἐπιβολαὶ ἡμῶν καὶ
ἐξηγήσεις ἄπιστοί εἰσιν· ἐπὶ στόματα δύο καὶ τριῶν μαρτύρων σταθήσεται πᾶν
ῥῆμα, μᾶλλον ἁρμόζει ἐπὶ τῶν διηγήσεων ἢ ἐπὶ τῶν ἀνθρώπων, ἵνα στήσω τὰ
ῥήματα τῆς ἑρμηνείας, λαβὼν μάρτυρας δύο ἀπὸ καινῆς καὶ παλαιᾶς διαθήκης,
λαβὼν μάρτυρας τρεῖς ἀπὸ εὐαγγελίου, ἀπὸ προφήτου, ἀπὸ ἀποστόλου· οὕτως γὰρ
σταθήσεται πᾶν ῥῆμα.—p. 57. ed. Huet. Colon. 1685. Whitaker, in the text,
has taken the old Latin version, which is therefore followed in the translation.]

[2] Doctoribus ecclesiæ præbet exemplum, ut ea quæ loquuntur ad popu-

The same author, Hom. 25 in Matth., writes thus: "The temple of the glory of God is all inspired scripture, and the gold is the meaning lodged in it. We ought, therefore, in evidence of every word that we utter in teaching to produce the sense of scripture as a confirmation of the sense which we expound. For, as all the gold outside the temple is unsanctified, so every sense which is beside the holy scripture (however admirable it may seem) is not holy, because it is not contained by the sense of scripture, which sanctifies only that sense which it hath in itself, as the temple does its own gold. We ought not then in confirmation of our doctrine to swear our own meanings, and produce as it were in evidence what each of us understands and deems true, without shewing that it is sanctified by being contained in the holy scriptures as it were in the temples of God. Foolish and blind are those that know not that the temple, that is, the reading of the scripture, makes a sense great and venerable like consecrated gold[3]." The same author, Hom. 10 in Genes., writes thus upon the words, "Rebecca went daily to the well:" "This is the instruction of souls which instructs and teaches thee to come daily to the wells of scripture, the waters of the Holy Spirit, and to draw continually, and bring home a vessel full, as also did the holy Rebecca." And Hom. 3 in Gen. he writes thus: "Circumcised and clean is he, who always speaks the word of God, and brings forward sound doctrine fortified by the

lum, non propriis præsumta sententiis, sed divinis munita testimoniis proferant. Si enim ipse tantus et talis apostolus auctoritatem dictorum suorum sufficere posse non credit, nisi doceat in lege et prophetis scripta esse quæ dicit: quanto magis nos minimi hoc observare debemus, ut non nostras, cum docemus, sed Sancti Spiritus sententias proferamus!—Origen. Opp. T. iv. p. 504, Paris. 1733.]

[3 Templum gloriæ Dei est omnis scriptura divinitus inspirata, aurum autem positus sensus in ea. Debemus ergo ad testimonium omnium verborum, quæ proferimus in doctrina, proferre sensum scripturæ, quasi confirmantem quem exponimus sensum. Sicut enim omne aurum, quodquod fuerit extra templum, non est sanctificatum; sic omnis qui fuerit extra divinam scripturam (quamvis admirabilis videatur quibusdam) non est sanctus, quia non continetur a sensu scripturæ, quæ solet eum solum sensum sanctificare quem habet in se, sicut templum proprium aurum. Non ergo debemus ad confirmandam doctrinam nostram proprios sensus jurare, et quasi testimonia assumere, quos unusquisque nostrum intelligit, et secundum veritatem existimat esse, ni ostenderit eos sanctos esse ex eo quod in scripturis continetur divinis, quasi in templis quibusdam Dei. Stulti ergo et cæci omnes qui non cognoscunt, quoniam templum, id est, lectio scripturarum, magnum et venerabilem facit sensum, sicut aurum sacratum.—T. iii. p. 842.]

rules of the evangelists and apostles[1]." So much from Origen, to whose testimony, thus unembarrassed, clear and pertinent to the point, Bellarmine answers not a word.

Our third testimony is that of CONSTANTINE the great, as given by Theodoret, Lib. I. c. 7, who thus addressed the fathers assembled in the council of Nice: "The evangelic and apostolic books, together with the oracles of the old prophets, plainly instruct us what we ought to think on divine subjects. Let us then, laying aside all hostile discord, resolve the debated questions by the testimony of the inspired scriptures[2]." In these words two things deserve to be considered : first, that the scriptures of the old and new Testaments teach us, and that *plainly* ($\sigma\alpha\phi\hat{\omega}\varsigma$), what we should think concerning the things of God : secondly, that we ought, therefore, to decide every controversy by the words of inspiration.

Bellarmine objects, *first*, that Constantine was a great emperor, but not a great doctor. I answer : In the first place, I confess that he was not a bishop or doctor of the church ; but yet I affirm him to have been a pious and learned man, studious of religion and very useful to the church. This is plain from Theodoret, I. 24 : for when bishops were rending the church and disturbing its peace, he pre- served it with a tender and remedial solicitude. Secondly, no bishop, either of those present at the Nicene council or of those who afterwards flourished in the church, ever blamed these words uttered by Constantine in the midst of the Nicene fathers. Now if they were not orthodox, doubtless somebody would have either interfered upon the spot, or at some time or other warned the church against them. Constantine desires this dispute to be de- termined by the scriptures of the evangelists, apostles, and prophets. And Evagrius, *Histor.*, Lib. II.[3], testifies that similar expressions were used by John, bishop of Antioch, in the council of Ephesus ; which were also approved by Cyril of Alexandria. *Secondly*, he objects, that the confirmation of those dogmas which touch and

---

[1 Circumcisus et mundus est qui semper verbum Dei loquitur, et sanam doctrinam, evangelicis et apostolicis munitam regulis, profert.]

[2 εὐαγγελικαὶ γὰρ βίβλοι καὶ ἀποστολικαί, καὶ τῶν παλαιῶν προφητῶν τὰ θεσπίσματα, σαφῶς ἡμᾶς ἃ χρὴ περὶ τοῦ θείου φρονεῖν ἐκπαιδεύουσι. τὴν πολε- μοποιὸν οὖν ἀπελάσαντες ἔριν, ἐκ τῶν θεοπνεύστων λόγων λάβωμεν τῶν ζητουμένων τὴν λύσιν.—p. 25. D. ed. Vales. Paris. 1673.]

[3 The reference meant is, I suppose, Lib. I. c. 6. p. 261. D. Paris, 1673 ; where Cyril speaks of his joy at finding that John of Antioch and he had the same faith, ταῖς θεοπνεύστοις γραφαῖς καὶ παραδόσει τῶν ἁγίων ἡμῶν πατέρων συμβαίνουσαν.]

relate to the divine nature may be deduced from scripture, but that
the true sense of scripture depends upon the unwritten tradition of
the church. I answer : In the first place, perhaps the occasion of
his thus trifling arose from the words περὶ τοῦ θείου. And so indeed Harding, in the book which he wrote against the English Apology, seeks to elude this testimony. But Harding makes a shameful
mistake; and Bellarmine too, if he be in the same opinion, hath
fallen into a shameful hallucination. For περὶ τοῦ θείου denotes
not only, "concerning those things which pertain to the divine
nature," but also, as Cassiodorus hath translated it, "concerning
the divine will, or the divine law." The very translator whom
Bellarmine follows renders it, "concerning divine things;" and so
indeed it ought to be rendered. And Theodoret himself, in the
words immediately preceding, hath the expression περὶ τῶν θείων
πραγμάτων, that is, "of things relating to faith and religion."
Then he says that "we have the teaching of the Holy Spirit in a
written form," τοῦ παναγίου πνεύματος διδασκαλίαν ἀνάγραπτον
ἔχοντας. Besides, Constantine says, "Let us take from scripture
τῶν ζητουμένων τὴν λύσιν," that is, the solution not of this or
that question, but of all questions. Secondly, in asserting that
the true sense of scripture depends upon the unwritten tradition
of the church, he openly makes the scriptures inferior to the church,
of which yet he elsewhere indicates a disapproval. For if the true
sense of scripture depend upon the church, then it is plain that the
credit and authority of the church is greater than of scripture :
since the true sense of scripture follows the unwritten tradition of
the church ; and what else is scripture but the sense of scripture?
The falsehood of Bellarmine's *third* objection, that the Arians were
not convicted and condemned by the testimony of scripture, is clear
from c. 8,[4] of this same book of Theodoret, ἐξ ἐγγράφων μετ'
εὐσεβείας ἐννοουμένων λέξεων κατεκρίθησαν : and from Socrates,
Lib. I. c. 6, "We have often refuted them by unrolling (or explaining) the scriptures[5]." For, although Socrates wrote this not
of the Nicene council, but of that at Alexandria, composed only of
a few bishops and presbyters, yet every one sees that the Arians
were most plainly condemned by scripture : unless indeed it be
supposed that scripture had more efficacy at Alexandria than at

[4 Where, however, another reading is, ἐξ ἀγράφων μετ' εὐσεβείας νοουμέ-
νων.—p. 29. A. See Valesius' note.]

[5 καὶ ταῦτα λέγοντες καὶ ἀναπτύσσοντες τὰς θείας γραφὰς πολλάκις ἀνετρέ-
ψαμεν αὐτούς.—p. 11. B. ed. Vales.]

Nice. And what else did Athanasius do but condemn Arius out of scripture?

Our fourth testimony is taken from ATHANASIUS, in his book against the Gentiles or idols: "The scriptures are sufficient for every purpose of instruction or education in the truth[1]." Bellarmine replies, that Chemnitz hath added the word "every" out of his own head. I answer: He did indeed add, but he hath not thereby changed the sense: for that this is Athanasius' meaning, is apparent from the place itself, which occurs in the beginning of the book. In the next place, Bellarmine answers that Athanasius speaks in that book of only two dogmas: one of which is, that idols should not be worshipped; the other, Christ's twofold nature, or that Christ was truly both God and man. I answer: That these two points are indeed handled in the books to Macarius; but this is no reason for not extending it in its force and application to all other dogmas, or taking it in a general sense. Thirdly, he concedes that scripture is sufficient, but not *without the explication of the fathers.* I answer: But by this explication of the fathers Bellarmine means unwritten traditions. If he meant the interpretation of the fathers, we should feel less reluctant to admit it. And yet even the interpretations of the fathers are not simply necessary; because there was a time when there were no patristic interpretations, and nevertheless the scriptures were understood. And Athanasius himself writes expressly in that same place, that the truth of scripture is known, and " clearer than the sun." Then he subjoins, " the scriptures are sufficient;" and afterwards he says, that the fathers must be read on account of some men's perverseness, who will not receive what is plain and manifest. Whence it appears that he means, that the fathers are not universally or simply necessary to the understanding of the scriptures. The same author, in his third book against the Arians, says: " By hearing the scriptures we are led into faith." This is the very point which we have proved above, from Rom. x., " Faith is by hearing, and hearing by the word of God." And in his Synopsis he says, that " holy scripture contained in certain books is the anchor and support of our faith[2]." Therefore, our faith is not supported by traditions, but by the scriptures.

Our fifth testimony is that of BASIL the great, *de Confessione*

[1 αὐτάρκεις μὲν γάρ εἰσιν αἱ ἅγιαι καὶ θεόπνευστοι γραφαὶ πρὸς τὴν τῆς ἀληθείας ἀπαγγελίαν.—T. I. p. 1. Paris. 1598.]

[2 τῆς πίστεως ἡμῶν οἱονεὶ ἀκροθίνια ἢ ἄγκυραι καὶ ἐρείσματα.—T. II. p. 127.]

Fidei, where he writes thus : " It is a manifest piece of infidelity, and incurs a just charge of arrogance, either to reject what is written, or to add anything which is not written[3]." It is a very remarkable passage. Bellarmine replies that this place of Basil is meant to refer, not to apostolical traditions, but to those things which are contrary to scripture and invented by private persons. I answer : These words do most clearly confirm the perfection of scripture. For Basil had said a little before, " I am bound to propose to you those things which I have learned from the divinely inspired scripture, according to the good pleasure of God, for the common profit. For if the Lord himself, in whom the Father was well-pleased, in whom are hidden all the treasures of wisdom and knowledge, who hath received from the Father all power and all judgment, says, ' He gave me a commandment what I should speak and what I should say ; ' and again, ' Those things, therefore, which I speak unto you, as the Father hath said unto me, even so I speak ; ' and if the Holy Spirit speaketh not of himself, but whatsoever he heareth from him ; how much more is it at once pious and safe for us to think and do this in the name of our Lord Jesus Christ[4] !' " And afterwards he says : " If the Lord be faithful in all his words, and all his commandments are faithful, standing fast for ever and ever, done in truth and equity ; " then he subjoins the words which we previously introduced, namely :— " It is a manifest incurring of the crime of infidelity and arrogance, either to reject anything that is written, or add anything that is not written." Then follows : " Since our Lord Jesus Christ says, ' My sheep hear my voice,' premising, ' a stranger will they not follow, but flee from him, for they know not the voice of strangers;' and the apostle, by an example taken from the case of men, earnestly prohibits the adding to, or taking from, the scriptures of God, when he says, ' Though it were but a man's testament, yet,

[3 φανερὰ ἔκπτωσις πίστεως καὶ ὑπερηφανίας κατηγορία ἢ ἀθετεῖν τι τῶν γεγραμμένων, ἢ ἐπεισάγειν τῶν μὴ γεγραμμένων.—T. II. p. 251. A. Paris. 1618.]

[4 Κἀγὼ ἅπερ ἔμαθον ἐκ τῆς θεοπνεύστου γραφῆς, ταῦτα ὑμῖν παραθέσθαι κατὰ τὸ ἀρέσκον Θεῷ πρὸς τὸ κοινῇ συμφέρον ὀφειλέτης εἰμί. Εἰ γὰρ αὐτὸς ὁ Κύριος, ἐν ᾧ εὐδόκησεν ὁ πατήρ, ἐν ᾧ εἰσι πάντες οἱ θησαυροὶ τῆς σοφίας καὶ τῆς γνώσεως ἀπόκρυφοι, ὁ πᾶσαν μὲν τὴν ἐξουσίαν πᾶσαν δὲ τὴν κρίσιν λάβων παρὰ τοῦ πατρός, 'Εντολὴν δέδωκέ μοι, φησί, τί εἴπω καὶ τί λαλήσω· καὶ πάλιν, ἃ οὖν ἐγὼ λαλῶ, καθὼς εἴρηκέ μοι ὁ πατὴρ οὕτω λαλῶ· καὶ τὸ πνεῦμα τὸ ἅγιον ἀφ' ἑαυτοῦ οὐ λαλεῖ, ἀλλ' ὅσα ἂν ἀκούσῃ παρ' αὐτοῦ, ταῦτα λαλεῖ· πόσῳ μᾶλλον ἡμῖν εὐσεβές τε ὁμοῦ καὶ ἀσφαλὲς τοῦτο φρονεῖν καὶ ποιεῖν ἐν ὀνόματι τοῦ Κ. ἡ. Ι. X.—Ibid. pp. 249, 250.]

when it is confirmed, no man disannulleth or addeth thereto;' consequently, we know that now and always we should flee all words and sentiments alien from the doctrine of the Lord[1]."

Basil, therefore, testifies that all points of faith, whatever they may be, are found in the scriptures; and therefore that those persons violate the testament of God, who seek other doctrines outside the scriptures. He condemns, therefore, all others as strange and foreign, ξένα and ἀλλότρια. But Bellarmine observes that Basil, in that same place, says that he was compelled to use unwritten discourses against the heretics. I answer: he did indeed use unwritten (not discourses, but) expressions; yet such as were not foreign from scripture, and its orthodox sense. He employed no new doctrines, but new terms, and those such as introduced no new sense: for he says that these words are not "foreign from the pious meaning of scripture." Although those terms were strange in *expression*, yet they contained no *strange meaning*, but preserved the " sense which lay in the scriptures." Consequently, he determines those to be strange, and false, and deserving to be rejected, which have not the meaning which lies in the scriptures. He clearly refers therefore, not to dogmas, but to certain terms not actually used in scripture, such as Ὁμοούσιον, and others of the like sort, which he was accustomed to use in disputing against the heretics. There is another place, in his eightieth epistle to Eustathius the physician, where Basil writes as follows: " We do not think it just and equitable, that the manner of speaking which obtains amongst them should be made the rule and canon of orthodox doctrine. If custom be indeed the test to try right doctrine, let us by all means be permitted also to follow their example. Let us stand then by the arbitration of the holy scriptures, and let the sentence of truth be certainly adjudged to those with whom are found doctrines consonant to the oracles of God[2]." Bellarmine says that he is speaking

[1 τοῦ κυρίου ἡμῶν Ἰησοῦ Χριστοῦ εἰπόντος, τὰ ἐμὰ πρόβατα τῆς ἐμῆς φωνῆς ἀκούει· καὶ πρὸ τούτου δὲ εἰρηκότος, ἀλλοτρίῳ δὲ οὐ μὴ ἀκολουθήσωσιν, ἀλλὰ φεύξονται ἀπ' αὐτοῦ, κ. τ. λ. καὶ τοῦ ἀποστόλου ἐν ὑποδείγματι ἀνθρωπίνῳ σφοδρότερον ἀπαγορεύοντος τὸ προσθεῖναι ἢ ὑφελεῖν τι ἐν ταῖς θεοπνεύστοις γραφαῖς, δι' ὧν φησιν, κ. τ. λ. πᾶσαν μὲν οὖν ἀλλοτρίαν τῆς τοῦ Κυρίου διδασκαλίας φωνὴν καὶ ἔννοιαν οὕτως ἡμεῖς πάντοτε καὶ νῦν ἀποφεύγειν ἐγνώκαμεν. —Ibid. p. 251. B. C.]

[2 οὐ νομίζομεν δίκαιον εἶναι τὴν παρ' αὐτοῖς ἐπικρατοῦσαν συνήθειαν νόμον καὶ κανόνα τοῦ ὀρθοῦ ποιεῖσθαι λόγου. εἰ γὰρ ἰσχυρόν ἐστιν εἰς ἀπόδειξιν ὀρθότητος ἡ συνήθεια, ἔξεστι καὶ ἡμῖν πάντως ἀντιπροβαλέσθαι τὴν παρ' ἡμῖν ἐπικρατοῦσαν συνήθειαν. Εἰ δὲ παραγράφονται ταύτην ἐκεῖνοι, ἡμῖν πάντως ἀκολουθη-

not of any tradition received by the whole church, but of particular customs. I answer: It is an important question which is handled and discussed in this place; namely, whether we may say that there are three persons and one Godhead, τρεῖς ὑποστάσεις καὶ μίαν θεότητα. Some persons alleged and urged custom; but he says it is not fit that " custom should be the rule," νόμος καὶ κανὼν τοῦ ὀρθοῦ λόγου. Then he subjoins the sentence quoted above; wherein he shews, first, that the divine oracles and the scriptures are the same thing; secondly, that those doctrines which agree with the scriptures should be received, and all others rejected. And so much for the testimony of Basil.

Our sixth testimony is taken from some sentences of CHRYSO-STOM. In Hom. 1 in Matt. he says: " There is need of scripture, because many corrupt doctrine." In Hom. 13 in Genes.[3] he says: " Scripture does not permit the hearer of it to go wrong." Then he subjoins: " But, because most people lend an ear to those who handle these subjects, not in order to gain some edification from the holy scriptures, but to be amused; and, therefore, seek to hear not those who profit, but those who entertain them best; I beseech you therefore, that, closing your ears to all such, we may together follow the standard set by the canon of holy scripture." In his 3rd Homily upon 2 Thess.[4] he says that all necessary things are clear in the scriptures. To all these Bellarmine replies only by the question: " For what purpose are these alleged?" I answer, by shewing the purpose, thus: If the gospel was committed to writing lest it should be corrupted, then all parts of it are written, because no part of it should be corrupted. If the scriptures were written lest we should err, then all things are written, because we should not err in any thing. If all things ought to be referred to this canon of scripture, then scripture is the perfect rule of all our actions and articles of faith. If all necessary things are plain in the scriptures, then nothing beside the scriptures is neces-sary. The same author, *Opus Imperf. in Matt.* Hom. 49, writes thus: " Then, when ye shall see the abomination of desolation standing in the holy place, that is, when ye shall see impious heresy, which is the army of antichrist, standing in the holy places

---

τέον ἐκείνοις. οὐκοῦν ἡ θεόπνευστος ἡμῖν διαιτησάτω γραφή· καὶ παρ᾽ οἷς ἂν εὑρεθῇ τὰ δόγματα συνῳδὰ τοῖς θείοις λόγοις, ἐπὶ τούτοις ἥξει πάντως [ἡ θεία] τῆς ἀληθείας ψῆφος.—T. II. p. 901. B.   Whitaker has, as the reader will perceive, omitted a whole clause in his translation of this passage.]

[3 Tom. IV. p. 103.]   [4 Tom. XI. p. 528.]

of the church ; then let those that are in Judæa flee to the mountains ; that is, let those who are in Christianity betake themselves
to the scriptures. For as the true Jew is the Christian, (according to the saying of the apostle, ' He is not a Jew who is one out-
wardly, but he who is one inwardly,') so the true Judæa is
Christianity, the name Judæa being, by interpretation, confession.
Now the mountains are the scriptures of the apostles and prophets,
concerning which it is said, ' Thou givest wonderful light from the
eternal mountains;' and again, it is said of the church, ' Her foundations are on the holy hills'[1]."

Bellarmine replies, that not Chrysostom, but some heretic, was
the author of these homilies. I answer : Some do, indeed, suppose that these homilies were written by one Maximus, who was
an Arian ; yet the book is an useful one, and this opinion is a
pious one, consonant not only with the scriptures, but with the
other fathers. Augustine, *de Pastoribus*, c. 12, says : " Hear
the voice of the Shepherd : draw to the mountains of the holy
scripture." And the reason which he uses, and which follows
in that same place, proves the truth of this sentence. " And
wherefore does he bid all Christians to betake themselves to the
scriptures ? Because at this time, since heresy hath prevailed in
those churches, there can be no other proof of true Christianity,
no other refuge for true Christians, who desire to know the truth
of faith, save the scriptures of God. Formerly it was shewn
in many ways, what was the true church of Christ, and what
paganism ; but now those who wish to know what is the true
church of Christ, have no other means of knowing but the holy
scriptures. Why so ? Because, even those churches which are in

[1] Tunc cum videritis abominationem desolationis stantem in loco
sancto, id est, cum videritis hæresim impiam, quæ est exercitus antichristi,
stantem in locis sanctis ecclesiæ ; in illo tempore, qui in Judæa sunt, fugiant
ad montes, id est, qui sunt in Christianitate conferant se ad scripturas. Sicut
enim verus Judæus est Christianus, dicente apostolo, Non qui in manifesto
Judæus est, sed qui in occulto ; sic vera Judæa Christianitas est, cujus
nomen intelligitur *confessio*. Montes autem sunt scripturæ apostolorum
aut prophetarum, de quibus dictum est, Illuminas tu mirabiliter a montibus æternis; et iterum de ecclesia dicit, Fundamenta ejus in montibus
sanctis.—Chrys. Opp. T. vi. col. 204. Paris. 1718—38. The quotation,
"Illuminas tu mirabiliter," &c., is from the Vulgate version, Ps. lxxvi. 4,
which here, as usual, follows the LXX. φωτίζεις σὺ θαυμαστῶς ἀπὸ ὀρέων
αἰωνίων. They probably conjectured that מֶרֶף should be read מֵרֹם. This
piece is falsely ascribed to Chrysostom.]

schism have all things which truly belong to Christ: they have churches
as well as we; the holy scriptures themselves as well as we; bishops
and the other orders of the clergy as well as we; baptism as well
as we; the eucharist as well as we, and all the rest; finally, they
have Christ himself.   If, then, one desires to know which is the
true church of Christ, where the points of resemblance are so confounded, whence can he know it but from the holy scriptures[2].?"
And more to the same purpose follows in the same writer.

There is another passage of Chrysostom's, in his homily on Ps.
xcv., where he writes thus: " We should not say any thing without
evidence, out of the mere device of our own minds.   If any thing be
spoken without proof from scripture, the thoughts of the hearers
stumble, now assenting, now hesitating, sometimes turning from the
discourse as frivolous, sometimes receiving it as specious.   But when
the testimony of the voice of God is uttered from the scripture, it
confirms at once the discourse of him who speaks, and the mind of
him who hears."   Thus Chrysostom.   Nothing therefore must be
said beside the scripture, lest the thoughts of the hearer should
halt or vacillate.   Bellarmine replies, that what is here prohibited
is the saying any thing *out of our own inventions*, because what is
so said does not so easily win assent as that which is confirmed by
scripture.   I answer: What a ridiculous subterfuge is this! For
that which is said out of our own inventions would be utterly
rejected.   But what Chrysostom says is, that nothing should be
said without evidence, merely of our own thoughts, and without
scripture; intimating, that every thing which is said without the
testimony of scripture is spoken merely from our own thoughts,
without evidence, and of our own invention.   For if any thing of

[2 Audite vocem pastoris; colligite vos ad montes scripturæ sanctæ. . . . Et
quare jubet hoc tempore omnes Christianos conferre se ad scripturas? Quia
in tempore hoc, ex quo obtinuit hæresis illas ecclesias, nulla probatio potest
esse veræ Christianitatis, neque refugium potest esse Christianorum aliud,
volentium cognoscere fidei veritatem, nisi scripturæ divinæ.   Antea enim
multis modis ostendebatur, quæ esset ecclesia Christi et quæ gentilitas.
Nunc autem nullo modo cognoscitur volentibus cognoscere quæ sit vera
ecclesia Christi, nisi tantummodo per scripturas.   Quare?   Quia omnia quæ
sunt proprie Christi in veritate, habent et hæreses illæ in schismate, similiter ecclesias, similiter et ipsas scripturas divinas, similiter episcopos
ceterosque ordines clericorum, similiter baptismum, similiter eucharistiam,
et cetera omnia; denique ipsum Christum.   Volens ergo quis cognoscere
quæ sit vera ecclesia Christi, unde cognoscat in tanta confusione similitu-
dinis, nisi tantummodo per scripturas?—T. IX. p. 279, et seqq.]

686THE FIRST CONTROVERSY.[CH.

this sort be said, it will be uncertain, and bring the minds of the
hearers into doubt and hesitation. The same Chrysostom, Hom.
13 in 2 Corinth. writes thus: "How can it be other than absurd to
refuse to trust others in the matter of money, and to count and
reckon it ourselves, and yet in far more important matters to
follow simply other men's opinions; especially when we have, in the
sentence of the divine laws, the most exact balance, and standard,
and rule of all things? Therefore, I beseech and implore you to
leave asking what this man or the other thinks, and to seek the
resolution of all these inquiries from the scriptures[1]." Bellarmine
brings a pitiable and foolish reply. He says, that Chrysostom
speaks of those who prefer riches to poverty, whereas scripture
teaches the contrary. I answer: Chrysostom speaks not of this
only, but says that we have the most exact balance and perfect
rule of *all things*, ἁπάντων, in the declaration of the laws of God,
ἀπόφασιν τῶν θείων νόμων. How he understands this, is shewn
by his subjoining, παρὰ τῶν γραφῶν ταῦτα πάντα πυνθάνεσθε.
Therefore he admonishes us not to be anxious about the opinions of
the many, but to *examine* all things for ourselves; and he illustrates it by a comparison: ' We examine money by counting and
reckoning it: now we ought to be much more careful about such
matters as these.'

Our seventh testimony is from EPIPHANIUS, *Hæres.* 61. This
is produced by Bellarmine. But there is a still clearer testimony,
Hæres. 69, where Epiphanius assigns the reason why he gives the
title Ἀγκυρωτός to his book,—because he collected the doctrine of
God out of the whole scripture, to be as it were an anchor[2].
Therefore the scripture is the anchor of our faith. And a little
after, in the same place, he says, that Christ is called the corner-
stone, because "he hath constructed for us the new and the old
Testaments[3]."

Our eighth testimony is that of CYRIL, in his book, *De Fide ad*

[1 Πῶς γὰρ οὐκ ἄτοπον ὑπὲρ μὲν χρημάτων μὴ ἑτέροις πιστεύειν, ἀλλ' ἀριθμῷ
καὶ ψήφῳ τοῦτο ἐπιτρέπειν, ὑπὲρ δὲ πραγμάτων ψηφιζομένους ἁπλῶς ταῖς ἑτέ-
ρων παρασύρεσθαι δόξαις, καὶ ταῦτα ἀκριβῆ ζυγὸν ἁπάντων ἔχοντας καὶ γνώμονα
καὶ κανόνα τῶν θείων νόμων τὴν ἀπόφασιν. διὸ παρακαλῶ καὶ δέομαι πάντων
ὑμῶν, ἀφέντες τί τῷ δεῖνι καὶ τῷ δεῖνι δοκεῖ περὶ τούτων, παρὰ τῶν γραφῶν
ταῦτα ἅπαντα πυνθάνεσθε.—Chrysost. Comment. T. v. pp. 636, 7. Paris.
1633.]
[2 c. xxvii. p. 751—2. ed. Petav. T. I.]
[3 διὰ τὸ ἐπισφίγξαι παλαιὰν καὶ νέαν διαθήκην.—Ib. c. xxxv. p. 758. D.]

Reginas, where he hath these words : " It is needful for us to follow the holy scriptures, and in nothing to depart from what they prescribe." Bellarmine says that he only affirms that no new dogmas should be broached contrary to the scriptures. I answer : Cyril refers us to the directions of scripture as perfect. For he plainly affirms the sufficiency of scripture, Lib. xii. in Joann. c. 68. : " All things which the Lord did are not written, but those which the writers thought sufficient, both for practice and for doctrine; that we, resplendent with the glory of orthodox faith and works and virtue, might attain to the kingdom of heaven[4]." The same author, Hom. 5 in Levit. writes as follows : " I (as far as the capacity of my judgment permits me to form an opinion) suppose that in these two days we may understand the two Testaments, wherein it is lawful that every word pertaining to God (for this is meant by sacrifice) should be searched out and examined, and that the understanding of all things should be taken from these; but if any thing remain, which the scripture of God determines not, that no other third scripture should be received for the confirmation of our knowledge (which is here called the third day), but we should commit what remains to the fire, that is, reserve it for God[5]." Bellarmine hath two replies : first, that Cyril was not the author of these homilies, but Origen, or somebody else, who (says he) everywhere destroys the letter to establish his own mystical sense. I answer : It makes no difference whether the piece be Cyril's or Origen's : the authority of both is equal. This author does indeed pursue allegories, as the other fathers do ; yet this sentence is true and orthodox. Secondly, he says, that it is not all unwritten doctrine, but any third scripture pretending to be divine, when it is really human, that is here condemned. I answer : The words are plain. He not only rejects any third scripture, but distinctly

[4 Non igitur omnia quæ Dominus fecit conscripta sunt, sed quæ scribentes tam ad mores quam ad dogmata putarunt sufficere; ut recta fide et operibus ac virtute rutilantes ad regnum cœlorum perveniamus.—Col. 220. Paris. 1508.]

[5 Ego (prout sensus mei capacitas habet) in hoc biduo puto duo testamenta posse intelligi, in quibus liceat omne verbum, quod ad Deum pertineat (hoc enim est sacrificium), requiri et discuti, atque ex ipsis omnem rerum scientiam capi : si quid autem superfuerit, quod non scriptura divina decernat, nullam aliam debere tertiam scripturam ad auctoritatem scientiæ suscipi, quæ hic dies tertia nominatur, sed igni tradamus quod superest, id est, Deo reservemus.—This passage is taken almost word for word from Origen, Hom. 5. in Levitic. 66. D.]

affirms that in the two Testaments " every word pertaining to
God may be sought." Therefore, those things which cannot be
found in these two Testaments, do in no way pertain to God.
To whom then shall we suppose that written traditions pertain ?

Our ninth testimony is that of Theophilus Alexandrinus, who
in his 2nd Paschal writes thus: "It is the fruit of a diabolic spirit to
think that there is aught divine without the authority of the sacred
scriptures[1]." Bellarmine says that he is speaking of apocryphal
books, which some sought to introduce. I answer : The words are
plain,—that nothing is divine without the scriptures. Now, traditions are without the scriptures : therefore, they are not divine.

Our tenth testimony is that of Apollinaris, mentioned by
Eusebius, Lib. v. c. 15. He says that he had deferred for a long
time writing against Montanus, lest he should seem to add something to the word of the gospel[2]. Bellarmine replies, firstly, that
these words are not found in all the books. I answer : They are
found in the Greek copies, c. 16; in the versions of Christopherson
and Musculus, c. 15; and the books which have them not are
faulty. Secondly, Bellarmine remarks that he does not say, to
the *written* word of the gospel of God, but simply, to the word of
the gospel of God. I answer : But he means the written word, as
is plain from his expressions. For he says that he feared lest he
should seem ἐπισυγγράφειν, or ἐπιδιατάσσεσθαι τῷ τῆς καινῆς
διαθήκης λόγῳ· that is, to add anything to the written gospel.
Besides, he could not possibly fear adding anything by writing to
an unwritten teaching, but only to written books. Thirdly, Bellarmine says that he means any dogma contrary to scripture,—that
he was careful not to write anything repugnant thereto. I answer :
He might easily have guarded against the danger of writing anything contrary to scripture; but what he dreaded was, lest any one
should suppose that the book which he wrote added anything to
the canon, in the same way as Montanus added many things. Then
he subjoins : "No one can neither add to, or diminish from, the
scriptures of the old and new Testaments," μήτε προσθεῖναι μήτε
ἀφελεῖν δυνατόν. Therefore it is certain that the doctrine delivered in the scriptures is perfect.

[1 Diabolici spiritus est, extra scripturarum sacrarum authoritatem divinum aliquid putare.—In Bibliothec. Patrum. Paris. 1589. T. iii. col. 519.]

[2 δεδιὼς δὲ καὶ ἐξευλαβούμενος μή πη δόξω τισιν ἐπισυγγράφειν ἢ ἐπιδιατάσσεσθαι τῷ τῆς τοῦ εὐαγγελίου καινῆς διαθήκης λόγῳ, ᾧ μήτε προσθεῖναι μήτ᾽
ἀφελεῖν δυνατόν.—T. ii. pp. 73, 74. ed. Heinich.]

Our eleventh testimony is that of TERTULLIAN (for I come now to the Latin fathers) in his books against the heretic Hermogenes, where these words occur: " I adore the fulness of scripture, which shews me at once the Creator and the creatures. But in the gospel I find still further, the Word, who is the minister and mediator of the supreme governor. But that all things were made out of any subject-matter, I have nowhere yet been able to read. Let the shop of Hermogenes teach us where this is written, or fear that woe which is destined for those who add to or diminish from the scripture[3]." In these words there are two things to be considered: the first is, that the scripture is full and perfect, which appears from the words, " I adore the plenitude of scripture ; " the other, that whoever add or deliver anything that is not written, have to dread that *woe* which is denounced, Rev. xxii. 18. He would not have those only to fear it, who bring forward anything contrary to scripture, but those also who bring forward anything that is not written. Bellarmine says that Tertullian is only speaking of a single dogma, namely, that God made all things out of nothing, without any pre-existent matter. The scripture, says he, is perfect enough to prove this. I answer : Tertullian does indeed handle that question in this book ; but these words are general and refer to all religious questions ; nor apply merely to this alone, but to all others. Indeed he would have said nothing, unless what he said should apply to all questions : for Hermogenes might have objected to him that we need not in every question recur to scripture ; and to what end should he have admonished the heretic to fear that *woe* denounced against all who add or diminish, unless he could shew that what he said was written, unless he himself had taken it for granted that all was written ? Tertullian disputes from the authority of scripture *negatively*. Hermogenes cannot shew that this is written ; therefore let him fear that *woe*: which argument would have no force at all in it, unless it were certain that the scriptures are absolutely full and perfect, and that no dogma should be received which is not delivered in the scriptures.

The same author also elsewhere, in his Prescriptions against

[3 Adoro scripturæ plenitudinem, quæ mihi factorem manifestat et facta. In evangelio vero amplius et ministrum atque arbitrum rectoris invenio Sermonem. An autem de aliqua subjacenti materia facta sint omnia, nusquam adhuc legi. Scriptum esse doceat Hermogenis officina, aut timeat vœ illud adjicientibus aut detrahentibus destinatum.—cap. 22, p. 19. ed Leopold. Lips. 1841.]

[WHITAKER.]

44

heretics, writes thus : " We are not permitted to indulge our own
caprice in anything, nor to choose what any shall introduce of his own
will. We have as our authorities the apostles of the Lord, who themselves chose not anything to be introduced at their own pleasure,
but faithfully consigned to all nations that instruction which they
received from Christ. Consequently, though even an angel from
heaven should preach unto us any other gospel, we should pronounce
him accursed[1]." The apostles delivered the instruction of Christ
faithfully to the *nations,* not to a few particular persons, but to all.
And a little after he says, that "all the Lord's sayings are set forth
for all[2]." Therefore not some for some, (as the Jesuit pretends) but
all for all. The same father, in his book *de Resurrectione Carnis,*
calls the heretics *shunners of the light of scripture, lucifugas
scripturarum.* This title suits our papists most aptly : for they
hate the light of scripture, and, whether writing or disputing, seek
to take us off from the scriptures to the fathers, or tradition, or
some other testimony. And in the same book he says : " Take
away from the heretics what they have in common with pagan wisdom, so as to make them support all their opinions by scripture
only, and they cannot stand[3]." The same may be said of the
papists : for if they are compelled to support all their dogmas by
the scriptures, it is all over with tradition and the whole of popery.
Thus Tertullian, as long as he was a catholic, everywhere asserts
the perfection and authority of the scriptures. In his book, *de
Carne Christi,* he says : " If they do not prove it, for indeed it is
not written[4]." And presently after : " But there is nothing certainly known, because scripture exhibits nothing[5]." And again :
" I do not admit what you add beside the scripture out of your
own head[6]."

Our twelfth testimony is that of CYPRIAN, *Ep.* 74 *ad Pompeium,*

[1 Nobis vero nihil ex nostro arbitrio indulgere licet, sed nec eligere quod
aliquis de arbitrio suo induxerit. Apostolos Domini habemus auctores, qui
nec ipsi quicquam ex suo arbitrio, quod inducerent, elegerunt, sed accep-
tam a Christo disciplinam fideliter nationibus adsignaverunt. Itaque etiam
si angelus de cœlis aliter evangelizaret, anathema diceretur a nobis.—c. 6,
p. 4.]

[2 Omnia quidem dicta Domini omnibus posita sunt.—c. 8, p. 7.]

[3 Aufer hæreticis quæ cum ethnicis sapiunt, ut de solis scripturis quæstiones suas sistant, et stare non possunt.—c. 3.]

[4 Si non probant, quia nec scriptum est.—c. 6, p. 69.]

[5 Certum est ; sed nihil de eo constat, quia scriptura non exhibet.—Ibid.]

[6 Non recipio, quod extra scripturam de tuo infers.—c. 7, p. 70.]

against Stephen, concerning the rebaptization of those who returned to the church from heresy. In that epistle he writes thus : " Whence is that tradition ? Descends it from the authority of the Lord and the gospel, or from the commandments and letters of the apostles ? That we should do what is written, is what God testifies, proposing this to Joshua the son of Nave, where he says : ' The book of this law shall not depart out of thy mouth, but thou shalt meditate therein day and night, that thou mayest observe to do all the things which are written therein.' In like manner the Lord, when he sends his apostles, commands that the nations should be baptized and taught to observe all things whatsoever he commanded them." Then he subjoins : " If therefore it is either enjoined in the gospels, or contained in the apostolic epistles or Acts, that those who come from any heresy should not be baptized, but only have hands laid upon them in token of repentance, let this divine and holy tradition be observed[7]." In these words we must observe two things : first, that every evangelical and apostolic tradition should be sought in the Gospels, Acts, or Epistles; secondly, that all things which cannot be found in these books should be rejected and despised. Bellarmine replies, in the *first* place, that Cyprian, when he wrote this epistle, was in error, and defended that error ; and that consequently he reasoned as men in error do. I answer : He erred indeed, but he advanced a good argument to support a bad cause : he was wrong in the minor, not in the major premiss. For thus he reasoned : Things unwritten should not be received. So far was true. Then he assumed that what Stephen held,— namely, that those baptized by heretics should not be rebaptized,— was not written. Now this was false : so that it was a good argument applied to a bad cause. *Secondly*, Bellarmine says, that Augustine refutes this epistle, *de Baptismo c. Donat.* Lib. v. c. 23. I answer : He does refute it, and censures it, not on account of this opinion, but on account of the drift of the epistle, because

[7 Unde est ista traditio ? Utrumne de dominica et evangelica auctoritate descendens, an de apostolorum mandatis atque epistolis veniens ? Ea enim facienda esse quæ scripta sunt, Deus testatur, et proponit ad Jesum Nave, dicens, Non recedet liber legis hujus ex ore tuo, sed meditaberis in eo die ac nocte, ut observes facere omnia quæ scripta sunt in eo. Item Dominus apostolos suos mittens mandat baptizari gentes et doceri, ut observent omnia quæcunque ille præcepit. Si ergo aut in evangelio præcipitur, aut in apostolorum epistolis aut actibus continetur, ut a quacunque hæresi venientes non baptizentur, sed tantum manus illis imponatur in pœnitentiam, observetur divina hæc et sancta traditio.—p. 211, ed. Fell.]

44—2

Cyprian therein contends that those who were baptized by heretics should be rebaptized. Yea, Augustine approves and praises this opinion of Cyprian's : for in this same book, c. 26, he says, " This is excellent which Cyprian hath said, ' Let us return to the fountain-head.'" If Cyprian had done what he himself says ought to have been done, that is, had entirely betaken himself to the tradition of canonical scripture, he would never have persisted in this opinion, or have contended for the repetition of a baptism performed by ever so gross a heretic. Bellarmine's argument therefore is a sophism—*a non causa ad causam.* His *third* reply is to this effect : Although Cyprian condemns this tradition, yet he condemns not other traditions. I answer : Cyprian condemns not merely one, but all traditions which cannot be established by the scriptures of the evangelists and apostles. And in *Ep.* 63 *ad Cœcilium*, he says that "Christ only should be heard," and none beside ; that we should do what he did and commanded to be done : where he refers us to the voice of Christ, and that consigned in writing. And in the same epistle he says that we should take care, that when Christ comes " he may find us holding what he admonished us of, observing what he taught, doing what he did." And a little before he says that we should follow the tradition of the Lord. Now he means no other tradition than the scripture, as in the epistle to Pompeius. Therefore, if we would keep the tradition of the Lord, we must always return to the scriptures alone.

I come now to Jerome and Augustine, who alone remain of those enumerated by Bellarmine. Our thirteenth testimony, then, is that of JEROME, Comment. in Tit. i. ; Comment. in Matth. xxiii. ; in Aggæum ; in Psalm. lxxxvi. ; and elsewhere. Those which we have enumerated are the only testimonies of Jerome to which Bellarmine replies. In the first of them Jerome says : " Garrulity unsupported by the authority of scripture hath no credit[1]." Bellarmine says that this fits us exactly ; meaning that garrulous men obtain no credit with any, unless they seek to confirm their errors by scripture. I answer : But in these words traditions are plainly set aside, and those are pronounced mere talkers, who maintain anything without authority of scripture ; which even Bellarmine's own interpretation of the passage proves. Would heretics seem mere talkers, when they teach anything without scriptural proof, and gain credit with nobody, unless every doctrine required to be confirmed by the authority of scripture ?

[1 Sine auctoritate scripturarum garrulitas fidem non habet.]

XVII.]   QUESTION THE SIXTH.   693

The second place from Jerome is contained in his Commentary on Matth. xxiii. : "That which hath no authority from scripture is as easily rejected as approved[2]." He speaks of Zacharias who was slain between the temple and the altar, and whom some made the father of John the Baptist on the authority of tradition. Bellarmine replies that he speaks of a particular tradition taken from some apocryphal book. I answer: Yet he speaks generally, that all those things may be easily rejected, which rest not upon scripture. For what, if that tradition was written in an apocryphal book, does it therefore follow that it ought to be rejected? As if any popish traditions were contained in canonical books!

Jerome's third testimony is found in his Commentary on Haggai i. The words are these: "And other things also, which they find or invent out of their own heads, as if it were an apostolic tradition, without the authority and testimony of scripture, the sword of God strikes through[3]." By the sword of God he means the scriptures. Bellarmine replies, that he is dealing with those who devise something out of their own heads, and would have it thought apostolical. The same reply is given by Harding in his book against the English Apology. I answer: This testimony pinches and opposes the papists mightily ; for they have invented many things which cannot be established by the authority of scripture, and which nevertheless they desire should be esteemed apostolical. And, to make Jerome's meaning still plainer, he subjoins, that all their labours, and fastings, and various observances, and lyings on the ground (χαμευνίας) are here condemned. These things are not plainly contrary to scripture, and yet he says that these are stricken by the sword of God! Now the papists use all these, and make a great part of piety and religion consist in them. It is manifest therefore that Jerome condemns all things which cannot be proved by plain testimonies of scripture.

The other passage of Jerome is upon Ps. lxxxvi. ; although Erasmus and others suppose that those commentaries on the Psalms are not Jerome's, but of some other writer. However, Bellarmine does not avail himself of that exception, or deny the authority of

[2 Hoc quia de scripturis non habet auctoritatem, eadem facilitate contemnitur, qua probatur.—T. IX. p. 57. Francof. 1684.]

[3 Sed et alia, quæ absque auctoritate et testimoniis scripturarum quasi traditione apostolica sponte reperiunt atque confingunt, percutit gladius Dei.—T. VI. p. 184.]

this piece. Thus then writes Jerome in that place: "Mark what he
says: 'Those who *were,*' not those who *are:* so as that, with the
exception of the apostles, whatever else may be said afterwards, is
cut off and deprived of authority. Although therefore a man be
holy after the apostles, although he be eloquent, he hath no authority, because, 'The Lord relates in the scripture of the people, and
of those princes who *were* in her[1]." Bellarmine replies, that those
things are rejected which are contrary and repugnant to the scriptures, and nothing else. I answer: The words of the psalm which
Jerome treats of are these: "The Lord shall relate in the scripture
of the people and of those princes who were in her." But how,
says Jerome, will he relate? Not by word of mouth, but in
scripture. Therefore every unwritten word must be amputated and
cut off. But Bellarmine hath omitted these words, because they
make against himself. But, says Jerome, why is scripture called
the scripture of *the people?* Because it is read *by all people,* that
all may understand it. Why of the *princes?* Because the apostles
and evangelists, the princes of the church, wrote these things.
And he says, "They *were,*" not they *are,* to shew that nothing
can now be added.

I come now to AUGUSTINE, from whom our divines allege many
testimonies. *De Doctr. Christ.* Lib. II. c. 9, he writes thus:
"Amongst those things which are plainly set down in scripture
are found all those which contain faith and manners, that is, hope
and charity[2]." Bellarmine replies, that Augustine speaks of those
things which are simply necessary to all. I answer: We have
already discussed this. Indeed it is a mere and a miserable subterfuge; for Augustine speaks of those doctrines which are necessary
not only for all, but for every one. He says, in the beginning of
this very chapter: "In all these books those who fear God, and

---

[1 Videte quid dicat: Qui fuerunt, non qui sunt: ut, exceptis apostolis,
quodcunque aliud postea dicetur, abscindatur, non habeat postea auctoritatem. Quamvis ergo sanctus sit aliquis post apostolos, quamvis disertus sit,
non habet auctoritatem: quoniam Dominus narrat in scriptura populorum
et principum horum, qui fuerunt in ea.—T. VIII. p. 163.

The quotation is from Ps. lxxxvii. 6, according to the Vulgate, following the Seventy: Κύριος διηγήσεται ἐν γραφῇ λαῶν καὶ ἀρχόντων τούτων τῶν
γεγενημένων ἐν αὐτῇ. They seem to have brought up וְשָׂרִים from v. 7, and
to have read it וְשָׂרִים.]

[2 In iis enim quæ aperte in scripturis posita sunt, inveniuntur illa omnia quæ
continent fidem moresque vivendi, spem scilicet atque caritatem.—T. III. p. 12.]

are endued with the meekness of piety, seek the will of God[3]."
And, to enable us the better to seek the will of God, he delivers
two rules: the first is, to know, read, and even commit to memory the canonical books; the second, to investigate those things
which are plainly expressed in them. Then he subjoins these
words: "For amongst those things which are plainly set down in
scripture are found all those which contain faith and manners, that
is, hope and charity." However, it is no despicable concession on
Bellarmine's part, that he confesses all dogmas simply necessary
for all to be contained in scripture: from which we may gather,
that no traditions are simply necessary for all persons. But Augustine plainly concedes, that whatever things simply contain faith
and morals, are perspicuously delivered in the scriptures. Now,
how impious and repugnant to sound theology is it to maintain that
some things are simply necessary to all for salvation, and some not
to all! As if the faith of prelates were one thing, and the faith
of the people another! To the same effect is what Augustine, *de
peccat. Merit. et Remiss.* Lib. II. c. ult.: "I believe that upon this
subject also the authority of the divine oracles would be abundantly
clear, if a man could not be ignorant of it without the loss of the
promised salvation[4]." Where he affirms that those things, whereof
we cannot be ignorant without the loss of our salvation, are plainly
found in scripture. He is speaking of a very difficult question,
how we can prove that God is not the author of the guilt of sin, if
the soul be not *ex traduce.* From this place of Augustine I draw
two inferences: one, that in every obscure question between us
and the papists, or any other adversaries who discourse upon
religion, we should suspend our assent unless the point be established by certain and clear testimonies of scripture; (for so says
Augustine in the words immediately preceding: "Where the dispute is about a matter of great obscurity, and clear and certain
instruction is not lent us by the holy scriptures, human presumption
should restrain itself and lie still, inclining to neither side[5]:" hence

[3 In his omnibus libris timentes Deum et pietate mansueti quærunt
voluntatem Dei.]

[4 Illud tamen credo, quod etiam hinc divinorum eloquiorum clarissima
auctoritas esset, si homo illud sine dispendio promissæ salutis ignorare non
posset.—T. VII. p. 304.]

[5 Ubi de re obscurissima disputatur, non adjuvantibus divinarum scripturarum claris certisque documentis, cohibere se debet humana præsumptio,
nihil faciens, in partem alteram declinando.—Ibid.]

it follows as a corollary, that all things must be proved by scripture :) the other, that there are plain testimonies in scripture to all
those things which we cannot be ignorant of without peril of our
salvation.   Farewell then traditions, as things no way necessary to
salvation ! Another passage of Augustine is, *contra Lit. Petil.* Lib.
III. c. 6, where he writes thus : " Therefore, if there be a question
concerning Christ, or his church, or any other matter appertaining
to our faith or practice, I say not if we—who are by no means
comparable to him who said, 'Though we,'—but I do say certainly
what he goes on to subjoin—' or an angel from heaven, preach any
thing to you beside what ye have received in the scriptures of the
law and the gospel, let him be accursed'[1]." Bellarmine replies :
" I have shewn already that the word *beside* is equivalent to *opposed to*." I answer : And I have shewn already, that all dogmas
which rest not on the scriptures of the law and the gospel are here
condemned.

Our divines produce besides other testimonies from Augustine,
as *Civit. Dei.* Lib. XIX. c. 18, where he writes thus : " The city
of God believes also in the holy scriptures, as well the old as
the new, which we style canonical; whence that faith is conceived
by which the just man lives, by which we walk without doubting
so long as we sojourn absent from the Lord, and which faith
remaining safe and certain, we may doubt, without incurring just
censure, about some things which we perceive neither by sense
nor reason, which are not revealed to us by the canonical scriptures, nor have come to our knowledge upon the testimony of
witnesses whose credit it would be absurd to question[2]." They
produce, moreover, many more testimonies, as from *Tract. 2. in Ep.
Joann., Epist.* 163, *de Pastor.* c. 14, *de Confess.* Lib. VI. c. 5.
To all these testimonies Bellarmine replies, that nothing is therein

[1 Proinde sive de Christo, sive de ejus ecclesia, sive de quacunque alia
re quæ pertinet ad fidem vitamque nostram, non dicam si nos, nequaquam
comparandi ei qui dixit, Licet si nos, sed omnino quod sequutus adjecit, si
Angelus de cœlo vobis annunciaverit præterquam quod in scripturis legalibus
et evangelicis accepistis, anathema sit.—T. IX. p. 301.]

[2 Credit etiam scripturis sanctis, et veteribus et novis, quas canonicas
appellamus, unde fides ipsa concepta est, ex qua justus vivit, per quam sine
dubitatione ambulamus, quamdiu peregrinamur a Domino, qua salva atque
certa de quibusdam rebus, quas neque sensu neque ratione percipimus,
neque nobis per canonicam scripturam claruerunt, nec per testes quibus non
credere absurdum est, in nostram notitiam pervenerunt, sine justa repre-
hensione dubitamus.]

said against traditions; but that Augustine merely affirms, that where scriptural evidences can be had for the confirmation of doctrines, we should use them rather than others. Surely a noble answer! The scriptures are to be produced when they can be produced! It is indeed thus that the papists act in defence of their cause. When they have scripture (which seldom happens), they produce it. But what must be done when the testimony of scripture cannot be produced? Why, forsooth, according to this reply, we need not feel much more care or solicitude what testimonies we use. But Augustine desires that in every case testimonies should be adduced from scripture, as appears plainly from the passages themselves, which we shall set forth every one, to manifest the futility and falsehood of this reply.

In the first, that taken from the *City of God*, Lib. xix. c. 18, he says that the church of God believes in the books of the old and new Testaments, "by which that faith whereby the just man lives is engendered." They therefore seek some new faith, who seek anything beside the scripture, forasmuch as this is the faith which all Christians hold who are Christians in reality as well as in profession.

In the second testimony, taken from the second Tractate on the Epistles of John, he says, that " God designed to lay a foundation against insidious errors in the scriptures, against which no man dares to speak who desires to seem a Christian in any sense." The end of scripture, therefore, is to defend us against errors.

In the third testimony, taken from Epist. 163, he says that the canonical books ought to be beside us, "from which, in preference to all others, if any evidence can be alleged on either side, the matter may be examined to the end."

In his book *de Pastoribus*, c. 14, (from which the fourth testimony is taken), he writes thus: "Read me this from the prophets, or from the Psalms; quote it from the law, quote it from the gospel, quote it from an apostle. From these sources I can quote the fact of the church diffused over the whole world, and the Lord saying, 'My sheep hear my voice, and follow me'[3]." And a little after he says: "Away with human writings! let us hear God's words." That divine voice, then, which the sheep of Christ hear,

[3 Lege hoc mihi de propheta, lege de Psalmo, recita de lege, recita de evangelio, recita de apostolo. Inde ego recito ecclesiam toto orbe diffusam, et Dominum dicentem, Quæ sunt oves meæ vocem meam audiunt et sequuntur me . . . Auferantur chartæ humanæ; sonent voces divinæ.—T. ix.]

sounds in the scriptures, and unwritten traditions deserve no esteem from his flock.

In his *Confessions*, Lib. VI. c. 5, he says, that he was drawn away from the Manichees by this conviction, amongst others, that he had begun to believe that God would never have given the scripture so eminent an authority throughout all lands, unless he had meant it to be the means whereby we should believe in him, and seek him.

Another passage of Augustine cited by Bellarmine is from his book *de bono Viduitatis*, c. 1, and is as follows: "The holy scripture hath fixed the rule of our doctrine, that we may not presume to be wise beyond what is meet, but may be wise (as the apostle says) unto sobriety, according as God hath dealt to every man the measure of faith. Let me not then consider that in teaching you I am doing anything more than expounding the great Teacher's words, and discoursing of what he hath given[1]." Bellarmine maintains that Augustine speaks only of one single dogma,—namely, that of the profession of widowhood. I answer: Augustine's expressions are general, laying down that holy scripture fixes for us the rule of doctrine in reference to all sound dogmas. He says not that it hath fixed the rule of this or that dogma, but of our doctrine, lest we presume to be wise above what is meet. This, says Bellarmine, is spoken against those who feign anything out of their own heads. But Augustine says that the rule of doctrine is fixed in scripture: therefore, if we teach anything that is not laid down in scripture, whether of our own invention or otherwise, it is foreign from the rule of doctrine.

Another passage of Augustine is contained in his treatise *C. Max. Arian.* Lib. III. c. 14. The words are these: "Neither should I allege the council of Nice, nor you that of Rimini, as if we would prejudge the question. You are not bound by the authority of the one, nor I by that of the other. With authorities from the scriptures, evidence not peculiar to either but common to both, let us compare matter with matter, cause with cause, reason with reason[2]."

[1 Sancta scriptura nostræ doctrinæ regulam figit, ne audeamus sapere plus quam oportet sapere, sed sapiamus, (ut ipse ait) ad temperantiam, sicut unicuique Deus partitus est mensuram fidei. Non sit ergo mihi aliud te docere, nisi verba tibi Doctoris exponere, et de iis, quod Dominus dederit, disputare.]

[2 Sed nunc nec ego Nicenum, nec tu debes Ariminense, tanquam præ-judicaturus proferre concilium. Nec ego hujus auctoritate, nec tu illius

Bellarmine replies, that these words may seem to make something against the authority of councils, but not against traditions. I answer: When Augustine appeals from councils to the scriptures, he certainly much more rejects traditions; because the authority of councils ranks next after that of scripture. And if (as the papists pretend) traditions have an equal authority with scripture, then Augustine would have mentioned them, and said, "with authorities from scripture and tradition." For so Augustine frequently rejects all other standards, and requires scripture to be produced. In his commentary on Psalm lvii. Augustine writes thus: "Away with our writings! Let the Book of God come forth: hear Christ teaching: hear Truth speaking [3]"—where he counts everything but scripture to be the voice of man. There are similar expressions in his book *de Unitate Ecclesiæ,* capp. 3, 6, 10, 16, 20; and another passage, *de Merit. et Remiss. Pecc.* Lib. II. c. ult. which hath been already cited. These are the testimonies, the force of which our opponent seeks to elude.

We might easily produce many more, as well from Augustine as from others; and therefore Bellarmine's *first* remark is of no weight against us: for he says, in the first place, that he hath cited twice as many testimonies for traditions as we bring against them. I answer: Firstly, the victory rests not with the multitude and number, but with the truth of testimonies. We read that a thousand men have been often routed by a hundred. Secondly, I say that we also could bring twice as many testimonies as he hath produced. In the *second* place, Bellarmine observes that the testimonies on their side *expressly teach* that traditions ought to be received; while ours do not teach that they should be rejected *expressly,* but only by wrong consequences which we draw from them. I answer: I confess that the fathers often mention traditions, but these four things are to be noted in their testimonies: first, that the name of tradition sometimes denotes written doctrine, and some article depending on the sure testimony of scripture: secondly, that those traditions mentioned by the fathers are generally free customs, and not necessary dogmas: thirdly, that the fathers themselves were often deceived: (this, perhaps, may seem reproachful to the fathers; but

detineris: scripturarum auctoritatibus, non quorumque propriis, sed utrisque communibus testibus, res cum re, causa cum causa, ratio cum ratione concertet.—T. VI. p. 306.]

[3 Auferantur de medio chartæ nostræ; procedat in medium codex Dei; audi Christum docentem, audi veritatem loquentem.]

the matter of fact is manifest, inasmuch as they differ among themselves :) fourthly, that many of the traditions mentioned by the fathers are now abrogated by the papists themselves. Some of these four observations will suffice to obviate every one of the testimonies from the fathers. *Finally*, Bellarmine remarks, that we concede that tradition is defended by the fathers, while they do not concede that it was opposed by them. I answer : We concede that traditions were defended by the fathers, but in the sense already explained : and his assertion, that the fathers do not oppose traditions, is false; for they who say that the scriptures are perfect and sufficient, and that all religious doctrines should be drawn from the scriptures, do really reject traditions.

However, since he taunts us with the paucity of testimonies, I am disposed to proceed a little further, and accumulate additional evidence. Origen, in Rom. xvi. 1. 10, writes thus : " Behold, how those men stand upon the brink of peril, who neglect to exercise themselves in holy scripture, from which alone"—so he proceeds— " the discernment of this examination can be learned[1]." Chrysostom, Hom. 58, on the beginning of John x. writes thus : " He justly calls the scriptures the door, because they lead us to God, and disclose to us the knowledge of him. They make us his sheep, they guard us, and permit not the irruption of the wolves. For, like a gate of exceeding strength, they repel heretics, place us in safety, and suffer us not to wander as we please." Then he subjoins : " He who does not use the holy scripture, but climbeth up some other way, the same is a thief[2]." Surely, there is a noble encomium upon scripture in this passage. He says that it is the door of the knowledge of God ; that it makes us of the flock and keeps us so ; that we are directed by it so as not to fall into error; that it protects us from heretics and repels them; lastly, that those who climb up some other way,—that is, who use any other

---

[1 Vide quam proximi periculis fiant hi, qui exerceri in divinis literis negligunt, ex quibus solis hujusmodi examinationis agnoscenda discretio est.—Origen. Opp. P. II. p. 412, G. Paris. 1604.]

[2 εἰκότως δὲ θύραν τὰς γραφὰς ἐκάλεσεν. αὗται γὰρ ἡμᾶς προσάγουσι τῷ Θεῷ καὶ τὴν θεογνωσίαν ἀνοίγουσιν· αὗται πρόβατα ποιοῦσιν· αὗται φυλάττουσιν, καὶ τοὺς λύκους οὐκ ἀφιᾶσιν ἐπεισελθεῖν· καθάπερ γάρ τις θύρα ἀσφαλὴς, οὕτως ἀποκλείει τοῖς αἱρετικοῖς τὴν εἴσοδον, ἐν ἀσφαλείᾳ καθιστῶσα ἡμᾶς περὶ ὧν ἂν βουλώμεθα πάντων, καὶ οὐκ ἐῶσα πλανᾶσθαι..... ὁ γὰρ μὴ ταῖς γραφαῖς χρώμενος, ἀλλὰ ἀναβαίνων ἀλλαχόθεν, τουτέστιν, ἑτέραν ἑαυτῷ καὶ μὴ νενομισμένην τέμνων ὁδὸν, οὗτος κλέπτης ἐστίν.—Chrysostom. Comment. T. II. p. 371. Paris. 1633.]

evidence—are thieves. What then, I beseech you, are the papists? The same father, Hom. 9. on the Colossians, says: "Wait not for another master. Thou hast the oracles of God. None can teach thee like them." And, a little after: "Ignorance of scripture is the source of all evils[3]." Where then are those who refuse to be satisfied with scripture, when Chrysostom bids us expect no other master? whereby he indicates pretty plainly, that all necessary things are found in scripture. Jerome, at the end of his epistle to Ctesiphon, writes thus: "I have not time at present to write about the rest, and it was a letter you asked of me and not a book; which must be dictated at leisure, and wherein all the calumnies of these men shall be, with Christ's help, refuted: and this cause must be asserted by the testimonies of holy scripture, wherein God speaks daily to believers[4]." From which words I gather two conclusions: first, that all things which any doctor asserts must be brought to the test of scripture; secondly, that God speaks still in the scriptures. The same father, in his commentary on Micah i., says, that the church hath "the cities of the law, of the prophets, of the gospel, and of the apostles, and hath not gone beyond its boundaries, which are the holy scriptures." Here he writes expressly, that the church is circumscribed by the bounds of scripture, and not permitted to transgress them.

Ambrose, Comment. in Luc. xvi., explaining the words of the woman of Canaan to Christ, "Truth, Lord; yet the dogs eat of the crumbs that fall from their masters' table," writes thus: "These are crumbs of that bread; and since that bread is the word, and faith is exercised upon the word, the doctrines of faith are as it were crumbs[5]." Now, lest any one should explain this of the unwritten word, Aquinas, in his *Catena Aurea*, upon these words, adopting the very same allegory, says that the table figuratively denotes the holy scripture, and the crumbs the least precepts or internal

[3 μηδὲ περιμείνῃς ἕτερον διδάσκαλον· ἔχεις τὰ λόγια τοῦ Θεοῦ· οὐδείς σε διδάσκει ὡς ἐκεῖνα.... τοῦτο πάντων αἴτιον τῶν κακῶν, τὸ μὴ εἰδέναι τὰς γραφάς.—T. VI. p. 224.]

[4 De ceteris non est hujus temporis scribere; neque enim a me librum sed epistolam flagitasti, qui dictandus est ex otio, et omnes oblatrationes eorum Christi auxilio destruendæ, quod nobis sanctarum scripturarum testimoniis asserendum est, in quibus quotidie credentibus loquitur Deus.— Hieron. Opp. T. I. coll. 1035, 6. Veronæ. 1734.]

[5 Micæ istæ de illo pane sunt, et quia panis verbum est, et fides verbi est, micæ velut quædam dogmata fidei sunt.—Exposit. in Luc. Lib. VIII. §. 15. T. V. p. 351. Paris. 1838.]

mysteries, on which the holy church feeds; and that the dogs are the faithful. The sense therefore is, that the faithful are fed by the precepts of faith, but only such as fall from the table of the Lord, that is, are taken from the holy scriptures. Consequently, the faithful feed only on those doctrines which are delivered in the word of God, that is, in scripture. The same Ambrose, *De Fide, ad Gratian.* Lib. I. c. 6, writes as follows : " I would not have your sacred majesty trust mere argument, or any reasoning of mine. Let us ask the scriptures, let us ask the apostles, let us ask the prophets, let us ask Christ[1]."

Augustine, Epist. 112, writes thus : " If it be confirmed by the clear authority of the scriptures of God, (those, I mean, which are called canonical in the church,) it should be believed without any doubt. But you may repose greater or less faith in all other witnesses or testimonies, which are urged as persuasions to belief, in proportion as we find them to have or to want the weight which is proper to produce belief[2]." Thus Augustine : In which words he teaches us that the authority of scripture is singular in its kind, so as that whatever is by it confirmed must be immediately received; but that all other witnesses and testimonies are destitute of such an authority, requiring to be examined, and to have just so much credit assigned to them as we find upon examination to be their due. Absolutely false, then, is the assertion of our adversaries, that the authority of scripture and tradition is the same; since we must believe scripture without any hesitation, while all other testimonies, of what kind soever, must be diligently weighed and examined. The same author elsewhere, *De Natura et Gratia,* c. 91, writes thus : " I owe an absolute assent only to the canonical scriptures[3]." What value, may I ask, did this father set upon traditions, when he declared that he owed an absolute assent to nothing but the canonical scriptures ?

Vincentius Lirinensis, an ancient author in whose book the papists have great confidence, speaks thus : c. 41, " The canon

[1 Sed nolo argumento credas, sancte imperator, et nostræ disputationi: scripturas interrogemus, interrogemus apostolos, interrogemus prophetas, interrogemus Christum.—T. VI. pp. 15, 16.]

[2 Si divinarum scripturarum, earum scilicet quæ canonicæ in ecclesia nominantur, perspicua firmatur auctoritate, sine ulla dubitatione credendum est. Aliis vero testibus vel testimoniis, quibus aliquid credendum esse suadetur, tibi credere vel non credere liceat, quantum ea momenti ad faciendam fidem vel habere vel non habere perpenderis.—Paris. 1635.]

[3 Quia solis canonicis debeo sine recusatione consensum.—T. VII. p. 322.]

of scripture alone is self-sufficient for all[4]." Still more plainly, c. 2: "The canon of scripture alone is sufficient, and more than sufficient for all things[5]." I do not see how he could have spoken more plainly: he says that the canon of scripture is sufficient, and more than sufficient; sufficient for all things, and sufficient alone. Theodoret, Dialog. 2. c. *Hæret.*, speaks thus: " I dare not say any thing upon which scripture is silent[6]." Those, therefore, are presumptuous, who say any thing beside the scripture. Damascene, *de Fide Orthodoxa*, c. 1, writes thus: "We receive, acknowledge, honour and approve all things delivered by the law, the prophets, the apostles, and the evangelists;" then he subjoins, "seeking nothing else beside these[7]." The same author, Lib. iv. c. 18, writes thus: "Like a tree planted by the streams of water, so the soul, irrigated by the holy scripture, is enriched, and brings forth seasonable fruit, even orthodox faith, and is adorned with foliage ever green, that is, with works well pleasing to God. For we become apt for zealous work and pure contemplation by the scriptures; since we find in them what encourages us to all virtue and turns us from all vice[8]."

Hugo de Sancto Victore, Prol. in Lib. i. *de Sacr*, c. 1,[9] compares Christ to a king who walks, as princes use, between his attendants, the sacraments of the old and new Testaments: he says that the matter of scripture is works of restoration, and that the works of restoration are the incarnation of the Word with all its sacraments. Wherein he expressly testifies that all the sacraments are contained in scripture, in opposition to the papists who derive some sacraments from tradition. In the same book, c. 7, he says that the sayings of the fathers are not reckoned part of the body of the text, and that they add nothing to the scripture, but only explain

[4 Solus scripturæ canon sibi ad universa sufficit.]

[5 Solus canon scripturæ ad omnia satis superque sufficit.]

[6 ΟΡΘΟ. Ἐγὼ μὲν οὐκ ἂν φαίην ἀνθρωπίνοις πειθόμενος λογισμοῖς. οὐ γὰρ οὕτως εἰμὶ θρασὺς ὥστε φάναι τι σεσιγημένον παρὰ τῇ θείᾳ γραφῇ.—Theodoret. Dialog. Tiguri. 1593, p. 107.]

[7 πάντα τοίνυν τὰ παραδεδομένα ἡμῖν διά τε νόμου καὶ προφητῶν καὶ ἀποστόλων καὶ εὐαγγελιστῶν δεχόμεθα καὶ γινώσκομεν καὶ σέβομεν, οὐδὲν περαιτέρω τούτων ἐπιζητοῦντες.—Damascen. Opp. T. i. p. 123. Paris. 1712.]

[8 ὥσπερ γὰρ δένδρον παρὰ τὰς διεξόδους τῶν ὑδάτων πεφυτευμένον, οὕτω καὶ ἡ ψυχὴ, τῇ θείᾳ ἀρδευομένη γραφῇ πιαίνεται καὶ καρπὸν ὥριμον δίδωσι, πίστιν ὀρθόδοξον, καὶ ἀειθαλέσι τοῖς φύλλοις, ταῖς θεαρέστοις φημὶ ὡραΐζεται πράξεσι. —c. 17, p. 282.]

[9 Divina scriptura materiam habet opera restaurationis.—Opp. T. iii. Mogunt. 1617.]

more clearly, and handle more largely, what is contained in scripture. He teaches us, therefore, not to seek in the fathers any thing else but what is in scripture, because they only interpret scripture, not add to it any thing of their own. Scotus, in his Prologue to Lombard, says that "Scripture contains sufficiently the doctrine necessary for a Christian in this life[1]." So Thomas, Comment. in 2 Tim. iii., says that the scriptures make the man of God perfect. Antoninus, *Summa*, P. III. Tit. 18, c. 8 : " The suitable matter of preaching is the holy scripture. For God speaketh once, says Job, xxii. and it is in the sacred scripture that God speaks : and that so copiously (as Gregory explains it, Moral. 22), as that he needs not say any thing necessary a second time, since all things are therein contained[2]." Driedo, *De Catal.* Lib. I. c. 1, says that scripture is called an *instrument*, because it *instructs* man what he should believe, hope, and do[3].

Thus have we come to the close of this controversy, and suppose that, in what hath been said, we have sufficiently explained that sentence of scripture which we laid down at the commencement as our text. Hitherto we have refuted those errors of the papists which relate to the prophetic office of Christ. Those follow, in the next place, which regard his royal functions.

[1 Quæstio II. p. 40, inter Scoti Opp. T. III. p. 1. Lugdun. 1639. Scotus proposes the question, Utrum cognitio supernaturalis necessaria viatori sit sufficienter tradita in sacra scriptura? and resolves it in the affirmative.]

[2 Materia congrua prædicationis est sacra scriptura. Semel enim loquitur Deus (inquit Job. xxii.); loquitur autem Deus in scriptura sacra, et ita copiose, ut Gregorius exponit 22 Moral., quod non oportet Deum iterum loqui aliquid nobis necessarium, cum ibi omnia habeantur.—Antoninus, Summa Summarum, P. III. Lugdun. 1639.]

[3 Earundem scripturarum canonem eruditissimi viri instrumentum vocant, quia illic instruitur quisque pro sua salute, quid credere, quid sperare, quid agere debeat.—Dried. Opp. fol. 2. Lovan. 1500.]

TO THE CHRISTIAN READER.

IF ever any heretics have impiously outraged the holy scripture of God, we may justly rank the papists of our time with this class of men, who pervert things the most sacred. For, not to mention how insultingly most of them speak, and how meanly they think, of the scriptures, and to pass by at present the insane slanders of certain of them, (because I would not hurt your pious ears with the foul speeches these men have uttered,) there are especially six opinions concerning scripture which they now hold and obstinately defend, that are eminently absurd, heretical, and sacrilegious.

The first concerns the number of canonical and truly inspired books of scripture; since, not content with those which in the old Testament were published by the prophets, in the new by the apostles and evangelists—the chosen organs of the Spirit, they add to this fair and perfect body of canonical scripture, not only the Wisdom of Solomon, Ecclesiasticus, Judith, Tobit, but even the history of the Maccabees, the apocryphal stories of Susanna and Bel and the Dragon, and fragments of Esther, than which nothing more spurious can be imagined.

The second is, their placing the authentic scripture in the old Latin translation, which they call the Vulgate, and not in the sacred Hebrew and Greek originals: which is not merely, as Glaucus with Diomede[4], to exchange gold for brass, but to prefer the work of man to that of God. Who can doubt that Glaucus was a wise man compared with these? Brasen arms are as fit for all warlike purposes as golden; but who would not choose to learn true religion from the words of the Holy Ghost rather than from those of a translator—especially such a translator, and draw the water which he drinks from a spring, and not a cistern? Besides, in forbidding the people to read the scriptures, and performing their service in a strange language, they plainly take away all mutual converse of God with the people, and the people with God, and interrupt the intercourse and communion of the Deity with man.

[4 Iliad, VI. 234—236.]

The third is, their determining that the authority of scripture depends upon the voice and testimony of the church, and their teaching that the scripture is no scripture to us except on account of the sentence of the church; which is just the same as Tertullian formerly so wittily charged upon the heathen, Apol. c. 5 : " With you divinity depends on human choice. God is no God, unless it so pleases man. Man must now be kind to God[1]." It is absolutely thus that the papists maintain, that the scriptures would be no scriptures to us, if the church did not give them their authority, and approve them by her judgment.

The fourth is, their complaining of the incredible obscurity of the scriptures, not for the purpose of rousing men to diligence in studying and perusing them, but to bring the scriptures into hatred and subject them to wicked suspicions : as if God had published his scriptures as Aristotle did his books of Physics, for no one to understand. " Know that they are published, and yet not published ; for they are only intelligible to those who have heard myself[2]."

The fifth is their refusal to have controversies decided by scripture, or to allow scripture to be its own interpreter, making the pope of Rome the sole judge of controversies and interpreter of scripture : as if scripture were of no force without the pope, could hold no sense but what it received from the pope, nor even speak but what the pope saw good; or as if God did not speak to us, but only by the pope as his interpreter.

The sixth is, their asserting the doctrine of scripture, which is most full and absolutely perfect, to be incomplete ; and therefore not only joining innumerable unwritten traditions, whereof there was no mention in the bible, with scripture, but even setting them on a level with scripture in dignity, utility, authority, credit, and necessity : wherein they fall under the weight of just so many anathemas from Christ as the traditions are which they add to scripture. Who can adequately conceive the greatness of this insult, that these rotten popish traditions, whereof there is not one syllable in scripture, should be counted equal to the scriptures ?

[1 Apud vos de humano arbitratu divinitas pensitatur. Nisi homini Deus placuerit, Deus non erit : homo jam Deo propitius esse debebit.—T. I. p. 62. Lips. 1839.]

[2 ἴσθι . . . . αὐτοὺς καὶ ἐκδεδομένους καὶ μὴ ἐκδεδομένους· ξυνετοὶ γάρ εἰσι μόνοις τοῖς ἡμῶν ἀκούσασιν.—Aristot. ad Alex. ap. Aul. Gell. Noct. Attic. L. xx. c. 5.]

These monstrous errors of the papists, courteous reader, we refute in this book, not only by arguments and testimonies drawn from scripture, but also by those other proofs in which our adversaries principally confide; nor do we produce merely the ancient fathers of the church as witnesses on our side, but also the schoolmen and classic authors of the papists, who though, as the apostle says, they "held the truth in unrighteousness," yet left it not without witness.

We publish this controversy by itself (though we mean not to follow the same course with the rest), and that for very great and satisfactory reasons. The style is that which was used in delivering them orally, scholastic and concise, suitable not for expansion (which was little suited to our design), but for argument. They are published as they were taken down by some of my constant and attentive auditors, and have been afterwards reviewed by myself.

FAREWELL.

INDEX.

in the Jewish canon, 93; does not treat the Decretal Epistles of the popes as holy scripture, 109; supposed Hebrew to have been the primitive language, 112, 113; his opinion of the Septuagint, 119; his opinion of the old Italic, 128; reads *ipsa* corruptly in Gen. iii. 15, 164; supposed John's first epistle to be written to the Parthians, 218; does not say that the scriptures were read in only three languages, 220; his opinion of the Punic language, 223; his testimony to the use and value of vernacular versions of scripture, 245; recognises the necessity of an inward teacher, 290, 357; says that comparatively few prophets left any writings, 302; does not make the whole difference between canonical and apocryphal writings depend on the judgment of the church, 309, 310, 315; meaning of his declaration, *non crederem evangelio, nisi me catholicæ ecclesiæ commoveret auctoritas*, 319, &c.; his reasons for the partial obscurity of scripture, 365, &c.; his testimony to the perspicuity of scripture, 393, &c.; to what church he refers doubters, 442; did not believe that the rule of faith contains anything not delivered in scripture, 487; his rules for interpreting scripture, 492-495; how far his decision about apostolical traditions may be admitted, 507; considers Christ as the author of the books of the new Testament, 527: his reasons for rejecting spurious Acts and Gospels, 523; his ignorance of the reasons of Christ's descent into hell, 537; his exposition of 2 Thess. ii. 5, misrepresented by Stapleton, 553; his testimony in favour of traditions considered, 594, &c.; his testimony to the sufficiency of scripture, 694, &c.

Augustinus Steuchus, 495.

Authentic, what the word means, 332; the Vulgate so declared by the Council of Trent, 111; in the fullest sense, no version can be, 138; protestants allow only the originals of scripture to be such, 140.

B.

Baptism, of infants, may be proved from scripture, 506; and so admitted by Bellarmine, 540; heretical, not to be repeated, *ib.* 507; Augustine's opinion respecting, 608, 609.

Baruch, book of, its claims to canonicity considered, 67-70.

Basil, his adventure with Demosthenes the cook, 233; his account of faith, 357; advises a reference to the bishop of Rome, 439; his rules for interpreting scripture, 491; what he means by παράδοσις, 493, 498; did not deem the perpetual virginity of Mary an article of faith, 502; his testimony in favour of traditions considered, 588, 593; his testimony to the sufficiency of scripture, 681.

Basil, the emperor, 438.

Bellarmine, his character, 5, 6; has deserted several old points of defence, 7; sometimes misrepresents the opinions of protestants, 9, 514; and garbles quotations from the fathers, 374; contradicts himself, 163, 540, 672, 673; borrows arguments from the old heretics, 614; pronounces all the histories of the old Testament unnecessary, 660; his strange interpretations of scripture, 668.

C.

Cajetan, cardinal, his judgment concerning the apocryphal books, 48, 66; vehemently censured for it by the popish writers, 49; deemed that only sacred scripture which the apostles wrote or approved, 53; what books of the new Testament he rejected, 105; admits many faults in the Vulgate version, 169; admits that matrimony cannot be proved a sacrament from Eph. v. 32, 197, nor extreme unction from James v. 15, 199; dislikes the use of Latin in the mass, 274; his remarks on Deut. xvii. 12, 420; doubts the genuineness of the works of Dionysius the Areopagite, 576.

Calvin, vindicated, in his objections to the Vulgate Psalter, against Bellarmine, 181, &c.; defended against Stapleton, 340, &c.

Canon of scripture, the papists cannot assign the period when it was defined, 63; was, according to Augustine, fixed in the apostles' times, and therefore cannot be altered or increased by the church in after ages, 310, 311; power of fixing, how incident to the apostolic office, 311; the fathers generally do not attribute the power of consigning it to the church, 323, &c.

the papists reject his authority, 573; his
errors, 573, 574.

Interpretation of scripture, means of assigned by protestants, Quest. v. c. 9; by
papists, Quest. v. c. 3; by scripture,
Quest. v. c. 13.

Irenæus, 30, 31, 34, 35; cites the Shepherd
of Hermas, 68; whether he cites the
Epistle to the Hebrews as Paul's, 107;
says that Matthew wrote his Gospel in
Hebrew, 126; wrote his books in Greek,
217; what he relates of Anicetus, *ib.*;
what obscurities he admits in scripture,
370, 371; Bellarmine misrepresents his
meaning, 438, 439; thinks that scripture
may be interpreted by itself, 491, 492;
says that some barbarous nations retained
the truth without the scriptures, 520;
his testimony to traditions considered,
583-585; his testimony to the sufficiency
of scripture, 670-675.

Itala, Vetus, the version so called, 128.

J.

Jerome, 18, 19, 20, 33, 35; thought that the
evangelists might sometimes make a mistake, 37; uses *canonical* in a different
sense from Augustine, 45; the judgments
of councils and doctors subject to his
correction, according to Cajetan, 48; rejects the Apocrypha, 60, 77, 79, &c.;
thinks Hebrew the mother of all languages, 113, 114; says that Ezra changed
the Hebrew letters, 116; thinks that he
saw the Hebrew original of Matthew's
Gospel, 126; made a copy of it, 127;
complains of the variety of texts in the
Latin versions, 128; not the author of
the *Vetus Itala*, 128, 129; nor of the
whole present Vulgate, 129, 130; censures the readings of the present Vulgate
132-135; it is preferred by the fathers
to other Latin versions, but not to the
originals, 137; Vulgate version of the
Psalms not his, 180, &c.; says that the
Septuagint varied widely from the Hebrew, 183; whether he translated the
Bible into Dalmatian, 221; says that the
Psalms were chanted at Paula's funeral
in Syriac, 222; thinks the Punic nearly
the same as the Phœnician, 223; complains of the audacity of ignorant persons
in expounding scripture, 233, 234; the

Commentary on Colossians not his, 239;
his testimony to the free use of the scriptures, 244, 245; rejects the apocryphal
pieces attributed to Peter, 304; what he
says of the obscurity of scripture, 367;
admits the necessity of divine help for
the understanding of scripture, 368, and
the use of a human teacher, 368-369, 373;
does not say that Justin and Irenæus
wrote commentaries on the Apocalypse,
391; why he consulted the Bishop of
Rome upon the use of the word *hypostasis*, 442, 443; differed from Augustine
upon the meaning of the passage, 1 Tim.
iii. 2, 455; says that the Roman Church
rejected the Epistle to the Hebrews, 505;
corrects a mistake of Chrysostom's, 525;
says there is but one genuine Epistle of
Clement, 566; his testimony for traditions, 605; his testimony to the sufficiency of scripture, 692-694.

Jesuits, description of that order, 3-5.

Job, Book of, some Anabaptists said to
reject it, 33; some of the Rabbins treat it
as a fiction, *ib.*

Judge of controversies, question concerning, Quest. v. c. 8.

Judges, Book of, written by several prophets, 302.

Judgment of individuals assisted by the
Holy Spirit, not to be censured as mere
private judgment, 460, 461.

Judith, Book of, Jerome does not say posi-
tively that the Council of Nice received
it as canonical, 82; shewn by Jerome to
be apocryphal on two grounds, 83; the
times referred to in it hard to be fixed,
83, &c.; cannot be referred to the time
of Manasseh, 84, 85; what led Bellarmine
to cast it in those times, 85; nor to those
of Zedekiah, 86.

L.

Latin version, whether the present be Jerome's, 128; many things in it blamed by
Jerome, 132; Bellarmine's replies with
respect to them considered, 134; the
Scholastics have drawn many absurd conclusions from it, 140, 141; sentiments of
Clarius and Erasmus concerning, 207;
arguments of the papists for its superiority to the Hebrew proposed and refuted, 135-140; arguments of the Rhemish

translators, 141, &c.; arguments of Melchior Canus, 140; arguments of protestants against its authority, 160, &c.; places so corrupt that no papist has defended them, 173, &c.; of the new Testament, corruptions in pointed out, 193, &c.; preferred to the Greek and Hebrew by the Rhemists, Lindanus, &c., 111; declared authentic by the Council of Trent, *ib.*; could not be made really authentic, 157, &c.; barbarous, and full of solecisms, *ib.*; in many places evidently corrupt, *ib.*; instances of corruption indicated, *ib.*; of the Psalms, not Jerome's, 180; made not from the Hebrew, but the Greek, *ib.*; worse than the Greek, *ib.*; our objections to it supported against Bellarmine's replies, 181, &c.; versions, formerly numerous, 128; versions, other besides Jerome's used in the church before and after Gregory the Great, 129.

Latin language, not now the most common, 227.

Language, one only spoken before the building of the tower of Babel, 112, 113; vulgar, the Council of Trent forbids the use of in saying mass, 250; arguments in defence of that decree refuted, 251, &c.

Law, by that term, Ps. xix. 8, the whole doctrine delivered in the old Testament is described, 641; in what sense there said to be perfect, *ib.*; mysteries of, not concealed by Moses, 611.

Lent, said by Bellarmine to be instituted by the apostles, not by Christ, 501; defended by Ambrose not from tradition, but scripture, 604.

Luther, no more erroneous in rejecting some canonical books than some catholic churches formerly, or some fathers, and even papists themselves, 105; distinguishes between the obscurity of passages and the obscurity of dogmas in scripture, 361; unjustly blamed by Stapleton, 362; distinguishes between the external and internal perspicuity and obscurity of scripture, 363.

M.

Maccabees, books of, arguments for their canonicity refuted, 93-96; rejected by Jerome and Gregory the Great, &c. 96-97; contain doctrinal errors, 97; and fabulous

stories, 98; contradictory statements, 98-100; whether written by Josephus, 96; second book of, an epitome of a larger work by Jason of Cyrene, 98; evidently written by a human spirit, 100-102.

Manichees, rejected the whole old Testament, 30; said that the books of the apostles and evangelists were full of falsehoods, 34.

Marcion, rejected the law and the prophets, 30, 31; a disciple of Cerdon, 34.

Marcionites, what epistles they rejected, 35.

Mary, the blessed Virgin, her perpetual virginity proved from scripture by the fathers, 502, 539; not an article of faith according to Basil, *ib.*; her rights to the title θεοτόκος, 538; story of her assumption fabulous, 579, 580.

Matrimony, not a sacrament, 197, 489, 490.

Melchizedek, did not execute a priestly office in bringing forth bread and wine, 167, 168; how a type of Christ, 168, 169.

Moses, the earliest writer, 114; not a priest after the unction of Aaron, 417; some say that there were scriptures before his time, 114, 516; books of, in respect of the sum of their doctrine, nothing added to them by the apostles and prophets, 618, 619.

N.

Nice, Councils of, see *Councils.*

Nicholas, H. 298.

Nicolaitans, rejected the book of Psalms, 31.

O.

Ὁμοούσιον, vindicated from scripture by the fathers, 534, 535, &c.; whether the bishops at Rimini understood that term, 139.

Origen, his labour in collecting versions of scripture, 124, 125; what books he received as canonical, 57; whether he defended the history of Susanna, 78; rejected the apocryphal parts of Daniel, 79; would have *all* search the scriptures, 247; admits obscurities in scripture, 371; his rules for interpreting scripture, 403, &c.; recommends the collation of parallel places, 493; thinks that the darkness at the crucifixion was not caused by an eclipse, 578; could not have been known